The Historical Guide to North American Railroads

COMPILED BY GEORGE H. DRURY

Editor: Bob Hayden   Copy Editor: Marcia Stern   Art Director: Lawrence Luser

On the cover: It's a minute or two after 11:15 on an April morning in 1965. Gulf, Mobile & Ohio train 1, *The Limited*, has just begun its trip from Chicago to St. Louis, while on the adjacent track the Pennsylvania Railroad's *Manhattan Limited*, heavy with mail and express, is under way for Pittsburgh and New York. Photo by George H. Drury. Inset: New York Central 4-6-4 No. 5271. NYC photo.

KALMBACH **k** BOOKS

INTRODUCTION

As I compiled the first edition of *The Train-Watcher's Guide to North American Railroads* in 1983 I recognized a need for a companion volume to document the railroads that have gone out of existence in recent years. The railroad scene has changed so much and so many famous names have disappeared that a reader needs a guidebook to keep it all straight.

A start at documenting recently departed railroads was made by David P. Morgan and J. David Ingles in a series of articles titled "Fallen Flags" in TRAINS Magazine. Those articles reviewed the major railroads that had vanished since World War Two, and their theme was the genesis of this book.

Which railroads are in this book?

A book describing *all* the railroads that have vanished would be the size of an unabridged dictionary — hardly handy for quick reference. The two principal criteria for inclusion in this book are that the railroad disappeared after 1930 and was more than 50 miles long.

The year 1930 represents the end of the Roaring Twenties and is a historical watershed. Railroads had already reached the peak of their extent and were feeling the competition of automobiles, trucks, paved highways, and airplanes; they would soon be affected by the events of Black Tuesday — October 29, 1929 — and the Great Depression. The diesel was a novelty and streamlining was in the future.

Canada's railroad history does not divide nicely at 1930. The Canadian government began taking over railroads before World War One, and by the early 1920s Canadian National Railways was an established concern. A discussion of the history of Canadian National's predecessors begins on page 50.

Length was the major part of the other criterion. Was the railroad more than an incidental part of the continent's rail network? To the 50-mile minimum I added the requirement of significance or conspicuousness. I also considered longevity. Some of the short lines created to operate cast-offs of the Rock Island and Conrail sprouted, flourished, withered, and died in a single season or two.

What is a railroad?

Railroads have four components: fixed plant (track, right of way, and buildings), rolling stock, human organization, and financial structure. The human organization operates the rolling stock over the fixed plant, and the financial structure supports the operation. But what we call a railroad does not necessarily have all four components. Amtrak began operation with a financial structure and few people; it rented cars, locomotives, and personnel from other railroads. Today's Buffalo, Rochester & Pittsburgh has financial structure and fixed plant, but Chessie System operates the BR&P with Chessie System employees and rolling stock. The Clinchfield Railroad of recent years was an unincorporated organization of people and rolling stock that operated the fixed plant of the Carolina, Clinchfield & Ohio Railway for its joint lessees, Atlantic Coast Line and Louisville & Nashville. There are many reasons for separation of the components, among them state laws and financial and operational convenience. Remembering that the components can be separated may make it easier to understand the more complex railroad organizations.

As with *The Train-Watcher's Guide*, the question of subsidiaries arose. In general, the Texas subsidiaries are with their parents — until 1967 the state of Texas required railroads operating within its boundaries to be incorporated there. Also with their parent companies are subsidiaries that were listed in *The Official Guide* on the same pages — the railroads of the New York Central System, for example. However, subsidiaries with a distinctive identity are shown separately. Sacramento Northern, for example, was quite different from its parent Western Pacific.

I dealt with still-active subsidiaries and railroads similarly. Today's Cotton Belt is for the purposes of the enthusiast simply a division of Southern Pacific, but in 1930 that was not so — it had a personality of its own. The Baltimore & Annapolis and East Broad Top still exist today and are doing business at the same location, but it's not the same business. Today's Norfolk Southern is completely different from the Norfolk Southern of a few years ago, and it includes the older NS, to further complicate the matter. For that matter, Baltimore & Ohio and Chesapeake & Ohio still exist — but "Chessie System" is how they appear in *The Official Guide* and that is what is painted on their cars and locomotives. That sentence may contain the criterion for inclusion in this book.

I have omitted most of the interurbans. The electric railway industry, well into its decline by 1930, has been extensively documented. The best treatise on the industry itself, with histories of the individual lines, is *The Electric Interurban Railways in America*, by George W. Hilton and John F. Due, published in 1960 by the Stanford University Press, Stanford, CA 94305. I have included the major traction lines that hung on into the 1950s, usually by virtue of a healthy freight business.

Also included are some major abandoned portions of still-active railroads, such as Milwaukee Road's line to the Pacific Coast and the narrow gauge portions of the Denver & Rio Grande Western, and a few entities other than railroads, like the Pullman Company and the Interstate Commerce Commission, that were important factors in North American railroad development. A few railroads not meeting my criteria sneaked in anyway. I let them stay.

What about them?

The entry for each railroad begins with its history. A railroad's history is not necessarily proportional to its length or its life span. The Great Northern, largely the creation of one man, James J. Hill, built its line through territory far distant from any competitor. For its right of way through the mountains it did not have to fight the Santa Fe — only bears and topography. The Western Pacific was involved with the Gould empire early in its existence but it had a simple existence afterward. In contrast the New Haven dated from 1831, endured a succession of flamboyant and shady managements, and had more history per route-mile than any three western roads put together.

I have tried to follow a middle path between the financial history that gives details of every stock and bond issue and the anecdotal history that tells the story of the railroad from the point of view of the locomotive engineer, the station agent, or the canal boat captain whose business the railroad took away. Enthusiasts of those types of history will find plenty of each out there. Of necessity the histories are brief, and I make no apology for that.

Following the history are a number of data elements, facts, and statistics. My primary information sources were:

• Railroad name and location of headquarters — *The Official Guide*, January 1930. I have omitted "Company" and "Corporation," and I have used the ampersand (&) instead of "and," whether or not the railroad did.

• Miles of railroad operated, number of locomotives, passenger cars, freight cars, and company service cars — *Poor's Railroads* and *Moody's Transportation Manual*. The figures for mileage and rolling stock are as of December 31 of the year shown. *The Official Railway Equipment Register* and Poor and Moody often disagree on equipment counts, but for consistency I've stuck with Poor and Moody, and to the figure for equipment as reported to the ICC — often other figures appear for "in service" and "owned." For roads that turned over passenger service to Amtrak, final passenger car counts are as of December 31, 1970. Cabooses are included with freight cars; business cars are included with company service equipment. In recent years Moody has lumped together the figures for freight and company service cars.

• Reporting marks — *The Official Railway Equipment Register*. For roads that did not have officially assigned reporting marks I have shown the initials used on the cars. In recent years the ampersand has disappeared from the official reporting marks, even if it still lingers on car sides.

• Notable named passenger trains — This is my own opinion. Trains with a nice matched set of streamlined equipment had a better chance of nomination.

• Historical and technical societies — The criterion for inclusion is receipt of some publication from the society by the Kalmbach Publishing Co. library during the past year.

• Recommended reading — I have cited what I think are the best books for further information on the railroad. Some have long been out of print but can still be found on library shelves or in used-book stores. I have provided the current address of the publisher.

• Subsidiaries and affiliated railroads — These are shown as of the end of the railroad's existence. I have included major line-haul railroads but omitted most terminal and switching roads.

• Successors — A successor railroad marked "TWG" is described in *The Train-Watcher's Guide to North American Railroads*.

• Portions still operated — My basic resource was a three-way comparison of the *1928 Handy Railroad Atlas*, the current *Handy Railroad Atlas*, and the map of the successor railroad in *The Official Guide*. For the most part I listed only major main lines, not minor branches. Omission of this entry means either "none" or "most lines are still in operation" — the text should make clear which.

- Map and photo — The map shows the railroad as it was in 1930 or in the year it came into being. The purpose of the map is to show how the railroad fit into the North American railroad scene, not to document each curve and station. Connecting railroads are shown to the extent that they help locate the railroad under discussion. Dashed lines indicate major abandoned lines or lines that need to be differentiated. The photo is representative, not exhaustive — one photo is as inadequate as one sentence to describe a railroad.

The omission of a data element can usually be interpreted as "none."

As you read this book, you will probably want to have at your side a copy of the *1928 Handy Railroad Atlas of the United States* — but it shows only lines that had passenger service in 1928. *The Train-Watcher's Guide to North American Railroads* gives you a good view of the current railroad situation. Both books are published by Kalmbach Publishing Co., 1027 North Seventh Street, Milwaukee, WI 53233. Other references that will provide useful and interesting supplemental information are:

- *Railroad Names*, compiled and published by William D. Edson, 10820 Gainsborough Road, Potomac, MD 20854 — names of railroads, the dates they were active, predecessors, and successors.
- *Handy Railroad Atlas of the United States*, published every few years by Rand McNally & Company.
- A standard atlas or map showing the major rivers and mountain ranges of North America.

Acknowledgments: Each entry was reviewed by knowledgeable people — experts on the railroad in question. They read copy, made corrections, suggested additions, offered encouragement — and brushed aside the term "expert." I couldn't have done this book without their help, and I am grateful for it. They are listed at the end of the index.

GEORGE H. DRURY

Milwaukee, Wisconsin
September 1985

A BRIEF HISTORY OF NORTH AMERICAN RAILROADING

North America's railroads did not develop in isolation. They connected with each other, shared many characteristics, and were shaped by the events of their time. A quick general review of North America's railroad history furnishes a framework for the individual railroad histories and affords an understanding of why and when things happened. For a more complete discussion of U. S. railroad history read *American Railroads*, by John F. Stover, published in 1961 by the University of Chicago Press. An interesting view of the influence of the railroad between 1880 and 1930 is presented by John R. Stilgoe in *Metropolitan Corridor*, published in 1983 by Yale University Press, 92A Yale Station, New Haven, CT 06520 (ISBN 0-300-03042-8).

First blossom, 1827-1850

Completion of the Erie Canal gave a boost to the city of New York and made other Atlantic port cities recognize the need for improved transportation to the interior. Baltimoreans could see that a canal to the west would be impractical and therefore chartered the Baltimore & Ohio Railroad on February 28, 1827, to build to the Ohio River and funnel commerce to Baltimore. The B&O was the first railroad in the U. S. — "railroad" meaning an incorporated common carrier offering freight and passenger service on regular schedules rather than a simple mine or quarry tramway. Ground was broken for the road on July 4, 1828, by Charles Carroll, last surviving signer of the Declaration of Independence.

The laying of the first stone of the Baltimore & Ohio on July 4, 1828, is depicted in this painting done a century later by Stanley Arthurs.

In 1828 the commonwealth of Pennsylvania chartered the Main Line of Public Works, a system of railroads and canals — and an ancestor of the Pennsylvania Railroad — to link Philadelphia with the Ohio River. Within a decade railroads also pushed inland from Boston and Charleston, South Carolina, and west from Albany parallel to the route of the Erie Canal. Railroad development along the coast was almost as rapid. By 1838 it was possible to travel from New York to Washington by a combination of boats and trains, using horse-drawn omnibuses to cross Philadelphia and Baltimore. In 1852 the B&O reached its goal at Wheeling, West Virginia, and rails connected Philadelphia to Pittsburgh. In early 1854 rails from the East Coast reached to the Mississippi River at Rock Island, Illinois. Three years later a Charleston, S. C.,-Memphis rail route was opened.

To the Pacific! 1850-1885

California joined the United States in 1850. A railroad was necessary to connect it to the rest of the nation and to bring to the marketplaces of the East Coast the legendary wealth of the Orient (then, jade, spices, and silk; later, Toyotas). Five routes were surveyed between 1853 and 1855: a northern route, later followed by Northern Pacific and Great Northern; a central route from Omaha to San Francisco following the Platte River across Nebraska and passing through Salt Lake City, the route ultimately chosen (and later followed by highway I-80); a route from Kansas City to San Francisco across southern Colorado and then into California either over Tehachapi Pass or along the Pit River, a route for the most part never used by a railroad; a route from Fort Smith, Arkansas, to Los Angeles, followed by the Rock Island and the Santa Fe (and later, I-40); and a route across central Texas through El Paso to Los Angeles, followed by the Texas & Pacific and the Southern Pacific. The Civil War settled the question of the route. When the South seceded the advocates of the southern routes went with it. On July 1, 1862, President Abraham Lincoln signed an act authorizing the construction of a railroad from the Missouri River to the Pacific, and in 1863 he signed another setting its track gauge at 4 feet 8½ inches, later to become standard for North America.

"Standard gauge" was not standard in the beginning. Early railroads were built to almost any track gauge. The 4-foot-8½-inch gauge was the most common in the North; railroads in the South were usually built to a 5-foot gauge (they were changed to standard gauge in 1886). Narrower gauges, such as 3 feet and 2 feet, were chosen for reasons of economy; wider gauges, such as the 6-foot gauge of the Erie, were adopted for more obscure reasons. As often as not, the reason for choosing a different gauge was so that cars could not be interchanged with a neighboring railroad. It was some time before railroads realized that interchanging cars was easier than unloading and loading freight.

Central Pacific broke ground in Sacramento in January 1863 and Union Pacific did the same near Omaha at the end of that year. Construction went slowly because of the lack of capital and because of the Civil War, which was occupying the resources of the nation. It was the first war in which strategic use was made of railroads for moving troops and supplies and also the first in which railroads were targets for destruction.

B&O

After the last spike was driven into the last tie at Promontory, Utah, on May 10, 1869, the two locomotives, Central Pacific *Jupiter* and Union Pacific 119, moved forward to touch pilots, and everyone lined up for the photographer.

The railroads of the South had been built primarily to tie inland areas to the coast rather than to connect with each other. Southern railroads seemed loath to arrange through service or even use joint stations in a city — all of which had to be hastily corrected during the Civil War. At the end of the war in 1865 the railroads of the South were demolished. Not all were rebuilt — some weak lines were pruned, with the result that later the South did not have the network of redundant lines found in the Northeast and the Midwest.

Construction of the Union Pacific got under way in earnest with the laying of the first rails in July 1865. By then Central Pacific had progressed as far east as Colfax, Calif., out of the foothills and into the Sierra Nevada. The last spike, a gold one, was driven on May 10, 1869, at Prom-

ontory, Utah. The first transcontinental railroad was complete. (The term "transcontinental" in U. S. railroad usage refers only to the west half or third of the continent — Omaha to Sacramento, for example, or even Salt Lake City to Oakland, as in the case of the Western Pacific.)

Many of the railroads that opened the West received land grants, alternate sections of federally owned land on each side of the track. Attackers of the railroads have been quick to pounce on this seeming magnanimity of the government, but the nation got its money's worth. The land was almost valueless without the railroads, but if the railroad provided access and transportation, the government could double the price of the land it retained. A stipulation of the land grants was that the railroads had to provide reduced-rate transportation for government property, mail, and employees; this provision was not repealed until 1946. By then the government had gotten back more than ten times the value of the land it had granted.

The 1870s and 1880s saw a tremendous increase in railroad mileage. It was as if a skeleton were suddenly fleshed out to obesity. Every town needed a railroad; two were better than one. If capital were not available locally, it was in Europe, especially from prosperous industrial England, which had more capital than it could invest at home. The railroads of the western U. S. and Canada got more than capital in Europe — they also recruited colonists to inhabit the land they were opening.

Several rail routes to the Pacific were completed in the early 1880s. The Santa Fe met the Southern Pacific at Deming, New Mexico, in 1881, and 1883 saw the completion of Santa Fe's own route across northern New Mexico and Arizona, SP's line between New Orleans and Los Angeles, and the Northern Pacific route from Duluth, Minnesota, to Portland, Oregon. A year later the Union Pacific route to Oregon opened. Canadian Pacific's route across Canada was completed in 1885 — and this is a good time for side trips across the northern and southern borders of the U. S. for summaries of Canadian and Mexican railroad history.

Canada

Canada's first railroad was the Champlain & St. Lawrence Railroad, opened in 1836 between the south bank of the St. Lawrence at Laprairie and St. Johns, Quebec, head of open-water navigation on the Richelieu River, which drains Lake Champlain. Railroads soon spread down the St.

Lawrence River into the Maritime Provinces and westward into Ontario.

When British Columbia joined the confederation in 1871, the Canadian government promised a railroad to link the new province with the rest of the country. The principal railroad in Quebec and Ontario, the Grand Trunk, was not interested in a western extension, so the Canadian Pacific Railway was incorporated in 1881 to build from Callander, Ont., near North Bay, to the Pacific at what is now Vancouver. The builders of the railroad were faced with 1,300 miles of wilderness — forests, swamps, and rivers — across northern Ontario, 1,000 miles of prairie, and 500 miles of rugged mountains. Construction of the line along the north shore of Lake Superior was extremely difficult, but nationalistic feeling prohibited a detour through the U. S. The crossing of the Rockies called for 4.5 percent grades, replaced later by a pair of spiral tunnels. The line was completed on November 7, 1885. Even while it was constructing its line to the west, the CPR (initials of Canadian roads almost invariably include the "R" for "Railway") was extending eastward to Ottawa and Montreal. By 1890 the road's eastern lines stretched from Windsor, Ont., opposite Detroit, through Montreal and across the state of Maine to Saint John, New Brunswick. CPR spread an extensive network of branches across the wheatlands between Winnipeg and Calgary after 1900, and in 1916 a secondary main line was opened through the Kootenay region just north of the British Columbia-Washington boundary. Part of that line was financed by the government in exchange for a permanent reduction in grain shipping rates — the Crows Nest Pass Agreement of 1897, only recently amended. CPR's railroad family inclúdes the Dominion Atlantic in Nova Scotia, the Quebec Central, the Toronto, Hamilton & Buffalo, the Esquimault & Nanaimo on Vancouver Island, and a majority interest in the Soo Line.

Most of eastern Canada's railroads were part of one predecessor or another of Canadian National Railways — see page 50. Financial difficulty brought these roads under government control between 1915 and 1923. The 3-foot-6-inch-gauge Newfoundland Railway was added to CNR in 1949 when Newfoundland joined the confederation. In recent years CNR has pushed several lines north from the prairies into the subarctic area.

The provinces of Ontario and British Columbia are in the railroad business through ownership of the Ontario Northland and British Columbia railways. The province of Alberta owned several railroads that were purchased by CNR and CPR jointly in 1929 to form Northern Alberta Railways, now part of CNR.

Mexico

Mexico's railroads are owned by the government, and the National Railways of Mexico (Ferrocarriles Nacionales de Mexico) operates most of the country's rail mileage. Mexico's first major railroad was one of the last to be nationalized (in 1946), the Ferrocarril Mexicano. It was built between 1864 and 1873 by British interests to connect Mexico City with the Gulf of Mexico at Veracruz. To counteract FCM's monopoly, Mexican president Porfirio Diaz offered concessions or subsidies to railroads between the interior and the coast, preferring at least for a few years to avoid connections with the U. S. railroad system.

National Railways of Mexico was incorporated in 1908 as successor to the National Railroad of Mexico, a company in which the Mexican government held a majority interest. National Railways of Mexico acquired the Mexican Central in 1909. During the late 1930s, a period of governmental upheaval, control of the railroad was tossed back and forth among the government, a syndicate of railroad workers, and the railroad's own management.

Both of NdeM's main lines from the U. S. border to Mexico City were built by companies receiving concessions from the government. NdeM's main line south from Ciudad Juarez, across the Rio Grande from El Paso, Tex., through Chihuahua, Torreon, Aguascalientes, and Queretaro, was built by Santa Fe interests as the Mexican Central. It was completed in 1884.

The line from Laredo was begun in 1881 as the 3-foot-gauge Mexican National by Gen. William Jackson Palmer, builder of the Denver & Rio Grande. It was completed to Mexico City in 1888 via Monterrey, Saltillo, San Luis Potosi, Acambaro, and Toluca, with branches from Monterrey to Matamoros and from Acambaro to Uruapan. It was standard-gauged as far south as Escobedo in 1903 and a new line was built through Queretaro to Mexico City, roughly parallel to the Mexican Central. National of Mexico operates the two Queretaro-Mexico City lines as double track; both lines are now being replaced by a new double-track electrified line. The line through Toluca was widened to standard gauge in 1949.

There are two lines from Mexico City to Veracruz, on the Gulf of Mexico. The line via Orizaba is the former Ferrocarril Mexicano; the line via Jalapa is the former 3-foot-gauge Ferrocarril Interoceanico, standard-gauged in 1948.

Three of the non-NdeM lines are on the West Coast. The Ferrocarril del Pacifico, from Nogales, on the Arizona border, to Guadalajara, is the former Southern Pacific of Mexico, completed in 1927. The Chihuahua Pacific, the former Kansas City, Mexico & Orient, cuts diagonally across northwestern Mexico from Ojinaga on the Texas border to Los Mochis on the Gulf of California. It was completed in 1961. The Sonora-Baja California, from Mexicali to a connection with the Pacifico at Benjamin Hill, was built by the government and opened in 1948.

The remaining non-NdeM road is the United Southeastern Railways, which was formed by the 1969 merger of the United Railways of Yucatan and the Southeastern Railway. The first portion of the UdeY was opened in 1881; the road developed into a system of both standard and narrow gauge lines linking much of the state of Yucatan with its capital, Merida, and extending southwest into the neighboring state of Campeche. The UdeY was isolated until the government completed the Southeastern Railway from Allende in the state of Veracruz to the city of Campeche in 1950.

Narrow gauge fever, 1870-1890

Part of the overall railroad boom, the narrow gauge boom ran from roughly 1870 to 1890. The reason usually given for preferring narrow gauge to standard gauge was economy: Smaller locomotives and cars cost less. Another view is that narrow gauge railroads were fresh and new at a time when standard gauge railroads had fallen out of favor with the public (the 6-foot-gauge Erie was worst of all). The advantage of standard gauge was that it was standard (and in 1886 the railroads of the South, which had been built to a 5-foot gauge, were converted to standard gauge). Financially successful narrow gauge railroads were soon standard-gauged, unless the cargo carried would have to be transloaded anyway (as in the case of the East Broad Top, where cleaning of coal was done at the point where it was moved from narrow gauge cars to standard gauge cars) or the terrain made the cost of standard-gauging greater than any benefits of through operation.

Time of technology, 1870-1910

The basic items of railroading, rails and rolling stock, came first and refinements later. The first rails were strap iron on top of wooden stringers. Iron rails were introduced in 1830, and steel rails were first used in 1863. The first cars were basically stagecoaches and wagons on flanged wheels. The first double-truck car is sometimes credited to Ross Winans of the Baltimore & Ohio in 1831, but Gridley Bryant constructed one for the Granite Railroad in Quincy, Massachusetts, in 1826. The first locomotives were simple four-wheel machines; one of the first improvements was the lead truck, which helped guide the locomotive around curves.

The pioneers of railroading were more concerned with going than with stopping. Steam-operated locomotive brakes and hand brakes on the cars were a considerable advance over what the first trains used, which included sticks thrust between wheel spokes. George Westinghouse patented an air brake in 1869; others had previously done so. Westinghouse's most significant contribution, a later refinement, was the triple valve that made the system fail-safe.

The first trains were held together by chains. Chains were succeeded by the link-and-pin coupler, which required a man to hold a link in position as the cars came together and remove his hand at the right instant, lest the couplers do so. Eli Janney's automatic coupler of 1873, approved by the Master Car Builders' Association in 1887, made railroading a much safer occupation.

In the 1880s steam heat and electric lights began to replace stoves and oil and gas lamps, which were ready sources of fire in case of an accident — cars were constructed almost entirely of wood. Automatic block signals and electric locomotives appeared in the 1890s, and all-steel cars came in the early 1900s.

Nor was technology limited to the railroads. A few minutes difference in sun time between neighboring cities made little difference when the cities were a day's travel apart. Railroads reduced the time between cities to hours, and the telegraph that accompanied them provided instant communication. To eliminate the confusion caused by a railroad having to use the time of city A in city B, in 1883 the railroads divided the U. S. into four zones with uniform times an hour apart. Gradually others adopted the standard time of the railroads.

Robber barons, regulation, and competition, 1880-1920

The U. S. was fast becoming an industrial nation in the late 1800s. Men were building industrial empires and railroad empires — ambitious men who would let nothing block them. It was the era of Titans of Industry. Men such as Jay Gould and E. H. Harriman built railroad systems, buying control of connecting lines to extend their systems, buying parallel lines to control competition, and sometimes just buying up railroads for the parts. The amount of publicity accorded these titans (or robber barons) is due in part to their accomplishments and in part to the fact that railroads were larger and more conspicuous businesses than anything else. These industrial empires and their leaders occupied newspapers and magazines the way rock stars now fill TV screens.

Regulation had its roots in the Midwest and West. Farmers there were far more dependent than those in the East on railroads to move their products to market. They complained that rates were so high they left little profit and that they were unfair. Favored shippers were receiving rebates, and rates were often higher where one railroad had a monopoly. (For a look at railroad rates from the viewpoint of the farmer, read Frank Norris's *The Octopus*.)

Illinois passed legislation in 1871 and 1873 regulating freight rates and passenger fares, and Minnesota did so in 1874. By 1880 pressure for regulation, particularly from the Grange — the National Grange of the Patrons of Husbandry — had shifted to the national level and resulted in the Interstate Commerce Act of 1887.

At first the railroads' only competition was stagecoaches and canal and river boats. The first practical electric streetcar appeared in 1888 and quickly evolved into the electric interurban railway. It was what we now call light rail technology: rolling stock smaller than standard railroad dimensions, track sometimes in the streets and sometimes on private right of way, and emphasis on local service. The steam railroads were suddenly paralleled by competing electric railways. Some steam roads recognized that the electric lines were going after local traffic, the service steam roads found most expensive to operate, and they encouraged neighboring electric lines. For the most part hostility existed between the two types of railroads. (Like "transcontinental," "steam railroad" is a flexible term. It implies standard dimensions and being an independent company — or a

subsidiary of some other steam road — rather than a division of a power and light company. The term does not preclude electric locomotives — the Pennsy's New York-Washington line, GG1s and all, was a "steam railroad." To the steam railroads, the electric railway was a lesser breed without the law, not quite our kind of railroad.)

The interurban wasn't the only competition for long. Paved highways took away the interurbans' business — the interurban era was over by 1930 — and then began eating into the traffic of the steam railroads. Many railroads responded by forming bus and truck lines; a few even offered air service.

USRA and the Roaring Twenties, 1917-1930

The U. S. entered World War One on April 6, 1917. Five days later a group of railroad executives pledged their cooperation in the war effort, creating the Railroad War Board. Among the problems the board had to deal with were labor difficulties, a patriotic rush of employees to join the Army, and a glut of supplies for the war effort choking East Coast yards and ports.

The efforts of the board were not enough for the government. On December 26, 1917, President Woodrow Wilson placed U. S. railroads under the jurisdiction of the United States Railroad Administration, whose director was William G. McAdoo, Secretary of the Treasury, Wilson's son-in-law, and, some years previous, builder of the Hudson & Manhattan Railroad (now the Port Authority Trans-Hudson line between New York, Hoboken, and Newark). The government guaranteed the railroads a rental based on their net operating income for the previous three years. Essentially the government was renting the railroads as one would rent a house, with responsibility for anything lost or damaged. Among McAdoo's acts were the discharge of all railroad presidents, elimination of all rail competition, and a flat $20 wage increase for all employees earning less than $46 a month. The USRA ordered and assigned to railroads more than 2,000 locomotives and 50,000 freight cars of standardized design.

USRA control ended March 1, 1920. The USRA's net operating income for the 26 months of control fell short of the guaranteed payments by $714 million and railroad damage claims were an additional $677 million. One happy legacy of the USRA was its set of 12 standardized locomo-

Atlantic Coast Line 494 is a USRA light Pacific.

tive designs. Steam locomotives were built to these specifications as late as 1944.

In 1920 Congress asked the ICC to prepare a plan for merging U. S. railroads into a limited number of systems, preserving competition and existing routes of trade and, where possible, subject to the other requirements, grouping the railroads so the cost of transportation on competing routes would be the same — or in the ICC's words, to equitably parcel out the weak sisters. In 1929 the ICC published its recommendation: 19 systems for the U. S., leaving the affiliates of the Canadian roads with Canadian National (Central Vermont and Grand Trunk Western) and Canadian Pacific (Soo Line, Spokane International, and Duluth, South Shore & Atlantic). Generally, subsidiaries would stay with their parents and short lines would be assigned to the connecting trunk line. A few railroads were assigned jointly to more than one system. The systems would have been (system name in **boldface**):

1. **Boston & Maine**; Maine Central; Bangor & Aroostook; Delaware & Hudson
2. **New Haven**; New York, Ontario & Western; Lehigh & Hudson River; Lehigh & New England
3. **New York Central**; Rutland; Virginian; Chicago, Attica & Southern
4. **Pennsylvania**; Long Island
5. **Baltimore & Ohio**; Buffalo, Rochester & Pittsburgh; Buffalo & Susquehanna; Chicago & Alton; Central of New Jersey; Reading; Monon (½); Detroit & Toledo Shore Line (½); Detroit, Toledo & Ironton (½)

6. **Chesapeake & Ohio-Nickel Plate**; Hocking Valley; Erie; Pere Marquette; Lehigh Valley; Delaware, Lackawanna & Western; Bessemer & Lake Erie; Chicago & Illinois Midland; Detroit & Toledo Shore Line (½)
7. **Wabash-Seaboard Air Line**; Lehigh Valley; Wheeling & Lake Erie; Pittsburgh & West Virginia; Western Maryland; Akron Canton & Youngstown; Norfolk & Western; Detroit, Toledo & Ironton (½); Toledo, Peoria & Western; Ann Arbor; Winston-Salem Southbound (½)
8. **Atlantic Coast Line**; Louisville & Nashville, Nashville, Chattanooga & St. Louis; Clinchfield; Atlanta, Birmingham & Coast; Gulf, Mobile & Northern; New Orleans Great Northern; Monon (¼); Winston-Salem Southbound (½)
9. **Southern**; Norfolk Southern; Tennessee Central (east of Nashville); Florida East Coast; Monon (¼)
10. **Illinois Central**; Central of Georgia; Minneapolis & St. Louis; Tennessee Central (west of Nashville); Cotton Belt; Atlanta & St. Andrews Bay
11. **Chicago & North Western**; Chicago & Eastern Illinois; Litchfield & Madison; Mobile & Ohio; Columbus & Greenville; Lake Superior & Ishpeming
12. **Great Northern-Northern Pacific**; Spokane, Portland & Seattle; Butte, Anaconda & Pacific (½)
13. **Milwaukee Road**; Escanaba & Lake Superior; Duluth, Missabe & Northern; Duluth & Iron Range; Butte, Anaconda & Pacific (½); trackage rights on SP&S to Portland
14. **Burlington**; Colorado & Southern; Fort Worth & Denver; Green Bay & Western; Missouri-Kansas-Texas; Trinity & Brazos Valley (½); Oklahoma City-Ada-Atoka
15. **Union Pacific**; Kansas City Southern
16. **Southern Pacific**
17. **Santa Fe**; Chicago Great Western; Kansas City, Mexico & Orient; Missouri & North Arkansas; Midland Valley; Minneapolis, Northfield & Southern
18. **Missouri Pacific**; Texas & Pacific; Kansas, Oklahoma & Gulf; Denver & Rio Grande Western; Denver & Salt Lake; Western Pacific; Fort Smith & Western
19. **Rock Island-Frisco**; Alabama, Tennessee & Northern; Louisiana &

Arkansas; Meridian & Bigbee; Trinity & Brazos Valley (½)

The plan caused great discussion, usually beginning with "The Pennsylvania is already big enough." No one, not even its creators, was happy with all facets. By 1932 most of the Wabash-Seaboard system had been parceled out among the others, because both principals had entered receivership (Seaboard was left unallocated) and because it was pointed out that most of the railroads in the Wabash-Seaboard system were controlled by the Pennsylvania. Any tinkering to correct an imbalance here resulted in three imbalances there. Congress withdrew the matter in 1940. It is interesting to compare the 1929 ICC proposal with mergers that have taken place recently.

Depression and the diesel, 1930-1939

The Great Depression was no easier for the railroads than for anyone else. As business declined, railroads had less freight and fewer passengers to carry. Locomotives and cars were stored or scrapped. Dozens of railroads declared bankruptcy, including such major lines as Frisco, Missouri Pacific, Milwaukee Road, and New Haven. Only the strongest survived unscathed.

During the 1920s a few railroads and a few locomotive builders had experimented with internal combustion engines in gas-electric passenger cars and diesel-electric switch engines. The former could replace a two- or three-car local passenger train and be operated with fewer men; the latter had the advantages over steam of cleanliness and instant availability — it could be turned on and off as needed. In both, an internal combustion engine (gasoline or diesel) drove a generator, which in turn produced electric current for traction motors that drove the wheels.

In the early 1930s two railroads and two carbuilders ventured combinations of internal combustion and streamlining. Two trains emerged in 1934, Union Pacific's aluminum *M-10000*, built by Pullman-Standard, and Burlington's stainless steel *Zephyr*, built by Budd. Both had power plants built by Electro-Motive Corporation, a subsidiary of General Motors: the UP train a spark-ignition distillate engine, the Burlington train a diesel. Both trains toured the country, and the *Zephyr* made a dawn-to-dark run from Denver to Chicago. The trains captured the attention of the public and of the railroad industry. UP and Burlington quickly acquired fleets of diesel streamliners, and so did other railroads. The

TRAINS Collection

In the late 1930s America's first two streamliners both served Kansas City. Union Pacific's M-10000, operating as the *City of Salina*, made a daily round trip between Kansas City and Salina, Kans., with an additional midday turn to Topeka, and Burlington's *Pioneer Zephyr* made a Lincoln-Omaha-Kansas City round trip each day.

streamliners were of lighter-weight construction than conventional passenger trains; two mechanical innovations they included were air conditioning and roller bearings on the axles. The use of roller bearings soon spread to freight cars.

The diesel proved to be separable from the train. In 1935 Baltimore & Ohio and Santa Fe bought diesels from Electro-Motive to pull conventional trains, and EMC passenger diesels became the usual power for the new streamliners.

In 1939 Electro-Motive produced a four-unit, 5400-horsepower freight diesel demonstrator, No. 103, a locomotive TRAINS editor David P. Morgan called "the most significant piece of motive power since Stephenson's *Rocket*." (The *Rocket*'s success in the trials at Rainhill in 1830 caused the directors of the infant Liverpool & Manchester Railway to choose the steam locomotive to power their trains.) EMC 103 demonstrated and sold. More than any other locomotive it is responsible for the dieselization of American railroads.

R. V. Nixon

In the Northern Pacific yards at Missoula, Mont., on March 6, 1940, all attention is on Electro-Motive 103, which has just arrived on a demonstration run. Behind the four-unit diesel is NP's dynamometer car.

War and wither away, 1940-1960

During World War Two U. S. railroads remained in control of their affairs. Freight traffic doubled and passenger business quadrupled. Then the war was over. Detroit set out to satisfy a populace that hadn't seen a new automobile in five years, and the railroads tried to erase the memory of wartime travel conditions with fleets of new cars and trains and innovations like the Vista-Dome. By the mid-1950s the local train had become a victim of the automobile, and the Interstate highway system and the passenger jet airplane would soon start the decline of the long distance train. Losses from passenger trains caused the railroads to cut back services and discontinue trains; the public responded by riding less and less. The decline accelerated in the late 1960s when the Post Office withdrew mail from most passenger trains in favor of trucks, planes, and a new sorting system. By 1970 train riding was only for the most determined.

On May 1, 1971, the National Railroad Passenger Corporation, doing business under the name Amtrak, took over most of the nation's passenger trains. The government company immediately discontinued approximately two-thirds of the remaining passenger trains and set out to beef up business on those that remained.

The Interstate highway system was as beneficial for trucks as it was for cars. The railroads soon lost their less-than-carload merchandise traffic, though much of that was picked up by freight forwarders who filled trailers and towed them across town to the railroad's trailer-on-flat-car terminal. Perishable and livestock traffic declined.

Innovative equipment, though, increased other categories of freight business. Years before the railroads had lost the new-automobile business, but they brought it back, using bilevel and trilevel rack cars twice as long and half again as high as the automobile box cars they replaced. Box cars the same size as the rack cars were developed for auto parts, which are light but bulky. Grain began to move in huge covered hopper cars, easier to load and unload than box cars, and like coal, it moved in unit trains, solid trains moved intact from origin to destination. Piggyback traffic — trailers and containers on flat cars — became the hottest commodity the railroads moved.

The merger era, 1957-1985

Some date the modern merger era from the spring of 1947, when three mergers occurred: Gulf, Mobile & Ohio and Alton; Denver & Rio Grande Western and Denver & Salt Lake; and Chesapeake & Ohio and Pere Marquette. Others choose as the kickoff date August 30, 1957, when Louisville & Nashville merged Nashville, Chattanooga & St. Louis. At first it seemed only the smaller, regional roads were disappearing. Then in 1963 Chesapeake & Ohio acquired control of Baltimore & Ohio. C&O had traditionally been associated with Erie and Nickel Plate. A year later the Norfolk & Western merged the Nickel Plate, leased the Wabash and the Pittsburgh & West Virginia, and acquired control of the Akron, Canton & Youngstown. N&W and Wabash had long been affiliates of the Pennsylvania. Then N&W and C&O announced the possibility of merger.

As confirmation that traditional alliances were out, rivals Pennsylvania and New York Central announced their impending merger to form Penn Central. In 1964 Union Pacific, which for years had relied on Chicago & North Western to forward its *City* streamliners to and from Chicago and in 1955 switched them to Milwaukee Road, proposed merger with the Rock Island. The ICC proceedings on the UP-RI merger were the longest in history, and by the time they were done, the Rock Island was in such poor shape that UP didn't want it anymore.

Symbolic of today's railroading is a train of containers and trailers moving on welded rail — a Cotton Belt train on former Rock Island track.

Meanwhile, Penn Central lasted little more than two years before becoming the biggest single bankruptcy in U. S. history. From its wreckage and that of several smaller roads the federal government formed Consolidated Rail Corporation on April 1, All Fools' Day, 1976. Conrail eventually lived down its birthday and began to show profits in 1981. As this book goes to press the federal government is seeking a buyer for the railroad.

Other major recent mergers include Southern and Norfolk & Western to form Norfolk Southern; Atlantic Coast Line and Seaboard Air Line to form Seaboard Coast Line, which merged with Louisville & Nashville to form Seaboard System; Union Pacific, Western Pacific, and Missouri Pacific; and Santa Fe and Southern Pacific.

Deregulation and renaissance, 1980

On October 14, 1980, President Jimmy Carter signed into law the Staggers Rail Act (named for Rep. Harley O. Staggers of West Virginia). It was massive deregulation of the railroads, including provisions to raise any rate that falls below 160 percent of out-of-pocket costs (later 180 percent) and to enter into contracts with shippers to set price and service, both without ICC approval.

Railroads are no less important and no less interesting now than they were in 1930. Even though the railroads' share of the intercity freight business has dropped in the intervening years from three-quarters to a bit more than one-third, ton-miles have doubled — railroads are carrying

the same amount of cargo twice as far (or twice the amount the same distance). Statistics comparing U. S. Class 1 railroads in 1930 and 1980 shed light on the nature of the changes:

	1930	1980	Notes
Trackage operated (miles)	429,883	290,000	1
Locomotives in service	56,582	28,396	
Freight cars in service	2,276,867	1,710,827	
Average freight car capacity (tons)	46.6	80.4	
Loaded freight cars moved	45,877,974	21,613,063	
Revenue ton-miles (millions)	383,450	918,621	
Passenger cars in service	52,130	4,347	2
Revenue passenger miles (millions)	26,815	11,500	
Average trip per passenger (miles)	38.11	37.97	3
Average trip per Amtrak passenger (miles)		216.7	

Notes:

1. 1980 figure is for mileage owned, which includes sidings, yards, additional main tracks.

2. 1980 figure is based on reports to ICC and does not include several hundred commuter cars.

3. Figures are for all classes of railroads.

This says that railroads of today are using a little more than half the hardware they did in 1930 to create more than twice as much of their product, which is ton-miles. The commuter business dominates the passenger statistics; the passenger-car count reflects the sleeping car of 1930, which held 27 passengers if all the upper berths were sold (and usually they weren't), and the commuter coach of 1980, which will seat 100 passengers or more.

There are fewer railroad companies today than in 1930, but they are as fascinating as they used to be and considerably more colorful. The Atlantic Coast Line and the New Haven and the Rock Island are gone. Start turning the pages to find out where they went and what they were — and perhaps how much remains of them.

ADIRONDACK RAILWAY

In 1972 storm damage caused Penn Central to abandon its Lake Placid line, formerly New York Central's Adirondack Division, north of Remsen, N. Y. The line had been built by William Seward Webb, son-in-law of William H. Vanderbilt. Webb had taken over the Herkimer, Newport & Poland, a narrow gauge line through the towns of its name, standard-gauged it, and extended it north as the Adirondack & St. Lawrence — later Mohawk & Malone. It and its Montreal extension, the St. Lawrence & Adirondack, became part of the New York Central in the early 1900s. NYC had a short branch from Lake Clear Jct. to Saranac Lake; from there to Lake Placid its trains ran on Delaware & Hudson rails, the tail end of a former narrow gauge line from Plattsburg. By the time Penn Central began operation, the Lake Clear Jct.-Malone line had been abandoned; a line from Tupper Lake Jct. to Ottawa had been taken up many years before.

The New York State Department of Transportation purchased PC's right of way and track in 1975. The Adirondack Railway was incorporated in 1976 to rehabilitate the line and restore service, with an eye to the 1980 Winter Olympic Games at Lake Placid. The Adirondack Railway inaugurated regularly scheduled passenger service between Utica and Lake Placid on October 9, 1979, using Conrail track between Utica and Remsen.

Despite extensive and expensive track rehabilitation, derailments were frequent. The state shut the railroad down after its seventh derailment, on August 6, 1980. Service was resumed between Tupper Lake Jct. and Lake Placid the next month, but the state revoked the operating contract in February 1981. The rolling stock and other equipment were sold at auction in April 1982.

Location of headquarters: Old Forge, New York
Miles of railroad operated: 118
Number of locomotives: 4
Number of passenger cars: 21
Predecessor railroads in this book:
New York Central
Penn Central

TRAINS: J. David Ingles

An Alco RS3 leads an Adirondack Railway passenger train through the woods on the way to Lake Placid. The diesel was purchased from Canada's Roberval & Saguenay Railroad, the coaches are ex-Pennsylvania P70s, and the diner came from Chesapeake & Ohio.

AKRON, CANTON & YOUNGSTOWN RAILWAY

The Akron, Canton & Youngstown was incorporated in 1907 and completed a line from Mogadore to Akron, Ohio, 8 miles, in 1913. In 1920 the AC&Y obtained control of the Northern Ohio Railway from the Lake Erie & Western. The Northern Ohio had a 161-mile route from Akron west to Delphos, Ohio. AC&Y also purchased outright a 9-mile portion of the Northern Ohio from Akron to Copley Junction. Akron was noted for the manufacture of tires, and over the years tires and inner tubes moving from Akron to Detroit via the Detroit, Toledo & Ironton interchange at Columbus Grove constituted a significant part of AC&Y's freight traffic.

On January 14, 1944, the AC&Y and the Northern Ohio were consolidated as the Akron, Canton & Youngstown Railroad. In 1947 AC&Y considered extending its line east to Youngstown for access to the steel industry there and also to serve as a route around the congestion of Cleveland, but nothing came of it.

In 1949 AC&Y's president proposed a 130-mile Ohio River-to-Lake Erie two-way conveyor belt. AC&Y was, understandably, the only railroad to support the proposal or to advocate passage of bills by the Ohio legislature granting right of eminent domain to the conveyor belt company.

Norfolk & Western purchased the AC&Y in 1964 at the time it merged with the Nickel Plate and leased the Wabash. N&W dissolved the AC&Y on January 1, 1982.

Location of headquarters: Akron, Ohio
Miles of railroad operated: 1929 — 171; 1964 — 171
Number of locomotives: 1929 — 25; 1964 — 18
Number of passenger cars: 1929 — 5
Number of freight cars: 1929 — 223
Number of company service cars: 1929 — 28
Number of freight and company service cars: 1964 — 1,687
Reporting marks: ACY
Subsidiaries and affiliated railroads, 1964:
Akron & Barberton Belt (25%)
Successors: Norfolk & Western (TWG)
Portions still operated: Mogadore-Sycamore: Norfolk & Western

Two Akron, Canton & Youngstown hood units, both products of Fairbanks-Morse, assemble a train at Carey, Ohio, about 1963.

Roger Meade

ALABAMA, TENNESSEE & NORTHERN RAILROAD

The Carrollton Short Line Railway was chartered in 1897. By 1906, when its name was changed to Alabama, Tennessee & Northern Railroad, it had built a line from Reform, Ala., through Carrollton to Aliceville and was pushing slowly down the western edge of Alabama toward the Gulf of Mexico. The company underwent foreclosure and reorganization in 1918, and by 1920 the road reached south to Calvert, Ala., where the Southern Railway offered a connection to Mobile.

In 1928 AT&N completed its own line from Calvert to Mobile and that same year entered into an agreement with the Saint Louis-San Francisco Railway (which had just built a line from Aberdeen, Mississippi, to Pensacola, Florida, making a connection with the AT&N at Aliceville) for joint handling of through traffic between the Port of Mobile and points on the Frisco.

AT&N's finances were again reorganized in October 1944. On December 28, 1948, Frisco purchased 97.2 percent of AT&N's common stock (later increasing its holdings to 100 percent) and unified AT&N's operations with its own. The Alabama, Tennessee & Northern was merged with the Frisco on January 1, 1971. Frisco itself became part of Burlington Northern on September 21, 1980.

Location of headquarters: Mobile, Alabama
Miles of railroad operated: 1929 — 224; 1970 — 214
Number of locomotives: 1929 — 19; 1970 — 1
Number of passenger cars: 1929 — 14
Number of freight cars: 1929 — 419; 1970 — 1
Number of company service cars: 1929 — 8; 1970 — 17
Reporting marks: AT&N
Historical and technical society: Frisco Modelers Information Group, 2541 West Allen Drive, Springfield, MO 65807
Successors:
St. Louis-San Francisco
Burlington Northern (TWG)
Portions still operated: Mobile-Aliceville, Ala.: Burlington Northern

Grady W. Robarts Jr.: Collection of Louis A. Marre

Burdened by the enormous volume of wartime traffic moving through the Port of Mobile, AT&N obtained War Production Board clearance for diesel purchases. Eleven Alco RS1s like No. 102 and two small GE switchers allowed the road to completely dieselize by 1946, one of the first roads its size to do so.

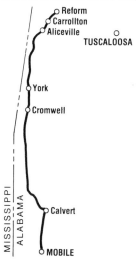

16

ALTON RAILROAD

The Alton & Sangamon Railroad was chartered in 1847 to build a railroad connecting the agricultural area centered on Springfield, Illinois, with Alton, on the east bank of the Mississippi River 20 miles north of St. Louis. The railroad opened in 1851. During the ensuing decade it was extended north through Bloomington to Joliet and was renamed the St. Louis, Alton & Chicago Railroad. The Chicago & Alton Railroad was organized in 1861 to purchase the StLA&C.

In 1864 the Chicago & Alton leased the Joliet & Chicago Railroad to gain access to Chicago. Timothy B. Blackstone, president of the Joliet & Chicago, became president of the C&A. In 1870 the C&A leased the Louisiana & Missouri River Railroad (Louisiana, Mo., to the north bank of the Missouri River opposite Jefferson City) and in 1878 it leased the Kansas City, St. Louis & Chicago Railroad (Mexico, Mo.-Kansas City), creating the shortest Chicago-Kansas City route. (The Santa Fe line, 32 miles shorter, was not opened until 1888.)

By the end of the nineteenth century the road had attracted the notice of Gould, Rockefeller, and Harriman, each of whom could find a place in his rail empire for the C&A. Harriman formed a syndicate of railroad financiers who were able to meet Blackstone's terms (basically $175 per $100 share of common stock and $200 per share for preferred; Blackstone controlled one-third of the stock), and in 1899 the syndicate purchased 95 percent of the stock. The Chicago & Alton then issued bonds, which the stockholders bought cheap and resold dear to the public, and the railroad used the proceeds of the bond sale to issue a 30 percent cash dividend on its stock.

The Chicago & Alton Railway was incorporated April 2, 1900, to take over a line from Springfield to Peoria; the following day it leased the Chicago & Alton Railroad. The two companies were consolidated as the Chicago & Alton Railroad in 1906. In 1904 control passed to the Union Pacific and the Rock Island, and in 1907 to the Toledo, St. Louis & Western (the Clover Leaf, later part of the Nickel Plate). In 1912 the Chicago & Alton began a string of deficit years that continued almost unbroken to 1941. It lost much of the coal traffic it had carried to Chicago, and the cattle trade from Kansas City disappeared (Blackstone had been one of the developers of the Chicago Union Stockyards). In 1922 the Chicago & Alton entered receivership.

The Baltimore & Ohio purchased the road at a foreclosure sale in 1929. B&O incorporated the Alton Railroad on January 7, 1931, and on July 18 of that year the Alton purchased the property of the Chicago & Alton Railroad. For 12 years the Alton was operated as part of the B&O, but on March 10, 1943, B&O restored its independence (Alton had filed for reorganization on November 25, 1942). Several midwestern railroads considered purchasing the Alton but declined; Gulf, Mobile & Ohio offered merger. In 1945 GM&O paid B&O approximately $1.2 million for all its claims against the Alton and all its Alton stock. The effective date of the merger was May 31, 1947.

Location of headquarters: Chicago, Illinois
Miles of railroad operated: 1929 — 1,028; 1945 — 959
Number of locomotives: 1929 — 292; 1945 — 193
Number of passenger cars: 1929 — 232; 1945 — 112
Number of freight cars: 1929 — 13,066; 1945 — 5,362

Continued on next page

Number of company service cars: 1929 — 571; 1945 — 391
Reporting marks: C&A
Notable named passenger trains: *Alton Limited, Abraham Lincoln, Ann Rutledge* (Chicago-St. Louis)
Historical and technical society: Gulf, Mobile & Ohio Historical Society, P. O. Box 24, Bedford Park, IL 60499
Recommended reading:
The Gulf, Mobile and Ohio, by James Hutton Lemly, published in 1953 by Richard D. Irwin, Inc., Homewood, IL 60430

GM&O North, by Robert P. Olmsted, published in 1976 by Robert P. Olmsted
Successors:
Gulf, Mobile & Ohio
Illinois Central Gulf (TWG)
Portions still operated: Chicago-East St. Louis; Springfield-Kansas City; Jacksonville-Murrayville, Ill.; Roodhouse-Godfrey, Ill.; Mexico-Fulton, Mo.: Illinois Central Gulf

Alton's motive-power policy was doubtless influenced by that of its parent, Baltimore & Ohio, one of the first railroads to use diesels in passenger service. Alton's E7s, built in early 1945, were among the very first of that model. Two are shown here soon after they arrived on the property bringing the southbound *Ann Rutledge* across the tracks of the Peoria & Eastern (nearer the camera) and the Nickel Plate into Bloomington, Illinois.

Henry J. McCord

ANN ARBOR RAILROAD

The history of the Ann Arbor began with two companies organized in 1869 and 1872 to build a railroad between Toledo, Ohio, and Ann Arbor, Michigan, about 45 miles. The Panic of 1873 killed one of those two companies; it took another 20 years and 12 companies, most of them named Toledo, Ann Arbor & something, for the railroad to reach the eastern shore of Lake Michigan at Frankfort, Mich. (The Toledo-Frankfort line was the road's sole route until the late 1960s, when it acquired its only branch, a 4-mile New York Central remnant from Pittsfield to Saline, Mich.) From Elberta, across a small inlet from Frankfort, the Ann Arbor operated car ferry lines to Kewaunee and Manitowoc, Wisconsin, and Menominee and Manistique, Mich. The Ann Arbor Railroad was incorporated in 1895 as a reorganization of the Toledo, Ann Arbor & North Michigan Railroad.

The Detroit, Toledo & Ironton obtained control of the Ann Arbor in 1905 but sold its interests in 1910. In 1911 the Ann Arbor purchased all the capital stock of the Manistique & Lake Superior Railroad, which extended north from Manistique, Mich., to connections with the Duluth, South Shore & Atlantic and the Lake Superior & Ishpeming.

In 1925 the Wabash, which was controlled by Pennsylvania Railroad interests, acquired control of the Ann Arbor. By 1930 it held more than 97 percent of Ann Arbor's stock. Ann Arbor was in receivership from December 4, 1931, to January 1, 1943, but did not reorganize.

Never a major passenger carrier, Ann Arbor discontinued its last passenger train in 1950 and gave its full attention to freight service, which was largely made up of through freight using the Lake Michigan ferries to bypass Chicago and take advantage of lower rates. The road was completely dieselized by 1951.

In 1963 Wabash sold the Ann Arbor to the Detroit, Toledo & Ironton (which was owned by the Wabash and the Pennsy). The Manistique & Lake Superior and the connecting 100-mile car ferry route were abandoned in 1968. In 1970 the ICC authorized abandonment of the ferry route between Frankfort and Menominee (80 miles) and the facilities at Menominee.

On October 16, 1973, Ann Arbor declared bankruptcy. Ann Arbor ceased operation as a railroad on April 1, 1976. Conrail took over operation that day. The state of Michigan then purchased the railroad from the DT&I and arranged for its operation by Michigan Interstate Railway. The remaining car ferry lines from Frankfort to Manitowoc (79 miles) and Kewaunee (60 miles) ceased operation in April 1982. In 1983 because of disputes over terms and payments, the operation was split among three railroads: Michigan Interstate, Tuscola & Saginaw Bay, and Michigan Northern. In 1984 T&SB took over Michigan Northern's portion of the Ann Arbor.

Continued on next page

Location of headquarters: Toledo, Ohio
Miles of railroad operated: 1929 — 294; 1972 — 300
Miles of car ferry route: 1929 — 319; 1972 — 139
Number of locomotives: 1929 — 50; 1972 — 15
Number of passenger cars: 1929 — 25
Number of freight cars: 1929 — 2,082
Number of company service cars: 1929 — 97
Number of freight and company service cars: 1972 — 454
Number of car ferries: 1929 — 6; 1972 — 3
Reporting marks: AA

Historical and technical society: Ann Arbor Railroad Technical & Historical Association, P. O. Box 51, Chesaning, MI 48616
Successors:
Michigan Interstate (TWG)
Michigan Northern
Tuscola & Saginaw Bay (TWG)
Portions still operated:
Toledo-Ann Arbor; Pittsfield-Saline, Mich.: Michigan Interstate
Ann Arbor-Frankfort: Tuscola & Saginaw Bay

Behind a pair of Alco FA2s painted like those of parent Wabash, a local freight works north out of Ann Arbor bound for Owosso, the road's operating headquarters, in 1952.

Robert A. Hadley

20

ATLANTA & WEST POINT RAIL ROAD
WESTERN RAILWAY OF ALABAMA
GEORGIA RAILROAD

R. D. Sharpless

Atlanta & West Point 427, a light Mikado of USRA design, leads a north-bound freight between semaphore signals between Newnan and Palmetto, Ga., in March 1949.

The Atlanta & West Point and the Western Railway of Alabama were together known as the West Point Route. They were affiliated with the Georgia Railroad, which was not a corporation but rather the representative of the Louisville & Nashville and the Atlantic Coast Line as lessees of the railroad properties of the Georgia Railroad & Banking Co. The Georgia Railroad & Banking Co. held substantial interests in the two West Point Route railroads. (Ownership and control of these three railroads was particularly convoluted; for most purposes it is sufficient to say they were in the Atlantic Coast Line family.) The West Point Route and the Georgia shared officers and *Official Guide* pages and were for most purposes considered a single entity.

The Georgia Railroad was chartered in 1833 and amended its name to include "& Banking Company" in 1836. Its charter specified exemption from state and local taxation except for a small tax on net earnings. Construction was begun at Augusta, Ga., in 1835, and chief engineer J. Edgar Thomson completed the 171-mile 5-foot-gauge main line to Atlanta in 1845. (Two years later Thomson became chief engineer of the Pennsylvania Railroad.) In 1878 the Georgia Railroad absorbed the Macon & Augusta, which formed a branch from Camak to Macon.

The Georgia Railroad acquired stock in the Atlanta & West Point and in 1875 purchased the Western of Alabama jointly with the Central Rail-road & Banking Co. of Georgia. In May 1881 William Wadley leased the Georgia Railroad and its holdings in the West Point Route. He assigned the lease jointly to the Louisville & Nashville and the Central of Georgia. CofG's interest later passed to the L&N, which assigned it to Atlantic Coast Line.

Atlanta & West Point: The Atlanta & La Grange Rail Road was chartered in 1847. In 1854 it opened a 5-foot-gauge line from East Point, Ga., 6 miles from Atlanta, through La Grange to West Point, Ga., on the Alabama state line. It obtained trackage rights into Atlanta on the Macon & Western. In 1857 the road was renamed Atlanta & West Point.

Early in its existence the road contracted with the Georgia Railroad to maintain its rolling stock at Georgia's Atlanta shops. When the latter road concentrated its facilities at Augusta, A&WP took over Georgia's shops for a few years before arranging with the Western Railway of Alabama for maintenance. In 1889 the A&WP constructed its own line from East Point to Atlanta, and in 1909 made an agreement with Central of Georgia, successor to the Macon & Western, to operate Atlanta & West

Point's and Central of Georgia's East Point-Atlanta lines as paired track.

Western Railway of Alabama: The Montgomery Rail Road was organized in 1834 to build from Montgomery, Ala., east to West Point, Ga. It built 32 miles of standard gauge track (rather than 5-foot gauge, which was almost universal in the South) before running into financial problems. It was taken over in 1843 by the Montgomery & West Point Rail Road. The remainder of the 88-mile route between Montgomery and West Point was constructed by slave labor and opened in 1851. A branch from Opelika to Columbus, Ga., was opened in 1854. During the Civil War the track gauge kept the road's rolling stock at home. An attack by Union forces in 1864 did not put the road out of business, but another in 1865 a few days after Lee's surrender destroyed enough equipment to shut down the railroad. Reconstruction began, and the road converted to 5-foot gauge in 1866. In 1870 the company was taken over by the Western Rail Road of Alabama.

The Western of Alabama had opened a line from Montgomery west to Selma, 44 miles, and acquisition of the line to West Point more than tripled its size. Financial troubles continued, and in 1875 the road was sold under foreclosure jointly to the Georgia Railroad & Banking Co. and the Central Railroad & Banking Co. of Georgia.

In 1881 the WofA came under control of the Central Railroad and Banking Co. when William Wadley leased the Georgia Railroad and its interests in the A&WP and WofA. That same year the Opelika-Columbus branch was leased to the Columbus & Western; it later became part of the Central of Georgia. In 1883 the Western Rail Road of Alabama was reorganized as the Western Railway of Alabama to untangle the various leases. During the 1890s the Central of Georgia (Central Railroad & Banking Co.) interests in the Wadley lease passed to the Louisville & Nashville, which assigned them to Atlantic Coast Line, but CofG retained ownership of some WofA stock until 1944.

The roads were standard-gauged in 1886, as were most railroads in the South. By the turn of the century they were firmly in the Atlantic Coast Line-Louisville & Nashville family, serving a rich agricultural area and working as a bridge route. For many years Southern Railway's premier train, the New York-New Orleans *Crescent Limited*, was operated between Atlanta and New Orleans not on Southern's own rails but over those of the West Point Route between Atlanta and Montgomery and Louisville & Nashville between Montgomery and New Orleans. Georgia Railroad's passenger service was more plebian, but its mixed trains lasted until 1983, when newly formed Seaboard System bought the Georgia Railroad from the bank and merged it. The West Point Route corporate shells remain in existence. Little if any of the trackage of these three railroads has been abandoned.

Location of headquarters: Atlanta, Georgia

Atlanta & West Point

Miles of railroad operated: 1929 — 91; 1981 — 91
Number of locomotives: 1929 — 24; 1981 — 11
Number of passenger cars: 1929 — 26; 1970 — 4
Number of freight cars: 1929 — 581; 1981 — 400

Number of company service cars: 1929 — 46; 1981 — 19
Reporting marks: A&WP, AWP
Western Railway of Alabama
  Miles of railroad operated: 1929 — 133; 1981 — 133
  Number of locomotives: 1929 — 29; 1981 — 14
  Number of passenger cars: 1929 — 21; 1970 — 11
  Number of freight cars: 1929 — 852; 1981 — 298
  Number of company service cars: 1929 — 44; 1981 — 13
  Reporting marks: WofA, WA
Georgia Railroad
  Miles of railroad operated: 1929 — 329; 1981 — 329
  Number of locomotives: 1929 — 68; 1981 — 31
  Number of passenger cars: 1929 — 72; 1970 — 2
  Number of freight cars: 1929 — 1,512; 1981 — 810
  Number of company service cars: 1929 — 70; 1981 — 57
  Reporting marks: GA
Notable named passenger trains: *Crescent Limited* (New York-New Orleans, operated north of Atlanta by Southern and Pennsylvania and south of Montgomery by Louisville & Nashville)
Recommended reading: *Steam Locomotives and History: Georgia Railroad and West Point Route*, by Richard E. Prince, published in 1962 by Richard E. Prince
Successors: Seaboard System (TWG)

Victor Hand

Georgia Railroad train 1 rolls west through Robinson, Ga., on its run between Augusta and Atlanta, two days after Christmas, 1965. Mail, baggage, and express revenue obviously will outstrip passenger receipts today.

ATLANTA, BIRMINGHAM & COAST RAILROAD

The Waycross Air Line Railroad was incorporated as a logging railroad in 1887. By the end of 1904 it had become the Atlantic & Birmingham Railway, a common carrier with a line from Brunswick to Montezuma, Georgia, and branches to Thomasville and Waycross, Ga. At Montezuma the Central of Georgia offered connections to Macon, Atlanta, and Birmingham.

In 1906 the newly created Atlanta, Birmingham & Atlantic Railroad absorbed the Atlantic & Birmingham. The new road built westward to Manchester, Ga., and from there to Atlanta and to Birmingham, reaching both cities in 1908 (until 1910, when it completed its own line into Birmingham, AB&A used Louisville & Nashville rails for the last few miles). By then the AB&A was in receivership, largely because of the cost of the marine terminal it had built at Brunswick.

The Atlanta, Birmingham & Atlantic Railway took over the operation at the beginning of 1916, but it fared little better financially. It was in receivership by 1921. The Atlanta, Birmingham & Coast Railroad was incorporated November 22, 1926, to acquire the properties of the Atlanta, Birmingham & Atlantic Railway; the Atlantic Coast Line was firmly in control of the AB&C. AB&C offered ACL entries to Atlanta and Birmingham, connections with ACL affiliates Louisville & Nashville and Nashville, Chattanooga & St. Louis, and a chance to participate more fully in Midwest-to-Florida traffic. ACL merged the AB&C on December 31, 1945.

Location of headquarters: Atlanta, Georgia

Miles of railroad operated: 1929 — 640; 1945 — 639
Number of locomotives: 1929 — 30; 1945 — 59
Number of passenger cars: 1929 — 51; 1945 — 39
Number of freight cars: 1929 — 1,948; 1945 — 908
Number of company service cars: 1929 — 128; 1945 — 129
Reporting marks: AB&C
Recommended reading: *Atlantic Coast Line Railroad Steam Locomotives, Ships, and History*, by Richard E. Prince, published in 1966 by Richard E. Prince
Successors:
Atlantic Coast Line
Seaboard Coast Line
Seaboard System (TWG)
Portions still operated: Birmingham-Manchester, Ga.; Atlanta-Waycross; Sessoms-Alma, Ga.; Moultrie-Thomasville, Ga.: Seaboard System
Map: See page 22

In 1936 AB&C began hosting Chicago-Florida passenger trains, and the streamlined *Dixie Flagler* inaugurated in 1940 called for a streamlined engine to match. AB&C's Fitzgerald shops shrouded a former Florida East Coast 4-6-2 for the every-third-day train. On other days No. 79 was available for duties such as train 1, an all-day Atlanta-Waycross mixed train.

David W. Salter

ATLANTIC & DANVILLE RAILWAY

The Atlantic & Danville Railway was chartered in 1882. Its line from Portsmouth to Danville, Virginia, was completed and opened in 1890. Short branches from main line led to West Norfolk, Hitchcock Mills, and Buffalo Lithia Springs, Va., and a 50-mile narrow gauge line ran from Emporia, junction with the Atlantic Coast Line, northeast to Claremont, on the James River.

In 1899 the Southern Railway leased the Atlantic & Danville for 50 years. The A&D provided a good connection from Southern's Washington-Atlanta main line at Danville to the port area of Norfolk and Portsmouth. The narrow gauge branch was abandoned in 1934, and the Hitchcock Mills and Buffalo Lithia Springs branches were taken up in the early 1940s, but the main line and the West Norfolk branch remained intact. When the lease expired in 1949, Southern weighed the cost of operating the A&D and the limitations of its track, mostly 60- and 85-pound rail, against the cost of trackage rights over Atlantic Coast Line from Selma, North Carolina, to Norfolk. Southern did not renew the lease.

Atlantic & Danville resumed operation on its own August 1, 1949. A&D filed for bankruptcy on January 19, 1960, after the ICC turned down its request to guarantee a loan for capital expenditures and the purchase of freight cars.

On October 31, 1962, the railroad was purchased at auction by the Norfolk & Western, which organized the Norfolk, Franklin & Danville Railway, a wholly owned subsidiary, to operate the line. The merger of Norfolk & Western and Southern rendered the Norfolk-Danville route redundant. The western third of the NF&D has been abandoned, and the remainder was absorbed by N&W on December 30, 1983.

Location of headquarters: Norfolk, Virginia
Miles of railroad operated: 1949 — 203; 1961 — 203
Number of locomotives: 1949 — 8; 1961 — 7
Number of freight cars: 1949 — 139; 1961 — 271
Number of company service cars: 1949 — 8; 1961 — 8
Reporting marks: AD
Successors:
Norfolk, Franklin & Danville
Norfolk & Western (TWG)
Portions still operated: Norfolk-South Hill, Va.; West Norfolk-Suffolk: Norfolk & Western

Continued on next page

Atlantic & Danville scheduled a single daily freight train in each direction. Here the two trains, both powered by Alco RS2s, meet at Franklin, Va.

Mallory Hope Ferrell

ATLANTIC & EAST CAROLINA RAILWAY

The Atlantic & North Carolina Railroad was organized at New Bern, North Carolina, in 1854. It was to be the eastern portion of a state-owned system of three railroads that would cross North Carolina from west to east, tapping the commerce and agriculture of the state for the port of Morehead City — trade that the rivers of the area were taking to Norfolk, Virginia, and Charleston, South Carolina. Morehead City never became the rival of New York, Baltimore, and Norfolk that its boosters predicted, and the three railroads continued as separate entities. The North Carolina Railroad and the Western North Carolina Railroad both wound up in the Southern Railway family, and in 1904 the Atlantic & North Carolina was leased to the Norfolk & Southern.

The lease was forfeited in 1934 for nonpayment of rent and the A&NC began operating on its own in November 1935. On April 20, 1939, the stockholders voted to lease the road to H. P. Edwards, who organized the Atlantic & East Carolina Railway to operate the railroad. Within two years the A&EC was making a profit. The road dieselized in 1946 with two Electro-Motive F2s, an SW1, and a General Electric 44-ton switcher.

In February 1957 the Interstate Commerce Commission authorized the Southern Railway to purchase all the capital stock of the A&EC. By January 1958 the A&EC was listed under the Southern Railway in *The Official Guide*, and it still exists as a subsidiary of the Southern. The Atlantic & North Carolina also still exists; 70 percent of its stock is held by the state of North Carolina.

The Beaufort & Morehead Railroad, an independent short line at one

The newness of Electro-Motive F2 No. 401 contrasts with the antiquity of the wooden cars as the daily train crosses the Trent River at New Bern, N. C.

time in the Norfolk Southern fold, was (and is) essentially a 3-mile extension of the A&EC from Morehead City to Beaufort.

Location of headquarters: New Bern, North Carolina
Miles of railroad operated: 1939 — 96; 1956 — 96
Number of locomotives: 1939 — 11; 1956 — 7
Number of passenger cars: 1939 — 10; 1956 — 9
Number of freight cars: 1939 — 41; 1956 — 128
Number of company service cars: 1939 — 5; 1956 — 7
Reporting marks: AEC
Predecessor railroads in this book: Norfolk Southern
Successors: Southern Railway (TWG)
Map: See page 25

ATLANTIC & YADKIN RAILWAY

The Cape Fear & Yadkin Valley Railway was an 1879 reorganization of the Western Railroad of North Carolina, which was opened in 1860 from Fayetteville to Cumnock, 6 miles north of Sanford. By 1890 the CF&YV had a line from Wilmington through Fayetteville, Sanford, and Greensboro to Mount Airy and another from Fayetteville southwest to Bennettsville, South Carolina. The road entered receivership in 1894.

In 1899 it was sold at foreclosure and split between the Atlantic Coast Line, which acquired the Wilmington-Sanford and Fayetteville-Bennettsville lines, and the Southern Railway, which organized the Atlantic & Yadkin Railway to take over the remainder from Sanford to Mount Airy. It was operated by the Southern Railway, which controlled it, until July 1, 1916, when it assumed its own operation. The Southern merged the company and resumed operation of the road on January 1, 1950.

Location of headquarters: Greensboro, North Carolina
Miles of railroad operated: 1929 — 163; 1949 — 152
Number of locomotives: 1929 — 24; 1949 — 13
Number of passenger cars: 1929 — 6

Number of freight cars: 1929 — 10; 1949 — 11
Number of company service cars: 1929 — 10; 1949 — 7
Successor companies: Southern Railway (TWG)
Portions still operated: Sanford-Greensboro, Walnut Cove-Mount Airy: Southern
Map: See page 25

Richard E. Prince Jr.

Atlantic & Yadkin Ten-wheeler No. 113, shown at Sanford in 1936, was acquired from Richmond, Fredericksburg & Potomac in 1929.

ATLANTIC COAST LINE RAILROAD

The history of the Atlantic Coast Line begins in 1830 with the organization of the Petersburg Railroad, which opened in 1833 between its namesake city in Virginia and the north bank of the Roanoke River opposite Weldon, North Carolina. The Richmond & Petersburg Railroad was organized in 1836 and formed a connection with the Petersburg road in 1838, after an initial period during which the two roads interchanged freight and passengers with riverboats but not with each other.

In 1840 the Wilmington & Raleigh was opened from Wilmington, N. C., north 161 miles to Weldon. Its initial destination had been Raleigh, but the citizens of the state capital were not interested in the project. It was renamed Wilmington & Weldon in 1855. The Wilmington & Manchester, from Wilmington west into South Carolina, was opened in 1853. Connecting with it at Florence, S. C., was the North Eastern, whose line to Charleston, S. C., opened in 1857.

After the Civil War William T. Walters of Baltimore gradually acquired control of the Wilmington & Weldon, Wilmington & Manchester, North Eastern, Petersburg, and Richmond & Petersburg railroads, forming a route known as the Atlantic Coast Line — an association of more or less independent railroads. In 1889 Walters formed a holding company to control them; it was renamed the Atlantic Coast Line Company in 1893.

The railroads acquired a number of smaller lines, and one major piece of construction was the Fayetteville Cutoff between Wilson, N. C., and Pee Dee, S. C., built by the Wilmington & Weldon between 1885 and 1892. Sixty-two miles shorter than the line through Wilmington, it became the main route of the railroad.

The Richmond & Petersburg merged the Petersburg in March 1898 and in November of that year was renamed the Atlantic Coast Line Railroad of Virginia. In April 1900 it merged the Norfolk & Carolina (Norfolk, Va.-Tarboro, N. C.), the Wilmington & Weldon, the Southeastern (an 11-mile line from Elrod, to Ashpole, N. C.), and the ACL of South Carolina and was renamed simply the Atlantic Coast Line Railroad. The new railroad stretched from Richmond and Norfolk, Va., to Charleston, S. C., and Augusta, Georgia.

After the turn of the century Atlantic Coast Line grew quickly into a large system of railroads, some leased, some controlled, some wholly owned. With the acquisition in 1902 of the Plant System (the Savannah, Florida & Western Railway and its leased lines and subsidiaries, plus steamship lines and hotels), ACL expanded south from Charleston, S. C., into Georgia and Florida. Henry B. Plant had been superintendent of Adams Express at the beginning of the Civil War. In 1861 he organized Southern Express, which much later became a component of Railway Express Agency. In 1879 Plant acquired the Atlantic & Gulf Railroad, whose main line ran from Savannah to Bainbridge, Ga. He reorganized it as the Savannah, Florida & Western and constructed several lines: west from a point a few miles east of Bainbridge to Chattahoochee, Fla., to connect with a Louisville & Nashville predecessor; southeast from Waycross, Ga., to Jacksonville, Fla.; and south from Live Oak, Fla., to Gainesville. In 1893 the Plant System absorbed the South Florida (Sanford-Port Tampa) and in 1899, the Jacksonville, Tampa & Key West (Jacksonville-Sanford). Among the other components of the Plant System were the Charleston & Savannah, the Brunswick & Western (Brunswick through Waycross to Albany, Ga.), and the Alabama Midland (Bainbridge to Montgomery, Alabama). All three were merged with the Savannah, Florida & Western in 1901. That same year a cutoff was constructed from Jesup to Folkston, Ga., bypassing Waycross.

Continued on next page

August A. Thieme Jr.

Typical of Atlantic Coast Line is the pair of Pacifics, considered passenger power on most other roads, on a southbound freight leaving Richmond, Va., in March 1947.

Also in 1902 ACL acquired control of the Louisville & Nashville, which in turn controlled the Nashville, Chattanooga & St. Louis. Later ACL and L&N jointly leased the Carolina, Clinchfield & Ohio and formed the Clinchfield Railroad to operate it. ACL and L&N also leased the railroad property of the Georgia Railroad & Banking Company (closely affiliated with the Atlanta & West Point and the Western Railway of Alabama) and formed the Georgia Railroad to operate it. In 1926 ACL acquired control of the newly reorganized Atlanta, Birmingham & Coast, which gave it lines from Waycross to Atlanta and Birmingham, where it connected

with L&N. ACL merged the Atlanta, Birmingham & Coast in 1945.

Another member of ACL's family was the Charleston & Western Carolina (Port Royal, S. C., through Augusta, Ga., to Anderson, Greenville, and Spartanburg, S. C., connecting with the Clinchfield at Spartanburg). The first portion of the road, between Augusta and the coast, was financed by the Georgia Railroad & Banking Co. However, the Central Railroad & Banking Co. (Central of Georgia) gained control in 1881 not so much to stop the flow of traffic from Georgia to Port Royal as to tap inland South Carolina for the port of Savannah. Central of Georgia lost the road in 1894; ACL gained control in 1897. By 1930 the C&WC shared officers with parent ACL; an attempt to merge the C&WC in 1930 was protested by neighboring roads. Although the C&WC was operated independently, its appearance was Atlantic Coast Line — secondhand ACL steam locomotives, including Pacifics for freight service, and silver and purple diesels. ACL finally merged the Charleston & Western Carolina in 1959. Connecting with the C&WC at Laurens, S. C., was another road controlled by ACL, the Columbia, Newberry & Laurens Railroad, a 75-mile line joining the three cities of its name.

Atlantic Coast Line was considered one of the three strong roads of the South (the other two were the Louisville & Nashville and the Southern). It carried the majority of Florida-bound passengers, turning Miami passengers over to Florida East Coast at Jacksonville but carrying west coast passengers all the way — to Tampa, St. Petersburg, Sarasota, Fort Myers, and Naples. ACL also participated in most of the Midwest-to-Florida passenger train routes. The opening of the Perry Cutoff in 1928 between Thomasville, Ga., and Dunellon, Fla., shortened considerably the route between the Midwest and west coast points.

Atlantic Coast Line advertised itself as the Standard Railroad of the South, and its route between Richmond and Jacksonville was fully signalled and mostly double track, much more than parallel Seaboard Air Line could boast. As with the Pennsylvania, which advertised itself as the standard railroad of the world, there were some nonstandard items. Two are notable. ACL was one of few railroads to consider the Pacific a dual-purpose engine, but the profile of its main line was such that a 4-6-2 could move freight at good speed. The other was the color choice for its diesels — purple (president Champion McDowell Davis liked purple).

30

ACL's first streamliner was the New York-Miami *Champion*, inaugurated in 1939 in conjunction with the Pennsylvania, the Florida East Coast, and the Richmond, Fredericksburg & Potomac railroads. In 1946 the train was joined by the *West Coast Champion* to Tampa and St. Petersburg. The postwar equipment is shown here on a publicity run for the press.

ACL

The 4-6-2s yielded to Es for passengers and Fs for freight, and purple on the diesels eventually gave way to black.

In 1958 Atlantic Coast Line and Seaboard Air Line announced they were considering merger, and in 1960 they petitioned to merge as the Seaboard Coast Line Railroad. The two roads served much the same territory, and they had 75 common points. The principal argument for merger was the elimination of duplicate lines and facilities. The merger was approved and took effect on July 1, 1967.

Location of headquarters: Wilmington, North Carolina until 1961; then Jacksonville, Florida

Miles of railroad operated: 1929 — 5,155; 1966 — 5,743

Number of locomotives: 1929 — 1,007; 1966 — 629

Number of passenger cars: 1929 — 786; 1966 — 361

Number of freight cars: 1929 — 32,644; 1966 — 31,284

Number of company service cars: 1929 — 1,852; 1966 — 1,116

Reporting marks: ACL

Notable named passenger trains: *Florida Special* and *Champion*

(New York-Miami; operated north of Richmond by Pennsylvania and Richmond, Fredericksburg & Potomac, and south of Jacksonville by Florida East Coast), *West Coast Champion* (New York-Tampa, Jacksonville-St. Petersburg)

Historical and technical society: Southeastern Railroad Technical Society, 1552 Highcrest Drive, Valrico, FL 33594

Recommended reading: *Atlantic Coast Line Railroad Steam Locomotives, Ships, and History*, by Richard E. Prince, published in 1966 by Richard E. Prince

Subsidiaries and affiliated railroads, 1965:

Clinchfield (50%, jointly with Louisville & Nashville)

Columbia, Newberry & Laurens

Louisville & Nashville

Georgia Railroad

Atlanta & West Point

Western Railway of Alabama

Winston-Salem Southbound (50%, jointly with Norfolk & Western)

Continued on next page

Richmond-Washington Co. — which owns controlling interest in Richmond, Fredericksburg & Potomac (16.7%)
Predecessor railroads in this book: Atlanta, Birmingham & Coast
Successors:
Seaboard Coast Line
Seaboard System (TWG)
Portions still operated: Most of the ACL is still operated by Seaboard

System. A list of all lines that have been trimmed would be cumbersome; the major routes that have been cut at one point or another are: Suffolk, Va.-Tarboro, N. C.; Wilmington-Fayetteville-Sanford, N. C.; Wilmington, N. C.-Pee Dee, S. C.; Bennettsville-Sumter, S. C.; Wadesboro, N. C.-Florence, S. C.; McCormick-Anderson, S. C. (ex-C&WC); Brunswick-Sessoms, Ga. (ex-AB&C); Fitzgerald-Moultrie, Ga. (ex-AB&C); Jacksonville-St. Petersburg, Fla.

auto-train

AUTO-TRAIN CORPORATION

Auto-Train Corporation was incorporated on April 11, 1969, by Eugene Kerik Garfield. Its purpose was to establish an automobile-carrying train service between the cities of the Northeast and Florida. Inspiration for the project had come from a Department of Transportation report — such services have been common in Europe for years. The route chosen for the service was from Lorton, Virginia, just south of Washington, to Sanford, Florida, using Richmond, Fredericksburg & Potomac as far south as Richmond and then Seaboard Coast Line's ex-Atlantic Coast Line route. The concept was aimed at the vacationer who wanted a car in Florida but didn't want to drive it there. The northern terminal was chosen because clearances in and north of Washington would restrict the ex-Canadian National auto carriers the corporation had purchased and also because Washington is no more than a day's drive from most of the densely populated Northeast. Sanford was convenient to Walt Disney World and the Kennedy Space Center, two of the biggest tourist attractions in Florida.

To carry the passengers, Auto-Train purchased dome cars from Santa Fe, Union Pacific, and Western Pacific and converted them to deluxe coach seating; the domes were soon augmented by refurbished sleeping cars for passengers who would rather sleep in a bed for the overnight trip. At the head of the train were General Electric U36Bs. The diesels and the cars alike were painted white with brilliant red and purple striping.

Service began on December 6, 1971, with a daily train in each direction. The service was well patronized from the beginning, and trains of more than 30 cars were usual. The trains made no intermediate stops other than for engine crew changes and for servicing at Florence, South Carolina.

In May 1974 Auto-Train expanded to include a route between Louisville, Kentucky, and Sanford via Nashville, Montgomery, and Waycross. The company mentioned other expansion plans, including Chicago-Denver and San Diego-Seattle plus service in Mexico. The Louisville service was not as successful as the original train, partly because of longer running time and partly because of the longer drive needed to reach the line's northern terminal from its major market, Chicago (and perhaps because Kentucky is perceived as part of "The South" and it can't be that much farther to drive the rest of the way). From October 31, 1976, to September 4, 1977, the Louisville Auto-Train and Amtrak's Chicago-Florida *Floridian* were combined between Louisville and Sanford, permitting daily service on that route. Daily service wasn't a sufficient attraction for passengers, and Auto-Train discontinued service to Louisville on September 4, 1977. (The *Floridian* was discontinued October 1, 1979.)

In addition to the losses from the Louisville service, at the same time Auto-Train encountered financial trouble. Derailments destroyed two locomotives and a large number of the auto carriers, reducing the capacity of the trains, and insurance costs rose. Discount airline fares eroded traffic, and the company fell into arrears on lease and operating payments, employee withholding taxes, and customer refunds. Auto-Train filed for bankruptcy on September 7, 1980.

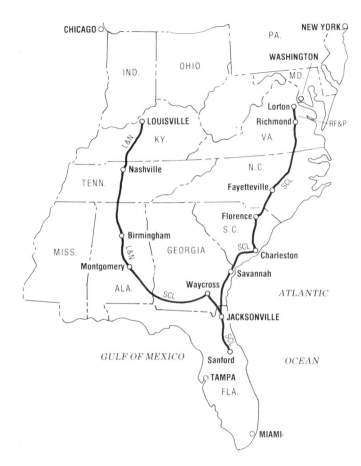

Auto-Train is only a few miles from the end of its northbound journey as it crosses Occoquan Creek at Woodbridge, Va. Behind the trio of white, purple, and red U36Bs is a long string of enclosed auto carriers.

April 30, 1981 — exactly 10 years after the last passenger trains of so many railroads departed on the eve of Amtrak — marked the last departure of Auto-Train. The rolling stock was sold at auction in December 1981. On October 30, 1983, Amtrak began triweekly Auto Train service between Lorton and Sanford.

Location of headquarters: Washington, D. C.

Miles of railroad operated: 1971 — 856; 1981 — 856

Number of locomotives: 1974 — 15; 1980 — 15

Number of passenger cars: 1974 — 88; 1980 — 93

Number of auto carriers: 1974 — 69; 1980 — 110

Number of company service cars (heater, caboose, etc.): 1974 — 9; 1980 — 16

BALTIMORE & ANNAPOLIS RAILROAD

The first train of the Annapolis & Baltimore Short Line ran on May 9, 1887, between the two Maryland cities of its name. In 1907 Maryland Electric Railways took over the railroad and electrified it using a 6600-volt AC system; in 1914 it was converted to 1200 volts DC. In 1921 the Washington, Baltimore & Annapolis acquired control of the line — WB&A had a line between Baltimore and Washington with a branch from Fort Meade to Annapolis.

After World War One ridership dropped as the state improved the highways. The combined system was sold at foreclosure in 1935. The AB&SL bondholders bought the Annapolis-Baltimore route and organized the Baltimore & Annapolis Railroad to operate it. Baltimore & Ohio electrified a short stretch of its track with overhead wire to allow B&A trains to use the upper level of Camden Station, B&O's principal Baltimore station (Camden's lower level had been electrified in 1895 as part of B&O's Howard Street Tunnel project). B&O also lent money for repair of bridges along the line, in return for a percentage of B&A's revenue.

World War Two brought an upsurge of traffic, but ridership declined

Car 97 rolls across the Severn River trestle on the last lap of its trip from Baltimore to Annapolis in June 1948.

William D. Middleton

again after the war. In November 1949 the road petitioned to discontinue rail passenger service: The entire physical plant of the road needed renewal, and there was no money for it. The last passenger train left Baltimore on February 5, 1950. In December 1961 the road briefly operated an experimental passenger service using Budd Company's RDC demonstrator, No. 2960.

The B&A ceased operating freight service in 1972 because of flood damage, but in 1976 it resumed operation between Clifford Jct., where it connects with Baltimore & Ohio, and Glen Burnie. B&A ceased operating scheduled bus service in 1975 (it began in 1941) but continues to operate charter bus service, which far overshadows its rail freight business.

Location of headquarters: Baltimore, Maryland
Miles of railroad operated: 1935 — 32; 1984 — 6
Number of locomotives: 1984 — 1
Number of passenger cars: 1949 — 22
Reporting marks: BLA
Portions still operated: Baltimore-Glen Burnie: Baltimore & Annapolis

BALTIMORE & OHIO RAILROAD

The Baltimore & Ohio was not the first railroad in the U. S., but it was the first common carrier railroad, the first to offer scheduled freight and passenger service to the public. The most important U. S. seaports in the early 1800s were Boston, New York, Philadelphia, Baltimore, and Charleston. Baltimore had an advantage in being farther inland than the others, located almost at the head of navigation on Chesapeake Bay, which is the estuary of the Susquehanna River. New York gained an advantage in 1825 with the opening of the Erie Canal, permitting navigation all the way to Lake Erie, and in 1826 the commonwealth of Pennsylvania chartered a system of canals to link Philadelphia with Pittsburgh. Baltimore responded to the competition of the other cities by chartering the Baltimore & Ohio Railroad on February 28, 1827. The B&O was to build a railroad from Baltimore to a suitable point on the Ohio River.

Continued on next page

Such a project would be challenging today — and we know where the Ohio River is, we know something about the intervening territory, and we know what a railroad is. Today's equivalent of the chartering of the B&O might be the establishment of a company to operate scheduled freight and passenger service to the moon. Baltimore's only alternative, though, was to build a canal, and the only route for that was south to Washington and up the Potomac, where the Chesapeake & Ohio canal was already under construction. Such a canal, too, would lead quickly to the Alleghenies, and mountains and canals are mutually exclusive.

R. H. Kindig

B&O's assault on the Alleghenies required far more massive locomotives than rivals Pennsylvania and New York Central. Number 7170, a 2-8-8-0, shown here climbing Newburg Grade near Austen, W. Va., in July 1949 with a 54-car coal train, has help from two similar Mallets pushing at the rear.

Ground was broken for the railroad with great celebration on July 4, 1828. The first stone was laid by 90-year-old Charles Carroll of Carrollton, Maryland, the last surviving signer of the Declaration of Independence. A route was laid out to follow the Patapsco and Monocacy rivers to the Potomac, and work began. The line was opened for scheduled service to Ellicott's Mills on May 24, 1830. On December 1, 1831, the road was opened to Frederick, 60 miles. The B&O opened a branch from Relay (then called Washington Jct.) to Washington in August 1835. Two years later a bridge was completed across the Potomac to Harpers Ferry, West Virginia. (The separation of the western portion of Virginia did not occur until 1863, but for clarity I'll use present state names.) At Harpers Ferry the B&O connected with the Winchester & Potomac, thus forming the first junction of two railroad companies in the U. S. The line continued west through Cumberland, Md., to Grafton, W. Va., where it turned northwest to reach the goal of its charter at Wheeling, W. Va., 379 miles from Baltimore, on January 1, 1853, almost 25 years after commencing construction. Another line was pushed west from Grafton to reach the Ohio at Parkersburg, W. Va., in 1856.

The railroad continued westward in 1866 by leasing the Central Ohio, a line from Bellaire, Ohio, across the Ohio River from Wheeling, through Newark to Columbus, and in 1869 by leasing a line from Newark to Sandusky, Ohio. From a point on that line called Chicago Jct. (now Willard) a subsidiary company, the Baltimore & Ohio & Chicago, built west to Chicago between 1872 and 1874.

Under the leadership of John W. Garrett the B&O expanded in several directions at once. In 1871 the Pittsburgh & Connellsville Railroad completed a Cumberland-Pittsburgh line and leased it to the B&O the following year. The Metropolitan Branch, from Washington to a connection with the main line at Point of Rocks, Md., was opened in 1873. The line into Pittsburgh put B&O into Pennsylvania Railroad territory, and even in 1871 the Pennsy was something of a bully. Washington-New York passenger service in the 1870s was operated jointly by the B&O between Washington and Baltimore, the Philadelphia, Wilmington & Baltimore between Baltimore and Philadelphia, and the Pennsylvania between Philadelphia and Jersey City. In 1872 the Pennsylvania built a line of its own from Baltimore to Washington. B&O rerouted its trains off the Pennsylvania to the Reading-Central Railroad of New Jersey route between Philadelphia and Jersey and proposed to construct terminal facilities of its own on Staten Island. Both B&O and Pennsy wanted control of the Philadelphia, Wilmington & Baltimore — Pennsy managed to get it in 1881. B&O set out to build its own line from Baltimore to Philadelphia, parallel to the PB&W and no more than a few miles from it. Pennsy responded in 1884 by refusing to handle B&O trains east of Baltimore. B&O opened its new line to Philadelphia in 1886.

Garrett died in 1884 and was succeeded by his son Robert for two years, Samuel Spencer for one, and then Charles F. Mayer. Mayer undertook to improve the road and at the same time keep its financial situation from crumbling. The most significant improvements were control of the Pittsburgh & Western (Pittsburgh-Akron), construction of a line from Akron, Ohio, to Chicago Jct.; control of a route from Parkersburg, W. Va., through Cincinnati to St. Louis (the Baltimore & Ohio Southwestern, which included the former Ohio & Mississippi, completed in 1857); construction of a line through, around, and under Baltimore to connect the Philadelphia route with the rest of the B&O; and electrification of the Baltimore Belt, the first mainline electrification in North America.

The financial situation was more difficult. The B&O had a large debt. Freight and passenger rates were low and revenues were dropping — in 1889 B&O handled 31 percent of the country's tidewater soft coal traffic; in 1896, that had dropped to just 4 percent because of competition from other roads. The B&O cut back on expenditures for maintenance and quickly acquired a reputation for unreliability. The Panic of 1893 was well under way, and business was in bad shape nationwide. B&O entered receivership in 1896.

Baltimore & Ohio came out of receivership in 1899 still under its original charter, which included tax exemption privileges. In 1901 the Pennsylvania managed to buy a large block of B&O stock and appoint Leonor F. Loree president of the road. Loree undertook a line improvement program that reduced grades and curves and added many miles of double track, and he secured for B&O a large interest in the Reading, which in turn controlled the Central Railroad of New Jersey. The Pennsylvania sold some of its B&O stock to Union Pacific in 1906 and traded the remainder to UP for Southern Pacific stock in 1913. UP eventually distrib-

James P. Gallagher

Baltimore & Ohio's early construction was characterized by heavy stone viaducts, most impressive of which was (and is) the Thomas Viaduct at Relay, Md. A trio of Electro-Motive EAs and EBs, the first streamlined passenger diesels that were separate from the train, leads a typical heavyweight and partly streamlined B&O passenger train across the viaduct in 1952.

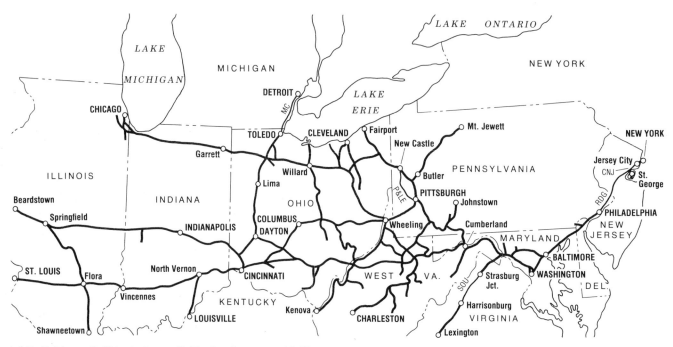

uted its Baltimore & Ohio stock as a dividend to its own stockholders.

Daniel Willard became president of the B&O in 1910. More than anyone else he is responsible for the road's conservative, courteous personality in the mid-twentieth century. Further expansion included the purchase in 1910 of the Chicago Terminal Transfer Railroad, a belt line that was renamed the Baltimore & Ohio Chicago Terminal; the acquisition in 1917 of the Coal & Coke Railway from Elkins to Charleston, W. Va.; and acquisition that same year of portions of the Cincinnati, Hamilton &

Dayton and its leased lines to form a route from Cincinnati to Toledo.

In 1927 B&O celebrated its centennial with the Fair of the Iron Horse, a pageant and exhibition at Halethorpe, Md. Much of the rolling stock exhibited there was from B&O's museum collection, which formed the nucleus of the B&O Museum in Baltimore, one of the earliest and best railroad museums.

The ICC merger plan of the 1920s put B&O into an expansionist mood. In 1926 B&O purchased the Cincinnati, Indianapolis & Western's line

DANIEL WILLARD (1861-1942) was born in North Hartland, Vermont. He was educated in the local schools, taught school in his hometown, and attended Massachusetts Agricultural College for a year before going to work for the Central Vermont as a track laborer in 1879. He soon hired on as a fireman with the Connecticut & Passumpsic Rivers Railroad, later becoming an engineer. In 1883 and 1884 he was a locomotive engineer

for the Lake Shore & Michigan Southern at Elkart, Indiana, and from 1884 to 1898 he rose from brakeman to superintendent of the Soo Line, where he met F. D. Underwood, general manager of the Soo. Willard followed Underwood to the Baltimore & Ohio in 1899 and became assistant general manager; in 1901 he went to the Erie as Underwood's assistant. From 1904 to 1910 Willard was second vice-president in charge of operation and maintenance of the Burlington. He returned to the B&O in 1910 to become its president.

Willard served as president or chairman of numerous railroad industry boards and committees, among them the American Railway Association, Eastern Railroads' President's Committee, Railroad War Board, and the War Industries Board.

In 1931 Willard, then 70 years old, offered his resignation; the board of directors of the B&O continued to elect him president. He resigned as president on June 1, 1941, and was elected chairman of the board. He died on July 6, 1942, and was buried in the cemetery of the Federated Church, Hartland, Vt., between the graves of his two sons.

Willard was best known for his liberal position on labor relations, a blend of innovation and conservatism in the passenger business (B&O was one of the first railroads to adopt air conditioning and diesel power, but rejected lightweight cars), and the Fair of the Iron Horse at Baltimore in 1927 (a celebration of B&O's centennial). He had an industrywide reputation for fairness, honesty, and sincerity.

Recommended reading: *Daniel Willard Rides the Line*, by Edward Hungerford, published in 1938 by G. P. Putnam's Sons, New York

---

from Hamilton, Ohio, to Springfield, Illinois. In 1927 it acquired an 18 percent interest in the Wheeling & Lake Erie and began to purchase Western Maryland stock. In 1929 B&O bought the Chicago & Alton, reorganized it as the Alton Railroad, and operated it as part of the B&O. (Alton regained independence in 1943 and merged with Gulf, Mobile & Ohio in 1947.) In 1932 B&O acquired the Buffalo, Rochester & Pittsburgh from the Van Sweringens in exchange for its interest in the W&LE and also purchased the Buffalo & Susquehanna. In 1934 B&O arranged for trackage rights on Pittsburgh & Lake Erie's water-level route between McKeesport and New Castle, Pa., bypassing the curves and grades of its own route (which remained in service for local business). B&O's through passenger trains moved to P&LE's Pittsburgh station across the Monongahela River from the B&O station.

For many years B&O competed with Pennsylvania and New York Central in the New York-Chicago and New York-St. Louis passenger markets and with Pennsy on the New York-Washington run. B&O's trains were slower, partly because of their longer route through Washington, but they were dieselized a decade before the competition. Many preferred B&O's New York-Washington trains to Pennsy's, but the most frequently stated reason for preferring B&O — "You could always get a seat" — was the reason B&O dropped its passenger service east of Baltimore in 1958.

In 1960 Chesapeake & Ohio began to acquire B&O stock. New York

Central made a bid, but B&O's stockholders approved C&O control, and on May 1, 1962, so did the ICC. By early 1964 C&O owned 90 percent of B&O's stock. In 1967 the ICC authorized C&O and B&O to control Western Maryland; B&O's WM stock had long been held in a nonvoting trust. On June 15, 1973, B&O, C&O, and WM were made subsidiaries of the newly created Chessie System. There has been no great surge of track abandonment, because in most areas B&O and C&O were complementary rather than competitive. In 1981 B&O leased the former Rock Island track from Blue Island to Henry, Ill.

Technically, then, B&O still exists: Locomotives and freight cars are marked with its initials if not with the full name, and the road maintains some identity within Chessie System.

Location of headquarters: Baltimore, Maryland
Miles of railroad operated: 1929 — 5,658; 1972 — 5,491
Number of locomotives: 1929 — 2,364; 1972 — 995
Number of passenger cars: 1929 — 1,732; 1972 — 23
Number of freight cars: 1929 — 102,072
Number of company service cars: 1929 — 3,092
Number of freight and company service cars: 1972 — 56,305
Reporting marks: BO
Notable named passenger trains: *Capitol Limited* (New York-Chicago), *National Limited* (New York-St. Louis), *Royal Blue* (New York-Washington), *Cincinnatian* (Baltimore-Cincinnati, later Detroit-Cincinnati)

Historical and technical societies:
Baltimore & Ohio Railroad Historical Society, P. O. Box 13578, Baltimore, MD 21203
Affiliation for Baltimore & Ohio System Historical Research, 536 Clairbrook Avenue, Columbus, OH 43228
Recommended reading: *Impossible Challenge*, by Herbert H. Harwood Jr., published in 1979 by Barnard, Roberts & Co., 6655 Amberton Drive, Baltimore, MD 21227
Subsidiaries and affiliated railroads, 1972:
Baltimore & Ohio Chicago Terminal (100%)
Staten Island Rapid Transit Railway (100%)
Reading Company (38.3%)
Western Maryland (43.3%)
Washington Terminal (50%, jointly with Pennsylvania)
Richmond-Washington Co. (16.7%)
Monongahela (33.3%)
Predecessor railroads in this book:
Buffalo & Susquehanna
Buffalo, Rochester & Pittsburgh
Successors: Chessie System (TWG)

BAMBERGER ELECTRIC RAILROAD

In 1891 Simon Bamberger began construction of the Great Salt Lake & Hot Springs Railway to serve the farming area between Salt Lake City and Ogden, Utah. It was to be a local railroad parallel to the Union Pacific and the Denver & Rio Grande Western, both of which were more concerned with through business. The new railroad's initial destination was Beck's Hot Springs, four miles north of Salt Lake City. On March 17, 1896, the road was reorganized as the Salt Lake & Ogden Railway, with plans to build north to Ogden and then southeast into Weber Canyon to a coal mining area. The SL&O reached Ogden in 1908 but abandoned the idea of continuing to the coal mines, already served by the UP.

The SL&O was electrified in 1910 and penetrated farther into its terminal cities on public streets — the two principal characteristics of an interurban. At Ogden SL&O made arrangements to use the Utah-Idaho Central terminal, and at Salt Lake City the road teamed up with the Salt Lake & Utah to acquire property on Temple Square for a temporary terminal (which was replaced by a monumental structure in 1923).

In 1917 the Salt Lake & Ogden took as its official name the nickname the public had given it — Bamberger Electric Railroad. It was one of very few railroads to carry the name of its founder. In 1924 the Bamberger began to interchange freight with UP and soon afterwards with the other steam railroads in the area. In 1927 it organized a subsidiary bus company. The road was in receivership from 1933 to 1939, emerging without "Electric" in its name.

Business surged during World War Two. The Ogden Ordnance Depot requested special train service at the same time the Office of Defense Transportation ordered the bus subsidiary to cease operation so its buses could be used elsewhere. The Bamberger scrabbled around for used cars and electrical equipment and purchased a diesel locomotive, an Alco RS1.

After the war rail passenger traffic drifted to the highways — to Bamberger's buses, back in business, and to automobiles. Bamberger's neighbor to the south, the Salt Lake & Utah, was abandoned in 1946, and the Utah-Idaho Central, its northern connection, was abandoned in 1947. The Bamberger gradually shifted its emphasis to buses. It built a new rail and bus station in Ogden and sold the Salt Lake City terminal to Greyhound, which remodeled it to serve long-distance bus travelers, keeping two tracks for Bamberger's remaining trains.

A shop fire in March 1952 destroyed much of the equipment used to maintain the passenger cars, and a substation fire three months later aggravated the situation. Bamberger's last electric operations, passenger and freight, took place on September 6, 1952, and less than a year later Bamberger sold its bus line, becoming a diesel-operated, freight-only

In this September 1950 scene at Ogden, Bullet car 128, purchased in 1939 from the Fonda, Johnstown & Gloversville, is about to leave as an extra train to Salt Lake City. In the background two of Bamberger's original electric cars, much rebuilt, show off the striping arrangement for both ends of Bamberger's orange and cream livery.

Fred H. Matthews Jr.

short line. Abandonment was authorized by the ICC on November 25, 1958, and took effect at the end of the year. A 4-mile portion of the main line in Salt Lake City was sold to the Denver & Rio Grande Western, and approximately 8 miles of the main line at the north end were sold to Union Pacific to maintain service to Hill Air Force Base. Union Pacific also acquired locomotive 570, the RS1 that had been repowered by EMD in 1952.

Location of headquarters: Salt Lake City, Utah
Miles of railroad operated: 1929 — 36; 1958 — 37
Number of locomotives: 1929 — 4; 1958 — 2
Number of motor cars: 1929 — 18
Number of other cars: 1929 — 75
Number of freight cars: 1958 — 15
Number of company service cars: 1958 — 4
Reporting marks: B
Recommended reading: *Interurbans of Utah*, by Ira L. Swett, published in 1954 by Interurbans, P. O. Box 6444, Glendale, CA 91205
Portions still operated:
Ogden: Union Pacific
Salt Lake City: Denver & Rio Grande Western

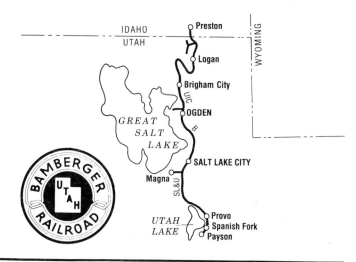

BUFFALO & SUSQUEHANNA RAILROAD

In 1885 Frank Goodyear, a fuel and lumber dealer in Buffalo, New York, bought a large tract of timberland in northwestern Pennsylvania. He organized the Sinnemahoning Valley Railroad to build a line from Keating Summit (on what later became the Pennsylvania Railroad line to Buffalo) to Austin, Pa., where he had a sawmill. Goodyear formed a partnership with his brother Charles in 1887 and began to expand their empire. By 1893 his railroad system reached east to Galeton and Ansonia, and the various railroad companies were consolidated as the Buffalo & Susquehanna Railroad. At the beginning of 1896 it extended northwest from Galeton to Wellsville, N. Y., and in 1898 the Goodyears purchased the Addison & Pennsylvania, a former narrow gauge line from Galeton to Addison, N. Y. The Goodyears pushed their railroad southwest through Du Bois to Sagamore, with the thought of continuing to Pittsburgh. Coal became the mainstay of the south end of the railroad, and lumber and leather (many tanneries were located on the line) were the principal commodities carried at the north end. The Goodyear lumber and railroad empire prospered, and by the early 1900s it included lumber mills in the South and the New Orleans Great Northern Railroad.

In 1906 the Goodyears built the Buffalo & Susquehanna Railway from

Wellsville to Buffalo, nearly 90 miles. A year later Frank Goodyear died; his brother Charles died in 1911, and the Goodyear empire began to fall apart. The expense of constructing the line to Buffalo began to cause financial difficulty, and the road laid aside plans to extend its line to Pittsburgh and to relocate its line to eliminate the four switchbacks over the mountains between Galeton and Wharton. The Buffalo & Susquehanna Railway leased the Buffalo & Susquehanna Railroad, but that didn't forestall receivership. After a brief period of operation as the Wellsville & Buffalo, the Buffalo extension was scrapped in 1916. The remainder of the system was reorganized as the Buffalo & Susquehanna Railroad Corporation.

In 1932 the Baltimore & Ohio purchased the B&S with the thought of using the Du Bois-Sinnemahoning portion as part of a new freight line across Pennsylvania. In July 1942 a flood washed out much of the line south of Galeton. B&O abandoned the line between Sinnemahoning and Burrows, just south of Galeton, isolating the Wellsville-Galeton-Addison portion from the rest of the B&O. Because of declining traffic and the problems of isolation, B&O considered selling or abandoning the northern part of the B&S. To simplify sale, in 1954 B&O merged the B&S and two smaller roads that it had leased since the turn of the century. On January 1, 1956, B&O sold the northern portion of the former Buffalo & Susquehanna to Murray M. Salzberg, who organized the Wellsville, Addison & Galeton Railroad to operate it.

The WA&G was abandoned in stages, with the last piece going in 1979. The last portion of the south end of the B&S, B&O's branch from Du Bois to Weedville, disappeared from B&O's map in the 1970s. None of Buffalo & Susquehanna's lines remains in service.

Location of headquarters: Wellsville, New York
Miles of railroad operated: 1929 — 254; 1931 — 254
Number of locomotives: 1929 — 47; 1931 — 46
Number of passenger cars: 1929 — 12; 1931 — 12
Number of freight and company service cars: 1929 — 2,833; 1931 — 1,482
Reporting marks: B&S
Historical and technical societies:
Baltimore & Ohio Railroad Historical Society, P. O. Box 13578, Baltimore, MD 21203
Affiliation for Baltimore & Ohio System Historical Research, 536 Clairbrook Avenue, Columbus, OH 43228
Recommended reading: *The History of the Buffalo & Susquehanna*, by Paul Pietrak, published by Paul Pietrak, North Boston, NY 14110
Successors:
Baltimore & Ohio
Wellsville, Addison & Galeton
Map: See next page

Mike Runey

When Baltimore & Ohio took over Buffalo & Susquehanna, B&S's Atlantics remained at the head of the passenger trains, though with new B&O numbers. Number 1485 is on the daily trip from Galeton to Addison and a connection with the Erie.

BUFFALO, ROCHESTER & PITTSBURGH RAILWAY

Rochester, New York, in 1869 had a well-developed flour-milling industry. The Genesee River furnished power to drive the mills; wheat came from the fertile Genesee Valley south of Rochester in boats on the Genesee Valley Canal. To provide better grain transportation and, more important, to bring coal from Pennsylvania, the Rochester & State Line Railroad was incorporated in 1869 to build up the valley of Genesee to the Pennsylvania state line — the destination was later changed to the town of Salamanca, N. Y. The railroad was completed in 1878. Most of its stock was owned by William H. Vanderbilt, of the New York Central system. However, Vanderbilt lost interest in the railroad about the time it began having financial difficulties, and he sold his stock to a New York syndicate.

The road was reorganized as the Rochester & Pittsburgh Railroad in 1881. It extended its line south to Punxsutawney, Pa., and contracted with the Pennsylvania Railroad for access to Pittsburgh. At the same time the Buffalo, Rochester & Pittsburgh Railroad was organized to build a branch to Buffalo, and several other roads were chartered.

In 1884 the R&P was sold to Adrian Iselin, a New York financier also connected with the Mobile & Ohio. After some corporate manipulations he consolidated the railroads as the Buffalo, Rochester & Pittsburgh Railway in 1887. The BR&P built branches into the coalfields of western Pennsylvania and constructed a line north from Rochester to the shore of Lake Ontario to connect with a car ferry to Cobourg, Ont. In 1893 a branch was opened to Clearfield, Pa., where it connected with the New York Central and, via the NYC, the westernmost part of the Reading. In 1898 the Allegheny & Western Railroad was incorporated to extend the BR&P from Punxsutawney west to Butler, Pa., and a connection with the Pittsburgh & Western (Baltimore & Ohio). Trackage rights from Butler to New Castle and Pittsburgh were included in the arrangement with the

B&O. The new line was opened in 1899, and BR&P finally linked the cities of its name.

BR&P developed into a well-run coal hauler. After the ICC merger plan of the 1920s was published, both Delaware & Hudson and Baltimore & Ohio petitioned for control of BR&P; the ICC approved B&O's application in 1930. Meanwhile the BR&P was sold to the Van Sweringen brothers (who owned the Nickel Plate and controlled the Chesapeake & Ohio) in 1928. B&O still wanted the BR&P, and the Van Sweringens wanted the Wheeling & Lake Erie, in which B&O held a minority interest. They

The year is 1945 and 2-6-6-2 7533 lugging 105 cars through Lewis Run, Pa., a few miles south of Bradford, carries Baltimore & Ohio identification, but the rails and the locomotive are both former Buffalo, Rochester & Pittsburgh property.

Gordon R. Roth

traded, and on January 1, 1932, Baltimore & Ohio acquired the BR&P.

Baltimore & Ohio was chiefly interested in assembling a shortcut with favorable grades for Chicago-New York freight (a railroad equivalent of Interstate 80) that would use BR&P from Butler to Du Bois, Buffalo & Susquehanna to Sinnemahoning and a new line connecting with the Reading, which B&O controlled, west of Williamsport. The Great Depression was not the time to do such things, though, and the project was shelved.

The Rochester branch was sold to the Genesee & Wyoming Railroad in 1985. Other than that, and except for a few branches that have been pruned back, the lines of the BR&P of 1930 are still intact and are operated by the Chessie System. The BR&P still exists as a corporation.

Location of headquarters: Rochester, New York
Miles of railroad operated: 1929 — 602; 1931 — 601
Number of locomotives: 1929 — 272; 1931 — 262
Number of passenger cars: 1929 — 96; 1931 — 94
Number of freight cars: 1929 — 11,152
Number of company service cars: 1929 — 359
Number of freight and company service cars: 1931 — 10,356
Reporting marks: BR&P
Historical and technical societies:
Baltimore & Ohio Railroad Historical Society, P. O. Box 13578, Baltimore, MD 21203
Affiliation for Baltimore & Ohio System Historical Research, 536 Clairbrook Avenue, Columbus, OH 43228
Recommended reading: *The Buffalo, Rochester & Pittsburgh Railway*, by Paul Pietrak, published in 1979 by Paul Pietrak, North Boston, NY 14110
Successors:
Baltimore & Ohio
Chessie System (TWG)

BURLINGTON-ROCK ISLAND RAILROAD

The Trinity & Brazos Valley Railway was chartered by the state of Texas on October 17, 1902, for 50 years. By the beginning of 1904 it had a line open between Cleburne and Mexia, Texas. In 1905 the Colorado & Southern purchased control of the T&BV; in 1906 C&S sold a half interest in the road to the Rock Island. The T&BV filled out its map in 1907: Mexia to Houston; trackage rights over Gulf, Colorado & Santa Fe from Houston to Galveston and from Cleburne north to Fort Worth; Teague to Waxahachie; trackage rights from Waxahachie to Fort Worth on Houston & Texas Central (Southern Pacific); and trackage rights from Waxahachie to Dallas on the Missouri-Kansas-Texas. The T&BV purchased a quarter interest in the Houston Belt & Terminal Railway, and T&BV's parents, C&S and Rock Island, jointly built the Galveston Terminal Railway. The T&BV constituted a Fort Worth-Houston-Galveston extension of the Burlington system and the Rock Island.

Texas in those days was not today's booming petrochemical complex.

Business did not meet expectations, and the T&BV entered receivership in 1914. During the receivership it lost its Santa Fe and Katy trackage rights; only the Fort Worth-Houston line via Waxahachie survived.

The Trinity & Brazos Valley emerged from receivership in July 1930 with a new name: Burlington-Rock Island Railroad (Chicago, Burlington & Quincy had gained control of the Colorado & Southern in 1908). It reestablished trackage rights from Waxahachie to Dallas over the Katy and from Cleburne to Fort Worth on the Santa Fe and acquired rights to Galveston over the Texas & New Orleans (Southern Pacific). In 1931 the Rock Island and the Fort Worth & Denver City (C&S) jointly leased the Dallas-Teague segment of the railroad and began operating it in alternate 5-year periods. In 1932 B-RI abandoned its line from Hillsboro to Cleburne and then dropped Santa Fe trackage rights to Fort Worth; by 1942 the branch, the original T&BV line, was cut back to Mexia. On June 1, 1950, B-RI ceased operation and its two parents made a new joint lease of the entire line with alternate 5-year operating periods. The Fort Worth & Denver and the Rock Island purchased the property of the B-RI in April

The *Sam Houston Zephyr* glides into Teague, Texas, in 1940. The trainset, No. 9901, one of the original *Twin Zephyrs*, is on lease from parent Chicago, Burlington & Quincy.

1964, and the corporation was dissolved in April 1965. Upon the demise of the Rock Island in 1980, the Burlington Northern assumed sole operation.

Location of headquarters: Houston, Texas
Miles of railroad operated: 1929 — 367; 1949 — 228
Number of locomotives: 1929 — 37
Number of passenger cars: 1929 — 20; 1949 — 3
Number of freight cars: 1929 — 721
Number of company service cars: 1929 — 186; 1949 — 36

Continued on next page

Reporting marks: BRI
Notable named passenger trains: *Sam Houston Zephyr, Texas Rocket* (Fort Worth-Dallas-Houston)
Historical and technical societies:
Burlington Route Historical Society, P. O. Box 456, LaGrange, IL 60525
Rock Island Technical Society, 8746 N. Troost, Kansas City, MO 64155
Recommended reading: *The Colorado Road*, by F. Hol Wagner Jr.,

published in 1970 by Intermountain Chapter, National Railway Historical Society, P. O. Box 5181, Denver, CO 80217
Successors:
Burlington Northern (TWG)
Chicago, Rock Island & Pacific
Fort Worth & Denver
Portions still operated: Dallas-Galveston: Burlington Northern

BUTTE, ANACONDA & PACIFIC RAILWAY

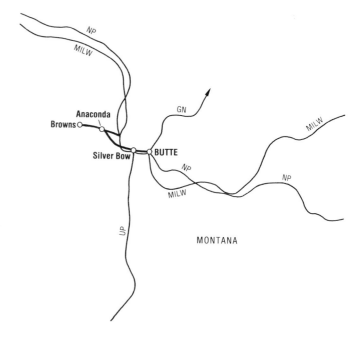

The Butte, Anaconda & Pacific was incorporated in 1892 to connect copper mines at Butte, Montana, with a smelter at Anaconda. The mines, the smelter, and the railroad were all owned by Marcus Daly. The railroad was opened in 1893.

By 1911 the Anaconda Copper Mining Co., Daly's company, had acquired considerable expertise using electric motors to drain and ventilate its mines. The BA&P electrified its line to take advantage of the economies that would result from electric operation of that aspect of the business as well. BA&P was the first road to electrify for purely economic reasons; moreover, the electrification project would demonstrate uses of the copper produced by its parent. The road was the first to use General Electric's 2400-volt DC system; electric locomotives started hauling trains in 1913.

Two electric locomotives were added to the original fleet of 28 in 1957; a few years earlier BA&P had replaced its few remaining steam locomotives with diesels for service on non-electrified track. In 1958 BA&P began operation over the Northern Pacific between Butte and Durant under a joint trackage agreement. Electric operation continued until 1967, when the installation of a new ore concentrator at Butte changed the road's traffic pattern. The seven GP7s and GP9s that had been working the non-electrified trackage took over all of BA&P's operation.

The 1980 closing of Anaconda's smelter in Anaconda again changed the road's traffic pattern — indeed, eliminated most of it — and BA&P's operations changed from daily to "as required." The mines themselves closed in 1983, and the railroad all but ceased operation. In 1984 owner Anaconda Minerals petitioned for abandonment and in March 1985 agreed to sell and donate the railroad properties to the state of Montana for operation by the Rarus Railway Co., a new short line.

Location of headquarters: Anaconda, Montana

Miles of railroad operated: 1929 — 69; 1982 — 43

Number of locomotives: 1929 — 7 steam, 28 electric; 1982 — 9

Number of passenger cars: 1929 — 8

Number of freight cars: 1929 — 1,422

Number of company service cars: 1929 — 22

Number of freight and company service cars: 1982 — 674

Reporting marks: BAP

Recommended reading: "Montana Copper Carrier," a chapter of *When The Steam Railroads Electrified*, by William D. Middleton, published in 1974 by Kalmbach Publishing Co., 1027 North Seventh Street, Milwaukee, WI 53233 (ISBN 0-89024-028-0)

Donald Sims

A trio of Butte, Anaconda & Pacific boxcabs brings a long train of empties along the main line near Silver Bow, west of Butte.

PREDECESSORS OF CANADIAN NATIONAL RAILWAYS

The two principal railroads in Canada today are the government-owned Canadian National Railways and the privately owned Canadian Pacific Railway. A paragraph on Canadian Pacific is a necessary preface to the history of Canadian National — but before that a few sentences on Canadian history are necessary.

The Dominion of Canada was created on July 1, 1867, by the union of the provinces of New Brunswick, Nova Scotia, and Quebec (whose two parts, Upper and Lower Canada, became present-day Ontario and Quebec, respectively). Canada's population was anything but homogeneous: Immigrants came from England, Scotland, Ireland, France, Germany, and the U. S., and they settled along the seacoast, the St. Lawrence River, and the shores of Lake Ontario and Lake Erie. North and west of Toronto lay a thousand miles of rocky forested wilderness, and beyond that were the prairies and the Rockies.

When British Columbia joined the confederation in 1871 (by then it included Manitoba), the Canadian government promised a railway to link British Columbia with the rest of Canada. The Canadian Pacific Railway was incorporated in 1881 to build from Callander, Ont., near North Bay, to the Pacific at what is now Vancouver. The company received extensive land grants and subsidies from the Canadian government in exchange for unifying Canada. CPR completed its main line on November 7, 1885, and then began to spread an extensive network of branches across the wheatlands between Winnipeg and Calgary. It became the dominant railroad on the prairies. In eastern Canada, though, Canadian Pacific was the minority railroad, with little more than a line east through Montreal and across Maine to Saint John, N. B., and another route southwest through Toronto to Windsor, Ont.

Canadian National was not built — it was gathered and assembled. Its five major components were Intercolonial Railway, National Transcontinental Railway, Canadian Northern Railway, Grand Trunk Pacific Railway, and Grand Trunk Railway.

Intercolonial Railway

The maritime provinces had far more communication and commerce with New England than with Quebec and Ontario. The government deemed a rail link necessary to tie the Maritimes to the rest of Canada and was willing to finance it. A commission headed by Sandford Fleming surveyed a route from Moncton, N. B., north to Mont Joli, Que., and then southwest along the south bank of the St. Lawrence to a connection with the Grand Trunk at Riviere du Loup, Que. For military reasons Fleming chose a route as far as possible from the U. S. border.

The Intercolonial began operation between Halifax and Riviere du Loup in 1896, and in 1879 it assumed operation of Grand Trunk's line from Riviere du Loup to just west of Levis, across the St. Lawrence from Quebec City. Canadian Government Railways took over operation of the Intercolonial in 1913.

National Transcontinental Railway

In the first few years of the twentieth century Grand Trunk, prompted by a spirit of expansionism, tried to team up first with Canadian Pacific and then with Canadian Northern. Neither attempt succeeded, so GT proposed a line between Callander, Ont., and Winnipeg well north of the Canadian Pacific line and then continuing west to the Pacific.

The Canadian Pacific was a product of Canada's Conservative Party; the Liberals, who came into power in 1896, decided to make their reputation with another transcontinental railroad. They seized GT's proposal, extended it eastward to Moncton, N. B., and laid out as direct a route as possible to Winnipeg, passing far to the north of Montreal, Ottawa, and Toronto. Except near Quebec City there was neither settlement nor population along the route (there is little more now), and the terrain was largely swamps and bare rock. The major engineering work on the NTR was the St. Lawrence River bridge at Quebec City, which collapsed twice during construction.

The line was to be constructed by Grand Trunk Pacific, a subsidiary of Grand Trunk, on behalf of the government; GTP would lease it from the government upon completion. The rental was to be based on the cost of construction — and that proved to be more than twice the estimate. Grand Trunk Pacific, already in financial trouble because of the cost of its own line west of Winnipeg, refused to take over the National Transcontinental upon its completion. Canadian Government Railways, which was

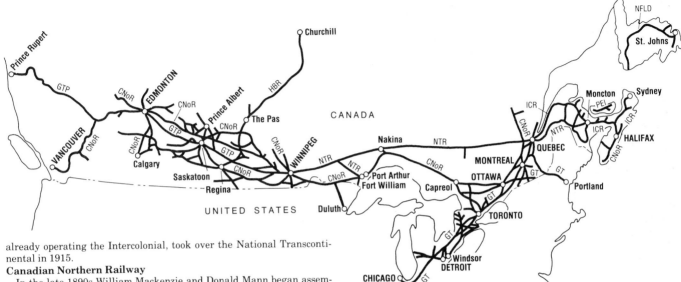

already operating the Intercolonial, took over the National Transcontinental in 1915.

Canadian Northern Railway

In the late 1890s William Mackenzie and Donald Mann began assembling the Canadian Northern system. It included a new line across the prairies from Winnipeg through Edmonton to Vancouver (not completed until 1915), several lines in Manitoba leased from the Northern Pacific, and lines in Ontario, Quebec, and Nova Scotia. By 1916 Canadian Northern had a main line from Toronto to Vancouver via Sudbury, Capreol, and Port Arthur-Fort William (now Thunder Bay), Ont.; Warroad, Minnesota; Winnipeg and Dauphin, Man.; Canora (named for the railroad), Warman, and North Battleford, Saskatchewan; Edmonton and Jasper, Alberta; and the canyons of the Thompson and Fraser rivers. The main line from Toronto to Quebec City ran via Napanee and Ottawa, Ont., and Joliette and Garneau, Que. A Capreol-Ottawa line was completed in 1917, and a line into Montreal via the Mount Royal Tunnel in 1918.

The Canadian Northern system included two orphan lines in Nova Scotia (the Halifax & Southwestern along the south shore, and a line to Inverness on Cape Breton Island); a long tentacle north to Chicoutimi, Que.; an extensive network of branches covering the prairies between Winnipeg and the Rockies; and the Duluth, Winnipeg & Pacific Railway from Fort Frances, Ont., to Duluth, Minn.

Canadian Northern ran out of money. The mother country couldn't help — World War One had stopped the export of capital from Britain. Because of loans and land grants the Canadian government found itself CNoR's major creditor. On September 6, 1917, CNoR management resigned and a new board appointed by the government took over. On December 20, 1917, all government-owned railways were brought under the new CNoR management, to be known as "Canadian National Railways."

Grand Trunk Pacific

The Grand Trunk Pacific Railway was incorporated in 1903 to build from Winnipeg to the Pacific at Prince Rupert, B. C., the Canadian port nearest the Orient. (Prince Rupert never developed into a major seaport. Land transportation rates were higher than those to and from Vancouver, and Prince Rupert's area had no population.) GTP was as deficient in branches as Canadian Northern was prolific, and GTP's Winnipeg-Saskatoon-Edmonton route lay between the Canadian Pacific and the Canadian Northern lines. From Edmonton to Yellowhead Pass, 250 miles, GTP and CNoR were parallel. During WWI the Canadian government ordered GTP to dismantle 200 miles of that portion of the line so the rails could be used in France. GTP was given running rights on CNoR's track, portions of which were later relocated on the GTP roadbed. From Yellowhead Pass GTP's line reached 700 miles northwest to Prince Rupert. The line was completed in 1914. GTP entered receivership in 1919 and came under the Canadian National umbrella in 1920.

Grand Trunk Railway

The Grand Trunk (whose lines included the former Champlain & St. Lawrence, Canada's first railway — 1836) was the last major addition to Canadian National Railways. It was conceived as a Canadian main line from Montreal through Toronto to Sarnia, Ont., where it would connect with a railroad to Chicago and there with a railroad to the Canadian West. At the time it was believed that the terrain north of Lake Superior would force any route to western Canada through Michigan. The project included two lines east from Montreal, one to the year-round port of Portland, Maine, and the other down the St. Lawrence to connect with a line from Halifax.

The Grand Trunk Railway was incorporated in 1852. By 1856 it was in operation between Quebec City (more accurately, Levis, on the south bank of the St. Lawrence River) and Windsor, Ont. In 1859 GT opened the Victoria Bridge across the St. Lawrence at Montreal — at a cost which sent GT to the government for funds.

At the time of confederation in 1867 it was proposed to extend the

HENRY W. THORNTON (1871-1933) was born in Logansport, Indiana. In 1894 he graduated from the University of Pennsylvania and joined the engineering department of the Pennsylvania Railroad. From 1911 to 1914 he was general superintendent of the Long Island Rail Road. His successful management of LI's commuter business led to his appointment in 1914 as general manager of England's Great Eastern Railway, whose commuter traffic out of London's Liverpool Street Station was the world's heaviest. He became a British citizen in 1919 and was knighted that year for his service in England and France during World War One.

On December 1, 1922, he became chairman and president of Canadian National Railways. He united the diverse components of CNR and at the same time created employee pride and public reputation for the railway. A change of government in 1930, the onset of the Great Depression, and even divorce and remarriage seemed to suddenly conspire against him. Hounded by critics, he resigned quietly from his post in July 1932. He died eight months later of cancer.

Grand Trunk west to the Pacific and east to New Brunswick and Nova Scotia at public expense. Public feeling was against the idea because of GT's debt and mismanagement, and GT was not interested because it could see little connection, either figurative or physical, between the existing GT system and the line to Vancouver. GT stuck to its original goal of Chicago, which it reached in 1880 by purchasing several short railroads (and in the process outfoxing William H. Vanderbilt). The Michigan lines were connected to the rest of the system by ferry until the completion of the St. Clair Tunnel in 1890.

In 1882 GT absorbed the Great Western, which had been opened in January 1854 from Niagara Falls through Hamilton to Windsor, Ont. Grand Trunk had acquired Central Vermont stock as part of a traffic agreement in the 1880s; to fend off advances into New England by Canadian Pacific and northward expansion by Boston & Maine, Grand Trunk increased its CV holdings so that by 1900 it owned a majority interest in the road. In 1914 GT purchased the Canada Atlantic Railway, which had a line from Alburgh, Vt., at the north end of Lake Champlain, through Coteau, Ottawa, and Algonquin National Park to the shores of Georgian Bay near Parry Sound.

Grand Trunk incurred an enormous debt for the construction of its subsidiary, Grand Trunk Pacific. Grand Trunk had an opportunity to turn over the GTP to the government, but GT's British board of directors rejected the government proposal. GT badly botched its own defense, and on May 21, 1920, the Canadian government took formal possession of Grand Trunk and Grand Trunk Pacific. Grand Trunk Pacific became part of Canadian National Railways almost immediately; Grand Trunk was absorbed in 1923. At that time GT's U. S. lines became separate companies: Grand Trunk Western (Port Huron and Detroit to Chicago) and Grand Trunk (Island Pond, Vt.-Portland, Me.). Central Vermont had not lost its identity in the Grand Trunk system.

Canadian National

Canadian National Railways was incorporated on June 6, 1919; the name had been in use for six months to conveniently refer to the combined Canadian Northern and Canadian Government railways. CNR also included two minor railways, the Prince Edward Island Railway, which the Canadian government had bailed out when Prince Edward Island

CNR

Grand Trunk Railway 4-6-2 No. 108 leads the first Grand Trunk Pacific train up to the Canadian Pacific station at Saskatoon on October 7, 1918.

joined the Confederation in 1873, and the Hudson Bay Railway, a line constructed to carry grain from the prairies north across the tundra to the ocean port (usable only three months each year) of Churchill, Man. Grand Trunk Pacific was brought into CNR in 1920 and Grand Trunk in 1923. The Newfoundland Railway became part of CNR when Newfoundland joined Canada in 1949.

Recommended reading: *History of the Canadian National Railways*, by G. R. Stevens, published in 1973 by The Macmillan Company, 866 Third Avenue, New York, NY 10022

CENTRAL OF GEORGIA RAILWAY

The opening in 1830 of the South Carolina Railroad between Charleston, S. C., and Augusta, Georgia, diverted traffic from the port of Savannah, Ga., to Charleston. To recapture that business, the citizens of Savannah organized the Central Rail Road & Canal Company in 1833 to build a railroad toward Macon. Lines were surveyed and construction began in

December 1835, about the same time the company's name was changed to Central Rail Road & Banking Company of Georgia. The railroad reached Macon, 191 miles from Savannah, in October 1843. By the Civil War the road had purchased or leased lines to Augusta and through Milledgeville (the state capital until 1867) to Eatonton.

In 1869 the CofG leased the South Western Railroad, which it had earlier helped finance, gaining lines from Macon to Columbus, Fort Gaines,

CENTRAL OF GEORGIA

In the summer of 1947 Central of Georgia inaugurated with great success two coach streamliners. In this July 1947 scene 4 miles out of Atlanta the *Nancy Hanks II* (left) has just begun its evening return to Savannah and the *Man o' War* (right) is nearly at the midpoint of its second daily Columbus-Atlanta round trip.

CofG

extended northwest from Columbus to Birmingham, Ala., and north through Rome to Chattanooga, Tennessee.

In 1888 the 2,600-route-mile CofG came under the control of the Richmond Terminal and was leased to the Georgia Pacific Railway, a subsidiary of the Richmond & Danville (a predecessor of the Southern Railway). In 1892 the CofG entered receivership. It soon lost the Port Royal system mentioned earlier and the Georgia Railroad and its affiliates. Sold at foreclosure and reorganized as the Central of Georgia Railway, the new CofG included several subsidiary companies which had been merged, two leased lines, the South Western and the Augusta & Savannah, and what was called the Auxiliary System — a land company, the steamship line, and several short lines. In 1900 the road opened a line southwest through Dothan and Hartford to Florala, Ala.; spurs of this line reached across the state line into Florida. In 1901 CofG regained its Chattanooga line, which had operated independently since the foreclosure sale, and acquired a branch west from Dover to Brewton, Ga. In 1905 the road widened its Columbus-Greenville, Ga., line from 3 feet to standard gauge and extended it to Newnan, forming a direct Atlanta-Columbus route in conjunction with the Atlanta & West Point.

In 1907 E. H. Harriman gained control of the Central of Georgia. Harriman's system already included Union Pacific, Southern Pacific, and Illinois Central. None of those roads connected with CofG, so Harriman quickly assembled a Jackson, Tenn.-Birmingham line for IC from 129 miles of trackage rights over Mobile & Ohio, Southern, and Frisco and 80 miles of new construction. In 1909 Harriman sold his interest in the CofG to the Illinois Central.

The Depression cut into CofG's traffic, and relocation of textile mills from New England to the South eliminated much of the business in cotton moving through the port of Savannah. The road entered receivership at the end of 1932 and was reorganized in 1948, out from under IC control and minus its holdings in the Georgia Railroad group. In 1951 CofG purchased the Savannah & Atlanta and in 1962 consolidated operations between Savannah and Waynesboro, Ga., with the S&A to allow abandonment of part of each road's line between those points.

The Central of Georgia was a desirable and strategic property. In 1956 the Frisco purchased control, subject to ICC approval — but the ICC dis-

and Albany, Ga., and Eufala, Alabama. In 1872 the road acquired a Savannah-New York steamship line and in 1875 purchased the Western Rail Road of Alabama jointly with the Georgia Railroad. The year 1879 saw the CofG enter Montgomery, Ala., through purchase of a controlling interest in the Montgomery & Eufala. In 1881 the Georgia Railroad and its interests in the Western of Alabama and the Atlanta & West Point were leased to William Wadley, president of the Central of Georgia. Wadley assigned half the lease to the CofG and half to the Louisville & Nashville. At the same time, CofG gained control of the Port Royal & Augusta and began development of a system to reach into western South Carolina. The state of South Carolina forced out the CofG a few years later; the Port Royal system became the Charleston & Western Carolina, a member of the Atlantic Coast Line family. In that same era CofG was

approved and ordered the Frisco to sell its interest in 1961. The ICC approved of Southern Railway's acquisition of CofG, and on June 17, 1963, the Central of Georgia Railway became a subsidiary of the Southern. The Central of Georgia Railroad was incorporated June 1, 1971, and immediately merged the Central of Georgia Railway and three smaller lines: the Georgia & Florida, the Savannah & Atlanta, and the Wrightsville & Tennille. The Central of Georgia Railroad today has little more identity within the Southern Railway System than Southern's other Class 1 subsidiaries, Alabama Great Southern and Cincinnati, New Orleans & Texas Pacific. To the casual observer the CofG exists only as reporting marks on freight cars and initials on locomotives.

Location of headquarters: Savannah, Georgia
Miles of railroad operated: 1929 — 1,944; 1970 — 1,729
Number of locomotives: 1929 — 331; 1970 — 131
Number of passenger cars: 1929 — 262; 1970 — 30
Number of freight cars: 1929 — 9,693
Number of company service cars: 1929 — 477
Number of freight and company service cars: 1970 — 8,296
Reporting marks: CG

Notable named passenger trains: *Nancy Hanks II* (Atlanta-Savannah), *Man o' War* (Atlanta-Columbus)
Recommended reading: *Central of Georgia Railway and Connecting Lines*, by Richard E. Prince, published in 1976 by Richard E. Prince
Subsidiaries and affiliated railroads, 1970:
Savannah & Atlanta
Wrightsville & Tennille
Successors: Southern Railway (TWG)
Portions still operated:
Dothan-Hartford, Ala.: Hartford & Slocomb
Atlanta-Oliver, Ga.; Dover-Metter, Ga.; Millen-Augusta, Ga.; Gordon-Eatonton, Ga.; Machen-Covington, Ga.; Macon-Athens, Ga.; Macon-Albany, Ga.; Albany-Dothan, Ala.; Smithville, Ga.-Clayton, Ala.; Americus-Columbus, Ga.; Fort Valley-Perry, Ga.; Fort Valley-Columbus, Ga.; Barnesville-Thomaston, Ga.; Griffin-Rome, Ga.-Chattanooga, Tenn.; Columbus-Greenville, Ga.; Columbus, Ga.-Andalusia, Ala.; Columbus, Ga.-Birmingham, Ala.; Opelika-Lafayette, Ala.; Union Springs-Montgomery, Ala: Central of Georgia Railroad (Southern Railway System)

CENTRAL RAILROAD OF NEW JERSEY

The earliest railroad ancestor of the Central of New Jersey was the Elizabethtown & Somerville Railroad, incorporated in 1831 and opened from Elizabethport to Elizabeth, N. J., in 1836. Horses gave way to steam in 1839, and the road was extended west, reaching Somerville at the beginning of 1842. The Somerville & Easton Railroad was incorporated in 1847 and began building westward. In 1849 it purchased the Elizabethtown & Somerville and adopted a new name: Central Railroad Company of New Jersey. The line reached Phillipsburg, on the east bank of the Delaware River, in 1852. It was extended east across Newark Bay to Jersey City in 1864, and it gradually acquired branches to Flemington, Newark, Perth Amboy, Chester, and Wharton.

The New Jersey Southern began construction in 1860 at Port Monmouth. The railroad worked its way southwest across lower New Jersey and reached Bayside, on the Delaware River west of Bridgeton, N. J., in 1871. The NJS came under the control of the Central of New Jersey in 1879. CNJ's influence briefly extended across the Delaware River in the form of the Baltimore & Delaware Bay Railroad, from Bombay Hook, Del., east of Townsend, to Chestertown, Maryland. That line became part of the Pennsylvania Railroad family in 1901.

The New Jersey Southern was connected to the CNJ by the New York & Long Branch Railroad, which was completed in 1881 between Perth Amboy and Bay Head Jct. The NY&LB, at least in modern times, had no equipment of its own; CNJ and the Pennsylvania, joint owners of the Long Branch, both operated on it by trackage rights.

CNJ's lines in Pennsylvania were built by the Lehigh Coal & Navigation Co. as the Lehigh & Susquehanna Railroad. The main line was completed between Phillipsburg, N. J., and Wilkes-Barre in 1866. A notable feature of the line was the Ashley Planes, a steep stretch of line (maxi-

mum grade was 14.65 percent) operated by cables driven by stationary engines, which remained in service until after World War Two. Central of New Jersey leased the Lehigh & Susquehanna in 1871. The line was extended to Scranton in 1888 by a subsidiary of the L&S, the Wilkes-Barre & Scranton; L&S leased the line upon completion and assigned the lease to the CNJ. The bulk of the traffic on the Pennsylvania lines was anthracite coal, much of it produced by subsidiaries of the railroad, until the Commodities Clause of the Interstate Commerce Act of 1920 forbade railroads to haul freight in which they had an interest.

From 1883 to 1887 the CNJ was leased to and operated by the Philadelphia & Reading, with which it formed a New York-Philadelphia route. CNJ resumed its own management after a reorganization in 1887. In 1901 the Reading Company (successor to Phildelphia & Reading) acquired control of the CNJ through purchase of a majority of its stock, and at about that same time Baltimore & Ohio acquired control of the Reading, gaining access to New York over Reading and Central of New Jersey rails.

In 1929 Central of New Jersey inaugurated the *Blue Comet*, a deluxe coach train operating twice daily between Jersey City and Atlantic City. It was painted blue from the pilot of its 4-6-2 to the rear bulkhead of its observation car, and its refurbished cars offered a level of comfort much higher than the usual day coach of the era. The train was the forerunner of the coach streamliners that blossomed nationwide in the late 1930s and the 1940s. Unfortunately it succumbed to automobile competition in 1941. Also in 1929 CNJ purchased a 30 percent interest in the Raritan River Railroad, a short line from Perth Amboy to New Brunswick. In 1931 it acquired total ownership of the Wharton & Northern and a partial interest in the Mount Hope Mineral Railroad from Warren Foundry & Pipe Corp.

The lines in Pennsylvania were organized as the Central Railroad of Pennsylvania in 1946 in an effort to escape taxation by the state of New Jersey. CNJ resumed its own operation of the Pennsylvania lines at the end of 1952. The CRP continued in existence as owner of the Easton & Western, four miles of track at Easton, Pa.

When the Lehigh & New England Railroad was abandoned in 1961 CNJ acquired a few of its branches and organized them as the Lehigh &

New England Railway. In 1963 Lehigh Coal & Navigation sold its railroad properties to the Reading, but the lease to the CNJ continued. In 1965 CNJ and Lehigh Valley consolidated their lines along the Lehigh River in Pennsylvania and portions of each road's line were abandoned; the anthracite traffic that had supported both roads had largely disappeared. CNJ operations in Pennsylvania ended March 31, 1972.

CNJ maintained a small carfloat terminal in the Bronx. It was the site of the first successful Class 1 railroad diesel operation. Over the years CNJ maintained an extensive marine operation on New York Bay, including a steamer line to Sandy Hook. CNJ's last marine service, the ferry line between Manhattan and CNJ's rail terminal at Jersey City, made its last run on April 30, 1967. It was also the last day for the terminal itself; the next day CNJ passenger trains began originating and terminating at the Pennsylvania Railroad station in Newark, where New York passengers could transfer to either PRR or Port Authority Trans-Hudson trains.

The years after WWII were not kind to the Central of New Jersey. Passenger traffic was almost entirely commuter business, requiring great amounts of rolling stock for two short periods five days a week. Three-fourths of CNJ's freight traffic terminated on line — the road was essentially a terminal carrier. In addition, heavy taxes levied by the state of New Jersey ate up much of CNJ's revenue. The state of New Jersey began subsidizing commuter service in 1964, and the tax situation changed in 1966; nonetheless, CNJ entered bankruptcy proceedings on March 22, 1967. The merger between Chesapeake & Ohio and Norfolk & Western that was proposed in 1965 to counter the impending Pennsylvania-New York Central merger was to have included CNJ, but the bankruptcy of Penn Central killed that prospect. CNJ drafted elaborate plans for reorganization; they came to naught as neighboring railroads collapsed. Conrail took over the railroad properties and freight operations of the Central of New Jersey on April 1, 1976; NJ Transit purchased the lines over which it now operates commuter service.

The Camelback locomotive was designed on the premise that the wide firebox necessary for slow-burning anthracite would restrict the forward view from a cab in the conventional location. The engineer rode in a cab astride the boiler and the fireman in a minimal shelter attached to the rear of the firebox. Central of New Jersey used Camelbacks later than any other major railroad, and the Camelback 4-6-0, as shown here on a local passenger train leaving Jersey City, was almost as much a CNJ trademark as the Statue of Liberty emblem.

William R. Frutchey

58

Location of headquarters: New York, New York
Miles of railroad operated: 1929 — 693; 1974 — 526
Number of locomotives: 1929 — 535; 1974 — 101
Number of passenger cars: 1929 — 917; 1974 — 157
Number of freight cars: 1929 — 22,978; 1974 — 2,232
Number of company service cars: 1929 — 674; 1974 — 51
Reporting marks: CNJ
Notable named passenger trains: *Blue Comet* (Jersey City-Atlantic City)
Historical and technical society: Anthracite Railroads Historical Society, P. O. Box 119, Bridgeport, PA 19405
Recommended reading: *Jersey Central Album*, by Warren B. Crater, published in 1963 by Warren B. Crater, 270 West Colfax Avenue, Roselle Park, NJ 07204
Subsidiaries and affiliated railroads, 1946-1952: Central Railroad of Pennsylvania
Predecessor railroads in this book: Lehigh & New England
Successors:
Conrail (TWG)
NJ Transit (TWG)
Portions still operated:
Elizabethport-High Bridge; Perth Amboy-Bay Head: NJ Transit
Elizabethport-Perth Amboy; Jersey City-Bayonne; Keyport-Matawan; Winslow Jct.-Bridgeton, Red Bank-Whitings: Conrail

---

CHESAPEAKE & OHIO RAILWAY

The primary avenues of transportation in Virginia in the 1830s were the rivers and the ocean. The early railroads connected the coast with inland points, and one of these was the Louisa Railroad, chartered in 1836 to run from Taylorsville, on the Richmond, Fredericksburg & Potomac just south of what is now Doswell, to points in Louisa County. At first the RF&P operated the railroad, but in 1847 the Louisa Railroad acquired its own rolling stock and took over its own affairs. By 1850 the railroad had been extended west to Charlottesville. That year it became the Virginia Central, and a year later over the protests of the RF&P it built its own line from Taylorsville to Richmond.

West of Charlottesville lay the Blue Ridge, the crossing of which required a series of tunnels. The state of Virginia undertook construction of that portion of the line as the Blue Ridge Railroad and on completion leased it to the Virginia Central (which later purchased it). Meanwhile, the Virginia Central leapfrogged its rails ahead to Clifton Forge. In 1853 the state chartered the Covington & Ohio Railroad to connect the Virginia Central and the James River & Kanawha Canal at Covington with the Ohio River.

The Civil War halted the westward expansion of the railroad, even though the line would have been valuable to the Confederacy. During the latter part of the war the Virginia Central pulled up parts of its line for supplies to maintain other parts. However, by 1865 the entire line was back in service. The Virginia Central and the Covington & Ohio were consolidated as the Chesapeake & Ohio Railroad in 1868.

In 1869 the C&O came under the control of C. P. Huntington, builder of the Central Pacific and the Southern Pacific. The C&O had run out of money, and its officers asked Huntington if he could finance the westward construction of the road. Huntington and his associates subscribed to mortgage bonds, and the C&O was reorganized with Huntington as its president.

On January 29, 1873, the C&O was completed from Richmond, Va., to the Ohio River a few miles east of the confluence of the Ohio and the Big Sandy — the latter river forms the border between West Virginia and Kentucky. The western terminus of the road was the new city of Huntington, W. Va. In 1875 C&O entered receivership and was foreclosed and reorganized as the Chesapeake & Ohio Railway; another reorganization followed in 1888.

Huntington envisioned the C&O as the eastern portion of a transcontinental system in conjunction with the Southern Pacific. He organized the Chesapeake, Ohio & Southwestern Railroad in 1877 to take over the

Memphis, Paducah & Northern Railroad, a line from Elizabethtown and Louisville through Paducah, Ky., to Memphis. Huntington's Louisville, New Orleans & Texas Railway provided the connection between Memphis and New Orleans, the east end of the Southern Pacific. In 1884 Huntington formed the Newport News & Mississippi Valley Co. to hold the Elizabethtown, Lexington & Big Sandy (opened in 1872 from the Big Sandy River to Lexington, Ky., with trackage rights to Louisville), the CO&SW, and the C&O itself.

William P. Price

A trainload of coal, Chesapeake & Ohio's principal commodity, leaves Ronceverte, W. Va., behind a 2-6-6-6; another Allegheny is pushing at the rear of the train.

C&O's line along the Ohio River to Cincinnati was opened in 1888 with the completion of the Maysville & Big Sandy Railroad from Ashland to Covington, Ky., opposite Cincinnati (the second Covington on C&O's main line), and the Covington & Cincinnati Elevated Railroad & Transfer & Bridge Co. — one of few three-ampersand railroads in the U. S. Both the M&BS and the C&CER&T&B were proprietary companies of the C&O.

Huntington's empire fell apart in 1888. The C&O was taken over and reorganized by Vanderbilt interests. It soon acquired the EL&BS and Lexington-Louisville trackage rights over Louisville & Nashville. Illinois Central, by then under the control of E. H. Harriman, purchased the Chesapeake, Ohio & Southwestern and the Louisville, New Orleans & Texas, consolidating the latter with the Yazoo & Mississippi Valley.

During the presidency of Melville Ingalls (also president of the Big Four), C&O undertook expansion at its eastern end. In 1882 it constructed a line east from Richmond to a new tidewater terminal at Newport News. In 1888 C&O leased (and later purchased) the Richmond & Allegheny Railroad, which followed the towpath of the James River & Kanawha Canal from Richmond through Lynchburg to Clifton Forge. Two years later the road arranged for access to Washington over the Virginia Midland Railway (later Southern Railway) from Gordonsville.

By the turn of the century C&O had become a major coal hauler, and the Midwest was becoming a better market for coal than the East. In 1903 the majority of the stock of the Hocking Valley Railroad (Toledo-Columbus-Athens and Gallipolis, Ohio) was purchased jointly by the C&O, Baltimore & Ohio, Erie, Lake Shore & Michigan Southern (New York Central), and Pennsylvania railroads. In addition, C&O and LS&MS acquired the Kanawha & Michigan (which had a line from Charleston, W. Va., through Gallipolis and Athens, Ohio, to Columbus) from the Hocking Valley, and LS&MS purchased most of the stock of the Toledo & Ohio Central (Toledo-Columbus-Corning). By 1911 C&O had acquired control of the Hocking Valley. To satisfy antitrust legislation, C&O was required to sell its interest in the Kanawha & Michigan to the T&OC in 1914.

To gain access to the Hocking Valley, C&O incorporated the Chesapeake & Ohio Northern Railway to build north from Limeville, Ky., a few

miles southeast of Portsmouth, Ohio. C&ON bridged the Ohio, built north to Waverly, Ohio, and arranged for trackage rights over Norfolk & Western for 62 miles to Valley Crossing, south of Columbus. The C&ON was opened in 1917. In the 1920s because of a limitation on the number of trains C&O could run on the N&W line and because grades on the N&W were steeper than those on C&O's main line, C&O constructed a parallel line — the Chesapeake & Hocking Valley Railway — between Greggs, near Waverly, and Valley Crossing. C&O leased the C&HV in 1926 and merged it (and also merged the Hocking Valley Railroad) in 1930.

On other fronts, in 1910 C&O purchased the Chicago, Cincinnati & Louisville Railroad, a line from Cincinnati to Hammond, Ind., and reorganized it as the Chesapeake & Ohio Railway of Indiana. About that same time C&O bought a one-sixth interest in the Richmond-Washington

Co., operator of the Richmond, Fredericksburg & Potomac. In 1918 C&O bought White Sulphur Springs, Inc. — it had controlled the company since 1910 — operator of the Greenbrier, a resort hotel at White Sulphur Springs, W. Va.

In 1923 Orris Paxton Van Sweringen and his brother Mantis James Van Sweringen, Cleveland real estate developers, purchased 30 percent of C&O's stock. The principal item in the Van Sweringens' empire was the Nickel Plate (more formally, the New York, Chicago & St. Louis Railroad), and they drafted proposals to merge C&O, NKP, Erie, Hocking Valley, and Pere Marquette to form a fourth eastern system of the magnitude of New York Central, Pennsylvania, and Baltimore & Ohio. By 1929 the Van Sweringens also hoped to include the Wheeling & Lake Erie, the Lackawanna, and the Chicago & Eastern Illinois, the last to furnish a

ROBERT R. YOUNG (1897-1958) was born at Canadian, Texas. His father and grandfather were local bankers. He distinguished himself in studies at Culver Military Academy; not so at the University of Virginia. In 1916 he married Anita O'Keeffe (sister of painter Georgia O'Keeffe) and settled down somewhat working for du Pont, Allied Chemical, and General Motors. He left GM in 1928 to go into finance. He anticipated the Depression successfully by selling short

NYC

before the market fell, and he acquired a seat on the New York Stock Exchange in 1931.

In 1937 Young purchased control of the Alleghany Corporation, which controlled several railroads: Chesapeake & Ohio, Erie, Pere Marquette, Nickel Plate, Wheeling & Lake Erie, and Missouri Pacific. He gained control of the Chesapeake & Ohio through a lawsuit and embarked on a career as gadfly to the railroad industry, basically berating the industry for conservatism and old-fashioned ways. He founded the Federation for Railway Progress as a counter to the Association of American Railroads; eventually FRP achieved a measure of respectability.

He then set out to gain control of New York Central, proposing merger with C&O. C&O stockholders saw that the Central would get more out of a merger than C&O and opposed the merger. Young sold his C&O holdings and began a proxy fight for NYC control. The purchasers of the NYC stock that C&O had held voted him in. He became chairman of NYC in 1954, appointed Alfred E. Perlman president, and then stepped back. NYC's stock rose as Perlman trimmed and rationalized, and then it fell during the recession of 1957 and 1958. Young committed suicide at his home in Palm Beach on January 25, 1958.

connection with the Missouri Pacific, in which they held a sizable interest. Later that year the Van Sweringens withdrew their applications as their empire began to collapse. Meanwhile, in 1928 C&O had received permission to control the Pere Marquette. In 1930 C&O and PM unified their operations.

In the depths of the Great Depression C&O inaugurated an all-air-conditioned passenger train, the *George Washington*, from Washington and Newport News to Louisville and Cincinnati and return. In 1933 C&O introduced the figure of a sleeping kitten in its advertising. "Chessie" is still in the first of her nine lives and has become the symbol — indeed the name — of a much larger railroad.

In 1937 Robert R. Young acquired 43 percent of the stock of Alleghany Corporation (briefly put, a holding company that controlled the Chesapeake Corporation, which was another holding company that controlled the C&O). By 1942 Young was chairman of the board of C&O, and in 1945 he proposed a merger of C&O, Pere Marquette, Nickel Plate, and Wheeling & Lake Erie, with the thought of adding western connections (likely prospects were Missouri Pacific, Rio Grande, and Western Pacific) to make a coast-to-coast railroad. The Nickel Plate objected to the proposal. As it fell out, C&O merged Pere Marquette on June 6, 1947, NKP purchased C&O's Wheeling & Lake shares about the same time, and C&O distributed its NKP shares to C&O stockholders as a dividend later that year.

Young also proposed takeover of the Association of American Railroads and the Pullman Company and became an advocate of coast-to-coast through sleeping car service with his famous ad headed "A hog can cross America without changing trains — but you can't!" Young intended to make C&O the top passenger railroad in the country. To this end, he ordered a steam-turbine-powered Vista-Dome streamliner, the *Chessie*, for daylight service between Washington and Cincinnati, and he sent an order to Pullman-Standard for 289 passenger cars, enough to completely re-equip all of C&O's other trains. By the time the *Chessie* arrived from the Budd Company, C&O had discovered (possibly by observing the patronage of Baltimore & Ohio's new *Cincinnatian*) that there was no market for a daytime Washington-Cincinnati train. Most of the *Chessie* cars were sold to other U. S. railroads; a dozen went to Argentina. Nearly half of the

Three blue-and-yellow E8s lead the eastbound *Sportsman* from Detroit and Cincinnati through Afton, Va., in 1965.

Pullman-Standard order was canceled or diverted to other railroads.

In 1947, while all that was happening, C&O acquired a large block of New York Central stock and became NYC's largest stockholder. Young proposed a merger of C&O, NYC, and Virginian. Young left the C&O in 1954 to take over management of the New York Central.

In 1960 C&O turned its attention to neighbor Baltimore & Ohio and offered to purchase its stock. The ICC approved C&O control of B&O at the end of 1962, and the actual exchange of C&O stock for B&O took place in February 1963. By 1973 C&O owned more than 90 percent of B&O's stock. B&O in turn owned nearly half the stock of Western Maryland and controlled Reading Company; the Reading controlled the Central Railroad of New Jersey. In 1966 the ICC approved C&O control of the Chicago South Shore & South Bend, an interurban-turned-commuter carrier with tracks through the industrial area just south of Lake Michigan.

The Chessie System was incorporated in 1973 to own the C&O. C&O in turn controlled B&O, and the two of them held more than 90 percent of

Western Maryland's stock. C&O, B&O, and WM did not merge immediately but became Chessie System Railroads: They traded their identities and colors for new paint and a new emblem featuring C&O's cat, Chessie. South Shore did not become a Chessie System Railroad but remained a stray in the alley behind Chessie's house until 1984, when it was purchased by the Venango River Corporation.

Location of headquarters: Richmond, Virginia, and Cleveland, Ohio
Miles of railroad operated: 1929 — 2,740; 1972 — 4,994
Number of locomotives: 1929 — 946; 1972 — 1,030
Number of passenger cars: 1929 — 427; 1970 — 92
Number of freight cars: 1929 — 53,518; 1972 — 74,962
Number of company service cars: 1929 — 1,641; 1972 — 1,850
Reporting marks: CO
Notable named passenger trains: *George Washington* (Washington/Newport News-Cincinnati/Louisville); *Chessie*
Historical and technical society: Chesapeake & Ohio Historical Society, P. O. Box 417, Alderson, WV 24910
Subsidiaries and affiliated railroads, 1972:

Baltimore & Ohio
Western Maryland
Chicago South Shore & South Bend
Predecessor railroads in this book: Pere Marquette
Successors: Chessie System (TWG)
Portions still operated: The C&O is for the most part still intact. Among the longer branches and secondary lines that have been abandoned are:

Lindsay-Strathmore, Va.
Covington-Hot Springs, Va.
Covington-Bess, Va.
North Caldwell-Durbin, W. Va.
Hocking Valley lines east of Diamond and south of Dundas, Ohio
C&O of Indiana between Cincinnati and Fernald, Ohio, and between Malden and Hammond, Ind. (that is, both ends of the Cincinnati-Hammond route — B&O lines are now used to bypass Cheviot Hill in Cincinnati and to go all the way into Chicago)
Pere Marquette north of Baldwin, Mich.

CHICAGO & EASTERN ILLINOIS RAILWAY

The earliest ancestor of the Chicago & Eastern Illinois was the Evansville & Illinois, chartered in 1849 to build north from Evansville, Indiana, on the Ohio River. The road reached Vincennes in 1853 and Terre Haute in 1854. By 1877 it had gone through several identities and was named the Evansville & Terre Haute Railway. That railroad controlled the Evansville & Indianapolis, a consolidation of several lines forming a second Evansville-Terre Haute route through Washington and Worthington, Ind., to the east of E&TH's own line.

The Evansville, Terre Haute & Chicago Railroad was chartered in 1869 and opened its line between Terre Haute and Danville in 1871. The Chicago, Danville & Vincennes Railroad, chartered in 1865, built south from Dolton, Ill., just south of Chicago, to Danville, completing the line in 1872. In 1873 it defaulted and in 1877 it was sold at foreclosure to become the Chicago & Eastern Illinois Railroad. In 1880 the C&EI leased the Evansville, Terre Haute & Chicago. In 1880 it began to build southwest from Danville, and by the turn of the century C&EI had, by construction and purchase, put together a line all the way to Thebes, Ill., on the Mississippi River.

A new Chicago & Eastern Illinois Railroad was incorporated June 6, 1894, as a consolidation of the previous C&EI and the Chicago & Indiana Coal Railway. The latter road had a line from Momence, Ill., on C&EI's main line, to Brazil, Ind., with a branch from Percy Jct. to La Crosse, Ind. The C&IC leased the Chicago & West Michigan (later Pere Marquette) line from La Crosse to New Buffalo, Mich. In the next five years Chicago & Eastern Illinois purchased the Evansville, Terre Haute & Chicago; the Chicago, Paducah & Memphis Railroad (Mt. Vernon to Marion, Ill., about 40 miles); the Eastern Illinois & Missouri River Railroad (Marion to

In 1940 nine railroads announced they would inaugurate coach streamliner service between Chicago and Miami. The trains would operate every third day on their respective railroads, giving daily service from Chicago and Miami. Chicago & Eastern Illinois teamed up with Louisville & Nashville; Nashville, Chattanooga & St. Louis; Atlanta, Birmingham & Coast; Atlantic Coast Line; and Florida East Coast to operate the *Dixie Flagler*. The cars had been built a year previously for Florida East Coast's *Henry M. Flagler*; C&EI sent a Pacific, No. 1008, to the shops to be streamlined for the train, shown here heading south on "the boulevard of steel."

Thebes); and the Indiana Block Coal Railroad (Terre Haute to Brazil).

In 1902 control of the C&EI was acquired by B. F. Yoakum's expanding St. Louis & San Francisco. To connect with the Frisco at its closest point, the C&EI built a 20-mile line from Findlay Jct. to Pana, Ill., and arranged for trackage rights on the Cleveland, Cincinnati, Chicago & St. Louis Railway (the Big Four, part of the New York Central System) from Pana to St. Louis. The C&EI also built a 62-mile line from Woodland Jct.

on the main line to Villa Grove, Ill., cutting off a dogleg through Danville. In 1911 the C&EI absorbed the Evansville & Terre Haute and the Evansville Belt Railway. About that same time the road purchased a number of coal mines and coal lands in southern Illinois and Indiana. In 1913 both the C&EI and its parent, the Frisco, entered receivership.

The Chicago & Eastern Illinois Railway was organized on December 13, 1920, to acquire the properties and franchises of the Chicago & Eastern Illinois Railroad, except for the coal properties and the following lines: the former Evansville & Indianapolis (which became the Evansville, Indianapolis & Terre Haute and eventually part of the New York Central); the Evansville & Richmond (which became part of Milwaukee Road's Chicago, Terre Haute & Southeastern); and the former Chicago & Indiana Coal Railway (which was incorporated as the Chicago, Attica & Southern). The new C&EI had hardly begun existence when a coal strike in 1922 resulted in southern Illinois coal pricing itself out of a shrinking market, and C&EI's traffic, largely based on coal, began to fall off. In 1927 the C&EI purchased the Chicago Heights Terminal Transfer Railroad, a switching line at Chicago Heights.

In 1928 the Van Sweringen brothers of Cleveland acquired control of C&EI through their Chesapeake & Ohio but did little to integrate it with the remainder of their empire (Chesapeake & Ohio, Missouri Pacific, Nickel Plate, Erie, Pere Marquette, and Wheeling & Lake Erie). Much of the plan for the reorganization of the C&EI was formulated by John W. Barriger III.

The Chicago & Eastern Illinois Railroad took over the business, assets, and property of the C&EI on December 31, 1940. At various times its leadership included John Budd (in his only period away from the Great Northern) and Downing B. Jenks, who later headed Missouri Pacific. In 1952 the CE&I acquired the Jefferson Southwestern, a 12-mile line at Mt. Vernon, Ill., and later transferred one-third of the shares to Missouri Pacific and one-third to Illinois Central. Through a lease agreement it acquired the abandoned St. Louis & O'Fallon in October 1954 for access to East St. Louis.

Missouri Pacific began merger discussions with C&EI in 1959. In 1961 both Mopac and Louisville & Nashville acquired C&EI stock and petitioned the ICC for permission to control the road; Illinois Central also pe-

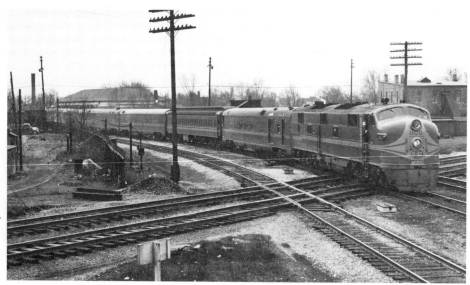

Union Switch & Signal

The *Whippoorwill* **leaves Danville north-bound for Chicago during its brief tenure (1946-1951) on the Evansville-Chicago route. The E7 on the point is crossing the Detroit-St. Louis line of the Wabash; the roof of C&EI's Danville station is visible above the coaches.**

titioned for control. In 1963 the ICC ruled in favor of Mopac with the condition that MP negotiate in good faith for sale of the Evansville line to L&N. The Woodland Jct.-Evansville line became L&N property in 1969; L&N purchased a half interest in the C&EI main line from there to Dolton Junction (Chicago) and half of C&EI's interests in the Chicago & Western Indiana and the Belt Railway of Chicago. L&N bought 48 diesel locomotives and 1,495 freight cars and cabooses from C&EI. Chicago & Eastern Illinois was merged with Missouri Pacific on October 15, 1976.

Chicago & Eastern Illinois was sometimes cited as an all-American average railroad, but it did have distinctions. For years it carried the majority of Florida-bound passengers out of Chicago on what was essentially a northern extension of Louisville & Nashville's passenger service —

trains such as the *Dixie Flyer*, *Dixie Limited*, and *Dixie Flagler*. C&EI's own passenger trains included two of the earliest and shortest-lived post-war streamliners, the *Whippoorwill* and the *Meadowlark*, on the Evansville-Chicago and Cypress-Chicago runs, respectively. C&EI's Chicago-St. Louis service succumbed shortly after World War Two to the competition of Wabash, Illinois Central, and Gulf, Mobile & Ohio. Service to southern Illinois, spruced up in the 1930s with ACF motorcars and taken over in the 1950s by an RDC, endured into the 1960s. C&EI discontinued passenger service south of Danville — the Evansville-Chicago portion of L&N's *Humming Bird* and *Georgian* — in 1968, shortly before L&N purchased the Evansville line. The last train, a Chicago-Danville local which briefly carried the name *Danville Flyer*, remained in service

until the start of Amtrak in 1971, though as an L&N train, ironically.

No other railroad surpassed C&EI in slogans: The Danville Route, The Evansville Route, The Modern Route, The Noiseless Route, The Boulevard of Steel, and one that could have been applied to several dozen roads, The Chicago Line.

Location of headquarters: Chicago, Illinois
Miles of railroad operated: 1929 — 946; 1975 — 644
Number of locomotives: 1929 — 334; 1975 — 49
Number of passenger cars: 1929 — 284
Number of freight cars: 1929 — 14,818
Number of company service cars: 1929 — 561
Number of freight and company service cars: 1975 — 7,210
Reporting marks: CEI
Historical and technical society: Missouri Pacific Historical Society, 9726 Whitestone Terrace, St. Louis, MO 63119
Subsidiaries and affiliated railroads, 1975:
Chicago Heights Terminal Transfer Railroad (100%)
Successors:
Chicago, Attica & Southern
Missouri Pacific (TWG)
Portions still operated:
Chicago-Woodland Junction, Ill.: Missouri Pacific and Seaboard System Woodland Jct., Ill.-Evansville, Ind.; Rossville-Brothers, Ill.; Otter Creek Jct.-Brazil, Ind.; Mt. Vernon Jct.-Mt. Vernon, Ind.: Seaboard System Woodland Jct.-St. Louis; Goodwine-Cissna Park, Ill.; Danville-Villa Grove, Ill.; Jamaica-Sidell Jct., Ill.; Findlay Jct.-Joppa, Ill.: Missouri Pacific

CHICAGO, ATTICA & SOUTHERN RAILROAD

The Chicago, Attica & Southern was a descendant of the grandly named Chicago & Great Southern, which by the mid-1880s had put together a line in northwestern Indiana from Fair Oaks, on the Monon between Rensselaer and Shelby, to Brazil, between Indianapolis and Terre Haute. It was reorganized as the Chicago & Indiana Coal Railway.

The C&IC extended itself north to Wilder and La Crosse to connect with what in later years became the Erie, the Chesapeake & Ohio, and the Pennsylvania, and acquired trackage rights north to New Buffalo, Michigan. The proprietor of the C&IC, Henry H. Porter, acquired control of the Chicago & Eastern Illinois and in 1888 constructed a connection

67

All of Chicago, Attica & Southern's power was bought used. Consolidation 320 came from Buffalo, Rochester & Pittsburgh in November 1928. It was built by Brooks in 1904 as BR&P 320. A rebuilding in BR&P's shop resulted in the unusual combination of Southern valve gear and inside valves.

John B. Allen

between his two roads from Percy Jct., near Goodland, Ind., northwest to Momence, Ill., on the C&EI main line. The C&EI leased and in 1894 merged with the Chicago & Indiana Coal Railway. "Coal Road" continued as an unofficial name of that portion of the C&EI.

In 1921 as part of its reorganization C&EI offered the Coal Road for sale. Edmund P. Kelly picked it up for $15,000 and assigned it to Stoddard M. Stevens Jr. Stevens sold the Brazil-West Melcher portion to the Cincinnati, Indianapolis & Western (later part of Baltimore & Ohio) for $137,500 and the remainder of the line to Charles F. Propst for $250,000.

Propst organized the Chicago, Attica & Southern Railroad, which started operation on December 7, 1922. He had hopes for local business and also for bridge traffic as a Chicago bypass. However, the CA&S faced formidable competition and had no money to rehabilitate its track. In the late 1920s there was an effort to lease the CA&S to the New York Central, but the Central said the cost of rehabilitation would not be worth the revenue that might come from operating the road. The CA&S entered receivership on August 5, 1931.

In June 1942 C&EI abandoned the portion of the connecting line from

Momence to the Illinois-Indiana state line, and in 1943 the Interstate Commerce Commission authorized abandonment of CA&S's portion of the connector, the line from Percy Jct. to La Crosse, and the line south of Veedersburg. What was left was a nowhere-to-nowhere (Morocco to Veedersburg) track that hung on through World War Two only because of the war effort. In April 1946 the ICC granted permission to abandon the rest of the CA&S.

Location of headquarters: Attica, Indiana
Miles of railroad operated: 1929 — 155; 1946 — 59
Number of locomotives: 1929 — 6; 1946 — 6
Number of freight cars: 1929 — 20; 1946 — 8
Number of company service cars: 1946 — 7
Reporting marks: CA&S
Recommended reading: *Ghost Railroads of Indiana*, by Elmer G. Sulzer, published in 1970 by Vane A. Jones Co., 6710 Hampton Drive East, Indianapolis, IN 46226
Predecessor railroads in this book: Chicago & Eastern Illinois
Map: See page 67

CHICAGO, AURORA & ELGIN RAILROAD

The Aurora, Elgin & Chicago Railway was incorporated in March 1901. By the autumn of 1902 it had opened a line from Aurora, Illinois, to Laramie Avenue in Chicago and a branch to Batavia; in May 1903 it opened a branch from Wheaton to Elgin. The line was unusual among interurbans in that current distribution was through a third rail rather than overhead wire, except in the streets, yards, and terminals. In March 1905 the AE&C extended its service over the rails of the Metropolitan West Side Elevated (the "L") to a terminal on Chicago's famous Loop at Wells Street.

The company was consolidated with several streetcar lines in the Fox River Valley in 1906 to form the Aurora, Elgin & Chicago Railroad. In 1910 a subsidiary built a line to West Chicago and Geneva; interurban cars continued from Geneva to St. Charles on streetcar tracks. The AE&C entered receivership in 1919. In 1922 the company's properties were separated into two parts: the Fox River Division, encompassing the streetcar lines in the Fox valley between Aurora and Elgin, and the Third Rail Division, the four-pronged line from Chicago to Aurora, Batavia, Geneva, and Elgin. The latter was sold to the Chicago, Aurora & Elgin Railroad, which took over the operation July 1, 1922.

Samuel Insull acquired control of the CA&E in 1926. He proposed a new line to bypass the congestion and local stations on the main line, much like the Skokie Valley line that the Chicago North Shore & Milwaukee opened that same year. The prospect of such a project for the CA&E was soon killed by the Depression. The CA&E entered another receivership in 1932. The West Chicago-Geneva-St. Charles line was abandoned in 1937 for lack of traffic. Private right of way and a new terminal in Aurora in 1939 replaced street running there, the last on the CA&E. The road was again in financial distress during World War Two. The physical plant was in poor condition, and the road lacked the resources to rebuild it. Even with a reorganization as the Chicago, Aurora & Elgin Railway in 1946, abandonment was inevitable.

The customary pattern of train operation was interesting. Originally local trains served Aurora and Elgin alternately; in the 1930s the service changed to alternate local trains to Wheaton and express trains with cars for Aurora, Elgin, and St. Charles — the expresses were divided and assembled at Wheaton. Shuttle cars operated between Batavia and Batavia Junction on the Aurora line. The road's business was primarily passengers — there was little industry on line and scant opportunity to participate in long-haul freight traffic.

The city of Chicago, Cook County, and state and federal highway administrations planned to build an expressway along the route of the "L" and move the Chicago Transit Authority tracks to its median strip. In September 1953 temporary track replaced the "L" so construction could begin. CA&E and CTA set up an interchange station at Desplaines Avenue. The loss of one-seat service to downtown Chicago only aggravated the loss of passengers resulting from service cuts and the postwar in-

Henry J. McCord

A Chicago limited rolls east through Villa Park. The first two cars are part of a batch of ten built by St. Louis Car Co. in 1945 — the last new cars CA&E purchased.

crease in automobile ownership. Half of CA&E's riders switched to parallel railroads or their own cars by December 1953, and the opening of the new highway only made the situation worse.

CA&E applied to discontinue passenger service in 1955. After the customary hearings and proceedings, passenger service ceased at noon on July 3, 1957. Track and rolling stock remained in place, and there was thought of reviving service on the new CTA route. However, CA&E trains could not operate into the new subway that replaced the "L" and there was no terminal the CA&E could use. Freight service continued until June 9, l959. Legal abandonment occurred on June 10, 1961.

Location of headquarters: Wheaton, Illinois
Miles of railroad operated: 1929 — 66; 1956 — 54
Number of locomotives: 1929 — 9; 1956 — 7
Number of passenger cars: 1929 — 87; 1956 — 89
Number of company service cars: 1929 — 2; 1956 — 12
Historical and technical society: Shore Line Interurban Historical Society, P. O. Box 346, Chicago, IL 60690
Recommended reading: *The Great Third Rail*, edited by George Krambles, published in 1961 by Central Electric Railfans' Association, P. O. Box 503, Chicago, IL 60690

70

CHICAGO, BURLINGTON & QUINCY RAILROAD

The Aurora Branch Railroad was chartered on February 12, 1849, to build a line from Aurora, Illinois, to a connection with the Galena & Chicago Union (forerunner of the Chicago & North Western) at Turner Jct. (West Chicago). Service began with G&CU's first locomotive, the *Pioneer*. In 1852 the road was renamed the Chicago & Aurora Railroad and received authority to build to Mendota, Ill., where it would connect with the Illinois Central. On February 14, 1855, it was again renamed, becoming the Chicago, Burlington & Quincy Railroad.

That same year a railroad was opened between Galesburg and the east bank of the Mississippi opposite Burlington, Iowa; a year later a string of railroads, including the CB&Q, linked Chicago with Quincy, Ill., via Galesburg. A Galesburg-Peoria line was opened in 1857. By 1865 the CB&Q had acquired all these lines, built its own line from Aurora to Chicago, and had undergone several consolidations to become the corporation that would endure until the Burlington Northern merger in 1970.

West of the Mississippi expansion proceeded on two fronts. The Hannibal & St. Joseph, chartered in 1847, began operation between its namesake cities in 1859. A short spur to a point opposite Quincy and a steamboat across the Mississippi created the first railroad from Chicago to the Missouri River. The Burlington & Missouri River Railroad began construction in 1855 at Burlington, Iowa, and followed an old Indian trail (later U. S. 34) straight across Iowa — very slowly. Not until November 26, 1869, did it reach the east bank of the Missouri River opposite Plattsmouth, Nebraska (Chicago & North Western reached Council Bluffs in 1867 and the Rock Island got there on May 11, 1869). By then CB&Q had bridged the Mississippi at Burlington and Quincy, both in 1868, and the Missouri in 1869 at Kansas City, as part of a line from Cameron, on the Hannibal & St. Joseph, to Kansas City.

The Burlington, in the form of the Burlington & Missouri River Rail Road In Nebraska, pushed beyond the Missouri River to Lincoln, Nebr., in 1870. It acquired the Omaha & South Western for access to Omaha and built west from Lincoln to a junction with the Union Pacific at Kearney. The road began a colonization program to increase the population along its lines and to sell off the lands it had been granted. CB&Q provided financial backing for the two B&MR (Iowa and Nebraska) companies and directors for their boards. Meanwhile the CB&Q was acquiring branch lines in Illinois and upgrading its plant: double track, steel rail to replace iron, and iron bridges to replace wood.

Jay Gould acquired control of the Hannibal & St. Joseph in 1871, and friction began to develop among the railroads in the Burlington family over such matters as routing of connecting traffic to and from the Union Pacific. To begin unifying the system, CB&Q leased the B&MR in 1872 and merged it in 1875. Gould gained control of Union Pacific in 1875 and then in quick succession got the Kansas Pacific (Kansas City-Denver), the Wabash (and extended it to Council Bluffs), and the Missouri Pacific. Burlington's Nebraska lines were surrounded by Gould lines, and the Wabash would be likely to get the largest share of eastbound traffic from the UP. In the summer of 1880 the CB&Q consolidated with the B&MRinN, acquired the Kansas City, St. Joseph & Council Bluffs, opened a bridge over the Missouri at Plattsmouth, and began an extension west to Denver, completed in May 1882.

In 1882 the growth of the Pacific Northwest and the construction of the Northern Pacific and the St. Paul, Minneapolis & Manitoba (Great Northern) prompted the Burlington to consider building a line up the east bank of the Mississippi River to St. Paul. It would be 25 miles longer than the Milwaukee Road and Chicago & North Western lines between Chicago and the St. Paul, but the grades would be easier. The Q extended its Chicago & Iowa line west to Savanna; the Chicago, Burlington & Northern (the Q owned one-third of its stock) built the line along the river. It was opened in 1886. Considerable friction ensued between parent and child: The CB&N wanted to cut rates to secure business, and the CB&Q knew that retaliation by the Milwaukee and the North Western would be directed at CB&Q systemwide, not just at the CB&N. The matter was eventually settled when CB&Q increased its CB&N holdings in 1890 and absorbed the road in 1899.

In May 1883 the Q regained control of the Hannibal & St. Joseph and soon found itself with increased competition in the Chicago-Kansas City market: Milwaukee Road in 1887 and Santa Fe in 1888.

Continued on next page

Over the years the Burlington considered extension to the Pacific coast and merger with nearly every other railroad. Between 1883 and 1886 it made surveys west of Denver but did no construction. The arrival at Pueblo of the Missouri Pacific in 1887 and the Rock Island in 1888 (on trackage rights from Colorado Springs) put the Burlington at a competitive disadvantage. The Rio Grande received the same amount for moving freight from Salt Lake City to Pueblo as it did from Salt Lake City through Pueblo to Denver (the Dotsero Cutoff was still nearly five decades in the future). Naturally Rio Grande preferred to interchange at Pueblo — it received nothing additional for the 119-mile haul from Pueblo to Denver. There was thought of the Burlington's acquiring James J. Hill's St. Paul, Minneapolis & Manitoba and vice versa. Burlington considered merger with the Pennsylvania; the two roads purchased interests in the Toledo, Peoria & Western. In 1893 the Burlington looked eagerly at the Oregon Short Line and Oregon Railway & Navigation Co. when their parent, Union Pacific, was in receivership. Other merger partners considered were Northern Pacific, Yazoo & Mississippi Valley, Missouri-Kansas-Texas, Chicago Great Western, Denver & Rio Grande, Kansas City Southern, Minneapolis & St. Louis, Chicago & Eastern Illinois, and St. Louis-San Francisco. With one exception the Q was content for a while to stay within its boundaries, marked by corner stakes at Chicago, St. Louis, Kansas City, Denver, Omaha, Galesburg, and St. Paul. That exception was a line opened in 1894 from Alliance, Nebr., northwest through the coalfields of eastern Wyoming to Billings, Montana.

Perhaps the most important event in the Burlington's history was the purchase effective July 1, 1901, of nearly 98 percent of its stock jointly by the Great Northern and the Northern Pacific. James J. Hill, builder of the Great Northern, saw in the Burlington the connection he needed from St. Paul to Chicago — the Chicago & North Western was largely held by New York Central, and the Milwaukee Road refused to consider the matter. At the same time Edward H. Harriman realized that the Burlington could bring his Union Pacific to Chicago from Omaha. Burlington realized it would be better off with the northern lines because of their on-line resources of coal and lumber, both lacking on the Union Pacific-Southern Pacific route to San Francisco. The battle for control was brief and in-tense. Control of the Burlington essentially moved from Boston to St. Paul. That same year Hill, with the backing of J. P. Morgan, his banker, acquired control of Northern Pacific. The next logical step was merger of the three railroads, a process that took 69 years of off-and-on petitioning, protesting, and arguing.

The Chicago, Burlington & Quincy Railroad was leased to the Chicago, Burlington & Quincy Railway for 99 years on September 30, 1901; that lease lasted until June 30, 1907, when the railroad resumed its own management. The Railroad and Railway companies had a number of officers and directors in common. Of the railway company during those years Moody's railroad manual simply says "The company has decided not to issue a report."

In 1908 the Burlington acquired control of the Colorado & Southern, gaining a route from Denver to the Gulf of Mexico at Galveston, Texas, and a route from Denver north into Wyoming. CB&Q extended a line down from Billings, Mont., to meet the C&S in 1914. Other extensions were to the coalfields of southern Illinois and on across the Ohio River to Paducah, Kentucky, and a line from Ashland, Nebr., north to a connection with the Great Northern at Sioux City, Iowa, in 1916.

The Burlington's growth leveled off during the 1920s. In 1930 the ICC authorized merger of Great Northern and Northern Pacific on the condition that they relinquish control of the Burlington; GN and NP withdrew their merger application in 1931 in favor of retaining joint control of the Q. The year 1932 saw the beginning of two significant projects: the Rio Grande's Dotsero Cutoff, which would give Denver a direct rail line west via the Denver & Salt Lake, and the ordering of a stainless-steel streamlined train from the Budd Company. The *Zephyr*, the country's first diesel-powered streamliner, was delivered in 1934 and was soon followed by a whole family of *Zephyrs*. In 1939 the Burlington teamed up with Rio Grande and Western Pacific to operate a through passenger train between Chicago and San Francisco via the Dotsero Cutoff — the *Exposition Flyer*. In 1945 Burlington built the first Vista-Dome coach. These elements achieved their ultimate synthesis in 1949 with the inauguration of the Vista-Dome-equipped *California Zephyr*, operated between Chicago and San Francisco by the Burlington, the Rio Grande, and the Western Pacific. The route was longer and slower than that of the compe-

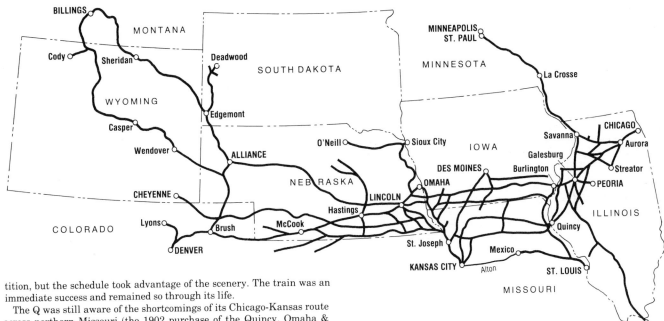

tition, but the schedule took advantage of the scenery. The train was an immediate success and remained so through its life.

The Q was still aware of the shortcomings of its Chicago-Kansas route across northern Missouri (the 1902 purchase of the Quincy, Omaha & Kansas City Railroad, a circuitous secondary local line between Quincy and Kansas City, largely abandoned in 1939, appears to have been an act of mercy on the Burlington's part). It first proposed a four-way deal that would give Santa Fe a route to St. Louis; Gulf, Mobile & Ohio a route of its own to Chicago (Q president Ralph Budd had been a member of the board of directors of GM&O predecessor Gulf, Mobile & Northern); and the foundering Alton a good home. GM&O would get the Alton, less its St. Louis-Kansas City line, which didn't fit into GM&O's north-south pattern; Burlington would take that line and swap trackage rights into St.

Louis to the Santa Fe for a shortcut across Missouri on Santa Fe's main line. The other roads serving St. Louis protested. GM&O merged the Alton, but the rest of the plan did not come to fruition. In the early 1950s Burlington built a new line across Missouri and coupled it with Wabash trackage rights to shorten its Chicago-Kansas City route by 22 miles. The line was further improved in 1960 with a new bridge at Quincy.

Burlington's *Zephyrs* introduced the combination of diesel power, streamlining, and stainless steel, and Burlington built the first streamlined dome car. The Q's pride in these trains was evident in its slogan, "Way of the Zephyrs." The *Twin Cities Zephyr*, shown crossing the Mississippi River at Minneapolis on Great Northern's James J. Hill Bridge, is headed by a shovel-nose power unit typical of the first *Zephyrs*; the consist includes five cars with Vista-Domes.

CB&Q

Merger with Great Northern, Northern Pacific, and Spokane, Portland & Seattle (jointly owned by GN and NP) was proposed once again in 1960 and finally became reality on March 2, 1970, with the creation of Burlington Northern.

Location of headquarters: Chicago, Illinois
Miles of railroad operated: 1929 — 9,367; 1969 — 8,430
Number of locomotives: 1929 — 1,575; 1969 — 665
Number of passenger cars: 1929 — 1,225; 1969 — 624
Number of freight cars: 1929 — 62,225; 1969 — 36,264
Number of company service cars: 1929 — 4,579; 1969 — 3,087
Reporting marks: CBQ, RBBQ, RBBX, BREX

Notable named passenger trains: *Denver Zephyr* (Chicago-Denver), *California Zephyr* (Chicago-Denver-Salt Lake City-San Francisco; operated jointly with Denver & Rio Grande Western and Western Pacific), *Twin Cities Zephyr* (Chicago-Minneapolis)
Historical and technical society: Burlington Route Historical Society, P. O. Box 456, LaGrange, IL 60525
Recommended reading: *Burlington Route*, by Richard C. Overton, published in 1965 by Alfred A. Knopf, New York, New York
Subsidiaries and affiliated railroads, 1969:
Colorado & Southern (74%)
Successors: Burlington Northern (TWG)

CHICAGO GREAT WESTERN RAILROAD

By the late 1870s the Upper Midwest was spiderwebbed with the lines of four major railroads: the Burlington, the Milwaukee Road, the Chicago & North Western, and the Rock Island. Even so, there were people who thought there was room for more. One of those was A. B. Stickney, who had been construction superintendent of the St. Paul, Minnesota, & Manitoba (forerunner of the Great Northern), general superintendent of the western portion of the Canadian Pacific, and an official of the Minneapolis & St. Louis. Stickney decided to build a railroad from St. Paul to Chicago. He acquired the franchise and outstanding stock of the Minnesota & Northwestern Railroad, which had been chartered in 1854 to build a line from Lake Superior through the St. Paul toward Dubuque, Iowa. The charter was particularly enticing to Stickney because of a tax limitation clause it contained.

Construction of the road started at St. Paul in September 1884, and a year later the line was open to the Iowa state line, where it connected with a road the Illinois Central had leased. Stickney, however, was intent on having his own line, so even before the Minnesota & Northwestern was completed he acquired and merged with it the Dubuque & Northwestern. That railroad had been incorporated in 1883 to build from Dubuque to Vancouver, British Columbia, or at least to a connection with the Northern Pacific. The M&NW met the Dubuque & Northwestern near Oneida, Iowa, in October 1886.

Meanwhile the Minnesota & Northwestern of Illinois was building west from what is now Forest Park, Ill. Completed in early 1888, the en-

gineering feat of the line was the longest tunnel in Illinois, the half-mile-long Winston Tunnel, named for the construction company that built the line.

Stickney realized that Minnesota & Northwestern was hardly an appropriate name for a railroad that began at St. Paul and went to Chicago. He renamed it the Chicago, St. Paul & Kansas City and set out for Kansas City. He acquired the Dubuque & Dakota Railroad, a short line from Sumner, Iowa, through Waverly to Hampton, and the Wisconsin, Iowa & Nebraska Railway, a line from Waterloo, Iowa, to Des Moines. The

Six F-units and their freight train are about to enter the west portal of Winston Tunnel. The summit of the grade up from the Mississippi River (the ruling grade of CGW's Chicago District) is just east of the tunnel.

Mark Nelson

WI&N was nicknamed "The Diagonal" for its direction across the state of Iowa. Stickney extended the WI&N east to connect with his main line at Oelwein and southwest to St. Joseph, Missouri, and Leavenworth, Kansas, arriving there in 1891. Trackage rights over a Missouri Pacific subsidiary carried CStP&KC trains to Kansas City.

Construction costs and rate wars began to adversely affect CStP&KC's financial situation — Stickney was an advocate of simplified freight rates and a practitioner of rate cutting. The road was reorganized in 1892 as the Chicago Great Western Railway. Stickney took advantage of de-

pressed prices during the Panic of 1893 to rebuild the road and erect new shops at Oelwein, the hub of the railroad. In 1901 the CGW leased the Wisconsin, Minnesota & Pacific Railroad, which had lines west out of Winona and Red Wing, Minn., and the Mason City & Fort Dodge Rail Road. The latter road (which had been controlled by James J. Hill since the late 1880s) served as a springboard for CGW's extension to Omaha. The route to Omaha, opened in 1903, led through largely unpopulated territory. A CGW subsidiary planned, developed, and sold towns at regular intervals along the line. About this same time the road planned and surveyed an extension to Sioux City but dropped the idea in 1906 because of the expense. CGW even set its sights briefly on Denver before turning its attention to a policy of encouraging the short lines, both steam and electric, with which it connected.

The CGW entered receivership in 1908. J. P. Morgan purchased it and reorganized it as the Chicago Great Western Railroad in August 1909. Samuel M. Felton, well known as a rehabilitator of weak railroads, replaced Stickney as president. During World War One USRA control diverted much business from the CGW, but government payment for damages helped finance postwar improvements. To cut passenger expenses, CGW replaced steam trains with motor cars. CGW had purchased several McKeen gasoline cars in the early 1900s, and it continued the motorization of its passenger trains with the purchase of Electro-Motive's first gas-electric car. In the mid-1920s CGW teamed up with Santa Fe to offer through Pullman car service from the Twin Cities to Texas and Los Angeles. In 1929 CGW converted three old McKeen cars to a deluxe gas-electric train, the *Blue Bird*, for service between Minneapolis and Rochester, Minn.

Felton retired in 1929 when a syndicate of industrial traffic managers led by Patrick H. Joyce acquired control of the CGW. The new management completely revised the operational structure of the railroad, closing down facilities and discharging employees. The Joyce administration got involved in a stock manipulation scheme — it included the Van Sweringen brothers of Cleveland and the Kansas City Southern — that resulted in CGW's bankruptcy in February 1935. More noteworthy fruits of the Joyce era were three dozen 2-10-4s for freight service and the inauguration in 1936 of piggyback service.

A 1941 reorganization created the Chicago Great Western Railway, which included a number of previously separate subsidiaries. Immediately after World War Two the road began to dieselize; dieselization was complete by 1950.

In 1948 a group of Kansas City businessmen began to invest heavily in the CGW. Among them were William N. Deramus, president of Kansas City Southern, and his son, William N., III. Within a few months the younger Deramus was president of the CGW. Under his direction the road caught up on deferred maintenance and improved its physical plant.

Passenger service was reduced to a single coach-only train each way between the Twin Cities and Kansas City, the Twin Cities and Omaha, and Chicago and Oelwein. With the intent of reducing train-miles, CGW began to run enormously long freight trains behind sets of six or more F-units. Service suffered as trains were held to reach maximum tonnage and through trains performed local work. The road consolidated its offices at Oelwein and Kansas City and closed its Chicago general offices. The last passenger trains, between the Twin Cities and Omaha, made their last runs on September 29, 1965. They lasted as long as they did because of mail and express traffic inherited when Chicago & North Western dropped its Twin Cities-Omaha trains.

Chicago Great Western did reasonably well during the 1950s and 1960s, but it became clear that it would have to merge to survive. As early as 1946 there had been a proposal to merge CGW with Chicago & Eastern Illinois and Missouri-Kansas-Texas, and during the Deramus era it was generally thought that Kansas City Southern and CGW would team up. CGW investigated merger with Rock Island, with Soo Line, and with Frisco, but it was with the rapidly expanding Chicago & North Western that CGW merged on July 1, 1968. The North Western subsequently abandoned most of the CGW.

Location of headquarters: Chicago, Illinois
Miles of railroad operated: 1929 — 1,495; 1967 — 1,411
Number of locomotives: 1929 — 237; 1967 — 139
Number of passenger cars: 1929 — 185
Number of freight cars: 1929 — 7,363
Number of company service cars: 1929 — 646
Number of freight and company service cars: 1967 — 3,540
Reporting marks: CGW
Historical and technical society: Chicago & North Western Historical Society, 17004 Locust Drive, Hazel Crest, IL 60429
Recommended reading: *The Corn Belt Route*, by H. Roger Grant, published in 1984 by Northern Illinois University Press, DeKalb, IL 60115 (ISBN 0-87580-095-5)
Successors: Chicago & North Western (TWG)
Portions still operated: Elmurst-Fox River, Ill.; Oelwein-Coulter, Iowa; Mason City-Somers, Iowa: Chicago & North Western

CHICAGO, INDIANAPOLIS & LOUISVILLE RAILWAY

The New Albany & Salem Rail Road was organized in 1847 to build a railroad from New Albany, Indiana, on the north bank of the Ohio River opposite Louisville, Kentucky, to the shore of Lake Michigan. The line's founder, James Brooks, chose Salem, Ind., for the destination in the road's title to provide an appearance of conservatism to attract investors. The line was opened to Salem in 1851, to Bedford and Bloomington in 1853, and to Gosport in early 1854. A branch was begun from Gosport toward Indianapolis, but financial problems stopped work on it before the grading was completed. (It was eventually built as part of the Pennsylvania Railroad system.) Finances also halted progress on the main line.

Meanwhile the Michigan Central was stymied at Michigan City in its effort to build west from Detroit to Chicago. The charter of the New Albany & Salem allowed construction anywhere in Indiana, and Brooks did some trading. Michigan Central built its line to the Illinois border using NA&S's franchise and bought a block of NA&S stock, providing the capital Brooks needed to finish the NA&S between Gosport and Crawfordsville. In 1852 NA&S had taken over the Crawfordsville & Wabash, which had a line from Crawfordsville to Lafayette. The NA&S line between Michigan City and Lafayette was opened in October 1853. The line was as level and straight (including a 65-mile tangent) as the south end of the NA&S was crooked and hilly.

A drought in 1856 adversely affected both farming along the railroad and the Ohio River steamboats with which the railroad connected. The New Albany & Salem defaulted on its interest payments and entered receivership in 1858. It was reorganized in 1869 as the Louisville, New Albany & Chicago Railway under the leadership of John Jacob Astor. The reorganization was declared illegal. There was another foreclosure sale to the same group of investors, and in 1873 the road made a second start as the Louisville, New Albany & Chicago Railway.

The road had lost any claim it might have had to Michigan Central's line into Chicago. The Indianapolis, Delphi & Chicago Railway was incorporated in 1865, then reincorporated in 1872 with the same name as part of a proposed railroad, the Chicago & South Atlantic, between Chicago and Charleston, South Carolina. It began construction in 1877 of a narrow gauge railroad. The first portion was opened a year later from Bradford (renamed Monon in 1879) to Rensselaer. A new company, the Chicago & Indianapolis Air Line Railway, took over in 1881, and it was merged with the LNA&C in 1883. The line was converted to standard gauge in 1881, and Chicago-Indianapolis trains began operating in 1883. Access to Chicago was over the rails of the Chicago & Western Indiana and entrance to Indianapolis was on the Indianapolis Union Railway. About the same time LNA&C gained access to Louisville from New Albany over the rails of the Pennsylvania and the Louisville & Nashville.

The LNA&C map now resembled an elongated X, with the Chicago-Indianapolis and Michigan City-Louisville lines crossing at the town of Monon. The "Monon Route" slogan was first used in 1882, and the nickname quickly eclipsed the official title of the road. The map showed few branch lines. In the 1880s the road acquired two, one from Orleans west to French Lick and the other from Bedford west toward (but not to) the western Indiana coalfields. In 1898 the Indiana Stone Railroad was incorporated to build a water-level bypass of the severe grades north of Harrodsburg — the old main line remained in service as a branch. A branch was constructed from Wallace Jct. to Victoria to reach the coalfields that the branch from Bedford had stopped short of. It was built by the Indianapolis & Louisville Railroad as part of a proposed Indianapolis-Evansville line — Wallace Jct.-Victoria was all that was built, though.

In 1889 and 1890 the Monon made an agreement to use the Kentucky & Indiana bridge over the Ohio River between New Albany and Louisville. It facilitated connections with the Louisville Southern, which extended east from Louisville to the Cincinnati, New Orleans & Texas Pacific (Southern Railway System). The Monon built a branch of the LS to Lexington and also built the Richmond, Nicholasville, Irvine & Beattyville east toward the coalfields of eastern Kentucky. Early in 1890 Astor died. Dr. William L. Breyfogle of New Albany pulled a shareholders' coup, unseated the management, and aborted the extension into Kentucky. The Louisville Southern became part of the Southern system, and

J. P. Lamb Jr.

Monon train 11, the southbound Chicago-Indianapolis *Tippecanoe*, crosses its namesake river at Monticello, Ind., in April 1959, less than a week before the train's last run.

the RNI&B became part of the L&N. The Monon was reorganized as the Chicago, Indianapolis & Louisville Railway in 1897, and J. P. Morgan acquired control in 1899.

In 1902 the Southern and the Louisville & Nashville acquired most of the Monon's common stock and more than three-quarters of the preferred. In the early 1900s the road did well enough to consider doubletracking the line between Monon and Chicago. To that end it acquired the Chicago & Wabash Valley, a short line parallel to and east of the main line across northwestern Indiana. Nothing came of the project. In

1916 the Monon merged that line and two other roads that formed Monon branches, the Indiana Stone Railroad and the Indianapolis & Louisville.

By the 1920s the Monon had begun to stagnate. The road served little of the industrial area of Indianapolis, and the through business on the route was largely in conjunction with the ne'er-do-well Cincinnati, Hamilton & Dayton. Baltimore & Ohio acquired CH&D's Cincinnati-Toledo line in 1917 and cast off the Hamilton-Indianapolis-Springfield, Ill., line as the Cincinnati, Indianapolis & Western. B&O acquired that in 1927, drying up connecting traffic — B&O could move Cincinnati-Chicago traf-

JOHN W. BARRIGER III (1899-1976) was born in Dallas and grew up in St. Louis. He began railroad service as a laborer in the Pennsylvania Railroad shops at Altoona. He soon left to attend the Massachusetts Institute of Technology, but he continued to work for the Pennsy during vacations. After graduation in 1921 he returned to the Pennsy full time in various capacities until 1927 when he joined the financial firm of Kuhn, Loeb & Co. From 1933 to 1941 Barriger was chief of the railroad division of the Reconstruction Finance Corporation. By the time he came to the Monon he had been reorganization manager of the Chicago & Eastern Illinois, federal manager of the Toledo, Peoria & Western, vice-president of the Union Stock Yards in Chicago, and manager of the Diesel Locomotive Division of Fairbanks-Morse.

Fabian Bachrach

After rebuilding the Monon Barriger spent brief periods as vice-president of the New Haven and the Rock Island, and from 1956 to 1964 he was president of Pittsburgh & Lake Erie, which came as close to his concept of super railroad as any of his railroads. At the end of 1964 Barriger retired from that post, and in March 1965 he became chairman and chief executive officer (his business card read "Traveling Freight Agent and President") of the Missouri-Kansas-Texas, which had fallen on hard times. After retirement from the Katy at age 70, Barriger briefly became chief executive officer of the Boston & Maine, and then in 1973, a consultant for the Federal Railroad Administration, retiring in 1975. (In 1984 Federal Railroad Administrator John Riley said "You didn't worry about missing one of JWB's retirement parties. You knew there'd be another.") He then was asked to return to the Rock Island as Senior Traveling Freight Agent, the position he held at the time of his death.

Barriger was an enthusiastic railroader. In 1976 when he went to the Rock Island, he said, "They could charge me money to let me work as a railroader and I'd still do it. For me, railroading comes under the heading of organized sport." During his life he amassed an excellent railroad library, which his family donated in 1982 to the Mercantile Library of St. Louis to create the John W. Barriger III Railroad Library.

fic on its own rails all the way via Deshler, Ohio. The Indiana coalfields were at a competitive disadvantage with the Appalachian ones. The demand for building stone, which at times constituted nearly a quarter of Monon's freight traffic, diminished as construction activity dropped during the Depression. Both the railroads with which the Monon connected at Louisville, Southern and L&N, had more expeditious connections for Chicago business and did not particularly favor the Monon, even though they controlled it.

In an effort to avert bankruptcy, Monon applied to the Reconstruction Finance Corp. for a loan in December 1933. John W. Barriger III, head of the agency, recognized that the road's finances needed reorganization and refused the loan. The Monon filed for bankruptcy on December 30, 1933. It cut passenger service to the minimum and abandoned the branch west of Bedford and the former Chicago & Wabash Valley. The trustees even considered total abandonment — the Monon had the longest route between an Ohio River crossing and Chicago and was the hardest to operate — but the road struggled through World War Two.

On May 1, 1946, a new Chicago, Indianapolis & Louisville Railway took over, with John W. Barriger III as president. Barriger was an advocate of the Super Railroad — flat, straight, fast, multiple track, heavy duty — and the Monon was its antithesis. Nonetheless, Barriger replaced steam with diesel, purchased war-surplus hospital cars to convert to streamlined passenger cars (cheaper and quicker than ordering new cars), restored passenger trains, solicited freight business, bought freight cars by the hundreds, and caught up on 20 years of deferred maintenance. Concluding that the south end of the railroad needed to be totally relocated, which was impossible, he limited relocation efforts to replacement of the Wabash River bridge at Delphi and a bypass of a bottomless bog at Cedar Lake. He was unable to relocate the Monon out of city streets at New Albany, Bedford, Lafayette, and Monticello. When Barriger departed at the end of 1952 to assume a vice-presidency of the New Haven he left behind a well-maintained and well-operated railroad with black ink on its ledgers.

Barriger was succeeded by Warren Brown, during whose tenure the railroad changed its name to Monon Railroad. In 1959 the Monon dropped its Indianapolis passenger trains; the Chicago-Louisville train lasted until 1967, largely because of business generated by Purdue University at Lafayette and Indiana University at Bloomington.

When the Louisville & Nashville purchased the eastern half of the Chicago & Eastern Illinois in 1969, the Monon approached the Southern Railway on the matter of merger. Southern had just upgraded its line into Cincinnati and was content to interchange Chicago business there rather than acquire its own line north from the Ohio River. Louisville & Nashville was much more receptive to merger, seeing the Monon as a useful alternate route and also eyeing Monon's interests in Chicago & Western In-

diana, Belt Railway of Chicago, and Kentucky & Indiana Terminal. The Louisville & Nashville merged the Monon on July 31, 1971.

Location of headquarters: Chicago, Illinois
Miles of railroad operated: 1929 — 648; 1970 — 541
Number of locomotives: 1929 — 174; 1970 — 44
Number of passenger cars: 1929 — 91
Number of freight cars: 1929 — 6,356; 1970 — 3,078
Number of company service cars: 1929 — 256; 1970 — 98
Reporting marks: CIL, MON
Historical and technical society: Monon Railroad Historical-Technical Society, 410 South Emerson Street, Mt. Prospect, IL 60056
Recommended reading: *Monon Route*, by George W. Hilton, published in 1978 by Howell-North Books, 850 North Hollywood Way, Burbank CA 91505
Subsidiaries and affiliated railroads, 1970:
Chicago & Western Indiana (20%)
Belt Railway of Chicago (8.33%)
Kentucky & Indiana Terminal (33.3%)
Successors:
Louisville & Nashville
Seaboard System (TWG)
Portions still operated: Chicago-Louisville; Monon-Delphi; Medaryville-Monon: Seaboard System

CHICAGO, MILWAUKEE, ST. PAUL & PACIFIC RAILROAD: PACIFIC EXTENSION

The Chicago, Milwaukee & St. Paul Railway of 1900 was considered one of the most prosperous, progressive, and enterprising railroads in the U. S. Its main lines ran from Chicago to Minneapolis, Omaha, and Kansas City, and its network of secondary lines and branches covered most of that portion of Wisconsin, Iowa, and Minnesota between the Omaha and Minneapolis lines and much of eastern South Dakota. Lines reached west to the Missouri River at Running Water, Chamberlain, and Evarts, S. Dak. Indeed, except for the last few miles into Kansas City and operation over Union Pacific rails from Council Bluffs to Omaha, the Missouri

River formed the western boundary of the Milwaukee Road ("Milwaukee Road" as a name or nickname did not come into use until the late 1920s; "St. Paul Road" was sometimes used as a nickname, but the railroad's advertising used the full name).

The battle over control of the Northern Pacific and the Burlington in 1901 made the Milwaukee Road aware that without its own route to the Pacific it would be at its competitors' mercy — a commodity the railroad industry was singularly short of. At the same time the Milwaukee Road was experiencing a change in its traffic from dominance by wheat to a

Little Joes E74 and E75 lead freight 263, running ahead of its schedule as an extra train, westward through Ringling, Mont. The high prairie is cattle country.

more balanced mix of agricultural and industrial products. Arguments against extension westward included the possibility of the construction of the Panama Canal and the presence of strong competing railroads: Union Pacific, Northern Pacific, and Great Northern. Arguments for the extension banked heavily on the growth of traffic to and from the Pacific Northwest.

In 1901 the president of the Milwaukee Road dispatched an engineer west to estimate the cost of duplicating Northern Pacific's line. His figure was $45 million. Such an expenditure required considerable thought; not until November 1905 did Milwaukee's board of directors authorize construction of a line west to Tacoma and Seattle.

In 1905 and 1906 the Milwaukee Road incorporated subsidiaries in

South Dakota, Montana, Idaho, and Washington. The Washington company was renamed the Chicago, Milwaukee & Puget Sound Railway, and it took over the other three companies in 1908. It was absorbed by the CM&StP in 1912.

The extension began with a bridge across the Missouri River three miles upstream from Evarts, S. Dak., at a point named Mobridge. Roadbed and rails pushed out from several points into unpopulated territory. The work went quickly, and the road was open to Butte, Mont., in August 1908. The route from Harlowton to Lombard was that of the Montana Railroad, the "Jawbone." Its mortgage was held by James J. Hill and the Great Northern Railway. Taking advantage of Hill's absence on a trip to England, the Milwaukee Road advanced the owner the funds required to pay off the mortgage and bought the railroad through the CM&PS.

Construction was also under way eastward from Seattle. The last spike on the line was driven near Garrison, Mont., on May 14, 1909. The cost of the extension was $234 million. Local passenger service was established later that year; through passenger service was inaugurated in May 1911.

The Milwaukee Road began carfloat service on Puget Sound to connect the railroad with a pair of isolated branches, one on the Olympic Peninsula and the other east from Bellingham, Wash. (The latter had rail connections, but not directly with the main line of the Milwaukee.)

In 1912 the Milwaukee Road decided to electrify much of the new line. The terrain of the five mountain ranges (the Belt, Rocky, Bitter Root, Saddle, and Cascade ranges), the possibility of hydroelectric power, the

difficulties associated with operating steam locomotives through tunnels and in severe winter weather, and an increase in traffic all suggested electrification. The section from Harlowton, Mont., to Avery, Idaho, was completely turned over to electric operation in late 1916. Early in 1917 the road decided to electrify the portion of the line from Othello, Wash., to Tacoma. Electric operation on the Coast Division began in 1919, and overhead wires reached Seattle, on a 10-mile branch off the main line, in 1927. The electrification cost $23 million, but in 1925 the road reported that the savings over steam operation had already amounted to more than half that sum.

The boom in the Pacific Northwest ended about 1910, and the Panama Canal opened in 1914. Traffic on the Milwaukee Road's route to the Pacific fell off, but the debt incurred in building it remained. In 1921 the Milwaukee Road leased the Chicago, Terre Haute & Southeastern to gain access to the coalfields of southern Indiana, and a year later it acquired the Chicago, Milwaukee & Gary to gain access to the CTH&SE. Both smaller roads were heavily in debt. In 1925 the Milwaukee Road entered receivership; the Chicago, Milwaukee, St. Paul & Pacific Railroad took over in early 1928. The road declared bankruptcy again in 1935 and was reorganized in 1945.

Through this period there was little change in Milwaukee's lines west of the Missouri River. North America's longest electrification continued unchanged — in the same two disconnected portions, with steam and later diesel power hauling trains over the 212 miles of nonelectrified track between Avery, Idaho, and Othello, Wash. With dieselization of the Milwaukee Road after World War Two it appeared that the electrification, by then 30 years old, would be dismantled, but the road purchased a dozen electric locomotives that had been built by General Electric for Russia and embargoed because of tensions between the U. S. and Russia. Milwaukee Road regauged the "Little Joes" from 5 feet to standard and equipped two with steam generators for passenger service. They went into service between Harlowton and Avery.

The electrification soldiered on for another two decades, but diesels showed up under the wires more and more often, sometimes running in multiple with the electrics. By the early 1970s passenger service had long since been discontinued, many of the original electric locomotives had been scrapped, and much of the hardware of the electrification needed replacement. The traffic density on the line did not justify rebuilding the electric plant — and the road did not have the funds to do so. The Milwaukee Road de-energized the catenary over the Coast Division in 1972 and ended electric operation on the Rocky Mountain Division on June 16, 1974.

The Milwaukee Road once again entered reorganization proceedings in 1977. A major aspect of that reorganization was abandonment of everything west of Ortonville, Minn., so management could concentrate on making the core of the railroad — specifically Chicago-Twin Cities-Duluth, Chicago-Kansas City, and Chicago-Louisville — viable. In March 1980, the Milwaukee Road ceased service between Miles City, Mont., and the Pacific Coast, and at the end of March 1982 pulled back to Ortonville. A few lines along Puget Sound and north and south of Spokane have been taken over by other railroads, but nearly a thousand miles of the former main line across Montana, Idaho, and Washington are gone.

Miles of railroad operated west of Mobridge, S. Dak.: 1929 — 3,074; 1979 — 3,064

Notable named passenger trains: *Olympian, Olympian Hiawatha* (Chicago-Seattle-Tacoma)

Historical and technical society: Milwaukee Road Railfans Association, 7504 West Ruby Avenue, Milwaukee, WI 53218

Recommended reading: *The Electric Way Across The Mountains*, by Richard Steinheimer, published in 1980 by Carbarn Press, Tiburon, CA 94920 (ISBN 0-934406-00-6)

Portions still operated:
Mobridge-Terry, Mont.; Lewistown to Geraldine, Heath, and Moore, Mont.; Bovill, Idaho-Palouse, Wash.; Warden-Royal City, Wash.; Maple Valley-Easton, Wash.: Burlington Northern
Avery-St. Maries, Idaho: Potlatch Corp.
Bovill-Plummer, Idaho: St. Maries River
Spokane-Newport, Wash.: Union Pacific
Newport-Metaline Falls, Wash.: Pend Oreille Valley
Tacoma-Chehalis Jct., Frederickson-Morton, Wash.: Chehalis Western
Port Townsend-Port Angeles, Wash.: Seattle & North Coast (discontinued 1984)

CHICAGO NORTH SHORE & MILWAUKEE RAILROAD

In 1891 the Waukegan & North Shore Rapid Transit Co. was incorporated — a trolley line for the city of Waukegan, Illinois, on the shore of Lake Michigan, 36 miles north of Chicago. In 1897, by which time it reached 6 miles south to Lake Bluff, it was sold and reorganized as the Chicago & Milwaukee Electric Railway. The line was extended south through the towns along the lake to Evanston, where it connected with a branch of the Milwaukee Road to Chicago. It also built a line west from Lake Bluff to Libertyville in 1903 and to what is now Mundelein in 1905.

Construction northward from Lake Bluff began in 1904 following steam-railroad standards of grade and curvature — the line to Evanston was typical of suburban trolley line construction. In December 1905 the line reached Kenosha, Wisconsin, where it connected with the Milwaukee Light, Heat & Traction Co. At the same time the Milwaukee Road connection at Evanston was replaced by the Northwestern Elevated Railroad. An all-electric Chicago-Milwaukee trip became possible — it took five hours, considerably more than on the parallel Chicago & North

A. C. Kalmbach

An *Electroliner* rolls north at speed through Woodridge, Illinois, on the Skokie Valley line.

Western or Milwaukee Road, but the fare was less. The Chicago & Milwaukee pushed its own rails north, reaching Milwaukee (and bankruptcy) in 1908. Operation began, nonetheless, and immediately included limited-stop express trains with parlor car and dining service.

In 1916 the Insull interests purchased the railroad, reorganized it as the Chicago North Shore & Milwaukee Railroad, and immediately began a modernization program. Business nearly doubled during the first year of new management. In 1919 the North Shore made arrangements to operate to the Loop in downtown Chicago over the rails of the elevated (the "L") and constructed new terminals in Chicago and Milwaukee. Business flourished on the 85-mile route, even with the competition of two very healthy steam roads. The North Shore quickly developed into the definitive interurban.

In the early 1920s traffic between Waukegan and Evanston reached the saturation point of the line, which was handicapped by stretches of

SAMUEL INSULL (1859-1937) was born in London, England. In 1881 he became the private secretary of Thomas Edison, and by 1886 he was manager of Edison's Schenectady, New York, plant. In 1892 when Edison's operations were merged with other companies to form General Electric, Insull set out on his own. He became president of Chicago Edison, a small electric power company; he merged it with Commonwealth Electric to form Commonwealth Edison in 1907.

In 1914 Insull began to acquire holdings in electric railroads. Eventually his companies controlled the elevated lines in Chicago, the three major Chicago interurbans (Chicago North Shore & Milwaukee; Chicago South Shore & South Bend; and Chicago, Aurora & Elgin — Insull is notable for his modernization of these three

lines), some of the major interurbans in Indiana, and electric companies that generated one-tenth of the nation's electricity.

To finance expansion of his utility companies Insull began selling stocks on a large scale to small investors. In the stock market crash of 1929 many of these investors were wiped out. Although none of Insull's companies failed during the Depression, Insull's empire began to collapse in 1932, when a New York bank refused to renew a loan. He was forced out of the management of his other companies and fled to Europe. Insull, who had been a symbol of the boom of the 1920s, became a scapegoat for the Depression. A campaign against him welled up, and he was seized in Istanbul and returned to the U. S. for trial for mail fraud, embezzlement, and violations of the Bankruptcy Act — he was acquitted on all three charges. He died in 1937 of a heart attack in a Paris subway station.

Recommended reading: *Insull*, by Forrest McDonald, published in 1962 by The University of Chicago Press, Chicago, IL 60637

street running. The railroad saw that a new line a few miles west along the right of way of one of Insull's power companies would be cheaper than just the construction of temporary track needed to reconstruct the existing line. The first 5-mile portion of the new Skokie Valley Line was opened in 1925 and operated by Chicago Rapid Transit, which continued to operate local service until 1948; the entire line was opened in 1926 and became the new main route. The Shore Line, as the original route was termed, was relegated to local service. The new route was much faster, materially helping the North Shore to compete with the steam roads. North Shore quickly became America's fastest interurban. In addition, the North Shore emphasized its parlor and dining service — it was perhaps the only interurban to have much success with such operations.

In 1931 the Great Depression finally got a grip on the North Shore. The line declared bankruptcy in September 1932. Even so, the road continued

to operate fast, frequent trains. It cooperated with parallel Chicago & North Western and public agencies in a line relocation project through Glencoe, Winnetka, and Kenilworth, eliminating grade crossings and street running. In 1939 the North Shore ordered a pair of streamliners from St. Louis Car Co.: the *Electroliners*. No other trains of the streamliner era had such disparate elements in their specifications as capacity for 85-mph speed (North Shore's schedules called for start-to-stop averages of 70 mph) and the ability to operate around the 90-foot radius curves of the Chicago "L." World War Two brought increased traffic, and the North Shore emerged from bankruptcy in 1946 — just as competition from automobiles and strikes by employees began to cut into the road's business. Waukegan and North Chicago streetcar services were taken over by buses in 1947, dining car service on trains other than the *Electroliners* was dropped in 1949, local streetcar service in Milwaukee was discontinued in 1951, and the Shore Line was abandoned in 1955.

By then the North Shore was owned by the Susquehanna Corporation, a holding company that found the road's losses useful for tax purposes — ditto for tax credits from abandonment. In 1959 an ICC examiner recommended abandonment, and the 1960 completion of the Edens Expressway took passengers away by the thousands. Protests and renewed petitions prolonged the struggles of the line until January 21, 1963.

North Shore's freight business consisted of less-than-carload traffic carried in merchandise despatch cars (motor baggage cars) and intermediate traffic, received from one steam road and delivered to another. North Shore inaugurated piggyback service in 1926, but improved parallel highways led to its discontinuance in 1947.

Remnants of the North Shore exist. Many of its standard steel passenger cars are in trolley museums across the country, and the two *Electroliners* are at Illinois Railway Museum at Union, Ill., and Shade Gap Electric Railway, Orbisonia, Pennsylvania, after putting in several years of service on the Philadelphia & Western between 69th Street Terminal and Norristown, Pa. North Shore's right of way is still visible, and part of the Shore Line has become a bicycle path. Chicago Transit Au-

thority restored service to the south end of the Skokie Valley Route in 1964 — the *Skokie Swift*, a nonstop service between Howard Street in Chicago and Dempster Street in Skokie.

Location of headquarters: Highwood, Illinois
Miles of railroad operated: 1929 — 138; 1962 — 107
Number of locomotives: 1929 — 7; 1962 — 8
Number of passenger cars: 1929 — 214; 1962 — 135
Number of motor freight cars: 1929 — 42
Number of freight cars: 1929 — 211; 1962 — 17
Number of company service cars: 1929 — 58; 1962 — 32
Reporting marks: CNS&M
Notable named passenger trains: *Electroliner* (Chicago-Milwaukee)
Historical and technical society: Shore Line Interurban Historical Society, P. O. Box 346, Chicago, IL 60690
Recommended reading: *North Shore*, by William D. Middleton, published in 1964 by Golden West Books, P. O. Box 80250, San Marino, CA 91108
Portions still operated: Howard Street, Chicago-Dempster Street, Skokie: Chicago Transit Authority

CHICAGO, ROCK ISLAND & PACIFIC RAILWAY

In 1847 the Rock Island & La Salle Rail Road was chartered to build between Rock Island, Illinois, on the Mississippi River, and La Salle, where connections would be made with the Illinois & Michigan Canal to Chicago. Contractor Henry Farnam persuaded the organizers to extend the railroad all the way to Chicago to connect with other railroads. The charter was so amended, and the railroad was renamed the Chicago & Rock Island. Construction began in 1851. The first train ran southwest from Chicago to Joliet, 40 miles, on October 10, 1852. Its power was a 4-4-0 named *Rocket*.

The line was opened to Rock Island on February 22, 1854, and the contractors turned the line over to the corporation in July of that year. By

then the railroad had an agreement with the Northern Indiana Railroad (later part of the New York Central) for joint terminal facilities in Chicago; a branch from Bureau, Ill., south to Peoria was nearly complete (it was opened in November 1854); and the Mississippi & Missouri Railroad had been chartered in Iowa to build a railroad from Davenport, across the Mississippi River from Rock Island, to Council Bluffs, with branches south through Muscatine and north through Cedar Rapids.

Money to finance construction of the Mississippi & Missouri was hard to come by. Both Iowa City, then the state capital, and Muscatine wanted the railroad first. Iowa City offered a bonus if a train arrived by midnight, December 31, 1855. Muscatine got its railroad first, on November 20, 1855, but (if we are to believe contemporary accounts) a frozen locomotive was pushed over hastily laid and barely spiked rails into Iowa City as church bells rang in the New Year, securing the bonus and providing the perfect scenario for a multitude of grade-B novels and movies.

A bridge across the Mississippi was necessary to connect the Chicago & Rock Island and Mississippi & Missouri railroads. The Mississippi had not yet been spanned, and the immediate reaction to the proposed railroad bridge was that it would be a hazard to navigation. However, the bridge was built, and it was officially opened on April 21, 1856. On the evening of May 6 the steamboat *Effie Afton*, which usually plied the New Orleans-Louisville run, cleared the open draw span and then veered aside, turned around, rammed one of the piers, then suddenly and suspiciously burst into flames. The case of the bridge soon became one of railroad advocates versus steamboat advocates. The latter felt that even a single bridge would set an unfortunate precedent and soon there would be bridges every 40 or 50 miles along the length of the river. The railroad's case, argued by Abraham Lincoln, went one way and the other in successive courts, but in 1866 the U. S. Supreme Court held for the railroad. Several other railroads immediately applied to bridge the Mississippi at other locations.

The Mississippi & Missouri, far behind its construction schedule, was sold to the newly incorporated Chicago, Rock Island & Pacific on July 9, 1866. On August 20 that company consolidated with the Chicago & Rock Island to form a successor Chicago, Rock Island & Pacific Railroad. The line reached Des Moines a year later and arrived at Council Bluffs on May 11, 1869 — one day after the completion of the Union Pacific and Central Pacific railroads from Council Bluffs to the West Coast. The Rock Island was not the first railroad into Council Bluffs; the Cedar Rapids & Missouri (later part of the Chicago & North Western) had reached there more than two years earlier and established ties with the Union Pacific.

In the 1870s the road extended its Muscatine line southwest across Iowa and northwestern Missouri to Leavenworth, Kansas, and later negotiated trackage rights over the Hannibal & St. Joseph from Cameron, Mo., to Kansas City. Also during the 1870s the road acquired a couple of "firsts" — the first dining cars and Jesse James's first train holdup. The 1880s saw some corporate simplification, the acquisition of the Keokuk & Des Moines and the St. Joseph & Iowa, and control of the Burlington, Cedar Rapids & Northern, which had a line from Burlington, Iowa, through Cedar Rapids and Cedar Falls to Plymouth, near Mason City, with a branch through Iowa Falls and Estherville to Watertown, South Dakota. The BCR&N later acquired lines west out of Davenport and Clinton, Iowa, and lines to Decorah, Iowa, Worthington, Minn., and Sioux Falls, S. Dak.

On December 5, 1883, the Rock Island made a tripartite agreement with Union Pacific and the Milwaukee Road for interchange of business at Omaha. The Chicago & North Western, which had been UP's preferred connection, quickly became a party to the agreement, as did the Wabash, St. Louis & Pacific (a predecessor of the Wabash). The Burlington & Missouri River in Nebraska (part of the Burlington) protested the agreement. UP suddenly found itself in financial difficulties, and Rock Island decided to build its own extensions west rather than rely on interchange traffic with UP. Two years later the Chicago, Kansas & Nebraska Railroad was chartered to build from St. Joseph and Atchison southwest across Kansas to Wichita, and another railroad of the same name was incorporated in Nebraska to build from the southeast tip of the state to Kearney. The two companies merged and were leased to the St. Joseph & Iowa Railroad, a subsidiary of the Rock Island. A charter was approved for the extension of the southwest line from Wichita to Galveston, Texas, and from Liberal, Kans., to El Paso, Tex. By the end of 1887 rails reached to Caldwell, on the southern border of Kansas, and in February 1888 they reached Liberal. A year later the Rock Island had built west across northern Kansas and Colorado to Colorado Springs. RI made arrangements to use Denver & Rio Grande track north to Denver and south to Pueblo; in 1889 RI began using Union Pacific tracks from Limon, Colo., to Denver.

Rock Island's Chicago-Colorado route via St. Joseph was circuitous. To assemble a route through Omaha, RI constructed a line from Omaha to Lincoln and in 1890 traded McPherson-Hutchinson, Kans., trackage rights to Union Pacific for trackage rights on UP between Lincoln and Beatrice and use of UP's Missouri River bridge between Council Bluffs and Omaha. RI began Chicago-Colorado service via Omaha on August 16, 1891, and later built its own line west of Lincoln. Also in 1891 Rock Island acquired the property of the Chicago, Kansas & Nebraska. Subsidiary Chicago, Rock Island & Texas reached Fort Worth in 1893.

In 1901 control of the Rock Island was taken over by the Reid-Moore syndicate: Daniel G. Reed, William H. Moore, his brother James H.

Moore, and William Leeds, men who had put together the National Biscuit, Diamond Match, and American Can companies. The road continued to burgeon. It acquired the Choctaw, Oklahoma & Gulf Railroad, a line from Memphis, Tennessee, through Little Rock, Arkansas, and Oklahoma City to Elk City in western Oklahoma, and the 70-mile St. Louis, Kansas City & Colorado Railroad (which the Santa Fe at one point had considered acquiring for an entrance to St. Louis). Expansion continued: 1902 — lease of the Burlington, Cedar Rapids & Northern for 999 years, and extension of the southwestern line from Liberal to Santa Rosa, New Mexico, to connect with the El Paso & Northeastern, a Southern Pacific predecessor (the new track included the second longest stretch of straight track in the U. S., nearly 72 miles between Guymon, Okla., and Dalhart, Tex.); 1903 — Chicago, Rock Island & Gulf completed a line between Fort Worth and Dallas; 1904 — the Choctaw line was extended west to Amarillo, Tex., and the Kansas City-St. Louis line was opened; 1905 — the road began assembling and constructing a line south from Little Rock to Eunice, Louisiana, with the intent of reaching New Orleans; and 1906 — RI acquired a half interest in the Trinity & Brazos Valley Railway (Dallas-Houston-Galveston, later the Burlington-Rock Island Railroad) from the Colorado & Southern.

At the same time the controlling syndicate, which now included B. F. Yoakum, was busy acquiring control of the Chicago & Alton, the Chicago & Eastern Illinois, the Toledo, St. Louis & Western, and the St. Louis-San Francisco through holding companies and exchanges of stock. By 1909, though, the interest due on SLSF bonds far exceeded dividends received on SLSF stock — none. B. F. Yoakum bought Rock Island's Frisco stock at a considerable loss to the Rock Island.

Rock Island created a Twin Cities-Kansas City route in 1913 by leasing the St. Paul & Kansas City Short Line Railroad and building a line between Allerton and Carlisle, Iowa, a few miles south of Des Moines. In 1914 red ink caused by debt interest appeared on Rock Island's ledgers, and on April 20, 1915, the road entered receivership. On June 22, 1917, the road was out of receivership and back in the hands of its stockholders. Shortly afterward the United States Railroad Administration took over management for the duration of World War One.

New management took over in the 1920s and placed considerable emphasis on paying of stock dividends to the detriment of maintaining the property. Edward N. Brown, chairman of the board of the Frisco, began to buy Rock Island stock with the thought of using dividends to bolster the Frisco's situation. Soon Brown was chairman of Rock Island's executive committee. In 1927 Rock Island declared a stock dividend of 5 percent; in 1928, 6 percent; and in 1929, 7 percent — even though Rock Island's annual interest on its debt was nearly $14 million. In 1930 Brown began to secretly acquire Frisco stock for the Rock Island. Revenues dropped as the depression deepened. Then Rock Island's territory was struck with wheat crop failures and dust storms. The Rock Island declared bankruptcy on June 7, 1933.

Edward M. Durham, vice-president of Missouri Pacific, took over as chief executive office in December 1935. He brought in John D.

A westbound *Rocket* powered by an Electro-Motive TA, a model unique to the Rock Island, overtakes a 2-8-2 and its freight train just east of Bureau, Illinois, in September 1940.

Farrington, general manager of the Fort Worth & Denver, as operating officer in May 1936. Farrington started a scrap drive to finance a rail relay program and purchased ten diesel switchers and six diesel-powered *Rocket* streamliners. His program included line relocations between Davenport and Kansas City and a new bridge over the Cimarron River just east of Liberal, Kans. The road turned a profit in 1941. Durham retired in July 1942, and Farrington took over as chief executive officer.

The Chicago, Rock Island & Pacific Railroad emerged from a long and acrimonious reorganization on January 1, 1948. Farrington was still leading the company and pursuing a program of dieselization, line improvement, and industrial development. Rock Island rolled on through the 1950s and into the 1960s doing decently, although surrounded by stronger railroads. Its freight traffic was largely agricultural; its passenger trains for the most part would take you anywhere the Burlington or the Santa Fe could, but not as quickly nor with quite as much style.

In 1964 Ben Heineman, chairman of the Chicago & North Western, proposed merging the C&NW, the Rock Island, and the Milwaukee Road into an Upper Midwest system and selling the lines south of Kansas City to Santa Fe. Union Pacific made a counterproposal: merger, which would put the UP into Chicago. That year — 1964 — was Rock Island's last year of profitability.

The proposal turned into the longest, most complicated merger case ever handled by the Interstate Commerce Commission. Most of the other railroads west of Chicago protested one aspect or another of the merger, petitioned for inclusion, or asked for a piece of the Rock Island. In 1970 the Milwaukee Road, which had fallen on hard times, entered the case, asking for inclusion in Union Pacific or Southern Pacific. In 1973 the ICC proposed a restructuring of the railroad systems of the West around four systems: Union Pacific, Southern Pacific, Burlington Northern, and Santa Fe. The railroads involved in the merger case other than the two principals petitioned the ICC to dismiss the case and start over.

The ICC finally approved the merger on November 8, 1974, with several conditions: Southern Pacific would be allowed to purchase the Kansas City-Tucumcari line (that had been part of the UP merger proposal from the beginning); the Omaha-Colorado Springs line would be sold to the Denver & Rio Grande Western; and Santa Fe would be permitted to buy the Choctaw Route (Memphis-Amarillo) only if it would absorb the bankrupt and decrepit Missouri-Kansas-Texas. Union Pacific said it would have to re-evaluate the merger, since the Rock Island of 1974 wasn't the Rock Island of 1964. Rock Island filed for bankruptcy on March 17, 1975, and on August 4 of that year UP withdrew its merger offer. The ICC dismissed the case on July 10, 1976.

By then the Rock Island was in terrible shape. A new management headed by John W. Ingram did its best, introducing a new image of skyblue and white and appointing John W. Barriger III, by then 76 years old, as Senior Traveling Freight Agent (Barriger's own title) and consultant.

Rock Island's clerks walked off their jobs on August 28, 1979, over a pay dispute, and United Transportation Union members followed the next day. President Jimmy Carter issued an order September 20 creating an emergency board to settle the dispute. The UTU members then re-turned to their jobs, but members of the Brotherhood of Railway and Airline Clerks stayed off. On September 26 the Kansas City Terminal was ordered by the ICC to operate the railroad. KCT's owners plus Denver & Rio Grande Western and Southern Pacific began operating the Rock Island. On March 2, 1980, the ICC refused to extend its directed service order, and the Rock Island ceased operation March 31, 1980.

The railroad industry had never before seen an abandonment of the magnitude of Rock Island. Other railroads had been abandoned in their entirety, but they were roads like the New York, Ontario & Western (541 miles, 1957; it had always been sickly and shouldn't have been built), Fort Smith & Western (250 miles, 1939; it didn't go anywhere and shouldn't have been built), and the Colorado Midland (338 miles, 1918; it had steep grades and shouldn't have been built — and 1918 was ancient history anyway). The 7,000-mile Rock Island connected big cities like Chicago, Denver, Minneapolis, Houston, and Kansas City. It had no major operating handicaps, like mountains. It had long routes, so it wasn't another Reading or Central of New Jersey. Industry reaction to the abandonment ranged from "Someone has to take it over and run it" to "Can I have the Kansas City-Minneapolis line?"

When the dust began to settle it turned out that what was abandoned was the operating company and the financial structure, not the physical plant. Rock Island's light-blue freight cars showed up with reporting marks like C&NW and BM underneath the slogan "The Rock," and the fixed plant of the railroad was parceled out to other railroads, as detailed below.

Location of headquarters: Chicago, Illinois
Miles of railroad operated: 1929 — 8,158; 1978 — 7,021
Number of locomotives: 1929 — 1,453; 1978 — 660
Number of passenger cars: 1929 — 1,075; 1978 — 79
Number of freight cars: 1929 — 43,751
Number of company service cars: 1929 — 3,489
Number of freight and company service cars: 1979 — 26,592
Reporting marks: RI, ROCK
Notable named passenger trains: *Golden State Limited* (Chicago-Kansas City-El Paso, Texas-Los Angeles; operated west of Tucumcari, N. Mex., by Southern Pacific); *Rockets* (Chicago-Peoria, Chicago-Des

Rock Island

Two GP7s wearing the new-image blue and white and lettered "The Rock" and two U25Bs in the old maroon livery lead a westbound freight across Iowa between Homestead and South Amana in September 1976.

Moines-Omaha-Colorado Springs/Denver, Minneapolis-Kansas City-Dallas-Houston, and others)

Historical and technical society: Rock Island Technical Society, 8746 North Troost, Kansas City, MO 64155

Major portions still operated:

Chicago-Colorado route and branches:

Chicago-Joliet, Ill.: Regional Transportation Authority (passenger)

Chicago-Blue Island, Gresham-Pullman Jct.-Calumet Harbor, Ill.: Chicago Rail Link (La Salle & Bureau County)

Chicago-Omaha; branches to Pella, Audubon, and Oakland, Iowa: Iowa Interstate

Blue Island-Joliet-Bureau-Henry, Ill.: Chessie System (Baltimore & Ohio)

Peoria-Mossville, Peoria-Keller, Ill.: Peoria & Pekin Union

Iowa Junction (Peoria)-Hollis, Ill.: Chicago & North Western
Davenport-Iowa City: Milwaukee Road (trackage rights)
Clinton-Davenport-Muscatine-Washington, Iowa: Milwaukee Road
Cedar Rapids-Manly; Vinton-Dysart, Iowa: Iowa Northern
Iowa Falls-Estherville; Bricelyn-Estherville-Ocheyedan; Dows-Forest City; Palmer-Royal, Iowa: Chicago & North Western
Hallam-Fairbury, Nebr.: Union Pacific
Clay Center-Belleville, Kans.; Mahaska, Kans.-Limon, Colo.: Kyle Railroad
Limon-Cimarron Hills, Colo.: Cadillac & Lake City

Golden State route:
St. Louis-Owensville, Mo; Kansas City-Tucumcari, N. Mex.: Cotton Belt (Southern Pacific)
Tucumcari-Santa Rosa, N. Mex.: Southern Pacific (long operated by SP)
Liberal, Kans.-Stinnett, Tex.; Morse Jct.-Etter, Tex.: Texas Northwestern

Mid-Continent route:
Inver Grove, Minn.-Des Moines-Kansas City: Chicago & North Western
Salina-Herington-Wichita, Kans.-El Reno, Okla.-Fort Worth: Oklahoma,

Kansas & Texas (subsidiary of Missouri-Kansas-Texas)
North Enid-Ponca City, Okla.: Enid Central
Fort Worth-Dallas: Missouri-Kansas-Texas
Dallas-Houston-Galveston: Burlington Northern (previously operated jointly with BN)

Choctaw route:
Memphis-Brinkley, Ark.: Cotton Belt
Hazen-Little Rock, Ark.: Missouri Pacific
Little Rock-Perry, Ark.: Little Rock & Western
McAlester-Council, Okla.: Missouri-Kansas-Texas
Shawnee-Oklahoma City: Atchison, Topeka & Santa Fe (trackage rights)
Weatherford-Elk City, Okla.: Farmrail Corp.

"Little Rock" lines:
Haskel-Hot Springs-Malvern, Ark.: Missouri Pacific
Fordyce-Whitlow Jct., Ark.: Fordyce & Princeton
El Dorado, Ark.-Lillie, La.: East Camden & Highland
Hodge-Winnfield-Alexandria, La.: Central Louisiana & Gulf

Recommended reading: *Iron Road to Empire*, by William Edward Hayes, published in 1953 by Simmons-Boardman Publishing Corp.

CHICAGO, SPRINGFIELD & ST. LOUIS RAILWAY
JACKSONVILLE & HAVANA RAILROAD

The Chicago, Peoria & St. Louis and Jacksonville Southeastern system of the early 1890s was a sizable amalgamation (more than 400 miles) of several railroads in central Illinois. It had a line from Peoria through Springfield to St. Louis and another from Havana through Jacksonville to Mount Vernon, crossing the first at Litchfield. Receivership in 1893 separated the Jacksonville-Mount Vernon line about the same time the St. Louis, Chicago & St. Paul (a line from St. Louis to Springfield via Alton and Jerseyville) became part of the system. Around the turn of the century several lines were sold to other railroads: Springfield-Litchfield to the Illinois Central, Litchfield-Madison to the Litchfield & Madison,

and Jacksonville-Centralia to the Burlington. The remainder constituted a slow and circuitous route from Peoria through Springfield and Alton to St. Louis — through an area generally dominated by large, strong, straight railroads.

The CP&StL ambled in and out of receivership during the first two decades of the twentieth century. In 1921 Coverdale & Colpitts, a firm of railroad consultants, recommended sale in one piece, sale in parts, or abandonment as a way to raise funds to pay off the accumulated debt. A 1923 attempt to sell the road in one piece attracted no bidders; the road was sold piecemeal at foreclosure on November 20, 1924. The Chicago & Illinois Midland bought the north end of the road between Springfield and Pekin. The extreme south end between Grafton and East St. Louis, Ill., was purchased by the president of the Litchfield & Madison, itself an earlier CP&StL castoff. The new line was named the Alton & Eastern. It was soon leased to the Illinois Terminal and became part of that road.

Continued on next page

Zellmer Studio

The management of the two railroads bought three Brill motor cars, two for the CS&StL and one for the J&H, shown here at Havana.

Yet another group of investors purchased the two other parts of the Chicago, Peoria & St. Louis: from Havana to Jacksonville and from Springfield to Lock Haven (a few miles west of Alton). The former was incorporated as the Jacksonville & Havana Railroad; the latter as the Chicago, Springfield & St. Louis Railway. The J&H began operation August 8, 1926, and the CS&StL began service in December of that year. In 1927 the J&H arranged with the Burlington for trackage rights between Jacksonville and Waverly in order to connect with the CS&StL.

The new companies were no more successful than their predecessor. They entered receivership a week apart in early 1930, not long after the ICC had authorized their merger (which was never consummated). The

Jacksonville & Havana received ICC approval to abandon its line in September 1937, and its last train ran on October 12 of that year. The Chicago, Springfield & St. Louis hung on for another four years, until 1941.

Two small portions of the CS&StL survived longer. An eight-mile segment from Springfield to Curran was organized as the Springfield & Southwestern Railroad. It ran until January 31, 1946, when the coal mines it served shut down. The Jerseyville & Eastern Railroad was incorporated to serve industries on a half-mile portion of former CS&StL track at Jerseyville. Its four-wheel gasoline-powered Whitcomb locomotive broke down in late 1965, and the line was abandoned (quite possibly for that reason alone) in 1967.

Location of headquarters: Springfield, Illinois
Chicago, Springfield & St. Louis
  Miles of railroad operated: 1929 — 87; 1940 — 87
  Number of locomotives: 1929 — 3; 1940 — 4

Number of motor cars: 1929 — 2; 1936 — 1
Number of passenger cars: 1929 — 1
Number of company service cars: 1929 — 14; 1940 — 11 (includes cabooses)
Jacksonville & Havana
  Miles of railroad operated: 1929 — 60; 1936 — 60
  Number of locomotives: 1929 — 1; 1936 — 1
  Number of motor cars: 1929 — 1; 1936 — 1
  Number of passenger cars: 1929 — 1; 1936 — 1
  Number of freight cars: 1929 — 4; 1936 — 5
  Number of company service cars: 1929 — 10; 1936 — 10
Recommended reading: *Chicago & Illinois Midland*, by Richard R. Wallin, Paul H. Stringham, and John Szwajkart, published in 1979 by Golden West Books, P. O. Box 80250, San Marino, CA 91108 (ISBN 0-87095-077-0)

CINCINNATI & LAKE ERIE RAILROAD

The Ohio Electric Railway was formed in 1907 as a confederation of several companies. The main trunk of the system was a line from Cincinnati north through Dayton, Springfield, and Lima to Toledo; branches reached from Dayton to Richmond, Indiana, and Union City, Ohio, from Springfield through Columbus to Zanesville, and from Lima to Fort Wayne, Ind., and Defiance, Ohio. In 1918 the Cincinnati, Dayton & Toledo Railway pulled out of Ohio Electric and reorganized as the Cincinnati & Dayton Traction Co. Ohio Electric went bankrupt in 1921, and its other components resumed their own identities: Indiana, Columbus & Eastern; Dayton & Western; Columbus, Newark & Zanesville; Lima & Toledo; and Fort Wayne, Van Wert & Lima.

Dr. Thomas Conway, a professor of finance at the University of Pennsylvania's Wharton School of Finance, had become an expert in the electric railway industry and decided to put his theories to practice. In 1922 he took over the Chicago, Aurora & Elgin but quickly realized he wanted a system with more growing room and that offered greater challenge. In 1926 he purchased the Cincinnati & Dayton Traction Co. and reorganized

George Krambles

Running as the *Golden Eagle*, Cincinnati & Lake Erie "Red Devil" 125, one of the 1929 lightweights, pauses to receive passengers at Osborn, Ohio, on August 2, 1936.

it as the Cincinnati, Hamilton & Dayton Railway (not to be confused with a steam railroad of the same name that became part of the Baltimore & Ohio). Conway began rebuilding the railroad, beginning with the purchase of ten new interurban cars and ten new suburban cars. Conway looked for directions in which to expand. He acquired control of the Indiana, Columbus & Eastern Traction Co. and the Lima-Toledo Railroad, both remnants of Ohio Electric, and he coordinated their operation with CH&D. In the summer of 1929 CH&D ordered 20 passenger cars of a new low-slung, lightweight design and within a short time ordered 15 new freight motors and assorted freight trailers. At the end of 1929 CH&D was reorganized as the Cincinnati & Lake Erie Railroad and acquired the properties of the Indiana, Columbus & Eastern and the Lima-Toledo. The new railroad consisted of a main line from Cincinnati to Toledo and a branch from Springfield to Columbus.

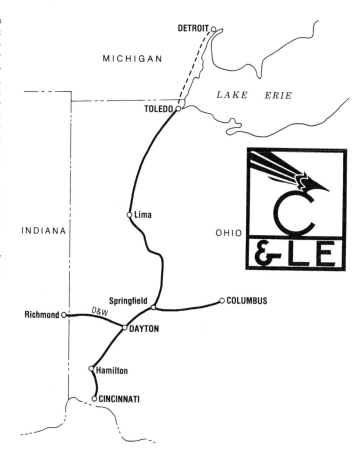

The new cars arrived and were tested. As a publicity stunt one of them raced an airplane over a mile and a half of specially groomed track. (The car won by a length.) The railroad began through service to Detroit in late 1930, but the connecting Eastern Michigan-Toledo Railway was abandoned in October 1932. Meanwhile, the Depression was deepening. Ridership and freight traffic dropped. Connecting interurban lines were dying, and to protect one of its connections, C&LE took over operation of the bankrupt Dayton & Western in 1931. Conway instituted economies such as cuts in executive salaries and one-man train crews. A rash of accidents in 1932 began to eat away at C&LE's rolling stock roster, and revenues continued to slide. The line entered receivership in 1932 with Conway as receiver.

Automobile competition increased. C&LE was unable to take up the slack with freight because of franchise restrictions on street trackage. Several fatal accidents in 1935 and 1936 drove away timid riders. In 1936 operation of the Dayton & Western was turned over to the Indiana Railroad. In November 1937 C&LE abandoned its line between Springfield and Toledo. In 1938 a road-widening project caused the south end of the line to be cut back (C&LE's cars had never gone farther south than Cumminsville in northwestern Cincinnati, because Cincinnati's streetcar system was broad gauge and used dual overhead wires). In October of that year service ceased between Columbus and Springfield. The high-speed lightweights were sold to Lehigh Valley Transit and the Cedar Rapids & Iowa City. In May 1939 more service was abandoned, leaving only a suburban line in Dayton — and that was abandoned in September 1941. The company's bus affiliate continued in service and was purchased by Greyhound in 1947.

Location of headquarters: Dayton, Ohio
Miles of railroad operated: 1930 — 270
Number of locomotives: 1930 — 1

Number of passenger cars: 1930 — 106
Number of freight motors: 1930 — 40
Number of freight trailers: 1930 — 175
Number of company service cars: 1930 — 19
Recommended reading: *Cincinnati & Lake Erie Railroad*, by Jack Keenan, published in 1974 by Golden West Books, P. O. Box 80250, San Marino, CA 91108

CLINCHFIELD RAILROAD

A railroad running north and south across the Blue Ridge Mountains in eastern Tennessee and western North Carolina had been proposed early in the railroad era, but until the end of the 1800s only bits and pieces of such a railroad were built. In 1900 the only piece of the future Clinchfield in existence was the Ohio River & Charleston, which meandered a few miles south from a connection with the Southern Railway at Johnson City, Tennessee.

The South & Western Railroad was incorporated in 1905 and was almost immediately purchased by a syndicate as part of a plan to mine coal in western Virginia and eastern Tennessee. By 1908, the year it was renamed the Carolina, Clinchfield & Ohio Railway, it was open between Johnson City, Tenn., and Marion, North Carolina. By the end of 1909 the CC&O had extended north from Johnson City to Dante, Va., and south from Marion to Spartanburg, South Carolina. In 1915 the road opened an extension north from Dante to a connection with the Chesapeake & Ohio at Elkhorn City, Kentucky.

In 1924 the Atlantic Coast Line and Louisville & Nashville railroads jointly leased the properties of the CC&O. The two lessees named the Clinchfield Railroad Company, an unincorporated entity, as the operating organization. The Clinchfield's original mission was to haul coal. Its strategic location and its relatively easy grades and curves — the result of construction late enough to take advantage of modern construction machinery and methods — led to Clinchfield's development into a fast

During World War Two the Clinchfield turned to 4-6-6-4s to power its fast freights. The first batch followed Delaware & Hudson specifications; one of this group gets a northbound freight under way at Ridge, N. C., in August 1952. A second group of Challengers was built for Union Pacific, diverted to the Rio Grande by the War Production Board, and sold by Rio Grande to Clinchfield.

Floyd A. Bruner

freight route between the Midwest and the Piedmont area. At Spartanburg, S. C., it connected with the Southern Railway and with Atlantic Coast Line's Charleston & Western Carolina subsidiary, and at Elkhorn City, Ky., it connected with C&O. The Clinchfield was unusual in that it had no significant branches, just the single main stem.

The creation of the Seaboard System Railroad on December 29, 1982, by the merger of Seaboard Coast Line and Louisville & Nashville rendered unnecessary a separate company to operate the Clinchfield. On January 1, 1983, the Clinchfield Railroad became the Clinchfield Division of the Seaboard System Railroad. On March 1, 1984, the Clinchfield Division was abolished and the former Clinchfield Railroad split between the Corbin and Florence divisions of the Seaboard. The entire line is still in service.

Location of headquarters: Erwin, Tennessee
Miles of railroad operated: 1929 — 309; 1982 — 296
Number of locomotives: 1929 — 86; 1982 — 98
Number of passenger cars: 1929 — 38
Number of freight cars: 1929 — 7,562
Number of company service cars: 1929 — 87
Number of freight and company service cars: 1982 — 5,291
Reporting marks: CRR
Successor companies: Seaboard System (TWG)

COAHUILA & ZACATECAS RAILWAY (Ferrocarril Coahuila y Zacatecas)

The Coahuila & Zacatecas was built in 1898 by the Mazapil Copper Co., a British concern, from Saltillo, in the Mexican state of Coahuila, to Concepcion del Oro, just across the Zacatecas state line. The purpose of the railroad was to serve copper, lead, zinc, and iron mines. The builders chose the same 3-foot track gauge as that of the Mexican National, which passed through Saltillo. (Mexican National standard-gauged its line in 1903.) The route paralleled the Mexican National to Carneros, 25 miles south of Saltillo, before turning southwest. In 1903 the C&Z added a short branch from Avalos, near the south end of the line, to new mines at San Pedro Ocampo. Other short branches were built at various times.

The road was badly damaged by revolutionary forces in 1914, but it was returned to service, still narrow gauge. In 1959 Mazapil Copper Co. was sold to Mexican interests; the railroad entered bankruptcy and was taken over by Mexico's Secretariat of Communication and Transport. SCT began rehabilitation of the road, bringing in three National of Mexico 2-8-0s as a stopgap. Diesel power came in 1963 in the form of three Electro-Motive GA8 units; later one was replaced by an almost identical GA18. The road also began building new freight cars.

Continued on next page

Donald E. Smith

Diesel power contrasts with wooden coaches as mixed train No. 1 of the Coahuila & Zacatecas rolls south near Carneros behind GA8 801 in 1969.

In 1972 the C&Z was taken over by National Railway of Mexico. The narrow gauge line was replaced by a new standard gauge line from Gomez Farias to a point five miles east of Concepcion del Oro.

Location of headquarters: Saltillo, Coahuila, Mexico
Miles of railroad operated: 1929 — 95; 1961 — 98
Number of locomotives: 1961 — 12; 1971 — 3

Number of passenger cars: 1961 — 8
Number of freight cars: 1961 — 158
Recommended reading: *Mexican Narrow Gauge*, by Gerald M. Best, published in 1968 by Howell-North Books, 850 North Hollywood Way, Burbank, CA 91505

COLORADO & SOUTHERN RAILWAY
FORT WORTH & DENVER CITY RAILWAY

The Colorado & Southern was an amalgamation of standard gauge and narrow gauge lines radiating in almost every direction from Denver. After 1908 C&S was controlled by the Chicago, Burlington & Quincy, but in its early years it had no relation at all with the Burlington.

Lines west of Denver

The earliest part of the Colorado & Southern was the standard gauge line from Denver to Golden, opened in 1870 as the Colorado Central Railroad. From Golden it pushed a 3-foot-gauge line up Clear Creek Canyon to Black Hawk (1872) and Central City (1878) and to Georgetown (1877). To allow its narrow gauge trains access to Denver, the road three-railed the original portion in 1879. In 1881 the road made plans to continue west to Leadville. The few miles from Georgetown to Silver Plume required a complete loop — a much-publicized engineering feat — to gain altitude. A tunnel under the Continental Divide was begun but little work was done on it. (The tunnel was eventually bored and opened in 1971 for Interstate highway 70.)

Lines north of Denver

Meanwhile, with financial help from Union Pacific the road built a line north from Golden through Boulder. The goal of the line was Julesburg on the Union Pacific main line in the northeast corner of the state, but construction halted at Longmont when the Panic of 1873 caused financial difficulty for the UP. In 1877 UP resumed construction of the Colorado Central, this time with a line south from Cheyenne, and in 1879 leased the CC. In 1882 the line was complete between Julesburg and La Salle.

At the latter town it connected with the Denver Pacific (UP's present Denver-Cheyenne line). By then UP owned the Denver Pacific and its parent Kansas Pacific (which forms UP's present Kansas City-Denver line). The Julesburg line gave UP a short route into Denver from the east, necessary to compete with the Burlington, whose rails reached Denver in May 1882.

Union Pacific built a connecting line between Greeley and Fort Collins in 1882, and in 1886 Colorado Central built a direct line between Denver and Boulder. Two portions of the CC that were considered roundabout and redundant were abandoned in 1889: the Colorado Central north of Fort Collins and most of the old Golden-Boulder line.

Cheyenne interests began building the Cheyenne & Northern Railway in 1886 to head off a Chicago & North Western subsidiary at Douglas. The North Western line reached Douglas the next year, and the C&N stopped at Wendover, Wyoming. It was extended north to a connection with the C&NW at Orin Jct. a few years later.

Lines southwest of Denver

In 1873 the Denver, South Park & Pacific began constructing a 3-foot-gauge line southwest from Denver. Progress was slowed by the Panic of 1873, and it was not until 1880 that the line reached the Arkansas River at Buena Vista. By then Jay Gould had gained control of Union Pacific and a half interest in the Denver & Rio Grande. He acquired control of the South Park in 1880 and sold it to Union Pacific, which made it part of the Colorado Central.

The DSP&P bored a tunnel — Alpine Tunnel, 1,805 feet long and the highest railroad tunnel in the U. S. — under the Continental Divide in 1881 to extend its line to Gunnison in 1882. Neither the South Park nor

the Rio Grande was happy with the DSP&P's trackage rights over Rio Grande from Buena Vista to Leadville, so in 1884 the South Park completed a Como-Leadville line that crossed the Continental Divide twice over Boreas and Fremont passes. The South Park entered receivership in 1889 and was reorganized as the Denver, Leadville & Gunnison Railway, still under UP control. Union Pacific itself entered receivership in 1893. DL&G regained independence as part of the UP reorganization in 1894.

Lines southeast of Denver

In 1881 John Evans, who had been the first governor of Colorado, incorporated the Denver & New Orleans Railroad to build a line to Fort Worth, Texas. The goal was later changed to a connection with Fort Worth & Denver City Railway, which had started construction northwest from Fort Worth. Evans's line built southeast from Denver through Parker, Elizabeth, and Fountain to Pueblo, with a 10-mile spur west to Colorado Springs from Manitou Jct. The Denver, Texas & Fort Worth was organized to build south of Pueblo; initially it used trackage rights on the Denver & Rio Grande as far as Trinidad. In 1888 it met up with the Fort Worth & Denver City. Soon afterward the DT&FW, itself having come under UP control, acquired control of the FW&DC and the Denver, Texas & Gulf, a reorganization of the Denver & New Orleans.

The north-south roads were brought together in 1890, when the Union Pacific, Denver & Gulf was formed by the UP to consolidate the Colorado Central, the Cheyenne & Northern, the Denver, Texas & Gulf, the Denver, Texas & Fort Worth, and several short lines. When the Union Pacific entered receivership in 1893, a separate receiver was appointed for these lines, Frank Trumbull, who was also to become receiver of the Denver, Leadville & Gunnison.

Colorado & Southern

The reorganization committees of the DL&G and the UPD&G (which by then owned the FW&D) arranged for the sale of their roads at foreclosure in 1898, and they were consolidated as the Colorado & Southern Railway. The only portion of the predecessors that was not included was the Julesburg-La Salle line, which was sold to Union Pacific. C&S made agreements with Santa Fe for joint use of terminal facilities in Denver, Colorado Springs, and Pueblo, and for trackage rights between Denver and Pueblo. C&S abandoned its own line from Manitou Junction to

Colorado & Southern 3-foot-gauge Mogul No. 8 stands on three-rail track in Denver Union Station awaiting departure in the 1930s.

L. C. McClure

Pueblo. However, that line was not dismantled until World War One.

C&S had its corporate eye on the boom town of Cripple Creek. The initial plan was to extend the former South Park line south to a connection with the Colorado Midland, and to that end C&S acquired control of Colorado Midland jointly with Rio Grande Western in 1900. In 1905 C&S purchased control of the Colorado Springs & Cripple Creek District Railway, which operated a steam railroad between Colorado Springs and Cripple Creek and an electric line between Cripple Creek and Victor. The mining boom declined, however: C&S sold its Colorado Midland interest in 1912 (CM was abandoned in 1921), and the CS&CCD, which had remained a separate operation, was abandoned in 1922.

In that same era C&S organized its own electric subsidiary, the Denver & Interurban, which built a line between Denver and Boulder and a streetcar system in Fort Collins. D&I entered receivership in 1918. The Fort Collins system was sold to the city (when service ended in 1951 it was the last city streetcar system in Colorado and the last in the U. S. to operate four-wheel Birney cars) and the Denver-Boulder line wandered in and out of receivership until 1926, when it was abandoned.

Control by the Burlington

In 1901 Great Northern and Northern Pacific acquired joint control of the Chicago, Burlington & Quincy. The three roads saw the C&S as an outlet to the Gulf of Mexico. In 1905 C&S bought control of the Trinity & Brazos Valley, gaining access to the port of Galveston (see the entry for Burlington-Rock Island), and in 1908 CB&Q bought nearly two-thirds of

Richard F. Lind

"Company service cars" includes the rolling stock that a railroad uses in maintaining its track and structures. An assortment of C&S company service cars trails 2-10-2 No. 900 at Boulder, Colo., on July 20, 1959.

the common stock of the C&S. In the ensuing years, though, C&S and Fort Worth & Denver maintained a degree of independence, even if their image soon became that of the Burlington.

In 1911 C&S restored the abandoned Fort Collins-Cheyenne link and teamed up with the Denver & Rio Grande to build a new double-track line between Pueblo and Walsenburg. That same year C&S abandoned the former South Park line west of Buena Vista. The mining industry was declining and paved highways were beginning to penetrate the Rockies. The last major portion of the South Park, between Denver and Climax, was abandoned in 1937; the Clear Creek lines to Idaho Springs and Black Hawk were torn up in 1941. The Leadville-Climax line, orphaned in 1937, was standard-gauged in 1941 and eventually was the home of C&S's last steam operation. Floods in May 1935 destroyed much of the original Denver & New Orleans line from Denver to Falcon, east of Colorado Springs, and that line was stubbed off just outside Denver.

Fort Worth & Denver

The history of the Texas lines is considerably simpler. The Fort Worth & Denver City Railway was chartered in 1873, and construction began in 1881. The line reached Wichita Falls in 1882 and met up with the line from Colorado on March 14, 1888.

The Wichita Valley Railway was chartered in 1890 to build southwest from Wichita Falls. It developed into a Wichita Falls-Abilene main stem with several branches owned by several different railroads, all operated as Wichita Valley Lines.

In 1939 the Burlington proposed leasing the Fort Worth & Denver City to the C&S and closing offices and shops in favor of C&S's facilities in Denver. There was loud protest in Fort Worth and Childress, and the ICC denied the request. In 1961 the Fort Worth & Denver ("City" was dropped in 1951) proposed leasing the C&S south of Denver (lines north of Denver would be leased to the Burlington) and routing traffic between Denver and Amarillo over the Santa Fe via Las Animas, Colo., to permit abandonment of the C&S line between Trinidad, Colo., and Folsom, N. M. Parent Burlington had its mind on the BN merger at the time and nothing came of the proposal.

FW&D and Rock Island purchased the Burlington-Rock Island in 1964; FW&D took over its operation upon the demise of the Rock Island.

Burlington Northern

Ownership of C&S was transferred to Burlington Northern when it was created in 1970, and by 1981 BN owned more than 92 percent of Colorado & Southern's stock. C&S was merged into Burlington Northern on December 31, 1981, and its line south of Denver was transferred to the Fort Worth & Denver. Exactly a year later Fort Worth & Denver was merged into BN. Traffic on the line has increased in recent years: Coal moves over the main line from Wyoming to Texas and the branch to Golden serves the Coors brewery, which a few years ago switched the bulk of its traffic from truck to rail.

Location of headquarters: Denver, Colorado

Miles of railroad operated: 1929 — 2,004; 1980 — C&S, 678; FW&D, 1,181

Number of locomotives: 1929 — 255; 1980 — C&S, 235; FW&D, 24

Number of passenger cars: 1929 — 164

Number of freight cars: 1929 — 10,093; 1980 — C&S, 2,329; FW&D, 1,443

Number of company service cars: 1929 — 559; 1980 — C&S, 65; FW&D, 105

(1929 figures include Fort Worth & Denver and the Wichita Valley lines)

Reporting marks: C&S, CX, RBCS, FW&D, FWDX

Notable named passenger trains: *Texas Zephyr* (Denver-Dallas)

Historical and technical society: Burlington Route Historical Society, P. O. Box 456, LaGrange, IL 60525

Recommended reading: *The Colorado Road*, by F. Hol Wagner Jr., published in 1970 by Intermountain Chapter, National Railway Historical Society, P. O. Box 5181, Denver, CO 80217

Subsidiaries and affiliated railroads, 1980:

Fort Worth & Denver (99.9%)

Galveston Terminal (50%, jointly with Rock Island)

Predecessor railroads in this book: Burlington-Rock Island

Successors: Burlington Northern (TWG)

Portions still operated: Orin Jct., Wyo.-Galveston, Tex.; Fort Collins-Greeley, Colo.; Denver-Golden; Denver-Sheridan; Denver-Connors; Climax-Leadville, Colo.; Estelline-Lubbock, Tex.; Sterley-Dimmitt, Tex.; Childress-Wellington, Tex.; Wichita Falls-Abilene, Tex.

COPPER RANGE RAILROAD

The Copper Range Railroad was incorporated in 1899 as successor to the Northern Michigan Railroad. It was controlled by the Copper Range Corporation, second largest producer of copper in the Lake Superior district. The line was opened from Gay to McKeever, Mich., that same year.

The railroad was reorganized in 1930. In 1944 it reinstated passenger service (only mixed train service had been offered for some years) with a new train called the *Chippewa*. It ran between Houghton and McKeever, where it connected with Milwaukee Road's *Chippewa*, providing daytime service between the Keweenaw Peninsula and Chicago. The service was a wartime measure, and it was discontinued in late 1946.

The Copper Range Railroad made its last run on October 27, 1972, and the road was torn up soon after; Soo Line's ex-Duluth, South Shore & Atlantic line to Houghton lasted less than a decade longer.

Location of headquarters: Houghton, Michigan
Miles of railroad operated: 1929 — 108; 1971 — 53
Number of locomotives: 1929 — 20; 1971 — 3
Number of passenger cars: 1929 — 16
Number of freight cars: 1929 — 637; 1971 — 35
Number of company service cars: 1929 — 11
Reporting marks: CR, COPR
Map: See page 123

Baldwin switcher No. 101 leads a train of pulpwood cars across the Firesteel River bridge north of McKeever, Mich., in the summer of 1972, shortly before the Copper Range Railroad was abandoned.

Clinton Jones Jr.

COPPER RIVER & NORTHWESTERN RAILWAY

The gold rush in Alaska at the end of the 1890s was followed by the discovery of copper, coal, and oil. In 1905 the Copper River & Northwestern was incorporated to build a railroad from tidewater near the mouth of the Copper River to copper mines in southeastern Alaska. The road was completed on March 29, 1911, from Cordova to Kennecott. A week later the first trainload of ore moved over the railroad.

Copper mining peaked in 1916. There were proposals to extend branches to the Bering River coalfield and north to the Yukon River, but nothing came of them, nor of a proposal to sell the railroad to the U. S. government. By the early 1930s the copper mines had been worked out

and the railroad had accumulated a long string of deficit years. Its owner, Kennecott Copper Corp., petitioned for abandonment, and the last train ran on November 11, 1938 — except for a brief period during World War Two when a few miles of the line at Cordova were reactivated for the construction of an airfield.

Location of headquarters: Seattle, Washington
Miles of railroad operated: 1929 — 195; 1936 — 195
Number of locomotives: 1929 — 15; 1936 — 13
Number of passenger cars: 1929 — 6; 1936 — 6
Number of freight cars: 1929 — 219; 1936 — 199
Number of company service cars: 1929 — 132; 1936 — 128
Recommended reading: *The Copper Spike*, by Lone E. Janson, published in 1975 by Alaska Northwest Publishing Co., Box 4-EEE, Anchorage, AK 99509 (ISBN 0-88240-066-5)

A. E. Hegg Collection

Consolidation No. 22 leads the first trainload of ore — 20 gondolas — to travel the Copper River & Northwestern.

CUMBERLAND & PENNSYLVANIA RAILROAD

Between 1844 and 1846 the Mount Savage Railroad was built from Cumberland, Maryland, northwest to coal and iron mines at Mount Savage. In 1854 the properties of the railroad were conveyed to the recently incorporated Cumberland & Pennsylvania Railroad, and in 1860 the C&P became the property of Consolidation Coal Company. In 1863 the C&P bought the George's Creek Railroad, which had built northeast toward Mount Savage from the Potomac River at Westernport, Md., and Piedmont, West Virginia. The C&P began a long career of carrying coal down to the Baltimore & Ohio and the Western Maryland.

In 1845 and 1846 the Maryland Mining Co. constructed a railroad from Eckhart Mines to Cumberland Narrows. The mining company became the property of Consolidation Coal Co. in 1870, and its railroad became part of the C&P in 1915.

In 1944 Consolidation Coal Co. was in financial difficulty and sold the Cumberland & Pennsylvania to the Western Maryland. WM quickly integrated C&P's operations into its own, but the smaller road's corporate existence continued until 1953, when it was merged into Western Maryland.

Location of headquarters: Cumberland, Maryland
Miles of railroad operated: 1929 — 50; 1944 — 49

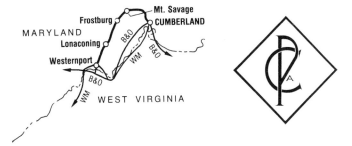

Number of locomotives: 1929 — 16; 1944 — 11
Number of passenger cars: 1929 — 11
Number of freight cars: 1929 — 933; 1944 — 5
Number of company service cars: 1944 — 21
Reporting marks: C&PA
Recommended reading: *Rails to the Big Vein,* by Deane Mellander, published in 1981 by Potomac Chapter, National Railway Historical Society, P. O. Box 235B, Kensington, MD 20895
Successors:
Western Maryland
Chessie System (TWG)
Portions still operated: Mt. Savage-Frostburg, Lonaconing-Westernport: Chessie System

C. A. Brown

Cumberland & Pennsylvania 2-8-0 No. 33, built by the road's Mt. Savage shops in 1917, leads a train of hoppers under Western Maryland's line near Cumberland in June 1944.

107

DELAWARE, LACKAWANNA & WESTERN RAILROAD

The Lackawanna's history, like that of many Eastern railroads, is one of mergers, consolidations, and leases. The oldest portion was the Cayuga & Susquehanna Railroad, completed in 1834 between Owego and Ithaca, New York. Lackawanna's corporate structure dates from the incorporation of the Liggett's Gap Railroad in 1849. That line was built north from Scranton, Pennsylvania, to the Susquehanna River and a connection with the Erie at Great Bend, Pa. It was renamed the Lackawanna & Western in 1851, and it opened later that year.

Also incorporated in 1849 was the Delaware & Cobb's Gap Railroad to build a line from the Delaware River over the Pocono Mountains to Cobb's Gap, near Scranton. It was consolidated with the Lackawanna & Western in 1853 to form the Delaware, Lackawanna & Western Railroad. It was completed in 1856 and almost immediately made a connection with the Central Railroad of New Jersey at Hampton, N. J., through the Warren Railroad, which was leased by the DL&W in 1857.

The Morris & Essex Railroad was chartered in 1835 to construct a line from Morristown, N. J., to New York Harbor. By 1860 it extended west to the Delaware River at Phillipsburg, N. J. The Lackawanna leased it in 1869 to avoid having to use the Central of New Jersey. Also in 1869 the Lackawanna bought the Syracuse, Binghamton & New York Railroad, leased the Oswego & Syracuse, and incorporated the Valley Railroad to build a connection from Great Bend to Binghamton to avoid having to use Erie tracks. In 1870 DL&W leased the Utica, Chenango & Susquehanna Valley and the Greene Railroad. Thus in the space of a couple of years the Lackawanna grew to extend from tidewater to Utica, Syracuse, and Lake Ontario.

On March 15, 1876, the Lackawanna converted its lines from 6-foot gauge (chosen because of the Liggett's Gap Railroad's connection with the Erie) to standard gauge. That year also marked the beginning of a short period of financial difficulty — not enough to cause reorganization, receivership, or bankruptcy, but enough for suspension of dividend payments. In 1880 Jay Gould began buying Lackawanna stock. His empire reached as far east as Buffalo, east end of the Wabash, and he saw that the Lackawanna would be an ideal route to New York if the gap between Binghamton and Buffalo could be closed. Lackawanna management prevented Gould from acquiring control of the road, but Gould's proposed extension to Buffalo was built: The New York, Lackawanna & Western was incorporated in 1880 and leased to the DL&W in 1882, changing the DL&W from a regional railroad to a New York-Buffalo trunk line.

The 1880s brought diversification in Lackawanna's traffic. Anthracite, much of it from railroad-owned mines, had been the reason for the Lackawanna's existence. During the 1880s the coal traffic increased one-third, but Lackawanna's general merchandise traffic increased five times that amount. In addition the DL&W was rapidly becoming a commuter carrier at its east end.

William H. Truesdale became president of the Lackawanna in 1899 and embarked on a rebuilding and upgrading program. The two major items were a 28-mile cutoff straight across western New Jersey between Slateford and Port Morris that bypassed some 40 miles of slow, curvy, hilly track, and a new line north of Scranton. Both new lines were characterized by massive cuts and fills and graceful reinforced-concrete viaducts — Tunkhannock, Paulins Kill, Martins Creek, and Kingsley. Lackawanna's suburban territory came in for track elevation, grade-crossing elimination, and new stations, all as prelude to the 1930 electrification of lines to Dover, Gladstone, and Montclair.

By the late 1930s the New York Central had purchased 25 percent of the Lackawanna's stock, giving it working — but unexercised — control of the DL&W. During World War Two the Lackawanna merged a number of its subsidiaries and leased lines for tax purposes. After the war the Lackawanna began to purchase Nickel Plate stock with an eye to possible merger, but Nickel Plate and New York Central were both opposed to it.

In 1949 Phoebe Snow returned to the Lackawanna. In the early part of the century she had been Lackawanna's symbol. Hers was the gown that stayed white from morn till night upon the Road of Anthracite — anthracite was much cleaner-burning than the bituminous coal used by other roads. Phoebe Snow's return to the road was in the form of a diesel-powered maroon and gray streamliner for daytime service between Hoboken and Buffalo.

In 1954 the Lackawanna and parallel rival Erie began to explore the idea of cooperation. The first results were the elimination of duplicate freight facilities at Binghamton and Elmira, and then in 1956 and 1957 the Erie moved its passenger trains from its old Jersey City terminal to Lackawanna's somewhat newer one at Hoboken. The two roads eliminated some duplicate track in western New York. The discussions of cooperation turned into merger talks, at first including the Delaware & Hudson.

Meanwhile DL&W's financial situation took a turn for the worse. Hurricanes in 1955 damaged Lackawanna's line through the Poconos; the cost of repairs no doubt contributed to deficits which occurred in 1958 and 1959. DL&W threatened to discontinue all suburban passenger service if the state of New Jersey would not alleviate the losses and rectify the tax situation. The state responded with a minimal subsidy.

DL&W and Erie merged as the Erie-Lackawanna on October 17, 1960.

Location of headquarters: New York, New York
Miles of railroad operated: 1929 — 998; 1959 — 926
Number of locomotives: 1929 — 683; 1959 — 212
Number of passenger cars: 1929 — 899; 1959 — 610
Number of freight cars: 1929 — 26,195; 1959 — 11,719
Number of company service cars: 1929 — 872; 1959 — 437
Reporting marks: DLW
Notable named passenger trains: *Phoebe Snow* (Hoboken-Buffalo)
Historical and technical societies:
Anthracite Railroads Historical Society, P. O. Box 119, Bridgeport, PA 19405
Erie Lackawanna Historical Society, 22 Duquesne Court, New Castle, DE 19720
Recommended reading:
The Delaware, Lackawanna & Western Railroad in the Nineteenth Century, by Thomas Townsend Taber, published in 1977, and *The Delaware, Lackawanna & Western Railroad in the Twentieth Century* (two volumes), by Thomas Townsend Taber and Thomas T. Taber III, published in 1980 by Thomas T. Taber III, 504 South Main Street, Muncy, PA 17756
Successors:
Erie Lackawanna

Continued on next page

Charles Phelps Cushing

The freight train atop Tunkhannock Viaduct at Nicholson, Pa., provides some idea of the size of the structure: 2,375 feet long and 240 feet high. It is the world's largest reinforced concrete viaduct.

Lackawanna Railroad

Gray-and-maroon E8s lead Lackawanna's *Phoebe Snow* through Milburn, N. J., on January 1, 1956. The train is about half an hour out of Hoboken on its run to Buffalo. Lackawanna's electric suburban trains draw their power from the catenaries overhead.

Don Wood

Conrail (TWG)
NJ Transit (TWG)
Portions still operated:
Hoboken-Morristown-Netcong; Roseville Avenue-Montclair; Summit-Gladstone; Hoboken-Paterson; Mountain View-Denville: NJ Transit
Netcong-Phillipsburg, N. J.; Martins Creek-Scranton, Pa.; Wind Gap-Martins Creek Jct., Pa.; Pittston Jct.-Taylor, Pa.; Binghamton-Vestal, N. Y.; Jamesville-Oswego, N. Y.; Painted Post-Bath, N. Y.; Greigsville-North Alexander, N. Y.; Lancaster-East Buffalo, N. Y.: Conrail
Chester Jct.-Succasunna, N. J.: Morristown & Erie

Northumberland-Hicks Ferry, Pa.: North Shore
Taylor, Pa.-Binghamton, N. Y.: Delaware & Hudson
Kingston-Pittston Jct., Pa.: Pocono Northeast
Binghamton-Jamesville; Chenango Forks-Utica, N. Y.: New York, Susquehanna & Western
Richfield Jct.-Richfield Springs, N. Y.: Central New York
Bath-Wayland, N. Y.: Bath & Hammondsport
Groveland-Greigsville, N. Y.: Genesee & Wyoming
Moscow-Scranton, Pa.: Steamtown, U. S. A. (museum operation)
Map: See page 133

110

DENVER & RIO GRANDE WESTERN RAILROAD — NARROW GAUGE LINES

Most of the Denver & Rio Grande Western was originally built with a 3-foot track gauge. The reason for preferring narrow gauge to standard gauge was economy: Smaller locomotives and cars cost less, the track could follow sharper curves, and the smaller rolling stock could squeeze through smaller tunnels and cuts.

The Denver & Rio Grande Railway was incorporated in 1870 to build south from Denver to Pueblo, Colorado, west along the Arkansas River and over Poncha Pass into the San Luis Valley, and then south along the Rio Grande to El Paso, Texas. The silver rush at Leadville in 1877 and skirmishes in 1878 with the Santa Fe over occupancy of Raton Pass and of the Royal Gorge of the Arkansas River changed the D&RG's goal from El Paso to Salt Lake City.

By 1880 the Denver & Rio Grande had lines from Denver to Pueblo, from Pueblo to Leadville, and from Pueblo through Walsenburg and Alamosa to Chama, New Mexico. In 1881 Rio Grande pushed its rails west to Gunnison and Durango. It added a third rail between Denver and Pueblo, both to accommodate standard gauge Santa Fe trains and to facilitate shipments from the steel mill at Pueblo. Between 1887 and 1890 D&RG created a standard gauge line between Pueblo and Ogden, Utah, by standard-gauging the Tennessee Pass-Colorado River route west of Leadville and adding a third rail east of Leadville. Standard gauge rails moved west to Alamosa in 1899 concurrent with a line relocation over La Veta Pass. The middle rail (for narrow gauge trains) was removed between Denver and Pueblo in 1902 and between Pueblo and Salida in 1911. The line from Grand Junction to Montrose and Somerset was widened in 1906, effectively pushing back the western end of the original narrow gauge main line; from Montrose south to Ridgway the line remained narrow gauge until the demise of the Rio Grande Southern.

By 1921 (the year the road became the Denver & Rio Grande Western Railroad) Rio Grande had two major narrow gauge routes: the original narrow gauge main line between Salida and Montrose via Marshall Pass, and the line from Alamosa west to Durango and Silverton, with a branch south from Antonito to Santa Fe, N. Mex. Connecting the eastern ends of the two routes was a line from Salida to Alamosa that included a 53-mile

tangent. On the west, completing a narrow gauge circle, was the Rio Grande Southern between Durango and Ridgway. D&RG had acquired control of the RGS in 1894.

A few branches were dismantled in the late 1920s and the 1930s, but there were no major abandonments until the 1940s. The Antonito-Santa Fe route, the "Chili Line," was removed in 1942 for lack of traffic. The

Dates are those of abandonment, conversion to standard gauge, installation of third rail, or sale.

WILLIAM JACKSON PALMER
(1836-1909) was born near Leipsic in
Kent County, Delaware, and grew up
in Philadelphia. He began his railroad
career as a surveyor at the age of 17,
and eventually became the private
secretary of Pennsylvania Railroad
president J. Edgar Thomson. During
the Civil War he rose to the rank of
brigadier general in the Union army.
His Civil War service over, Palmer decided on a career with a western railroad and selected the Union Pacific
Eastern Division (later Kansas Pacific). He was in charge of surveying parties that were investigating routes westward from El
Paso and Albuquerque and became fascinated with the Southwest
and its mineral wealth.

Kansas Pacific's tracks arrived in Denver in 1870, and Palmer
set off on his own. Even before then, he had espoused the idea of a
railroad south from Denver along the Front Range of the Rockies.
A chance encounter with New York attorney William Proctor
Mellen resulted in both financing and a wife — Mellen's daughter.

Palmer incorporated the Denver & Rio Grande Railway in 1870
as a Denver-El Paso railroad. To exploit coal deposits near Canon
City and Walsenburg, Palmer incorporated a coal company which
eventually became Colorado Fuel & Iron Co. (now CF&I Steel).
Palmer left the D&RG in 1883 as a result of stockholder dissatis-
faction and subsequent changes in the board of directors. He continued as president of the Denver & Rio Grande Western Railway,
which was building the western extension of the Denver & Rio
Grande from the Colorado-Utah border to Salt Lake City. In 1889
Palmer organized the Rio Grande Western Railway to acquire the
D&RGW and standard-gauge it.

Meanwhile Palmer had received concessions from the Mexican
government to build railways from Mexico City to the Pacific
Ocean and to the U. S. border at Laredo, Texas. In 1881 he began
work on the Mexican National Railway, built as a narrow gauge
line from Laredo to Mexico City. Palmer sold his Mexican interests in 1902.

In 1901 George Gould, who controlled the Denver & Rio Grande,
acquired the Rio Grande Western. Palmer retired from railroading
and closed out his life with a period of quiet philanthropy in Colorado Springs, the city he had founded. Despite a riding accident in
1906 that left him paralyzed from the waist down, he remained active to the point of hosting a reunion of the Fifteenth Pennsylvania Cavalry and traveling once more to England before his death
in 1909.

Recommended reading: *A Builder of the West*, by John S.
Fisher, published in 1939 by The Caxton Printers, Ltd., Caldwell,
ID 83605

next major portion to go was the Marshall Pass route between Sapinero
and Cedar Creek, 11 miles east of Montrose, abandoned in 1949 because
of land slippage near Cerro Summit. Removal of that line broke the narrow gauge circle. Two years later in 1951 the abandonment of the Mears
Jct.-Hooper line left the Rio Grande with three isolated narrow gauge
segments. One of those, from Montrose to Ridgway, was standard-gauged
in 1953 as soon as the Rio Grande Southern was dismantled; the
Ridgway-Ouray and Montrose-Cedar Creek portions were abandoned at
the same time. The Marshall Pass line west of Poncha Jct. was abandoned in 1955, as were the Crested Butte and Baldwin branches, which
D&RGW had acquired from Colorado & Southern in 1937. Continued
traffic from a limestone quarry at Monarch was the reason for standard-
gauging the Salida-Monarch line in 1956.

That left only the Alamosa-Durango main line and the branches from
Durango to Silverton and Farmington. Materials for pipeline construction and oil-drilling equipment kept traffic brisk on the Farmington

Mikado 482 has the westbound *San Juan* moving at Bountiful, Colo., in three-rail territory between Alamosa and Antonito in April 1950. The *San Juan* was the last narrow gauge passenger train in the U. S. to display its name on a drumhead sign and the last to offer first-class service — the rear car is a parlor-buffet car with kitchen and dining room. The regularly assigned coaches had reclining seats.

Donald Duke

Branch until 1956. (The Durango-Farmington line was completed in 1905 as an isolated standard gauge line to head off a proposed Southern Pacific line. It was narrowed in 1923, becoming one of the few lines ever to be narrowed to less-than-standard gauge.) During the winter of 1964 and 1965 the line over Cumbres Pass was closed for five months — there was no traffic to make it worth opening — and in 1967 D&RGW ceased all narrow gauge operations except on the Silverton Branch. The Chama-Durango-Farmington line was abandoned in 1968, and the Antonito-Chama portion was sold to the states of Colorado and New Mexico in 1970 for operation as a tourist railroad.

The Silverton Branch was embarrassingly successful. Rio Grande had discontinued the *San Juan* in 1951 but continued to run a weekly mixed train between Durango and Silverton. Tourists began to ride the train. Frequency of operation was increased — weekend operation began in the mid-1950s, and in the summer of 1964 the railroad had to schedule two trains each day and build new cars for the line. Rio Grande continued to operate the Silverton line until 1979, when it sold the line to Charles Bradshaw, who continues to operate it.

Location of headquarters: Denver, Colorado
Miles of railroad operated: 1929 — 805; 1978 — 46
Number of locomotives: 1929 — 91; 1978 — 10
Number of passenger cars: 1929 — 80; 1978 — 21
Number of freight cars: 1929 — 2,783; 1969 — 862
Number of company service cars: 1929 — 201
Reporting marks: D&RGW
Notable named passenger trains: *San Juan* (Alamosa-Durango)
Recommended reading: *Rio Grande to the Pacific*, by Robert A. LeMassena, published in 1974 by Sundance Limited, 100 Kalamath Street, Denver, CO 80223 (ISBN 0-913582-10-7)
Portions still operated:
Durango-Silverton: Durango & Silverton Narrow Gauge Railroad
Antonito, Colo.-Chama, N. Mex.: Cumbres & Toltec Scenic Railroad

DENVER & SALT LAKE RAILWAY

When the Union Pacific pushed westward in the 1860s the city of Denver was the largest center of population between the Missouri River and the Pacific. The railroad to the Pacific did not pass through Denver, though, because the Rocky Mountains immediately west constituted an almost insurmountable barrier. Routes had been surveyed, but all were at considerably higher elevations than the route UP selected across Wyoming — and all of them would require much tunneling in the bargain. The Denver Pacific Railroad was organized to connect Denver with Cheyenne, Wyoming, on the UP line; treasurer of the enterprise was David H. Moffat, a Denver businessman and banker. Its first train arrived in Denver on June 24, 1870, drawn by a locomotive named for Moffat. For the next 30 years Moffat was involved at one time or another with most of Denver's railroads as he tried to plan and build a railroad directly west from Denver.

In 1902 Moffat decided to build a steam railroad, the Denver, Northwestern & Pacific Railway, west from Denver to serve as a connection from the Burlington and the Rock Island at Denver to the San Pedro, Los Angeles & Salt Lake at Salt Lake City. Construction began almost immediately. The line was and is one of the most spectacular in North America. In June 1904 the DNW&P began operating trains to Tolland and almost simultaneously was ousted from Denver Union Station, which was controlled by the Union Pacific and the Denver & Rio Grande. By September of that year rails had reached the top of Rollins Pass on what was intended to be a temporary line until a tunnel could be bored under the divide.

Later that autumn Moffat met a foe far more formidable than either the UP or the D&RG — snow. The summit of the pass was 11,680 feet above sea level, and it was reached by 4 percent grades and tight curves. The road was shut down for much of that winter after its new rotary snowplow became snowbound.

Late in the summer of 1905 DNW&P rails reached Hot Sulphur Springs, and soon afterward Moffat ran out of money. (Earlier Moffat had met with E. H. Harriman to discuss takeover of the road, but he could not accept Harriman's terms.) In 1907 a group of Denver men formed a company to construct an extension of the road to Steamboat Springs, which was completed in December 1908. A more important goal was the coalfields near Oak Creek, because the D&NWP penetrated largely unpopulated territory with little potential for freight traffic. Moffat by then had exhausted his fortune. On March 17, 1911, he received a promise of financial support and, a day later, word of withdrawal of that support. The turn of events killed Moffat.

In July 1912 the Moffat Road was reorganized as the Denver & Salt Lake Railroad; the new company entered receivership in January 1913. In November 1913 D&SL rails reached Craig, in northwestern Colorado. They were to go no farther. The D&SL struggled along and entered receivership again in 1917. In 1918 the employees went on strike for seven months after years of low, and sometimes unpaid, wages.

Things got worse. A tunnel fire and the subsequent collapse of the tunnel in South Boulder Canyon in March 1922 threatened to shut down the road permanently. However, the city of Denver recognized the importance of the road and pressed for the construction of a tunnel under the Continental Divide. The state legislature passed a bill in 1922 that provided funds for the boring of a 6-mile tunnel.

The authorization of the tunnel (which would take six years to build) wasn't an immediate help — wrecks, rockslides, and fires continued to plague the line — but finally, as northwestern Colorado developed, freight traffic began to increase. The D&SL made a profit for the first time in 1925, and capital was becoming less scarce. The road emerged from reorganization as the Denver & Salt Lake Railway in 1926. The Moffat Tunnel opened on February 26, 1928, vastly improving the operation of the railroad and shortening the route by approximately 23 miles. The line over the pass was abandoned.

Thought was given to the road's goal of Salt Lake City. A more practical route than one west from Craig was to follow the Colorado River 38 miles downstream to a connection with the Denver & Rio Grande Western at Dotsero, where the Eagle River joins the Colorado. The D&SL incorporated the project in 1924 as the Denver & Salt Lake Western, but the Rio Grande fought for the right to build the new cutoff, knowing that the owner of the cutoff would control the route. The ICC, after considering the financial condition of both roads, granted the right to the Rio

DAVID H. MOFFAT JR. (1839-1911) was born in Washingtonville, Orange County, New York, a town founded by his grandfather. At the age of 12 he went to New York City, began working as a bank messenger, and quickly rose to the post of assistant teller. In 1855 much of the Moffat family moved from Washingtonville to Des Moines, Iowa. David went with them and found a job in a bank there, but a year later moved west to the new city of Omaha, Nebraska. Moffat prospered until a business panic in 1860 wiped out both his bank and his real estate speculation. He moved farther west to Denver (which had just been settled) where he established a book and stationery store. In 1861 he moved the store to larger quarters, became postmaster, and traveled back to Washingtonville to marry Frances Buckhout. Moffat prospered and entered the banking business in Denver. He soon became involved with Denver's railroads, and gradually the creation of a railroad directly west from Denver became the goal of his life.

State Hist. Soc. of Colorado

Moffat had been involved with a proposed railroad up Clear Creek — the main purpose of the road had been to spur the Colorado Central into action — and he was one of the organizers of the Denver, South Park & Pacific, which had been diverted from the goal of its name to Leadville by news of the discovery of silver there. In 1880 Moffat sold his holdings in several Denver railroads and invested in the Denver, Utah & Pacific, which was to build west over Rollins Pass and then follow the Fraser and Colorado rivers west to connect with the Rio Grande Western at Grand Junction. The Burlington bought the DU&P but abandoned the proposed road in 1886. In 1885 Moffat became president of the Denver & Rio Grande. To counter the construction of the Colorado Midland west from Colorado Springs, he extended Rio Grande's Leadville line over Tennessee Pass and down to the Colorado River, and he surveyed the mountains west of Denver for a pass that would allow a direct line from Denver to Leadville. The directors of the Rio Grande were not interested in such a project and discharged Moffat in 1891.

Moffat's association with the Denver streetcar system had acquainted him with the potential of electric motive power. In 1901 he and others incorporated the Denver & Northwestern Railway, to be an electric railroad to coal mines a few miles west of Denver and eventually into northwestern Colorado. In 1902 Moffat decided to build a steam railroad west from Denver, the Denver, Northwestern & Pacific, predecessor of the Denver & Salt Lake. In the next decade Moffat spent most of his fortune building and maintaining the railroad and battling for its survival. On March 17, 1911, he was in New York and received a promise of the financing he needed to complete his railroad west to Salt Lake City. Word leaked back to Union Pacific (the stories are unclear and conflict) and the help was withdrawn the next morning. Moffat died shortly after learning of the broken promise.

Recommended reading: *The Giant's Ladder*, by Harold A. Boner, published in 1962 by Kalmbach Publishing Co., 1027 North Seventh Street, Milwaukee, WI 53233

Low-drivered Ten-Wheeler No. 302 leads Denver & Salt Lake train 1, the Denver-Craig local at Tolland, a few miles east of the Moffat Tunnel in November 1939.

R. H. Kindig

Grande. Construction began in late 1932, and in June 1934 the route was opened, cutting 175 miles out of D&RGW's Denver-Salt Lake City route. The east end of the cutoff was at Orestod (Dotsero spelled backwards), and a new station named Bond was designated on the cutoff just west of Orestod. The Rio Grande acquired trackage rights on the D&SL from Denver to Orestod. D&RGW began to acquire D&SL stock and finally merged the D&SL on April 11, 1947. The entire line is still in service, and coal traffic from mines along the western portion of the line has increased in recent years.

Location of headquarters: Denver, Colorado
Miles of railroad operated: 1929 — 238; 1945 — 232

Number of locomotives: 1929 — 58; 1945 — 39
Number of passenger cars: 1929 — 25; 1945 — 9
Number of freight cars: 1929 — 1,020; 1945 — 590
Number of company service cars: 1929 — 164; 1945 — 179
Reporting marks: D&SL
Recommended reading: *Rails That Climb*, by Edward T. Bollinger, published in 1979 by the Colorado Railroad Historical Foundation, P. O. Box 10, Golden, CO 80401
Successors: Denver & Rio Grande Western (TWG)
Map: See page 111

DETROIT & TOLEDO SHORE LINE RAILROAD

The Pleasant Bay Railway was incorporated in Toledo, Ohio, on March 29, 1898. A year later it purchased the Toledo & Ottawa Beach Railway, acquiring a substantial debt along with it, and was renamed Detroit & Toledo Shore Line Railroad. The original plans were to create a fast electric line between Detroit and Toledo. Track reached from Toledo north to Trenton, Michigan, about three-fourths of the distance to Detroit, when the stockholders sold the line jointly to the Grand Trunk and the Toledo, St. Louis & Western (the Clover Leaf) in 1902. The acquisition was a logical one for both roads, giving Grand Trunk a connection to Toledo and the Clover Leaf a connection to Detroit. The road was opened in 1903.

Detroit & Toledo Shore Line carried no passengers and originated very little freight — it was principally a bridge route for its owners. The two principal commodities it carried were coal to fuel the automobile factories of Detroit, and automobiles.

The Clover Leaf half interest passed to the Nickel Plate in 1923 and then to Norfolk & Western when N&W merged NKP in 1964. In April 1981 Grand Trunk Western purchased Norfolk & Western's half interest in the D&TSL, merged the road, and integrated D&TSL operations with its own.

Location of headquarters: Detroit, Michigan
Miles of railroad operated: 1929 — 50; 1980 — 50
Number of locomotives: 1929 — 31; 1980 — 16
Number of freight cars: 1929 — 402
Number of company service cars: 1929 — 68
Number of freight and company service cars: 1980 — 604
Reporting marks: D&TS
Successors: Grand Trunk Western (TWG)
Map: See next page

John Uckley

A pair of Detroit & Toledo Shore Line diesel switchers pushes a cut of cars over the hump at Lang Yard in Toledo, Ohio, in September 1979.

DETROIT, TOLEDO & IRONTON RAILROAD

In May 1905 two bankrupt railroads, the Detroit Southern and the Ohio Southern, merged to form the Detroit, Toledo & Ironton Railway. The Detroit Southern, previously the Detroit & Lima Northern, extended southwest from Detroit to Lima, Ohio. Ohio Southern's antecedents included the Springfield, Jackson & Pomeroy, a 3-foot-gauge coal hauler that was intended to become part of a narrow gauge system stretching from Toledo, Ohio, to Mexico City. The new railroad then took control of the Ann Arbor to gain entry to Toledo. Ann Arbor regained independence in 1910, and the DT&I was reorganized in 1914 as the Detroit, Toledo & Ironton Railroad.

In 1920 Henry Ford wanted to straighten the shipping channel through which Great Lakes freighters reached his new River Rouge plant at Dearborn, Michigan. The project included a new bridge for DT&I, and DT&I management suggested that Ford lend them the money in exchange for DT&I bonds. Ford decided instead to purchase the railroad. He rebuilt it, instituted some unusual labor practices (wages considerably higher than average, white caps and clean overalls required, beards and mustaches not allowed, and no trains on Sundays), electrified a 17-mile portion between the Rouge Plant and Carleton, Mich., and built a 46-mile cutoff between Dundee, Mich., and Malinta, Ohio.

In 1929 Ford sold the railroad to the Pennroad Corporation, which was closely associated with the Pennsylvania Railroad. The 1930s saw the end of passenger service, except for a Springfield-Jackson, Ohio, mixed train that lasted until 1955, and the purchase of a number of modern Berkshires and Mikados. Dieselization began in the late 1940s and was complete by the end of 1955.

In 1951 the Pennsylvania Company, a subsidiary of the Pennsylvania Railroad, and the Wabash Railroad purchased Pennroad's stock in DT&I; in 1965 Wabash sold its share, 18 percent, to Pennsylvania Company (which held 87 percent of the stock of the Wabash). In 1963 DT&I purchased the Ann Arbor Railroad from the Wabash. Ann Arbor went bankrupt in 1973, and portions of its line have been sold to the state of Michigan; DT&I retained trackage rights from Diann, Mich., to Toledo.

With the formation of Conrail in 1976 DT&I acquired trackage rights

DT&I was intimately tied to the economic activity of the automobile industry. In 1975 the road took delivery of eight brand-new GP38-2s that had been ordered when traffic was high. Seven of them, shown here, were immediately placed in storage at Flat Rock, Mich., to await better times.

MODEL RAILROADER: Jim Hediger

over Conrail from Springfield, Ohio, to Cincinnati. The Pennsylvania Company, by then a subsidiary of Penn Central, put the DT&I up for sale. Grand Trunk Western, a subsidiary of Canadian National Railways, offered to purchase the DT&I, and Chessie System and Norfolk & Western offered a joint counterproposal. The ICC approved the sale to Grand Trunk; the sale was consummated on June 24, 1980. On December 31, 1983, DT&I was merged with GTW.

Location of headquarters: Dearborn, Michigan
Miles of railroad operated: 1929 — 517; 1981 — 623
Number of locomotives: 1929 — 67; 1981 — 72

Number of passenger cars: 1929 — 11
Number of freight cars: 1929 — 2,746
Number of company service cars: 1929 — 133
Number of freight and company service cars: 1981 — 3,778
Reporting marks: DTI
Successors: Grand Trunk Western (TWG)
Portions still operated: Detroit-Jackson, Ohio; Flat Rock-Dearborn, Mich.; Diann, Mich.-Toledo; Cincinnati-Maitland, Ohio; Malinta-Napoleon, Ohio: Grand Trunk Western

119

DULUTH & IRON RANGE RAIL ROAD

Collection of H. L. Broadbelt

The largest locomotives on the Duluth & Iron Range were the class N-2 Mikados, built in 1923. The deep-arched cab roof and the Vanderbilt tender are reminiscent of Erie motive power.

In the late 1860s gold was discovered — so the reports said — at Vermilion Lake in the wilderness north of Duluth, Minnesota. The gold turned out to be iron pyrites, often called fool's gold, but it led to a more important discovery — an immense deposit of high-grade iron ore, the Vermilion Range.

The Duluth & Iron Range Rail Road was chartered on December 21, 1874, to build a line from Duluth to Babbitt. The Minnesota legislature granted the company land through the wilderness, but the railroad remained no more than a charter.

The iron ore interested two Philadelphians, Charlemagne Tower and George C. Stone. Stone acquired ore lands from the public domain for Tower's Minnesota Iron Co., and Tower formed the Duluth & Iron Mountain Railroad in 1881. Tower was unable to get a land grant for his railroad, so he acquired control of the D&IR and vested its ownership in the Minnesota Iron Co.

Surveys and construction got under way, and the company built an ore dock at Agate Bay (now Two Harbors). The first trainload of iron ore rolled down to the docks at Two Harbors on July 31, 1884. In 1886 the road constructed a 26-mile extension southwest along the shore of Lake Superior to Duluth.

Illinois Steel Co. developed a mine at Ely, 20 miles northeast of the Minnesota Iron Co. operation at Tower and Soudan, and proposed to build a railroad from Duluth. Tower sold Minnesota Iron and the D&IR to Illinois Steel, whose backers included Henry H. Porter, Marshall Field, Cyrus McCormick, and John D. Rockefeller. (Porter had built the Chicago & Illinois Coal Railway and acquired control of the Chicago & Eastern Illinois for Illinois Steel.) The discovery of the iron ore deposits of the Mesabi Range in 1890 spurred D&IR to construct a branch from Allen Jct. west to the city of Virginia and several short branches to mines.

Illinois Steel was succeeded by Federal Steel, and Federal Steel by United States Steel Corporation. In 1901 U. S. Steel acquired the Duluth & Iron Range and also its neighbor to the west, the Duluth, Missabe & Northern. The two railroads retained their autonomy at first but gradually began to move toward unification, starting by sharing officers. On January 1, 1930, the DM&N leased the D&IR and immediately consolidated operations with an eye toward the economies that would result from joint use of equipment and eliminating duplicate facilities. On

March 22, 1938, the Duluth, Missabe & Iron Range, successor to the DM&N, acquired the assets and property of the D&IR.

Location of headquarters: Duluth, Minnesota
Miles of railroad operated: 1929 — 308
Number of locomotives: 1929 — 85
Number of passenger cars: 1929 — 21
Number of freight cars: 1929 — 5,313
Number of company service cars: 1929 — 49
(Operations were consolidated with DM&N January 1, 1930.)
Reporting marks: D&IR
Historical and technical society: Missabe Railroad Historical Society, 719 Northland Avenue, Stillwater, MN 55082

Recommended reading:
The Missabe Road, by Frank A. King, published in 1972 by Golden West Books, P. O. Box 80250, San Marino, CA 91108 (ISBN 87095-040-1)
Locomotives of the Duluth, Missabe & Iron Range, by Frank A. King, published in 1984 by Pacific Fast Mail, P. O. Box 57, Edmonds, WA 98020 (ISBN 0-915713-11-X)
Successors:
Duluth, Missabe & Northern
Duluth, Missabe & Iron Range (TWG)
Portions still operated: Two Harbors-Embarrass; Wales-Jordan; Allen Jct.-Gilbert: DM&IR
Map: See next page

DULUTH, MISSABE & NORTHERN RAILWAY

The iron mines of Minnesota's Vermilion Range had been in production for more than 20 years when the mammoth deposits of high-grade hematite ores of the Mesabi Range were discovered in 1890. (There are several spellings of "Mesabi," a Chippewa word meaning "giant.") Neither of the nearby railroads, the Duluth & Iron Range to the east and the Duluth & Winnipeg (later Great Northern) to the southwest, was interested in extending to the Mesabi Range, so on June 3, 1891, the Merritt brothers of Duluth, who had acquired tracts of land at Mountain Iron and Biwabik, incorporated their own railroad: the Duluth, Missabe & Northern Railway. Surveying and construction soon began, and on October 18, 1892, the first carload of Mesabi ore rolled into Duluth. The Merritts contracted with the Duluth & Winnipeg to use its line south of Brookston and its ore docks at Allouez (Superior), Wisconsin, but in 1893 they decided to build their own line into Duluth and construct ore docks there. The Merritts incurred considerable debt in doing so, and the Panic of 1893 didn't help matters. By February 1894 John D. Rockefeller was in control of their Lake Superior Consolidated Iron Mines and the DM&N.

Business rebounded. The Mesabi Range quickly outstripped the Vermilion Range, and DM&N, located at the center of the range, prospered. Traffic required a second ore dock at Duluth, then a third. In 1901 Rockefeller sold the DM&N to the newly formed United States Steel Corporation, which in the same year acquired the Duluth & Iron Range. DM&N entered an era of improving its physical plant: steel ore cars, Mallet locomotives, double track, extensions to other mines.

At first U. S. Steel made no moves to consolidate its two railroads, but after tentative steps were made in that direction, on January 1, 1930, DM&N leased the D&IR and integrated the operations of the two roads. The economies that resulted from eliminating duplicate facilities and sharing equipment were welcome during the Depression. Ore traffic in 1932 fell to almost nothing.

On July 1, 1937, the DM&N consolidated with the Spirit Lake Transfer Railway, part of a short connecting line from Adolph, Minn., to Itasca, Wis., to form the Duluth, Missabe & Iron Range Railway (DM&N had leased the Spirit Lake line since 1915). On March 22, 1938, DM&IR ac-

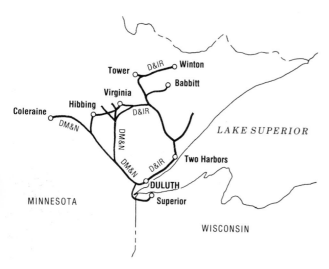

DM&IR

Duluth, Missabe & Northern 2-8-8-2 No. 207 hauls a string of empty ore hoppers back to the Mesabi Range in a scene that predates the 1930 rebuilding of the Mallet into a single-expansion articulated.

quired the assets and property of the Duluth & Iron Range and the Interstate Transfer Railway (the other portion of the connecting line, also leased by DM&N since 1915). The names of the two predecessors survived as designations for the two divisions of the DM&IR, Iron Range and Missabe.

Location of headquarters: Duluth, Minnesota
Miles of railroad operated: 1929 — 313; 1937 — 539
Number of locomotives: 1929 — 101; 1937 — 131
Number of passenger cars: 1929 — 29; 1937 — 22
Number of freight cars: 1929 — 8,917
Number of company service cars: 1929 — 128
Number of freight and company service cars: 1937 — 13,759
(1937 figures reflect the combining of DM&N and DM&R operations)

Reporting marks: DM&N
Historical and technical society: Missabe Railroad Historical Society, 719 Northland Avenue, Stillwater, MN 55082
Recommended reading:
The Missabe Road, by Frank A. King, published in 1972 by Golden West Books, P. O. Box 80250, San Marino, CA 91108 (ISBN 87095-040-1)
Locomotives of the Duluth Missabe & Iron Range, by Frank A. King, published in 1984 by Pacific Fast Mail, P. O. Box 57, Edmonds, WA 98020 (ISBN 0-915713-11-X)
Subsidiaries and affiliated railroads, 1937: Duluth & Iron Range
Successors: Duluth, Missabe & Iron Range (TWG)
Portions still operated: Duluth-Mountain Iron; Wolf-Virginia; Iron Jct.-Sparta; Keenan-Hibbing; Calumet-Coleraine; Adolph, Minn.-South Itasca, Wis.: DM&IR

DULUTH, SOUTH SHORE & ATLANTIC RAILWAY

The backers of the Duluth, South Shore & Atlantic Railway proposed to build a railroad from Duluth, Minnesota, east through the iron country of Wisconsin and the Upper Peninsula of Michigan to Sault Ste. Marie, with branches to St. Ignace, Mich., on the Straits of Mackinac, and Houghton, Mich., in the copper-mining country of the Keweenaw Peninsula. The DSS&A was incorporated in 1887 as a consolidation of several railroads serving the iron ore region of Michigan's Upper Peninsula: Mackinaw & Marquette; Sault Ste. Marie & Marquette; Wisconsin, Sault Ste. Marie & Mackinac; and Duluth, Superior & Michigan. The first-named, the Mackinaw & Marquette, was successor to the Detroit, Mackinac & Marquette, which opened a line in 1881 between St. Ignace and Marquette.

The DSS&A reached Sault Ste. Marie in September 1887 and Duluth in September 1888, the latter by using Northern Pacific tracks west of Iron River, Wis. About the same time it acquired control of the Mineral Range Railroad, which reached north from Hancock. Control of the DSS&A was acquired in 1888 by Canadian Pacific.

DSS&A extended its own rails west from Iron River to Superior in 1892. When the Lake Superior & Ishpeming arrived in the iron-mining area in 1896 it took much of the ore business away from the South Shore, leaving it largely dependent upon forest products. The road carried on — several issues of *Moody's Railroads* refer to it as "one of the least prosperous of the Canadian Pacific Railway's subsidiaries." By 1930 the road was sharing officers with Soo Line, also a CPR subsidiary. South Shore filed for bankruptcy in 1937, emerging in 1949 as the Duluth, South Shore & Atlantic Railroad, which included the old South Shore and the Mineral

Range Railroad (which ran from Houghton to Calumet and Lake Linden).

In the late 1930s the South Shore abandoned its main line west of Marengo, Wis., in favor of trackage rights from there to Ashland on Soo Line and from Ashland to Superior on Northern Pacific. Passenger service dwindled to a St. Ignace-Marquette round trip, operated with an RDC, discontinued in 1958, and the north end of the Chicago-Calumet *Copper Country Limited*, operated in conjunction with the Milwaukee Road.

On January 1, 1961, the Soo Line Railroad was created by the merger of the DSS&A, the Minneapolis, St. Paul, & Sault Ste. Marie (the old Soo Line), and the Wisconsin Central, which had long been operated by the Soo Line. The new railroad used DSS&A's corporate structure.

123

Location of headquarters: Minneapolis, Minnesota
Miles of railroad operated: 1929 — 574; 1960 — 544
Number of locomotives: 1929 — 62; 1960 — 24
Number of passenger cars: 1929 — 58
Number of freight cars: 1929 — 2,709
Number of company service cars: 1929 — 154
Number of freight and company service cars: 1960 — 1,720
Reporting marks: DSS&A, DSA
Historical and technical society: Soo Line Historical & Technical Society, 3410 Kasten Court, Middleton, WI 53562
Successors: Soo Line Railroad (TWG)
Portions still operated: Marengo, Wis.-White Pine, Mich.; Nestoria-St. Ignace, Mich.: Soo Line

Kalmbach Publishing Co.: A. C. Kalmbach

Duluth, South Shore & Atlantic train 1 pauses at Marquette, Mich., in September 1951 on its journey from Mackinaw City to Calumet. Power is Pacific 556. On the next track 2-8-0 No. 92 makes up train 7, the overnight to Duluth. Both locomotives are 1924 products of Alco's Brooks Works.

DURHAM & SOUTHERN RAILWAY

The Durham & Southern was incorporated in 1906 as a reorganization and extension of the Cape Fear & Northern Railway. The CF&N had been built by a lumber company between Apex and Dunn, North Carolina, and the D&S would extend the line north to Durham. The purpose of the road was to connect Durham with the main lines of Atlantic Coast Line and Seaboard Air Line to the south.

The Duke family had been associated with the railroad from the beginning, and in 1930 control passed to the Duke Power Co., which also owned the Piedmont & Northern. The two roads were put under the same management, and a connection between the two was proposed, but it was rejected by the ICC. In 1954 management of the two roads was separated,

Durham & Southern 2-10-0 No. 202, which was built by Baldwin in 1933, rolls into Apex, N. C., with a freight train from Durham in September 1952.

Philip R. Hastings

and Durham & Southern came under the control of the Nello Teer Co., a Durham construction company.

The Durham & Southern was noteworthy from the standpoint of motive power: an assortment of Decapods, including one of only two common-carrier steam locomotives built in the U. S. during 1933, and an ex-Norfolk & Western Twelve Wheeler in steam days; an array of Baldwin diesel road-switchers; and finally orthodoxy in the form of four GP38-2s.

Seaboard Coast Line bought the railroad in 1976 and dissolved the corporation on September 15, 1981.

Location of headquarters: Durham, North Carolina
Miles of railroad operated: 1929 — 59; 1980 — 59

Number of locomotives: 1929 — 9; 1980 — 4
Number of passenger cars: 1929 — 9
Number of freight cars: 1929 — 1; 1980 — 50
Number of company service cars: 1929 — 11
Reporting marks: DS
Successors:
Seaboard Coast Line
Seaboard System (TWG)
Portions still operated: Durham-Apex; Erwin-Dunn, N. C.: Seaboard System
Map: See page 25

125

EAST BROAD TOP RAILROAD & COAL CO.

The East Broad Top was the last narrow gauge common carrier in the U. S. east of the Mississippi. It was better known than most other roads of its size and remoteness. Strictly speaking it should not be in this book, because it still exists.

The East Broad Top Railroad & Coal Company was chartered in 1856 to mine and transport coal from Broad Top Mountain, a plateau in Pennsylvania south of the Juniata River and about halfway between Philadelphia and Pittsburgh. Construction did not begin until 1872, after the road's directors had chosen a track gauge of 3 feet. The line was opened from Mount Union, on the main line of the Pennsylvania Railroad, south to Orbisonia in 1873 and extended farther south to Robertsdale in 1874. By then the Rockhill Iron & Coal Company had been organized by the same management.

The Shade Gap Railroad was incorporated in 1884 to handle business that was sure to result from the construction of the South Pennsylvania Railroad, a line across the state backed by New York Central interests. A year later the Pennsylvania Railroad and the New York Central called a truce, and the half-dug tunnels of the South Penn were abandoned for the next 50 years.

The East Broad Top had a long career of carrying mostly coal but also limestone, lumber, and bark; its history is peppered with strikes by mine workers and flooding rivers and creeks. The EBT hit on hard times in the 1890s and was rehabilitated in the early 1900s. The road adopted automatic couplers in 1908 and air brakes in 1913; in 1912 it ordered its first all-steel hopper cars. In 1919 the road was purchased by Madeira, Hill & Co., a coal mining firm. The chief improvements under that management were a coal-cleaning plant at Mount Union and facilities for changing the trucks of standard gauge cars so they could move on the EBT. In 1934 Madeira, Hill underwent voluntary bankruptcy and in 1937 went bankrupt again.

In 1938 the road's bondholders bought the East Broad Top and the mining company and reorganized them as the Rockhill Coal Company. The Shade Gap branch finally got the traffic for which it had been built when the long-abandoned roadbed of the South Penn was used as the founda-

tion for the Pennsylvania Turnpike, construction of which began in 1939.

After World War Two rising labor costs and shorter work days increased EBT's operating expenses, and frequent strikes called by John L. Lewis, head of the United Mine Workers, resulted in less coal moving over the railroad (and decreased revenue). However, the road remained in business and went so far as to ask General Electric about diesel power. The demand for coal dropped as oil and gas took its place in homes and in-

John Krause

Loaded and empty East Broad Top coal trains meet at Kimmel, Pa., between Saltillo and Robertsdale, in March 1956, shortly before the line was abandoned.

dustries. The Rockhill Coal Co. decided to close its mines and offered the EBT to the Pennsylvania Railroad at scrap prices, but Pennsy declined the offer. The ICC approved the abandonment petition, to be effective March 31, 1956, and the last train ran on April 13, 1956, just three days short of the centennial of the chartering of the railroad. Nothing was scrapped immediately; the locomotives and cars were stored on the property.

The railroad and the coal company were purchased by Kovalchick Salvage Co., a scrap dealer. Nick Kovalchick, its president, petitioned to postpone dismantling the railroad and the mine facilities, and mining activity resumed in 1957, but the coal moved in trucks. In 1960 Kovalchick was asked if the railroad could be reactivated for the celebration of the bicentennial of Orbisonia. It could, and the East Broad Top reopened August 13, 1960. EBT has operated since then as a tourist railroad during the summer season. In 1963 standard gauge tracks were laid on a short

portion of the Shade Gap branch by Railways to Yesteryear, which operates a trolley museum at Orbisonia.

Location of headquarters: Philadelphia, Pennsylvania
Miles of railroad operated: 1929 — 51; 1955 — 38
Number of locomotives: 1929 — 12; 1955 — 8
Number of passenger cars: 1929 — 18; 1955 — 4
Number of freight cars: 1929 — 402; 1955 — 311
Number of company service cars: 1929 — 20; 1955 — 8
Recommended reading: *East Broad Top*, by Lee Rainey and Frank Kyper, published in 1982 by Golden West Books, P. O. Box 80250, San Marino, CA 91108 (ISBN 0-87095-078-9)
Portions still operated:
Orbisonia-Colgate Grove: East Broad Top Railroad
Orbisonia: Shade Gap Electric Railway (standard gauge)

127

EAST TENNESSEE & WESTERN NORTH CAROLINA RAILROAD

The East Tennessee & Western North Carolina Railroad was chartered in 1866 and built a few miles of five-foot gauge track (then standard for the South) before stopping for breath and refinancing. In 1879 a group of investors led by Ario Pardee (who was connected with the East Broad Top Railroad) bought the line and resumed construction with a track gauge of three feet. The line was opened in 1882 between Johnson City, Tennessee, and Cranberry, North Carolina. At Cranberry were mines that produced high-grade ore used in the production of tool steel.

In 1913 the ET&WNC purchased the Linville River Railway, a logging railroad with which it connected at Cranberry. The line was extended a few miles at a time until it reached Boone, 33 miles from Cranberry, in 1918. In the 1930s ET&WNC turned to tourism to fill its trains — the mountains had been logged off, the mines were running out, and highways were taking passengers away. The mountains and the Doe River Gorge attracted excursionists, and during that era the road received its nickname, "Tweetsie." In 1940 rains washed out much of the Linville River line, and it was abandoned in 1941.

The ET&WNC was busy during World War Two because of the increased demand for steel and because of gasoline and tire rationing. At the end of the war the mines were depleted; without the ore traffic there was little need for the narrow gauge railroad. The last narrow gauge train ran on October 16, 1950.

The railroad had installed a third rail for standard gauge traffic between Johnson City and Elizabethton in 1906. That portion remained in service after the narrow gauge line was abandoned and was operated with steam locomotives until 1967, when the last two Consolidations, Nos. 207 and 208, were replaced with a pair of Alco road-switchers from the Southern Railway. The two Consolidations returned to the Southern, their former owner, and regained their old numbers, 630 and 722, for Southern's steam excursion service.

In September 1983 the East Tennessee Railway Corporation took over operation of the line between Johnson City and Elizabethton.

Robert B. Adams

Ten-Wheeler No. 11 of the East Tennessee & Western North Carolina brings a train of ore around Pardee Point in the Doe River Gorge.

Location of headquarters: Johnson City, Tennessee
Miles of railroad operated: 1929 — 36; 1949 — 34
Number of locomotives: 1929 — 7; 1949 — 6
Number of passenger cars: 1929 — 18
Number of freight cars: 1929 — 278
Number of company service cars: 1929 — 21
Number of cars: 1949 — 69
Historical and technical society: Friends of the East Tennessee &

Western North Carolina, c/o Jim Teese, P. O. Box 37029, Charlotte, NC 28237
Recommended reading: *Tweetsie Country*, by Mallory Hope Ferrell, published in 1976 by Pruett Publishing Co., 3235 Prairie Avenue, Boulder, CO 80301 (ISBN 0-87108-082-6)
Successors: East Tennessee Railway
Portions still operated: Johnson City-Elizabethton: East Tennessee
Map: See page 97

ERIE RAILROAD

When the Erie Canal was built across upstate New York between Albany and Buffalo, DeWitt Clinton, governor of New York, promised the people of the Southern Tier of the state some kind of avenue of commerce by way of appeasement. William Redfield proposed a direct route from the mouth of the Hudson to the Great Lakes, but it was Eleazar Lord who was instrumental in the chartering of the New York & Erie Railroad by the New York state legislature in April 1832. Among the conditions of the charter were that the railroad lie wholly within New York and that it not connect with any railroads in New Jersey or Pennsylvania without permission of the legislature. A track gauge of 6 feet ensured that even if it did connect, its cars and locomotives wouldn't stray onto foreign rails. The terminals were fixed: The town of Dunkirk offered land for a terminal on Lake Erie, and Lord lived at Piermont, on the Hudson River just north of the New Jersey state line. The New York & Harlem was willing to extend a line north to a point opposite Piermont, which would have given the New York & Erie an entrance to Manhattan, but the new road refused the offer.

The surveyed route included two detours into Pennsylvania, one because the Delaware & Hudson Canal had already occupied the New York side of the Delaware River above Port Jervis, and the other to follow the Susquehanna River to maintain an easy grade.

Ground was broken on November 7, 1835, near Deposit, N. Y. Shortly afterwards fire destroyed much of New York and wiped out the fortunes of many of the road's supporters; then a business panic struck the nation.

Construction got under way in 1838, and the first train ran in 1841. Much of the railroad was built on low trestlework rather than directly on the ground; the resulting construction and maintenance costs drove the railroad into bankruptcy soon after it opened. Construction continued, however. The line that had been built east a few miles from Dunkirk was taken up to provide rails for the extension from Goshen, N. Y., to Middletown. Standard-gauging the line was proposed while it would still be relatively inexpensive to do so, but the road chose to stay with its broad gauge. The New York & Erie reached Port Jervis, N. Y., on the Delaware River 74 miles from Piermont, on December 31, 1847; just a year later it was into Binghamton. The whole road from Piermont to Dunkirk was opened in May 1851 with an inspection trip for dignitaries from U. S. President Millard Fillmore and Secretary of State Daniel Webster on down and the customary eating, drinking, and speechifying.

The road grew a few branches: at the east end to Newburgh, N. Y., on the Hudson, and at the west end to Rochester and to Buffalo. The latter soon replaced Dunkirk as the principal western terminal of the road.

In 1833 the Paterson & Hudson River Rail Road was chartered to build between Paterson, N. J., and Jersey City, and the Paterson & Ramapo Railroad north to the New York state line at Suffern. The two lines provided a shortcut between New York City and the New York & Erie at Suffern, even though they did not connect directly — passengers walked the mile between the two. The New York & Erie fought the situation until 1852, when it leased the two railroads, built a connecting track, and

ERIE

Compared to its rivals in the New York-Chicago business, Erie was basically a freight railroad and one concerned more with through traffic than with local trade. Here a fast freight rolls down the Delaware Valley west of Port Jervis, N. Y., bound for Jersey City, behind one of Erie's massive Berkshires.

made that the main route, supplanting the original line to Piermont.

The New York & Erie came upon hard times in the 1850s. Cornelius Vanderbilt, the "Commodore," and Daniel Drew both lent the road money, and in 1859 it entered receivership and was reorganized as the Erie Railway. Drew and two associates, James Fisk and Jay Gould, engaged in some machinations, with the result that in the summer of 1868 Drew, Fisk, and Vanderbilt were out and Gould was in as president of the Erie.

In 1874 the Erie leased the Atlantic & Great Western, which had been opened 10 years earlier between Salamanca, N. Y., on the Erie, and Dayton, Ohio. The A&GW entered Cincinnati over the Cincinnati, Hamilton & Dayton, which laid a third rail to accommodate A&GW's broad gauge equipment. At Cincinnati the A&GW connected with the broad gauge Ohio & Mississippi to St. Louis. (The two connecting roads later became part of Baltimore & Ohio.) The lease to the Erie did not last long. A&GW entered receivership and was reorganized as the New York, Pennsylvania & Ohio. To obtain access to Cleveland and Youngstown, the NYP&O leased the Cleveland & Mahoning Valley in 1880. The Erie leased the Nypano (as it was known) in 1883, acquired all its capital stock in 1896, and acquired its properties in 1941.

Hugh Jewett became president of the Erie in 1874. His first task was to lead the road through reorganization; it became the New York, Lake Erie & Western Railroad. On June 22, 1880, the entire system was converted to standard gauge. That same year the Chicago & Atlantic was completed between Hammond, Indiana, and Marion, Ohio, where it connected with the Atlantic & Great Western. Access to Chicago was over the rails of the Chicago & Western Indiana, a terminal road. Jewett also double-tracked the Erie from Jersey City to Buffalo. The road was bankrupt again by 1893 and reorganized in 1895 as the Erie Railroad.

In 1899 Frederick Underwood began a 25-year term as president of the Erie. He had been associated with James J. Hill, and he was a friend of E. H. Harriman. Both Hill and Harriman had considered the Erie as a possible eastern extension of their respective systems. Neither man did much toward acquiring it, although Harriman became a member of Erie's board of directors and arranged financing for it. In 1905 the Erie briefly acquired the Cincinnati, Hamilton & Dayton and the affiliated Pere Mar-

It's the evening rush hour at Erie's riverfront terminal in Jersey City, with Vanderbilt-tendered Pacifics and Stillwell coaches in profusion. The New York skyline is visible across the Hudson.

ERIE

quette from J. P. Morgan, Erie's banker. Investigation revealed that CH&D's financial condition was not as advertised, so Underwood asked Morgan to take the two roads back — which he did. Two days later the CH&D and the PM entered receivership. Underwood is remembered for rebuilding the Erie. His projects included double-tracking the remainder of the main line and building several freight bypasses with lower grades, making the line east of Meadville, Pa., largely a water-level route. In 1907 Erie electrified passenger operations on its branch between Rochester and Mt. Morris, N. Y. Electric operation lasted until 1934.

In the 1920s the Van Sweringen brothers began buying Erie stock, seeing the road as a logical eastern extension of their Nickel Plate Road. By the time they were done, they owned more than 55 percent of Erie's stock along with their interests in Chesapeake & Ohio, Pere Marquette, and Hocking Valley.

The Erie family included several short lines. The Erie began to buy New York, Susquehanna & Western stock in 1898 and leased the line that same year. The Susquehanna entered bankruptcy in 1937 and resumed life on its own in 1940. Bath & Hammondsport was controlled by the Erie from 1903 to 1936, when it was sold to local businessmen. Much of Erie's commuter business out of Jersey City was over subsidiary lines that Erie operated as part of its own system: New York & Greenwood Lake, Northern Railroad of New Jersey, and New Jersey & New York.

The Erie held its own against the Great Depression until January 18, 1938, when it entered bankruptcy. Its reorganization, accomplished in December 1941, included purchase of the leased Cleveland & Mahoning Valley, swapping high rent for lower interest payments, and purchase of subsidiaries and leased lines. To the surprise of many, Erie began paying dividends. Prosperity continued until the mid-1950s, but then began to decline. Erie's 1957 income was less than half that for 1956; in 1958 and 1959 the road posted deficits.

The business recession of the 1950s prompted Erie to explore the idea of cooperation with Delaware, Lackawanna & Western. The first results were the elimination of duplicate freight facilities at Binghamton and Elmira, and in 1956 and 1957 Erie moved its passenger trains from its old Jersey City terminal to Lackawanna's newer one at Hoboken. The discussions of cooperation turned into merger talks, at first including the Delaware & Hudson. An agreement was worked out with the Lackawanna, and the two roads merged as the Erie-Lackawanna on October 17, 1960.

Location of headquarters: New York, New York; after 1931 Cleveland, Ohio

Miles of railroad operated: 1929 — 2,316; 1959 — 2,215

Number of locomotives: 1929 — 1,122; 1959 — 484

Number of passenger cars: 1929 — 1,368; 1959 — 535

Number of freight cars: 1929 — 44,916; 1959 — 20,028

Number of company service cars: 1929 — 1,619; 1959 — 605

Reporting marks: ERIE

Notable named passenger trains: *Erie Limited* (Jersey City-Chicago)

Historical and technical society: Erie Lackawanna Historical Society, 22 Duquesne Court, New Castle, DE 19720

Recommended reading: *Men of Erie*, by Edward Hungerford, published in 1946 by Random House, New York, N. Y.

Subsidiaries and affiliated railroads, 1959:

Akron & Barberton Belt (25%)

Buffalo Creek (50%, jointly with Lehigh Valley)

Niagara Junction (25%)

New Jersey & New York (84%)

Successors:

Erie Lackawanna

Conrail (TWG)

NJ Transit (TWG)

Portions still operated:

Hoboken, N. J.-Port Jervis, N. Y.; Hoboken-Spring Valley, N. Y.: NJ Transit

Jersey City, N. J.-Rittman, Ohio; Burbank-Ontario, Ohio; Kenton-Alger, Ohio; Aurora-Cleveland, Ohio; Maitland-Dayton, Ohio; Jersey City-Orangeburg, N. Y.; Hornell-Buffalo, N. Y.; Carrolton, N. Y.-Bradford, Pa.; Meadville-Oil City, Pa.: Conrail

Lackawaxen-Honesdale, Pa.: Lackawaxen & Stourbridge

Buffalo-Gowanda, N. Y.: Buffalo Southern

Gowanda-Waterboro, N. Y.; West Dayton-East Salamanca, N. Y.: New York & Lake Erie

Lima-Glenmore, Ohio: Spencerville & Elgin

Monterrey-North Judson, Ind.: Tippecanoe

Passaic Jct., N. J.-Campbell Hall, N. Y.-Binghamton: New York, Susquehanna & Western (trackage rights)

Map: See opposite page

ERIE LACKAWANNA RAILROAD

The Erie-Lackawanna Railroad was formed by the merger of the Erie Railroad with the Delaware, Lackawanna & Western on October 17, 1960. (A minor renaming occurred in late 1963 when the hyphen was dropped.) The new railroad took after its parent Erie; the largest amount of Lackawanna influence seemed to be paint. Both of EL's parents entered the merger after a couple of years of deficit operations, and EL continued their record, except for 1965 and 1966.

EL quickly consolidated its passenger services, with most trains follow-

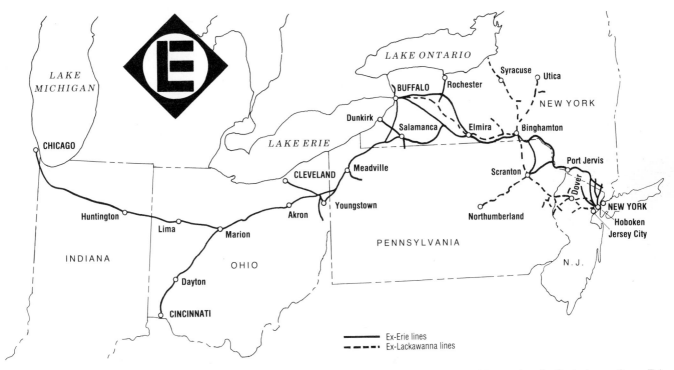

```
——— Ex-Erie lines
- - - Ex-Lackawanna lines
```

ing the ex-Lackawanna route east of Binghamton and the ex-Erie route west. Long-distance passenger trains were gradually cut back during the 1960s, and the last Hoboken-Chicago train was discontinued in 1970, leaving EL with a single daily commuter round trip between Cleveland and Youngstown and its extensive New Jersey commuter services. In 1967 the state of New Jersey began subsidizing the service and in 1970

began to acquire new cars and locomotives for the trains on the ex-Erie routes and the nonelectrified Lackawanna lines (the Lackawanna electric cars would continue running until 1984). The Cleveland-Youngstown train lasted until 1977.

In 1960 Chesapeake & Ohio began acquiring Baltimore & Ohio stock, and in November 1961 New York Central and Pennsylvania announced their intention to merge. In 1964 Norfolk & Western teamed up with Nickel Plate, Wabash, Pittsburgh & West Virginia, and Akron, Canton & Youngstown. Erie Lackawanna was suddenly surrounded, or thought it would be when all the mergers were approved, and asked to be included in the Norfolk & Western system. In 1965 Norfolk & Western and Chesapeake & Ohio announced their merger plan, which would include EL and several other smaller eastern railroads, to be held by a wholly owned subsidiary holding company named Dereco. The N&W-C&O merger didn't take place, but on March 1, 1968, Dereco and the Erie Lackawanna Railway were both incorporated. Dereco exchanged its shares for Erie Lackawanna Railway's 1,000 shares. On April 1, 1968, the Erie Lackawanna Railway merged with the Erie Lackawanna Railroad. Stockholders of the

Erie Lackawanna Railroad received Dereco shares. To put it in simpler language, Norfolk & Western bought the Erie Lackawanna at arm's length.

Hurricane Agnes hit the East on June 22, 1972. After estimating that damage to the railroad, principally between Binghamton and Salamanca, N. Y., amounted to $9.2 million, EL filed for bankruptcy on June 26, 1972. During the reorganization of the eastern railroads, it was thought that EL might be able to reorganize on its own, and there was a proposal by Chessie System to buy a portion of the EL. However, Chessie canceled the agreement and EL asked to be included in Conrail.

Consolidated Rail Corporation took over EL's operations on April 1, 1976. Conrail's map excluded most of the former Erie main line west of

Symbol freights CX-99 and NE-74, Erie Lackawanna's hottest westbound and eastbound freights, meet at Rood's Creek, N. Y., in the early 1970s. Two SD45s are in charge of NE-74, waiting at the right; two SDP45s and an SD45 head CX-99.

J. J. Young Jr.

Marion, Ohio. The Erie Western was formed to operate the 152 miles from Decatur to Hammond, Indiana, with subsidy from the state of Indiana. The road operated for a brief period in 1978 and 1979, but the subsidy was withdrawn and on-line traffic wasn't sufficient to support the operation. Other shortline operators have taken over various parts of EL with more success; they are listed in the entries for the Erie and the Lackawanna. As an odd valedictory for EL, parent Norfolk & Western donated its 1,000 shares of Erie Lackawanna stock and the corporate records to the University of Virginia in 1983.

Location of headquarters: Cleveland, Ohio
Miles of railroad operated: 1960 — 3,189; 1975 — 2,807
Number of locomotives: 1960 — 695; 1975 — 516
Number of passenger cars: 1960 — 1,098; 1975 — 407
Number of freight and company service cars: 1960 — 29,905; 1975 — 19,162
Reporting marks: EL
Historical and technical society: Erie Lackawanna Historical Society, 22 Duquesne Court, New Castle, DE 19720

Recommended reading: *Erie Lackawanna East*, by Karl R. Zimmermann, published in 1975 by Quadrant Press, 19 West 44th Street, New York, NY 10036 (ISBN 0-915276-12-7)
Subsidiaries and affiliated railroads, 1975:
Akron & Barberton Belt (25%)
Buffalo Creek (50%, jointly with Lehigh Valley)
Chicago & Western Indiana (20%)
Lackawanna & Wyoming Valley (86%)
New Jersey & New York (84%)
Predecessor railroads in this book:
Delaware, Lackawanna & Western
Erie Railroad
Successors:
Conrail (TWG)
NJ Transit (TWG)
Portions still operated: See entries for Delaware, Lackawanna & Western and Erie

FLORIDA EAST COAST RAILWAY — KEY WEST EXTENSION

When Henry M. Flagler's Florida East Coast Railway reached Miami from the north in 1896, Flagler was not content to rest. The Florida Keys, a string of islands, reach more than 100 miles southwest from the southern tip of mainland Florida. The outermost, only 90 miles from Havana, Cuba, is Key West. Until the 1950s there was a great deal of freight and passenger traffic between the U. S. and Cuba; in addition Key West was nearer the Panama Canal, then under construction, than any other U. S. port. In 1904 Flagler decided to extend his railroad to Key West.

The construction problems were formidable and labor turnover was high. The first portion of the line, from Homestead to Key Largo, was across swamp. The dredging of drainage canals provided material for the roadbed. Along Key Largo the problem was not terrain but insects. Worse than either terrain or insects was the weather: A hurricane in September 1906 destroyed the initial work on the Long Key Viaduct and killed more than 100 laborers. In 1907 the opening of Long Key Viaduct, more than 2 miles of concrete arches (it became FEC's trademark), allowed service to begin to Knights Key, where a marine terminal was built.

Hurricanes in 1909 and 1910 wiped out much of the completed railroad. After both hurricanes, work resumed at a faster pace — Flagler was getting old and wanted to ride all the way to Key West on his railroad. He did so on January 22, 1912.

Regular service began the next day, with through sleepers between New York and Key West and connections at Key West with passenger steamers and carferries for Havana.

A hurricane on September 2, 1935, washed away 40 miles of the Key West Extension. Florida East Coast was unwilling to repair a line that had never repaid its construction cost — an unknown figure only hinted at by the federal valuation of $12 million. The concrete viaducts survived

Continued on page 137

HENRY MORRISON FLAGLER

(1830-1913) was born in Hopewell, New York. At the age of 22 he began a business career in Ohio, though he had little education or money. His success led to a partnership with John D. Rockefeller; eventually they formed the Standard Oil Company. Soon the two men controlled much of the oil industry in the U. S.

In 1878 (some accounts say 1883) Flagler went to Florida hoping the climate there would help his ailing wife,

Collection of Seth Bramson

Mary. She died in 1881; Flagler then married her nurse. He recognized the state's potential as a tourist attraction. To open Palm Beach and Miami to winter vacationers he built the Florida East Coast Railway. He took over a narrow gauge line between Jacksonville and St. Augustine (where he built a hotel, the Ponce de Leon, and, for his second wife, Alice, a mansion), standard-gauged it, and extended it south, reaching Miami in 1896. When Alice became insane and was committed to an institution, Flagler doubled his efforts to develop Florida. Shortly after divorcing Alice in 1901, Flagler remarried. He built a new mansion for third wife, Mary Lily, at Palm Beach, where he lived out the last years of his life. He died in May 1913.

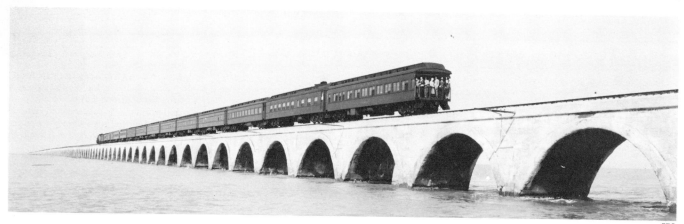

FEC

Passengers enjoy the fresh sea air on the observation platform as the *Havana Special* rolls across Long Key Viaduct on the way to Key West.

to become the bridges of U. S. Highway 1, and the railroad was cut back to Florida City, 30 miles south of Miami.

Miles of railroad operated: 1929 — 156

Notable named passenger trains: *Havana Special* (New York-Key West, operated north of Jacksonville by Atlantic Coast Line, Richmond, Fredericksburg & Potomac, and Pennsylvania Railroad)

Recommended reading:

The Railroad That Died At Sea, by Pat Parks, published in 1968 by the Stephen Greene Press, Brattleboro, VT 05301

Speedway to Sunshine, by Seth Bramson, published in 1984 by Boston Mills Press, 98 Main Street, Erin, Ontario N0B 1T0, Canada (ISBN 0-919783-12-0)

Portions still operated: Miami-Florida City: Florida East Coast

---

FORT DODGE, DES MOINES & SOUTHERN RAILROAD

In 1893 the Boone Valley Coal & Railroad Company was formed to build a railroad from coalfields northwest of Des Moines, Iowa, to a connection with the Minneapolis & St. Louis Railway. Within a decade it was part of the Newton & Northwestern, a line from Newton, Iowa, northwest to Rockwell City. A notable feature of the line was the long, high trestle over Bass Point Creek, a tributary of the Des Moines River near Boone.

The Fort Dodge, Des Moines & Southern Railroad was incorporated in 1906 and built three lines branching off the Newton & Northwestern: from Hope north to Fort Dodge, from Midvale south to Des Moines, and

William D. Middleton

Car 72 operating as train 2 from Fort Dodge to Des Moines crosses the Fort Dodge Line's famous high bridge near Boone, Iowa, in April 1955.

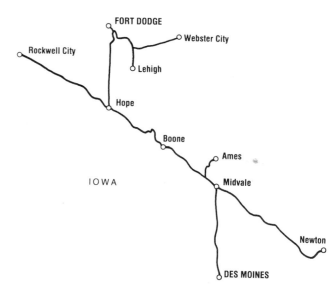

from Kelly to Ames. The road purchased existing streetcar companies in Fort Dodge and Ames, and it connected with the Inter-Urban Railway (later part of the Des Moines & Central Iowa) for access to downtown Des Moines. The Des Moines and Fort Dodge lines were electrified from the beginning, and trolley wires were erected over the Newton & Northwestern between Midvale and Hope.

The N&NW entered receivership in 1908 and was purchased in 1909 by the FDDM&S; a year later the FDDM&S also entered receivership, which lasted until 1913, when the road was sold at foreclosure to another company of the same name. The Rockwell City line was electrified, and the line from Midvale to Newton was dismantled in 1917 after several years of disuse. About that same time the FDDM&S built and acquired lines from Fort Dodge east to Webster City and Lehigh to tap coal and gypsum mines.

From the beginning the railroad was primarily a freight carrier. The road was listed in the 1930 edition of Poor's — unusual for an electric line — which said, "Road is electrically operated, but is of standard steam railroad construction . . . and operates under the steam railroad laws of Iowa." Passenger service on the branches was discontinued in the 1920s, and by 1930 mainline passenger service was down to four trips a day in each direction. That was reduced to two each way from 1935 until the early 1940s, when four trips were again scheduled.

The Fort Dodge, Des Moines & Southern entered receivership again in 1930; the Fort Dodge, Des Moines & Southern Railway took over the property in 1943. The Iowa Commerce Commission permitted abandonment of passenger service in 1952, but the passenger trains continued to operate until 1955. Dieselization began in 1949, and the road was temporarily totally dieselized for three months in the summer of 1954 because of floods. Electric operation ended when passenger service ceased.

The Des Moines & Central Iowa was successor in 1922 to the Inter-Urban Railway. Its main lines ran from Des Moines east to Colfax and northwest to Perry. It abandoned the Colfax line and went bankrupt in 1946. In 1949 it was purchased by Murray Salzberg, who ended passenger service on the Perry line and dieselized the road. Chicago & North Western acquired control in 1969.

In 1954 control of the FDDM&S was acquired by the Des Moines & Central Iowa. Most of the Fort Dodge Line's branches were abandoned in the 1960s. C&NW leased the FDDM&S in 1971 and quickly took over its operations. In 1983 most of the main line was abandoned. The Boone Railroad Historical Society purchased 11 miles of the line from Boone to Wolf Crossing, including the famous High Bridge, for operation as the Boone & Scenic Valley Railroad, a tourist carrier.

Location of headquarters: Boone, Iowa
Miles of railroad operated: 1929 — 151; 1970 — 112
Number of locomotives: 1929 — 12; 1970 — 9
Number of passenger cars: 1929 — 19
Number of freight cars: 1929 — 683; 1970 — 202
Number of company service cars: 1929 — 23; 1970 — 17
Reporting marks: FtDDM&S
Historical and technical societies:
Boone Railroad Historical Society, 1024 Eighth Street, Boone, IA 50036
Chicago & North Western Historical Society, 17004 Locust Drive, Hazel Crest, IL 60429
Recommended reading: *Iowa Trolleys*, edited by Norman Carlson, published in 1975 by Central Electric Railfans' Association, P. O. Box 503, Chicago, IL 60690
Successors: Chicago & North Western (TWG)
Portions still operated:
Boone-Wolf Crossing: Boone & Scenic Valley Railroad

FORT SMITH & WESTERN RAILWAY

The Fort Smith and Western Railroad was incorporated in Arkansas in 1899 and opened its first 20 miles of line between Coal Creek and McCurtain, Oklahoma, at the end of 1901. (The road used trackage rights on Kansas City Southern from Fort Smith, Ark., headquarters of the line, to Coal Creek.) The end of 1903 saw the entire line open between Coal Creek and a connection with the Santa Fe at Guthrie, Okla., at that time the territorial capital. The line served no major population centers, and

the lack of business put the road into receivership. In 1915 FS&W acquired trackage rights on the Missouri-Kansas-Texas from Fallis, Okla., to Oklahoma City, which had become the state capital in 1910. The road teamed up with Missouri, Oklahoma & Gulf, with which it connected at Dustin, to offer through passenger service between Oklahoma City, Muskogee, and Joplin, Mo. A major portion of the road's freight traffic was metallurgical-grade coal from mines near McCurtain and cotton.

Continued on next page

Fort Smith & Western's freight was moved by light Mikados such as Baldwin-built No. 25. Air reservoirs atop the boiler were an FS&W trait.

Charles E. Winters

The Fort Smith & Western Railway was incorporated on January 10, 1921, to purchase and operate the property of the Fort Smith & Western Railroad. It began operation on February 1, 1923. The early 1920s were good years for the FS&W. Oil was discovered near Okemah, and the road made a successful effort to solicit bridge traffic — traffic received from one railroad and delivered to another. Prosperity, however, managed to elude FS&W's grasp. On June 1, 1931, the Central United National Bank of Cleveland, Ohio, brought suit for foreclosure and appointment of a receiver (corporate headquarters of the road were in Cleveland, and several of the road's directors were connected with the Nickel Plate Road). The Great Depression had the same effect on the FS&W that it did on other roads; in addition, droughts during the early 1930s destroyed much of the agriculture along the FS&W. The road faced other problems too: Its equipment was old and worn out; many of its management people, who had been with the road since its construction, were in the same condition; the approach to the Canadian River bridge was washed out twice in the late 1930s, requiring expensive repairs and detours over other railroads; and Katy withdrew trackage rights into Oklahoma City. Operations ceased on February 9, 1939, and permission to abandon was granted five months later. Kansas City Southern subsidiary Fort Smith & Van Buren acquired the original portion of the road from Coal Creek to McCurtain.

From 1907 to 1922 the Fort Smith & Western controlled the St. Louis, El Reno & Western Railway, whose line from Guthrie to El Reno, Okla., gave the FS&W a connection with the Rock Island. It was dismantled in 1926.

Location of headquarters: Fort Smith, Arkansas
Miles of railroad operated: 1929 — 250; 1938 — 250
Number of locomotives: 1929 — 26; 1938 — 11
Number of passenger cars: 1929 — 21; 1938 — 6
Number of freight cars: 1929 — 1,063; 1938 — 136
Number of company service cars: 1929 — 64; 1938 — 6
Reporting marks: FS&W
Recommended reading: *Railroads in Oklahoma*, edited by Donovan L. Hofsommer, published in 1977 by the Oklahoma Historical Society, 2100 North Lincoln, Oklahoma City, OK 73105
Portions still operated: Coal Creek-McCurtain, Okla.: Kansas City Southern
Map: See page 190

GEORGIA & FLORIDA RAILROAD

John Skelton Williams, former president of the Seaboard Air Line, proposed in 1906 to assemble a railroad from Columbia, South Carolina, to a port to be developed on the Gulf of Mexico in Florida. To form the Georgia & Florida Railway he acquired four short lines: the Augusta & Florida Railway (Keysville-Swainsboro, Ga.); the Millen & Southwestern Railroad (Millen-Pendleton-Vidalia, Ga.); the Douglas, Augusta & Gulf Railway (Hazlehurst-Nashville-Sparks, Ga.); and the Valdosta Southern Railway (Valdosta, Ga.-Madison, Fla.). In addition the four roads included several branches and leased lines. He connected these by constructing four segments of track totaling 84 miles: Swainsboro-Pendleton, Vidalia-Hazlehurst, Garent-Douglas Jct., and Nashville-Valdosta. In addition, he secured trackage rights between Augusta and Keysville over the Augusta Southern.

By 1910 a line was complete between Augusta, Ga., and Madison, Fla. In 1911 the G&F reached Moultrie, Ga., by purchase and completion of a short branch and a few miles of trackage rights. In 1919 the road purchased the Augusta Southern at foreclosure, gaining a line to Sandersville and Tennille, Ga. In 1924 the road leased the Midland Railway of Georgia, which formed a branch to Statesboro (the Midland had begun life as a Savannah-Chattanooga proposal and had gone through several identities).

The Georgia & Florida entered receivership in 1915. Skelton became receiver of the G&F in 1921, and it was reorganized as the Georgia & Florida Railroad shortly after Skelton's death in 1926. The road began construction of an extension north to Greenwood, S. C., completed in 1929. The cost of construction and the effects of the Depression put the G&F into receivership again in 1929. In March 1954 the road sold the Valdosta-Madison line to the Valdosta Southern Railroad — a new company, not the one acquired by Skelton.

In February 1962 the Southern Railway formed the Georgia & Florida Railway to acquire the road and then sell it to three other roads controlled by the Southern: Live Oak, Perry & Gulf; Carolina & North Western; and South Georgia. Transfer of the G&F to the three roads occurred July 1, 1963. On June 1, 1971, the Georgia & Florida Railway was

merged into the Central of Georgia Railroad, another subsidiary of the Southern. The South Carolina portion was abandoned in the early 1970s; most of the main line remains in service.

Location of headquarters: Augusta, Georgia
Miles of railroad operated: 1929 — 502; 1961 — 321

Continued on next page

Number of locomotives: 1929 — 32; 1961 — 12
Number of passenger cars: 1929 — 29
Number of freight cars: 1929 — 635; 1961 — 513
Number of company service cars: 1929 — 49; 1961 — 43
Reporting marks: G&F
Recommended reading: *Central of Georgia Railway and Connecting Lines*, by Richard E. Prince, published in 1976 by Richard E. Prince
Successors: Southern Railway (TWG)
Portions still operated:
Midville-Valdosta, Ga.: Central of Georgia (Southern Railway System)
Valdosta-Clyatteville, Ga.: Valdosta Southern
Adel-Moultrie, Ga.: Georgia Northern

Georgia & Florida's largest steam locomotives were three 4-8-2s originally built for New Orleans Great Northern in 1927 and purchased from Gulf, Mobile & Ohio in 1947. They proved too heavy for the track south of Augusta and were soon restricted to the South Carolina portion of the line.

T. Blasingame

GEORGIA NORTHERN RAILWAY

In 1891 a private logging railroad that extended a few miles north from Pidcock, Georgia, was organized as the Boston & Albany Railroad of Georgia. Within two years it had been extended north to Moultrie and it had entered receivership. J. N. Pidcock, who owned lumber mills in the area, purchased the railroad and reorganized it as the Georgia Northern Railway. In 1905 the railroad relocated the southern 4 miles of the line to terminate at Boston, east of Pidcock, and that same year completed the line north to Albany, 68 miles from Boston.

The Flint River & Northeastern was completed between Pelham and Ticknor, 23 miles, in 1904. By 1908 Pidcock had acquired an interest in the road and was operating it as part of the Georgia Northern. In 1922 Pidcock organized the Georgia, Ashburn, Sylvester & Camilla Railway to take over a 50-mile portion of a sub-subsidiary of the Southern Railway between Ashburn and Camilla.

The Albany & Northern was organized in 1895 to take over a 35-mile line between Albany and Cordele. In 1910 the Georgia, Southwestern & Gulf, which had been incorporated to build a line from Albany southwest to St. Andrews Bay on the Gulf of Mexico, purchased control of the Albany & Northern, leased it, and operated it as the Georgia, Southwestern & Gulf. (The line to the Gulf never became reality.) The GSW&G entered receivership in 1932, and Pidcock was appointed receiver in 1939. In 1942 the GSW&G was dissolved, the lease was canceled, and the Albany & Northern resumed its own operation.

The roads shared many officers. Georgia Northern, GAS&C, and FR&N were listed together in *The Official Guide* and shared general offices at Moultrie. Offices of the Albany & Northern and the Georgia, Southwestern & Gulf were at Albany.

The Flint River and Northeastern was abandoned in 1946. Southern Railway acquired control of Georgia Northern, Albany & Northern, and GAS&C in 1966. The roads were merged on January 1, 1972; Georgia Northern exists today as a subsidiary of the Southern Railway. It operates the remains of the Pidcock system and also a short portion of the for-

Georgia Northern SW8 No. 13 leads a Georgia, Ashburn, Sylvester & Camilla freight through a sea of dry grass between Camilla and Bridgeboro.

Jim Boyd

mer Georgia & Florida Railroad extending from Moultrie to Adel, Ga.

Georgia Northern
Location of headquarters: Moultrie, Georgia
Miles of railroad operated: 1929 — 68; 1965 — 68
Number of locomotives: 1929 — 5; 1965 — 3
Number of passenger cars: 1929 — 7; 1965 — 1
Number of freight cars: 1929 — 49; 1965 — 3
Number of company service cars: 1929 — 2; 1965 — 5

Georgia, Ashburn, Sylvester & Camilla
Location of headquarters: Moultrie, Georgia
Miles of railroad operated: 1929 — 50; 1965 — 51
Number of locomotives: 1929 — 1; 1965 — 2
Number of cars: 1929 — 10; 1965 — 1

Flint River & Northeastern
Location of headquarters: Moultrie, Georgia
Miles of railroad operated: 1929 — 23; 1945 — 23
Number of locomotives: 1929 — 2; 1945 — 2
Number of cars: 1929 — 4; 1945 — 3
Reporting marks: FR&N

Albany & Northern
Location of headquarters: Albany, Georgia
Miles of railroad operated: 1929 — 35; 1962 — 35
Number of locomotives: 1929 — 5; 1962 — 2
Number of passenger cars: 1929 — 7
Number of freight cars: 1929 — 13; 1962 — 2

Georgia, Southwestern & Gulf
Location of headquarters: Albany, Georgia
Miles of railroad operated: 1929 — 35; 1938 — 35
Number of locomotives: 1929 — 5; 1938 — 5
Number of passenger cars: 1929 — 7; 1938 — 4
Number of freight cars: 1929 — 13; 1938 — 9

Recommended reading: *Central of Georgia Railway and Connecting Lines,* by Richard E. Prince, published in 1976 by Richard E. Prince
Successors: Southern Railway (TWG)
Portions still operated: Pavo-Albany; Camilla-Sylvester: Georgia Northern (Southern Railway System)
Map: See page 141

GREAT NORTHERN RAILWAY

In 1857 the Minnesota & Pacific Railroad was chartered to build a line from Stillwater, Minnesota, on the St. Croix River east of St. Paul, through St. Paul and St. Cloud to St. Vincent, in the northwest corner of the state. The road defaulted after completing a roadbed between St. Paul and St. Cloud, and its charter was taken over by the St. Paul & Pacific Railroad, which ran its first train between St. Paul and St. Anthony (now Minneapolis) in 1862. For financial reasons the railroad properties were reorganized as the First Division of the St. Paul & Pacific. Both StP&P companies were soon in receivership, and Northern Pacific, with which the StP&P was allied, went bankrupt in the Panic of 1873.

In 1878 James J. Hill and an associate, George Stephen, acquired the two St. Paul & Pacific companies and reorganized them as the St. Paul, Minneapolis & Manitoba Railway (often referred to as "the Manitoba"). By 1885 the company had 1,470 miles of railroad and extended west to Devils Lake, North Dakota. In 1886 Hill organized the Montana Central Railway to build from Great Falls, Montana, through Helena to Butte, and in 1888 the line was opened, creating in conjunction with the StPM&M a railroad from St. Paul to Butte.

In 1881 Hill took over the 1856 charter of the Minneapolis & St. Cloud Railroad. He first used its franchises to build the Eastern Railway of Minnesota from Hinckley, Minn., to Superior, Wisconsin, and Duluth. Its charter was liberal enough that he chose it as the vehicle for his line to the Pacific. He renamed the road the Great Northern Railway; GN then leased the Manitoba and assumed its operation. Hill decided to extend his railroad from Havre, Mont., west to the Pacific, specifically to Puget Sound at Seattle, Washington. He had briefly considered building to Portland, but it was already served by the Oregon-Washington Railroad & Navigation Co. and the Northern Pacific.

Hill's surveyors found an easy route through the Rockies over Marias Pass. Later there was considerable advocacy for creating a national park in the Rockies of northern Montana, and GN — in particular, Louis W. Hill, son of James J. and president of GN from 1907 to 1912 and 1914 to 1919 — soon joined the forces urging the establishment of Glacier National Park. GN developed the park, and for many years furnished the

only transportation to it. The park, in turn, drew passengers to the railroad-owned hotels and provided the railroad with a herald, a Rocky Mountain goat (actually a species of antelope). GN sold its Glacier Park hotel properties in 1960.

The Cascade Range in the state of Washington was a far more formidable barrier to the Great Northern. The Northern Pacific had originally detoured to the south, using Oregon-Washington rails along the Columbia River. Hill, however, saw the vast stands of timber on the slopes of the mountains as a resource, and his engineer, John Stevens, found a pass (it now bears his name) that could afford a route from the interior of Washington to the tidewater of Puget Sound.

The Great Northern was opened through to Seattle in 1893 using a temporary line over Stevens Pass. In 1900 the first Cascade Tunnel, 2.63 miles long, provided relief from the switchbacks and the 4 percent grades of the temporary line and lowered the summit of the line from 4,068 feet to 3,383 feet. The tunnel was electrified with a 2-wire, 3-phase system in 1909. The electrification was replaced with a more conventional system in 1927 as a prelude to the opening of the 7.79-mile second Cascade Tunnel in 1929. The new tunnel, the longest in the Western Hemisphere, lowered the maximum elevation of the line to 2,881 feet and eliminated 8 miles of snowsheds and more than 5 complete circles of curvature. The tunnel project included other line relocations in the area and the extension of the electrified portion of the line east to Wenatchee and west to Skykomish.

Even before completion of the route from St. Paul, the Great Northern had opened a line along the shore of Puget Sound between Seattle and Vancouver, British Columbia, in 1891. In the years that followed Hill pushed a number of lines north across the international boundary into the mining area of southern British Columbia in a running battle with Canadian Pacific. In 1912 GN traded its line along the Fraser River east of Vancouver to Canadian Northern for trackage rights into Winnipeg. GN gradually withdrew from British Columbia after Hill's death. In 1909 the Manitoba Great Northern Railway purchased most of the property of the Midland Railway of Manitoba (lines from the U. S. border to Portage la Prairie and to Morden), leaving the Midland, which was jointly controlled by GN and NP, with terminal properties in Winnipeg. Manitoba

Great Northern disposed of its rail lines — later abandoned — in 1927.

In 1907 the Great Northern purchased the properties and assets of the St. Paul, Minneapolis & Manitoba and of a number of its proprietary companies, such as the Eastern Railway of Minnesota and the Montana Central. In 1928 there was another spate of such activity. The result was that GN was a large railroad with very few subsidiaries, unlike, for example, the Southern Railway.

Among the major branches and lines added to the system were the Surrey Cutoff between Fargo and Minot, N. Dak., shortening the route between St. Paul and Seattle by about 50 miles, opened in 1912; an interurban system, the Spokane, Coeur d'Alene & Palouse, east and south from Spokane (absorbed by GN in 1943); and an extension of the Oregon Trunk from Bend, Oreg., south to a connection with the Western Pacific at Bieber, California, completed in 1931 (Chemult to Klamath Falls, Oreg., n Southern Pacific rails).

The Great Northern changed little in the modern era — from the 1920s

through the 1960s — apart from the industry-wide change from steam to diesel. A ventilating system allowed dieselization of the Cascade Tunnel in 1956 and eliminated the electrification. In November 1970 the Cascade Tunnel acquired a rival, the Flathead Tunnel, shorter by only 70 yards, as part of a line relocation necessitated by construction of a dam at Libby, Mont. Most of the construction was done by GN; only the last portion and the actual opening of the tunnel were done by Burlington Northern.

On July 1, 1901, the Great Northern and the Northern Pacific jointly purchased more than 97 percent of the stock of the Chicago, Burlington & Quincy to ensure a connection between St. Paul and Chicago. GN and NP backed construction of the Spokane, Portland & Seattle, a line to Portland, Oreg., from Spokane; SP&S in turn sponsored the construction of the Oregon Trunk Railway from Wishram, Wash., on the Columbia River, south to Bend, Oreg. GN got another route to Portland by acquiring trackage rights on Northern Pacific from Seattle.

Continued on next page

The 69-inch drivers of Great Northern class O-8 Mikado 3381 have a freight train moving at a mile a minute across the prairie near Benson, Minn. Great Northern and Pennsylvania were the only two railroads in the U. S. to favor the Belpaire boiler on their steam locomotives.

Frank A. King

Hill soon acquired control of Northern Pacific with the intent of merging GN, NP, Burlington, and Spokane, Portland & Seattle into a single railroad. As a start, he formed Northern Securities as a holding company, but the ICC quickly ruled against such a merger. In 1927 the Great Northern Pacific Railway was incorporated to merge GN and NP and lease SP&S and the Burlington. The ICC approved the merger upon the condition that GN and NP divest themselves of the Burlington — a condition the two Northerns were unwilling to meet. More than four decades passed before the merger went through on March 2, 1970 — with the Burlington included and indeed half the name of the merged company.

Location of headquarters: St. Paul, Minnesota
Miles of railroad operated: 1929 — 8,368; 1969 — 8,274
Number of locomotives: 1929 — 1,164; 1969 — 609
Number of passenger cars: 1929 — 946; 1969 — 415

Number of freight cars: 1929 — 55,777; 1969 — 36,300
Number of company service cars: 1929 — 2,766; 1969 — 2,268
Reporting marks: GN
Notable named passenger trains: *Empire Builder* (Chicago to Seattle and Portland; operated east of St. Paul by the Chicago, Burlington & Quincy, and between Spokane and Portland by the Spokane, Portland & Seattle)
Historical and technical society: Great Northern Railway Historical Society, 6161 Willow Lake Drive, Hudson, OH 44236
Recommended reading: *The Great Northern Railway: A Pictorial Study*, by Charles and Dorothy Wood, published in 1979 by Pacific Fast Mail, P. O. Box 57, Edmonds, WA 98020
Subsidiaries and affiliated railroads, 1969:
Spokane, Portland & Seattle (50%, jointly with Northern Pacific)

Continued on page 148

JAMES J. HILL (1838-1916) was born in Rockwood, Ontario, west of Toronto. He grew up on a farm and worked as a store clerk before leaving at the age of 18 for New York, where he intended to get work on a ship bound for the Orient. He changed his mind and returned west to St. Paul, Minnesota, a new town that was rapidly becoming the gateway to the opening Northwest. He went to work immediately with a shipping agent and then held a succession of various jobs, mostly connected with shipping on the Mississippi River and later the railroads.

In 1867 Hill married Mary Mehegan and began to produce a family that eventually numbered 10 children. His business interests expanded to encompass trade and shipping along the Red River of the North and a coal business in St. Paul and Minneapolis. In 1878 Hill acquired control of the St. Paul & Pacific and reorganized it as the St. Paul, Minneapolis & Manitoba. He quickly completed its line from St. Paul to St. Vincent, where it connected with a Canadian Pacific line to Winnipeg, and then added a number of branches to the system.

Hill recognized that the completion of the Northern Pacific between Duluth and Puget Sound meant his railroad would need a route to the Pacific. He purchased an interest in the Canadian Pacific Railway as a western outlet for the StPM&M — and also with the hope that construction of a railroad north of Lake Superior would prove so difficult that CPR would have to go through St. Paul. Hill did persuade the CPR to adopt a more southerly route across the prairies than originally proposed, but an all-Canadian route was necessary for political reasons. Hill resigned from the CPR board in 1883 to build his own line to the Pacific, the Great Northern.

In the 1890s the Northern Pacific was once again in financial trouble. Hill acquired working control of the railroad and began to coordinate the management of NP and GN. NP had briefly owned the Wisconsin Central, which had a line from the Twin Cities to Chicago, and Hill knew his roads would need access to Chicago. On July 1, 1901, the Great Northern and the Northern Pacific jointly purchased more than 97 percent of the stock of the Chicago, Burlington & Quincy to ensure a connection between St. Paul and Chicago. GN and NP backed construction of the Spokane, Portland & Seattle, which afforded access to Portland, Oregon, from Spokane; SP&S in turn sponsored the construction of the Oregon Trunk Railway from Wishram, Washington, on the Columbia River, south to Bend, Oreg.

Hill lived long enough to see his railroad attain most of its growth. In 1907 he turned over the presidency of GN to his son Louis, but he remained on the board of directors and maintained an active role in the management of the road until his death. Outside the railroad world Hill was deeply interested in art, particularly as a collector, and agriculture.

Recommended reading: *James J. Hill & the Opening of the Northwest,* by Albro Martin, published in 1976 by Oxford University Press, 200 Madison Avenue, New York, NY 10016

In 1951 Great Northern re-equipped the *Empire Builder*, which had received streamlined equipment only four years before. GN then used the 1947 *Empire Builder* cars to create a second Chicago-Seattle streamliner, the *Western Star*, shown here in Marias Pass on the southern boundary of Glacier National Park.

GN

Chicago, Burlington & Quincy (48.59%)
Oregon, California & Eastern (50%, jointly with Southern Pacific)
Successors: Burlington Northern (TWG)
Portions still operated: Only these major lines have been abandoned:

Sioux Falls-Yankton, S. Dak.; Basin-Butte, Mont.; Eureka-Ripley, Mont. (replaced by the Flathead Tunnel line); and most of the former Spokane, Coeur d'Alene & Palouse system. The remainder, except for short portions of a few branches, is operated by Burlington Northern.

GULF, MOBILE & NORTHERN RAILROAD

C. W. Witbeck

Gulf, Mobile & Northern standardized on the 2-10-0 for freight power. In 1934 Decapods made up one-third of its steam roster. The arched, brow-like device on the front of the smokebox is a Coffin feedwater heater.

In 1890 the Mobile, Jackson & Kansas City Railroad was chartered to tap the longleaf-pine areas of southern Mississippi. In 1898 it opened the first 50 miles of line northwest from Mobile, Alabama, to the new town of Merrill, Miss., named for one of the promoters of the railroad, and in 1902 reached Hattiesburg, Miss. New promoters bought the line and also purchased the 62-mile narrow gauge Gulf & Chicago between Middleton, Tennessee, and Pontotoc, Miss., and proceeded to fill in the 240 miles between the two railroads. The MJ&KC entered receivership in 1906 shortly after construction was completed; it emerged in 1909 as the New Orleans, Mobile & Chicago Railroad. In 1911 the Louisville & Nashville and the Frisco assumed joint control of the NOM&C with the thought of using the road as an entrance to New Orleans. In 1913 the railroad's finances collapsed again.

The Gulf, Mobile & Northern Railroad began operation on January 1, 1917, as a reorganization of the New Orleans, Mobile & Chicago. President of the road was Isaac B. Tigrett, a banker in Jackson, Tenn. One of the first items of business was to extend the road north 40 miles from Middleton, Tenn., to Jackson and connections with Illinois Central and Nashville, Chattanooga & St. Louis.

In 1926 GM&N began operating freight trains from Jackson, Tenn., north to Paducah, Kentucky, on trackage rights over NC&StL. At Paducah GM&N connected with the Chicago, Burlington & Quincy, with which it made a preferential traffic agreement, forming a Chicago-Gulf route that did not require a competing road, such as Illinois Central, to short-haul itself in order to give traffic to GM&N. (IC had considered GM&N a friendly connection until GM&N extended itself to Jackson, Tenn.) In 1928 GM&N merged with the 49-mile Birmingham & Northwestern, which ran from Jackson, Tenn., northwest to Dyersburg, Tenn. It shared a president — Tigrett — with the smaller road and had controlled it since 1924. In 1929 GM&N merged with the Meridian & Memphis (Union to Meridian, Miss.) and the Jackson & Eastern (Union, Miss., to Jackson, Miss.) — over the years the two Jacksons on GM&N's map, both of them important cities, must have created untold confusion for GM&N's ticket agents, traffic representatives, and historians. On December 30, 1929, GM&N acquired control of New Orleans Great Northern, whose line ran from Jackson, Miss., to New Orleans, and on July 1, 1933, GM&N leased the NOGN.

Continued on next page

149

GM&N got through the Depression by reducing wages, services, and maintenance, but subsidiary New Orleans Great Northern defaulted on bond interest and had to reorganize. In 1935 GM&N upgraded its through passenger service with the *Rebel* trains, the first streamliners in the South. The *Rebels* and the various types of rail motor cars GM&N had been using gave the road an all-motorized passenger service. In 1936 GM&N organized Gulf Transport, a bus and truck subsidiary to supplement rail service and replace money-losing local passenger trains; GM&N had been operating highway services for several years under its own banner.

On June 1, 1933, GM&N moved its Jackson, Tenn.-Paducah freight trains from the NC&StL to Illinois Central rails on a route 34 miles shorter. In 1934 the road began to study acquisition of bankrupt Mobile & Ohio, whose line paralleled GM&N from Mobile to Jackson, Tenn., and continued north from Jackson to St. Louis. A line to St. Louis would bypass the need for operating on the rails of competitor Illinois Central and would afford connections with railroads to the east, north, and west. Ralph Budd (who represented Burlington's stock interest, nearly 30 percent, on GM&N's board of directors) objected, because Burlington would lose its exclusive connection with GM&N and also collect a smaller portion of the freight revenue because its mileage on a through move would be less. M&O acquisition was given added impetus in 1936 when problems arose in connection with GM&N crews operating over IC rails. On June 30, 1938, a decree was rendered — GM&N trains would have to use IC crews within 20 days. GM&N quickly executed a traffic agreement with Mobile & Ohio and ceased operating to Paducah.

Despite the objections of the Burlington and the Illinois Central — IC said that one day it would buy GM&N and M&O — the merger of Gulf, Mobile & Northern and Mobile & Ohio took place on September 13, 1940.

Location of headquarters: Mobile, Alabama
Miles of railroad operated: 1929 — 734; 1940 — 827
Number of locomotives: 1929 — 77; 1940 — 55
Number of passenger cars: 1929 — 39; 1940 — 31
Number of freight cars: 1929 — 1,573
Number of company service cars: 1929 — 144
Number of freight and company service cars: 1940 — 1,647
Reporting marks: GM&N
Notable named passenger trains: *Rebel* (Jackson, Tenn.-Jackson, Miss.-New Orleans)
Historical and technical society: Gulf, Mobile & Ohio Historical Society, P. O. Box 24, Bedford Park, IL 60499
Recommended reading: *The Gulf, Mobile and Ohio,* by James Hutton Lemly, published in 1953 by Richard D. Irwin, Inc., Homewood, IL 60430
Subsidiaries and affiliated railroads, 1939:
Mississippi Export (25%)
New Orleans Great Northern (29%)
Predecessor railroads in this book: New Orleans Great Northern
Successors:
Gulf, Mobile & Ohio
Illinois Central Gulf (TWG)
Portions still operated:
Slidell, La.-Wanilla, Miss.; Slidell-Covington, La.; Mobile, Ala.-Carmichael, Miss.: Illinois Central Gulf
Laurel-Ackerman, Miss.; Woodland, Miss.-Middleton, Tenn.; Union-Walnut Ridge, Miss.: Gulf & Mississippi
Map: See next page

GULF, MOBILE & OHIO RAILROAD

The Gulf, Mobile & Ohio was incorporated in Mississippi on November 10, 1938, to acquire the properties of the Mobile & Ohio and the Gulf, Mobile & Northern. It acquired the M&O through foreclosure sale on August 1, 1940, and was consolidated with the GM&N on September 13, 1940.

All lines north of St. Louis are former Alton lines. South of St. Louis, solid lines indicate former Gulf, Mobile & Northern routes, and dashed lines indicate former Mobile & Ohio routes.

The new railroad extended from New Orleans, Louisiana, and Mobile and Montgomery, Alabama, north to St. Louis.

During World War Two GM&O trimmed a few branches from its system, consolidated shop facilities, and otherwise tightened up the organization. In 1944 the road began to investigate acquiring the bankrupt Alton Railroad, which extended from Chicago to St. Louis and from Springfield, Illinois, west to Kansas City. On May 31, 1947, GM&O merged with the Alton and became a Great Lakes-to-Gulf carrier.

At first GM&O planned to sell the Kansas City line, which was an east-west appendage to an otherwise north-south system. In 1948 GM&O, the Burlington, and the Santa Fe formulated a plan that would result in the sale of the Kansas City line to the Burlington, Santa Fe's use of that line and the connecting Burlington line at Mexico, Missouri, for access to St. Louis, and Burlington trackage rights over Santa Fe into Kansas City from the northeast. Several of the railroads serving St. Louis protested Santa Fe's part in the plan. As it fell out, Burlington acquired trackage rights over GM&O between Mexico and Kansas City and in 1952 opened 71 miles of new line across northern Missouri to shorten its own Chicago-Kansas City route. Santa Fe never gained access to St. Louis.

In 1949 and 1950 GM&O acquired the properties of three roads the Alton had leased, the Kansas City, St. Louis & Chicago Railroad; the Louisiana & Missouri River Railroad; and the Joliet & Chicago Railroad. The Mobile & Ohio had trackage rights on Southern and Illinois Central track between Memphis, Corinth, Miss., and Birmingham. In 1952 GM&O acquired trackage rights over Louisville & Nashville from Tuscaloosa to Birmingham and ceased its use of the Corinth-Birmingham route. GM&O was one of the first major railroads to dieselize completely. Its last steam operation was on October 7, 1949.

By 1947 GM&O's passenger service south of St. Louis consisted of the *Rebel* trains, the first streamliners in the South, between St. Louis and New Orleans and the St. Louis-Mobile *Gulf Coast Rebel*. In addition subsidiary Gulf Transport operated an extensive bus system between St. Louis and the Gulf Coast. Rail passenger service to New Orleans ended in 1954, and the St. Louis-Mobile train was discontinued in 1958.

North of St. Louis GM&O inherited an intensive passenger service from the Alton: seven trains daily between Chicago and St. Louis, a pair

Three GP30s and a GP35 lead a freight south through Scooba, Miss. GM&O's GP30s and 35s were distinctive on several counts: They rode on the trucks of traded-in Alco FAs, they wore an EMD-designed black and white paint scheme on a road traditionally associated with red and maroon liveries, and they seldom worked north of St. Louis before the ICG merger.

of St. Louis-Kansas City trains operated jointly with the Burlington, and a few motor-train locals and mixed trains on branches. The Bloomington, Ill.-Kansas City motor train run endured until 1960. When Amtrak took over the nation's passenger trains, GM&O was operating three trains daily between Chicago and St. Louis and a Chicago-Joliet commuter train. Amtrak continued the operation of the two daytime Chicago-St. Louis trains; the Chicago-Joliet train survived the ICG merger and now two Chicago-Joliet commuter trains are operated by Chicago's Regional Transportation Authority. Gulf Transport still operates buses from Springfield, Ill., St. Louis, and Memphis to Mobile and Pascagoula.

GM&O merged with Illinois Central on August 10, 1972, forming the Illinois Central Gulf Railroad.

Location of headquarters: Mobile, Ala.
Miles of railroad operated: 1940 — 1,808; 1971 — 2,734
Number of locomotives: 1940 — 180; 1971 — 258
Number of passenger cars: 1940 — 96; 1970 — 92
Number of freight and company service cars: 1940 — 6,255
Number of freight cars: 1971 — 12,699
Number of company service cars: 1971 — 567
Reporting marks: GM&O
Notable named passenger trains: *Rebel* (Jackson, Tenn.-New Orleans; later St. Louis-New Orleans); *Abraham Lincoln, Ann Rutledge, Alton Limited* (Chicago-St. Louis)
Historical and technical society: Gulf, Mobile & Ohio Historical Society, P. O. Box 24, Bedford Park, IL 60499
Recommended reading:
The Gulf, Mobile and Ohio, by James Hutton Lemly, published in 1953 by Richard D. Irwin, Inc., Homewood, IL 60430
GM&O North, by Robert P. Olmsted, published in 1976 by Robert P. Olmsted
Subsidiaries and affiliated railroads, 1971:
New Orleans Great Northern (98.17%)
Mississippi Export (25.5%)
Predecessor railroads in this book:
Alton Railroad
Gulf, Mobile & Northern

Mobile & Ohio
New Orleans Great Northern
Successors: Illinois Central Gulf (TWG)
Portions still operated:
Chicago-St. Louis; Jacksonville-Murrayville, Ill.; Roodhouse-Godfrey, Ill.; Springfield-Kansas City; Mexico-Fulton, Mo.; Slidell, La.-Wanilla, Miss.; Slidell-Covington, La.; Elton-Jackson, Miss., Jackson-Wells, Miss., Mobile, Ala.-Carmichael, Miss.; Corinth, Miss.-Kenton, Tenn.; Rives-Union City, Tenn.; Murphysboro, Ill.-East St. Louis: Illinois Central Gulf Mobile, Ala.-Corinth, Miss.; Artesia, Miss.-Tuscaloosa, Ala.; Laurel-Ackerman, Miss.; Woodland, Miss.-Middleton, Tenn.; Union-Walnut Ridge, Miss.: Gulf & Mississippi

HOOSAC TUNNEL & WILMINGTON RAILROAD

The Deerfield River Railroad was chartered in Vermont in 1884; on July 4, 1885, it celebrated the opening of 11 miles of 3-foot-gauge track from Readsboro, Vt., to a junction with the Fitchburg Railroad at the east portal of the Hoosac Tunnel in northwestern Massachusetts. (The 4.75-mile Hoosac Tunnel was opened in 1875 and is still used by the Boston & Maine.) In 1886 the proprietors of the railroad incorporated the Hoosac Tunnel & Wilmington Railroad in Massachusetts; it acquired the Massachusetts portion of the line and leased the Vermont part, with which it

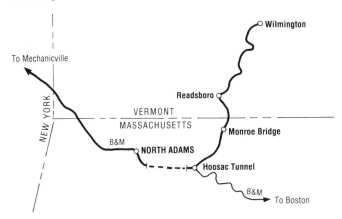

R. E. Tobey

Hoosac Tunnel & Wilmington No. 5 switches the Boston & Maine interchange track at Hoosac Tunnel, Mass. The Mogul came to HT&W secondhand from the Washington, Brandywine & Point Lookout in 1938.

153

SAMUEL M. PINSLY (1899-1977) was born in Cambridge, Massachusetts, and attended Northeastern University in Boston, where he received degrees in engineering and law. He served in the Army during World War One, then worked in the automobile business. In 1923 he married Jessie Salzberg, daughter of H. E. Salzberg, and six years later he joined Salzberg's company, which dealt in used railroad equipment. Salzberg bought the Hoosac Tunnel & Wilmington  Railroad in 1936 and sold it in 1938 to Pinsly, who brought it to profitability. His group of railroads eventually included several short lines cast off by the Boston & Maine:

- Saratoga & Schuylerville (Mechanicville to Saratoga and Schuylerville, New York — purchased 1945, abandoned 1956)
- Sanford & Eastern (Rochester, New Hampshire, to Westbrook, Maine — purchased 1949, abandoned 1961)
- Montpelier & Barre (Montpelier Jct. to Graniteville, Vermont — purchased 1957, sold 1980)
- Claremont & Concord (Claremont Jct. to Concord, N. H. — purchased 1954, still in operation from Claremont Jct. to Claremont)
- St. Johnsbury & Lamoille County (St. Johnsbury-Swanton, Vt. — purchased 1967, sold 1973)

Appropriately enough, Pinsly's headquarters for many years were located in Boston & Maine's general office building in Boston. He also owned two non-B&M lines, the Greenville & Northern (Greenville to Travelers Rest, South Carolina — purchased 1957) and the Frankfort & Cincinnati (Frankfort to Elsinore, Kentucky — purchased 1961). Both are still in operation. In 1956 Pinsly attempted to purchase the New York, Ontario & Western, and in 1958 he proposed to purchase the Old Colony lines of the New Haven to operate them for freight service. Neither project came to fruition. Pinsly was active in the American Shortline Railroad Association, several regional railroad associations, and numerous civic organizations.

After his death in 1977 the Pinsly organization continued in business. It expanded in 1982 with the acquisition from Conrail of former New Haven lines from Westfield to Easthampton and Holyoke, Mass., now operated as the Pioneer Valley Railroad.

was consolidated in 1892. By then the line had been extended north from Readsboro to Wilmington, another 13 miles. The entire line was converted to standard gauge in 1913.

The New England Power Company purchased the road in 1922 and began construction of a dam across the Deerfield River that required relocation of the north end of the line — after an initial proposal by the power company to substitute a carferry on the lake that the dam would create. The power company sold the railroad to local interests in 1926.

The world's first organized railroad fan trip was held on the HT&W. Members of the Railroad Enthusiasts chartered a train to ride the length of the line on Sunday, August 26, 1934. They were the first rail passengers on the line since floods in 1927 had caused the substitution of bus service for the passenger trains.

After more floods in early 1936 the railroad was sold to the H. E. Salzberg Co.; ownership soon passed to Salzberg's son-in-law, Samuel M. Pinsly. He abandoned the line north of Readsboro but thought the remainder could be operated profitably. A hurricane did substantial damage to the HT&W in September 1938, but Pinsly rebuilt the line. In 1941 the Hoosac Tunnel & Wilmington made its first profit in 15 years, and it continued to be a profit maker. Pinsly dieselized the line in 1949.

Business fell off in the mid-1950s and profits turned to deficits. In the late 1950s the HT&W received a new customer in the form of a nuclear power plant at Monroe Bridge. HT&W hauled in much of the material for construction on the plant. Another power plant, the Bear Swamp Project, would have required extensive relocation of the HT&W and resulted instead in abandonment on October 13, 1971.

Location of headquarters: Wilmington, Vermont, until 1937; then Readsboro, Vermont

Miles of railroad operated: 1929 — 24; 1970 — 11
Number of locomotives: 1929 — 3; 1970 — 2
Number of passenger cars: 1929 — 5
Number of freight cars: 1929 — 25; 1970 — 4
Recommended reading: *Hoot Toot & Whistle*, by Bernard R. Carman, published in 1963 by the Stephen Greene Press, Brattleboro, VT 05301

HUNTINGDON & BROAD TOP MOUNTAIN RAILROAD & COAL COMPANY

The Huntingdon & Broad Top Mountain was incorporated in 1852 to build a railroad into the coalfields along the west side of Broad Top Mountain south of Huntingdon, Pennsylvania. (The Pennsylvania Railroad had reached Huntingdon from Harrisburg two years before.) The first portion of the line was opened that same year, and in 1864 it was consolidated with the Bedford Railroad, which continued the line southward to Mt. Dallas. From there to Bedford, eight miles, the H&BTM operated over Pennsylvania Railroad tracks.

The line was prosperous for many years, but by the end of World War Two the road's future, which depended on coal mines along the railroad, was doubtful. The road had last paid dividends on preferred stock in 1922 and on common stock in 1906. Reorganization began in 1949 but without much success; in December 1953 the ICC granted permission for abandonment on March 31, 1954.

Upon the abandonment of the H&BTM, the Everett Railroad was organized to take over the segment of the line from Mt. Dallas through Everett to Tatesville, about four miles. It has since ceased operation.

Location of headquarters: Philadelphia, Pennsylvania
Miles of railroad operated: 1929 — 74; 1953 — 64
Number of locomotives: 1929 — 15; 1953 — 6
Number of passenger cars: 1929 — 9
Number of freight cars: 1929 — 659; 1953 — 70
Number of company service cars: 1929 — 16; 1953 — 14
Reporting marks: H&BT
Map: See page 126

Philip R. Hastings

Consolidation No. 37 leads Huntingdon & Broad Top Mountain train 3, consisting of a combine (a depowered gas-electric car) and a milk car, out of Bedford, Pa.

ILLINOIS CENTRAL RAILROAD

The Illinois Central was chartered in 1851 to build a railroad from Cairo, Illinois, at the confluence of the Ohio and Mississippi rivers, to Galena, in the extreme northwestern corner of the state, with a branch from Centralia (named for the railroad) to Chicago. A previous undertaking had resulted in a few miles of grading north of Cairo but nothing else; the IC was aided, however, by a land grant act signed by President Millard Fillmore in 1850. It was the first federal land grant to a railroad. The line was finished in 1856, giving Chicago a route to New Orleans by way of a railroad-operated steamboat line between Cairo and New Orleans.

In 1867 the IC, which by then had progressed beyond Galena and across the Mississippi to Dubuque, Iowa, leased the Dubuque & Sioux City Railroad, extending its western line to Iowa Falls. The line reached Sioux City in 1870.

The IC realized it was necessary to extend its rails south to the Gulf of Mexico. The railroad made a traffic agreement in 1872 with the New Orleans, Jackson & Great Northern Railroad (opened in 1858 from New Orleans, through Jackson, Mississippi, to Canton, Miss.) and the Mississippi Central Railway (completed in 1860 from Canton north to Jackson, Tennessee). A new railroad line would be necessary between Jackson, Tenn., and Cairo to replace the existing connection via the Mobile & Ohio from Jackson to Columbus, Kentucky, and a riverboat from Columbus to Cairo. The new line was completed in 1873. In 1874 the Illinois Central, principal bondholder of the other two lines, took them over and organized them as the New Orleans, St. Louis & Chicago Railroad. The NOJ&GN and Mississippi Central reorganized in 1877 as the New Orleans, Jackson & Northern and the Central Mississippi, respectively, and then consolidated as the Chicago, St. Louis & New Orleans Railroad, a subsidiary of the IC. Like most of the railroads in the South, the route from Cairo south to New Orleans was built to a 5-foot track gauge. The entire 550-mile route was converted to standard gauge in one day on July 29, 1881.

In the 1870s railroads began to penetrate the fertile Yazoo Delta along the western edge of the state of Mississippi. IC's entry was the Yazoo & Mississippi Valley Railroad, incorporated in 1882 to build a railroad westward from Jackson, Miss. Meanwhile, a rival route, the Louisville,

EDWARD H. HARRIMAN (1848-1909) was born in Hempstead, New York, son of an Episcopal clergyman. At age 14 he began work as an office boy in a New York brokerage house; 8 years later he bought his own seat on the New York Stock Exchange. In 1879 Harriman married Mary Averell, the daughter of the president of the Ogdensburg & Lake Champlain Railroad.

UP

In 1881 Harriman bought control of the Sodus Bay & Southern Railroad, a short line running south from the shore of Lake Ontario. He improved the line, then set the New York Central and the Pennsylvania bidding against each other for it. Pennsy bought it, and Harriman soon went after a larger railroad, the Illinois Central. By 1883 he was on IC's board of directors and within a few years he had left the brokerage house he had established and become vice-president of the road. He launched an expansion program for Illinois Central but, looking ahead, was able to curtail it so the railroad could weather the Panic of 1893.

In 1898 Harriman took over the Union Pacific, which at the time went no farther west than Ogden, Utah. He added to UP the Oregon Railway & Navigation Company and the Oregon Short Line, giving it access to the Pacific at Portland. In 1901 Harriman bought the Southern Pacific and shortly afterward bought the Central Pacific and a half interest in the San Pedro, Los Angeles & Salt Lake. He rounded out his system with the Chicago & Alton and the Central of Georgia. He attempted to buy first the Burlington and then the Northern Pacific but was thwarted by James J. Hill of the Great Northern. In 1908 he came to the rescue of the chronically troubled Erie and added that to his empire.

Harriman was not one to buy a railroad for a quick profit. He believed that the financial yield would be considerably greater if the railroad's property was improved and its affairs managed well. Harriman doubled-tracked the Union Pacific and gave it a new line over Sherman Hill; his improvements to Southern Pacific included the Lucin Cutoff across the Great Salt Lake and the Bayshore Cutoff south of San Francisco — and it was under his direction that SP rechanneled the Colorado River after it flooded California's Imperial Valley. Harriman established common standards for locomotives, cars, bridges, structures, signals, and even such items as paint and stationery.

In 1906 the ICC investigated Harriman's railroads. It found nothing to prosecute and concluded that the roads were well managed.

Harriman's financial interest in the Union Pacific passed to his son, W. Averell Harriman, who was chairman of Union Pacific's board from 1932 to 1946. The younger Harriman is well known for his work in politics and international relations.

Recommended reading: *E. H. Harriman — A Biography*, by George Kennan, published in 1922 by Houghton Mifflin Company, Boston, Mass.

New Orleans & Texas Railway, was under construction between Memphis and New Orleans via Vicksburg and Baton Rouge, west of IC's main line. That line obtained the backing of C. P. Huntington, who saw the route as a connection between his Southern Pacific at New Orleans and his Chesapeake, Ohio & Southwestern at Memphis. Huntington's forces completed the LNO&T in 1884 and then purchased the Mississippi & Tennessee Railroad, whose line from Grenada, Miss., to Memphis funneled traffic to IC. Saber rattling in the form of canceled traffic agreements ensued, but Huntington's empire was in trouble. IC purchased the LNO&T and the Mississippi & Tennessee and consolidated them with the

ILLINOIS CENTRAL

A posed Sunday-morning photo shows two sides of Illinois Central's passenger service: glossy orange, brown, and yellow streamliners and electric suburban trains at 35th Street in Chicago. The nearer streamliner is the *City of Miami*, and the farther one is the *City of New Orleans*, standing on the suburban line to be photographed just before entering service in April 1947.

IC

Yazoo & Mississippi Valley. The acquisition increased IC's mileage by 28 percent and greatly expanded IC's presence in the South. The southern lines were finally connected by rail to the northern part of the IC with the completion of the Ohio River bridge at Cairo in 1889. In 1893 IC purchased the Chesapeake, Ohio & Southwestern (Louisville to Memphis) and in 1895 built a line into St. Louis from the southeast.

In the late 1880s under the leadership of E. H. Harriman IC began expanding toward the west. The Chicago, Madison & Northern was incorporated in 1886 to build from Chicago to a connection with IC's western line at Freeport, Ill., then north to Madison and Dodgeville, Wisconsin. IC also constructed branches from its line across Iowa to Cedar Rapids, Iowa, Omaha, Nebraska, and Sioux Falls, South Dakota.

In 1900 a minor train wreck at Vaughan, Miss., achieved worldwide fame because an engine-wiper named Wallace Saunders wrote a song about the incident. The engineer, the only person killed, was one John Luther Jones, nicknamed "Casey."

Illinois Central continued to expand in the twentieth century. In 1906 the Indianapolis Southern Railroad, an IC subsidiary, completed a line from Effingham, Ill., to Indianapolis. Part of the line was new construction and part was a rework of existing narrow gauge lines. In 1908 IC assembled a route from Fulton, Ky., to Birmingham, Alabama, largely using trackage rights, and in 1909 IC purchased the Central of Georgia Railway. In 1926 IC electrified its suburban line along the Chicago lakefront. The suburban tracks were separate from the tracks used by mainline passenger and freight trains. In 1928 IC constructed a cutoff line between Edgewood, Ill., and Fulton, Ky., to bypass congestion at Cairo, the waist of its system, and also to avoid taxes levied on traffic moving on IC's original line.

After World War Two, IC began to simplify its corporate structure by purchasing and dissolving subsidiaries and neighboring short lines. Among the subsidiaries absorbed in 1945 and 1946 were the Gulf & Ship Island and the Yazoo & Mississippi Valley. Illinois Central lost its Central of Georgia holdings in 1948 when CofG reorganized after bankruptcy. The year 1951 saw the purchase of the Chicago, St. Louis & New Orleans (essentially everything south of Cairo not part of G&SI or Y&MV). Two years later IC acquired control of the Alabama & Vicksburg and the Vicksburg, Shreveport & Pacific, leased since 1926 by the Yazoo & Mississippi Valley. IC merged the A&V and the VS&P in 1959. IC and Rock Island jointly organized the Waterloo Railroad in 1956 to purchase the Waterloo, Cedar Falls & Northern; IC bought the Rock Island's half interest in 1968. Other short lines purchased by IC were the Tremont & Gulf (1959), the Peabody Short Line (1960, merged 1961), the Louisiana Midland (1967, regained independence 1974), and the Hopkinsville, Ky.-Nashville, Tenn., segment of the Tennessee Central (1968).

In 1972 IC merged with the parallel Gulf, Mobile & Ohio to form Illinois Central Gulf. In recent years ICG has been selling lines to trim its system to a Chicago-to-Gulf railroad.

Location of headquarters: Chicago, Illinois
Miles of railroad operated: 1929 — 6,712; 1971 — 6,760
Number of locomotives: 1929 — 1,762; 1971 — 766
Number of passenger cars: 1929 — 2,034; 1970 — 462
Number of freight cars: 1929 — 65,035; 1971 — 49,709
Number of company service cars: 1929 — 2,334; 1971 — 2,161
Reporting marks: IC
Notable named passenger trains: *Panama Limited, City of New Orleans* (Chicago-New Orleans), *Green Diamond* (Chicago-St. Louis), *City of Miami* (Chicago-Miami)
Historical and technical society: Illinois Central Historical Society, 556 South Elizabeth Drive, Lombard, IL 60148
Recommended reading: *Main Line of Mid-America*, by Carlton J. Corliss, published in 1950 by Creative Age Press, New York, N. Y.
Successors: Illinois Central Gulf (TWG)
Portions still operated:
Waterloo, Iowa-Albert Lea, Minn.: Cedar Valley
Chicago-Omaha; Fort Dodge-Sioux City; Manchester-Cedar Rapids: Chicago Central & Pacific
Most of the remainder of the Illinois Central is still being operated by Illinois Central Gulf. The major portions that have been abandoned are:

IC

In steam days Illinois Central kept its Paducah Shops busy rebuilding and upgrading motive power. Typical of IC's steam power is Mountain-type 2605 leading a long train of refrigerator cars full of bananas north across the Illinois prairie.

Cherokee-Onawa, Iowa; Waterloo-Cedar Rapids, Iowa (ex-Waterloo, Cedar Falls & Northern); Freeport, Ill.-Dodgeville, Wis.; Freeport, Ill.-Madison, Wis.; Herscher-Minonk, Ill.; Saxony-Barnes, Ill.; West Lebanon, Ind.-LeRoy, Ill.; New Holland-Havana, Ill.; Waggoner-Madison, Ill.; Centralia-Assumption, Ill. (part of the original main line); Murphysboro-Thebes, Ill.; Carbondale-Rosiclare, Ill.; Wilson-Princeton, Ky.; Hopkinsville, Ky.-Nashville, Tenn. (ex-Tennessee Central); Mayfield-Fulton, Ky.; Jackson, Tenn.-Coffeeville, Miss.; Grenada-Greenwood, Miss.; Durant-Tchula, Miss.; Lula, Miss.-Helena, Ark.; Coahoma-Metcalf, Miss.; Lambert-Moorehead-Yazoo City, Miss.; Silver City-Ball Ground, Miss.; Hollandale-Rolling Fork, Miss.; Greenville-Riverside Jct., Miss.; Jackson-Foster, Miss.; Mendenhall-Maxie, Miss.; Woodville, Miss.-Argue, La. Other lines up for sale: Louisville-Paducah; Evansville-Effingham; Freeport-El Paso, Ill.; Meridian, Miss.-Shreveport, La.

ILLINOIS TERMINAL RAILROAD SYSTEM

The Illinois Terminal had its beginning in the 1890 purchase of a streetcar system serving the neighboring towns of Urbana and Champaign, Illinois, by William B. McKinley. He sold it in 1893, bought it again, and within two decades expanded it into an interurban system from Danville and Peoria through Springfield to East St. Louis and across the Mississippi River on its own bridge to St. Louis, Missouri. His empire also included an interurban line between Joliet and Princeton, Ill., that was intended to form a Chicago extension of the system.

When McKinley was elected to Congress in 1904 the railway system was placed in the hands of Illinois Traction Co. ITC early recognized the importance of freight service: It built bypasses around most of the major cities to avoid running freight trains on city streets, and in 1909 it established joint rates with Chicago & Eastern Illinois and Frisco — similar arrangements with other steam roads soon followed.

In 1923 ITC formed a subsidiary, Illinois Power & Light, to hold the railroad properties, which were then consolidated as Illinois Traction System (the various parts of the system had been built by different companies, though all under the same ownership). Manager of the system was Clement Studebaker, of the South Bend, Indiana, automobile manufacturing family. In 1925 Illinois Traction acquired two steam railroads serving the industrial area east of the Mississippi, the St. Louis & Illinois Belt and the St. Louis, Troy, & Eastern. At the beginning of 1928 Illinois Power & Light Corporation acquired all the common stock of the Illinois Terminal Railroad, a line from Edwardsville to Alton. IT then leased the two steam roads and Illinois Traction. In 1930 the Alton & Eastern, a remnant of the Chicago, Peoria & St. Louis, was brought into the family, by then known as the Illinois Terminal Railroad System. The company was reorganized in 1937 as the Illinois Terminal Railroad Co.

Most railroad reorganizations involved minor changes of name, usually "Railroad" to "Railway" or vice versa. IT's history is different in the matter of names. The Purchaser Railroad was incorporated in 1945 to acquire the Illinois Terminal Railroad Co. On December 14, 1945, the old IT became the Liquidating Railway and the Purchaser Railroad was renamed the Illinois Terminal Railroad.

In 1954 the Illinois-Missouri Terminal Railway was incorporated by nine railroads: Baltimore & Ohio; Chicago & Eastern Illinois; Chicago, Burlington & Quincy; Gulf, Mobile & Ohio; Litchfield & Madison; Illinois Central; Nickel Plate; Frisco; and Wabash. The Illinois-Missouri Terminal purchased the IT in June 1956, whereupon the Illinois-Missouri Ter-

mainline passenger trains off the streets of the major cities (except Bloomington) and onto the freight belt lines. IT discontinued all of its city streetcar services in 1936, except for those in Peoria, which lasted another decade.

IT's passenger service was notable for several features: sleeping cars, parlor cars, and streamliners. Only three interurbans operated sleeping cars: Interstate Public Service (Indianapolis-Louisville), Oregon Electric (Portland-Eugene), and IT. IT's service was much more extensive and longer-lived than the other two and was operated largely with private-room cars. The principal sleeper route was between Peoria and St. Louis, a route with no steam-road competition. Peoria-St. Louis sleepers ran until 1940. For a short time a sleeper ran between Champaign and St. Louis, and a Springfield-St. Louis setout car lasted until 1934.

IT offered parlor-buffet car service on many of its day trains almost until the end of passenger service. After World War Two the road purchased three streamliners (eight cars — three cab-baggage-coach cars, two coaches, and three buffet-parlor-observation cars) for St. Louis-Decatur and St. Louis-Peoria service. Streamliner service to Decatur was discontinued after less than two years, and it never reached Peoria. IT's tracks in Peoria could not handle the new trains, so streamliner service was offered only as far as East Peoria, and the cars had to be uncoupled to be turned at East Peoria and St. Louis. The streamliners lost their names and their parlor-buffet cars in 1951. In 1955 passenger service was dropped north and east of Springfield; less than a year later Springfield-St. Louis passenger service was dropped, leaving only the St. Louis-Granite City suburban service, which lasted until June 1958.

In 1950 the IT began eliminating unproductive track, beginning with the line through Bloomington and most of the Granite City-Wood River-Alton-Grafton route. At the same time IT began dieselizing its freight service, and by the end of 1955 only passenger service — what little remained of it — was operated electrically. By 1980 IT's main lines were about two-thirds trackage rights on parallel railroads and one-third owned. The major portions of IT's own lines remaining in service were the former steam-powered lines in East St. Louis. In addition, IT purchased a former Pennsylvania line between Maroa and Farmdale in 1976, creating a Decatur-East Peoria route. Norfolk & Western purchased Illinois Ter-

Kalmbach Publishing Co. David A. Strassman

Car 270 loads passengers at Danville for the trip to Springfield in May 1950. It was the first interurban car in the U. S. to be air conditioned (in 1935).

minal was renamed the Illinois Terminal Railroad Co. and the previous Illinois Terminal was renamed the Liquidating Terminal. The Rock Island and the New York Central purchased interests in the IT later. IT could furnish the steam roads neutral access to the industrial area between East St. Louis and Alton.

IT was one of the last interurbans to offer passenger service. The 1930s saw the abandonment of branchline passenger service and the routing of

Three yellow-and-green GP7s lead a freight north along Chicago Street in Lincoln in 1961. The station building at the right belongs to the Gulf, Mobile & Ohio.

minal September 1, 1981. IT's corporate existence ended May 8, 1982.

Location of headquarters: St. Louis, Missouri

Miles of railroad operated: 1929 — 484; 1980 — 413

Number of locomotives: 1929 — 22 steam, 51 electric; 1980 — 46 diesel

Number of passenger cars: 1929 — 124

Number of freight and company service cars: 1929 — 2,055

Number of freight cars: 1980 — 2,624

Number of company service cars: 1980 — 4

Reporting marks: ITC

Historical and technical society: Illinois Terminal Railroad Historical Society, 417 Wagner Place, Washington, IL 61571

Recommended reading: *The Lincoln Land Traction*, by James D. Johnson, published in 1965 by The Traction Orange Co., P. O. Box 52, Wheaton, IL 60189

Successors: Norfolk & Western (TWG)

Portions still operated: St. Louis-Wood River, Ill.; Madison-Edwardsville-Wood River: Norfolk & Western

Henry L. Stuart Jr.

Interstate Railroad Mikado No. 15, once on the roster of the Pennsylvania Railroad, leads a long train through Tacoma, Va., heading for the Clinchfield interchange.

INTERSTATE RAILROAD

The Interstate was incorporated in 1896 and completed in 1909 from Stonega to Norton, Virginia, 16 miles. In 1913 it absorbed the Wise Terminal Co., and in 1923 it constructed a branch line from Norton to a connection with the Clinchfield near St. Paul, Va. That branch soon became the main line. Interstate's chief business was hauling coal for its parent, Virginia Coal & Iron Co. Whatever the goal implied by the name of the railroad, it never crossed the Virginia state line, though it got within a mile or two. The Southern Railway bought the Interstate in June 1961 and operates it as part of the Southern system.

Location of headquarters: Andover, Virginia

Miles of railroad operated: 1929 — 83 (with branches and sidings); 1960 — 88
Number of locomotives: 1929 — 12; 1960 — 10
Number of passenger cars: 1929 — 6
Number of freight and company service cars: 1929 — 3,052
Number of freight cars: 1960 — 2,812
Number of company service cars: 1960 — 11
Reporting marks: INT
Successor companies: Southern Railway (TWG)
Map: See page 97

INTERSTATE COMMERCE COMMISSION

The Constitution of the United States, Article I, Section 8, gave Congress the power to regulate commerce among the several states. In 1886 the Supreme Court of the U. S. ruled that the Illinois Railroad Act of 1871 (which established a commission to fix maximum rates) was in violation of the Fourteenth Amendment to the Constitution (no state may deprive a person of property without due process) and that therefore the states could not regulate interstate commerce.

The Interstate Commerce Act was passed in February 1887. The Act applied to all railroads engaged in interstate commerce, even if they were located entirely within one state, and it also applied to water carriers — riverboats, barges, ferries, and so forth — owned or controlled by railroads. The Act stated that rates charged by the railroads had to be "just and reasonable," but it set no standards for reasonableness. Railroads were forbidden to give preference, advantage, special rates, or rebates to any person, company, location, or type of traffic. Railroads were not allowed to charge more for a short haul than for a long haul under the same circumstances when the short haul was a segment of a longer haul — for example, a New York-Baltimore trip should not cost more than a New York-Washington trip. The act prohibited pooling, which is the sharing of revenue or freight. Railroads were required to publish their rates and give advance notice of change.

Finally, the Act created the Interstate Commerce Commission. Its members were to be appointed by the President; the commission was authorized to investigate violations of the Act and order the cessation of wrongdoing. However, ICC orders required an order by a federal court to become effective. The Interstate Commerce Act was the first important federal regulation of big business, and the ICC was the first independent regulatory body.

Initially the ICC had little power. In 1897 the Supreme Court ruled that the ICC had no power to fix rates and took most of the bite out of the clause stating that the short haul should cost no more than the long haul. The situation began to change around the turn of the century. The Elkins Act (1903) increased the penalties for rate discrimination and made those who sought rebates as guilty as the railroads that granted them. The Hepburn Act (1906) gave the commission the power to determine maximum rates and declared that any order of the ICC had the force of a court order. It also introduced new accounting methods and raised the number of commissioners to seven. The Mann-Elkins Act of 1910 set up a court to hear only ICC cases and gave the ICC authority to begin judicial proceedings against railroads without the need for the Attorney General to initiate the action. It gave the ICC power to suspend rate increases pending hearings and laid on the railroads the burden of proof that the rate — not just the increase — was just and reasonable. The 1910 Act also extended the ICC's jurisdiction to telephone and telegraph companies (that authority was transferred to the Federal Communications Commission in 1934).

The ICC soon grew to have authority over almost every aspect of railroading: locomotive boilers, passenger accounting, diameter of grab irons, and speed limits, to choose a few items at random. The railroads reached their peak in extent and influence about 1915, about the time the ICC was hitting its stride. Ironically, just as the railroads began to suffer from the competition of highways and waterways, the ICC set out to protect the public from the railroads.

The Transportation Act of 1920 contained a clause granting the railroads a fair return. The Act (which was repealed in 1933) also allowed the ICC to set minimum rates and instructed the ICC to prepare a plan to consolidate the railroads of the U. S. into a few large systems. By 1952 the ICC had jurisdiction over railroads, ferries, pipelines, bridges, internal and coastal shipping, trucks, and buses, except that the majority of internal waterway traffic and truck traffic was, by virtue of one law or another, exempt from ICC control. The ICC's authority over the railroads extended to the setting of maximum and minimum rates, approving or disapproving consolidations and mergers, authorizing construction and abandonment of lines, and issuance of securities — indeed, every aspect of the railroad business but labor relations.

The Transportation Act of 1958 gave the ICC jurisdiction over passenger train discontinuances, previously under the authority of the state commissions (state authorities had allowed discontinuance of through trains within states — such as allowing a New York-Chicago train to be discontinued within Ohio, to use a hypothetical example). The ICC earned a reputation for capriciousness in the matter of passenger-train discontinuances. For example, it denied Milwaukee Road's petition to drop a coach-only Chicago-Minneapolis local service on a route that had three other trains, yet it permitted the discontinuance of Chicago & Eastern Illinois' well-patronized *Georgian-Humming Bird*. It was the last passenger train on the Chicago-Danville-Terre Haute-Evansville run, and it was far less a local train than it was the north end of Chicago-Atlanta and Chicago-Nashville-Mobile service operated jointly with Louisville & Nashville.

In the matter of mergers the ICC functioned at a glacial pace. Proceedings in connection with the proposed merger of Rock Island and Union Pacific dragged on for ten years, during which the Rock Island fell apart and ceased to be the desirable merger partner that UP had courted. (Some of the blame can be laid on the other railroads. The usual reaction of a railroad company upon learning of a proposed merger between two of its competitors is not "We're good enough to give them a run for their money even if they merge" but "They'll run us out of business.")

Regulation of railroads reached the point that the ICC could (and did) require railroads to continue operations that lost money — or to look at it

On the northwest corner of 12th Street and Constitution Avenue in Washington, D. C., stands the Interstate Commerce Commission building.

Don Phillips

another way, the ICC was depriving the railroads of property without due process. In 1962 President John F. Kennedy delivered a message on transportation to Congress in which he criticized the regulatory structure, but it fell to his successor, Lyndon B. Johnson, to establish the Department of Transportation in 1966. The DOT was to develop and coordinate policies that would encourage a national transportation system. Some rate-making and regulatory functions remained with the ICC, though. The Federal Railroad Administration is the agency of the DOT that deals with railroads.

Deregulation finally came on October 14, 1980, when President Jimmy Carter signed into law the Staggers Rail Act (named for Rep. Harley O. Staggers of West Virginia). It was massive deregulation of the railroads, including the provisions to raise any rate that fell below 160 percent of out-of-pocket costs (later 180 percent) and to enter into contracts with shippers to set price and service, both without ICC approval.

Recommended reading:

Enterprise Denied, by Albro Martin, published in 1971 by Columbia University Press, 440 West 110th Street, New York, NY 10025 (ISBN: 0-231-03508-X)

Transportation: The Domestic System, by Robert C. Lieb, published in 1978 by Reston Publishing Co., Reston, VA 22090 (ISBN: 0-87909-843-0)

KANSAS CITY, MEXICO & ORIENT RAILWAY
(Ferrocarril Kansas City, Mexico y Oriente)
MEXICO NORTH-WESTERN RAILWAY
(Ferrocarril Nor-Oeste de Mexico)

In the 1880s Albert Kimsey Owen proposed a railroad that would form a land bridge for traffic between Europe and the Far East. The two North American ports to be connected by the railroad were Norfolk, Virginia, and Topolobampo, Mexico — if you extend the Arizona-New Mexico border about 400 miles south, it will hit the Gulf of California just about at Topolobampo. Owen incorporated the Texas, Topolobampo & Pacific Railroad, but little more came of his proposal.

In 1897 Enrique Creel, governor of the state of Chihuahua, incorporated the Ferrocarril Chihuahua al Pacifico, a railroad to run from the city of Chihuahua to the Pacific coast. The railroad opened its first section, 124 miles from Chihuahua to Miñaca, on March 31, 1900.

The Rio Grande, Sierra Madre & Pacific Railroad was incorporated on June 11, 1897, to build a line between Ciudad Juarez, across the Rio Grande from El Paso, Texas, to the Pacific at Tijuana. The railroad worked southwest through Casas Grandes into timber country, eventually stopping at Madera, just west of the Continental Divide. The Chihua-

hua al Pacifico built a branch north from La Junta to Temosachic, and the ChP and the RGSM&P teamed up to organize the Sierra Madre & Pacific to construct the line between Madera and Temosachic, 54 miles. In 1909 the Sierra Madre & Pacific, the Rio Grande, Sierra Madre & Pacific, and the Chihuahua al Pacifico were consolidated as the Ferrocarril Nor-Oeste de Mexico (Mexico North-Western Railway). The entire Ciudad Juarez-Chihuahua route was open by 1912.

Arthur E. Stilwell built the Kansas City, Pittsburg & Gulf Railroad (now the Kansas City Southern) from Kansas City directly south to the Gulf of Mexico at Port Arthur, Tex. Ousted by new management in 1899, he proposed a railroad from Kansas City to the nearest Pacific port, Topolobampo — to be called Port Stilwell. The rail distance would be less than 1,700 miles (Kansas City-Los Angeles via the Santa Fe is 1,780 miles). Creel granted Stilwell trackage rights from Chihuahua to Miñaca and also the federal concessions of the Chihuahua al Pacifico. Stilwell met with Owen and secured the rights and lands of the Texas, Topolobampo & Pacific.

On April 30, 1900, Stilwell incorporated the Kansas City, Mexico & Orient Railway. By mid-1903 lines were open from Milton, Kansas, near Wichita, to Carmen, Oklahoma; from Chihuahua to a point 34 miles east; and from Topolobampo to El Fuerte. By early 1912 the U. S. portion of the line reached from Wichita to Girvin, Tex., on the Pecos River, traversing a barren, uninhabited area for most of its length. Also by 1912 Mexico was deep in a revolution. Neither the desolate country in the U. S. nor the situation in Mexico was conducive to revenue. The road entered receivership in March 1912, and Stilwell was once again a former railroad president.

The newly organized Kansas City, Mexico & Orient Railroad purchased the KCM&O on July 6, 1914. The first reorganization plan was rejected and a second receiver, William T. Kemper, was appointed in 1917. The Orient scraped along, adding an extension to Alpine, Tex., and a connection with Southern Pacific. During World War One the USRA at first rejected the KCM&O but later took over its operation at Kemper's request. In the early 1920s things began to look better for the Orient — the Mexican government said it would extend the line east from Chihuahua toward the border at Presidio to compensate for damage sustained during

the revolution, and oil was discovered in west Texas. In 1924 a U. S. government loan came due. The KCM&O was unable to repay it, and the government directed that the railroad be sold at auction. Kemper was the successful bidder, and he organized the Kansas City, Mexico & Orient Railway, the second company of that name. However, pipelines had begun to cut into the Orient's oil traffic, and Kemper realized he could never afford to extend the line from Wichita to Kansas City, much less connect the three disjointed Mexican portions of the railroad. He sought a buyer, first in the Missouri Pacific, which had financial difficulties of its own, then the Santa Fe.

On September 24, 1928, the Santa Fe purchased the Orient (merger came on June 30, 1941, except for the Texas portion, which was merged in 1964). Santa Fe then sold the three Mexican portions of the road to B. F. Johnston and the United Sugar Co. of Los Mochis. Johnston combined the operations of the Mexican portion of the KCM&O with those of the Mexico North-Western, whose rails joined the eastern and middle portions of the KCM&O. In October 1930 the eastern portion of the line was opened to Ojinaga. Santa Fe extended its line from Alpine to Presidio and bridged the Rio Grande that same year, opening a new gateway for traffic between the U. S. and Mexico.

In 1940 the Mexican government purchased the FKCM&O from United Sugar and also purchased the La Junta-Miñaca portion of the Mexico North-Western. Operations of the two railroads were separated. The government announced that the two portions of the KCM&O would be connected. Separating the two portions between Creel and San Pedro was Mexico's Sierra Madre range, some of the roughest and least known topography in North America. Surveys were made and some construction was undertaken, then suspended, then resumed, and so on. In 1952 KCM&O took over operation of the Rio Mayo Railway, a 38-mile line from Yavaros, on the shore of the Gulf of California, to Navojoa, on the Southern Pacific of Mexico 86 miles north of Sufragio, where KCM&O crossed the SPdeM. Three years later the Rio Mayo line became part of the Ferrocarril del Pacifico, successor to SPdeM.

In 1952 the Mexico North-Western was taken over by the Mexican government and in 1955 it was merged with the Ferrocarril Kansas City, Mexico y Oriente to form the Ferrocarril de Chihuahua al Pacifico. The

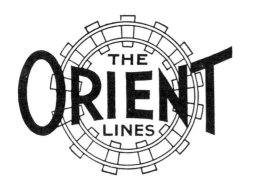

Edward C. Spalding

A 2-8-0 once on Santa Fe's roster leads an eastbound way freight at Pichachos, between Chihuahua and Ojinaga.

pace of construction accelerated. Laying of rail on the new line began in 1960, and the line connecting Chihuahua with the coast was opened by Mexico's president on November 23, 1961.

Kansas City, Mexico & Orient

Location of headquarters: El Paso, Texas; later Ciudad Juarez, Chihuaua; then Chihuahua, Chih.

Miles of railroad operated: 1929 — 349 (122 miles joint with Mexico North-Western); 1954 — 384

Number of locomotives: 1929 — 11; 1954 — 15

Number of passenger cars: 1929 — 11; 1954 — 18

Number of freight cars: 1929 — 255; 1954 — 356

Number of company service cars: 1929 — 15; 1954 — 15

Reporting marks: FKCM&O

Successors:

Atchison, Topeka & Santa Fe (TWG)

Chihuahua Pacific (TWG)

Portions still operated:

Wichita-Viola, Kans.; Harper-Anthony, Kans.; Cherokee, Okla.-Mary-neal, Tex.; Sayard, Tex.-Ojinaga, Chih.: Atchison, Topeka & Santa Fe Ojinaga, Chih.-Topolobampo, Sinaloa: Chihuahua Pacific

Mexico North-Western

Location of headquarters: Ciudad Juarez, Chihuahua

Miles of railroad operated: 1929 — 497; 1954 — 476

Number of locomotives: 1929 — 27; 1954 — 41

Number of passenger cars: 1929 — 21; 1954 — 32

Number of freight cars: 1929 — 935; 1954 — 1,099

Number of company service cars: 1929 — 8; 1954 — 81

Reporting marks: N-O de M

Successors:

Chihuahua Pacific (TWG)

Portions still operated: Ciudad Juarez-La Junta, Chih.: Chihuahua Pacific

Recommended reading: *Destination Topolobampo*, by John Leeds Kerr and Frank P. Donovan Jr., published in 1968 by Golden West Books, P. O. Box 80250, San Marino, CA 91108

LEHIGH & HUDSON RIVER RAILWAY

The Warwick Valley Railroad was chartered in 1860 to build a line from Warwick, New York, to Greycourt, on the New York & Erie. It was opened in 1862, and until 1880, when it narrowed its tracks from 6 feet to standard gauge, it was operated with Erie cars and locomotives.

The line was extended southwest to serve iron mines, then all the way to the Delaware River at Belvidere, New Jersey, as the Lehigh & Hudson River Railroad. The two railroads were consolidated as the Lehigh & Hudson River Railway in 1882. The construction of the Poughkeepsie Bridge across the Hudson River prompted a 10-mile extension from Greycourt to Maybrook, N. Y., opened in 1890. (The bridge was begun by Pennsylvania Railroad interests; by the time it was opened it was part of the Central New England, which soon came under control of the Reading.) At the other end of the line, the Delaware River was bridged and the L&HR and the Pennsylvania traded trackage rights: L&HR over Pennsy between Belvidere and Phillipsburg, N. J., and Pennsylvania over L&HR to reach the Poughkeepsie Bridge.

Initially traffic was agricultural, but soon coal became predominant. The principal industry on the L&HR was a mine and crushing plant of the New Jersey Zinc Co. near Franklin. The purchase of the Central New England and its bridge at Poughkeepsie by the New Haven turned the L&HR into a bridge route. At the insistence of the New Haven, the LH&R was purchased in 1905 by several major railroads to ensure the New Haven's connections with those roads.

The only major change in ownership between 1929 and 1975 was that the 20 percent interest held by Lehigh Coal & Navigation Co., owner of the Lehigh & New England, passed more or less equally to Lehigh Valley and Pennsylvania about 1950. Ownership in 1975, just before the property passed to Conrail, was Central of New Jersey, 16.75 percent; Reading, 13.44 percent; Penn Central, 14.43 percent; Erie-Lackawanna, 32.73 percent; and Lehigh Valley, 22.16 percent.

Traffic patterns began to change in the 1960s. The merger of Erie and Lackawanna shifted traffic off the L&HR to the former Erie line, which connected directly with the New Haven. With the creation of Penn Central, traffic between New England and the South that had moved over the

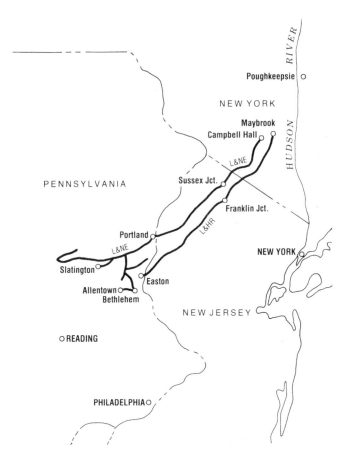

Lehigh & Hudson River No. 94, a massive 2-8-0 with a wide firebox for burning anthracite and a 12-wheel tender for carrying it, brings a Maybrook-Allentown freight through Lake, N. Y., 5 miles northeast of Warwick.

Donald W. Furler

Poughkeepsie Bridge was rerouted through Selkirk, near Albany, via the ex-New York Central West Shore and Boston & Albany lines. L&HR filed for bankruptcy protection on April 18, 1972. What little traffic remained disappeared when the Poughkeepsie Bridge burned in 1974. L&HR's property was transferred to Conrail on April 1, 1976.

Location of headquarters: Warwick, New York
Miles of railroad operated: 1929 — 97; 1975 — 90
Number of locomotives: 1929 — 34; 1975 — 6
Number of passenger cars: 1929 — 14
Number of freight cars: 1929 — 398; 1975 — 2
Number of company service cars: 1929 — 66; 1975 — 9

Reporting marks: LHR
Historical and technical society: Anthracite Railroads Historical Society, P. O. Box 119, Bridgeport, PA 19405
Recommended reading: *The Northeast Railroad Scene, Vol. 2: The Lehigh & Hudson River*, by Bob Pennisi, published in 1977 by Railroad Avenue Enterprises, P. O. Box 114, Flanders, NJ 07836
Successors: Conrail (TWG)
Portions still operated:
Warwick, N. Y.-Franklin, N. J.: New York, Susquehanna & Western
Maybrook-Warwick, N. Y.; Franklin-Belvidere, N. J.: Conrail

LEHIGH & NEW ENGLAND RAILROAD

The Lehigh & New England's oldest ancestor was the South Mountain & Boston, chartered in 1873 to construct a railroad between Harrisburg, Pennsylvania, and Boston, Massachusetts. Several reorganizations finally produced the Pennsylvania, Poughkeepsie & Boston, which completed a line from Slatington, Pa., on the Lehigh River, to Pine Island, New York, using the tracks of the New York, Susquehanna & Western between Hainesburg Jct. and Swartswood Jct., New Jersey. In 1891 the Philadelphia & Reading leased the road, but canceled the lease when the PP&B entered receivership in 1893. Yet another reorganization in 1895 produced the Lehigh & New England Railroad. After 1904 most of the L&NE's stock was owned by the Lehigh Coal & Navigation Co.

In 1926 the L&NE and the Reading agreed to a lease of the L&NE by the Reading, but the ICC denied the application. In 1929 the Baltimore & Ohio and the Chesapeake & Ohio both asked for four-way control of the L&NE by B&O, C&O, New York Central, and Pennsylvania; that same year the Wabash asked to control the road. All three applications were withdrawn in 1930. The ICC's merger plan of 1929 assigned the road to the New Haven.

Declining traffic, first in anthracite, then in cement, made the L&NE's fate obvious to its owner. In 1960 the road — which was still solvent — petitioned for abandonment. The Central Railroad of New Jersey organized the Lehigh & New England Railway to buy and operate the portions of the line between Hauto and Tamaqua, Pa., and from Bethlehem and Allentown through Bath to Martins Creek, Pa., about 40 miles total. The remainder of the L&NE was abandoned in 1961. In 1972 CNJ transferred its own Pennsylvania lines to the Lehigh Valley but continued to operate the L&NE remnants. In 1974 the ICC assigned operation of the line out of Bethlehem to the LV and the Hauto-Tamaqua line to the Read-

General Electric

Black-and-white Alco freight units wearing Lehigh & New England's "fried egg" herald lead a train of hopper cars through the Lehigh River Gorge.

ing. Two years later both of those railroads were taken over by Conrail.

Location of headquarters: Philadelphia, Pennsylvania
Miles of railroad operated: 1929 — 217; 1960 — 177
Number of locomotives: 1929 — 61; 1960 — 32
Number of passenger cars: 1929 — 12
Number of freight cars: 1929 — 3,457
Number of company service cars: 1929 — 63
Number of freight and company service cars: 1960 — 2,608
Reporting marks: LNE
Historical and technical society: Anthracite Railroads Historical So-

ciety, P. O. Box 119, Bridgeport, PA 19405
Recommended reading: *The Lehigh and New England Railroad*, by
Ed Crist, published in 1980 by Carstens Publications, P. O. Box 700,
Newton, NJ 07860
Successors:
Central Railroad of New Jersey

Lehigh Valley
Reading
Conrail (TWG)
Portions still operated: Tamaqua-Hauto, Pa.; Bethlehem-Bath-Belfast, Pa.: Conrail
Map: See page 169

LEHIGH VALLEY RAILROAD

Anthracite coal was discovered at Mauch Chunk, Pennsylvania, in
1791 (Mauch Chunk was renamed Jim Thorpe in 1954). The only practical means to transport the coal to a sizable market was to boat it down the
often unnavigable Lehigh River. A canal was constructed, and by the
1820s the Lehigh Coal & Navigation Co. had a near-monopoly on the
mining and transportation of coal in the region. To break the monopoly
and also to improve transportation, the Delaware, Lehigh, Schuylkill &
Susquehanna Railroad was incorporated in 1846 to build a line from
Mauch Chunk to Easton, Pa., where the Lehigh River flows into the Delaware. Construction did not begin until 1851; then with the management
and the financing of Asa Packer work began in earnest. The railroad was
renamed the Lehigh Valley Railroad in 1853, and it was opened from
Easton to Mauch Chunk in September 1855.

The railroad began to grow both by new construction and by consolidating with existing railroads. In 1866, the year the Lehigh & Mahanoy
merged with Lehigh Valley, Alexander Mitchell, master mechanic of the
L&M, designed a freight locomotive with a 2-8-0 wheel arrangement and
named it "Consolidation" — the name became the standard designation
for that wheel arrangement. The Lehigh Valley reached north into the
Wyoming Valley to Wilkes-Barre in 1867, the same year that Lehigh
Coal & Navigation's Lehigh & Susquehanna Railroad, originally a White
Haven-to-Wilkes-Barre line, opened a line south along the Lehigh River
to Easton, in places on the opposite bank of the Lehigh River from the LV
and in other places sharing the same bank.

In 1865 Packer purchased a flood-damaged canal, renamed it the Pennsylvania & New York Canal & Railroad, and used its towpath as roadbed.

The P&NY was completed to a connection with the New York & Erie at Waverly, New York, in 1869, giving the Lehigh Valley an outlet to the west. In 1876 Lehigh Valley furnished the material and the money necessary for Erie to lay a third rail to accommodate standard gauge trains on its line from Waverly to Buffalo, to eliminate the need to transfer freight and passengers at Waverly. Lehigh Valley leased the P&NY in 1888.

At its eastern end Lehigh Valley saw its connecting routes taken over by rival railroads: The Lackawanna acquired the Morris & Essex in 1868, and the Central of New Jersey, formerly considered friendly, leased the Lehigh & Susquehanna in 1871, getting a line parallel to the Lehigh Valley all the way from Easton to Wilkes-Barre. LV bought the Morris Canal across New Jersey chiefly for its property on New York Harbor at Jersey City. It assembled a line to Perth Amboy in 1875, but not until 1899 did LV reach its Jersey City property on its own rails.

Lehigh Valley's use of Erie rails (or, more accurately, one of its own and one of Erie's) to reach Buffalo was not completely satisfactory. In 1876 LV got control of the Geneva, Ithaca & Sayre Railroad, which put it into Geneva, N. Y. In the early 1880s LV built a terminal railroad and a station in Buffalo and established a Great Lakes shipping line (whose flag became the emblem of the railroad). Construction of a line from Geneva to Buffalo and a freight bypass to avoid the steep grades on the Geneva, Ithaca & Sayre began in 1889. In 1890 LV merged the companies involved in building the new line as the Lehigh Valley Rail Way. The Buffalo extension was opened in September 1892.

LV lines in western New York included a branch from the new line to Rochester; the former Southern Central Railroad from Sayre to North Fair Haven on Lake Ontario; and the Elmira, Cortland & Northern Railroad, which meandered from Elmira through East Ithaca, Cortland, and Canastota to Camden — nothing came of a proposal to extend the line to Watertown, N. Y. In 1896 LV opened a short bypass around Buffalo for traffic to and from Canada.

A few years earlier Archibald A. McLeod had started the Philadelphia & Reading on a course of expansion with the backing of financiers J. P. Morgan and Anthony Drexel. The Reading negotiated quietly with the Lehigh Valley, which had a Great Lakes outlet for Reading's anthracite as well as its own. The financial arrangement seemed beneficial to LV,

too, which had just spent a lot of money getting to Buffalo and was noticing a decline in anthracite traffic. In February 1892 the Reading leased the Lehigh Valley (and also the Central of New Jersey). Morgan and Drexel were suddenly alarmed by the growth of the Reading (it was pursuing the Boston & Maine by then) and withdrew their support. The Reading collapsed into receivership. The lease of the Lehigh Valley was terminated in August 1893.

J. P. Morgan agreed to fund the LV. He moved its general offices from Philadelphia to New York and began rebuilding the road. The independent stockholders of the line protested the diversion of money from dividends into physical plant and regained control in 1902. Several other railroads bought blocks of LV stock — New York Central, Reading, Erie, Lackawanna, and Central of New Jersey — and the road became part of William H. Moore's short-lived Rock Island system. In 1903 the company underwent some corporate simplification, merging and dissolving a number of subsidiaries.

In 1913 LV's passenger trains were evicted from the Pennsylvania Railroad's Jersey City terminal and moved to the Central of New Jersey station; in 1918 under the direction of the USRA they were moved into Pennsylvania Station in New York. It remained LV's New York terminus until the end of passenger service. Several events during the teens adversely affected LV's revenues: a munitions explosion on Black Tom Island on the Jersey City waterfront in 1916, the divestiture of the Great Lakes shipping operation in 1917 (required by the Panama Canal Act), the divestiture of the coal mining subsidiary (required by the Sherman Antitrust Act), and a drop in anthracite traffic as oil and gas became the dominant home heating fuels.

The ICC merger proposal of the 1920s called for four major railroad systems in the East. The response of Leonor F. Loree, president of the Delaware & Hudson, was a proposal for a fifth system, to include D&H; LV; Wabash; Wheeling & Lake Erie; and Buffalo, Rochester & Pittsburgh. Loree purchased large amounts of LV stock but not enough to gain control. He was later able to sell his shares in Wabash and Lehigh Valley to the Pennsylvania Railroad, which suddenly found itself with 31 percent of LV's common stock, enough to keep LV from falling into the hands of the New York Central. However, the Pennsylvania Railroad exercised no

In the late 1930s and early 1940s Lehigh Valley streamlined several of its named passenger trains and adopted a new livery of black and Cornell red with white trim. Train 28, the eastbound *John Wilkes*, is shown near Glen Onoko, Pa., not long after its 1939 streamlining.

Wayne Brumbaugh

noticeable influence on the policies and operations of the Lehigh Valley.

Lehigh Valley entered the Depression with its physical plant in good shape and with little debt of its own maturing in the next few years. However, the maturation of bonds of the Lehigh Valley Coal Co., New Jersey state taxes, and interest on debt soon had the railroad in debt to the federal government for nearly $8 million. Highways were taking away passenger and freight business. LV began to prune its branches, starting with the former Elmira, Cortland & Northern. At the end of the 1930s LV made a valiant effort to attract passenger business by hiring designer Otto Kuhler to streamline its old cars and locomotives. World War Two brought a tremendous surge of business to on-line Army bases and LV's

port facilities, but LV's decline resumed quickly when the war was over.

The route chosen for the New York State Thruway in Buffalo lay along LV's right of way, so after first considering renting facilities from another railroad LV constructed and opened a new terminal in Buffalo in 1955. That same year Hurricane Diane inflicted severe damage on much of LV's line in Pennsylvania, with attendant costs of rebuilding. The next year, 1956, was to be LV's last profitable year.

On the New York-Buffalo run LV's passenger trains competed with the much newer and faster ones of the Lackawanna and the New York Central — to say nothing of the new Thruway. In May 1959 LV discontinued all but two of its mainline passenger trains, and those two, the New York-

Lehighton *John Wilkes* and the New York-Toronto *Maple Leaf*, lasted less than two years longer. LV was one of the first major railroads to offer only freight service.

Relief from passenger losses made no difference. LV's financial situation continued to worsen. In 1961 the Pennsylvania Railroad bought all the outstanding stock to protect its previous investment in the Lehigh Valley. LV continued to prune branches and reduce double track to single and teamed up with Central of New Jersey to eliminate duplicate lines between Easton and Wilkes-Barre. In 1972 Lehigh Valley took over all of Central of New Jersey's operations in Pennsylvania.

One of the conditions of the creation of Penn Central was that Lehigh Valley be offered to Norfolk & Western and Chesapeake & Ohio. Neither wanted it. Penn Central declared bankruptcy on June 21, 1970, and Lehigh Valley filed for bankruptcy protection three days later. LV's situation got no better during the next six years, and its properties were taken over by Conrail on April 1, 1976. Most of the track west of Sayre, Pa., was considered redundant and abandoned.

Location of headquarters: New York, New York
Miles of railroad operated: 1929 — 1,362; 1974 — 988
Number of locomotives: 1929 — 725; 1974 — 149
Number of passenger cars: 1929 — 673
Number of freight cars: 1929 — 26,443; 1974 — 3,965

Number of company service cars: 1929 — 1,578; 1974 — 161
Reporting marks: LV
Historical and technical society: Anthracite Railroads Historical Society, P. O. Box 119, Bridgeport, PA 19405
Recommended reading: *Lehigh Valley Railroad*, by Robert F. Archer, published in 1977 by Howell-North Books, 850 North Hollywood Way, Burbank, CA 91505
Subsidiaries and affiliated railroads, 1974:
Buffalo Creek Railroad (50%, jointly with Erie Lackawanna)
Ironton (50%, jointly with Reading)
Niagara Junction (25%)
Successors: Conrail (TWG)
Portions still operated:
Jersey City-Newark, N. J.-Easton-Pittston, Pa.-Waverly-Ithaca-Ludlowville, N. Y.; Lansdown-Clinton, N. J.; Penn Haven Jct.-Hazleton-Tomhicken, Pa.; Kendaia-Geneva, N. Y.; P&L Jct.-Batavia, N. Y.; Niagara Jct.-Williamsville, N. Y.: Conrail
Towanda-Monroeton, Pa.: Towanda-Monroeton Shippers' Lifeline
Pittston Jct.-Wilkes-Barre, Pa.: Pocono Northeast
Owego-Harford, N. Y.: Delaware & Hudson
Manchester-West Victor, N. Y.: Ontario Central

LITCHFIELD & MADISON RAILWAY

The Litchfield & Madison was incorporated March 1, 1900, to take over an orphaned line of the Chicago, Peoria & St. Louis between Litchfield and Madison, Illinois. The CP&StL continued to operate the road for four years, but then L&M took charge of its own affairs. In 1926 L&M completed a short connection from DeCamp to the Chicago & North Western south of Benld, Illinois.

The L&M was primarily a terminal road that also served coal mines near DeCamp, Ill. It was the St. Louis entrance for Illinois Central's line from Gilman, Ill., and, more important, for Chicago & North Western's line south from Nelson, Ill. By 1957 Chicago & North Western had ac-

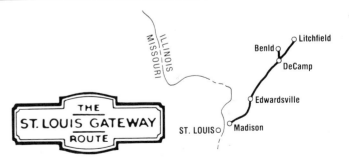

R. J. Foster

Litchfield & Madison 201, a 2-10-2 once on Union Pacific's roster, waits in the siding at Glen Carbon, Illinois, with a coal train, while Mikado 159 approaches on the main line.

quired more than 97 percent of L&M's stock. C&NW merged the Litchfield & Madison on January 2, 1958. The Litchfield-Mt. Olive portion of the line was abandoned in 1961, and the Mt. Olive-DeCamp portion in 1970.

Location of headquarters: Edwardsville, Illinois
Miles of railroad operated: 1929 — 44; 1956 — 44
Number of locomotives: 1929 — 10; 1956 — 4
Number of freight cars: 1929 — 1,047; 1956 — 305
Number of company service cars: 1929 — 4; 1956 — 6
Reporting marks: LM
Historical and technical society: Chicago & North Western Historical Society, 17004 Locust Drive, Hazel Crest, IL 60429
Successors: Chicago & North Western (TWG)
Portions still operated: Madison-DeCamp, Ill.: Chicago & North Western

LOUISIANA MIDLAND RAILWAY

The Lousiana Midland was incorporated in 1945 to purchase a branch of the Louisiana & Arkansas between Packton and Vidalia, Louisiana (the last nine miles to Vidalia were on Missouri Pacific rails). It teamed up with Mississippi Central on the east and L&A on the west to form a bridge route called "The Natchez Route." (The term "bridge route" is perhaps inaccurate in one sense, in that the crossing of the Mississippi between Vidalia and Natchez was by ferry.) Locomotives of the L&A and Kansas City Southern operated through on the LM, and the road shared some officers with KCS and L&A. The road shared pages in *The Official Guide* with the Mississippi Central. The railroad was purchased by Illinois Central on March 28, 1967.

The Louisiana Midland resumed independent operation on March 28, 1974, exactly seven years later. For a brief period in late 1980 and early 1981 the road operated the former Rock Island line between Hodge and Winnfield, La. That line is now operated by the Central Louisiana &

Gulf. In 1984 the Louisiana Midland was embargoed because of flood and fire damage, and its abandonment petition was approved in July 1985.

1945-1967
Location of headquarters: Baton Rouge, Louisiana
Miles of railroad operated: 1945 — 77; 1966 — 77
Number of locomotives: 1947 — 4; 1966 — 2
Number of freight cars: 1966 — 7
Reporting marks: LM

1974-1985
Location of headquarters: Jena, Louisiana
Miles of railroad operated: 1974 — 75; 1984 — 75
Number of locomotives: 1974 — 3; 1984 — 3
Number of freight cars: 1974 — 40; 1984 — 73
Reporting marks: LOAM

Map: See page 194

C. W. Witbeck

Louisiana Midland Ten-Wheeler 503 (ex-Louisiana & Arkansas 503) is on familiar L&A rails leaving Minden, La., in July 1948. Home rails are 80 miles ahead at Packton.

Louis Saillard

RS1 No. 1111, once on the roster of Gulf, Mobile & Ohio with the same number, switches a pulpwood yard at Rhinehart, La., in January 1976.

LOUISVILLE & NASHVILLE RAILROAD

In the 1840s Louisville, Kentucky, was developing into a river port and distribution center — except during seasons of low water in the Ohio River. The growing city needed more dependable transportation. Tennessee was already building railroads from Memphis and Nashville to Chattanooga, and the Western & Atlantic Railroad opened from Chattanooga to Atlanta, Georgia, in 1850. Nashville interests proposed a railroad north toward but not into Louisville to capture the trade that moved through Louisville. That proposal spurred Louisville to action: In 1850 the Kentucky legislature chartered the Louisville & Nashville Railroad to build between the cities of its name, with branches to Lebanon, Ky., and Memphis, Tenn. The state of Tennessee issued a charter for the southern portion of the line, with the condition that the railroad come no closer to Nashville than the north bank of the Cumberland River — any freight for Nashville would have to enter the city by wagon.

Work went slowly because of problems with financing, disputes over the route, and low water that kept materials from arriving at Louisville. In March 1850 the road was opened between Louisville and Lebanon. The segment between Nashville and Bowling Green opened in August 1859, and two months later the line was completed, including a bridge across the Cumberland into Nashville and another over the Green River at Munfordville, Ky., that was the longest iron bridge in America at the time. The line to Memphis was opened in April 1861. It was a joint effort by the L&N, the Memphis & Ohio, and the Memphis, Clarksville & Louisville railroads.

By then the Civil War had begun, with Kentucky on one side and Tennessee on the other. During the war Union and Confederate forces fought up and down the L&N, destroying as they went. By mid-1863 the major action of the war had moved to the Southeast. L&N began to pick up the pieces and get back to business — and there was enough business that L&N prospered.

With the war over, L&N began to find its territory invaded by competing railroads. On the west the Evansville, Henderson & Nashville was completed in 1872 and sold to the St. Louis & Southeastern Railway, and to the east the city of Cincinnati was busy planning and building the Cin-

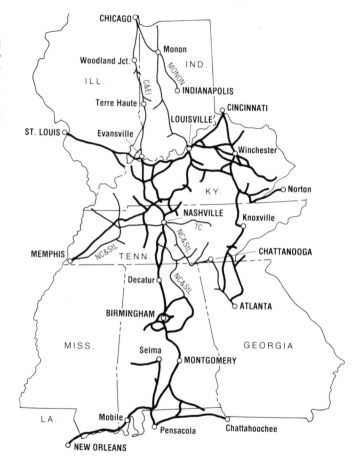

L&N

The year and the engine number are the same as one of L&N's M-1 class Berkshires leads an Atlanta-bound freight out of Decoursey (Ky.) Yard a few miles south of Cincinnati.

cinnati Southern Railway (now operated by the Southern Railway but still owned by the city).

To the south, though, L&N faced little competition. By 1860 several railroad companies had put together a line from Nashville to Decatur, Alabama — they were consolidated in 1866 as the Nashville & Decatur Railroad — and by 1870 a rail line was open from Montgomery, Ala., through Mobile to New Orleans. The Nashville & Decatur proposed a lease to the L&N if L&N would guarantee the completion of the South & North Alabama, which was under construction from Mobile north through the infant industrial center of Birmingham to Decatur. The Lou-

179

isville-Montgomery route was completed in 1872. L&N also began extending its Lebanon branch southeastward toward Knoxville and Cumberland Gap.

In 1875, therefore, L&N had a main line from Louisville to Montgomery and branches from Lebanon Jct. to Livingston, Ky., from Richmond Jct. to Richmond, Ky., and from Bowling Green, Ky., to Memphis. L&N began expanding in earnest. It purchased the Evansville, Henderson & St. Louis at foreclosure in 1879, gaining a second route from the Ohio River to Nashville. EH&StL's owner, the St. Louis & Southeastern, had been in receivership since 1874; its line from East St. Louis to Evansville was purchased by the Nashville, Chattanooga & St. Louis. On the southern front, L&N purchased the Montgomery & Mobile and the New Orleans, Mobile & Texas, obtaining a route to New Orleans; along with the Montgomery & Mobile came routes into western Florida. L&N was alarmed at the sudden expansion of the NC&StL that promised a bridge over the Ohio, a link between Owensboro and Evansville, and leases of the Western & Atlantic and Central of Georgia. L&N began buying NC&StL stock, soon acquiring virtual control over its rival. L&N quickly took the East St. Louis-Evansville line from NC&StL and added it to its own system.

One of L&N's major acquisitions was the "Short Line" between Louisville and Cincinnati. The Louisville & Frankfort and Lexington & Frankfort railroads completed a line from Louisville to Lexington in 1851. There were proposals to extend that line from Lexington to Cincinnati and to build a new short, direct line from Louisville to Cincinnati. The latter was built in 1869 by the Louisville & Frankfort in the face of rivalry between the cities of Louisville and Cincinnati, debate over the gauge (and thus over which city would have the freight transfer business), and even the route into Louisville — the city council advocated a route that the railroad said could be damaged by floods, and when the railroad knuckled under to the city and sent surveyors out, they found the proposed route deep under water. The two railroads consolidated in 1869 to form the Louisville, Cincinnati & Lexington Railroad, over the protests of the city of Frankfort that it would become simply a way station. L&N purchased the Louisville, Cincinnati & Lexington in 1881.

Another major acquisition was the Kentucky Central Railway, purchased from the C. P. Huntington interests in 1892. The road consisted of a main line from Covington, Ky., across the Ohio River from Cincinnati, south to a junction with L&N's Lebanon Branch just north of Livingston, Ky., and a line from Lexington to Maysville, Ky., crossing the main line at Paris, Ky.

L&N had made a connection with the Southern Railway at Jellico, Tenn., for traffic to and from Knoxville, but shortly after the turn of the century decided to build its own line south to Knoxville and Atlanta. In 1902 L&N acquired the Knoxville Southern and the Marietta & North Georgia railroads, which formed a line from Knoxville to Marietta, Ga., 20 miles northwest of Atlanta on the Western & Atlantic. This line ran through an area rich in copper and marble — and through mountainous territory that required a pair of sharp curves between Whitestone and Talking Rock, Ga. — the "Hook" — and a complete loop between Farner and Appalachia, Tenn. — the Hiwassee Loop or "Eye." In 1906 L&N constructed a line with easier grades and curves between Etowah, Tenn., and Cartersville, Ga., west of the Hook & Eye line.

In 1898 L&N became the sole lessee of the Georgia Railroad and the affiliated Western Railway of Alabama and Atlanta & West Point but almost immediately assigned a half interest in the lease to Atlantic Coast Line.

In April 1902 Edwin Hawley and John W. Gates acquired a large block of L&N stock which they sold within a few weeks to J. P. Morgan & Co. Before the year was over Morgan sold his L&N interest — 51 percent — to the Atlantic Coast Line Railroad. In May 1902 L&N and Southern, both under J. P. Morgan's control, jointly purchased the Chicago, Indianapolis & Louisville (Monon). Many pieces of the Seaboard System were in place 80 years before the creation of that railroad.

L&N was one of only a few railroads to build its own locomotives in any great numbers. Between 1905 and 1923 L&N's South Louisville Shops constructed more than 400 Consolidations, Pacifics, Mikados, and Eight-Wheel switchers. Although L&N was the largest coal hauler south of Virginia it began dieselizing relatively early. At the beginning of World War Two L&N purchased 14 Berkshires for freight and passenger service and simultaneously began dieselizing passenger trains with a fleet of Electro-Motive E6s. L&N had already purchased its first road freight diesels, al-

A single E6 leads the Cincinnati-New Orleans *Humming Bird* through Turner, Ky., in 1948. A rebuilt heavyweight sleeping car trails the original six lightweight cars of the streamliner.

beit for helper service, when 22 more 2-8-4s came from Lima in 1949 for service in the eastern Kentucky coalfields at a time when L&N was undertaking a great deal of branchline construction in that area. In 1950 L&N began to dieselize freight service in earnest, finishing the job by the end of 1956.

The upgrading of passenger service after WWII centered on two coach streamliners, the Cincinnati-New Orleans *Humming Bird* and the St. Louis-Atlanta *Georgian*, placed in service in 1946. Both trains soon acquired sleeping cars and through cars to Chicago via the Chicago & Eastern Illinois — Chicago traffic on the *Georgian* quickly outstripped that on its original route. The New York-New Orleans *Crescent Limited*, considered the premier train of the Southern Railway, but operated between Montgomery and New Orleans by L&N, was streamlined in 1950. In 1949

L&N and Seaboard teamed up to offer the Jacksonville-New Orleans *Gulf Wind*. L&N was a key link in the busiest Chicago-Florida passenger route, the "Dixie Route" (C&EI-L&N-NC&StL-ACL), and also forwarded the Pennsylvania Railroad's Chicago-Florida trains south of Louisville.

L&N merged the Nashville, Chattanooga & St. Louis on August 30, 1957 — a date some consider the beginning of the modern railroad merger era (others say it began a decade earlier when Pere Marquette, Denver & Salt Lake, and Alton were merged into larger systems). In either case, it was the beginning of L&N's modern expansion era: In 1969 L&N purchased the Woodland, Ill.-Evansville, Indiana, line of the Chicago & Eastern Illinois and acquired 140 miles of the abandoned Tennessee Central from Nashville to Crossville, Tenn. In 1971 L&N merged the Monon Railroad to obtain a second route from the Ohio River to Chicago. (L&N's financial interest in the Monon had been eliminated in Monon's 1946 reorganization.)

L&N's ownership by Atlantic Coast Line included a joint lease of the Carolina, Clinchfield & Ohio Railway (operated by the Clinchfield Railroad) and the railroad properties of the Georgia Railroad & Banking Co. (Georgia Railroad, Western Railway of Alabama, and Atlanta & West Point Rail Road). Atlantic Coast Line merged with Seaboard Air Line in 1967 to form Seaboard Coast Line Railroad. In the mid-1970s SCL began to refer to the "Family Lines" in its advertising, and the ad usually included a list of the members. It wasn't an official railroad name, but it indicated probable merger in the future. On November 1, 1980, Seaboard Coast Line Industries, parent of SCLRR, merged with Chessie System to form CSX Corporation, and on December 29, 1982, Seaboard Coast Line Railroad merged with L&N to form the Seaboard System Railroad.

Location of headquarters: Louisville, Kentucky
Miles of railroad operated: 1929 — 5,250; 1982 — 10,396
Number of locomotives: 1929 — 1,350; 1982 — 1,086
Number of passenger cars: 1929 — 1,006; 1970 — 113
Number of freight cars: 1929 — 64,134; 1982 — 53,095
Number of company service cars: 1929 — 2,584; 1982 — 1,554
Reporting marks: LN
Historical and technical society: Louisville & Nashville Historical Society, P. O. Box 541, Glenwood, IL 60425

Continued on next page

Recommended reading: *Louisville & Nashville Railroad, 1850-1963*, by Kincaid A. Herr, published in 1964 by the Public Relations Department, Louisville & Nashville Railroad, Louisville, Ky.
Predecessor railroads in this book:
Chicago, Indianapolis & Louisville (Monon)
Nashville, Chattanooga & St. Louis

Successors: Seaboard System (TWG)
Portions still operated: The only major routes of the "old" L&N (before the NC&StL merger) that have been cut or abandoned are the Bowling Green-Memphis line and some redundant lines between Louisville and Winchester and Richmond, Ky. For the status of Monon, NC&StL, and Tennessee Central see the entries for those roads.

MACON, DUBLIN & SAVANNAH RAILROAD

The Macon, Dublin & Savannah began construction southeast from Macon, Georgia, in 1885, the year of its incorporation. The line reached Dublin in 1891 and the decision was made not to build all the way to Savannah but only to Vidalia, where the MD&S could connect with the Georgia & Alabama Railway. The Georgia & Alabama became part of the Seaboard Air Line in 1900, forming its Savannah-Montgomery line, and the MD&S served as a Macon branch of that route.

In 1904 the Atlantic Coast Line purchased the outstanding stock and bonds of the MD&S but soon realized that the railroad was many miles from the nearest ACL track, an orphan. In 1906 ACL sold its holdings to the Seaboard. In 1930 SAL owned somewhat less than half of MD&S's stock but in the mid-1940s acquired the remainder. SAL absorbed the MD&S on March 1, 1958. The entire line is still in operation.

Location of headquarters: Macon, Georgia
Miles of railroad operated: 1929 — 94; 1957 — 93
Number of locomotives: 1929 — 11; 1957 — 8
Number of passenger cars: 1929 — 7
Number of freight cars: 1929 — 21
Number of company service cars: 1929 — 11
Number of freight and company service cars: 1957 — 107
Reporting marks: MD&S
Successors:
Seaboard Air Line
Seaboard System (TWG)
Portions still operated: Macon-Vidalia: Seaboard System
Map: See Seaboard Air Line

Truman Blasingame

In 1946 Macon, Dublin & Savannah acquired an ex-Western Maryland Pacific from its parent Seaboard Air Line. The much-traveled Baldwin is shown at Dublin, Ga., on the daily passenger train. MD&S's diesel fleet comprised a Baldwin VO1000 and seven Alco RS2s.

MASTER CAR BUILDERS' ASSOCIATION

As North America's railroads developed into a transcontinental network, mechanical standardization became necessary. The interchange of cars among railroads raised the problem of repairs. Why should a Southern Pacific shop foreman in California fix a broken truck frame on a New Haven boxcar? What kept a car man on the East Coast from tipping an Espee gondola into the dump as unserviceable for some minor fault? The answer was an industry-wide reciprocal agreement for repairs; without it, North America's rail system might have evolved quite differently.

The Master Car Builders' Association was founded in 1867. The initial purpose of the organization was to facilitate the interchange of cars among railroads. In 1876 it established rules for prompt interchange of cars, repairs to damaged and defective cars, and billing and payment for the repairs. The association established standards for car parts, with the result that from 1882 to 1918 the number of different axles and journal boxes used was reduced from more than 50 to 5. The MCB adopted automatic couplers in 1887 and automatic air brakes in 1888.

The association also attacked the problem of confusion in part names. In 1871 it appointed a committee to prepare a dictionary of car-building terms. Published in 1879 by *The Railroad Gazette*, the dictionary defined everything from "adjustable-globe lamp" to "yoke" in words and pictures. *The Car Builder's Dictionary* became *The Car Builders' Dictionary and Cyclopedia* in 1919, *The Car Builders' Cyclopedia of American Practice* in 1922, and *The Car and Locomotive Cyclopedia of American Practice* in 1966.

In 1918 the USRA asked that the various railroad associations be amalgamated. The American Railway Master Mechanics' Association and the Master Car Builders' Association were consolidated as Section III, Mechanical, of the American Railroad Association, which was a reorganization of the American Railway Association (by mid-1920 the "R" in "ARA" again stood for "Railway"). One immediate difference was that where MCB's rules had been recommendatory, ARA's were mandatory. In 1934 The Association of American Railroads was formed by the consolidation of the American Railway Association and the Association of Railway Executives; several other associations soon joined the AAR.

MEXICAN RAILWAY (Ferrocarril Mexicano)

The Mexican Railway was projected as early as 1837 and originally chartered in 1855 as a transcontinental line from Veracruz, on the Gulf of Mexico, through Mexico City to Acapulco, on the Pacific, a straight-line distance of approximately 300 miles. The first piece of the line, three miles out of Mexico City, was opened in 1857. The route to Veracruz was then surveyed, and by 1861 a few miles of track had been laid west from Veracruz.

Then Mexico defaulted on the interest payments on its European debts. Great Britain and Spain joined with France to collect the debts by force. Britain and Spain withdrew their troops from Mexico, but the French remained. Napoleon III of France established a monarchy in Mexico and placed the emperor Maximilian on the throne in 1864. Mexico demanded that France withdraw, and at the end of the U. S. Civil War the U. S. government moved troops to the border to support Mexico's demands. Napo-

leon III withdrew, leaving Maximilian to face capture and execution.

The situation eventually stabilized sufficiently that the railway could attract British capital, and it was registered in England as the Imperial Mexican Ry. Co., Ltd. Construction resumed and at the end of 1872 the road was opened from Veracruz to Mexico City, 264 miles. It was never extended beyond Mexico City.

The line was notable for its engineering. In the 48 miles from Veracruz to Paso del Macho the line climbed from sea level to 1,560 feet. That averages to a little over 30 feet a mile; FCM's maximum grade there was 1.7 percent. From Mexico City east to Esperanza the line lay across a plateau, with grades of no more than 1.5 percent. But the 64 miles between Esperanza, at an elevation of 8,045 feet, and Paso del Macho included ruling grades of 4.7 percent and curves of 16.5 degrees (or 347-foot radius) — the Maltrata Incline. Mexicano's initial solution to the problem of motive

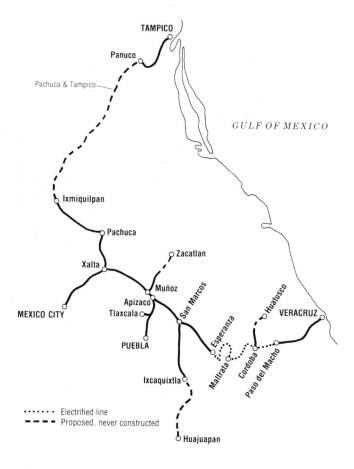

TAMPICO

Panuco

Pachuca & Tampico

GULF OF MEXICO

Ixmiquilpan

Pachuca

Zacatlan

Xalta

Muñoz

San Marcos

Huatusco

MEXICO CITY

Apizaco

VERACRUZ

Tlaxcala

Esperanza

PUEBLA

Maltrata

Cordoba

Paso del Macho

Ixcaquixtla

Huajuapan

······· Electrified line

– – – Proposed, never constructed

power that could cope with such grades was the Fairlie articulated — a pair of swiveling engine units beneath a double-ended center-firebox boiler. The second solution was to electrify the line. The first segment of the electrification, between Orizaba and Esperanza, was opened in 1923, and the wires extended east to Paso del Macho by 1928. The electrification was still in service as late as the end of 1968, but it was discontinued in the early 1970s. Other noteworthy motive power was a group of 3-cylinder Pacifics, 4 built in 1928 by Alco and 3 in 1938 by Montreal, and 10 2-8-0s turned out by Baldwin in 1946.

The Mexicano had five principal branch lines with four different gauges. Two were purchased in 1909, the 34-mile, 30-inch-gauge Zacatlan Railway and the 20-mile, 2-foot-gauge Cordoba Huatusco Railway. In 1913 FCM bought the 57-mile, 3-foot-gauge San Marcos & Huajuapan De Leon Railway. The Huatusco Branch was abandoned in 1951, and the Zacatlan and Huajuapan branches were abandoned in 1958. All three narrow gauge branches were named for towns they never reached. The standard gauge line from Apizaco to Puebla remains in service; the standard gauge branch from Xalta to Pachuca, opened in 1890, was abandoned in 1956. In 1921 FCM began construction of the line between Pachuca and Tampico that would cut in half the distance from Mexico City to Tampico; the project was abandoned in 1931 after two short stubs out of Pachuca and Tampico had been constructed. A 6-mile branch from Santa Ana, on the Puebla Branch, to Tlaxcala, was operated in 1930 with Ford motor cars, according to Moody's manual for that year. That branch was abandoned in 1944.

The Mexicano was purchased by the Mexican government in 1946. In 1959 it ceased to exist as a separate company and its operations were merged with National Railways of Mexico. The main line is still in service, but the Orizaba-Esperanza section of the line is being augmented by a new line with easier grades. The new line will have the highest double-track railroad bridge in the world.

Location of headquarters: Mexico City, Mexico
Miles of railroad operated: 1929 — 490; 1959 — 292
Number of steam locomotives: 1929 — 93; 1959 — 75
Number of electric locomotives: 1929 — 12; 1959 — 12
Number of passenger cars: 1929 — 110; 1959 — 59

Ferrocarril Mexicano No. 32, an 0-6-6-0 named *Orizava*, was built in 1872. The plate on the tank at the far end reads "Fairlie's Patent."

Number of freight cars: 1929 — 1,153; 1959 — 644
Number of company service cars: 1929 — 94; 1959 — 85
Reporting marks: FCM
Recommended reading: *Mexican Narrow Gauge*, by Gerald M. Best, published in 1968 by Howell-North Books, 850 North Hollywood Way, Burbank, CA 91505
Successor companies: National Railways of Mexico (TWG)
Portions still operated: Mexico City-Veracruz; Apizaco-Puebla: National Railways of Mexico

Mexicano B-B-B electric 1011 helps a pair of National of Mexico F units bring the Veracruz-Mexico City day train to the top of the Orizaba-Esperanza grade in 1961.

MICHIGAN NORTHERN RAILWAY

The Michigan Northern was formed in December 1975 to take over operation of the Grand Rapids & Indiana line of the former Pennsylvania Railroad between Grand Rapids and Mackinaw City, Michigan. Since the line was not slated for inclusion in Conrail, the Michigan Department of Transportation purchased it to maintain rail service in the area. Michigan Northern began operation on April 1, 1976.

In 1982 Michigan Northern inaugurated seasonal passenger service into the resort areas along its line. In 1983 the railroad purchased the Chesapeake & Ohio (ex-Pere Marquette) lines from Grawn to Williamsburg and from Petoskey to Charlevoix and took over operation of the state-owned Ann Arbor Railroad from Alma to Frankfort.

The state of Michigan withdrew its subsidy from Michigan Northern, and on October 1, 1984, the Tuscola & Saginaw Bay took over operation of all the Michigan Northern lines except from Pellston, where a truck-rail transfer facility was established for Algoma Steel, to Petoskey, where the loads were turned over to T&SB. Service was discontinued south of Reed City.

Location of headquarters: Cadillac, Michigan
Miles of railroad operated: 1976 — 250; 1983 — 432
Number of locomotives: 1976 — 2; 1983 — 8
Number of freight cars: 1983 — 22
Reporting marks: MIGN
Predecessor railroads in this book:
Ann Arbor
Pennsylvania Railroad
Pere Marquette
Successors: Tuscola & Saginaw Bay (TWG)
Portions still operated:
Petoskey-Pellston: Michigan Northern
Reed City-Petoskey-Charlevoix; Alma-Frankfort; Walton Jct.-Traverse City; Grawn-Williamsburg: Tuscola & Saginaw Bay

Byron C. Babbish

In the last month of Michigan Northern service south of Petoskey, a pair of GP7s leads a freight train at Boyne Falls. The lead unit is still in the paint of its former owner, Toledo, Peoria & Western; the other is an ex-Algoma Central unit wearing Michigan Northern's own livery.

MIDLAND TERMINAL RAILWAY

The name "Midland Terminal" refers to the road's original purpose as a switching road between mines at Cripple Creek and a mainline railroad, the Colorado Midland — and also refers to the terminal phase of the Colorado Midland's existence. A brief history of the CM is a necessary prelude to discussion of the Midland Terminal. In 1883 a line drawn through Denver, Pueblo, and Trinidad, Colo., would have been the demarcation between standard gauge and narrow gauge railroading in the state. It was surprising, therefore, when a standard gauge railroad from Colorado Springs over Ute Pass into the South Park was proposed and incorporated in November 1883 — the Colorado Midland Railway, to build from Colorado Springs to Leadville and Salida. It was to be primarily a local railroad; the Rock Island's line into Colorado Springs from the east was still five years in the future.

Financial backing for the new railroad came from James J. Hagerman, who had been instructed by his physician to find a climate better for his health than that of Milwaukee. Hagerman owned mines near Aspen and Glenwood Springs, and he proposed building a western extension of the CM first because of the traffic those mines would furnish. When the two established roads in Colorado, the Denver & Rio Grande and the Union Pacific, doubled their rates on rails carried to Leadville, Hagerman decided to start from Colorado Springs. Construction of the hastily surveyed route over Ute Pass began in 1886, and the line was completed to Glenwood Springs in December 1887. It included the Hagerman Tunnel west of Leadville, 2,060 feet long at an elevation of 11,530 feet.

By then Grand Junction, Colo., and Ogden, Utah, were CM's goals. (The present Rio Grande line west of Grand Junction was the independent Rio Grande Western at the time.) CM continued its line down the south bank of the Grand River (the pre-1921 name of the Colorado River east of Grand Junction), reaching New Castle about the same time the Denver & Rio Grande rails on the north bank did. The two rivals formed the Rio Grande Junction Railway to build the line to Grand Junction. In 1890 that line was completed, Denver & Rio Grande finished standard-gauging its main line, and Santa Fe purchased the Colorado Midland.

Also in 1890 gold was discovered west of Pikes Peak. Colorado Midland proposed a branch south from the main line at the summit of Hayden Divide to Midland, there to connect with a new 2-foot-gauge line, the Midland Terminal Railway, to go the last few miles to Victor and Cripple Creek. The Midland Terminal built the whole line from Divide to Cripple Creek. The knowledge that the narrow gauge Florence & Cripple Creek was building north from a connection with the narrow gauge Denver & Rio Grande caused a change to standard gauge, since MT's only connection would be the standard gauge CM. The line was opened to Victor in December 1894 and to Cripple Creek a year later. Traffic was outbound ore for processing in the mills at Colorado Springs and inbound merchandise and supplies.

The panic of 1893 was caused in part by the closing of the mints of India to silver coinage. The resulting silver glut was doubly hard on Colorado: The U. S. was on a bimetallic money standard (until silver was demonetized in late 1893), and silver mining was one of Colorado's major industries. CM's traffic fell off. The company defaulted on its bond interest and soon found itself in receivership. Reorganization occurred in 1897.

Also in 1893 the Busk-Ivanhoe Tunnel under Hagerman Pass was opened, eliminating 575 feet of elevation and more than five complete circles from CM's line. The tunnel was owned by a separate company, and

after a dispute over tolls in 1897 CM reopened its old line over the pass. Blizzards in early 1899 tied up the Leadville-Glenwood end of the road for more than two months. CM purchased the Busk-Ivanhoe Tunnel in 1899.

That same year the Colorado & Southern and the Rio Grande Western jointly purchased the Colorado Midland; two years later Denver & Rio Grande, CM's principal competitor, bought the RGW and with it RGW's half interest in the Colorado Midland. Initially CM's fears that its traffic would be diverted to the D&RG proved groundless. Rio Grande routed traffic over CM while rebuilding and upgrading its own line, but took the traffic itself once it had the capacity to move it. Colorado & Southern was

purchased by the Burlington, which was in turn part of the Hill empire — of which the CM was an insignificant piece. CM defaulted on its Rio Grande Junction obligations, Rio Grande bought CM's half interest, and CM entered receivership again in 1912.

In 1917 Albert E. Carlton purchased the Colorado Midland at foreclosure. He proposed an extension to Utah, using the Uintah Railway as part of the new line (but bypassing the 7.5-percent grades and 66-degree curves of Baxter Pass). During World War One the USRA noted on its maps CM's short route across Colorado and routed a great deal of traffic over the line — until the road choked up and the USRA withdrew all traf-

Midland Terminal bought six 0-6-0s from the U. S. Army in 1946 and rebuilt three of them as Moguls. All three are shown here with an ore train near Bull Hill in October 1948.

Donald Duke

188

fic. The road closed down in August 1918. Carlton delayed dismantling the line while the Santa Fe considered purchasing it, but scrapping began in 1921. Carlton gave the right of way to the state for highways, except for the Busk-Ivanhoe Tunnel, which became first a toll highway tunnel, then a conduit to bring western slope water into the Arkansas Valley for irrigation.

For a few years in the late teens all the railroads in Cripple Creek — the Midland Terminal, the Colorado Springs & Cripple Creek District, and the remains of the Florence & Cripple Creek — were united as the Cripple Creek & Colorado Springs under Carlton. Upon the demise of the Colorado Midland, the Midland Terminal took over the CM line from Divide to Colorado Springs. Within a few years it was the sole railroad serving the dying mining industry of Cripple Creek. There was a brief revival in 1933 when the government revised gold prices, but for the most part the trend was just as much downhill as the journey the ore made from Cripple Creek and Victor to the mill at Colorado Springs. Finally a new mill near Victor removed the last reason for the existence of the railroad. The Midland Terminal ceased operation in February 1949.

Location of headquarters: Colorado Springs, Colorado
Miles of railroad operated: 1929 — 56; 1948 — 56
Number of locomotives: 1929 — 9; 1948 — 7
Number of passenger cars: 1929 — 15
Number of freight cars: 1929 — 240; 1948 — 279
Number of company service cars: 1929 — 25; 1948 — 20
Reporting marks: MTR
Historical and technical societies: Colorado Midland Quarterly, 1731 North Cooper, Colorado Springs, CO 80907
Recommended reading: *The Cripple Creek Road*, by Edward M. "Mel" McFarland, published in 1984 by Pruett Publishing Co., 3235 Prairie Avenue, Boulder, CO 80301 (ISBN 0-87108-647-6)

MIDLAND VALLEY RAILROAD
KANSAS, OKLAHOMA & GULF RAILWAY
OKLAHOMA CITY-ADA-ATOKA RAILWAY

These three railroads were controlled by the Muskogee Company and were operated jointly; in later years most of the rolling stock was lettered for all three roads.

The Midland Valley was incorporated in 1903 and completed its line from Hoye, Arkansas, south of Fort Smith, through Muskogee and Tulsa, Oklahoma, to Wichita, Kansas, in 1906. MV reached Fort Smith by exercising trackage rights over the Frisco; the road owned considerable coal land in that area of Arkansas and adjoining Oklahoma. In 1926 MV made a joint facility and operation agreement with the Kansas, Oklahoma & Gulf and in 1930 did the same with the Oklahoma City-Ada-Atoka. In 1930 the Muskogee Company acquired control of the MV.

The Kansas, Oklahoma & Gulf was incorporated in 1918 as a successor to the Missouri, Oklahoma & Gulf. The MO&G was built between

Preston George

Kansas, Oklahoma & Gulf 2-10-2 No. 500 brings a freight across the Katy crossing at Durant, Okla., in December 1948.

1903 and 1913 from Muskogee northeast to Joplin, Mo., and southwest to Denison, Texas. The only major town it served was Muskogee, and at nearly every town it faced competition from the long-established Frisco and Katy. It was proposed to extend the line north to Pittsburg, Kans., then to Kansas City on trackage rights over Kansas City Southern to form a connection between the Union Pacific at Kansas City and the Houston & Texas Central (Southern Pacific) at Denison; the proposed extension was mentioned well into the 1920s, but it was never built. The MO&G was sold at foreclosure and reorganized as the Kansas, Oklahoma & Gulf in July 1919.

The KO&G entered receivership in 1924 and was acquired by Midland Valley interests in 1925. The KO&G and MV worked out joint facility agreements, and KO&G developed into a bridge route for Kansas-Texas traffic between the Missouri Pacific and the Texas & Pacific. About 1960 MP and T&P rerouted such traffic to remain on MP and T&P rails all the way, which dried up much of KO&G's traffic. In 1962 KO&G abandoned the northern 105 miles of its line between Baxter Springs, Kans., and Okay (North Muskogee), Okla.

The Oklahoma City-Ada-Atoka was incorporated in 1923 to acquire the Shawnee Division of the Missouri-Kansas-Texas, which was undergoing reorganization. The line ran from Oklahoma City to Atoka, Okla. In 1930 OCAA acquired the Oklahoma City-Shawnee Interurban Railway. Muskogee Co. acquired control in 1929.

Muskogee also owned the Foraker Co., which in turn owned the 18-mile Osage Railway, which connected with the Midland Valley at Foraker in northern Oklahoma. The Osage was abandoned in 1953.

In 1962 the Muskogee Co. authorized the sale of all its railroad stocks to the Texas & Pacific. In September 1964 T&P acquired control of the three Muskogee roads but immediately sold the OCAA to the Santa Fe. OCAA was merged with Santa Fe on December 1, 1967. Midland Valley was merged into T&P on April 1, 1967, and the same happened to KO&G exactly three years later. The Muskogee Company was dissolved in 1964 after its properties were sold.

Location of headquarters: Muskogee, Oklahoma
Midland Valley
   Miles of railroad operated: 1929 — 363; 1966 — 333
   Number of locomotives: 1929 — 26
   Number of passenger cars: 1929 — 19
   Number of freight cars: 1929 — 295

Number of company service cars: 1929 — 73; 1966 — 2
Reporting marks: MV
Kansas, Oklahoma & Gulf
Miles of railroad operated: 1929 — 327; 1969 — 206
Number of locomotives: 1929 — 28; 1969 — 15
Number of passenger cars: 1929 — 3
Number of freight cars: 1929 — 255
Number of company service cars: 1929 — 48
Number of freight and company service cars: 1969 — 468
Reporting marks: KO&G
Oklahoma City-Ada-Atoka
Miles of railroad operated: 1929 — 129; 1966 — 101
Number of passenger cars: 1929 — 7

Number of company service cars: 1929 — 6
Recommended reading: *Railroads in Oklahoma*, edited by Donovan L. Hofsommer, published in 1977 by the Oklahoma Historical Society, 2100 North Lincoln, Oklahoma City, OK 73105
Successors:
Texas & Pacific
Missouri Pacific (TWG)
Atchison, Topeka & Santa Fe (TWG)
Portions still operated:
MV — Muskogee-Barnsdall, Okla.: Missouri Pacific
KO&G — Durant-Muskogee-Okay, Okla.: Missouri Pacific
OCAA — Shawnee-Ada, Okla.: Atchison, Topeka & Santa Fe

MINNEAPOLIS & ST. LOUIS RAILROAD

The Minneapolis & St. Louis began with the chartering of the Minnesota Western Railroad in 1853. The name was changed to Minneapolis & St. Louis Railway in 1870, and the company built a line that reached from White Bear, Minn., south through Minneapolis to Albert Lea and by 1881 to Fort Dodge, Iowa. By 1884 a tentacle stretched west from Minneapolis to Watertown, South Dakota, and in 1900 a line was opened from Winthrop, Minn., on the Watertown line, south to Storm Lake, Iowa. In 1905 the Minnesota, Dakota & Pacific Railway extended the Watertown line west to Leola and Le Beau, S. Dak., with the thought of eventual extension to the Pacific. M&StL purchased the MD&P in 1912.

Meanwhile the Iowa Central, after reorganizations and renamings, had assembled a railroad from Albia east through Oskaloosa to Peoria, Illinois, and from Oskaloosa north across Iowa to a connection with the M&StL at Northwood, Iowa, south of Albert Lea.

In 1896 Edwin Hawley became president of the M&StL and soon afterward president of the Iowa Central. Hawley also became involved with the Alton and the Toledo, St. Louis & Western (the Clover Leaf), and for a brief season around 1911 the four roads were under common management. Hawley also invested in the Chesapeake & Ohio, the Missouri-

Time freight 19 rolls past the station at Eldora, Iowa, behind a 3-unit set of F3s delivered in January 1947. M&StL numbered its diesels with the month and year of their acquisition.

Kansas-Texas, and the Kansas City, Mexico & Orient in the hope of assembling a coast-to-coast railroad system. Such a system never materialized — the only thing to come out of it was the purchase of the Iowa Central by the M&StL on January 1, 1912, a month before Hawley's death.

The third major portion of the M&StL was the Des Moines & Fort Dodge-Des Moines Valley system, a route from Des Moines through Perry and Fort Dodge to Ruthven, Iowa, and by trackage rights over Milwaukee Road to Spencer, on M&StL's Winthrop-Storm Lake line. In later years trackage rights over the Burlington between Oskaloosa and Des Moines connected the south end of this portion of the road with the rest of the M&StL.

The M&StL ran into financial trouble and entered receivership in 1923. The bondholders elected Walter Colpitts of Coverdale & Colpitts, the railroad engineering firm, as chairman of their reorganization committee. He appointed Lucian Sprague as receiver. Sprague took over at the beginning of 1935 in the face of numerous proposals to dismember, parcel out, and abandon the M&StL. He sold antiquated rolling stock as scrap to realize immediate cash, modernized the road's locomotives, and opened traffic offices and began soliciting business at a time when other railroads were pulling back.

In 1942 the road was sold — after 42 previous efforts to auction it off — to Coverdale & Colpitts, the firm that had managed its reorganization. The reorganized M&StL encompassed a new Railway Company (the main lines), a new Railroad Corporation (the branches), and the old Railroad Company, all titled Minneapolis & St. Louis. The separation of the branch lines was found unnecessary by 1944. The M&StL began dieselization in 1938 and was fully dieselized by 1950.

In May 1954 a group of stockholders led by attorney Ben Heineman took over the M&StL, and Heineman replaced Sprague as chairman of the board. Heineman's only previous railroad experience was in representing a group of stockholders in a dividend case against the Chicago Great Western. Heineman revived an old idea of a belt route around Chicago and began negotiating to purchase Toledo, Peoria & Western stock. His purchase of a block of Monon stock apparently alerted the Santa Fe and the Pennsylvania, which jointly purchased the TP&W to block Heineman.

In 1956 the M&StL acquired all the stock of the Minnesota Western Railway (Minneapolis to Gluek, Minn., 115 miles; a 1924 reorganization of the Electric Short Line Railway and a sometime affiliate of the Minneapolis, Northfield & Southern) and renamed it the Minneapolis Industrial Railway. It was abandoned in the early 1970s.

Heineman gave the M&StL a modern-thinking, aggressive management before he moved on to the Chicago & North Western in 1956. Chicago & North Western purchased the railroad assets of the M&StL on November 1, 1960.

Location of headquarters: Minneapolis, Minnesota
Miles of railroad operated: 1929 — 1,628; 1959 — 1,391
Number of locomotives: 1929 — 218; 1959 — 74
Number of passenger cars: 1929 — 122; 1959 — 10
Number of freight cars: 1929 — 6,581; 1959 — 4,178
Number of company service cars: 1929 — 310; 1959 — 116
Reporting marks: M&StL, MSTL
Historical and technical societies: Chicago & North Western Historical Society, 8242 North Knox Avenue, Skokie, IL 60076
Recommended reading: *Mileposts On the Prairie*, by Frank P. Donovan, published in 1950 by Simmons-Boardman Publishing Corporation, 1809 Capitol Avenue, Omaha, NE 68102
Successors: Chicago & North Western (TWG)
Portions still operated: Peoria-Middle Grove, Ill.; Albia, Iowa-Waseca, Minn.; Montgomery-Minneapolis, Minn.; Belmond-Kanawha, Iowa; Des Moines-Rippey, Iowa; Grand Jct.-Mallard, Iowa; Norwood-Madison, Minn.: Chicago & North Western

MISSISSIPPI CENTRAL RAILROAD

In 1896 the Pearl & Leaf Rivers Railroad was incorporated. It was a logging road from Hattiesburg to Sumrall, Mississippi, 19 miles. The western goal of the railroad was Natchez, across the state on the Mississippi River. In 1905 after a reorganization the railroad was renamed the Mississippi Central Railroad, and the line was completed in 1908 (the western portion was built by the Natchez & Eastern Railway, absorbed by Mississippi Central in 1909). The road's plans to extend its line to the Gulf of Mexico were never fulfilled, but in 1921 MSC leased a branch of the Gulf, Mobile & Northern from Hattiesburg to Beaumont and acquired trackage rights to Mobile over GM&N. In 1924 GM&N sold off the branch, which became the Bonhomie & Hattiesburg Southern, and MSC pulled back to Hattiesburg.

Mississippi Central ran its last passenger train in 1941. Just before the beginning of World War Two the Army announced it would reopen Camp Shelby, south of Hattiesburg. Mississippi Central had torn up its branch line to Camp Shelby some years previously, but the road hastily relaid 7

MISSISSIPPI CENTRAL

C. W. Witbeck

Mississippi Central 2-8-2 No. 131 assists in the cleanup of a mishap at Cobbs, west of Brookhaven. Both of the Mike's bells — a characteristic of the road's steam locomotives — are nicely polished.

miles of track in the interests of national defense and freight revenue.

MSC's business held up well after the war, and the road participated in east-west bridge traffic in cooperation with the Louisiana Midland, a new road created from a Louisiana & Arkansas branch west of the Mississippi River. The route was a joint Louisiana & Arkansas-Louisiana Midland-MSC project using the name "Natchez Route." Profits turned to deficits in the early 1960s and MSC looked for a buyer. At first Illinois Central rejected the offer, but the prospect of a new paper mill between Wanilla and Silver Creek changed the situation. IC purchased the Mississippi Central on March 29, 1967. Illinois Central Gulf still operates the entire line.

Location of headquarters: Hattiesburg, Mississippi
Miles of railroad operated: 1929 — 151; 1966 — 148

Number of locomotives: 1929 — 21; 1966 — 9
Number of passenger cars: 1929 — 19
Number of freight cars: 1929 — 698; 1966 — 165
Number of company service cars: 1929 — 69; 1966 — 18
Reporting marks: MSC
Recommended reading: *Natchez Route — A Mississippi Central Railroad Album*, by David S. Price and Louis R. Saillard, published in 1975 by Mississippi Great Southern Chapter, National Railway Historical Society, 306 Bay Street, Hattiesburg, MS 39401
Successors:
Illinois Central
Illinois Central Gulf (TWG)

MISSOURI & NORTH ARKANSAS RAILWAY

After the Civil War, Eureka Springs in northwest Arkansas developed as a health resort. To provide easier access to the resort the St. Louis & San Francisco chartered the Missouri & Arkansas Railroad in 1882 to build from Seligman, Mo., to Beaver, Ark., on the White River, a distance of 13 miles. That same year the Eureka Springs Railway was chartered to build roughly 5 miles of railroad from the M&A to Eureka Springs, and the two railroads were consolidated under the Eureka Springs name. The line was completed in February 1883.

The towns of the Ozark area beyond Eureka Springs were clamoring for rail service, so in May 1899 the St. Louis & North Arkansas Railroad was chartered to purchase the Eureka Springs and extend it east to Harrison, reaching there in March 1901. In 1906 the road was reorganized as the Missouri & North Arkansas Railroad. It arranged for trackage rights on the Frisco between Seligman and Wayne, Mo., and on the Kansas City Southern between Neosho and Joplin, Mo. It built a line from Wayne to Neosho, 32 miles, and started construction southeast across Arkansas to Helena, on the Mississippi River. The M&NA hoped to serve as a bridge route between the KCS and Frisco and the Yazoo & Mississippi Valley (Illinois Central) for traffic moving between Kansas City and New Orleans. There were proposals to change M&NA's eastern terminus from Helena to Little Rock or to Memphis and to extend construction to Pensacola, but the management of the road stuck with Helena. The line was completed from Neosho to Helena in 1909. By then Frisco had a Kansas City-Memphis line that connected directly with IC, and KCS reached the Gulf of Mexico at Port Arthur, Texas — most M&NA bridge traffic would require that the connecting roads shorthaul themselves. In addition, the M&NA lay between two Missouri Pacific routes. It soon became clear that the Missouri & North Arkansas would have to rely on local business, and there wasn't much of that. The road entered receivership in 1912.

On August 5, 1914, a southbound M&NA gas-electric car collided with a KCS passenger train just south of Joplin on KCS rails. It was the first recorded accident involving a gas-electric. The car's fuel tanks contained more than 100 gallons of gasoline, and 47 people were crushed or burned in the resulting fire. The financial loss to the railroad was considerable.

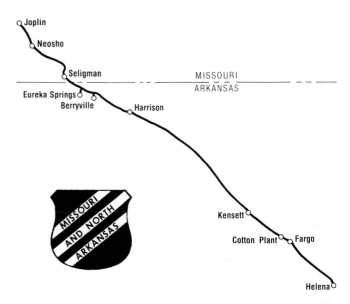

The United States Railroad Administration took over operation of the M&NA in 1918 and raised employee wages, which had been low, to industry standards. M&NA requested and got release from USRA control, then quickly returned the railroad to the agency until 1920. Upon release from the USRA, management returned wages to their old levels, and the employees walked out on February 26, 1921. During the 23-month work stoppage the railroad was plagued with bridge fires, track damage, and acid in its locomotive boilers, and at least one employee was murdered.

The railroad was reorganized as the Missouri & North Arkansas Railway in 1922. It entered receivership in 1927 and was sold at foreclosure

M. B. Cooke

The Missouri & Arkansas purchased a pair of ACF *Motorailers* in 1938 to revive passenger service along the line. Car 705, named *Thomas C. McRae* (governor of Arkansas from 1921 to 1925), pauses at Harrison, the road's headquarters, while running as train 202 from Kensett, Ark., to Neosho, Mo.

Johnnie M. Gray

The fancy paint and striping on the wood caboose matches that on the 70-ton diesel pulling an Arkansas & Ozarks freight past the spur to the Eureka Springs station.

in 1935 to become the Missouri & Arkansas Railway. The new railroad managed to turn a profit for a few years, but fires in 1941 destroyed the offices and the shops, and floods in 1945 wiped out part of the south end of the railroad. In 1946 the employees demanded a wage increase and threatened a strike. Management retaliated with the threat of abandonment. The employees walked out on September 6, 1946, and the Missouri & Arkansas was abandoned.

The Arkansas & Ozarks Railway was incorporated on March 4, 1949, to operate the line between Seligman, Mo., and Harrison, Ark., the oldest part of the M&A. It began operations in February 1950 and was abandoned in April 1961, because of flooding and also condemnation of part of the line by the U. S. Army Corps of Engineers for dam construction.

The portion of the line from Cotton Plant, Ark., to Helena was revived as the Helena & Northwestern Railway. Operation began in September 1949; after a foreclosure suit the last train operated on October 18, 1951. The Cotton Plant-Fargo Railway was chartered in February 1952 to operate the six miles of line between those two towns. It ceased operation in 1977.

Location of headquarters: Harrison, Arkansas
Miles of railroad operated: 1929 — 365; 1945 — 365
Number of locomotives: 1929 — 32; 1945 — 22
Number of passenger cars: 1929 — 14; 1945 — 11 (3 motor cars)
Number of freight cars: 1929 — 394; 1945 — 53
Number of company service cars: 1929 — 53; 1945 — 46
Reporting marks: M&NA (Missouri & North Arkansas), MA (Missouri & Arkansas)
Historical and technical society: Missouri & Arkansas Railroad Museum, Box 83, Beaver, AR 72613
Recommended reading: *The North Arkansas Line*, by James R. Fair Jr., published in 1969 by Howell-North Books, 850 North Hollywood Way, Burbank, CA 91505
Successors:
Missouri & Arkansas
Arkansas & Ozarks
Helena & Northwestern
Cotton Plant-Fargo

The 2-8-2 was Mobile & Ohio's principal freight locomotive. Number 408, built by Baldwin in 1913, was one of 21 similar light Mikados. Following them on the roster were 37 heavier Mikes of USRA design.

MOBILE & OHIO RAIL ROAD

The original purpose of the Mobile & Ohio was to tap the trade of the Mississippi, Missouri, and Ohio rivers for the port of Mobile, Alabama. It would do this by connecting the city with the Ohio and the Mississippi at their confluence at Cairo, Illinois. Cities, counties, and states along the route bought stock and aided the project financially, and Congress passed a land grant bill in 1850 to aid the M&O (and also the Illinois Central). The first 30 miles of the M&O from Mobile to Citronelle, Ala., opened in 1852, and the line was completed to Columbus, Kentucky, on the east bank of the Mississippi a few miles south of Cairo, on April 22, 1861. River steamboats connected Columbus with the south end of the Illinois Central at Cairo, and the St. Louis & Iron Mountain was planning a terminal at Belmont, Missouri, across the river from Columbus.

The road was completed just 10 days after the Confederates fired on Fort Sumter. The Civil War negated any salutary effect the road might have had on the city of Mobile — in addition to pretty much using up the rolling stock and track. The cost of rebuilding the railroad combined with its previous debt sent the M&O into receivership in 1875.

The Iron Mountain did not reach Belmont until 1871, and by then M&O had decided to extend its line north to East Cairo, about 20 miles, but because of M&O's financial difficulties the extension was not completed until 1882. In 1886 M&O acquired the 3-foot-gauge St. Louis & Cairo, which ran between East St. Louis and Cairo, and quickly stan-dard-gauged it. The importance of the terminal at Columbus, Ky., declined, and soon M&O abandoned the spur to the river there. In 1898 the road opened a line from Artesia and Columbus, Miss., to Montgomery, Ala.

The M&O recognized that it was not as strong a railroad as the Illinois Central or the Louisville & Nashville and accepted Southern Railway's offer of an exchange of securities in 1901 — Southern had its eye on M&O's route between Mobile and St. Louis. Merger of Southern and M&O nearly occurred, but the bill allowing the merger was vetoed by the governor of Mississippi. Southern control continued, though. In the late 1920s traffic fell off, and deficits appeared on M&O's ledgers in 1930. Southern was unable to provide financial assistance. M&O entered receivership on June 3, 1932.

M&O pursued its own course, but Southern ownership continued until 1938, when Southern had to sell its M&O bonds to meet other financial commitments. Gulf, Mobile & Ohio purchased the Mobile & Ohio on August 1, 1940 (GM&O was consolidated with Gulf, Mobile & Northern a month later).

Location of headquarters: St. Louis, Missouri
Miles of railroad operated: 1929 — 1,159; 1940 — 1,180
Number of locomotives: 1929 — 231; 1940 — 119
Number of passenger cars: 1929 — 112; 1940 — 31
Number of freight cars: 1929 — 8,368
Number of company service cars: 1929 — 361
Number of freight and company service cars: 1940 — 3,298
Reporting marks: M&O
Historical and technical society: Gulf, Mobile & Ohio Historical Society, P. O. Box 24, Bedford Park, IL 60499
Recommended reading: *The Gulf, Mobile and Ohio*, by James Hutton

Lemly, published in 1953 by Richard D. Irwin, Inc., Homewood, IL 60430
Successors:
Gulf, Mobile & Ohio
Illinois Central Gulf (TWG)
Portions still operated:
Mobile-Whistler, Ala.; Corinth, Miss.-Lawrence, Tenn.; Rives-Union City, Tenn.; Murphysboro, Ill.-East St. Louis: Illinois Central Gulf
Whistler, Ala.-Corinth, Miss.; Artesia, Miss.-Tuscaloosa, Ala.: Gulf & Mississippi
Maplesville-Autauga Creek, Ala.: Southern
Autauga Creek-Montgomery, Ala.: Seaboard System
Lawrence-Kenton, Tenn.: West Tennessee
Map: See page 151

MONTPELIER & WELLS RIVER RAILROAD

The Montpelier & Wells River was incorporated in 1867 to connect the city of Montpelier, the capital of Vermont, with several Boston & Maine predecessors at Wells River, Vt., and Woodsville, New Hampshire. The railroad was opened in November 1873 and entered receivership almost immediately. It was reorganized by its original officers in 1877. In 1883 the M&WR financed the construction of the Barre Branch Railroad from Montpelier to Barre, six miles, to compete with an existing Central Vermont line. The Barre Branch was opened in 1889 and immediately leased to its parent; it was merged in 1913.

In 1911 Boston & Maine took control of the road through its subsidiary, the Vermont Valley, but in 1926 B&M withdrew from management of the M&WR and returned it to local management, though retaining ownership. By then passenger service, which had once included through trains between Burlington, Vt., and the White Mountains of New Hampshire and through sleepers between Montpelier and Boston, had dwindled to mixed trains. Mail and milk traffic were more important to the road than passengers. The principal item of freight was granite from quarries along the line, particularly on the Barre Branch.

In December 1944 the properties of the M&WR were acquired by the

William Moedinger Jr.

Montpelier & Wells River train 1 leads off with an ex-Boston & Maine 2-8-0 built in 1911. Following is a milk car, and bringing up the rear is a wood combine.

Jim Shaughnessy

Barre & Chelsea Railroad, with which it had long been affiliated and which also was a member of the Vermont Valley family. The B&C had been incorporated in 1913 as a consolidation of the Barre Railroad and the East Barre & Chelsea Railroad. The chief traffic of the B&C was granite from quarries in and around Barre. The road was notable for 5-percent grades, a switchback, and a locomotive roster consisting exclusively of saddle-tankers.

After absorbing the Montpelier & Wells River, the Barre & Chelsea dieselized with three GE 70-tonners and continued in existence until 1956, when the ICC authorized abandonment because of operating losses (the Montpelier-Wells River line produced 5 percent of the revenue and was charged with 40 percent of the operating cost). In 1957 the newly organized Montpelier & Barre Railroad, owned by Samuel Pinsly, purchased the portion of the line from Montpelier through Barre to Graniteville, 14 miles, and two of the diesels. In 1958 the Montpelier & Barre purchased the Central Vermont's branch from Montpelier Jct. through Montpelier to Barre and combined that line with its own parallel track.

Montpelier & Barre received ICC permission to abandon in 1980. The state of Vermont purchased the tracks, and operation of the line was taken over by the Washington County Railroad.

Location of headquarters: Montpelier, Vermont
Miles of railroad operated: 1929 — 44; 1944 — 44
Number of locomotives: 1929 — 9; 1944 — 6
Number of passenger cars: 1929 — 7; 1944 — 1
Number of freight cars: 1929 — 9; 1944 — 2
Number of company service cars: 1929 — 16; 1944 — 19
Reporting marks: M&WR
Successors:
Barre & Chelsea
Montpelier & Barre
Washington County
Map: See Rutland

A Barre & Chelsea 70-tonner eases a train of granite-laden flat cars down the hill from South Barre to Barre.

NASHVILLE, CHATTANOOGA & ST. LOUIS RAILWAY

The Nashville & Chattanooga Railroad was incorporated in 1845. The first nine miles of the line out of Nashville were opened in 1851, and by 1853 the line had crossed Cumberland Mountain and reached the Tennessee River at Bridgeport, Alabama. The next year the N&C arrived in Chattanooga, where a connection to Atlanta was made with the Western & Atlantic, owned by the state of Georgia. Floods in 1862 destroyed much of the N&C before retreating Confederate and advancing Union forces could tear it up, but each army demolished one of the two Tennessee River bridges. The N&C was rebuilt — and destroyed again — before the Civil War was over; in 1864 and 1865 the United States Military Railroad thoroughly rebuilt the road and returned it to its owners.

In 1870 the road leased from the state of Tennessee the Nashville & Northwestern Railroad, a line from Nashville to Hickman, Kentucky, on the Mississippi River, and in 1873 N&C purchased the line. The N&C was renamed the Nashville, Chattanooga & St. Louis Railway in 1873. During the 1870s the road acquired several short lines which became branches off the N&C's single main line from Hickman through Nashville to Chattanooga.

In 1879 the road's president, Edwin W. Cole, attempted to make the NC&StL into a St. Louis-Atlanta route. He obtained control of the incomplete Owensboro & Nashville, which was building a line from the Ohio River toward Nashville, and purchased the Illinois and Indiana portion of the St. Louis & Southeastern, which had been in receivership since 1874. Evansville, Ind., the eastern terminus of the StL&SE, was about 30 miles west, or down the Ohio River, from Owensboro, Ky. Cole then initiated negotiations (but didn't complete them) to lease the Western & Atlantic and the Central of Georgia.

Louisville & Nashville reacted quickly to this expansionist policy by buying 55 percent of NC&StL's stock and transferring the East St. Louis-Evansville line to its own system. In 1896 L&N acquired and leased to NC&StL the Paducah, Tennessee & Alabama Railroad (Paducah, Ky.-Bruceton-Lexington, Tenn.) and the Tennessee Midland Railway (Memphis-Lexington-Perryville, Tenn.). This gave NC&StL a route north to

the Ohio River at Paducah and a route southwest to Memphis, a considerably more important destination than Hickman, Ky., NC&StL's original western terminal.

NC&StL teamed up with the Burlington to build a connecting railroad and a bridge over the Ohio River between Paducah, Ky., and Metropolis, Ill., opened in 1917. In 1924 the two roads sold a one-third interest in the Paducah & Illinois Railroad to the Illinois Central, which used the P&I as part of a freight line (the Edgewood Cutoff) it was building to bypass its own congested Ohio River crossing at Cairo, Ill. IC also participated in another, and unusual, bridge construction project in the 1940s. The Tennessee Valley Authority project widened the Tennessee River at Johnsonville, Tenn., creating the need for a longer bridge for NC&StL's track. Downstream, IC's line east of Paducah was rerouted along the top of a dam, rendering its bridge unnecessary. Its spans were barged upstream and raised into place to make a new bridge for NC&StL.

NC&StL was the middle link in several Midwest-Southeast routes, most notably the "Dixie Route" Chicago-Florida passenger trains operated in conjunction with Chicago & Eastern Illinois and L&N north of

Nashville and Atlanta, Birmingham & Coast or Central of Georgia, Atlantic Coast Line, and Florida East Coast south of Atlanta.

After nearly 60 years of control, parent Louisville & Nashville merged the Nashville, Chattanooga & St. Louis on August 30, 1957.

Location of headquarters: Nashville, Tennessee
Miles of railroad operated: 1929 — 1,223; 1956 — 1,043
Number of locomotives: 1929 — 249; 1956 — 132
Number of passenger cars: 1929 — 219; 1956 — 106
Number of freight cars: 1929 — 8,510; 1956 — 6,761
Number of company service cars: 1929 — 775; 1956 — 517
Reporting marks: N&C

Successors:
Louisville & Nashville
Seaboard System (TWG)
Portions still operated:
Memphis-Cordova, Tenn.; Dresden-Bruceton, Tenn.; Bruceton-Paducah, Ky.; Bruceton-Atlanta; Wartrace-Shelbyville, Tenn.; Tullahoma-Sparta, Tenn.; Decherd-Fayetteville, Tenn.; Elora, Tenn.-Hobbs Island, Ala.; Guntersville-Gadsden, Ala.; Cowan-Coalmont, Tenn.; Bridgeport, Ala.-Pikeville, Tenn.: Seaboard System
Colesburg-Hohenwald, Tenn.: South Central Tennessee

The first section — coaches and express cars — of the *Dixie Flyer* starts out of Sherwood, Tenn., in March 1946. The Mikado in the lead has just coupled on to help the semistreamlined Dixie (NC&StL's name for its 4-8-4s) lift the train up to Cumberland Tunnel.

Hugh M. Comer

NEVADA COUNTY NARROW GAUGE RAILROAD

The Nevada County Narrow Gauge Railroad was incorporated in 1874 to connect the gold-mining towns of Nevada City and Grass Valley, California, with the newly constructed Central Pacific at Colfax. The incorporators specified 3-foot gauge after learning of the construction costs of the standard gauge Central Pacific. Construction got under way in early 1875, and rolling stock was ordered. The principal engineering features of the line were tall trestles over the Bear River and Greenhorn Creek. Rails reached Grass Valley in early 1876; regular service began in April of that year to Grass Valley and in May to Nevada City.

In 1908 a line relocation eliminated the trestles and You Bet Tunnel but required a high steel bridge, as impressive as the trestles had been, over the Bear River. The NCNG was also notable in having a woman, Sara Kidder, as president from 1901 to 1913 — she inherited the majority of the road's stock from her husband, the previous president.

The railroad went through the usual crises of poor management and competition from trucks, buses, and automobiles. It was reorganized in 1927 under local management. One response to competition was to acquire a number of tank cars to carry oil and gasoline from the Southern

The Bear River Bridge of 1908 was the engineering highlight of the Nevada County Narrow Gauge. When the road was abandoned, the cost of dismantling the bridge exceeded its scrap value, so the bridge remained in place until it was blown up in 1963 to make way for a dam.

Jim Morley

202

Pacific connection at Colfax to Grass Valley and Nevada City. NCNG was unusual among narrow gauge railroads in that it purchased two second-hand gasoline switchers in 1936.

On May 16, 1937, the railroad hosted a railfan excursion, first on the West Coast. In 1938 the road discontinued rail passenger service; the road's own buses had taken most of the passengers. The NCNG became profitable in the late 1930s and even paid dividends. As World War Two began, though, the scrap value of the railroad outstripped its transportation value, and the federally ordered closing of the gold mines clinched the matter. The last revenue train ran on July 10, 1942.

Location of headquarters: Grass Valley, California
Miles of railroad operated: 1929 — 21; 1939 — 21
Number of locomotives: 1929 — 4; 1939 — 3
Number of passenger cars: 1929 — 5
Number of freight cars: 1929 — 43; 1939 — 66
Number of company service cars: 1939 — 3
Recommended reading: *Nevada County Narrow Gauge*, by Gerald M. Best, published in 1965 by Howell-North Books, 850 North Hollywood Way, Burbank, CA 91505

NEVADA NORTHERN RAILWAY

Mining in Nevada meant gold or silver — until the electrical industry began to grow. Then copper, which had been treated almost as a waste material, became valuable. A large deposit of copper ore was discovered near Ely, in eastern central Nevada many miles from the nearest railroad. Proposals for a railroad to Ely involved standard-gauging the Eu-

reka & Palisade and extending it 75 miles eastward from Eureka, Nev., to Ely over four mountain ranges. In 1905 the Nevada Consolidated Copper Co., which had been created the previous year by merger of several companies active in the area, incorporated the Nevada Northern Railway to build a line from Ely north through the Steptoe Valley to a connection with the Southern Pacific's line between Reno, Nev., and Ogden, Utah. NN's route was almost twice as long as the proposed line from Eureka,

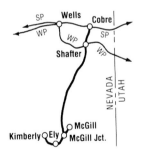

An RS2, No. 101 on the roster of Nevada Northern's parent Kennecott Copper, leads a freight southward through the sagebrush.

Ted Benson

but the only obstacle was sagebrush. The railroad was completed in 1906.

Nevada Consolidated Copper Co. became a subsidiary of Utah Copper Co. in 1909; Kennecott Copper Corp. acquired control in 1923 and still owns the Nevada Northern. In the Ely area the Nevada Northern was used by the mine trains of its parent, but the major portion of the road saw only a triweekly freight train. In mid-1983 Kennecott shut down its smelter at McGill, Nev.; for lack of traffic, NN suspended operation.

Location of headquarters: East Ely, NV 89315
Miles of railroad operated: 1929 — 166; 1981 — 149
Number of locomotives: 1929 — 8; 1981 — 1
Number of passenger cars: 1929 — 13
Number of freight cars: 1929 — 37; 1981 — 58
Number of company service cars: 1929 — 17
Reporting marks: NN

NEWFOUNDLAND RAILWAY

The Newfoundland Railway was chartered in 1881. A track gauge of 3'6" was chosen both for reasons of economy and because that gauge was traditionally associated with railroads in British colonies. Construction got under way at St. John's, capital of Newfoundland, and the line reached Harbour Grace, almost to its goal, Carbonear, in November 1884. By then it was in financial difficulty and was taken over by the government of the colony. In 1886 the government began work on a line from Whitbourne to Placentia; that was completed in 1888. The government found that railroad construction was expensive, so for the next extension, 280 miles west, bids were let. Robert Reid won the contract. He received a land grant and contracted to operate both the railroad he was to construct and those lines already under government control.

The plans for the railroad were eventually revised to make the western terminal Port-aux-Basques, on the southwest tip of the island, about 110

CNR

Newfoundland Railway Mikado 1024 prepares to lead the westbound *Caribou* out of St. John's. The 2-8-2 was built by Montreal Locomotive Works in 1949, just before the road became part of Canadian National Railways.

miles from the mainland port of North Sydney, Nova Scotia. The line was completed from St. John's to Port-aux-Basques in 1898. During the next 20 years several branches were added.

In 1920 the Reid Newfoundland Company, as the railroad had become, began to have financial problems. The government took over the railway in 1923, calling it first the Newfoundland Government Railway and later, in 1926, simply Newfoundland Railway. Many of the branches built during the early years of the century were pruned in the 1930s.

The colony itself was nearly bankrupt by the mid-1930s; World War Two brought activity and prosperity to Newfoundland, closest North American point to Europe. Newfoundland became Canada's tenth province in 1949, and the Newfoundland Railway became part of Canadian National Railways.

CNR tried a number of ways to cut the cost of operating its only narrow gauge line: It completed dieselization of the line in 1957, instituted procedures for carrying standard gauge freight cars on narrow gauge trucks, replaced the cross-island *Caribou* (or *Newfie Bullet*) with buses in 1969, and in 1979 created a separate organization, Terra Transport, to operate CNR's various Newfoundland services. As this book goes to press, the future of the line is uncertain.

Location of headquarters: St. John's, Newfoundland
Miles of railroad operated: 1929 — 968; 1949 — 717
Number of locomotives: 1949 — 63
Notable named passenger trains: *Caribou* (Port-aux-Basques-St. John's)
Recommended reading: *Narrow Gauge Railways of Canada*, by Omer Lavallée, published in 1972 by Railfare Enterprises Limited, Box 33, West Hill, ON, Canada M1E 4R4
Successors: Canadian National Railways (TWG)
Portions still operated: Port-aux-Basques-St. John's; Brigus Jct.-Carbonear; Placentia Jct.-Placentia-Argentia; Notre Dame Jct.-Lewisporte: Canadian National

NEW ORLEANS GREAT NORTHERN RAILROAD

The New Orleans Great Northern began, like many other railroads in southern Mississippi and adjacent Louisiana, as a logging railroad, but it was constructed to considerably better standards than most other such roads and it was planned to be a permanent railroad. It was part of the lumbering empire of Frank and Charles Goodyear of Buffalo, New York — another piece was the Buffalo & Susquehanna Railroad. The NOGN was incorporated in Louisiana and Mississippi in 1905, and the Mississippi company was merged into the Louisiana one the following year. Also in 1905 the NOGN purchased the East Louisiana Railroad, which had a network of lines in the area north of Lake Pontchartrain and reached New Orleans by trackage rights over the New Orleans & Northeastern (later Southern Railway) from Slidell, La. NOGN opened its line north to Jackson, Miss., in 1909. Passenger traffic on the NOGN declined after World War One, but freight business prospered until the mid-1920s.

Thomas T. Taber: Collection of Louis A. Marre

New Orleans Great Northern 4-4-0 No. 105 stands in Jackson, Miss., on September 3, 1923, after bringing train 102 from New Orleans.

New Orleans Great Northern's route between Jackson, Miss., and New Orleans was important to Gulf, Mobile & Northern's traffic agreement with the Burlington. Accordingly, GM&N took control of NOGN on December 30, 1929. NOGN entered receivership on November 7, 1932, with Isaac B. Tigrett, president of GM&N, as receiver. It was reorganized as the New Orleans Great Northern Railway and leased to GM&N on July 1, 1933. The lease was assumed by Gulf, Mobile & Ohio and later by Illinois Central Gulf.

Location of headquarters: New Orleans, Louisiana
Miles of railroad operated: 1929 — 277; 1933 — 263
Number of locomotives: 1929 — 28; 1933 — 14
Number of passenger cars: 1929 — 29; 1933 — 14
Number of freight cars: 1929 — 1,354
Number of company service cars: 1929 — 48

Number of freight and company service cars: 1933 — 407
Reporting marks: NOGN
Historical and technical societies: Gulf, Mobile & Ohio Historical Society, P. O. Box 24, Bedford Park, IL 60499
Recommended reading: *The Gulf, Mobile and Ohio*, by James Hutton Lemly, published in 1953 by Richard D. Irwin, Inc., Homewood, IL 60430
Successors:
Gulf, Mobile & Northern
Gulf, Mobile & Ohio
Illinois Central Gulf (TWG)
Portions still operated: Slidell, La.-Wanilla, Miss.; Slidell-Covington, La.; Elton-Jackson, Miss.: Illinois Central Gulf
Map: See page 151

NEW YORK CENTRAL SYSTEM

The New York Central was a large railroad, and it had several subsidiaries whose identity remained strong, not so much in cars and locomotives carrying the old name but in local loyalties: If you lived in Detroit, you rode to Chicago on the Michigan Central, not the New York Central; Conrail's line across Massachusetts is still known as "the Boston & Albany."

NYC's history is easier to digest in small pieces: first New York Central followed by its two major leased lines, Boston & Albany and Toledo & Ohio Central; then Michigan Central and Big Four (Cleveland, Cincinnati, Chicago & St. Louis). By the mid-1960s NYC owned 99.8 percent of the stock of Michigan Central and more than 97 percent of the stock of the Big Four. NYC leased both on February 1, 1930, but they remained separate companies to avoid the complexities of merger.

In broad geographic terms, the New York Central proper was everything east of Buffalo plus a line from Buffalo through Cleveland and Toledo to Chicago (the former Lake Shore & Michigan Southern). NYC included the Ohio Central Lines (Toledo through Columbus to and beyond Charleston, West Virginia) and the Boston & Albany (neatly defined by

its name). The Michigan Central was a Buffalo-Detroit-Chicago line and everything in Michigan north of that. The Big Four was everything south of NYC's Cleveland-Toledo-Chicago line other than the Ohio Central.

The New York Central System included several controlled railroads that did not accompany NYC into the Penn Central merger. The most important of these were (with the proportion of NYC ownership in the mid-1960s):

● Pittsburgh & Lake Erie (80 percent owned by NYC — now independent)

● Indiana Harbor Belt (NYC, 30 percent; Michigan Central, 30 percent; Chicago & North Western, 20 percent; and Milwaukee Road, 20 percent — now half Conrail and half Milwaukee Road)

● Toronto, Hamilton & Buffalo (NYC, 37 percent; MC, 22 percent; Canada Southern, 14 percent; and Canadian Pacific, 27 percent — CP became sole owner in 1977)

New York Central: The Erie Canal, opened in 1825 between Albany and Buffalo, New York, followed the Hudson and Mohawk rivers between Albany and Schenectady. The 40-mile water route included several locks and was extremely slow; in consequence, stagecoaches plied the 17-mile direct route between the cities. In 1826 the Mohawk & Hudson Rail Road

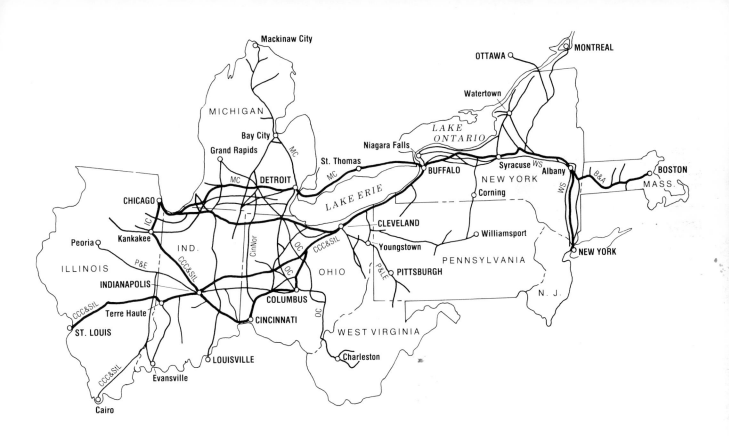

Mackinaw City

MICHIGAN

Bay City

Grand Rapids

MC

DETROIT

MC

CHICAGO

St. Thomas

Niagara Falls

LAKE ERIE

BUFFALO

LAKE ONTARIO

OTTAWA

MONTREAL

Watertown

Syracuse WS Albany

Corning

NEW YORK

WS

B&A

BOSTON

MASS.

Peoria

Kankakee

IC

IND.

CinNor

OC

CCC&StL

CLEVELAND

Youngstown

WILLIAMSPORT

PENNSYLVANIA

NEW YORK

ILLINOIS

P&E

CCC&StL

INDIANAPOLIS

Terre Haute

OC

OHIO

P&LE

PITTSBURGH

N. J.

CCC&StL

ST. LOUIS

COLUMBUS

CINCINNATI

OC

LOUISVILLE

WEST VIRGINIA

Charleston

Evansville

CCC&StL

Cairo

207

CORNELIUS VANDERBILT (1794-1877) was born into a farming family on Staten Island. He received little education and went to work early. At 16 he bought a small boat and began ferry service between Staten Island and Manhattan. In 1813 he married Sophia Johnson, a cousin, and began to build a family that eventually numbered nine daughters and four sons (one of whom died in infancy). Vanderbilt's ferry business expanded and prospered, first to a New York-New

NYC

Brunswick (New Jersey) line, then out Long Island Sound to Stonington, Connecticut. His shipping interests later included a system of ships and stagecoaches from New York to California via Nicaragua and a transatlantic route. Vanderbilt's shipping activities got him the nickname "Commodore."

His shipping activities also brought him into contact with railroads, and he held directorships of several of the railroads that connected with his boats. In 1857 he acquired control of the New York & Harlem Railroad. It was a weak railroad; its chief asset was its line the length of Manhattan Island. In 1863 Vanderbilt bought control of the Hudson River Railroad, which competed with the New York & Harlem, and in 1864 he bought a block of New

York Central stock. Vanderbilt attempted to gain control of the Erie in 1867 but failed; the event was his only unsuccessful bid to acquire a railroad. Throughout his later years he continued to buy NYC stock to maintain control of the road.

In his declining years the Commodore took up a belief in spiritualism, attending seances and asking the spirits for information on the future of the stock market. His wife Sophia died in 1868 after a long period during which they had grown apart; not long afterward the Commodore married Miss Frank Crawford, thirtyish, of Mobile, Alabama. The hero of the Commodore's early years, William Henry Harrison, had been replaced in his esteem by George Washington. Vanderbilt proposed an enormous monument to Washington in New York's Central Park, but his wife's pastor suggested to him that it would be more practical to endow a university. In 1873 Vanderbilt gave a million dollars to Central University in Nashville, Tennessee; the university changed its name to Vanderbilt in his honor.

The Commodore was concerned about the future of his railroad empire, and he arranged his will so that nearly all of his $100 million estate went to his son William H. and to William's sons, in particular Cornelius II. The Commodore died in 1877 and was buried in the family vault in a Moravian cemetery on Staten Island.
Recommended reading: *Commodore Vanderbilt*, by Wheaton J. Lane, published in 1942 by Alfred A. Knopf, New York, N. Y.

---

was incorporated to replace the stages between Albany and Schenectady. The railroad opened in 1831; its first locomotive was named *DeWitt Clinton* after the governor of the state when the M&H was incorporated. Within months there was a proposal for a railroad all the way from Albany to Buffalo, but the subject was touchy — the state was still deeply in debt for the construction of the Erie Canal.

One by one, railroads were incorporated, built, and opened westward from the end of the Mohawk & Hudson: Utica & Schenectady, Syracuse &

Utica, Auburn & Syracuse, Auburn & Rochester, Tonawanda (Rochester to Attica via Batavia), and Attica & Buffalo. By 1841 it was possible to travel between Albany and Buffalo by train in just 25 hours (lightning speed compared with the canal packets); by 1851 the trip took a little over 12 hours. In 1851 the state passed an act freeing the railroads from the need to pay tolls to the Erie Canal, with which they competed; that same year the Hudson River Railroad was opened from New York to East Albany and the New York & Erie (later the Erie Railroad) was opened from

Piermont, on the Hudson River, west to Dunkirk, N. Y., on Lake Erie.

From the beginning the railroads between Albany and Buffalo had cooperated in running through service. In 1853 they were consolidated as the New York Central Railroad — the roads mentioned above or their successors plus the Schenectady & Troy, the Buffalo & Lockport, and the Rochester, Lockport & Niagara Falls — and two unbuilt roads, the Mohawk Valley and the Syracuse & Utica Direct.

The New York & Harlem Railroad was incorporated in 1831 to build a line in Manhattan from 23rd Street north to 129th Street between Third and Eighth avenues (the railroad chose to follow Fourth Avenue). At first the railroad was primarily a horsecar system, but in 1840 the road's charter was amended to allow it to build north toward Albany. In 1844 the rails reached White Plains and in January 1852 the New York & Harlem made connection with the Western Railroad (later Boston & Albany) at Chatham, N. Y., creating a New York-Albany rail route.

The Hudson was a busy river, and the towns along it felt no need of a railroad — except during the winter when ice prevented navigation. Poughkeepsie interests organized the Hudson River Railroad in 1847. In the autumn of 1851 the road was opened from a terminal on Manhattan's west side all the way to East Albany. By then the road had leased the Troy & Greenbush, gaining access to a bridge over the Hudson at Troy. (A bridge at Albany was opened in 1866.)

By 1863 Cornelius Vanderbilt controlled the New York & Harlem and had acquired a substantial interest in the Hudson River Railroad. In 1867 he obtained control of the New York Central, consolidating it with the Hudson River in 1869 to form the New York Central & Hudson River Railroad. (For simplicity I will refer to the NYC&HR as "NYC," "Central," or "New York Central.")

Vanderbilt wanted to build a magnificent terminal for the NYC&HR in New York and chose as its site the corner of 42nd Street and Fourth Avenue on the New York & Harlem, the southerly limit of steam locomotive operation in Manhattan. Construction of Grand Central Depot began in 1869 and took two years. The new depot was actually three separate stations serving the NYC&HR, the New York & Harlem, and the New Haven. Trains of the Hudson River line reached the New York & Harlem by means of a connecting track completed in 1871 along Spuyten Duyvil

Creek and the Harlem River (they have since become a single waterway).

That was the first of three Grand Centrals. The present station, Grand Central Terminal, was opened in 1913. Superlatives are inadequate; GCT has a total of 48 platform tracks on two subterranean levels; the project included depressing and decking over the tracks along Park Avenue and electrifying NYC's lines north to Harmon and White Plains. Even in the space age Grand Central remains awesome. (NYC had two other stretches of electrified line: the Detroit River Tunnel, opened in 1910, and Cleveland Union Terminal, opened in 1930. Diesels put an end to both those electrifications in 1953.)

The Watertown & Rome Railroad was chartered in 1832 to connect Watertown, N. Y., with the Syracuse & Utica, then only a proposal itself. The road opened in 1851, and in 1852 it was extended to Cape Vincent, where it connected with a ferry to Kingston, Ontario. In 1861 the W&R consolidated with the Potsdam & Watertown to form the Rome, Watertown & Ogdensburg. The RW&O built a line to Oswego and bought lines to Syracuse and Buffalo. The line to Buffalo was a mistake — it bypassed Rochester, had almost no local business, and was not part of any through route. The RW&O came under Lackawanna control briefly before a rehabilitation in the 1880s. New management extended the RW&O north to connect with a Grand Trunk line to Montreal and added the Black River & Utica (Utica to Watertown and Ogdensburg) to the system. NYC leased the RW&O in 1893. Meanwhile, NYC had built its own line north from Herkimer: the St. Lawrence & Adirondack (later Mohawk & Malone) of William Seward Webb, son-in-law of William H. Vanderbilt. NYC merged the Mohawk & Malone in 1911 and the RW&O in 1913.

Lake Shore & Michigan Southern: The Michigan Southern was chartered by the state of Michigan in 1837 to build from the head of navigation on the River Raisin west of Monroe across the southern tier of Michigan to the shore of Lake Michigan at New Buffalo. Under state auspices it got as far west as Hillsdale, Mich. It was sold to private interests which combined it with the Erie & Kalamazoo (opened in 1837 from Toledo, Ohio, to Adrian, Mich.) and extended it west to meet the Northern Indiana Railroad, which was building east from La Porte, Ind. The line was opened from Monroe to South Bend in 1851; by February 1852 it reached Chicago, where it teamed up with the Rock Island to build termi-

NYC

In 1892 New York Central built a replica of the *DeWitt Clinton* and its train, shown here with engineer, passengers, and crew carefully retouched in.

nal facilities (Northern Indiana's successors shared a Chicago station — La Salle Street — with Rock Island until 1968). The roads were combined as the Michigan Southern & Northern Indiana in 1855; by then a direct line between Elkhart, Ind., and Toledo had been constructed.

The railroad situation along the south shore of Lake Erie was complicated by Ohio's insistence on a track gauge of 4'10", Pennsylvania's reluctance to let a railroad from another state cross its borders, and the desire of the city of Erie, Pa., to have the change of gauge within its limits in the hope that passengers would spend money while changing trains there. (Such thinking continues today; oil companies put their gas stations at corners with traffic signals.) The NYC controlled the Buffalo & State Line and the Erie & North East railroads by 1853; they were combined as the Buffalo & Erie in 1867. The Cleveland, Painesville & Ashtabula was opened between Cleveland and Erie in 1852. In 1868 the CP&A took its familiar name, Lake Shore, as its official name, and a year later it absorbed the Cleveland & Toledo and joined with the Michigan Southern &

Northern Indiana to form the Lake Shore & Michigan Southern. Cornelius Vanderbilt acquired control of the LS&MS during a business panic about that time.

In 1914 the New York Central & Hudson River and the Lake Shore & Michigan Southern (and several smaller roads) were combined to form the New York Central Railroad — the second railroad of that name.

West Shore: In 1869 and 1870 several railroads were proposed and surveyed up the west bank of the Hudson River; in 1880 the New York, West Shore & Buffalo Railroad was formed to build a line from Jersey City to Albany and Buffalo, parallel to the New York Central. William Vanderbilt suspected the Pennsylvania Railroad was behind the project. The road opened to Albany and Syracuse in 1883 and reached Buffalo at the beginning of 1884. A rate war ensued. The West Shore entered bankruptcy, as did the construction company that built the line. West Shore cut its rates to beat those of the NYC, hoping the Central, with its far greater volume of business, would lose a lot more money than the West Shore. Central, however, had resources to withstand a temporary loss.

In retaliation Vanderbilt decided to revive an old survey for a railroad across Pennsylvania. The surveyed route was considerably shorter than that of the Pennsylvania Railroad. He enlisted the support of Andrew Carnegie and John D. Rockefeller. Meanwhile, Pennsy bought West Shore bonds. It took J. P. Morgan to work a compromise between the NYC and the Pennsylvania: The Central would lease the West Shore, and the Pennsy would get the South Pennsylvania and its partially excavated tunnels. In 1885 the West Shore was reorganized as the West Shore Railroad, wholly owned by the NYC and leased to it. (The roadbed of the South Pennsylvania was later used for the Pennsylvania Turnpike.) The Weehawken-Albany portion of the West Shore proved to be a valuable freight route for NYC and more so for its successors Penn Central and Conrail; most of the West Shore west of Albany has been abandoned. In 1952 NYC merged the West Shore.

Boston & Albany: The Boston & Worcester Railroad was opened between the cities of its name in 1835. Its charter had a clause prohibiting the construction of a parallel railroad within 5 miles for 30 years. The Western Railroad was opened in 1840 from Worcester west to Springfield and in 1841 across the Berkshire range to Greenbush, N. Y., on the east

WILLIAM HENRY VANDERBILT

(1821-1885) was the Commodore's oldest son. During his youth he was a considerable disappointment to his father, who considered him dull and backward. Soon after William married Maria Kissam his health failed, and the Commodore installed him on a marginal farm on Staten Island. When William made a success of farming and was able to enlarge the estate, his father began to think better of him. This paternal admiration increased when William negotiated for manure from the Commodore's stables at $4 a load. As William prepared to sail for Staten Island with a large scow loaded with manure, the Commodore asked how many loads were on the scow. William said "One." William later was made manager of the Staten Island Railroad, one of the Commodore's properties, and soon was brought onto the board of the New York & Harlem.

NYC

It was William, not the Commodore, who advocated the idea of extending the New York Central to Chicago. The Commodore was not in favor of the idea; he in effect harrumphed, "Chicago — next you'll want to extend the road to San Francisco or even to China."

In 1883 William resigned from the presidency of the NYC because of failing health — high blood pressure, a stroke, and blindness in one eye. He owned 87 percent of the stock of the railroad and asked J. P. Morgan if he could sell the majority of it without causing a panic. He did so with the condition that he or his nominee hold a seat on NYC's board. William retained his interest in the South Pennsylvania, however (see page 210). A few days after the South Penn-West Shore affair was finally resolved in 1885, William was conversing in his office with Robert Garrett, president of the Baltimore & Ohio, and suddenly collapsed and died.

A number of other members of the Vanderbilt family were active in New York Central affairs: William Henry's sons Cornelius II (1843-1899), William K. (1849-1920), and Frederick William (1856-1938); William K.'s sons William K. Jr. (1878-1944) and Harold S. (1884-1970), the last Vanderbilt to serve on NYC's board of directors; the Commodore's sons-in-law Daniel Torrance and Horace F. Clark; and William Henry's son-in-law William Seward Webb. William K.'s fourth son, George Washington (1862-1914), assembled and gave to the nation the Pisgah National Forest. Later Vanderbilts have been active in horse and yacht racing; artist and designer Gloria Vanderbilt is a granddaughter of Cornelius II.

bank of the Hudson opposite Albany. The two railroads shared some directors, but efforts at merging them were futile until 1863, when B&W's protection clause expired and the Western proposed building its own line from Worcester to Boston. The two roads were consolidated as the Boston & Albany Railroad in 1867.

The B&A had several minor branches and a few major ones: Palmer to Winchendon, Mass.; Springfield to Athol, Mass.; Pittsfield to North Adams, Mass.; and Chatham to Hudson, N. Y. — only short portions of them remain in service.

The B&A's principal connection was the New York Central at Albany.

The New York Central leased the B&A in 1900. The reason for B&A's willingness to forsake independence is probably that NYC would acquire the parallel Fitchburg Railroad (now Boston & Maine) were it unable to get the B&A, and B&A would be left with only local business. In 1961 NYC merged the Boston & Albany.

B&A maintained much more of its own identity than did other NYC subsidiaries. It had its own officers, and until 1951 its locomotives and cars were lettered "Boston & Albany" rather than "New York Central Lines," largely to appeal to local sensitivities. B&A's steam power was basically of NYC appearance but with occasional distinctive features, such as square sand domes on the Hudsons and offset smokebox doors on Pacifics. The profile of the B&A, definitely not the water level route NYC was so proud of elsewhere, called for heavy power in the form of 2-6-6-2s and 2-8-4s (the latter named for the Berkshires over which the line ran). Nearer Boston, B&A ran an intense suburban service powered by 2-6-6Ts and 4-6-6Ts, the latter looking like condensed, solid-pack NYC Hudsons.

Ohio Central Lines included the Toledo & Ohio Central Railway and three leased lines (merged in 1938), the Zanesville & Western Railway, the Kanawha & Michigan Railway, and the Kanawha & West Virginia Railroad. They formed a route from Toledo southeast through Columbus, across the Ohio River, and through Charleston to Swiss and Hitop, West Virginia. The line began as the Atlantic & Lake Erie, chartered in 1869. After a series of receiverships and a name change to Ohio Central the line managed to link Columbus with the Ohio River at Middleport in 1882. The road then pushed into the coalfields along the Kanawha River in West Virginia and extended itself northwest toward Toledo. It was renamed the Toledo & Ohio Central in 1885. The NYC acquired control of the T&OC by 1910 and began operating it as part of the New York Central System. NYC leased the road in 1922 and merged it in 1952. In recent years Penn Central revived the road's identity with the "TOC" reporting marks.

Michigan Central had its beginnings in the Detroit & St. Joseph Railroad, which was incorporated in 1832 to build a railroad across Michigan from Detroit to St. Joseph. Michigan attained statehood in 1837 and almost immediately chartered railroads to be constructed along three routes: the Northern, from Port Huron to the head of navigation on the Grand River; the Central, from Detroit to St. Joseph; and the Southern, from the head of navigation on the River Raisin, west of Monroe, to New Buffalo.

The state purchased the Detroit & St. Joseph to use as the basis for the Central Railroad. About the time the road reached Kalamazoo (in 1846) it ran out of money. It was purchased from the state by Boston interests led by John W. Brooks and was reorganized as the Michigan Central Railroad. Construction resumed in the direction of New Buffalo rather than St. Joseph, and in 1849 the line reached Michigan City, Ind., about as far as its Michigan charter could take it.

To reach the Illinois border the Michigan Central used the charter of the New Albany & Salem (a predecessor of the Monon) in exchange for which it purchased a block of NA&S stock. The MC continued on Illinois Central rails to Chicago, reaching there in 1852.

The Great Western Railway opened in 1854 from Niagara Falls to Windsor, Ont., opposite Detroit, and in March 1855 John Roebling's suspension bridge across the Niagara River was completed, creating with the New York Central a continuous line of rails from Albany to Windsor. The Great Western (which had a track gauge of 5′6″) installed a third rail for standard gauge equipment between 1864 and 1866. Vanderbilt, who had started buying Michigan Central stock in 1869, tried to purchase the Great Western. He did not succeed and turned his attention instead to the Canada Southern. It had been incorporated in 1868 as the Erie & Niagara Extension Railway to build a line along the north shore of Lake Erie and then across the Detroit River below the city of Detroit. He acquired the road in 1876; Michigan Central leased it in 1882. Conrail sold the Canada Southern to Canadian Pacific and Canadian National in 1985. New York Central leased the Michigan Central in 1930.

Cleveland, Cincinnati, Chicago & St. Louis (Big Four): The oldest predecessor of the Big Four (and a comparatively late addition to it) was the Mad River & Lake Erie. Ground was broken in 1835, and the line was opened from Sandusky to Dayton, Ohio, in 1851. It went through several renamings and became part of what later was the Peoria & Eastern before it was merged into the CCC&StL in 1890.

The Cleveland, Columbus & Cincinnati was chartered in 1836, broke ground in 1847, and opened in 1851 between Cleveland and Columbus. In 1852 it teamed up with the Little Miami and Columbus & Xenia railroads to form a Cleveland-Cincinnati route.

In 1848 the Indianapolis & Bellefontaine and the Bellefontaine & Indiana railroads were incorporated to build a line between Galion, Ohio, on the CC&C, and Indianapolis. The I&B and the B&I amalgamated and became known as "The B. Line." They were absorbed by the CC&C when it reorganized as the Cleveland, Columbus, Cincinnati & Indianapolis in 1868. The nickname of the new road was "The Bee Line." The Cleveland, Columbus, Cincinnati & Indianapolis reached Cincinnati with its own rails in 1872; that same year it opened a line from Springfield to Columbus. By then the Vanderbilts owned a good portion of the road's stock.

The Terre Haute & Alton Railroad was organized in 1852; its backers were certain that with a railroad to Indiana the Mississippi River town of Alton, Ill., could easily outstrip St. Louis a few miles south. It soon combined with the Belleville & Illinoistown Railroad (Illinoistown is now East St. Louis) as the Terre Haute, Alton & St. Louis. The Indianapolis & St. Louis was organized to build between Indianapolis and Terre Haute. It leased the St. Louis, Alton & Terre Haute, successor to the Terre Haute, Alton & St. Louis, and came under control of the CCC&I in 1882.

In the late 1840s and early 1850s several railroads were completed forming a route from Cincinnati through Indianapolis and Lafayette, Ind., to Kankakee, Ill., connecting there with the Illinois Central north to Chicago. In 1880 these roads were united as the Cincinnati, Indianapolis, St. Louis & Chicago — which some consider the first "Big Four." Heading the company was Melville Ingalls, and on its board was C. P. Huntington, whose Chesapeake & Ohio formed a friendly connection at Cincinnati.

NYC advertised itself as "The Water Level Route," so "Mountain" would hardly be an appropriate name for its 4-8-2 type. Thus it's a Mohawk wheeling freight west through Waterloo, Ind., 367 miles west of Buffalo, N. Y., in 1948.

Robert A. Hadley

213

NYC wasn't all four-track main lines and glossy streamliners. J-1 Hudson 5340 stops at Lake Orion, Mich., between Bay City and Detroit, at 3:22 p.m. on June 3, 1949. However, on the rear of this secondary-line local train is a new all-room streamlined sleeping car which will be in Grand Central Terminal tomorrow morning at seven.

Elmer Treloar

The Vanderbilts had invested in the first Big Four, and they were firmly in control of the new Big Four, the Cleveland, Cincinnati, Chicago & St. Louis, which was formed in 1889 by the consolidation of the old Big Four (Cincinnati, Indianapolis, St. Louis & Chicago) and the Bee Line (Cleveland, Columbus, Cincinnati & Indianapolis).

In the late 1880s Ingalls and the Vanderbilts gathered in a group of railroads between Cairo and Danville, Ill.; added to them the St. Louis, Alton & Terre Haute; and then added them all to the Big Four. The line from Danville north to Indiana Harbor was a comparatively late addition to the system: It was built in 1906 and became part of the New York Central rather than the Big Four.

The Peoria & Eastern was formed in 1890 from several small roads. At one time its predecessor briefly included the former Mad River & Lake Erie and a line from Indianapolis east to Springfield, Ohio, before settling down to be simply a Peoria-Bloomington-Danville-Indianapolis route. In 1902 the Big Four bought the Cincinnati Northern, a line that had been proposed in 1852 and finally constructed in the 1880s from Franklin, Ohio, between Dayton and Cincinnati, to Jackson, Mich. In 1920 the Big

Four acquired the Evansville, Indianapolis & Terre Haute, a castoff from the Chicago & Eastern Illinois in southwestern Indiana. The New York Central leased the Big Four in 1930.

The New York Central System was the largest of the eastern trunk systems from the standpoint of mileage and second only to the Pennsylvania in revenue. It served most of the industrial part of the country, and its freight tonnage was exceeded only by the coal-carrying railroads. In addition it was a major passenger railroad — with perhaps two-thirds the number of passengers as the Pennsylvania, but NYC's average passenger traveled one-third again as far as Pennsy's. NYC did not share as fully in the postwar prosperity because of rising labor and material costs and an extensive improvement program, especially for passenger service.

In 1946 and 1947 Chesapeake & Ohio purchased a block of NYC stock (6.4 percent), becoming the road's largest stockholder. Robert R. Young gained control of New York Central and became its chairman in 1954 as part of a maneuver to merge it with C&O. One of his first acts was to put Alfred E. Perlman in charge of the Central.

Under Perlman NYC slimmed its physical plant, reducing long stretches of four-track line to two tracks under Centralized Traffic Control, and developed an aggressive freight marketing department. At the same time NYC's passenger operations were de-emphasized. On December 3, 1967, just before NYC and Pennsy merged, the Central reduced its passenger service to a skeleton, combining its New York-Chicago, New York-Detroit, New York-Toronto, and Boston-Chicago services into a single train and dropping all train names (including that of the *Twentieth Century Limited*, once considered the world's finest train) except for, curiously, that of the Chicago-Cincinnati *James Whitcomb Riley*.

The Central's archrival was the Pennsylvania Railroad. West of Buffalo and Pittsburgh the two systems duplicated each other at almost every major point; east of those cities the two hardly touched. Both roads had physical plant not being used to capacity (NYC was in better shape); both had a heavy passenger business; neither was earning much money. In 1957 NYC and Pennsy announced merger talks.

The initial industry reaction was utter surprise. "Who? Why?" Every merger proposal for decades had tried to balance the Central against the Pennsy and create two, three, or four more-or-less equal systems in the east. Traditionally Pennsy had been allied with Norfolk & Western and Wabash; New York Central with Baltimore & Ohio, Reading, and maybe the Lackawanna; and everyone else swept up with Erie and Nickel Plate. Tradition also favored end-to-end mergers rather than those of parallel roads.

Planning and justifying the merger took nearly ten years, during which time the eastern railroad scene changed radically, in large measure because of the impending merger of NYC and PRR: Erie merged with Lackawanna, Chesapeake & Ohio acquired control of Baltimore & Ohio, and Norfolk & Western took in Virginian, Wabash, Nickel Plate, Pittsburgh & West Virginia, and Akron, Canton & Youngstown. Tradition aside, though, the New York Central and the Pennsylvania merged on February 1, 1967, to form Penn Central.

Location of headquarters: New York, New York

New York Central, including Boston & Albany and Ohio Central
    Miles of railroad operated: 1929 — 6,915
    Number of locomotives: 1929 — 3,472
    Number of passenger cars: 1929 — 3,866
    Number of freight cars: 1929 — 138,199
    Number of company service cars: 1929 — 9,533

Michigan Central
    Miles of railroad operated: 1929 — 1,858
    Number of locomotives: 1929 — 500
    Number of passenger cars: 1929 — 337
    Number of freight cars: 1929 — 16,303
    Number of company service cars: 1929 — 1,187

Big Four, including Peoria & Eastern
    Miles of railroad operated: 1929 — 2,399
    Number of locomotives: 1929 — 925
    Number of passenger cars: 1929 — 615
    Number of freight cars: 1929 — 40,996
    Number of company service cars: 1929 — 1,137

New York Central
    Miles of railroad operated: 1967 — 9,696
    Number of locomotives: 1967 — 1,917
    Number of passenger cars: 1967 — 2,085

Number of freight cars: 1929 — 78,172
Number of company service cars: 1967 — 2,650
Reporting marks: NYC, B&A, CASO, CCC&StL, MCRR, P&E, P&LE, PMcK&Y, CRI, IHB
Notable named passenger trains: *Twentieth Century Limited, Commodore Vanderbilt, Pacemaker* (New York-Chicago), *Mercury* (Detroit-Cleveland, Detroit-Chicago), *Detroiter* (New York-Detroit), *Cleveland Limited* (New York-Cleveland), *Empire State Express* (New York-Buffalo-Cleveland/Detroit), *New England States* (Boston-Chicago), *Southwestern Limited* (New York-St. Louis), *Ohio State Limited* (New York-Cincinnati), *James Whitcomb Riley* (Cincinnati-Chicago)

Historical and technical societies: New York Central System Historical Society, P. O. Box 745, Mentor OH 44060
Recommended reading: *The Road of the Century*, by Alvin F. Harlow, published in 1947 by Creative Age Press, New York, New York
Predecessor railroads in this book: Ulster & Delaware

The Boston & Albany was an exception to NYC's water-level profile. Two E8s are working hard to lift train 27, *The New England States*, over the summit of the Berkshires in western Massachusetts in the early 1950s.

Jim Shaughnessy

Successors:
Penn Central
Conrail (TWG)
Metro-North (TWG)
Major portions operated by roads other than Conrail and *major portions abandoned*:
(The size and complexity of the NYC calls for a slightly different format here. This is not an exhaustive list of what is gone and what remains. In some cases I have shown an entire line as abandoned, even though short stubs remain where it crossed other lines.)
New York Central
Hannibal-Webster, N. Y.: Ontario Midland
Pittsfield-Saline, Mich.: Michigan Interstate (Ann Arbor)
Litchfield-Hillsdale-Steubenville, Ind.: Hillsdale County
East View-Brewster, N. Y. (Putnam Division); Millerton-Chatham, N. Y. (New York & Harlem); Herkimer-Remsen, N. Y.-Adirondack Jct., Que.; Tupper Lake Jct., N. Y.-Ottawa, Ont.; Philadelphia-Ogdensburg, N. Y.; Carthage-Cape Vincent, N. Y.; Pulaski-Oswego, N. Y.; Webster-Niagara Falls, N. Y.; Batavia-North Tonawanda, N. Y.; Fredonia, N. Y.-North Warren, Pa.; Litchfield-Lansing, Mich.; Otsego-Grand Rapids, Mich.; Ypsilanti-Pittsfield, Mich.; Saline-Hillsdale, Mich.; Jackson-Bankers, Mich.; Steubenville-Fort Wayne, Ind.
West Shore
Kingston-Oneonta (ex-Ulster & Delaware); South Amsterdam-Utica;
Utica-Rochester; Rochester-Oakfield, N. Y.
Boston & Albany
North Adams Jct.-North Adams, Mass.: Boston & Maine
Post Road Crossing-Rensselaer, N. Y.: Amtrak
South Barre-Winchendon; Ludlow-Athol, Mass.; Chatham-Claverack, N. Y.
Ohio Central
Fostoria-Thurston, Ohio; St. Marys-Peoria, Ohio
Michigan Central
Bay City-Mackinaw City: Detroit & Mackinac
Kalamazoo, Mich.-Michigan City, Ind.: Amtrak
Canada Southern lines: Canadian National and Canadian Pacific
Carleton-Marshall, Mich.; Battle Creek, Mich.-Shipshewana, Ind.; Monroe-Hillsdale, Mich. (original Michigan Southern route)
Big Four
Brookville, Ind.-Valley Jct., Ohio: Indiana & Ohio
Sheldon-Kankakee, Ill.: Kankakee, Beaverville & Southern
Mt. Carmel-Cairo, Ill.: Southern
Mitchell-Pana, Ill.: Missouri Pacific
Springfield, Ohio-Shirley, Ind.; Greensburg-Nabb, Ind.; New Castle-Brookville, Ind.; Goshen, Ind.-Niles, Mich.; Paris-Pana, Ill.; Hillsboro-Alton, Ill.; Kankakee-Seneca, Ill.
Bloomington-Tremont, Ill. (Peoria & Eastern)
Greenville, Ohio-Jackson, Mich. (Cincinnati Northern)

NEW YORK, CHICAGO & ST. LOUIS RAILROAD

In 1879 and 1880 a syndicate headed by George I. Seney, a New York banker, assembled the Lake Erie & Western Railway, a line from Fremont, Ohio, to Bloomington, Illinois. After a dispute with the New York Central System about the routing of freight, Seney decided to build a line to connect the LE&W to Cleveland. He incorporated the New York, Chicago & St. Louis Railway in 1881 as a Buffalo-Chicago project. About this time it was referred to by a Norwalk, Ohio, newspaper as the "great double-track nickel-plated railroad" and the nickname stuck. (That's one

theory about the name; another hinges on the pronunciation of "NYCL.")

The line was completed in August 1882. William H. Vanderbilt offered to buy off Seney during its construction and then threatened to starve it of traffic — from Cleveland to Buffalo it was parallel to Vanderbilt's Lake Shore & Michigan Southern. Jay Gould began to negotiate to purchase the road; to block Gould, Vanderbilt purchased it instead and installed his son William K. Vanderbilt as president in 1883. Then he wondered what to do with it — benign neglect is what happened. Even

O. P. Van Sweringen

ORIS PAXTON VAN SWERING-EN (1879-1936) and brother **MAN-TIS JAMES VAN SWERINGEN** (1881-1935) were born near Wooster, Ohio. Their father, injured in the Civil War, never held a job for long, and their mother died in 1886. Soon afterward the family moved to Cleveland. The boys — indeed the entire family — were supported by an older brother, Herbert, and raised by an older sister. O. P. and M. J., as they were known, attended school through the eighth grade, then had a succession of odd jobs. The brothers had long been intrigued by the real estate business. They began in a small way, buying and quickly reselling one house. They rapidly expanded their business on capital provided by others — a characteristic of the Vans' financial dealings. Within a few years they were subdividing large blocks of properties on Cleveland's east side to create upper-class suburbs. Chief among these was Shaker Heights, an elegant, well-planned community.

Shaker Heights needed transportation. The Vans could not persuade the Cleveland Railway to extend streetcar service, so they purchased a right of way along a ravine between Shaker Heights and downtown Cleveland, bought property for a terminal on Cleveland's Public Square, and organized the Cleveland & Youngstown Railroad. The Vans did not have money to build the

though it was no more than a secondary line in the Vanderbilt system, it gained a reputation for fast movement of perishables, particularly meat.

In 1916 Cleveland real estate developers Oris Paxton Van Sweringen and Mantis James Van Sweringen bought NYC's interest in the Nickel Plate. NYC recognized that the Clayton Antitrust Act would require selling NKP; selling it to the Van Sweringen brothers would keep it out of the clutches of the Lackawanna or the Pennsylvania. The Van Sweringens were suddenly in the railroad business, and to run their railroad they chose John Bernet of the NYC. Bernet worked a thorough upgrading of NKP's locomotives and track, with the result that by 1925 the road had doubled its freight tonnage and average speed, halved its fuel consumption per ton mile, and led all U. S. roads in car miles per day.

The ICC merger plan of the 1920s grouped NKP with Lake Erie & Western; Toledo, St. Louis & Western; Wheeling & Lake Erie; Lehigh Valley; and Pittsburgh & West Virginia. In 1922 the Van Sweringens ac-

quired both the LE&W, an unprofitable ward of the NYC, and the TStL&W (the Clover Leaf), which was in receivership because it had defaulted on the bonds it issued to gain control of the Alton.

Lake Erie & Western: The Lake Erie & Western Railway was formed in 1879 to consolidate smaller railroads between Fremont, Ohio, and

218

railroad, but they negotiated with Alfred H. Smith of the New York Central to trade portions of their right of way for financing.

Then O. P. and M. J. ran into the Nickel Plate Road, which owned property where they wanted to locate their transit line. NYC owned the Nickel Plate, which paralleled NYC for its entire length. At the time, the U. S. Justice Department was concerned about monopolies and trusts. The Van Sweringens made an offer for the

M. J. Van Sweringen

Nickel Plate, and NYC decided they would be a far better purchaser than someone like the Pennsylvania Railroad. In 1916 the Vans had a railroad.

Cleveland had long wanted and needed a Union Station; the Van Sweringens proposed building such a station to serve all the interurbans and steam railroads on their Public Square property. After lengthy debate and negotiation, construction of Cleveland Union Terminal, owned by Nickel Plate, New York Central, and Big Four, began in 1923. The terminal opened in 1930.

The various merger plans proposed by the ICC in the early 1920s set the Vans in motion toward a railroad empire. In 1922 they acquired the Toledo, St. Louis & Western (the Clover Leaf) for access to St. Louis. That same year they purchased the Lake Erie & Western from the New York Central to put the Nickel

Plate into Peoria. The Vans set up a new holding company, Vaness Company, for their properties, and they managed to get an enlarged Nickel Plate which included the Clover Leaf and the LE&W past the ICC. They kept going, acquiring the Chesapeake & Ohio and with it the Hocking Valley, the Pere Marquette, the Erie, the Wheeling & Lake Erie, the Buffalo, Rochester & Pittsburgh, the Chicago & Eastern Illinois, and the Missouri Pacific. They formed the Alleghany Corporation to hold their railroad interests.

These purchases were not made with cash, and the Vans accumulated a debt of millions. As the Depression deepened, railroad earnings and stock prices fell; there was no money to pay interest on the debt, and the stocks were of no value as collateral for more loans. Shuffling of securities from holding company to railroad and back to holding company could not mitigate the financial problems. With an infusion of new capital, though, the Vans were able to buy back much of their empire at an auction sale in 1935.

In spite of being a major force in Cleveland, the two brothers led an almost secluded private life. In December 1935 M. J. died of heart disease. O. P. tried to carry on the business alone, but the ICC began investigating the management of the railroads, and in 1936 several of the Van Sweringen companies declared bankruptcy. In November of that year O. P. died of a heart attack while en route to New York. He was buried next to M. J.

Recommended reading: *The Van Sweringens of Cleveland*, by Ian S. Haberman, published in 1979 by Western Reserve Historical Society, Cleveland, Ohio (ISBN 0-911704-20-5)

Bloomington, Ill. In 1880 the LE&W extended its line east from Fremont to Sandusky to replace boats on the lower stretches of the Sandusky River and teamed up with the Lake Shore to offer through freight and passenger service. The Lake Shore's lack of cooperation in the matter of westbound traffic was the reason LE&W's backers built the Nickel Plate.

The LE&W nearly died during the 1880s, but the discovery of natural gas and oil along the line in Ohio and Indiana revived it. In 1887 it was reorganized and extended west to Peoria, Ill. That same year it acquired a Michigan City-Indianapolis line that crossed its main line at Tipton, Ind., and in 1890 it acquired a line from Fort Wayne to Connersville and

Rushville, Ind., a line which crossed the Lake Erie & Western at Muncie.

In 1895 the LE&W proposed assembling a line to the East Coast by using the Reading, the Buffalo, Rochester & Pittsburgh, and the Pittsburgh, Akron & Western, a former narrow gauge line from Akron to Delphos, Ohio. The PA&W was reorganized that year as the Northern Ohio and leased to the LE&W.

In 1899 the LS&MS purchased a majority interest in the LE&W and proceeded to let it decline gently. In 1920 LE&W sold the Northern Ohio to the Akron, Canton & Youngstown.

Toledo, St. Louis & Western: The Toledo, Delphos & Indianapolis was organized in 1877 and that year opened a 3-foot-gauge line a few miles north from Delphos, Ohio. Two years later it became part of the Toledo, Delphos & Burlington, a consolidation of four railroads. The TD&B had as its goal a 3-foot-gauge line from Toledo to Burlington, Iowa. The line was opened from Toledo to Kokomo, Ind., in 1880. It began extending south, buying up railroads to form a line south through Dayton to Cincinnati and Ironton, Ohio. Then it got caught up in a proposal to assemble a narrow gauge line all the way from Toledo to Mexico City.

The line was opened from Toledo to East St. Louis, Ill., in 1883 and collapsed soon afterwards. The lines south of Delphos to Cincinnati and Ironton were spun off to eventually become standard gauge pieces of the Cincinnati, Hamilton & Dayton, the Pennsylvania, and the Detroit, Toledo & Ironton. The Toledo-East St. Louis line was nearly dead when gas and oil were discovered along the line. It was reorganized as the Toledo, St. Louis & Kansas City Railroad, and it adopted a clover leaf as its emblem. Trackage east of Frankfort, Ind., was converted to standard gauge on June 25, 1887; the remainder of the line was converted two years later. The road developed a good freight business, particularly in eastbound livestock and perishables received from connections at East St. Louis.

The TStL&KC went bankrupt in 1893; the bankruptcy proceedings included William Howard Taft as judge and Benjamin Harrison as counsel. It was sold to its bondholders and became the Toledo, St. Louis & Western. The road continued as a fast freight line, particularly in competition with the Wabash. In contrast to many midwestern roads, the TStL&W got along well with neighboring interurbans, even filing joint passenger tariffs. In 1903 the Clover Leaf acquired a half interest in the Detroit &

Toledo Shore Line. In 1907 it purchased control of the Alton. The TStL&W issued bonds to finance the purchase; interest on the bonds brought on another receivership in 1914.

Nickel Plate: In 1923 the Nickel Plate, the Lake Erie & Western, and the Clover Leaf were consolidated as a new New York, Chicago & St. Louis Railroad. On the recommendation of Alfred H. Smith, president of the NYC, the Van Sweringens went after the Chesapeake & Ohio, for its coal traffic, and the Pere Marquette, for its automobile business. In 1925 the New York, Chicago & St. Louis Railway was incorporated to lease and operate the Nickel Plate, C&O, PM, Erie, and Hocking Valley. The railroad industry was in favor of the merger, but a small group of C&O stockholders fought it. In 1926 the ICC rejected the petition on financial grounds — it was in favor of it from the standpoint of transportation. Then the Van Sweringens tried again in 1926 — C&O applied to acquire PM, Erie, and Hocking Valley. The ICC rejected that in 1929.

The Van Sweringens moved Bernet to the Erie; taking his place was Walter Ross, who had been president of the Clover Leaf. He engineered an about-face for NKP's passenger service, which for years had been operated on the assumption there was no sense trying to compete with the NYC. Ross went after the long-haul passenger with comfort and personal service. The passenger renaissance lasted only until 1931, when the Depression occasioned cutbacks.

Nickel Plate came under Chesapeake & Ohio management in 1933, and Bernet was back in the presidency. He initiated a scrap drive to finance rebuilding of the Clover Leaf district, and he ordered the first 15 of a series of big 2-8-4 Berkshires that eventually numbered 80 to upgrade the road's freight power. The design of the new locomotives drew heavily on Chesapeake & Ohio's 2-10-4s. Other improvements of the late 1930s and the war years were strengthening the bridges east of Cleveland, introducing Centralized Traffic Control, and upgrading track and bridges on the Lake Erie & Western and the Clover Leaf to permit the Berkshires to work to Peoria and Madison (East St. Louis), Ill.

Nickel Plate resumed its own management in December 1942; Chesapeake & Ohio attempted merger in 1945, but NKP stockholders objected. Dieselization of passenger service began in the late 1940s, but freight continued to roll behind steam. In 1948 Nickel Plate tested a set of

A westbound Nickel Plate freight rolls along the shore of Lake Erie in April 1957 between Lorain and Vermilion, Ohio. The locomotive, Berkshire No. 779, was the last steamer built by Lima Locomotive Works.

John A. Rehor

Electro-Motive F3s and immediately ordered 10 more Berkshires (they proved to be Lima's last steam locomotives). A four-unit set of F3s could outperform the 2-8-4s, but fuel costs were greater; a Berkshire developed greater horsepower at speed than a three-unit set — and at speed was where Nickel Plate used most of its horsepower. NKP also tested General Electric's gas turbine-electric; EMD painted a pair of F7s blue and gray, like the PAs, for a demonstration on the former LE&W. Freight diesels finally began to arrive in the form of GP7s in 1951, but steam dominated mainline freight service until the business recession of 1957 and 1958. Nickel Plate was one of the last U. S. railroads to operate steam, and two of the Berkshires, 759 and 765, remain in excursion service.

In 1946 and 1947 NKP purchased approximately 80 percent of the stock of Wheeling & Lake Erie, and on December 1, 1949, NKP leased the W&LE. The Wheeling served the steel-and-coal area of Ohio and originated much of its tonnage, in contrast to NKP, thus providing balance to the NKP's bridge-route freight business. For years NKP's principal freight competitors had been the Erie and the Wabash; after 1954 the New York Central under Alfred Perlman began to become a lean, fast railroad. The Lackawanna proposed merger with Nickel Plate; NKP management rejected the union. When Lackawanna merged with Erie, it disposed of a large block of NKP stock. Norfolk & Western merged the Virginian, and the New York Central and the Pennsylvania announced their engagement. Nickel Plate, suddenly unattached, looked around, set up through freight trains with Lehigh Valley, and began merger negotia-

tions with Norfolk & Western. On October 16, 1964, N&W merged the Nickel Plate.

Location of headquarters: Cleveland, Ohio
Miles of railroad operated: 1929 — 1,691; 1963 — 2,170
Number of locomotives: 1929 — 465; 1963 — 408
Number of passenger cars: 1929 — 159; 1963 — 60
Number of freight cars: 1929 — 21,625; 1963 — 22,305
Number of company service cars: 1929 — 832; 1963 — 700
Reporting marks: NKP
Historical and technical society: Nickel Plate Road Historical & Technical Society, P. O. Box 10069, Cleveland, OH 44110
Recommended reading: *The Nickel Plate Story*, by John A. Rehor, published in 1965 by Kalmbach Publishing Co., 1027 North Seventh Street, Milwaukee, WI 53233
Subsidiaries and affiliated railroads, 1963: Detroit & Toledo Shore Line (50%, jointly with Grand Trunk Western)
Predecessor railroads in this book: Wheeling & Lake Erie
Successors: Norfolk & Western (TWG)
Portions still operated: Norfolk & Western operates all the former Nickel Plate except South Lorain-Wellington, Ohio; Massillon-Dalton, Ohio (ex-W&LE lines); Waterville-Douglas, Ohio (ex-Clover Leaf); Sandusky-Fostoria, Ohio; New Castle-Rushville, Ind; and Beesons-Connersville, Ind. (ex-LE&W). Indiana Hi-Rail Corp. operates New Castle-Rushville and Beesons-Connersville.

NEW YORK, NEW HAVEN & HARTFORD RAILROAD

The New York, New Haven & Hartford eventually gathered in nearly all the railroads in Connecticut, Rhode Island, and southeastern Massachusetts. Its four principal predecessors were the Old Colony, the New York & New England, the Central New England, and the New York & New Haven (for simplicity, the "New Haven"), which was the dominant corporation.

The Old Colony Railroad was opened in 1845 between Boston and

Plymouth, Mass. In 1854 it was consolidated with the Fall River Railroad, which had been formed in 1845 from three smaller roads to form a route from the port of Fall River, Mass., north to a junction with the Old Colony at South Braintree. In 1876 the Old Colony leased and in 1883 merged the Boston, Clinton, Fitchburg & New Bedford, which extended from New Bedford to Fitchburg, Mass., with a branch from Framingham to Lowell. The final addition to the Old Colony came in 1888 with the

PATRICK B. McGINNIS (1904-1973) was born in Palmyra, New York. After attending St. Lawrence University, Columbia University, and Brooklyn Law School, he worked in and was partner in various financial firms until 1947, when he became chairman of the board of the Norfolk Southern. He left in 1953 and, all in all, the Norfolk Southern was in better shape than when he found it. He was chairman of the board of the Central of Georgia briefly before he moved on to assume

Philip R. Hastings

the presidency of the New Haven in 1954. In 1956 he became president of the Boston & Maine, moving up to the position of chairman in 1962 and leaving the road in 1963.

Opinions on McGinnis's skill at railroad management differ widely. His careers with New Haven and B&M are remembered for the proxy contests that got him the jobs, new paint schemes designed by his wife Lucile, low-slung lightweight passenger trains that never fulfilled their promises (New Haven's were stored after a few months in Boston-New York service; B&M's Talgo was put immediately into commuter service), and financial dealings that culminated in a prison sentence for receiving kickbacks on the sale of B&M's streamlined passenger cars — ending McGinnis's career in railroading.

lease of the Boston & Providence. The B&P had been chartered in 1831 and completed in 1835 between the Massachusetts and Rhode Island cities of its name.

Most of the railroading in southeastern Massachusetts was now under the control of the Old Colony. The area was rich in industry, and the road's traffic included not only raw materials and finished goods but also coal distributed inland from the ports. The Old Colony had an intense passenger business, participating not only in an all-rail route to New York in conjunction with other lines beyond Providence but also connecting with steamers operating on Long Island Sound, principally between Fall River and New York.

Only fragments remain today of the New York & New England, which at its height reached from Boston and Providence through Hartford, Conn., to the Hudson River, with branches to Worcester and Springfield, Mass., and New London, Conn. Its oldest ancestor was the Manchester Railroad, chartered in 1833 to build east from Hartford, Conn., through Manchester to Bolton. The charter lay dormant for some years until a group of Providence, R. I., businessmen sought to build a railroad to the industrial towns of western Rhode Island and eastern Connecticut. The project quickly expanded, first taking over the Manchester charter

and then blossoming into a line from Providence to the Hudson River at Fishkill Landing (now Beacon), N. Y. The first part of the Hartford, Providence & Fishkill was opened in 1849, and by 1855 the line was in service between Providence and Waterbury, Conn.

Meanwhile two small railroads were building southwest out of Boston into the area between Providence and Worcester. The Norfolk County Railroad opened a line through Walpole to Blackstone, Mass., in 1849, and a combination of the Charles River Branch, the Charles River Railroad, and the New York & Boston assembled a line from Brookline, Mass., on the Boston & Albany, to Woonsocket, R. I., with the intention of building on through Willimantic, Conn., to New Haven. The Norfolk County became the Boston & New York Central and also headed for Willimantic, but to connect with the Hartford, Providence & Fishkill. It reorganized and changed its name several times. Among its names were Midland and Boston, Hartford & Erie, and under the latter it consolidated with the New York & Boston and the Hartford, Providence & Fishkill in 1864, creating a line chartered all the way from Boston to the Hudson River and in service from Boston to Mechanicsville, Conn. (just north of Putnam), and from Providence to Waterbury.

The BH&E entered bankruptcy in 1870 after a short period of control by the Erie Railroad and emerged as the New York & New England Railroad. NY&NE closed the Mechanicsville-Willimantic gap in eastern Connecticut in 1872 and completed the line west to the Hudson in December 1881. In 1884 the NY&NE inaugurated the *New England Limited*, a Boston-New York express operated in conjunction with the New Haven, which handled the train southwest of Willimantic. The train achieved a place in railroad lore as the "Ghost Train" in 1891 when the cars were painted white (some accounts add that the coal in the tender was sprayed with whitewash before departure each afternoon).

Every few miles NY&NE's route crossed a railroad offering a connection to New York — but nearly all those connections depended on the New Haven. The New Haven, feeling some anxiety about competition from the NY&NE, began to choke off the connections. The NY&NE turned first to the Housatonic Railroad to form a route to New York that included a ferry across Long Island Sound from Wilson's Point (south of Norwalk) to Oyster Bay and a connection with the Long Island Rail Road. The New Haven took over the Housatonic. NY&NE then turned to the New York & Northern, which it met at Brewster, N. Y. The New Haven and the New York Central had previously agreed not to compete with each other, so at the New Haven's request the New York Central acquired the New York & Northern (it became NYC's Putnam Division) to put itself briefly into and out of competition with the New Haven for Boston-New York business. The New York & New England was squeezed out again. In 1893 the Philadelphia & Reading acquired control of the NY&NE; the NY&NE was bankrupt by the end of that year. The New Haven acquired control of the New York & New England through J. P. Morgan and in 1898 leased the road.

Almost nothing remains of the Central New England. In the early 1890s under the presidency of A. A. McLeod the Philadelphia & Reading put together a group of small railroads as the Central New England & Western to form an outlet for anthracite coal. The new road took over the Hartford & Connecticut Western, which had a line reaching from Hartford to the northwestern corner of the state and then consolidated with the Poughkeepsie Bridge & Railroad Co. to form the Philadelphia, Reading & New England. In October 1893 the PR&NE gained control of the New York & New England and the Boston & Maine and even tried to

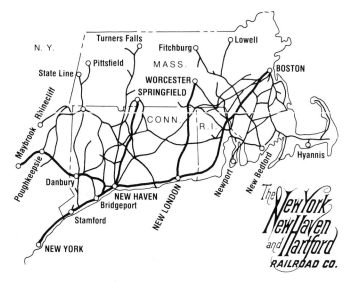

grab the Old Colony. By the end of 1893, the Philadelphia & Reading was bankrupt. The PR&NE was reorganized as the Central New England in 1899, still under Reading control. In 1904 the New Haven purchased the Central New England, thus acquiring the Poughkeepsie Bridge over the Hudson River (originally backed by the Pennsylvania; opened in 1888). The railroad was operated separately until 1927, when it was fully absorbed by the New Haven. Most of the Central New England other than the portion that formed NH's freight route to Maybrook, N. Y., was abandoned in 1938.

The New York & New Haven Railroad was a relative latecomer because of the adequacy of road and water transportation along the Connecticut coast — early railroad activity aimed inland. The Hartford & New Haven Railroad was chartered in 1833 and opened in 1839; by

Fresh out of the Readville, Mass., shops, streamlined Hudson 1402 breaks in on a Providence-to-Boston local. The 600-foot-long stone viaduct at Canton, Mass., completed in 1835, today carries trains of Amtrak and the Massachusetts Bay Transportation Authority.

1844 it had been extended north to Springfield, Mass. The Housatonic Railroad was chartered in 1836 to build up the river of that name from Bridgeport to the Massachusetts state line. In 1842 it reached a connection with the Western Railroad (later Boston & Albany). It was not until 1844 that the New York & New Haven Railroad was chartered in Connecticut; a New York charter was opposed by the New York & Harlem Railroad until arrangements were made to use the Harlem's tracks into New York City. The line was opened in 1848. That same year the first portion of the New Haven & Northampton was opened from New Haven north to Plainville, Conn., along the route of a canal. The New York & New Haven promptly leased the Canal Line to use as a competitive weapon against the Hartford & New Haven. The year 1848 also saw the chartering of the New Haven & New London Railroad which was opened in 1852 and soon extended to Stonington, Conn., with ferries taking whole trains across the Connecticut River at Saybrook and across the Thames at New London. The line was reorganized in 1864 as the Shore Line Railway and leased to the New York & New Haven in 1870. The Connecticut and the Thames were bridged in 1870 and 1889, respectively.

On August 6, 1872, the New York & New Haven and the Hartford & New Haven were consolidated as the New York, New Haven & Hartford Railroad. The new road had close affiliations with the Housatonic and Naugatuck lines (the latter followed the river of that name up to Waterbury and Winsted). It acquired control of the Canal Line in 1881 (the lease had ended in 1869), leased the Air Line (New Haven to Willimantic), and bought the Hartford & Connecticut Valley (Hartford to Saybrook) in 1882. In 1892 the New Haven leased the New York, Providence & Boston (which had leased the Providence & Worcester), and in 1893 leased the Old Colony, which was about the same size as the New Haven, completing an all-rail route under one management between Boston and New York.

In 1893 the New York & New England collapsed and NYNH&H began acquisition of its former rival. The New Haven also looked covetously at the concatenation of railroads that stretched up the Connecticut Valley from Springfield but contented itself with an agreement with Boston & Maine to split New England between them along the line of the Boston & Albany (B&M had no lines south of the B&A; NYNH&H had several tentacles reaching almost to the northern border of Massachusetts). By the turn of the century the New Haven had a virtual monopoly on the railroads and the steamboat lines in Connecticut, Rhode Island, and much of Massachusetts.

Enter Charles S. Mellen, a protege of J. P. Morgan. Mellen set out to gain control of all the railroads in New England. He bought the street and interurban railways in New Haven's territory, then bought control of Boston & Maine and Maine Central and, jointly with New York Central, the Rutland. He reached outside New England for control of the New York, Ontario & Western. He undertook the construction of the New

York, Westchester & Boston, an interurban line parallel to New Haven's own line from New York to Port Chester, with a branch to White Plains.

A long battle ensued between the Mellen interests and Justice Louis D. Brandeis of the U. S. Supreme Court over what was basically a violation of the Sherman Antitrust Act. A series of wrecks in 1911 and 1912 turned public feeling against the New Haven (and gained it mention in Clarence Day's play *Life With Father*). The costs of electrifying the line between New York and New Haven and of constructing the New York Connecting Railroad and its Hell Gate Bridge to connect with the Pennsylvania Railroad would have helped push the road into bankruptcy had it not been taken over by the United States Railroad Administration during World War One.

New Haven's electrification deserves special mention. Before the turn of the century NH electrified several branch lines using low-voltage DC systems, but for its main line between Woodlawn, N. Y., and New Haven the road chose the relatively unproven high-voltage AC system, even though the locomotives would have to be able to use New York Central's low-voltage DC system in Grand Central Terminal.

The New Haven's situation improved in the late 1920s. The Pennsylvania acquired nearly one-fourth of New Haven's stock and an interest in the Boston & Maine, and New Haven also acquired B&M stock, effectively regaining control of B&M. The New Haven struggled through the Depression as long as it could and entered bankruptcy on October 23, 1935.

In the ensuing reorganization NH pruned much of its branchline network, abandoned its steamship lines and the New York, Westchester & Boston, and upgraded the physical plant and rolling stock on its main lines. It inaugurated piggyback service in 1938 and dieselized many of its mainline trains with a fleet of Alco DL-109s. New Haven's traffic increased greatly during WWII. If the New Haven is remembered for nothing else it will be for a 1942 advertisement, "The Kid in Upper 4." The ad showed a young soldier lying awake in an upper berth on his way to war; the accompanying text, which told of his feelings, was a masterpiece.

The New Haven was heavy-duty, intense railroading as few other roads in North America have practiced it. The main passenger routes came from Pennsylvania Station and Grand Central Terminal to merge

Jim Shaughnessy

A train of the multiple-unit electric cars built in 1954 is overtaken at Stamford, Conn., by a pair of New Haven's unique FL9s on a New York-bound express. The FL9s could draw electric power from third rail, permitting the diesel engines to be shut down in the long tunnels leading to the Grand Central Terminal and Penn Station in New York. Both the M. U. cars (nicknamed "Washboards") and the FL9s wear the orange, black, and white livery of the McGinnis era.

at New Rochelle, N. Y., forming a four-track electrified line as far east as New Haven. From there double-track lines continued east to Boston and north to Springfield. The principal freight route was the line east from Maybrook, N. Y., where New Haven connected with Erie, Lehigh & Hudson River, Lehigh & New England, and New York, Ontario & Western; New Haven also interchanged a great deal of freight with the Pennsylvania via carfloats across New York harbor. The New Haven experimented very early with electrification of branch lines and was the first railroad with a long-distance mainline electrification. The road had three major bridges: the high bridge that carried the Maybrook Line across the Hudson at Poughkeepsie, N. Y., the vertical lift bridge, until 1959 the longest in the world, over the Cape Cod Canal at Buzzards Bay, Mass., and the Hell Gate Bridge (operated by New Haven, but owned by the New York Connecting Railroad, which was jointly owned by the New Haven and the Pennsylvania).

New Haven's reorganization was completed on September 18, 1947. Frederic C. Dumaine Sr. and others, including Patrick B. McGinnis, gained control in 1948. The experienced executives who had overseen the reorganization were dismissed, new management came in, and the road began another plunge into the depths. Frederic C. Dumaine Jr. took over upon his father's death in 1951 and immediately set about restoring the condition of the railroad and the morale of the employees.

In 1953 control passed from the preferred stockholders to the common stockholders. A proxy battle ensued and Patrick B. McGinnis won. He slashed maintenance and ordered experimental lightweight trains for Boston-New York service. Another McGinnis contribution was a new image of red-orange, black, and white. New paint or no, Connecticut commuters revolted at the imposition of parking charges at stations. Directors resigned. Hurricanes (not McGinnis's fault) in 1955 washed out a number of lines. Upon McGinnis's departure for the Boston & Maine in 1956 auditors found that New Haven's earnings for 1955 were less than half what McGinnis had been saying they were.

George Alpert became president just as the lightweight trains that McGinnis ordered arrived. One caught fire on the press run, and then derailed later that day. The piggyback traffic disappeared as the railroads serving New York initiated their own piggyback service and found that trailers could move into NH's territory by highway, especially the newly completed Connecticut Turnpike that paralleled NH from Greenwich to New London. In 1956 the New Haven decided to buy 60 FL9s, diesel locomotives that could also draw power from third rail in the New York terminals, in order to phase out its electrification — for which it had within the past year or so taken delivery of 10 new passenger locomotives and 100 new M. U. cars. A few years later, after the FL9s arrived, the New Haven purchased 11 nearly new electric freight locomotives from the Norfolk & Western.

Government loans guaranteed by the ICC kept the road afloat until July 7, 1961, when the New Haven went back into reorganization. The railroad sought local and state tax relief and petitioned for inclusion in the Pennsylvania-New York Central merger. The initial condition imposed by the two larger railroads was that NH be free of passenger service, but the ICC denied that request and on December 2, 1968, ordered Penn Central (which had come into being on February 1 of that year) to take over the New Haven by the beginning of 1969. On December 31, 1968, PC purchased New Haven's properties.

With all of its problems the New Haven soldiered on. Freight business suffered as much from the change in New England's economy and the shift from heavy industry to high technology as it did from truck competition. Until its inclusion in Penn Central the New Haven offered hourly passenger service between Boston and New York, with parlor and dining cars on nearly all trains, and almost as frequent service between New York, Hartford, and Springfield. Only in the past few years and by virtue of extensive track work has Amtrak managed to equal New Haven's Boston-New York running time.

Location of headquarters: New Haven, Connecticut
Miles of railroad operated: 1929 — 2,133; 1967 — 1,547
Number of locomotives: 1929 — 957; 1967 — 332
Number of passenger cars: 1929 — 2,110; 1967 — 855
Number of freight cars: 1929 — 24,033
Number of company service cars: 1929 — 1,049
Number of freight and company service cars: 1967 — 4,200
Reporting marks: NH
Notable named passenger trains: *Merchants Limited, Yankee Clip-*

To begin replacement of its aging fleet of Alco DL109s, in 1956 New Haven purchased 60 road-switchers — 30 GP9s, 15 RS11s, and 15 H-16-44s — for passenger and freight service. Representatives of all three types are shown in this 1960 photo leading a freight east out of Maybrook, N. Y.

per (New York-Boston); *Colonial, Senator, Patriot* (Washington-New York-Boston, operated jointly with Pennsylvania Railroad); *State of Maine, Bar Harbor* (Washington-New York-Portland-Ellsworth, operated with Boston & Maine and Maine Central), *Washingtonian, Montrealer* (Washington-New York-Montreal, operated with Pennsylvania, Boston & Maine, Central Vermont, and Canadian National)

Historical and technical society: New Haven Railroad Historical & Technical Association, P. O. Box 122, Wallingford, CT 06492

Recommended reading:

Steelways of New England, by Alvin F. Harlow, published in 1946 by the Creative Age Press, New York, New York

The New Haven Railroad — Its Rise And Fall, by John L. Weller, published in 1969 by Hastings House, New York, NY 10016

Subsidiaries and affiliated railroads, 1967:

Boston Terminal Corp. (70%)

New York Connecting Railroad (50%)

Union Freight Railroad (50%)

South Manchester Railroad (100%)

Successors:

Penn Central

Conrail (TWG)

Amtrak (TWG)

Providence & Worcester (TWG)

Pioneer Valley

Bay Colony (TWG)

Massachusetts Bay Transportation Authority (TWG)

Metro-North Commuter Railroad (TWG)

Portions still operated:

Boston-New York (Penn Station); Springfield-New Haven: Amtrak

Boston to Attleboro, Stoughton, and Franklin, Mass.: Massachusetts Bay Transportation Authority

New York (Grand Central) to New Haven, Waterbury, Danbury, and New Canaan, Conn.: Metro-North

New York-New Haven-Groton, Conn.; New Haven-Springfield, Mass.; Hartford to Manchester and East Windsor, Conn.; New Haven-Portland, Conn.; South Norwalk-New Milford, Conn.; Devon, Conn., to Poughkeepsie and Beacon, N. Y.; Highland-Maybrook, N. Y.; Providence-Boston; Mansfield to Fitchburg and Chelmsford, Mass.; Attleboro-Middleboro-Braintree, Mass.; Taunton to New Bedford, Mass., and Tiverton, R. I.; Readville-Franklin-Milford, Mass.: Conrail

Braintree-Hingham; Braintree to Rockland and North Plymouth; Middleboro to Falmouth, Hyannis, and South Dennis; Westport Factory-Watuppa; Medfield Jct. to Newton Highlands and West Roxbury, Mass.: Bay Colony

Holyoke-Easthampton, Mass.: Pioneer Valley

Worcester, Mass.-Providence, R. I.-Westbrook, Conn.; Worcester-Groton, Conn.; Plainfield-Willimantic, Conn.; Webster-Southbridge, Mass.; Providence-Washington, R. I.; Tiverton-Newport, R. I.: Providence & Worcester

Pittsfield, Mass.-Canaan, Conn.; Springfield, Mass.-New Haven, Conn.; Springfield-Hazardville, Conn.; Berlin-Waterbury, Conn.; Torrington-Waterbury-Derby, Conn.; Avon-Plainville-Mt. Carmel, Conn.: Boston & Maine

NEW YORK, ONTARIO & WESTERN RAILWAY

In 1866 the New York & Oswego Midland Railroad was incorporated to build a railroad from Oswego, N. Y., on the shore of Lake Ontario, to New York — or more specifically to the New Jersey state line and then to a point on the Hudson River opposite New York City. The road's first problem was finance. Cities and towns that refused to issue bonds to finance the line found themselves bypassed by the new railroad, with the result that the line went through few established places of any size and made unnecessary contortions, both horizontal and vertical. The state of New Jersey refused to allow such bonding, so the NY&OM struck a deal with the Middletown, Unionville & Water Gap and the New Jersey Midland (forerunners of the Middletown & Unionville and the New York, Susquehanna & Western). One of the incorporators of the railroad boasted that the line would run at right angles to the mountains, and after construction began the railroad discovered just what that meant in terms of bridges and tunnels.

The line was opened from Oswego to Norwich in 1869, and in 1872 the NY&OM leased roads that formed branches to Utica and Rome. In 1871 it opened a line known as the Auburn Branch — it straggled northwest, southwest, and northwest from Norwich through Cortland and Freeville to end at Scipio, about ten miles short of Auburn. The first train ran all the way from Oswego to Jersey City in July 1883; within weeks the railroad was bankrupt.

For a short period in early 1875 the NY&OM ceased operation entirely except for the portion from Sidney to Utica and Rome, which was operated by Delaware & Hudson, in much the same way as designated operators took over portions of the Rock Island a century later. While the line was idle, a number of local residents, fearing they would not be paid, simply tore up the track and reclaimed their land. Operation resumed, and the road was reorganized in 1879 as the New York, Ontario & Western Railway. Implicit in the new name was hope of a ferry connection across Lake Ontario and a continuation to the West. Missing from the map was the Auburn branch, dismantled except from Freeville through Cortland to De Ruyter, which became part of the Lehigh Valley. Soon added to the map was a line from Middletown east to Cornwall, on the Hudson River. NYO&W made arrangements with the West Shore for trackage rights south from Cornwall to West Shore's terminal at Weehawken, N. J. The West Shore soon came under the control of New York Central. NYO&W found NYC amenable to continued use of the Weehawken-Cornwall portion of the West Shore, but it put NYO&W firmly in the position of a feeder line, not part of a trunk route. The through route that NYO&W did participate in was hardly competitive with NYC: Rome, Watertown & Ogdensburg from Oswego to Buffalo, and Wabash from Buffalo to Chicago.

More important to NYO&W's future was the opening in 1890 of a 54-mile branch from Cadosia, N. Y., to Scranton, Pennsylvania, to tap the anthracite regions. The road converted a number of its locomotives to anthracite-burners, in the process changing them from conventional configuration to Camelbacks. In 1904 the New Haven purchased control of the NYO&W for its coal business (that same year NH purchased the Central New England, whose bridge across the Hudson at Poughkeepsie afforded access to several railroads at Maybrook and Campbell Hall, N. Y.). In 1912 the New York Central and the New Haven discussed trading their interests in Rutland and NYO&W, respectively; New Haven wound up with part of NYC's Rutland stock but retained its NYO&W control.

The 1920s saw a travel boom on the NYO&W as the Catskill Mountains became a resort area. The Depression killed much of that business; coal from the Scranton Branch provided a greater and greater portion of

the road's revenue, peaking in 1932. It was downhill from there. The coal mines in Scranton failed in 1937; NYO&W filed for reorganization in May of that year.

The road's trustee, Frederic Lyford, recognized that any future the NYO&W had lay in general merchandise traffic, not coal, and began a metamorphosis of the road into a bridge route between the west end of the New Haven at Maybrook and connections at Scranton. By this time passenger traffic to the Catskills was growing again. NYO&W couldn't afford a streamliner but asked designer Otto Kuhler to do what he could for $10,000 for the 1937 summer season. The result was *The Mountaineer*: streamstyling for a 4-8-2, slipcovers for the seats of the coaches, and ma-

Jim Shaughnessy

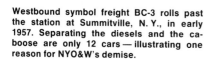

Westbound symbol freight BC-3 rolls past the station at Summitville, N. Y., in early 1957. Separating the diesels and the caboose are only 12 cars — illustrating one reason for NYO&W's demise.

230

ple armchairs replacing wicker in the parlor car, all painted maroon and black with orange trim — and matching uniforms for the crew. The New Berlin branch was sold in 1941 to the Unadilla Valley, and dieselization of the NYO&W began in 1941 and 1942 with five General Electric 44-ton switchers. Several sets of Electro-Motive FTs soon followed for freight service. One pair of FTs was financed by Standard Oil in exchange for detailed performance data over three years of operation.

The NYO&W enjoyed a brief postwar surge of business, but NYO&W's division of the revenue wasn't enough to keep the rest of the road in business. (The originating carrier gets most of the revenue from a freight move; to make money as a bridge carrier you need lots of business and a long haul — longer than the 145 miles from Scranton to Campbell Hall.) Passenger service was reduced to a single summer-only Weehawken-Roscoe round trip. A booster organization of shippers was formed but little of the road's freight originated on line. In 1952 the New Haven offered to purchase the road but soon withdrew its offer (and had financial problems of its own). Abandonment was loudly protested by towns along the line, which considered unpaid back taxes as an investment in the railroad. The New York state legislature passed a $1 million aid bill, citing the road as essential for civil defense, but the state civil defense commission rejected it. The federal government recommended liquidation. Finally operation ceased on March 29, 1957. The assets were auctioned off — the diesels found new owners, but everything else was scrapped. None of the road's lines remains in operation.

Location of headquarters: New York, New York
Miles of railroad operated: 1929 — 569; 1956 — 541
Number of locomotives: 1929 — 177; 1956 — 46
Number of passenger cars: 1929 — 401; 1956 — 12
Number of freight cars: 1929 — 5,077; 1956 — 152
Number of company service cars: 1929 — 253; 1956 — 71
Reporting marks: OW
Historical and technical society: Ontario & Western Railway Historical Society, P. O. Box 713, Middletown, NY 10940
Recommended reading: *O. & W.*, by William F. Helmer, published in 1959 by Howell-North Books, 850 North Hollywood Way, Burbank, CA 91505

NIAGARA JUNCTION RAILWAY

The Niagara Junction was established in 1892 as a subsidiary of the Niagara Falls Power Co., which was seeking to increase its business by attracting industry to the area. The new railroad connected the industrial area of Niagara Falls, New York, with the New York Central and the Erie. The line was electrified in 1913 — a logical enough move for a road owned by an electric power company. The road's freight business prospered.

In 1948 the NYC, the Erie, and the Lehigh Valley purchased the railroad. Conrail absorbed the Niagara Junction when it acquired the railroad properties of Penn Central, Lehigh Valley, and Erie Lackawanna. Electric operation ceased in 1979, and two of the locomotives (built by General Electric in 1952) were moved to the former New York Central electrified lines out of New York's Grand Central Terminal. The overhead wires were taken down, and Conrail diesels do all the work.

Location of headquarters: Niagara Falls, New York
Miles of railroad operated: 1929 — 6; 1975 — 11
Number of locomotives: 1929 — 5; 1975 — 7
Number of freight cars: 1929 — 14
Number of company service cars: 1929 — 4
Successors: Conrail

Ken Kraemer

NJ 16 has a respectable-length train in tow as it heads up the main line on a winter day in the 1970s. The locomotive is one of seven identical center-cab electrics built by General Electric in 1952.

NORFOLK SOUTHERN RAILROAD

Today's Norfolk Southern is quite a different railroad from the one that is the subject of this entry. True, this railroad is part of the present one, but only a small part. Perhaps the problem is the Southern Railway's historical penchant for reusing names.

The Elizabeth City & Norfolk Railroad was chartered in 1870; in 1880 construction began on its line from Berkley, Virginia, now part of Norfolk, along the east edge of the Dismal Swamp to Elizabeth City, North Carolina. The line was opened to Elizabeth City in June 1881 and extended a few miles farther to Edenton, on the shore of Albemarle Sound,

in December of that year. There steamers connected with the trains for points up the rivers and along the coast of North Carolina. The road got a new name, Norfolk Southern Railroad, in 1883.

The Norfolk Southern entered receivership in 1889 and was reorganized as the Norfolk & Southern Railroad in 1891. Included in the N&S was the Albemarle & Pantego Railroad, which had been organized in 1887 by the John L. Roper Lumber Co. to build from Mackey's Ferry, across the sound from Edenton, to Belhaven, N. C. In 1900 the N&S absorbed the Norfolk, Virginia Beach & Southern Railroad. The NVB&S had opened in 1883 as a 3-foot-gauge line from Norfolk to Virginia Beach; in 1899 it was standard-gauged and acquired a branch to Munden, in the extreme southeast corner of Virginia. In 1902 Chesapeake Transit Co.

opened an electric line from Norfolk to Cape Henry, Va. To meet the competition, N&S built a short branch from Virginia Beach to Cape Henry, electrified its line from Norfolk to Virginia Beach, and bought Chesapeake Transit — and the former management of Chesapeake Transit wound up in control of N&S. That same year N&S acquired the 3-foot-gauge Washington & Plymouth, which connected the North Carolina towns of its name, widened it to standard gauge, built a ten-mile link between Plymouth and Mackey's ferry, and installed the *John W. Garrett*, a ferry that had been on Baltimore & Ohio's roster, on the run between Edenton and Mackey's Ferry.

The Suffolk & Carolina Railway was chartered in 1873. By 1897 its 3′6″-gauge line reached from Suffolk, Va., to Ryland, N. C. In 1902 it was extended to Edenton; in 1904 it was standard-gauged and built a branch to Elizabeth City. In 1906 it was taken over by the Virginia & Carolina Coast. The V&CC bought the Roper Lumber Co. and built a line east from Mackey's Ferry to Columbia, N. C. In 1903 the Raleigh & Pamlico Sound was organized to build lines from Raleigh and New Bern to Washington, N. C., and the Pamlico, Oriental & Western began a line from New Bern to Oriental. The Atlantic & North Carolina is discussed on page 26; the Beaufort & Western was the predecessor of the Beaufort & Morehead.

In 1906 the Norfolk & Southern Railway was formed as a consolidation of the Norfolk & Southern Railroad, the Virginia & Carolina Coast Railroad, the Raleigh & Pamlico Sound Railroad, the Pamlico, Oriental & Western Railway, and the Beaufort & Western Railroad. The new N&S also held the lease of the Atlantic & North Carolina.

Expansion outpaced the railroad's finances in 1908. The road entered the hands of receivers that year and was reorganized as the Norfolk Southern Railroad in 1910. That same year a trestle was constructed across Albemarle Sound to replace the ferry that operated between Edenton and Mackey's Ferry. The expansion program continued. NS bought four railroads and undertook new construction, extending the main line from Raleigh to Charlotte with branches to Fayetteville, Aberdeen, and Asheboro. In 1920 the NS leased the Durham & South Carolina Railroad, gaining access to Durham.

The Depression drove the NS into receivership yet again in 1932. The electric passenger service to Virginia Beach and Cape Henry, primarily suburban in character, was replaced by gasoline-powered cars in 1935 (and discontinued in 1948). Also in 1935 the Atlantic & North Carolina withdrew its lease for nonpayment, and in 1937 the Beaufort & Western was sold to local interests to become the Beaufort & Morehead. In 1937 NS abandoned much of the Belhaven branch and in 1940 all of the former Virginia & Carolina Coast. The road was sold at foreclosure in 1941.

The Norfolk Southern Railway took over at the beginning of 1942. In 1947 a group of investors headed by Patrick B. McGinnis took control. The railroad acquired a pair of office cars, leased apartments or suites in New York, Washington, and Miami, lavishly entertained its shippers, and got investigated by the ICC. McGinnis resigned and moved on, eventually to the New Haven. New management took over in 1953. In the

In 1940 Norfolk Southern received five light 2-8-4s from Baldwin. They were the road's only steam locomotives with trailing trucks and were several orders of magnitude more modern than anything else on the NS. When NS dieselized the Berkshires were sold to National Railways of Mexico.

H. Reid

early 1960s NS constructed a branch to serve phosphate deposits between Washington and New Bern.

The Southern Railway purchased the Norfolk Southern in 1974. Southern merged it with the Carolina & Northwestern under the NS name. In 1981 the name was changed to Carolina & Northwestern so that the Norfolk Southern name could be used for a newly formed holding company as part of the Southern-Norfolk & Western merger.

Location of headquarters: Norfolk, Virginia; after 1961 Raleigh, North Carolina

Miles of railroad operated: 1929 — 933; 1973 — 622

Number of locomotives: 1929 — 105; 1973 — 37

Number of passenger cars: 1929 — 108

Number of freight cars: 1929 — 3,282; 1973 — 2,245

Number of company service cars: 1929 — 192; 1973 — 50

Number of electric locomotives: 1929 — 5

Number of electric passenger cars: 1929 — 42

Number of electric company service cars: 1929 — 2

Reporting marks: NS

Recommended reading: *Norfolk Southern*, by Richard E. Prince, published in 1972 by Richard E. Prince (SBN 9600088-5-3)

Successors:

Atlantic & East Carolina

Southern (TWG)

Portions still operated: Norfolk-Charlotte; Norfolk-Virginia Beach; Washington-Belhaven; Phosphate Jct.-Lee Creek; New Bern-Chocowinity; Bern; Varina-Fayetteville; Star-Aberdeen; Goldsboro-Morehead City (A&NC): Southern

NORTHERN ALBERTA RAILWAYS

The Northern Alberta Railways Co. was incorporated June 14, 1929, and was owned half-and-half by Canadian Pacific Railway and Canadian National Railways. On July 1, 1929, NAR purchased from the province of Alberta four railways: the Edmonton, Dunvegan & British Columbia; the Central Canada; the Pembina Valley; and the Alberta & Great Waterways.

Construction of the Edmonton, Dunvegan & British Columbia began in 1912. The line reached Dawson Creek, B. C., in 1930, by way of Smith, Slave Lake, McLennan, and Grande Prairie, Alta. The Central Canada was opened from McLennan north to Peace River, Alta., in 1916 and later extended to Hines Creek. The two roads were built by the J. D. McArthur Co. of Winnipeg. The construction company operated them until financial difficulties caused by World War One caused the provincial government to take control. It leased the ED&BC and the Central Canada in 1920 and contracted with Canadian Pacific to operate the two roads.

The Alberta & Great Waterways was chartered in 1909 and began construction in 1914 at Carbondale, just north of Edmonton on the ED&BC. The line reached Lac La Biche a year later and was completed to Waterways (Fort McMurray), Alta., in 1925. The government purchased the A&GW from the McArthur company and operated it through its Department of Railways and Telephones, but later turned it over to CP to operate with the other two provincially owned lines.

The government of Alberta chartered and built the Pembina Valley Railway, opening the 26-mile line from Busby, on the ED&BC north of Edmonton, to Barrhead in 1927.

The provincial government tried without success to sell its railroads to either CP or CN, and in November 1926 it took over operation from CP. In 1928 CP offered to purchase the railroads if CN would go halves. The arrangement was acceptable to the province, and Northern Alberta Railways, jointly owned by the two large roads, began operation.

The construction of the Alaska Highway north from Dawson Creek began in March 1942 and brought a great increase in traffic to NAR. Traffic remained at a high level after WWII. The opening of provincial highway 43 in 1955 provided a shortcut from Edmonton to the Dawson Creek and

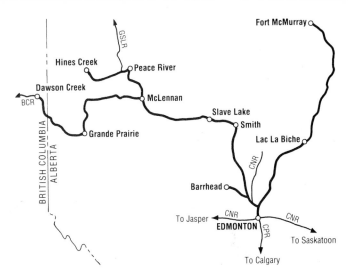

Peace River areas, and in 1958 the British Columbia Railway reached Dawson Creek from North Vancouver. Both the highway and BCR siphoned traffic from NAR. In 1962 the Canadian government began construction of the Great Slave Lake Railway north from Roma Junction, west of Peace River. The line, operated by Canadian National, was opened in 1964. It furnished much bridge revenue to NAR in the form of lead and zinc ores moving south to Trail, B. C., to supplement the grain that was NAR's principal commodity. Another provincially owned, CN-operated road, the Alberta Resources Railway, reached Grande Prairie from the south in 1969.

Canadian Pacific sold its share of NAR to Canadian National in 1980. Northern Alberta's operations were absorbed into CN on January 1, 1981, as part of a new CN operational unit, the Peace River Division. CN still offers mixed train service between Edmonton and Waterways, and a

Two GP9s bring Northern Alberta train 52 across the Toms Creek trestle at Dawson Creek, B. C., in 1976.

F. D. Shaw

group of boxcars painted gold to celebrate Northern Alberta Railways' fiftieth anniversary is still in service wearing NAR's name and markings.

Location of headquarters: Edmonton, Alberta
Miles of railroad operated: 1930 — 862; 1980 — 923
Number of locomotives: 1930 — 27; 1980 — 21
Number of passenger cars: 1930 — 39; 1980 — 9
Number of freight cars: 1930 — 225; 1980 — 100

Number of company service cars: 1930 — 202
Reporting marks: NAR
Recommended reading: *The Northern Alberta Railways*, by Colin Hatcher, published in 1981 by the British Railway Modelers of North America, 5124 33 Street N.W., Calgary, AB, Canada T2L 1V4 (ISBN 0-9690798-9-3)
Successors: Canadian National (TWG)

NORTHERN PACIFIC RAILWAY

In 1864 Abraham Lincoln signed the charter of a railroad to be built from the Great Lakes to Puget Sound — the Northern Pacific Railroad. The Philadelphia banking house of Jay Cooke & Co. undertook to sell the bonds, which were to yield 7.3 percent interest, and sold $30 million worth. Work began in 1870 at Carlton, Minnesota, 20 miles from Duluth on the Lake Superior & Mississippi Railroad. The LS&M had just been opened between St. Paul and Duluth, and in 1872 Northern Pacific leased the road. By 1873 the NP was completed between Duluth and Bismarck, North Dakota, as was an isolated section from Kalama, Washington, on the Columbia River, to Tacoma. The Panic of 1873 wiped out Cooke and work ceased on the railroad.

NP reorganized by converting the bonds to stock, and the Lake Superior & Mississippi was reorganized as the St. Paul & Duluth. In 1881 Henry Villard bought control of the railroad; he also controlled the Oregon Railway & Navigation Co. and the Oregon & California Railroad. The last spike on the line between Northern Pacific Jct. (Carlton, Minn.) and Wallula Jct., Wash., was driven at Gold Creek, Montana, near Garri-

son, on September 8, 1883. NP trains reached Portland on the rails of the OR&N; NP's own line to Tacoma resumed there, with a ferry crossing the Columbia River between Goble, Oreg., and Kalama, Wash.

Even before the completion of the line at Gold Creek, NP began construction of a direct line from Pasco, Wash., over the Cascade Range to Tacoma. The Puget Sound area was beginning to grow, and NP wanted to reach it with its own line rather than rely on OR&N. Indeed, soon after the last-spike ceremonies, Villard's empire collapsed and OR&N became part of Union Pacific (Southern Pacific got the Oregon & California). The Pasco-Tacoma line opened in 1887, with temporary switchbacks carrying trains over Stampede Pass until the opening of Stampede Tunnel in May 1888.

In 1889 NP contracted with the Wisconsin Central to operate through service to Chicago from the Twin Cities, and in 1890 NP leased the WC. NP organized a terminal company, the Chicago & Northern Pacific, and leased it to the WC. NP entered receivership in 1893 and defaulted on lease payments to Wisconsin Central, which in turned defaulted on the

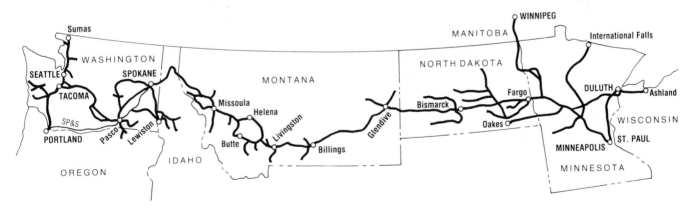

237

Northern Pacific was the first railroad to use the 4-8-4 wheel arrangement, and the type was named "Northern" for the railroad. NP 2601, second of the first group of Northerns, leads train 407 out of Tacoma on the last leg of its Portland-Seattle run.

F. Barry Thompson

238

C&NP lease. Wisconsin Central later became part of Soo Line, and the Chicago & Northern Pacific eventually became the Baltimore & Ohio Chicago Terminal.

The Superior & St. Croix Railroad, chartered in Wisconsin in 1870, provided the vehicle for the reorganization of the NP. It was renamed the Northern Pacific Railway in July 1896 and on September 1 of that year acquired the properties, rights, franchises, and lands of the Northern Pacific Railroad. The reorganization included the absorption of the St. Paul & Northern Pacific Railway (Brainerd and Staples, Minn., to St. Paul). In 1900 NP acquired the properties of the St. Paul & Duluth, and in 1901, the Seattle & International Railway (Seattle to Sumas, Wash.). Also in 1901 NP leased its Manitoba lines (Emerson-Winnipeg-Portage-la-Prairie and Morris-Brandon) to the Province of Manitoba. (They were sold to Canadian National Railways in 1946.)

In 1901 Northern Pacific and Great Northern gained control of the Chicago, Burlington & Quincy by jointly purchasing approximately 98 percent of its capital stock. That same year James J. Hill and J. P. Morgan formed the Northern Securities Co. as a holding company for NP and Great Northern. The U. S. Supreme Court dissolved Northern Securities in 1904. In 1905 the two roads organized the Spokane, Portland & Seattle, which was completed from Spokane through Pasco to Portland in 1908. GN and NP attempted consolidation in 1927, but the Interstate Commerce Commission made giving up control of the Burlington a requisite for approval.

In October 1941 NP purchased the property of the Minnesota & International Railway (Brainerd-International Falls, Minn.), which it had controlled for a number of years.

In image Northern Pacific was the most conservative of the three northern transcontinentals. (Great Northern was a prosperous, well-thought-out railroad; the Milwaukee Road was a brash newcomer.) Bulking large in NP's freight traffic were wheat and lumber. In the 1920s and 1930s NP suffered from smaller than usual wheat crops and competition from ships for lumber moving to the East Coast. Ship competition decreased during World War Two, and postwar prosperity brought an increase in building activity and population growth to the area NP served. NP was the oldest of the northern transcontinentals and had been instru-

R. V. Nixon

NP relied on Electro-Motive F units for both passenger and freight service and was one of the few roads ordering the F9, last of the type, in significant numbers. Five black-and-gold freight Fs (NP's passenger Fs were green) are shown here lifting a freight up the west slope of the Continental Divide at Elliston, Mont.

mental in settling the northern plains. It served the populous areas of North Dakota, Montana, and Washington. Its slogan was "Main Street of the Northwest," and its secondary passenger train of the 1950s and 1960s was the *Mainstreeter*.

In 1956 NP and Great Northern again studied merger of the two roads, the Burlington, and the Spokane, Portland & Seattle. In 1960 the directors of both roads approved the merger terms. On March 2, 1970, NP was merged into Burlington Northern along with Great Northern; Chicago, Burlington & Quincy; and Spokane, Portland & Seattle.

Location of headquarters: St. Paul, Minnesota
Miles of railroad operated: 1929 — 6,784; 1969 — 6,771
Number of locomotives: 1929 — 1,087; 1969 — 604
Number of passenger cars: 1929 — 933; 1969 — 192
Number of freight cars: 1929 — 50,960; 1969 — 34,961
Number of company service cars: 1929 — 2,924; 1969 — 3,970

Continued on next page

239

Reporting marks: NP, NPM
Notable named passenger trains: *North Coast Limited* (Chicago-St. Paul-Seattle and Portland; operated Chicago-St. Paul by Chicago, Burlington & Quincy and Pasco-Portland by Spokane, Portland & Seattle)
Historical and technical society: Northern Pacific Railroad Historical Association, 3314 Warehime Road, Millers, MD 21107
Recommended reading: *Northern Pacific Supersteam Era 1925-1945,* by Robert L. Frey and Lorenz P. Schrenk, published in 1985 by Golden West Books, P. O. Box 80250, San Marino, CA 91108 (ISBN 0-87095-092-4)
Subsidiaries and affiliated railroads, 1969:
Chicago, Burlington & Quincy (48.59%)

Spokane, Portland & Seattle (50%, jointly with Great Northern)
Camas Prairie (50%, jointly with Union Pacific)
Midland Ry. of Manitoba (50%, jointly with Great Northern)
Walla Walla Valley (100%)
Successors: Burlington Northern (TWG)
Portions still operated: Of the major lines of the Northern Pacific, only the following have been abandoned: Moose Lake-Duluth, Minn.; Glenwood-Brainerd, Minn.; Wadena-Breckenridge, Minn.; Red Lake-East Grand Forks, Minn.; Silesia-Red Lodge, Mont.; Livingston-Gardiner, Mont.; St. Regis, Mont.-Mullan, Idaho; Hartford-Sedro Woolley, Wash. The remainder, except for a few short branches, is operated by Burlington Northern.

NORTHWESTERN PACIFIC RAILROAD

The Northwestern Pacific still exists as a subsidiary of Southern Pacific. It has had no locomotives, passenger cars, or interchange freight cars of its own since 1960, and to the casual observer it appears to be simply another piece of the far-flung SP. The present company was incorporated in 1907 by the Southern Pacific and the Santa Fe to consolidate the San Francisco & North Pacific Railway, the North Shore Railroad, and several other smaller roads. In 1929 Southern Pacific purchased Santa Fe's interest and became sole owner.

NWP. gradually lost its identity in that of its parent, SP, much as Northern Pacific, Great Northern, and Burlington have lost their identity in Burlington Northern since March 2, 1970. The date is the difference. NWP still exists, and it has become a "paper railroad," a railroad that exists only on paper and has no rolling stock of its own. Since most of NWP's rolling stock was gone by the end of 1959, I will use that for an ending date for the mileage statistics. NWP equipment statistics in *Moody's Transportation Manual* for the 1950s and 1960s are as meaningless as the route description that has remained constant through the years, even in the 1984 edition: "Lines extend from San Francisco Bay at Sausalito northward to Eureka connecting by motor coach for the Red-wood Empire Tour to Grants Pass, Oregon, where connection is made with Southern Pacific Shasta Route trains for Portland."

San Francisco & North Pacific: The earliest ancestor of the NWP was the Petaluma & Haystack Railroad, which in 1864 opened a three-mile line from Petaluma, California, to a landing on Petaluma Creek and a connection with boats for San Francisco. A boiler explosion destroyed its locomotive in 1866 and the line reverted to horse power.

In the 1860s there were several rival proposals for railroads in Sonoma County, some aimed north at the redwood country and some aimed south toward San Francisco Bay. The San Francisco & North Pacific was the successor to most of these. By 1870 construction was in progress from Petaluma north toward Santa Rosa. In 1871 the California Pacific, which had lines from Vallejo to Sacramento, Marysville, and Calistoga, purchased the SF&NP and completed it to Healdsburg — and then made noises about building a line up the Feather River Canyon and over Beckwourth Pass to connect with the Union Pacific at Ogden. Central Pacific, already smarting because upstart California Pacific had built a shorter, faster route between San Francisco and Sacramento, snapped up California Pacific and considered making Sausalito its San Francisco Bay terminal. The SF&NP was extended to Cloverdale in 1872. At the beginning of 1873 Central Pacific sold the SF&NP back to its builder, Peter Donahue.

NORTHWESTERN PACIFIC

In 1874 the Sonoma & Marin was organized to build a line from Petaluma south to San Rafael. It purchased the Petaluma & Haystack, surveyed a line to San Rafael, and was taken over by the SF&NP. The S&M was opened and closed several times in 1878 and 1879. A tunnel cave-in was responsible for one closing, but the SF&NP was responsible for another — the new line in conjunction with the San Rafael & San Quentin and its ferry could provide a much faster trip to San Francisco than SF&NP's own steamer down winding Petaluma Creek. However, the growing commuter trade from San Rafael to San Francisco prompted SF&NP to extend the Sonoma & Marin south to Tiburon on San Fran-

Jack Farley

Train 1, the day train from Eureka, rolls through the hills of Marin County just a few miles north of San Rafael in March 1942. Powering the train is NWP Ten-Wheeler No. 143.

cisco Bay. The SF&NP also gained a branch to Sonoma that had been started as a monorail, then converted to narrow gauge. In 1886 a line was completed across the marshes to connect it to the rest of the SF&NP at Ignacio.

In 1886 SP (successor to Central Pacific) built a line to Santa Rosa from Napa Junction, finally establishing a rail connection between the lines north of San Francisco and the rest of the country. Mervyn Donahue, Peter's son and his successor as head of the SF&NP, discovered that SP had an option on the Eel River & Eureka (descendant of an 1854 logging railroad), which Donahue had anticipated using as the north end of the SF&NP. Donahue invoked the prospect of extending his system up the Feather River Canyon, and SP let its option drop. The younger Donahue died in 1890 and the road was sold. The new owners organized the California Northwestern and leased the SF&NP to it.

North Pacific Coast: In 1870 the standard gauge San Rafael & San Quentin Railroad was opened from San Rafael to the San Quentin ferry landing, three miles to the southeast.

In 1871 the North Pacific Coast Railroad was incorporated to build a line from Sausalito north through San Rafael to Tomales, on the coast, to serve a growing redwood lumber industry. The line was constructed with a gauge of three feet and was completed in 1875. Since its line bypassed San Rafael by a couple of miles, the NPC built a branch from what is now San Anselmo. It then leased the San Rafael & San Quentin, narrowed its gauge, and made that the main line rather than the route to Sausalito. In 1876 NPC rails reached the Russian River, and the road re-established Sausalito as its principal terminal after boring a tunnel at Corte Madera to replace a stiff climb over the hills, and in 1877 the road extended its rails north of the Russian River to Duncan Mills.

New management took over the NPC in 1902. They renamed it the North Shore Railroad and standard-gauged, double-tracked, and electrified it from Sausalito to Mill Valley and San Rafael.

Northwestern Pacific: In 1903 the Santa Fe acquired the Eel River & Eureka and the Albion & Southeastern (an isolated line extending inland from the coast) and Southern Pacific acquired the California Northwestern (by then its northern terminal was Willits) and the North Shore and started talking about building to Eureka. The battle lines were drawn.

B. H. Ward

A long train of wood, open-platform electric cars rolls toward Sausalito. Mt. Tamalpais is visible in the distance.

The principals, E. H. Harriman and Edward Ripley, soon recognized that the Eureka area could not support two railroads, and expensive ones at that. They formed the Northwestern Pacific Railway as a compromise; the Northwestern Pacific Railroad soon followed. Construction of a line along the Eel River canyon — inaccessible and prone to flood — was completed in 1914.

In 1929 SP assumed sole ownership of the NWP. The former NPC was standard-gauged as far as Point Reyes in 1920; the line from there north to the Russian River remained narrow gauge until its abandonment in 1930. The Manor-Point Reyes line was abandoned in 1933, and the Russian River branch was abandoned in 1935. The NWP bought the Petaluma & Santa Rosa, an interurban connecting the towns of its name, in 1932. P&SR discontinued its passenger service then and ended electric operation in 1947. The road was abandoned in 1984.

NWP's electric suburban service was discontinued on March 1, 1941, a casualty of bus service over the new Golden Gate Bridge, leaving a pair of San Rafael-Eureka trains as NWP's only passenger service. The day

Richard Steinheimer

Typical of the diesel freight era on the NWP is this pair of Southern Pacific SD7s leading train 77 south near Scotia in August 1956.

train was discontinued in May 1942. The overnight was replaced by the triweekly daytime *Redwood* in 1956, and that was cut back to a Willits-Eureka run handled by SP's sole RDC in 1958.

During the 1930s NWP began to lease steam locomotives from parent SP. The last of these was returned to SP in August 1953, leaving just five active NWP steamers; the last steam run was September 20, 1953. The diesels that took over were all SP property. NWP's last passenger cars left the roster in 1957, and the last interchange freight cars to carry NWP markings were gone by October 1958. A few cabooses carried NWP lettering until the 1970s.

A tunnel fire north of San Rafael in July 1961 cut off rail access to the south end of the NWP; traffic was maintained by Santa Fe carfloat to the slip at Tiburon. The tunnel was repaired in 1967 after a long legal battle. Floods in December 1964 washed out more than 100 miles of the line in the Eel River Canyon; replacement took six months. A fire in a tunnel north of Island Mountain severed the line again in September 1978; it was reopened a year later. In January 1980 heavy rains washed out the interchange yard at Schellville, NWP's only rail connection. SP closed the NWP north of Willits in April 1983, citing heavy expenses as its reason. In June of that year SP reopened the line but levied a $1200-per-car surcharge on each shipment. Another tunnel fire north of Willits in September 1983 again shut down the line — and SP threatened to make it permanent. A U. S. District Court ordered the line reopened, since it had been closed without ICC approval, and the line was reopened in March 1984. On November 1, 1984, the line north of Willits was sold to a new company, the Eureka Southern. SP continues to operate the NWP south of Willits. Subsidiary Petaluma & Santa Rosa was abandoned in 1984.

Location of headquarters: San Francisco, California
Miles of railroad operated: 1929 — 477; 1959 — 328
Number of locomotives: 1929 — 65
Number of passenger cars: 1929 — 207
Number of freight cars: 1929 — 1,234
Number of company service cars: 1929 — 322
Reporting marks: NWP
Recommended reading:
The Northwestern Pacific Railroad, by Fred A. Stindt and Guy L.

Dunscomb, published in 1964 by Fred A. Stindt, 3363 Riviera West Drive, Kelseyville, CA 95451

Electric Railway Pioneer, by Harre Demoro, published in 1983 by Interurban Press, P. O. Box 6444, Glendale, CA 91205 (ISBN 0-916374-55-6)

Subsidiaries and affiliated railroads, 1959: Petaluma & Santa Rosa

Successors:
Southern Pacific (TWG)
Eureka Southern
Portions still operated:
Schellville-Willits; Ignacio-San Rafael: Southern Pacific
Willits-Eureka: Eureka Southern

OAHU RAILWAY & LAND COMPANY

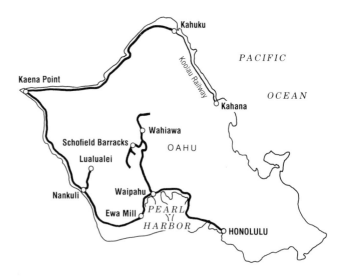

In September 1888 Benjamin F. Dillingham received a franchise from King Kalakaua to build a railroad from Honolulu to a sugar plantation at Ewa, about 20 miles west. Dillingham organized the Oahu Railway & Land Co., and construction of the 3-foot-gauge line began. The road opened for service on November 16, 1889 — the king's birthday — and the rails reached Ewa in May 1890. As Dillingham developed more sugar plantations the railroad was extended up the west coast of the island of Oahu, around Kaena Point, then east to Kahuku, 71 miles by rail from Honolulu (26 miles, air line distance).

In 1906 the railroad constructed an 11-mile branch north from Waipahu to a pineapple plantation being developed by James B. Dole at Wahiawa, with a spur added to the U. S. Army base at Schofield Barracks. The new branch included stretches of 3-percent grade.

The road prospered. Between 1908 and 1916 it thoroughly modernized its roster of locomotives and cars and installed block signals along the double-track line between Honolulu and Waipahu. In 1925 the road built a new station in Honolulu, and about that time it acquired four 2-8-2s (nearly identical to Rio Grande's K-28 Mikados) and built four motor cars for passenger service. By 1927 the company had retired all its bonds and was free of debt; the Depression merely reduced the dividend rate.

Passenger business dropped during the 1930s but freight traffic held up. When World War Two began traffic to Army and Navy bases increased, and the bombing of Pearl Harbor on December 7, 1941, brought a complete change of pace. The road found itself running 20-car commuter trains; to accommodate the traffic it acquired used cars and locomotives from the Pacific Coast Railway, the Nevada County Narrow Gauge, and

the Boston, Revere Beach & Lynn. A connection was built from Wahiahwa to Waialua in case the Japanese shelled the main line along the coast.

By the end of 1946 the servicemen had gone home and passenger traffic dropped 50 percent. As plantation owners scrapped their railroads and

Oahu Railway No. 70, a Mikado built by Alco in 1925, wheels a Kahuku-bound freight train along the edge of the Pacific east of Kaena Point.

turned to trucks, freight traffic on the Oahu Railway dropped. The railroad abandoned most of its line at the end of 1947. A short portion serving docks and canneries at Honolulu remained in operation until 1971. The U. S. Navy purchased the main line from Pearl Harbor to Nanakuli and operated it until 1970 to serve ammunition dumps at Lualualei. Some of the locomotives and cars were sold to El Salvador.

Hawaii's other common-carrier railroads were:
• Koolau Railway (3-foot gauge) from Kahuku to Kahana, 11 miles, on the northeast shore of Oahu, absorbed by a plantation railway
• Ahukini Terminal & Railway (30-inch gauge), approximately 12 miles on the eastern shore of Kauai, absorbed by a plantation railway
• Kauai Railway (30-inch gauge), 19 miles along the south shore of the island of Kauai, abandonment date uncertain
• Hawaii Railway (3-foot gauge) on the island of Hawaii, 18 miles, abandoned in 1945
• Hawaii Consolidated Railway (standard gauge), 77 miles of main line along the eastern shore of Hawaii, wiped out by a tidal wave April 1, 1946
• Kahului Railroad (3-foot gauge), 16 miles of main line along Maui's north shore, abandoned in 1966

The Koolau Railway connected with the Oahu Railway at Kahuku; none of the other common-carrier railroads connected with each other. There were also numerous plantation railroads in Hawaii. One last line deserves mention: The Lahaina, Kaanapali & Pacific Railroad along the west shore of Maui was built in 1970 as a tourist carrier. It can be considered a successor to the Kahului Railway in that it reused the rails of that line. It is still in operation.

Location of headquarters: Honolulu, Hawaii
Miles of railroad operated: 1929 — 88; 1945 — 93
Number of locomotives: 1929 — 30; 1945 — 26
Number of passenger cars: 1929 — 64; 1945 — 83
Number of freight cars: 1929 — 1,033
Number of company service cars: 1929 — 7
Number of freight and company service cars: 1945 — 1,308
Historical and technical society: Hawaiian Railway Society, P. O. Box 1208, Ewa Station, Ewa Beach, HI 96706
Recommended reading: *Railroads of Hawaii*, by Gerald M. Best, published in 1978 by Golden West Books, P. O. Box 80250, San Marino, CA 91108 (ISBN: 0-87095-049-5)

PACIFIC ELECTRIC RAILWAY

The 1900 census put the population of Los Angeles at 102,479 — it had more than doubled in the previous decade and would more than triple in the next. During the 1890s the city acquired a local trolley system, and in 1895 the Los Angeles & Pasadena Railway was opened from Los Angeles to Pasadena, 10 miles northeast. The line was successful and its owners opened another line the next year, the Pasadena & Pacific, from Los Angeles to Santa Monica. Both companies were reorganized in 1898 as the Pasadena & Los Angeles and the Los Angeles Pacific, respectively. The Pasadena & Los Angeles was purchased (and along with it the Los Angeles Consolidated Electric Railway) by a group of investors headed by Henry E. Huntington (nephew of Collis P. Huntington, one of the builders of the Southern Pacific).

Huntington incorporated the Pacific Electric Railway in 1901 to build a high-speed interurban line from Los Angeles to Long Beach (20 miles) — it was opened in 1902. PE's tracks quickly spread throughout the Los Angeles area. E. H. Harriman was concerned about the effect the interurban would have on his Southern Pacific. He opposed Huntington at first and then purchased a 45 percent interest in the PE. Huntington, who was at the time also a vice-president of SP, then incorporated the Los Angeles Inter-Urban Railway, entirely under his control. That company soon outgrew the PE. In 1908 Huntington leased the Los Angeles Inter-Urban to PE; in 1909 he sold several traction properties elsewhere in California to SP; and in 1910 he sold his Pacific Electric interests to Southern Pacific. He retained his ownership of the Los Angeles Railway, the 3-foot-6-inch-gauge local trolley system.

Donald Duke

Pacific Electric had a stretch of four-track main line from Los Angeles south to Watts. In this late-1950s scene the two inner tracks are occupied by a pair of "Blimps" (nearly 73 feet long, much longer than the usual interurban car, acquired secondhand from Northwestern Pacific) bound for Long Beach and a freight train behind a tiger-striped Southern Pacific diesel switcher equipped with trolley poles to activate grade-crossing signals.

A new Pacific Electric Railway was incorporated in 1911 to consolidate the old PE, the Los Angeles Pacific, the Los Angeles Inter-Urban, and several other traction lines. It was the largest electric railway in the country. In addition to interurban lines stretching from Santa Monica east to Redlands and from San Fernando south to Balboa, PE operated local trolley service in most of the cities and towns. By 1918 PE was the largest electric railway in the world, according to its advertisement in *The Official Guide*. PE's big red cars went nearly everywhere, and they were responsible for much of the development of southern California.

PE's local lines were gradually abandoned or converted to bus operation, but the interurban lines remained strong into the 1940s, operating from terminals in Los Angeles at Sixth and Main streets and on Hill Street near Fourth at the end of a mile-long subway for trains to Hollywood, Burbank, and Van Nuys. After World War Two the interurban lines disappeared one by one. In 1953 PE sold the remaining passenger operations (to Bellflower, Long Beach, San Pedro, Burbank, and Hollywood) to Metropolitan Coach Lines. The Burbank and Hollywood lines were abandoned in 1955. Metropolitan Transit Authority took over the system in 1958; the last line, the Long Beach route, ceased passenger service on April 8, 1961.

Pacific Electric remained in the freight business with diesel power. It was merged with parent Southern Pacific on August 13, 1965.

Location of headquarters: Los Angeles, California
Miles of railroad operated: 1929 — 575; 1964 — 316
Number of locomotives: 1929 — 64; 1960 — 42
Number of passenger cars: 1929 — 822
Number of freight cars: 1929 — 2,296; 1960 — 29
Number of company service cars: 1929 — 97; 1960 — 41
Reporting marks: PE
Recommended reading: Numerous books on all aspects of PE have been published by Interurban Press, P. O. Box 6444, Glendale, CA 91205
Portions still operated: Major portions of the Santa Monica, El Segundo, Torrance, Long Beach, Santa Ana, Yorba Linda, and San Bernardino lines are operated for freight traffic by Southern Pacific.

PEABODY SHORT LINE

Peabody Coal Company (currently the largest producer of coal in the U. S.) purchased the St. Louis & Belleville Electric Railway from Union Electric Company of St. Louis in 1956. The railroad was renamed the Peabody Short Line in December 1958 and adopted a new image of bright yellow and green. The colors were unexpected for a railroad whose business was the traditionally dirty one of moving coal — specifically from Peabody's River King Mine near Freeburg, Illinois, to an interchange

Two of Peabody Short Line's trio of yellow-and-green RS2s shift hopper cars in the four-track yard at Peabody Coal Co.'s River King mine near Belleville, Illinois.

J. P. Lamb Jr.

with the Terminal Railroad Association of St. Louis at East St. Louis.

The St. Louis & Belleville Electric Railway was at first a freight-only subsidiary and later a survivor of the East St. Louis & Suburban railway, an interurban system that was abandoned in 1932. It was dieselized in 1949.

Illinois Central acquired stock control of the line in 1960 and merged it in August 1961. Almost all the track has since been retired, except for that leading to the mine at Freeburg. Peabody Coal Co. has a number of mine operations in Illinois and Indiana that continue to use a similar yellow and green livery on their diesels and coal cars.

Location of headquarters: East St. Louis, Illinois
Miles of railroad operated: 1956 — 14; 1960 — 14
Number of locomotives: 1956 — 1; 1960 — 3
Number of freight cars: 1956 — 206; 1960 — 180
Reporting marks: PSL
Successors:
Illinois Central
Illinois Central Gulf (TWG)

PENN CENTRAL COMPANY

Penn Central came into existence on February 1, 1968. More accurately, it was incorporated in 1846 as the Pennsylvania Railroad; changed its name to Pennsylvania New York Central Transportation Co. on February 1, 1968, when it merged the New York Central; and adopted the name Penn Central Company on May 8, 1968. On October 1, 1969, it again changed its name, to Penn Central Transportation Company, and became a wholly owned subsidiary of a new Penn Central Company, a holding company.

The stockholders of the Pennsylvania and the New York Central approved merger of the two roads on May 8, 1962; nearly four years later the Interstate Commerce Commission approved the merger on the following conditions:

• The new company ("Penn Central" for convenience) had to take over the freight and passenger operations of the New Haven. That happened on December 31, 1968.

• Penn Central had to absorb the New York, Susquehanna & Western. PC and the Susquehanna could not agree on price, and eventually NYS&W became part of the Delaware Otsego System.

• Penn Central had to make the Lehigh Valley available for merger by either Norfolk & Western or Chesapeake & Ohio or, if neither of those roads wanted it, merge it into PC. Lehigh Valley struggled along on its own and entered bankruptcy only three days after Penn Central did.

The merger was not a success. Little thought had been given to unifying the two railroads, which had long been intense rivals and had different styles of operation. In the previous decade New York Central had trimmed its physical plant and assembled a young, eager management group under the leadership of Alfred E. Perlman. The Pennsy was a more conservative and traditional operation. Many of NYC's management people (the "green team") saw that Pennsy (the "red team") was dominant in Penn Central management and soon left for other jobs.

In addition to the problems of unification, the industrial states of the Northeast and Midwest were fast becoming "The Rust Bowl." As industries shut down and moved away, railroads found themselves with excess capacity. The Pennsylvania was worse than practically anyone else in having four or six tracks where one or two would do — track that was no longer needed but which was still on the tax rolls — and west of the Alleghenies Pennsy and Central duplicated each other's track nearly everywhere. The PC merger was like a late-in-life marriage to which each partner brings a house, a summer cottage, two cars, and several complete sets of china and glassware — plus car payments and mortgages on the houses.

Pennsy and New York Central came into the merger in the black, but Penn Central's first year of operation yielded a deficit of $2.8 million. In 1969 the deficit was nearly $83 million. PC's net income for 1970 was a deficit of $325.8 million. By then the railroad had entered bankruptcy proceedings — specifically on June 21, 1970. The nation's sixth largest corporation had become the nation's largest bankruptcy.

The reorganization court decided in May 1974 that PC was not

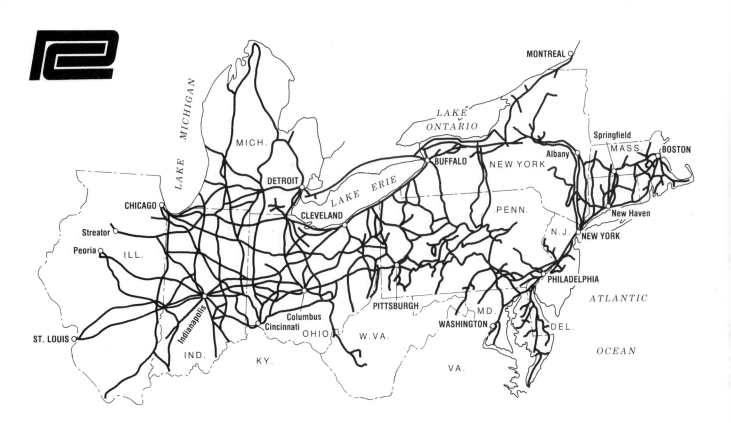

249

reorganizable on the basis of income. A U. S. government corporation, the United States Railway Association, was formed under the provisions of the Regional Rail Reorganization Act of 1973 to develop a plan to save Penn Central. The outcome was that Consolidated Rail Corporation, owned by the U. S. government, took over the railroad properties and operations of Penn Central (and six other railroads: Central of New Jersey, Erie Lackawanna, Lehigh Valley, Reading, Lehigh & Hudson River, and Pennsylvania-Reading Seashore Lines) on April 1, 1976. It was a major step toward nationalization of the railroads of the U. S. They had been nationalized briefly during World War One, but the U. S. had held out against a world-wide trend toward nationalization of railroads until the creation of Amtrak, which nationalized the country's passenger trains, on May 1, 1971.

PC participated in two passenger service experiments in cooperation with the U. S. Department of Transportation. Both were aimed at upgrading passenger service in the Northeast Corridor. Between New York and Washington PC inherited the Metroliner experiment that the Pennsy had begun — fast electric trains that were intended for a maximum speed of 160 mph. The inauguration of service was delayed several times, and when it did begin, it was not shown in *The Official Guide*. The Metroliner was not an absolute success, but it reversed a long decline in ridership on the New York-Washington run. On the Boston-New York run PC operated a United Aircraft TurboTrain in an effort to beat the 3-hour-55-minute running time of the New Haven's expresses of the early 1950s. Information about TurboTrain schedules was even more difficult for the public to obtain than Metroliner timetables. The combination of untested equipment, track that had been allowed to deteriorate, and the general incongruity of space-age technology and traditional railroad thinking made the services the butt of considerable satire. Most of the Metroliner cars are stored out of service, and the TurboTrains were scrapped. PC's intercity passenger service was taken over by Amtrak on May 1, 1971. The commuter service, which was already subsidized by local authorities, passed first to Conrail and then to other operating authorities.

The Penn Central bankruptcy was a cataclysmic event, both to the railroad industry and to the nation's business community. The PC and its

Jay Potter

Electro-Motive and General Electric diesels lead a Penn Central freight west on the former Pennsylvania Railroad Pittsburgh-St. Louis line at Mingo Junction, Ohio, in 1975.

problems have been the subject of more words than almost anything else in the railroad industry, everything from diatribes on the passenger business to analyses of the reason for its collapse. Oddly, almost nothing specifically aimed at the railroad enthusiast has been published about the Penn Central.

Location of headquarters: Philadelphia, Pennsylvania
Miles of railroad operated: 1968 — 20,530; 1975 — 19,300
Number of locomotives: 1968 — 4,411; 1975 — 4,033
Number of passenger cars: 1968 — 5,046; 1970 — 3,569

Number of freight cars: 1968 — 187,423; 1975 — 137,546
Number of company service cars: 1968 — 5,254; 1975 — 4,354
Reporting marks: PC
Recommended reading:
The Wreck of the Penn Central, by Joseph R. Daughen and Peter Binzen, published in 1971 by Little, Brown & Co., Boston, Mass.
No Way to Run a Railroad, by Stephen Salsbury, published in 1982 by McGraw-Hill, Inc., 1221 Avenue of the Americas, New York, NY 10020 (ISBN 0-07-054483-2)
Subsidiaries and affiliated railroads, 1975:
Akron & Barberton Belt (25%)
Ann Arbor (99.5%)
Cambria & Indiana (40%)
Detroit, Toledo & Ironton (100%)
Illinois Terminal (9%)
Indiana Harbor Belt (51%)
Lehigh Valley (97%)
Monongahela (66.7%)
Niagara Junction (75%)
Norfolk & Portsmouth Belt Line (12.5%)
Pennsylvania-Reading Seashore Line (66.7%)
Pittsburgh & Lake Erie (92.6%)
Toledo, Peoria & Western (50%, jointly with Santa Fe)
Toronto, Hamilton & Buffalo (72.9%)
Washington Terminal (50%, jointly with Baltimore & Ohio)
Predecessor railroads in this book:
Pennsylvania
New York Central
New York, New Haven & Hartford
Successors: PC's principal successor in the freight business is Conrail. The carriers that now operate former PC passenger routes are Amtrak, Metro-North, Massachusetts Bay Transportation Authority, Southeastern Pennsylvania Transportation Authority, and NJ Transit. All are described in *The Train-Watcher's Guide*. The short lines spun off to operate portions of former Penn Central track are too numerous to mention here.
Portions still operated: See entries for Pennsylvania, New York Central, and New Haven

PENNSYLVANIA RAILROAD SYSTEM

The Pennsylvania Railroad was originally a line from Philadelphia to Pittsburgh. Much of the road's subsequent expansion was accomplished by leasing or purchasing other railroads: the Pittsburgh, Fort Wayne & Chicago; the Pittsburgh, Cincinnati, Chicago & St. Louis; the Little Miami Railroad (to Cincinnati); the Northern Central (Baltimore to Sunbury, Pa.); the Philadelphia, Baltimore & Washington; and the Philadelphia & Trenton and the United New Jersey Railroad & Canal Company (to New York). I will deal with these separately.

Philadelphians were slow to recognize that the Erie Canal and the National Road (and later the Baltimore & Ohio Railroad) were funneling to New York and Baltimore commerce that might have come to Philadelphia. A canal was opened in 1827 between the Schuylkill and Susque-

hanna rivers, and another was proposed along the Susquehanna, Juniata, Conemaugh, and Allegheny (along with a four-mile tunnel under the summit of the Allegheny Mountains) to link Philadelphia and Pittsburgh. That project was declared impractical, and in 1828 the Main Line of Public Works was chartered to build a railroad from Philadelphia to Columbia, another across the mountains, and canals from Columbia and from Pittsburgh to the base of the mountains.

By 1832 canals were open from Columbia to Hollidaysburg and from Pittsburgh to Johnstown; in 1834 a railroad was opened from Philadelphia to Columbia and a portage railroad was opened over the mountains. The latter was a series of rope-operated inclined planes; canal boats were designed to be taken apart and hauled over the mountains.

The pace of the state's action increased when the Baltimore & Ohio requested a charter for a line to Pittsburgh. The B&O line was chartered,

Three Atlantics, a Cole compound, Pennsy class E29, one of two built for PRR in 1905, and two E3a-class 4-4-2s, lift the *Pennsylvania Limited* up the 1.45 percent grade around Horse Shoe Curve sometime before 1911.

but so was the Pennsylvania Railroad, on April 13, 1846 — to build a railroad from Harrisburg to Philadelphia with a branch to Erie. B&O's charter would be valid only if the Pennsylvania Railroad were not constructed.

The line was surveyed by J. Edgar Thomson, who had built the Georgia Railroad. His operating experience led him to lay out not a line with a steady grade all the way from Harrisburg to the summit of the mountains, but rather a nearly water-level line from Harrisburg to Altoona, where a steeper grade (but still less than that of the Baltimore & Ohio) began for a comparatively short assault on the mountains. This arrangement concentrated the problems of a mountain railroad in one area.

Construction began in 1847. In 1849 the Pennsy made an operating contract with the Harrisburg, Portsmouth, Mountjoy & Lancaster ("Har-

risburg & Lancaster" from here on), and by late 1852 rails ran from Philadelphia to Pittsburgh, via a connection with the Portage Railroad between Hollidaysburg and Johnstown. The summit tunnel was opened in February 1854, bypassing the inclined planes and creating a continuous railroad from Harrisburg to Pittsburgh. More than half the line had already been double-tracked.

The Main Line of Public Works was constructed with a much smaller loading gauge or clearance diagram than the Pennsylvania, and although the Pennsy was operating the Harrisburg & Lancaster, the road's own management was responsible for maintenance — and not doing much of it. In 1857 PRR bought the Main Line and in 1861 leased the Harrisburg & Lancaster, putting the entire Philadelphia-Pittsburgh line under one management.

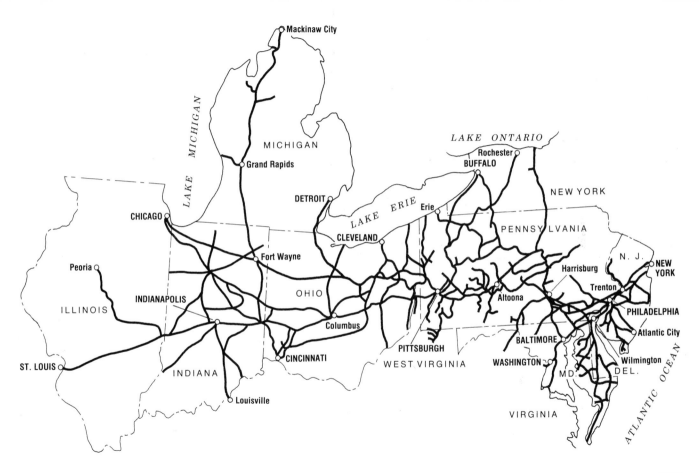

To protect its canal the state had included a tax on railroad tonnage in PRR's charter. When PRR purchased the Main Line, canals and all, it had to engage in a long battle to have the tax repealed, and then only with the provision that the funds for the unpaid taxes be used to aid short lines that connected with the Pennsy. PRR had at the time only one branch, a 3-mile line to Blairsville. Most of the railroads thus aided eventually became part of the PRR.

PRR also acquired two major railroads, the Cumberland Valley and the Northern Central. The Cumberland Valley was opened in 1837 from Harrisburg to Chambersburg, and it was extended by another company in 1841 to Hagerstown, Maryland. The Baltimore & Susquehanna was incorporated in 1828, not long after the Baltimore & Ohio got under way, to build north from Baltimore. Progress was slowed not by construction difficulties but because of the reluctance of Pennsylvania to charter a railroad that would carry commerce to Baltimore. The line reached Harrisburg in 1851 and Sunbury in 1858. By then the several railroad companies that formed the route had been consolidated as the Northern Central Railway. A block of its stock that had been held by John Garrett, president of the Baltimore & Ohio, was purchased by John Edgar Thomson, PRR's president, about 1860 and transferred to PRR ownership. Pennsy did not acquire majority ownership of the Northern Central until 1900.

The Pennsylvania Railroad expanded into the northwestern portion of the state by acquiring an interest in the Philadelphia & Erie Railroad in 1862 and assisting that road to complete its line from Sunbury to the city of Erie in 1864. The line to Erie was not particularly successful, but from Sunbury to Driftwood it could serve as part of a freight route with easy grades. The rest of that route was the Allegheny Valley Railroad, originally conceived as a feeder from Pittsburgh to the New York Central and Erie railroads. The Pennsylvania obtained control in 1868 and opened the low-grade route in 1874 — Harrisburg to Pittsburgh via the valleys of the Susquehanna and Allegheny rivers. PRR leased the Allegheny Valley in 1900.

Pittsburgh, Fort Wayne & Chicago

By 1847 the directors of the Pennsylvania were looking west into Ohio. In 1851 they discussed assisting the Ohio & Pennsylvania Railroad

which by then was open from Allegheny, Pa., across the Allegheny River from Pittsburgh (and now part of Pittsburgh), to Salem, Ohio. Projected west from the end of the O&P at Crestline, Ohio, was the Ohio & Indiana, which was building a line to Fort Wayne, with extensions to Burlington, Iowa, and, almost incidentally, Chicago.

In 1856 the Ohio & Pennsylvania, the Ohio & Indiana, and the Fort Wayne & Chicago were consolidated as the Pittsburgh, Fort Wayne & Chicago Rail Road. The Pennsylvania held an interest in the road, but not a controlling one. In 1858 the Fort Wayne connected its track with the Pennsylvania at Pittsburgh, and at the end of that year its rails reached into Chicago. In 1860 the Fort Wayne leased the Cleveland & Pittsburgh, a line from Cleveland through Alliance (where it crossed the Fort Wayne) to the Ohio River near Wellsville, Ohio, and then upstream to Rochester, Pa., where it again met the Fort Wayne.

In 1869 George Gould tried to get control of the Fort Wayne for the Erie. The Fort Wayne evaded him and was leased by the Pennsy that year. The lease included the Grand Rapids & Indiana, a line from Fort Wayne north through Grand Rapids, Michigan.

The Pennsylvania assembled a route into Toledo in 1873; it was nearly 50 years later that it extended the line, largely on trackage rights, to Detroit.

Pittsburgh, Cincinnati, Chicago & St. Louis

West of Pittsburgh lay a string of railroads — Pittsburgh & Steubenville, Steubenville & Indiana, Central Ohio, Columbus & Xenia, and Little Miami — that formed a route through Columbus to Cincinnati. The Pittsburgh & Steubenville was the last to be opened because the state of Virginia, which held a large interest in the B&O, refused to permit a railroad to be built across its narrow strip of territory (now the panhandle of West Virginia) between Pennsylvania and the Ohio River. The Pittsburgh & Steubenville was sold at foreclosure and a new company, the Panhandle Railway, took over in January 1868. In May of that year the Pennsylvania consolidated the Panhandle and the Steubenville & Indiana as the Pittsburg, Cincinnati & St. Louis Railway, but the nickname "Panhandle" stuck with it and its successors.

West of Columbus the Columbus, Chicago & Indiana Central Railway by 1863 had a line from Columbus to Indianapolis and another from Columbus through Logansport, Ind., to Chicago. The Pennsy leased the CC&IC in February 1869, snatching it from the clutches of George Gould.

Beyond Indianapolis lay the Terre Haute & Indianapolis and the St. Louis, Alton & Terre Haute. Because of a lack of agreement among several roads about division of traffic, the St. Louis, Vandalia & Terre Haute was constructed between 1868 and 1870 from East St. Louis to Terre Haute and leased by the Terre Haute & Indianapolis, which then made traffic agreements with the Panhandle and the Columbus, Chicago & Indiana Central. (The St. Louis, Alton & Terre Haute wound up in the New York Central System.)

The Little Miami Railroad was incorporated in 1836; by 1846 it had a line from Cincinnati through Xenia to Springfield, Ohio, and it grew by purchasing and leasing lines to Columbus and Dayton. It was a desirable property as far as the Pennsy was concerned. To force the issue of a lease, the Panhandle got control of the Cincinnati & Zanesville, a secondary line that would give it access to Cincinnati. The Panhandle leased the Little Miami in 1869.

In 1890 the Pittsburg, Cincinnati & St. Louis and several other lines were consolidated as the Pittsburgh, Cincinnati, Chicago & St. Louis Railway, and in 1905 the Vandalia Railroad was incorporated to consolidate the lines west of Indianapolis. The PCC&StL, the Vandalia, and several others were consolidated in 1916 as the Pittsburgh, Cincinnati, Chicago & St. Louis Railroad. At the beginning of 1921 the PCC&StL was leased to the Pennsylvania Railroad.

Pennsylvania Company

With the leases of 1869 the Pennsylvania suddenly had more than 3,000 miles of line west of Pittsburgh. Rather than try to manage it all from Philadelphia, the PRR organized the Pennsylvania Company to hold and manage the lines west of Pittsburgh. The new company also operated the Fort Wayne and its affiliate roads.

The division of the Pennsylvania system into several more or less autonomous divisions was not altogether successful, partly because the pieces all came together at Pittsburgh, where the yards and terminals were under three managements. The Pennsylvania Company ceased to be an operating company in 1918 and transferred its leases to the Pennsylvania Railroad.

GG1 No. 4831 stands at the head of the *Congressional* awaiting departure from Washington Union Station. The big electric was built in 1935; the sans-serif lettering dates from the same era.

Lines east of Philadelphia

Even with the loyalty to Philadelphia engendered by having its roots and headquarters there, the Pennsy could not ignore New York, both as a city and as a port. Any traffic from the west to New York had to be turned over to the Reading at Harrisburg because there was no through Philadelphia-New York route. In 1863 the PRR contracted with the Philadelphia & Trenton (which was built and opened in 1834), the Camden & Amboy (with lines from Camden to South Amboy and from Trenton to New

255

Pennsy's last stronghold of steam operation was suburban service on the New York & Long Branch, jointly operated with Central of New Jersey. K4 Pacific No. 5387 powers a local at Brielle, N. J., in June 1956.

R. E. Tobey

Brunswick, New Jersey), and the Delaware & Raritan Canal Co. In 1871 it leased the properties of these companies and the United Canal & Railroad Companies of New Jersey, acquiring lines northeast to Jersey City, south to Cape May, and north along the Delaware to Belvidere. In the 1880s PRR acquired lines from Philadelphia east across New Jersey to the shore and constructed lines up the Schuylkill Valley into Reading territory. The New Jersey lines were combined with a parallel line owned by the Reading in 1933 as the Pennsylvania-Reading Seashore Lines.

The New York Central had long had an advantage in passenger service to and from New York: It had a terminal, Grand Central, on Manhattan Island, and all the other roads (except the New Haven, which shared NYC's facilities) had to ferry their passengers across to Manhattan. Pennsy's desire for a rail terminal in Manhattan was given added impe-

tus by its acquisition of the Long Island Rail Road in 1900. After studying proposals for bridges and tunnels, PRR began construction in 1904 of Pennsylvania Station, between Seventh and Eighth avenues and 31st and 33rd streets; two tunnels under the Hudson River; four tunnels under the East River; and a double-track line across the Jersey Meadows to connect it to the main line east of Newark — all electrified. The new station opened in 1910.

In 1917 the New York Connecting Railroad, including the Hell Gate Bridge, was opened, creating a rail route from Bay Ridge in Brooklyn for freight service and from Penn Station for passenger service to a junction with the New Haven in the Bronx.

Lines south of Philadelphia

Baltimore & Ohio had a monopoly on traffic to and from Washington,

D. C. — and protection of that monopoly in its charter. B&O refused to make arrangements with the Northern Central or the Philadelphia, Wilmington & Baltimore for through ticketing of passengers and through billing of freight. The Pennsy bought the charter of the Baltimore & Potomac, a line which was to have run from Baltimore straight south to the Potomac River at Popes Creek, Md., but which had lain dormant since its chartering in 1853. The charter allowed the B&P to build branch lines no more than 20 miles long, and it was slightly less than that from Washington to Bowie, Md., on the B&P. The resulting Baltimore-Washington route, opened in 1872, was only three miles longer than B&O's. Congress authorized the Pennsylvania to continue its line through Washington and across the Potomac to connect with railroads in Virginia.

The Philadelphia, Wilmington & Baltimore was opened in 1838 between the cities of its name. The Pennsy was quick to connect it to the B&P in Baltimore (it had had no physical connection with the B&O), and in 1873 through service was inaugurated between Jersey City and Washington. Both Pennsy and B&O saw the strategic importance of the PW&B, which included lines down the Delmarva Peninsula; PRR got it in 1881. PRR soon extended the Delmarva lines southward by construction of the New York, Philadelphia & Norfolk RR to Cape Charles, Va., and where they connected with a ferry to Norfolk, Va.

In 1902 the PW&B and the B&P were consolidated as the Philadelphia, Baltimore & Washington Railroad. PB&W and Baltimore & Ohio teamed up to form the Washington Terminal Co., which constructed a new Union Station in Washington, opened in 1907. In 1917 the PB&W was leased to the Pennsylvania Railroad.

Turn of the century and after

Major additions to the Pennsylvania at the end of the nineteenth century were extension of the Grand Rapids & Indiana north to Mackinaw City, Mich. (1882); construction of the Trenton Cutoff, a freight line bypassing Philadelphia (1892); control of the Toledo, Peoria & Western (1893, sold 1927); and acquisition of the Western New York & Pennsylvania Railroad, which had lines from Oil City, Pa., to Buffalo, N. Y., and Emporium, Pa., and from Emporium to Buffalo and Rochester. By 1910 the Pennsylvania had achieved full growth: It has been described as a man with his head in Philadelphia, his hands in New York and Washing-

ton, and his feet in Chicago and St. Louis. The metaphor, which is unkind to Pittsburgh, requires for completeness a fishnet spread over the man with pins holding it down at Buffalo, Rochester, and Sodus Point, N. Y., Detroit and Mackinaw City, Mich., Marietta, Cincinnati, and Cleveland, Ohio, Madison, Ind., and Louisville, Kentucky. The hand in New York holds a large fish — Long Island — and resting on the other shoulder is another, the Delmarva Peninsula. Almost everywhere the Pennsy went it was the dominant railroad, the principal exception being the New York Central territory along Lake Ontario and the south shore of Lake Erie.

The Pennsylvania was also, by its own declaration, "The Standard Railroad of the World." The standardization was internal. Passenger trains moved behind a fleet of 425 K4s-class Pacifics; the road had hundreds of P70-class coaches built to a single design. Freight was hauled by 579 L1s-class Mikados (which used the same boiler as the K4s) and 598 I1s-class Decapods; PRR had thousands of X29-class 40-foot steel boxcars. Much of Pennsy's standardization was different from nearly everything else in North America: Belpaire boilers on steam locomotives; position-light signals giving their indications with rows of amber lights at different angles; tuscan red passenger cars instead of olive green.

At the turn of the century under the leadership of Alexander Johnston Cassatt, PRR purchased substantial interests in Norfolk & Western, Chesapeake & Ohio, Baltimore & Ohio, and (through B&O) Reading. Cassatt was vigorously opposed to the practice of rebating (returning a portion of the freight charge to favored shippers) and was in favor of an industry-wide end to the practice. Strong railroads would be able to resist pressure to grant rebates, but weaker ones would not — unless they were controlled by strong railroads. In 1906 PRR sold its B&O and C&O interests but increased its Norfolk & Western holdings.

In 1929 the Pennroad Corporation was formed as a holding company owned principally by PRR stockholders. Pennroad purchased sizable interests in Detroit, Toledo & Ironton; Pittsburgh & West Virginia; New Haven; and Boston & Maine. The Pennsylvania Railroad would have needed ICC approval to purchase interests in other railroads; it was not necessary for the holding company.

The biggest single improvement accomplished by the Pennsylvania Railroad in the 1920s and 1930s was the electrification of its lines from

New York to Washington and from Philadelphia to Harrisburg. The nucleus of the project was the 1915 electrification between Philadelphia and Paoli, Pa. That was extended south to Wilmington in 1928 and began working north to Trenton. PRR decided to change the New York terminal third-rail electrification to high-voltage AC to match the Philadelphia electrification and connect the two; that was completed in 1933, putting the New York-Wilmington line under wires. At the same time the road opened two new stations in Philadelphia, Suburban Station next to Broad Street Station in the city center and 30th Street, on the west bank of the Schuylkill, as the first steps in the elimination of Broad Street Station and the "Chinese Wall" elevated tracks leading to it. Two years later the electrification was extended through Baltimore and Washington to Potomac Yard in Alexandria, Va. Electrification was extended west from Paoli to Harrisburg in 1938, with the thought of eventually continuing it to Pittsburgh.

During World War Two Pennsy's freight traffic doubled and passenger traffic quadrupled, much of it on the eastern portion of the system. The electrification was of inestimable value in keeping the traffic moving. After the war Pennsy had the same experiences as many other railroads but seemed slower to react. PRR was slower to dieselize, and when it did so it bought units from every manufacturer. As freight and passenger traffic left the rails for the highways, Pennsy found itself with far more fixed plant than the traffic warranted or could support, and it was slow to take up excess trackage or replace double track with Centralized Traffic Control. PRR was saddled with a heavy passenger business, and it had extensive commuter services centered on New York, Philadelphia, and Pittsburgh — and lesser ones at Chicago, Washington, Baltimore, and Camden, N. J. It had gone through the Depression without going bankrupt — and bankruptcy can have a salutary effect on old debt. (The Pennsylvania Railroad had to its credit, though, the longest history of dividend payment in U. S. business history.)

Pennsylvania and New York Central surprised the railroad industry by announcing merger plans in November 1957. The two had long been rivals, and the merger would be one of parallel roads rather than end-to-end. The merger took place on February 1, 1968 — and Penn Central fell apart faster than it went together.

Herbert H. Harwood Jr.

Pennsy was by far Baldwin's best diesel customer. A four-unit set of "Shark Nose" freighters brings a Mingo Jct.-Crestline, Ohio, train under the Nickel Plate at Orrville in June 1960.

Location of headquarters: Philadelphia, Pennsylvania
Miles of railroad operated: 1929 — 10,512; 1967 — 9,538
Number of locomotives: 1929 — 6,152; 1967 — 2,211
Number of passenger cars: 1929 — 7,384; 1967 — 2,632
Number of freight cars: 1929 — 270,653; 1967 — 112,431
Number of company service cars: 1929 — 3,976; 1967 — 2,489
Reporting marks: PRR
Notable named passenger trains: *Broadway Limited, General, Trail Blazer* (New York-Chicago), *Liberty Limited* (Washington-Chicago), *Spirit of St. Louis, Jeffersonian* (New York-St. Louis), *Congressional*

(New York-Washington), *Senator* (Boston-Washington, operated north of New York by the New Haven), *South Wind* (Chicago-Miami), *Pittsburgher* (New York-Pittsburgh)

Historical and technical society: Pennsylvania Railroad Technical & Historical Society, P. O. Box 389, Upper Darby, PA 19082

Recommended reading: *Centennial History of the Pennsylvania Railroad Company,* by George H. Burgess and Miles C. Kennedy, published in 1949 by The Pennsylvania Railroad Company, Philadelphia, Pa.

Subsidiaries and affiliated railroads, 1967:

Lehigh Valley (97.33%)

New York & Long Branch (50%, jointly with Central of New Jersey)

New York Connecting (50%, jointly with New Haven)

Detroit, Toledo & Ironton (99.9%)

Wabash (86.7%)

Montour (50%, jointly with Pittsburgh & Lake Erie)

Toledo, Peoria & Western (50%, jointly with Santa Fe)

Pennsylvania-Reading Seashore Lines (66.7%)

Washington Terminal (50%, jointly with Baltimore & Ohio)

Successors:

Penn Central

Conrail (TWG)

Major portions operated by roads other than Conrail and *major portions abandoned*:

(The size and complexity of the Pennsy calls for a slightly different format here. This is not an exhaustive list of what is gone and what remains. In some cases I have shown an entire line as abandoned, even though short stubs remain where it crossed other lines.)

New York-Washington (Northeast Corridor)

New York-Washington; Philadelphia-Harrisburg: Amtrak

New York-Trenton, N. J.; Princeton Jct.-Princeton, N. J.; Rahway-Bay Head Jct., N. J.: NJ Transit

Philadelphia to Trenton, N. J., and Chestnut Hill, Manayunk, Marcus Hook, Paoli, and West Chester, Pa.: Southeastern Pennsylvania Transportation Authority

Wawa, Pa.-Colora, Md.: Octoraro

Pemberton-Bay Head Jct., N. J.; Hightstown-Fort Dix, N. J.; Kinkora-Fort Dix, N. J.; Newfield-McKee City, N. J.; Manumuskin-Cape May, N. J.; Trenton-Lambertville, N. J.

Delmarva Peninsula

Townsend, Del.-Centreville, Md.; Massey-Chestertown, Md.; Seaford, Del.-Cambridge, Md.; Hurlock-Preston, Md.; Frankford, Del.-Snow Hill, Md.: Maryland & Delaware

Pocomoke, Md.-Norfolk, Va.: Eastern Shore

Clayton, Del.-Oxford, Md.; Denton Branch Jct.-Love Point, Md.; Easton-Claiborne, Md.; Easton-Preston, Md.; Hurlock-Ocean City, Md.; Kings Creek-Crisfield, Md.; Snow Hill, Md.-Franklin City, Va.

Philadelphia-Pittsburgh

York-Hanover, Pa.: Maryland & Pennsylvania

Taneytown-Walkersville, Md.: Maryland Midland

Newark-Sodus Point, N. Y.: Ontario Midland

Doe Run, Pa.-Newark, Del.; York, Pa.-Cockeysville, Md.; Hanover, Pa.-Taneytown, Md.; Walkersville-Frederick, Md.; Marion-Mercersburg, Pa.; Williamsport, Pa.-Elmira-Newark, N. Y.; Oil City-Irvineton, Pa.; Warren, Pa.-Salamanca, N. Y.; Cuba Jct.-Rochester, N. Y.; Mayville-Brocton, N. Y.; Bedford-Hyndman, Pa.; Mifflinburg-Snow Shoe, Pa.; Washington-Waynesburg, Pa. (3-foot gauge); New Castle-Franklin, Pa.; Hollidaysburg-Gallitzin, Pa. (Mule Shoe Curve)

West of Pittsburgh

Petoskey-Pellston, Mich.: Michigan Northern

Reed City-Petoskey, Mich.: Tuscola & Saginaw Bay

Grand Rapids-Muskegon, Mich.: Grand Trunk Western

Logansport-Effner, Ind.: Toledo, Peoria & Western

Paris-Decatur, Ill.: Prairie Central

Maroa-Peoria, Ill.: Norfolk & Western (ex-Illinois Terminal)

Warren-Ashtabula, Ohio; Coshocton-Loudonville, Ohio; Bellaire-Zanesville, Ohio (Ohio River & Western, 3-foot gauge); Marietta-Oneida, Ohio; Bremen-Washington Court House, Ohio; Wilmington-Morrow, Ohio; Xenia-Cincinnati, Ohio; Cambridge City-Columbus-North Vernon, Ind.; Frankfort-Otter Creek Jct., Ind.; Richmond-Decatur, Ind.; Butler-Logansport, Ind.; South Bend-Logansport, Ind.; Frankton-Kokomo, Ind.; Kendallville-Lagrange, Ind.; Comstock Park-Reed City, Mich.; Pellston-Mackinaw City, Mich.

259

PENNSYLVANIA-READING SEASHORE LINES

The Philadelphia-Atlantic City, New Jersey, corridor was the setting for one of North America's most intense railroad rivalries — back long before the term "corridor" was applied to railroad routes. The two railroads were the Pennsylvania and the Reading — specifically Pennsy's West Jersey & Seashore Railroad and Reading's Atlantic City Railroad.

The West Jersey & Seashore had been formed in 1896 by the consolidation of several Pennsylvania Railroad properties in New Jersey, among them the Camden & Atlantic, which had a direct route from Camden to Atlantic City via Haddonfield and Winslow Junction; the West Jersey Railroad (Camden to Cape May through Newfield and Millville plus several branches to towns west of that line); and the West Jersey & Atlantic, which ran from Newfield to Atlantic City. In 1906 the West Jersey & Seashore electrified the more southerly of its two routes to Atlantic City (the Newfield route, which served a more heavily populated area and did more local business than the former Camden & Atlantic) with a 650-volt third-rail system. The Newfield-Atlantic City electrification was dismantled in 1931, but Camden-Millville electric trains lasted until 1949. The road's Camden-Philadelphia ferries were discontinued in 1952.

The Atlantic City Railroad had been built as a narrow gauge line from Camden to Atlantic City through Haddon Heights and Winslow Junction, parallel to the Camden & Atlantic and no more than a few miles from it — indeed, within sight much of the way. The narrow gauge line

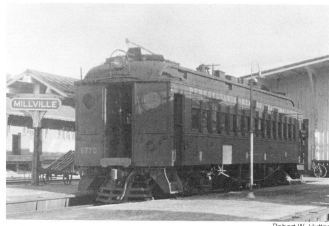

Robert W. Hutton

Car 6770 lays over between runs at Millville, the southern terminus of PRSL's third-rail electrification. The horizontal-barred pilot and the round end windows are Pennsy traits; the trolley poles are used for the last four miles into Camden, an area with many highway crossings.

went bankrupt and was acquired in 1883 by the Reading, which standard-gauged and double-tracked it. By the mid-1890s the Reading's subsidiary had reached Cape May, duplicating the West Jersey & Seashore route.

In the 1920s it was clear to all that the competition and duplication were ruinous, particularly for traffic, both freight and passenger, that could easily be diverted to the highways. Moreover, the business was seasonal — two-thirds of the revenue came from the summer trade traveling to and from the New Jersey shore. The two railroads agreed in 1932 to consolidate the operations. The Pennsylvania bought two-thirds of Reading's Atlantic City stock for $1 (the AC was piling up deficits because of taxes, interest on debt, and equipment rentals), and assigned its lease of

NEW JERSEY

PENNSYLVANIA

PHILADELPHIA ○ ○ Camden

○ Glassboro

Winslow Jct.

Salem ○

ATLANTIC CITY

ATLANTIC

OCEAN

○ Cape May

Until the diesel era, Pennsylvania-Reading Seashore Lines' equipment came from its two parents. In this 1955 scene a Pennsylvania B6 0-6-0 watches while train 756, a Pennsy P70 coach behind a 1948-built Reading G3 Pacific, arrives at Camden from Millville.

Philip R. Hastings

the West Jersey & Seashore to the Atlantic City. The consolidation was effective June 25, 1933, and the Atlantic City Railroad was renamed Pennsylvania-Reading Seashore Lines on July 15 of that year. The initial rationalization of the lines resulted in the abandonment of the Reading line east of Winslow Junction and the Pennsylvania line route south of Woodbine. Most of the Newfield-Atlantic City line was abandoned in the early 1960s.

PRSL's business, largely passenger, dwindled to a handful of Camden-Atlantic City and Camden-Cape May RDC runs, and they eventually terminated their runs at Lindenwold, end of the PATCO rapid transit line, instead of Camden. On July 1, 1982, the last of those runs were replaced by buses because of a federally imposed track speed limit of 15 mph. PRSL's properties were conveyed to Conrail on April 1, 1976.

Location of headquarters: Camden, New Jersey (officers shared with Pennsylvania and Reading were located in Philadelphia)
Miles of railroad operated: 1933 — 413; 1975 — 307
Number of locomotives: 1933 — 22; 1975 — 14
Number of passenger cars: 1933 — 216
Number of motor passenger cars: 1975 — 10

Number of cabooses: 1933 — 26; 1975 — 19
Number of company service cars: 1933 — 53
Reporting marks: PRSL
Historical and technical societies:
Anthracite Railroads Historical Society, P. O. Box 119, Bridgeport, PA 19405
Pennsylvania Railroad Technical & Historical Society, P. O. Box 389, Upper Darby, PA 19082
Reading Company Technical & Historical Society, P. O. Box 5143, Reading, PA 19612-5143
Recommended reading: *Atlantic City Railroad*, by W. George Cook and William J. Coxey, published in 1980 by West Jersey Chapter, National Railway Historical Society, P. O. Box 101, Oaklyn, NJ 08107
Successor companies: Conrail (TWG)
Portions still operated:
Camden-Atlantic City, Camden-Cape May, Camden-Dorchester, Glassboro-Mauricetown, Woodbury-Salem, Woodbury-Deep Water Point: Conrail
Atlantic City-McKee City, Pleasantville-Linwood: Shore Fast Line

PERE MARQUETTE RAILWAY

The Pere Marquette Railroad was formed on January 1, 1900, by the consolidation of the Chicago & West Michigan Railway, the Detroit, Grand Rapids & Western Railroad, and the Flint & Pere Marquette Railroad. The three railroads had been built to serve Michigan's lumber industry, and they were feeling the effects of the decline in lumber produc-

tion as the forests were logged off. Consolidation would make them into one larger, more powerful road.

The Chicago & West Michigan had a main line from La Crosse, Indiana, north to Pentwater, Mich., opened in 1872, and another line from Holland through Grand Rapids to Bay View, Mich. The Flint & Pere Marquette had a line (completed in 1874) from Monroe, Mich., through Flint and Saginaw, Mich., to the eastern shore of Lake Michigan at Ludington (originally called Pere Marquette). From Ludington the F&PM operated car ferries across Lake Michigan to Kewaunee, Manitowoc, and Milwaukee, Wisconsin. Also part of the F&PM was the former Port Huron & Northwestern, built between 1879 and 1882 as a 3-foot-gauge line from Port Huron to Saginaw. The F&PM acquired control of the PH&N in 1883 and merged it in 1889. The Detroit, Grand Rapids & Western, successor in 1897 to the Detroit, Lansing & Northern, had a line from De-

Robert A. Hadley

In common with the other Van Sweringen roads, Pere Marquette bought Berkshires to accelerate its freight trains. Number 1238, still wearing PM lettering in 1949, leaves Detroit bound for Saginaw. Visible in the background is the Ambassador Bridge to Windsor, Ontario.

troit to Grand Rapids and a network of branches north and east of Grand Rapids.

The Pere Marquette inherited substantial debt from its predecessors — all three had histories of receivership and foreclosure — and new management concentrated on absorbing short lines in the interior of Michigan rather than the logical step of extending the line to Chicago. Another new management in 1903 leased the Lake Erie & Detroit River Railway, which had lines from Walkerville (Windsor), Ontario, to St. Thomas and from Sarnia to Erieau and acquired trackage rights over the Michigan Central (ex-Canada Southern) from St. Thomas to Suspension Bridge, New York, and over New York Central from Suspension Bridge to Buffalo. The Pere Marquette of Indiana was chartered to build a line from New Buffalo, Mich., to Porter, Ind., 22 miles. That line was opened in 1903, and trackage rights on the Lake Shore & Michigan Southern (NYC) and Chicago Terminal Transfer Railroad (the predecessor of Balti-

more & Ohio Chicago Terminal) brought the PM the remaining 52 miles to Chicago.

An era followed in which the PM was tossed around like a volleyball. In July 1904 the Cincinnati, Hamilton & Dayton acquired most of the stock of the Pere Marquette and leased the railroad, but in December 1905 the CH&D annulled the lease. PM purchased the Chicago, Cincinnati & Louisville in 1904 and soon let it go — to eventually become Chesapeake & Ohio's line across Indiana. B&O briefly controlled the PM through the CH&D, and the road was briefly leased to the Erie. Meanwhile, the PM had entered receivership, from which it emerged in 1907. It again went into receivership in 1912.

Pere Marquette Railway was incorporated in 1917 to succeed the Pere Marquette Railroad. The automobile industry was beginning to grow, and PM was in the right places to serve it. The Van Sweringen brothers of Cleveland acquired control of the road in 1924, seeing that it could pro-

263

vide markets for coal from their Chesapeake & Ohio. Soon PM's largest source of traffic was the interchange with the Hocking Valley (controlled by C&O) at Toledo. In 1928 the ICC approved control of PM by C&O.

In 1932 Pere Marquette purchased the Manistee & Northeastern Railway, a lumber carrier that reached north from Manistee, Mich., to Traverse City and northeast to Grayling. PM began to develop into a bridge route. Despite the handicaps of a ferry transfer between Walkerville and Detroit and another much longer ferry run on Lake Michigan, the road was able to expedite freight service by avoiding the terminal congestion around Chicago. Chesapeake & Ohio merged the Pere Marquette on June 6, 1947. For several years thereafter it led an almost autonomous existence as the Pere Marquette District and later as part of C&O's Northern Region. Gradually the Pere Marquette name disappeared and was replaced by "Chesapeake & Ohio" and now "Chessie System." (Amtrak revived the Pere Marquette name in 1984 for a new Chicago-Grand Rapids train.)

Location of headquarters: Detroit, Michigan
Miles of railroad operated: 1929 — 2,241; 1945 — 1,949
Number of locomotives: 1929 — 388; 1945 — 283
Number of passenger cars: 1929 — 281; 1945 — 113
Number of freight cars: 1929 — 16,405; 1945 — 14,335
Number of company service cars: 1929 — 599; 1946 — 541

Reporting marks: PM
Notable named passenger trains: *Pere Marquette* (Detroit-Grand Rapids)
Historical and technical societies: Chesapeake & Ohio Historical Society, P. O. Box 417, Alderson, WV 24910
Recommended reading: *Pere Marquette Power*, by Thomas W. Dixon Jr. and Art Million, published in 1984 by the Chesapeake & Ohio Historical Society, P. O. Box 417, Alderson, WV 24910 (ISBN 0-87012-472-2)
Subsidiaries and affiliated railroads, 1945: Manistee & Northeastern
Successors:
Chesapeake & Ohio
Chessie System (TWG)
Portions still operated:
Buffalo-Chicago; Blenheim, Ont.-Port Huron-Saginaw, Mich.; Grand Ledge-Portland, Mich.; Elmdale-Greenville, Mich.; Grand Rapids-Baldwin, Mich.; Holland-Montague, Mich.; Berry-Fremont, Mich.; Holland-Hamilton, Mich.; Paw Paw-Hartford-South Haven, Mich.; New Buffalo, Mich.-La Crosse, Ind.; Toledo-Ludington, Mich.; Croswell-Saginaw-Edmore, Mich.; Palms-Harbor Beach, Mich.; Sandusky-Carsonville, Mich.; Bad Axe-Kinde, Mich.; Walhalla-Manistee, Mich.: Chessie System Grawn-Williamsburg, Mich.; Charlevoix-Petoskey, Mich.: Tuscola & Saginaw Bay

PIEDMONT & NORTHERN RAILWAY

When the American Tobacco Trust was dissolved in 1910 by the U. S. government, its founder, James B. Duke, turned his attention to general industry in the Piedmont area of North and South Carolina. Rivers flowing through the area could provide hydroelectric power, and Duke soon owned several power companies, which in turned owned streetcar systems in area cities.

In 1909 William S. Lee, vice-president of Southern Power & Utilities, proposed an interurban railroad system to connect the cities in the Piedmont area. Two companies were organized, the Piedmont Traction Company in North Carolina and the Greenville, Spartanburg & Anderson Railway in South Carolina, with Duke as president and Lee as vice-president. The railroads were planned for freight service from the outset and would use a 1500-volt DC catenary distribution system. The Piedmont Traction Co. was opened in 1912 as was the Greenwood-Greenville segment of the South Carolina company; the line to Spartanburg was opened in 1914. Also in 1914 the two railroads were consolidated as the Piedmont & Northern Railway.

Even while the railroad was under construction Duke proposed joining the two portions of the system with a 51-mile line between Spartanburg and Charlotte. He also proposed an extension to Norfolk, Virginia;

TRAINS: Linn H. Westcott

Of Piedmont & Northern's eight B-B + B-B freight motors, only one was not built in its own shops: No. 5611, a 1949 General Electric product is shown here switching near Gastonia in 1953.

through the years there were other proposals for extensions to Raleigh, Winston-Salem, and Atlanta, and even to take over and electrify the Georgia & Florida Railroad.

The P&N was taken over by the USRA during World War One; by the early 1920s it had rebuilt the line and begun a new emphasis on freight service. The connection between the two portions of the line was again proposed in 1924. The Southern Railway, whose main line ran between Spartanburg and Charlotte, opposed it, and the ICC ruled against it. Technically the ICC had no jurisdiction over an electric railway, but it ruled that the P&N was a Class 1 railroad that was electrified (basically, a "steam railroad"). The P&N went ahead with preliminary work; the ICC obtained an injunction, which the Supreme Court upheld.

During the Depression the management of the P&N was combined with that of the Durham & Southern, also owned by Duke interests. P&N dropped most of its passenger service, but because its franchise required

that a minimum service be offered, it reduced fares from 3.5 cents per mile to 1 cent per mile. The road had to restore some schedules and buy used passenger cars from the Pennsylvania and the Long Island to handle the resulting surge of business. Later in the 1930s the P&N actively solicited industries to establish plants along the line.

By 1950 the power distribution system needed replacement, and the road turned to diesel power. It dropped all passenger service in 1951 and ended electric operation in South Carolina that year. Mainline electric operation ended in North Carolina in 1954 but a short switching operation at Charlotte remained under wires until 1958.

In 1930 Charleston & Western Carolina and Clinchfield (both controlled by Atlantic Coast Line) and Piedmont & Northern proposed a tunnel under the Southern Railway main line at Spartanburg to connect the Clinchfield directly with the other two without involving the Southern for a half-mile move. The Southern protested, but in 1961 the Supreme

Court approved the project and the 750-foot tunnel was opened in 1963.

In 1965 P&N constructed a branch north from Mount Holly, N. C., to a new Duke Power Co. plant at Terrell. That same year the Duke interests decided to divest their P&N holdings and looked for a buyer. Seaboard Air Line was interested but was preoccupied by its merger with Atlantic Coast Line. Once that was accomplished, though, and over the protests of the Southern, Seaboard Coast Line merged the Piedmont & Northern July 1, 1969.

Location of headquarters: Charlotte, North Carolina
Miles of railroad operated: 1929 — 127; 1968 — 150
Number of locomotives: 1929 — 17; 1968 — 18
Number of passenger cars: 1929 — 30

Number of freight and company service cars: 1929 — 340; 1968 — 23
Reporting marks: PN
Historical and technical society: Piedmont & Northern Railway Historical Association, 6 Rockmont Road, Greenville, SC 29615
Recommended reading: *Piedmont and Northern*, by Thomas T. Fetters and Peter W. Swanson Jr., published in 1974 by Golden West Books, P. O. Box 80250, San Marino, CA 91108 (ISBN 0-87095-051-7)
Successors:
Seaboard Coast Line
Seaboard System
Portions still operated: Seaboard System operates all the former Piedmont & Northern except for the Belton-Anderson, S. C., branch.

PITTSBURG, SHAWMUT & NORTHERN RAILROAD

The Pittsburg, Shawmut & Northern was incorporated in 1899 to consolidate five small railroads, some standard gauge and some narrow gauge, in southwestern New York and northwestern Pennsylvania. The road's immediate task was to join the five separate parts with new construction and standard-gauge the narrow ones to form a route from Wayland and Hornell, N. Y., to Hyde, Pa., north of Brockway in the Shawmut area (a tract of coal land which had been named by a group of Boston industrialists).

The PS&N then organized the Brookville & Mahoning (which later became the Pittsburg & Shawmut Railroad) to extend the line southwest toward Pittsburgh (at the time, spelled without the "h"). P&S was leased to and operated by the PS&N until 1916, when it gained independence.

No sooner had the PS&N assembled its railroad than it found it could not pay the interest on the money borrowed to finance construction. It entered receivership in 1905. Even though the road earned a modest income in most years, it could not begin to repay its accrued debt, nor could it formulate an acceptable reorganization plan. The PS&N served no major industrial centers; the few towns of any appreciable size that it reached were well served by other roads. Coal and lumber formed the Shawmut's

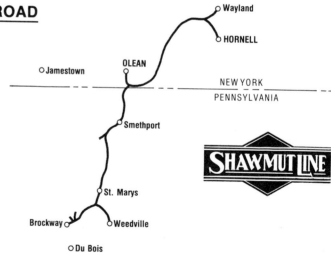

principal traffic, and both gradually disappeared as the mountains were logged off and the mines played out. In the mid-1940s the courts and the management decided that 40 years of receivership was enough, and the road was abandoned in its entirety in 1947.

Only PS&N's herald survives: In 1978 onetime affiliate Pittsburg & Shawmut began using the diamond-shaped "Shawmut Line" emblem in its advertising.

Location of headquarters: St. Mary's, Pennsylvania
Miles of railroad operated: 1929 — 198; 1945 — 190
Number of locomotives: 1929 — 33; 1945 — 16
Number of passenger cars: 1929 — 18
Number of freight cars: 1929 — 416; 1945 — 220
Number of company service cars: 1929 — 34; 1945 — 40
Reporting marks: PS&N
Historical and technical society: Pittsburg, Shawmut & Northern Railroad Historical Society, RD 1, Box 361, Alfred Station, NY 14803
Recommended reading: *Pittsburg, Shawmut & Northern*, by Paul Pietrak, published in 1969 by Paul Pietrak, North Boston, NY 14110

H. D. Runey

Pittsburg, Shawmut & Northern 2-8-0 No. 71 leads a southbound freight train between West Eldred and Corryville, Pa., in February 1947, just before the road was abandoned.

PITTSBURGH & WEST VIRGINIA RAILWAY

In 1881 Jay Gould acquired control of the barely begun Wheeling & Lake Erie. The Wheeling, a line from Toledo, Ohio, to Wheeling, West Virginia, was to be a link in a chain of railroads to connect the Wabash and the Central of New Jersey — and one link in the transcontinental system Gould sought to assemble. In the mid-1880s Gould lost much of his railroad empire, but he was able to pass the Missouri Pacific and the Wabash on to his son George.

George Gould saw that the Wheeling & Lake Erie put him within 60 miles of the industries of Pittsburgh. Spurred by a traffic agreement with Andrew Carnegie, who was feuding with the Pennsylvania Railroad, Gould built a railroad into Pittsburgh from the west to form an eastern extension of the Wheeling & Lake Erie and the Wabash. The easy locations for railroads had already been taken, so the new line was built from hilltop to hilltop and finally through Mount Washington, across the Mo-

nongahela on an immense cantilever bridge, and into an elaborate passenger terminal in downtown Pittsburgh. It was an expensive railroad. It was completed in 1904 and the three companies that had built the lines were consolidated as the Wabash Pittsburgh Terminal Railway, though it and the West Side Belt (a coal-hauling line around the southern part of Pittsburgh) were operated as an integral part of the W&LE.

By 1904 George Gould had acquired control of the Western Maryland and was trying, as his father had tried, to assemble a transcontinental railroad system. WM planned an extension from Cumberland, Maryland, to Connellsville, Pennsylvania, and WPT projected a 40-mile extension southeast to Connellsville.

The Panic of 1907, the cost of building the WPT, and an accord between Andrew Carnegie and the Pennsylvania put an end to Gould's plans. Both WPT and the Wheeling & Lake Erie entered receivership in 1909.

The Pittsburgh & West Virginia was incorporated in 1916 as successor under foreclosure to the Wabash Pittsburgh Terminal Railway. In the

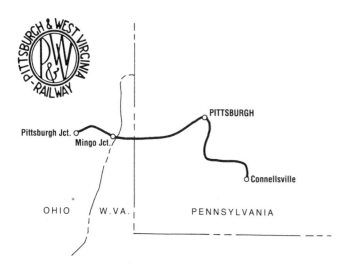

To aid in its transformation from coal-and-terminal road to bridge carrier, Pittsburgh & West Virginia fielded seven Belpaire-boilered 2-6-6-4s. One is shown here leading a freight across the Monongahela River bridge at Belle Vernon, Pa.

1920s Frank Taplin, president of the P&WV, made overtures to control the Wheeling & Lake Erie and the Western Maryland, but the ICC disapproved. In 1931 Taplin was able to complete the extension to Connellsville, where the Western Maryland had been waiting since 1912. About that time control of the P&WV was acquired by the Pennroad Corporation, a holding company that shared many officers with the Pennsylvania Railroad but which was a separate company.

During the late 1930s P&WV developed into a bridge railroad, part of the alphabet route between the Midwest and the East (Nickel Plate, Wheeling & Lake Erie, P&WV, Western Maryland, and Reading). P&WV pulled out of downtown Pittsburgh after its freight house burned in 1946 — the fire may well have sparked the redevelopment of downtown Pittsburgh. In 1949 the road tore down its nine-story passenger terminal (idle since 1931) and office building, dismantled its downtown Monongahela River bridge, and sealed the Mount Washington tunnel.

Pittsburgh & West Virginia was a natural eastern extension of the Wheeling & Lake Erie (later Nickel Plate), providing access to the industry of Pittsburgh, as Gould had intended so many years before. When Norfolk & Western merged the Nickel Plate in 1964 it leased the Pittsburgh & West Virginia.

Location of headquarters: Pittsburgh, Pennsylvania
Miles of railroad operated: 1929 — 89; 1963 — 132
Number of locomotives: 1929 — 30; 1963 — 25
Number of passenger cars: 1929 — 5
Number of freight cars: 1929 — 5,589; 1963 — 1,334
Number of company service cars: 1929 — 55; 1963 — 161
Reporting marks: P&WV
Successors: Norfolk & Western (TWG)
Portions still operated: Norfolk & Western operates the entire P&WV except for the 6-mile Donora branch, which is out of service.

PULLMAN COMPANY

George M. Pullman did not invent the sleeping car — what he did was develop the construction and operation of sleeping cars into a nationwide institution.

Sleeping cars existed before 1850, but most railroad routes were not long enough to require an overnight journey. But as railroads and railroad trips grew longer, the need developed for cars that combined day and night accommodations. Inventors strove to find ways to change seats into beds and vice versa. During the same period there was a shift in the way the cars were operated. Originally the railroads had operated the sleeping cars; gradually entrepreneurs — often the inventors or builders of the cars — took over their operation, essentially sparing the railroad the problems of running a hotel. The better-known sleeping car builders and operators included Theodore and Jonah Woodruff, William D'Alton Mann, and Webster Wagner.

In 1859 George M. Pullman, a cabinetmaker from Brocton, New York, and Benjamin Field remodeled two coaches into sleeping cars for the Chicago, Alton & St. Louis. In 1863 Pullman decided to go into the sleeping car business for himself and built a car named *Pioneer* that was larger and more luxurious than most cars of the era. Much legend and myth clings to *Pioneer*; it is fairly certain, though, that the car was part of the train that carried Abraham Lincoln's body home to Springfield, Illinois.

The Pullman Palace Car Company was chartered in 1867 and began its operations with 48 cars. The company grew as it acquired the cars and lines of other operators. The arrangement with the railroads was usually that Pullman provided the cars, furnished and staffed, and the railroad hauled them and provided heat and light. The railroad received the regular coach fare for each passenger, and Pullman received a supplemental fare and a charge for berth or seat occupancy. Some railroads owned the cars, either solely or jointly.

When Pullman died in 1897 the company had a virtual monopoly on operation of sleeping and parlor cars in the U. S. It owned the largest railroad car plant in the world and had, incidentally, an enormous cash surplus. Robert Todd Lincoln, son of President Abraham Lincoln, succeeded George M. Pullman as head of the company. The company changed its name to Pullman Company. It soon began building steel cars, spurred in part by the prohibition on wooden cars in New York's two subterranean terminals. It expanded into the manufacture of freight cars by acquiring other builders, among them Haskell & Barker and Standard Steel Car Company.

Pullman was known for standardization, both in its rolling stock and in its service. Although its car fleet comprised more than a hundred different floor plans, half the cars were of the 12-section-1-drawing-room configuration, and the various floor plans were combinations of a few standard accommodations. Even more standardized was the level of service on board. Everything the black porter and the Filipino lounge attendant did was governed by books of instructions, from the position of the pillows and the folding of the towels to the proper way to serve beer in the lounge car.

Pullman operated sleeping cars in Mexico just as it did in the U. S., but operations in Canada were limited to international routes and to routes that predated Grand Trunk's absorption into Canadian National Railways — for the most part, the Canadian roads operated their own sleeping car services.

At the height of the Roaring Twenties approximately 100,000 passengers slept in Pullman beds every night, but the Depression soon wrote losses in Pullman's ledgers. Only grudgingly did Pullman yield to pressure for streamlined cars and private-room accommodations; it balked at operating sleeping cars built by Budd. In 1940 the U. S. Department of Justice filed a complaint against Pullman's monopoly of the sleeping car business — Pullman was the sole operator and almost the sole builder of sleeping cars. It was a monopoly the railroads tolerated because Pullman's enormous pool of cars could move around the country to handle

Pullman accommodations: The basic Pullman space was the section, which consisted of two facing seats during the day. At night, the lower berth was formed by pulling the two seat cushions toward each other; the backs of the seats dropped down to a horizontal position. The upper berth was swung down from its stowed position against the upper wall of the car (during the day it provided storage space for the lower berth mattress, pillows, blankets, and curtains). Heavy curtains hung between the berths and the aisle; the passenger buttoned them together after he was in his berth, and that was the extent of privacy. Attached to the inside of the curtains were two coat hangers for each berth, and a net hammock slung lengthwise could hold anything that wouldn't slip through the mesh. The only space for luggage was under the seat (which explains the piece of luggage known as a Pullman case); toilets and washrooms were at either end of the car. Amtrak's Superliner economy room is much like a Pullman section in its basic principles.

Most sleeping cars had one or more private rooms in addition to the sections. These rooms were wider, forcing the aisle to the side of the car. A compartment had a standard section plus a basin and a toilet. A drawing room had a standard section plus a lengthwise couch along the corridor wall, with toilet and basin in a separate room. The term "bedroom" was originally applied to a room with a bed crosswise of the car, with or without an upper berth above it. The roomette, which first appeared in 1937, was a single-occupancy room that had a bed stowed in the wall behind the seat, plus a toilet and a basin. At night the bed was swung down, filling the room.

Some Pullman cars were part sleeper, part lounge, usually with a buffet or kitchenette for the service of beverages and meals. The terms "lounge car" and "club car" both meant lounge, but the lounge did not necessarily have an accompanying buffet. Nowadays "club car" means daytime first-class accommodation, what used to be called parlor car. Parlor cars were daytime Pullmans that had two rows of big revolving armchairs and often a private stateroom or drawing room.

traffic peaks: to Florida in the winter, to Maine in the summer, to Chicago for a Shriners' convention, to Washington for a presidential inauguration. In 1944 a ruling stated that Pullman must separate its carbuilding and its operating divisions.

Separation came in 1947. Pullman became Pullman, Inc., a builder of railroad cars, and sold the sleeping-car operation, the Pullman Company, to the 57 railroads over which its cars ran. There was still a market for long-distance travel, and business held up for a decade. Then one by one railroads pulled out of the Pullman operation. In 1957 the Pennsylvania Railroad began operating its own parlor cars, and in 1958 New York Central began to operate its own sleeping cars.

A more devastating development in 1958 was the beginning of commercial jet flight in the U. S. Jet flight took away the Pullman passenger just as the interstate highway system took away the coach passenger.

First-class passenger business collapsed, and the Pullman Company ceased operation of sleeping cars in the U. S. on December 31, 1968. The railroads took over operation of the few remaining sleeping car lines; Pullman continued to maintain and service the cars until August 1, 1969. Pullman service in Mexico ended about the same time.

Location of headquarters: Chicago, Illinois

Number of passenger cars: 1929 — 9,860; 1968 — 765 (leased) plus 387 cars in Mexican service

Recommended reading:

More Classic Trains, by Arthur D. Dubin, published in 1974 by Kalmbach Publishing Co., 1027 North Seventh Street, Milwaukee, WI 53233

The American Railroad Passenger Car, by John H. White Jr., published in 1978 by Johns Hopkins University Press, Baltimore, MD 21218 (ISBN 0-8018-1965-2)

A long train of heavyweight Pullmans — "battleships" — leaves Milwaukee on the Chicago & North Western in the summer of 1950. The rear car, *Lake James*, has ten sections, two compartments, and one drawing room.

Kalmbach Publishing Co.: Bill Wight

QUANAH, ACME & PACIFIC RAILWAY

The Acme, Red River & Northern was incorporated May 3, 1902, to build between Acme (five miles west of Quanah, the southwesternmost end of the Frisco) and Floydada, Texas. The railroad was renamed the Quanah, Acme & Pacific on January 28, 1909. QA&P projected a line west to El Paso, about 500 miles, and, although never built, the extension appeared on route maps as late as 1944.

The Saint Louis-San Francisco guaranteed some QA&P bonds in 1911 and eventually acquired full control of the road. By the early 1960s the

Donald Sims

Three Frisco GP7s lead a Quanah, Acme & Pacific freight across the open country of the Texas panhandle.

271

QA&P had no rolling stock of its own and relied on parent Frisco for its equipment, although three of Frisco's GP7s bore QA&P lettering when they were delivered.

The QA&P was a bridge line between the Frisco at Quanah (named for the last chief of the Comanches) and the Santa Fe at Floydada for traffic moving to and from the West Coast via Lubbock. In 1973 most of the transcontinental traffic moving over the QA&P was diverted through a direct Frisco-Santa Fe interchange at Avard, Oklahoma. The QA&P was merged with Burlington Northern on June 8, 1981. Merger of the Frisco with Burlington Northern rendered the Quanah Route redundant, and the western half of the line was abandoned in 1982.

Location of headquarters: Quanah, Texas

Miles of railroad operated: 1929 — 126; 1980 — 119
Number of locomotives: 1929 — 7
Number of freight cars: 1929 — 47
Number of company service cars: 1929 — 27
Reporting marks: QAP
Historical and technical societies: Frisco Modelers Information Group, 2541 West Allen Drive, Springfield, MO 65807
Successors:
St. Louis-San Francisco
Burlington Northern (TWG)
Portions still operated: Acme-Paducah: Burlington Northern
Map: See page 287

RAILWAY EXPRESS AGENCY

Express service is the prompt and safe movement of parcels, money, and goods at rates higher than standard freight rates. It is generally considered to have been started by William Harnden, who in 1839 began regular trips between New York and Boston carrying such items. Other early names in the express business are those of William G. Fargo, a New York Central freight clerk at Auburn, N. Y., and Henry Wells, a leather worker at Batavia, N. Y., who organized Wells Fargo & Co. in 1853; Henry B. Plant, who formed Southern Express; Alvin Adams; and John Butterfield. The express business flourished in the latter half of the nineteenth century, and by 1900 there were four principal express companies: Adams, Southern, American, and Wells Fargo. In 1913 the Post Office in-

Ward Kimball

Part of the scene at every station used to be Railway Express Agency's wagons, bright green with red wheels. Their loads — boxes and crates, baskets and milk cans — echoed the diversity of express traffic.

troduced parcel post, the first major competition for the express companies. Even so, express business continued to increase until 1920, then remained stable for a decade.

Under the USRA the four major companies were consolidated as American Railway Express, Inc., except for the portion of Southern Express that operated over the Southern Railway and the Mobile & Ohio (and that came into the organization in 1938). In March 1929, upon expiration of the initial contracts, the assets and operations of American Railway Express were transferred to Railway Express Agency, which was owned by 86 railroads in proportion to the express traffic on their lines — no one railroad or group of railroads had control of the agency. REA's arrangement with the railroads was that they provided terminal space and cars and moved the cars at their expense; REA paid its own expenses and divided the profit among the railroads in proportion to the traffic. Express service in Canada and Mexico was operated directly by the railroad companies.

Express revenues remained at profitable levels into the 1950s, albeit partly because of rate increases — express volume dropped substantially after World War Two. The railroads began to view express service as expensive business. REA negotiated a new contract in 1959 which allowed it to use any mode of transportation, and it acquired truck rights to allow continued service after passenger trains were discontinued. It tried piggyback and containers, but without much success.

In 1969, after several years of deficits, REA was sold to five of its officers and renamed REA Express. By then only ten percent of its business moved by rail and its entire business constituted less than one percent of all intercity parcel traffic. The company sued the railroads and United Parcel Service for various reasons and became involved in suits and countersuits with the clerks' union, and the Civil Aeronautics Board terminated REA's exclusive agreement with the airlines for air express. REA Express terminated operations in November 1975 and began liquidation — which was complicated by the trials of its officers for fraud and embezzlement.

RAILWAY MAIL SERVICE

The date mail first moved on trains in the U. S. is disputed, but in 1832 the first official route was authorized by the Postmaster General over the Camden & Amboy Railroad. In 1837 the Post Office Department appointed route agents to accompany mail shipments. In 1838 Congress declared all railroads to be post roads and that same year mail cars in which mail was sorted en route began running between Washington and Philadelphia.

What is generally acknowledged as the first Railway Post Office was established July 7, 1862, on the Hannibal & St. Joseph Railroad to expedite mail handling in connection with the Pony Express. George B. Armstrong of the Post Office Department undertook a reform of the mail service; part of that reform was the establishment of traveling post offices, to be called United States Railway Post Offices. The first official RPO was inaugurated between Chicago and Clinton, Iowa, over the Chicago & North Western on August 28, 1864. In July 1869 the Post Office Department established the Railway Mail Service with Armstrong as its first general superintendent. Among Armstrong's early innovations were standard mail cranes and catcher arms and overnight mail trains. Armstrong was followed after three years by George S. Bangs, who is credited with the establishment of fast long-distance mail trains.

The Congressional declaration that all railroads were post roads or mail routes meant that Railway Post Office cars soon were found everywhere rails went. Most through and local passenger trains carried mail — and until the 1920s there was no other practical way for mail to move.

In the 1930s trucks began to replace trains for short-distance transportation of mail and Highway Post Offices — buses or trucks outfitted for sorting mail — were introduced to replace branchline RPOs. The Railway Mail Service oversaw the introduction of air mail and made a few experiments with mail-sorting in flight and even with pickup and delivery

Pickup and delivery of mail at speed was a feature of Railway Post Office operation. Here New York Central train 406, the Chicago-Cincinnati *Carolina Special*, picks up a sack of mail at better than 70 miles per hour in May 1949.

Four clerks sort mail aboard Milwaukee Road train 15 between St. Paul, Minn., and Aberdeen, S. Dak., in 1968.

literally on the fly. In 1949 the Railway Mail Service was replaced by the Postal Transportation Service. The change of name forecast changes in service. First-class mail began to move by air, first as space was available, then regularly. The Post Office discontinued RPO runs because passenger trains were being discontinued, and the railroads dropped passenger trains because mail contracts were not being renewed. In 1963 the introduction of Zip Code and Sectional Center Facilities — in many ways a return to the mail distribution and sorting system in use in the early 1800s — meant the eventual end of sorting in transit. The last RPO route

in the U. S., between New York and Washington, made its last run on the night of June 30, 1977. Much mail still moves by rail, but for the most part in containers and trailers on flat cars.

Canada's Railway Mail Service was similar to that of the U. S.; generally speaking, RPO operation in Canada was discontinued before that in the U. S. Mexico's railroads also carried and sorted the mails — and still do. The Spanish term for "Railway Post Office" is *Oficina Postal Ambulante*, though the cars are lettered simply *Correo*.

READING COMPANY

The Philadelphia & Reading Railroad was chartered in 1833 and opened in 1842 from Philadelphia along the Schuylkill River through Reading to Pottsville, Pennsylvania. The purpose of the railroad was to carry anthracite to Philadelphia. The railroad grew by acquiring other roads. The P&R assisted construction of the Lebanon Valley Railroad from Reading to Harrisburg; in 1858 the Lebanon Valley was merged into the Philadelphia & Reading. By 1869 the P&R had acquired the East Pennsylvania Railroad between Reading and Allentown, and in 1870 the P&R leased the Philadelphia, Germantown & Norristown Railroad, which had been built between 1831 and 1835 from Philadelphia to Germantown and along the east bank of the Schuylkill to Norristown.

In 1869 Franklin B. Gowen became president of the P&R and began buying coal lands for the railroad. The Philadelphia & Reading Coal & Iron Co. acquired about 30 percent of the anthracite land in Pennsylvania, but the cost of the land put the railroad into receivership in 1880. During Gowen's administration the P&R acquired the North Pennsylvania Railroad, which ran from Philadelphia to Bethlehem and Yardley, and built the Delaware & Bound Brook from Yardley to a connection with the Central Railroad of New Jersey at Bound Brook, N. J. Between 1880 and 1890 the P&R reached out to Shippensburg, Pa., with a line that would eventually carry much of the road's bridge traffic, and extended a line from Bound Brook to a new port, Port Reading, on the New Jersey shore of Arthur Kill (the body of water which separates Staten Island from the mainland).

On its second attempt the railroad emerged from receivership, and Archibald A. McLeod became president in 1890. The P&R leased the Central Railroad of New Jersey (P&R had previously leased the CNJ between 1883 and 1887) and the Lehigh Valley; the three railroads transported more than half of the country's mined coal at the time. To get a better grip on the New England coal market, the P&R acquired control of the Poughkeepsie Bridge route, the Boston & Maine, and the New York &

New England. The P&R was reaching out for the Old Colony when it collapsed once again into receivership.

In the reorganization of 1896 the railroad and the coal company both became properties of the Reading Company, a holding company. In 1898 the Reading leased the Wilmington & Northern Railroad, a line from Reading to Wilmington, Delaware, and in 1901 the Reading acquired control of the Central of New Jersey. At that same time the Baltimore & Ohio Railroad purchased a controlling interest in the Reading.

The Philadelphia & Reading expanded into New Jersey in 1883 by purchasing the Atlantic City Railroad, a narrow gauge line from Camden to Atlantic City, N. J. P&R standard-gauged and double-tracked the line — Philadelphia-Atlantic City passenger traffic was growing — and extended it to Cape May.

At the end of 1923 the Reading Company merged a number of wholly owned railroads (the Philadelphia & Reading Railroad chief among them) and became an operating company.

By the 1930s traffic to the New Jersey seashore was declining on the Atlantic City Railroad and also on Pennsylvania Railroad's West Jersey & Seashore, which duplicated the Atlantic City Railroad at almost every point. In 1932 the Reading and the Pennsy agreed to consolidate operations. Pennsy bought two-thirds of Reading's Atlantic City stock and assigned its lease of the West Jersey & Seashore to the Atlantic City, which was renamed Pennsylvania-Reading Seashore Lines. The consolidation took effect June 25, 1933. During the same period, between 1929 and 1933, Reading electrified its Philadelphia suburban service.

Beginning in 1945 the Reading underwent a series of corporate simplifications, merging controlled and leased lines. In 1963 Reading acquired the Lehigh & Susquehanna Railroad from Lehigh Coal & Navigation — Central of New Jersey's lines in Pennsylvania — and in 1968 Reading acquired the Cornwall Railroad, a 12-mile line from Lebanon to Mount Hope, Pa., from Bethlehem Steel.

The Reading supplemented its coal traffic with overhead traffic between the Western Maryland at Shippensburg and connections at Allentown for New York and New England. Reading's passenger trains were deemed commuter trains and therefore were not taken over by Amtrak. Philadelphia-Reading-Pottsville and Philadelphia-Bethlehem service was

Reading 2-10-2 No. 3012 leads an anthracite train along the bank of the Schuylkill River at Tamaqua, Pa., in July 1953. Reading's K-1sb class Santa Fes, built by Baldwin in 1931, were the world's largest 2-10-2s.

discontinued in 1981. Philadelphia-New York service, once part of the Royal Blue Route operated in partnership with Baltimore & Ohio and Central of New Jersey, was down to a single Newark-West Trenton train when service ceased in November 1982.

The Reading entered bankruptcy proceedings on November 23, 1971; its operations were taken over by Conrail on April 1, 1976.

Location of headquarters: Philadelphia, Pennsylvania
Miles of railroad operated: 1929 — 1,460; 1975 — 1,149
Number of locomotives: 1929 — 988; 1975 — 225
Number of passenger cars: 1929 — 910; 1975 — 176
Number of freight cars: 1929 — 43,298; 1975 — 12,213

Number of company service cars: 1929 — 823; 1975 — 168

Reporting marks: RDG

Notable named passenger trains: *Crusader, Wall Street* (Philadelphia-Jersey City)

Historical and technical society:

Anthracite Railroads Historical Society, P. O. Box 119, Bridgeport, PA 19405

Reading Company Technical & Historical Society, P. O. Box 5143, Reading, PA 19612-5143

Recommended reading: *Reading Power Pictorial*, by Bert Pennypacker, published in 1973 by P&D Carleton, 158 Doretta Street, River Vale, NJ 07675

Subsidiaries and affiliated railroads, 1975:

Ironton (50%, jointly with Lehigh Valley)

Central Railroad of New Jersey (49%)

Pennsylvania-Reading Seashore Lines (33%)

Wilmington & Northern

Successors:

Pennsylvania-Reading Seashore Lines

Conrail (TWG)

Southeastern Pennsylvania Transportation Authority

Portions still operated:

Philadelphia-Bound Brook-Port Reading, N. J.; Philadelphia-Bethlehem, Pa.; Philadelphia-Reading-Tamaqua-Sunbury, Pa.; Winfield-Williamsport-Newberry Jct., Pa.; Norristown-Doylestown, Pa.; Pottstown-Boyertown, Pa.; Pottsville-St. Clair, Pa.; Schuylkill Haven-Good Spring, Pa.; Allentown-Reading-Harrisburg-Shippensburg, Pa.; Emmaus-Pennsburg, Pa.; Alburtis-Seiple, Pa.; Topton-Kutztown, Pa.; Sinking Spring-Akron, Pa.; Lititz-Columbia, Pa.; Lancaster Jct.-Lancaster, Pa.; Lebanon-Cornwall, Pa.: Conrail

Philadelphia to West Trenton, N. J., and Chestnut Hill, Doylestown, Newtown, Norristown, and Warminster, Pa.: Southeastern Pennsylvania Transportation Authority

Coatesville-Elsmere (Wilmington), Del.: Octoraro

Mount Holly Springs-Gettysburg, Pa.: Gettysburg

Warminster-New Hope, Pa.: New Hope & Ivyland

William D. Middleton

Silverliner multiple unit cars, built by Budd in 1963, approach the huge arched trainshed of Reading Terminal in Philadelphia while a train of Reading's original MU cars, built in 1931, awaits departure.

RIO GRANDE SOUTHERN RAILROAD

In 1882 the Denver & Rio Grande completed its line from Durango to Silverton, Colorado, and in 1887 it pushed a line south from Montrose to Ouray, a silver-mining center about 15 miles north of Silverton — straight-line distance, ignoring Red Mountain. Otto Mears surveyed and built a wagon road from Silverton over Red Mountain Pass. He then built the Silverton Railroad on much the same alignment as far as Albany, about 8 miles short of Ouray. To descend from Albany to Ouray the railroad would have to use stairs, not rails, or resort to extremely expensive construction to build a line that would be subject to rockslides part of the year and snowslides during the rest.

Mears knew that the ore-rich area west and northwest of Durango needed transportation, so he had a railroad surveyed from Dallas, north of Ridgway to Durango by way of Telluride, Rico, and Dolores. The Rio Grande Southern Railroad was incorporated in 1889 and completed in 1891. The route crossed four major summits, highest of which was Lizard Head Pass (10,250 feet), and included innumerable trestles and bridges.

The road basked briefly in the prosperity that resulted from the passage of the Silver Purchase Act in 1890. Repeal of the act in 1893, however, ended the prosperity, and the Rio Grande Southern entered receivership because of its construction debt. The Denver & Rio Grande gained control in 1893.

The RGS continued to exist as a separate entity on paper, but it was operated as a divison of its parent, eking out an existence carrying ore and livestock and battling snow and slides. Even though it operated at a profit, it never earned enough to cover interest on its bonds or issue a stock dividend. In 1929 it was again placed in the care of a receiver, Victor Miller.

In 1931 RGS assembled a motor rail car from Buick parts. It was successful enough that the road then built a fleet of motor cars from Pierce-Arrow parts. These cars, which acquired the nickname "Galloping Geese," replaced the mixed trains that had previously replaced the passenger trains. They became a symbol of the Rio Grande Southern. In 1942 the property of the RGS was purchased by the Defense Supplies Corporation — one of the road's cargoes during World War Two was uranium ore

Galloping Goose No. 4 — more properly, Motor No. 4 of the Rio Grande Southern — rolls north past Trout Lake, between the Lizard Head Pass and Ophir.

from mines at Vanadium. In spite of Galloping Geese and uranium, though, the Rio Grande Southern continued to decline. Its ailments and afflictions included floods and washouts, a fire that destroyed a large lumber mill, the explosion of the boiler of its rotary snowplow, a drop in zinc prices, and loss of the mail contract. The imposition of a surcharge on every car of freight drove away business. There were no formal protests to Rio Grande Southern's abandonment petition, and the last train ran on December 27, 1951.

Location of headquarters: Denver, Colorado
Miles of railroad operated: 1929 — 174; 1951 — 172
Number of locomotives: 1929 — 13; 1951 — 5
Number of motor cars: 1951 — 5
Number of passenger cars: 1929 — 5
Number of freight cars: 1929 — 9
Number of company service cars: 1929 — 33
Number of cars: 1951 — 84
Recommended reading: *Silver San Juan*, by Mallory Hope Ferrell, published in 1973 by Pruett Publishing Co., 3235 Prairie Avenue, Boulder, CO 80301 (ISBN 0-87108-057-5)
Map: See page 111

RUTLAND RAILROAD

The Rutland's early history is entwined with that of the Vermont Central (predecessor of today's Central Vermont) and with that of New England railroads in general. Two major themes in New England railroad history are the competition of the early railroads to build lines to the Great Lakes, and the consolidation of the multitude of small railroads into a few major ones. Rutland's development is easiest to understand considered route by route: the original Bellows Falls-Rutland-Burlington route diagonally across Vermont; the line south from Rutland through Bennington to Chatham, New York; and the tentacle from Burlington across the north end of Lake Champlain and the northern tier of New York to Ogdensburg, on the St. Lawrence River. Not until the turn of the century were the three routes united as one railroad.

The Champlain & Connecticut River Rail Road Company was incorporated November 1, 1843, to build a railroad between Bellows Falls and Burlington, Vt., as part of a route from Boston to Ogdensburg, N. Y. The enterprise was reorganized as the Rutland & Burlington Railroad in 1847, and the line was completed in December 1849. At Bellows Falls there were connections southeastward to Boston and south down the Connecticut River, but at Burlington the railroad fought and feuded with the Vermont Central for traffic and for connections with the Vermont & Canada at nearby Essex Junction. In 1854 the Rutland & Burlington defaulted on mortgage interest payments. It was reorganized in 1867 as the Rutland Railroad.

The Vermont Central leased the Rutland on December 30, 1870, partly to acquire Rutland's leases of the Vermont Valley (Bellows Falls to Brattleboro, Vt.) and the Vermont & Massachusetts (Brattleboro to Millers Falls, Massachusetts), which gave Vermont Central a connection to the New London Northern and a water route from New London, Connecticut, to New York. A more pressing reason for the lease was to forestall a move by the Rutland to construct a line around the south end of Lake Champlain, then north along the west shore of the lake to a connection west to Ogdensburg. The terms of the lease were particularly beneficial to the Rutland; the rental was better than the income the Rutland would earn operating independently. In 1887 Delaware & Hudson gained control of the Rutland, which was still leased to the Central Vermont (the successor in 1873 to the Vermont Central). The Rutland renewed its lease to the CV in 1890. Central Vermont entered receivership in 1896 and terminated the lease of the Rutland; in 1888 D&H had sold its interest in the Rutland to Percival W. Clement, a banker in Rutland (and later governor of Vermont).

The Western Vermont Railroad was chartered in 1845 to build south from Rutland to North Bennington, then west to a connection with the Troy & Boston at White Creek, N. Y. The railroad opened in 1853 and was leased to the T&B in 1857, forming a route, if a roundabout one, from Boston to the Hudson River in conjunction with the Rutland & Burlington, Cheshire, and Fitchburg railroads. The Western Vermont was renamed the Bennington & Rutland in 1865. When the Hoosac Tunnel in western Massachusetts was opened in 1875, the T&B gained a much shorter route to Boston and cast off the Bennington & Rutland. The B&R filed suit against the T&B; there was a small railroad war; and the B&R merged with the Lebanon Springs, a line that meandered north from Chatham, N. Y., to form the Harlem Extension Railroad — essentially a northward extension of what later became the Harlem Division of the New York Central. Vermont Central leased the Harlem Extension from 1873 to 1877. It emerged from the lease as two railroads, the Harlem Extension South, later Lebanon Springs, then Chatham & Lebanon Valley, and the Bennington & Rutland. The Rutland purchased the Bennington & Rutland in 1900 and the Chatham & Lebanon Valley in 1901.

Ogdensburg, N. Y., was at the eastern limit of Great Lakes and St. Lawrence River navigation. A railroad between Ogdensburg and Lake Champlain was discussed as early as 1830 as part of a Boston-to-Great Lakes route, but it was 1850 before the Northern Railroad (of New York) was opened between Ogdensburg and Rouses Point. It was extended east to connect with the Vermont & Canada in 1852, and it was reorganized as the Ogdensburg Railroad in 1858 and again as the Ogdensburg & Lake Champlain in 1864. A subsidiary, the Ogdensburg Transportation Company, operated a fleet of lake boats between Ogdensburg and Chicago. The O&LC was leased to the Vermont Central in 1870. Like the Rutland, it resumed independent operation after Central Vermont entered receivership in 1896. In 1901 the Rutland purchased the road.

To connect the O&LC with its own line the Rutland chartered the Rutland & Canadian Railroad, which quickly constructed a line from Burlington to Rouses Point. The line used the islands at the north end of Lake Champlain as stepping stones; a 3-mile causeway connected the islands with the mainland north of Burlington. The line was opened in 1901 and consolidated with the Rutland that same year.

By 1902 the Rutland extended from Chatham, N. Y., and Bellows Falls, Vt., north through Rutland, where the two lines joined, to Burlington and then west through Rouses Point and Malone, N. Y., to Ogdensburg. It participated in Boston-Montreal and New York-Montreal passenger traffic and in conjunction with its navigation line on the Great Lakes it offered freight service between New England and Chicago. It did a good business carrying Boston- and New York-bound milk out of Vermont.

Shortly after the turn of the century the New York Central & Hudson River and William Seward Webb, son-in-law of William H. Vanderbilt of the NYC&HR, began to buy Rutland stock. Webb became president of the Rutland in 1902, and by 1904 NYC interests owned more than half the capital stock of the Rutland. The railroad entered a period of New York Central control and prosperity.

About that same time the New Haven acquired control of the New York, Ontario & Western. The New Haven regarded New England as its own territory and was concerned with New York Central's acquisitions of the Boston & Albany and the Rutland; NYC for similar reasons was wary of NH's interest in the NYO&W. There was discussion of an exchange of subsidiaries. In 1911 the New Haven purchased half of the New York Central interest, over the protests of Rutland's minority stockholders, who recognized that NYC control was the best thing that had happened to the road in many years.

The Panama Canal Act of 1915 amended the Interstate Commerce Act to prohibit railroad ownership of a competing interstate water carrier. The Interstate Commerce Commission ruled that Rutland's boats between Ogdensburg and Chicago competed with parent New York Central. The boats were discontinued, and their traffic, which formed a large part of Rutland's freight business, wound up on NYC trains. Control by the United States Railroad Administration during World War One

Phillip R. Hastings

In 1946 Rutland purchased four 4-8-2s, the first new power on the line since 1929. By 1952 they had been retired in favor of diesels, but for six years they served admirably in freight and passenger service. Number 90, first of the series, doubleheads with Mikado No. 35 a few miles south of Rutland on a freight for Bellows Falls.

brought a great increase of traffic to the Rutland but at a considerable cost in deferred maintenance. Passenger traffic began to trickle away to the highways, and floods in 1927 washed out much of Rutland's line. The Rutland was strong enough financially to remain solvent through much of the Great Depression, but on May 5, 1938, the Rutland entered receivership.

Economy measures, wage cuts, tax reductions, and a "Save the Rutland" Club kept the railroad going. Symbolic of the effort was a new Bellows Falls-Norwood, N. Y., freight train, *The Whippet*, for which the road streamstyled and painted a 1913-vintage 2-8-0. Many different reorganization plans were proposed and discussed, but it was more than 12 years before a new company emerged — the Rutland Railway, which came into existence on November 1, 1950.

Heading the management committee of the new company was Gardner Caverly, a major bondholder. He scrapped 25 miles of sidings and branches, and used the scrap value of Rutland's roster of steam locomotives and the worst of the freight cars as a down payment on 15 diesels. He scrapped the Bennington-Chatham line to pay for 450 new box cars, which wore yellow and green paint and a new herald, plus 70 gondolas and 27 covered hopper cars. A short strike in the summer of 1953 had the beneficial effect of ridding the Rutland of its passenger trains, which were expensive to operate and ran almost empty. The entire physical plant of the railroad was modernized and the labor force was thinned. In 1957 the Rutland paid a dividend on its preferred stock.

Through all of this Rutland's employees were being paid less than the national standard, and in September 1960 they walked out. William Ginsburg, Caverly's successor, had cut all the costs he could; traffic, particularly milk, was declining, and the company had no cash reserve. An injunction brought the employees back to work 41 days after they struck, but the cooling-off period ended on September 25, 1961, and so did all service on the Rutland Railway. Neither management nor labor would compromise, and on December 4, 1961, the Rutland petitioned for abandonment. Hearings and appeals went on for more than a year, but the Rutland was dead.

The state of Vermont bought the Burlington-Bennington-White Creek and Rutland-Bellows Falls lines. The Vermont Railway began operation on the former on January 6, 1964, and the Green Mountain Railroad began freight service between Bellows Falls and Rutland in April 1965 after a season of steam passenger operation on the line by the Steamtown, U. S. A., museum at Bellows Falls. Service resumed on the Norwood-Ogdensburg portion of the former O&LC in 1967 following its acquisition by the Ogdensburg Bridge & Port Authority. That line is now operated by the St. Lawrence Railroad.

Location of headquarters: Rutland, Vermont
Miles of railroad operated: 1929 — 413; 1961 — 391
Number of locomotives: 1929 — 85; 1961 — 15
Number of passenger cars: 1929 — 138; 1953 — 42; 1961 — 3
Number of freight cars: 1929 — 1,778
Number of company service cars: 1929 — 231
Number of freight and company service cars: 1961 — 465
Reporting marks: R
Recommended reading: *The Rutland Road* (second edition), by Jim

Shaughnessy, published in 1981 by Howell-North Books, 850 North Hollywood Way, Burbank CA 91505
Portions still operated:
White Creek, N. Y.-Burlington: Vermont Railway
Bellows Falls-Rutland: Green Mountain Railroad
Norwood-Ogdensburg, N. Y.: St. Lawrence Railroad

SACRAMENTO NORTHERN RAILWAY

At one time Sacramento Northern offered the longest interurban ride in the world, 183 miles from San Francisco to Chico, California. The ride included the Bay Bridge between San Francisco and Oakland, a tunnel through the Oakland hills, a train ferry across Suisun Bay just west of the confluence of the Sacramento and San Joaquin rivers, a fast ride across California's delta country, and a long look at the agricultural Sacramento Valley. In recent years SN abandoned much of its main line, leaving odds and ends of track in the towns and cities it served, and it shared most of its officers with parent Western Pacific (or vice versa, to be more accurate). WP was acquired by Union Pacific in 1982, and by 1984 SN no longer had interchange freight cars of its own and most of its officials were in Omaha. I have used 1971 as an end date for SN because the 1972 issue of *Moody's Transportation Manual* is the last with any information on the road.

Northern Electric Company was incorporated in 1905 to build a railroad from Chico to Sacramento, 90 miles. Construction began at Chico, and service began between there and Oroville on April 25, 1906, a week after the San Francisco earthquake and fire. Construction then worked south from Oroville Junction through Marysville, reaching Sacramento, the state capital, in 1907. The extension to Sacramento was built with a 600-volt third rail for power distribution, except in the cities, where it used conventional trolley wire, and in 1909 Northern Electric converted the Oroville-Chico line to third rail. The line soon acquired branches to Hamilton City, Colusa, and Woodland. It proposed an extension north to Redding, and a subsidiary built an isolated line between Vacaville and Suisun as part of a proposed extension from Woodland to Vallejo.

In 1914 Northern Electric entered receivership. The Hamilton branch, which had a pontoon bridge over the Sacramento River, was abandoned in 1915 after only eight years of operation. A new company, the Sacramento Northern Railroad, took over the properties and operations in 1918, and in 1921 Western Pacific acquired control of the SN.

The Oakland, Antioch & Eastern was successor to the Oakland & Antioch Railway, which was incorporated in 1909. By early 1913 the line was open from Bay Point (now Port Chicago) south through the San Ramon Valley towns of Concord, Walnut Creek, and Lafayette to Oakland. The engineering feat of the line was a 3,600-foot tunnel through the Oakland hills. From 40th Street and Shafter Avenue in Oakland the O&A used Key System rails to reach the Key System pier and a ferry connection to San Francisco. In September of that year the line to Sacramento was opened. Trains were ferried across Suisun Bay; the railroad obtained permission from the U. S. War Department to build a bridge, but specifications for height and clear channel put it beyond OA&E's means. From the north shore of Suisun Bay the line made a straight shot through unpopulated country to Sacramento. A branch was constructed as far east as Pittsburg; the line never reached Antioch. OA&E's cars were equipped with pantographs to draw current from Key System's 600-volt overhead wire and trolley poles for OA&E's 1,200-volt overhead.

In 1920 the OA&E was succeeded by the San Francisco-Sacramento Railroad. In 1927 the Western Pacific bought control of the San Francisco-Sacramento with the idea of using its line to save 50 miles between Oakland and Sacramento. (WP's own line headed south out of Oakland before crossing the Coast Range to a point well south of Stockton.) On December 31, 1928, Sacramento Northern acquired all the properties of the San Francisco-Sacramento, creating a single railroad between Oakland and Chico.

The Sacramento Northern Railway was incorporated in 1921. In 1925 it purchased the properties of the Sacramento Northern Railroad and in 1928 it acquired the San Francisco-Sacramento. SN placed its emphasis on freight. For passengers SN offered no time advantage over Southern Pacific between San Francisco and Sacramento, and the opening of a bridge over the Carquinez Strait put SP well ahead. Paved highways began to siphon off SN's passengers, and the Depression put an end to any thought of acquiring additional all-steel passenger cars. Dining car and parlor car service ended in 1936 and 1938, respectively.

The Bay Bridge opened between San Francisco and Oakland for motor vehicles in 1936 and for Key System, Interurban Electric (SP), and SN trains in 1939. San Francisco-Sacramento through service lasted little more than a year before discontinuance on August 26, 1940; San Francisco-Pittsburg commuter service ran less than a year longer. Interurban service north of Sacramento ended October 31, 1940. There was almost no

Reginald McGovern

Motors 604 and 603 prepare to pull cars off the car ferry *Ramon* at Mallard, on the south shore of Suisun Bay, in 1951.

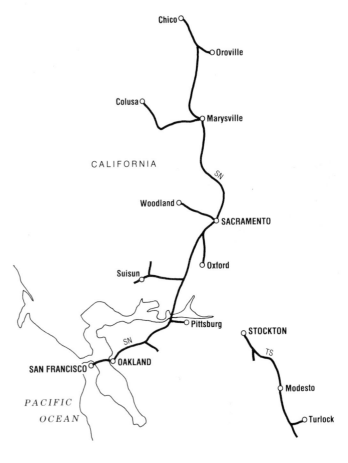

opposition to SN's petitions to cease passenger service. Marysville-Yuba City streetcar service was discontinued in 1942. Streetcar service in Chico ended in December 1947 — it was the last Birney car and the last nickel fare in California.

In 1929 SN opened a line south along the Sacramento River to Oxford, and the same year SN connected its isolated Vacaville-Suisun line, by then freight-only, with the rest of the system by building a line from Vacaville Junction east to Creed (construction of Travis Air Force Base later required a relocation of the line and a new junction at Dozier).

In December 1937 floods damaged the Feather River bridge at Oroville, severing the branch line. SN's presence in Oroville changed to that of a

Sacramento Northern car ferry *Ramon* approaches the slip at Chipps with cars bound for Sacramento. Locomotive and caboose await the boat's arrival.

Reginald McGovern

switching road for its parent WP. The Oroville line was dieselized in 1954 and discontinued in 1957.

SN dieselized its operation between Sacramento and Marysville in 1946. In 1951 a low trestle at Lisbon collapsed under a trainload of steel. Trains were rerouted over WP and Santa Fe between Sacramento and Pittsburg in an arrangement that became permanent when the ferry *Ramon* failed a Coast Guard inspection in 1954. When the trestle was repaired the line was de-electrified. Floods in 1955 washed out some of SN's line near Marysville and caused a rerouting to the WP line there. The Oakland-Walnut Creek line was abandoned in 1957, and the remaining Pittsburg-Walnut Creek segment was dieselized. SN's last electrified operation was at Marysville; as late as April 1965 it was possible to ride underneath live catenary in the domes of WP's *California Zephyr* and watch SN motors on the adjacent track.

Gradually SN was dismembered until its affairs were all but indistinguishable from those of Western Pacific. The absorption of WP by Union Pacific spelled the end of any separate existence for Sacramento Northern.

Location of headquarters: San Francisco, California
Miles of railroad operated: 1929 — 261; 1971 — 336
Number of locomotives: 1929 — 24; 1971 — 8
Number of passenger cars: 1929 — 82
Number of freight cars: 1929 — 315; 1971 — 229
Number of company service cars: 1929 — 64; 1971 — 18
Reporting marks: SN
Notable named passenger trains: *Comet, Meteor* (San Francisco-Chico)
Recommended reading: *Sacramento Northern* (Interurbans Special 26), edited by Ira L. Swett, published in 1962 by Interurban Press, P. O. Box 6444, Glendale, CA 91205
Successors: Union Pacific
Portions still operated: Clyde-Pittsburg; Dozier-Vacaville; Clarksburg-Sacramento; Sacramento-Woodland; Rio Linda-Sankey; Live Oak-Marysville-Reed; Colusa Jct.-Sutter; Durham-Chico: Union Pacific
Rio Vista Jct.-Dozier: leased to Bay Area Electric Railroad Association Inc. (Western Railway Museum)

The Bridge Road

The St. Johnsbury & Lamoille County diesel-ized with General Electric 70-tonners, such as No. 49, shown wheeling a short mixed train along freshly ballasted track.

Alco-GE

ST. JOHNSBURY & LAKE CHAMPLAIN RAILROAD

In 1869 ground was broken at St. Johnsbury, Vermont, for the Vermont Division of the Portland & Ogdensburg. The destination was Lake Champlain; the railroad was to be part of a bridge route between Portland, Maine, and the Great Lakes. The Portland & Ogdensburg Railroad building northwest from Portland met the independent Vermont Division at Lunenburg, Vt., east of St. Johnsbury on the New Hampshire boundary, in 1875. The line was pushed through to Swanton, Vt., almost to Lake Champlain, in 1877. Receivership followed within months.

The railroad was reorganized as the St. Johnsbury & Lake Champlain by its bondholders in 1880, and it built the last few miles to the shore of Lake Champlain at Maquam that year. In 1883, with the encouragement of the Ogdensburg & Lake Champlain, it built a short extension from Swanton to Rouses Point, New York, to connect with the O&LC, the last link in the Portland-to-Ogdensburg route. In the meantime the Central

Vermont took over the O&LC and refused to interchange traffic with the StJ&LC at Rouses Point, prompting abandonment of the now-useless new extension.

In 1880 Maine Central acquired the Portland & Ogdensburg and leased the portion of the StJ&LC that lay east of St. Johnsbury. Boston & Lowell obtained control of the StJ&LC in 1885; that control passed to Boston & Maine in 1895.

Boston & Maine guaranteed StJ&LC's bonds, but when the StJ failed to earn enough to pay the interest on them, B&M turned the line over to local management in 1925 — the same management that later operated the Montpelier & Wells River — in an experiment to see if local management could run the road better than B&M could from its Boston headquarters. The road struggled on into bankruptcy in 1944, and it was reorganized in 1948 as the St. Johnsbury & Lamoille County Railroad.

Boston & Maine soon sold the railroad to local interests. They in turn sold it in 1956 to the H. E. Salzberg Co.; it was sold again in 1967 to Samuel M. Pinsly, who like Salzberg was the owner of a group of short lines. Pinsly's rehabilitation of the railroad included abandonment of the western end of the railroad between Swanton and East Swanton (including the three-span covered bridge over the Missisquoi River at Swanton), purchase of a short piece of Central Vermont trackage from East Swanton to Fonda Jct., and replacement of two more covered bridges at Cambridge Jct. and west of Wolcott with steel bridges. The Fisher Bridge east of Wolcott was preserved by adding concealed reinforcement, retaining its appearance as a covered bridge, and it became the emblem of the railroad.

Pinsly had no more financial success with the road than had previous management. He petitioned for abandonment, embargoed the line, and proposed that the state of Vermont purchase it as it had the Rutland Railway. In 1973 the state purchased the railroad from Pinsly and awarded the operating contract to Bruno Loati of Morrisville, Vt. The road began operation as the Lamoille County Railroad, then reassumed its former name. Because of a dispute with the state over required track rehabilitation and a strike by maintenance of way employees, the state announced that Vermont Northern, a subsidiary of Morrison-Knudsen, would take over in October 1976.

Vermont Northern took over, but the state was still not satisfied with the operation of the railroad and refused to provide long-term subsidy. A local group that included the line's major shippers formed the Northern Vermont Corporation, bid in on the operation, and incorporated the Lamoille Valley Railroad, which took over the railroad on January 1, 1978.

In 1980 the Lamoille Valley and the Central Vermont agreed to interchange traffic at St. Albans rather than Fonda Jct., with LVRC operating between Sheldon Jct. and St. Albans on CV track and CV in turn serving the road's customers at Swanton and East Swanton. In 1985 the Lamoille Valley began operating passenger excursion service.

Location of headquarters: Montpelier, Vermont
Miles of railroad operated: 1929 — 96; 1972 — 98
Number of locomotives: 1929 — 9; 1972 — 10
Number of passenger cars: 1929 — 5
Number of freight cars: 1929 — 7; 1972 — 47
Number of company service cars: 1929 — 9; 1972 — 20
Reporting marks: SJL
Successors:
St. Johnsbury & Lamoille County
Lamoille County
Vermont Northern
Lamoille Valley (TWG)
Portions still operated: Sheldon Jct.-St. Johnsbury: Lamoille Valley
Map: See page 281

ST. LOUIS-SAN FRANCISCO RAILWAY

Ground was broken on July 19, 1853, at Franklin (now Pacific), Missouri, for the South-West Branch of the Pacific Railroad (now the Missouri Pacific). The line reached Rolla, Mo., 77 miles from Franklin, in 1860, but the Civil War brought a halt to construction. In 1866 the state of Missouri took over the railroad — separation from the parent road seemed desirable — and sold it to John C. Frémont, who reorganized it as the Southwest Pacific Railroad. Frémont was unable to keep up the payments, and the road was reorganized again as the South Pacific Railroad in 1868. The line continued to inch southwest. It reached Springfield in 1870 and was consolidated with the Atlantic & Pacific that same year.

The Atlantic & Pacific Railroad was chartered in 1866 to build a railroad from Springfield, Mo., to the Pacific. Its route lay roughly along the 35th parallel of latitude — west along the Canadian River to Albuquerque, then along the Little Colorado and Colorado rivers and west to the Pacific by a "practicable and eligible route," to quote the language of the act of incorporation. Among the provisions of the act were that the U. S. government would clear up the matter of Indian lands being granted to the railroad, the Southern Pacific Railroad would connect with it at the Colorado River, and the railroad had to be completed within 12 years to receive the land grant.

Financing was difficult to find, and the A&P entered receivership in 1875. The portion of the A&P within Missouri was sold to become the St. Louis & San Francisco Railway, and the 37-mile portion in Indian Territory (now Oklahoma) from the border to Vinita retained the Atlantic & Pacific name.

The SL&SF began expanding. Lines reached Wichita, Kansas, in 1880, Fort Smith, Arkansas, and Tulsa, Ind. Terr., in 1882, and St. Louis (to replace the use of Missouri Pacific track) in 1883. In 1887 an extension of the Fort Smith line reached Paris, Texas, and in 1888 a line was opened from Wichita to Ellsworth, Kans.

In 1879 Frisco, A&P, and Santa Fe signed an agreement under which Frisco and Santa Fe would jointly build and own the A&P west of Albuquerque. At the time Jay Gould was trying to gain control of the Frisco to head off its extension into Texas — and forestall competition with Gould's Texas & Pacific. Gould and C. P. Huntington acquired control of the Frisco in 1882. The A&P was completed in 1883 from Albuquerque to Needles, California, on the west bank of the Colorado River, where it connected with the Southern Pacific. The Santa Fe would not allow earnings from the completed portion to finance the construction of the line from Sapulpa, near Tulsa, to Albuquerque. In 1886 Congress voided A&P's land grant for the unbuilt part of the line. The Santa Fe purchased the Frisco in 1890, briefly creating the largest railroad in North America (measured in route-miles). During the Panic of 1893, though, Santa Fe

entered receivership. A new St. Louis & San Francisco Railroad, organized in 1896, bought the old Frisco and the Oklahoma portion of the A&P; the A&P from Albuquerque to Needles became part of Santa Fe.

The new Frisco extended its main line from Tulsa to Oklahoma City in 1898, and a subsidiary, the Kansas City, Osceola & Southern, completed a Kansas City-Springfield route that same year. In 1901 Frisco put in service a line from Sapulpa, Okla., near Tulsa, to Denison, Tex.; a year later the line reached Carrollton, Tex., within striking distance of Dallas and Fort Worth. Also in 1901 Frisco leased the Kansas City, Fort Scott & Memphis, which with subsidiaries formed a route from Kansas City

A 4-8-2 bearing such Frisco traits as coonskin-shaped number plate, air reservoirs atop the boiler, and ornate striping on cab and tender sides wheels a block of refrigerator cars east into Tulsa, Okla., in November 1946.

Preston George

through Springfield, Mo., and Memphis, Tennessee, to Birmingham, Alabama.

Benjamin F. Yoakum acquired control of the Frisco right after the turn of the century. His holdings included the Rock Island, the Chicago & Eastern Illinois, and a group of railroads stretching from New Orleans through Houston to Brownsville, Tex., later known as Gulf Coast Lines. Yoakum's empire collapsed in 1913, and the Frisco was reorganized in 1916 as the St. Louis-San Francisco Railway.

The new Frisco settled down to become a regional railroad, an X-shaped system with lines from St. Louis through Oklahoma to Texas, including the Quanah, Acme & Pacific, the west Texas tail of the system, and from Kansas City to Birmingham. In 1925 the Frisco purchased the Muscle Shoals, Birmingham & Pensacola Railway (Kimbrough, Ala.-Pensacola, Florida, successor in 1922 to the Gulf, Florida & Alabama Railway), and constructed a new line from Aberdeen, Mississippi, to Kimbrough. In 1928 Frisco purchased and absorbed the Kansas City, Fort Scott & Memphis and its subsidiaries.

The Frisco again entered receivership in 1932. In 1937 the road sold the Fort Worth & Rio Grande, a line from Fort Worth to Menard, Tex., to the Santa Fe. Revenues from increased traffic during World War Two helped boost Frisco out of receivership in 1947. In 1948 SL-SF acquired control of the Alabama, Tennessee & Northern, gaining a second Gulf port, Mobile. (Merger with AT&N occurred January 1, 1971.) Frisco dropped the last of its passenger trains in 1967.

In 1956 Frisco purchased control of the Central of Georgia, but the ICC disapproved and Frisco sold its interest to the Southern Railway in 1961. In 1964 Frisco acquired control of the Northeast Oklahoma Railroad, a one-time interurban — merger of NEO occurred January 1, 1967. About the same time Frisco talked merger with Chicago Great Western, then with Santa Fe, then with Southern. In 1966 the Burlington purchased a sizable block of Frisco stock. For about a decade there was no further substantive news of a Frisco merger, but in 1977 Burlington Northern and Frisco began discussions which led to merger on November 21, 1980.

Location of headquarters: St. Louis, Missouri
Miles of railroad operated: 1929 — 5,735; 1979 — 4,653
Number of locomotives: 1929 — 880; 1979 — 431
Number of passenger cars: 1929 — 669
Number of freight cars: 1929 — 34,009; 1979 — 17,392
Number of company service cars: 1929 — 1,964; 1979 — 933
Reporting marks: SLSF

Notable named passenger trains: *Texas Special* (St. Louis-San Antonio, operated south of Vinita, Okla., by the Missouri-Kansas-Texas); *Meteor* (St. Louis-Oklahoma City)

Historical and technical society: Frisco Modelers Information Group, 2541 West Allen Drive, Springfield, MO 65807

Recommended reading:

The St. Louis-San Francisco Transcontinental Railroad, by H. Craig Miner, published in 1972 by the University Press of Kansas, Lawrence, Kans. (SBN 7006-0081-7)

Frisco Power, by Joe G. Collias, published in 1984 by M M Books, P. O. Box 29318, Crestwood, MO 63126 (ISBN 0-9612366-0-4)

Subsidiaries and affiliated railroads, 1979: Quanah, Acme & Pacific

Predecessor railroads in this book: Alabama, Tennessee & Northern

Successors: Burlington Northern (TWG)

Portions still operated: St. Louis-Quanah, Tex.; Cuba-Salem, Mo.; Springfield-Bolivar, Mo.; Springfield-Kissick, Mo.; Monett, Mo.-Fort Smith, Ark.-Wister, Mo.; Greenland-Chester, Ark.; Pierce City, Mo.-Ellsworth, Kans.; Tulsa-Avard, Okla.; Enid-Davidson, Okla.; Sapulpa, Okla.-Irving, Tex.; Lakeside, Okla.-Hope, Ark.; Antlers, Okla.-Paris, Tex.; Kansas City-East Lynne, Mo.; Kansas City-Memphis, Tenn.-Birmingham, Ala.; Amory, Miss.-Pensacola, Fla.; Aliceville-Mobile, Ala.; Edward, Kans.-Afton Jct., Okla.; Red Plant, Mo.-Baxter Springs, Kans.; Arcadia-Parsons, Kans.: Burlington Northern

---

ST. LOUIS SOUTHWESTERN RAILWAY

The St. Louis Southwestern (usually called the Cotton Belt) is Southern Pacific's principal subsidiary, and it is scheduled to be absorbed by SP at the end of 1985 as one of the preliminaries of the Southern Pacific-Santa Fe merger. It has remained a separate railroad through more than half a century of SP control. The ICC approved control of Central Pacific by Southern Pacific in 1923 upon condition that SP solicit freight traffic for movement via Ogden, Utah, and the Union Pacific in preference to its own route across Texas. Cotton Belt traffic offices were not governed by that agreement and could solicit traffic to move over SP and SSW rails all the way to East St. Louis.

The Cotton Belt began as the 3-foot-gauge Tyler Tap Railroad, chartered in 1871 and opened in 1877 between Tyler, Tex., and a junction with the Texas & Pacific at Big Sandy. It was rechartered as the Texas & St. Louis Railway in 1879 under the leadership of James Paramore, a St. Louis financier, who sought an economical way to transport cotton from Texas to St. Louis. The road was extended to Texarkana and a connection with the St. Louis, Iron Mountain & Southern in 1880. A year later the west end of the railroad was extended to Waco.

In 1881 Jay Gould purchased the Iron Mountain (he already had the T&P), returning the Texas & St. Louis to one-connection status. At the same time Gould canceled the Iron Mountain's traffic agreements with the T&StL. The T&StL decided to fulfill its name. In 1882 it reached Birds Point, Missouri, across the Mississippi River from Cairo, Illinois. There it connected by barge with the narrow gauge St. Louis & Cairo, and by 1885 a continuous line of 3-foot-gauge railroads reached from Toledo, Ohio, to Houston, Tex., with intentions of heading for Laredo and eventually Mexico City.

In 1886 the T&StL was reorganized as the St. Louis, Arkansas & Texas Railway. It converted its lines to standard gauge, built branches to Shreveport, Louisiana, and Fort Worth in 1888, and entered bankruptcy in 1889. Jay Gould organized the St. Louis Southwestern Railway in 1891

R. S. Plummer

During World War Two the War Production Board rejected Cotton Belt's request for freight diesels but allowed the construction of five 4-8-4s by the road's Pine Bluff shops, which had built five such machines in 1937. The last of the series, 819, which entered service in February 1943, is shown here leaving Texarkana in 1951. The locomotive was retired to a park in Pine Bluff in 1955; it was restored and returned to operation in 1985.

and took over the StLA&T. Shortly thereafter the road gained access to Memphis, Tennessee, by way of trackage rights over the Iron Mountain. Cotton Belt acquired trackage rights over Missouri Pacific from Thebes, Ill., to St. Louis in exchange for letting MP operate over SSW between Illmo, Mo., and Paragould, Ark.; and joined with MP in 1905 to construct a bridge over the Mississippi between Thebes and Illmo. Passenger trains to and from Memphis were moved to Rock Island's Brinkley, Ark.-Memphis line in 1912; freight trains made the change in 1921.

After World War One overhead traffic (also called intermediate or bridge traffic — freight received from one railroad to be turned over to another) began to increase on the Cotton Belt. The Rock Island purchased a controlling interest in the road in 1925 and sold it almost immediately to Kansas City Southern. KCS proposed a regional system to include KCS, SSW, and the Missouri-Kansas-Texas, but the ICC refused approval. KCS lost interest in the Cotton Belt about the time Southern Pacific was looking for a connection to St. Louis from its Texas lines. SP applied for control and in 1932 took over. Cotton Belt weathered receivership between 1935 and 1947; in recent years it has been essentially a division of the SP, though its equipment is still lettered "Cotton Belt." The last diesels painted in Cotton Belt's yellow and gray were delivered in 1949; after that they wore SP colors.

Cotton Belt was never a major passenger carrier. The Dallas-Memphis *Lone Star* was discontinued in 1953, all passenger service in Texas ended in 1956, and Cotton Belt's last passenger train, a St. Louis-Pine Bluff coach-only local, made its last run November 30, 1959. As SSW's 4-8-4s had done, the passenger diesels and ten streamlined coaches moved west for service on SP lines.

In 1973 Cotton Belt purchased a half interest in the Alton & Southern, a belt line serving East St. Louis, Ill., from the Chicago & North Western. In 1980 SSW acquired the former Rock Island line from St. Louis through Kansas City to Santa Rosa, New Mexico. (RI owned the line between Santa Rosa and Tucumcari, N. Mex., but it had long been leased to SP.) Most of the St. Louis-Kansas City trackage is not being operated; from Kansas City west the road is a fast freight route in conjunction with parent SP from Tucumcari to El Paso. In 1982 SSW obtained another piece of the late Rock Island, the line from Brinkley, Ark., to the Mississippi

River bridge west of Memphis.
Location of headquarters: St. Louis, Missouri
Miles of railroad operated: 1929 — 1,809; 1983 — 2,375
Number of locomotives: 1929 — 248; 1983 — 307
Number of passenger cars: 1929 — 168
Number of freight cars: 1929 — 8,458
Number of company service cars: 1929 — 898
Number of freight and company service cars: 1983 — 17,407
Reporting marks: SSW
Historical and technical society: Cotton Belt Rail Historical Society, P. O. Box 2044, Pine Bluff, AR 71613
Recommended reading: *Cotton Belt Locomotives*, by Joseph A. Strapac, published in 1977 by Shade Tree Books, P. O. Box 2268, Huntington Beach, CA 92647
Subsidiaries and affiliated railroads, 1973: Alton & Southern (50%, jointly with Missouri Pacific)
Successors: Southern Pacific (TWG)
Portions still operated: St. Louis-Fort Worth; Malden-East Prairie, Mo.; Lilbourn-New Madrid, Mo.; Brinkley, Ark.-Memphis, Tenn.; Stuttgart-Gillett, Ark.; Altheimer-Little Rock, Ark.; Lewisville, Ark.-Shreveport, La.; Mount Pleasant-Lime City, Tex.; Tyler-Lufkin, Tex.: St. Louis Southwestern

SALT LAKE & UTAH RAILROAD

The Salt Lake & Utah was incorporated in 1912 to build a railroad south from Salt Lake City into the Utah Valley. The road was financed and constructed by A. J. Orem & Co. Several members of the Orem family were involved with the railroad, and it soon became known as the Orem Road. Construction began immediately in Provo. Service began between Salt Lake City and American Fork in March 1914 with Hall-Scott gasoline motor cars, and electric service was inaugurated between Salt Lake City and Provo, 49 miles, in July of that year. The line was extended 18 miles south to Payson in 1916, and shops were constructed

there. In 1917 SL&U opened a 9-mile branch west from Granger to Magna. About that same time Provo streetcar service began; it died from lack of patronage only 2 years later.

The Salt Lake & Utah entered receivership on July 24, 1925. New management gave the railroad a thorough overhaul and advertised its services — SL&U had interchanged freight with steam railroads from the beginning — and business increased, but not enough to keep the road going. In 1938 it was sold at foreclosure to the Eccles interests, which also owned the Utah-Idaho Central and the Amalgamated Sugar Co. The Salt Lake & Utah lost money during World War Two, when nearly every railroad in the country was experiencing gains in revenue, and the road's

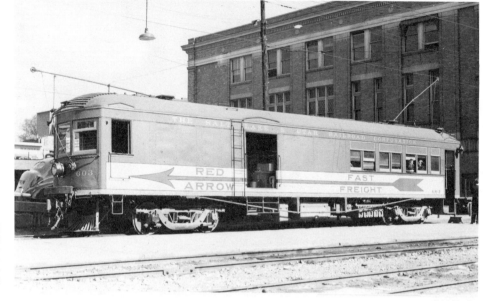

Car 603, one of Salt Lake & Utah's original passenger cars built by Niles in 1914, was badly damaged in a wreck in 1921. It was rebuilt with a much larger baggage compartment for express service and less-than-carload freight shipments. It is shown at Salt Lake City in 1939.

R. H. Kindig

poor condition got worse. Receivers took charge again in December 1945 and petitioned for abandonment. Service was suspended for lack of money on March 1, 1946, and the SL&U was officially abandoned June 8, 1946. The Bamberger Railroad bought SL&U's half of the Salt Lake City terminal, and the Denver & Rio Grande Western bought a few short pieces of SL&U track to serve industries.

Location of headquarters: Salt Lake City, Utah
Miles of railroad operated: 1929 — 76; 1941 — 75
Number of locomotives: 1929 — 6; 1941 — 7
Number of passenger cars: 1929 — 16 (11 motor cars); 1941 — 17 (11 motor cars)
Number of freight and company service cars: 1929 — 119 (2 motor cars); 1941 — 130 (1)
Reporting marks: SLU
Recommended reading: *Interurbans of Utah*, by Ira L. Swett, published in 1954 by Interurban Press, P. O. Box 6444, Glendale, CA 91205
Subsidiaries and affiliated railroads: Salt Lake Terminal Co. (50%, jointly with Bamberger)
Map: See page 42

SAN DIEGO & ARIZONA RAILWAY

In 1907 John D. Spreckels broke ground at San Diego, California, for a railroad that would give the city a direct route east. Financial backing for the San Diego & Arizona came from Spreckels and from E. H. Harriman of the Southern Pacific. The new railroad would bring SP into San Diego and break Santa Fe's monopoly there — a reversal of the usual situation in California in those days. The route of the railroad was south across the Mexican border to Tijuana, east to Tecate via the subsidiary Tijuana & Tecate Railway, back into the U. S. and north through awesome Carriso Gorge, and east to a connection with SP at El Centro, the principal town in California's Imperial Valley. In spite of revolution in Mexico and a ban on new construction during World War One, the last spike was driven in 1919.

In 1932 Spreckels sold his interest to Southern Pacific, which formed the San Diego & Arizona Eastern Railway to take over operations on February 1, 1933. In 1951 the SD&AE operated its last passenger train. The slow trip east to a connection with the secondary trains of SP's Golden State Route — and El Centro was not on the main line — was no match for Santa Fe's frequent *San Diegans* to Los Angeles and the best of Santa Fe's, Union Pacific, and Southern Pacific from there. In 1970 SP sold the Tijuana & Tecate to the Mexican government; it has become an isolated part of the Sonora-Baja California Railway. (SP retained trackage rights for through traffic.) A hurricane in September 1976 damaged a 40-mile stretch of the line, and Southern Pacific petitioned for abandonment of all but a few miles from El Centro to Plaster City.

In 1979 San Diego's Metropolitan Transit Development Board purchased three portions of the SD&AE: from Plaster City to the border, from San Diego south to the border between San Ysidro, Calif., and Tijuana, Baja California, and from San Diego east to El Cajon. MTDB began construction of a 16-mile transit line from the Amtrak (ex-Santa Fe) station in San Diego to the border. The trolley line, which was constructed without federal funds, shares track with the freight trains of the SD&AE. The trolleys began operating in July 1981.

MTDB contracted with Kyle Railways to operate freight service on the line. Kyle set up the San Diego & Arizona Eastern Transportation Co. for

that purpose. SD&AE also operates the Mexican segment of the line, not only to connect the two U. S. portions of its line but also to do local work for Sonora-Baja California. Operations were taken over by the San Diego & Imperial Valley on October 13, 1984.

San Diego & Arizona Railway
   Location of headquarters: San Diego, California
   Miles of railroad operated: 1929 — 201; 1975 — 199
   Number of locomotives: 1929 — 16; 1975 — 5
   Number of passenger cars: 1929 — 34
   Number of freight cars: 1929 — 173; 1975 — 3
   Number of company service cars: 1929 — 39; 1975 — 16
   Reporting marks: SDAE
San Diego & Arizona Transportation Co.
   Location of headquarters: San Diego, California
   Miles of railroad operated: 1983 — 60
   Number of locomotives: 1983 — 9
   Reporting marks: SDAE
Recommended reading: *San Diego & Arizona*, by Robert M. Hanft, published in 1984 by Trans-Anglo Books (Interurban Press), P. O. Box

6444, Glendale, CA 91205 (ISBN 0-87046-071-4)
Subsidiaries and affiliated railroads, 1969:
Tijuana & Tecate
Successors:
Southern Pacific (TWG)
San Diego & Arizona Eastern Transportation Co. (TWG)
San Diego & Imperial Valley
Portions still operated:
Seeley-Plaster City: Southern Pacific
San Diego-San Ysidro: San Diego Metropolitan Transit Board
San Diego-El Cajon; San Diego-Plaster City: San Diego & Imperial
Valley

East of San Diego is a land of mountains and desert, rocks and little else. The hostile topography dwarfs the railroad and its train.

C. D. Whittaker

SANDY RIVER & RANGELEY LAKES RAILROAD

The Sandy River was the most extensive 2-foot-gauge railroad in Maine. Its ancestry, like that of the state of Maine itself, lies in Massachusetts. In 1875 George Mansfield organized the Billerica & Bedford Railroad to build a 2-foot-gauge railroad between the towns of its name. Mansfield had visited the Festiniog Railway, a 23½-inch-gauge slate carrier in Wales, and he promoted the narrow gauge as economical. There was no traffic to support the B&B; it operated only from November 1877 through May 1878, then was abandoned and its equipment was sold at auction to a B. F. Brown.

Mansfield went north to Franklin County, Maine, which was having an attack of railroad fever and also had a growing lumber industry. Standard gauge rails, later to become a branch of the Maine Central, had reached the county seat of Farmington, about 80 miles north of Portland, in 1865. The Sandy River Railroad was organized in 1879 with Mansfield as its manager and a track gauge of two feet. Mansfield knew where he could get a complete 2-foot-gauge train set, slightly used, in exchange for Sandy River stock. On November 20, 1879, the first train arrived in Phil-

lips, 18 miles from Farmington — the town of Phillips had set that completion date as the deadline for the town's credit to be available to the railroad.

In 1883 the Franklin & Megantic Railroad was incorporated to build from Strong, 11 miles north of Farmington, to Kingfield, 15 miles. The line was completed in October 1884. Traffic on the F&M, as on the Sandy River, was dominated by lumber. In 1894 the owners of the Franklin & Megantic organized the Kingfield & Dead River Railroad to extend their line north to Carrabasset and, in 1900, to Bigelow. In 1892 Josiah Maxcy, a Gardiner, Me., banker, purchased the Sandy River, and in 1897 he purchased control of the F&M and the K&DR. He began operating the three roads as a single system.

In 1890 the Phillips & Rangeley was incorporated to build north from Phillips to Rangeley, 28 miles. In 1902 the P&R organized the Madrid Railroad to build a branch into the forests west of Madrid, and in 1903 the Eustis Railroad was chartered to build into the area northeast of Rangeley.

294

Linwood W. Moody

A Sandy River & Rangeley Lakes mixed train headed by No. 9, a Baldwin 2-4-4T, waits in the siding at Salem for a meet with a southbound railbus in July 1934.

In January 1908 Maxcy organized the Sandy River & Rangeley Lakes Railroad, which immediately took control of the Sandy River, the Franklin & Megantic, and the Kingfield & Dead River. In June of that year the SR&RL purchased the Phillips & Rangeley and the Madrid Railroad and leased the Eustis Railroad (and purchased it in 1911). Maine Central gained control of the SR&RL in 1911 and began to operate it as an extension of its Farmington Branch.

Traffic, chiefly pulpwood, was good on the narrow gauge through World War One, but in the early 1920s expenses began to outpace income, and a good portion of the expense was interest on the debt owed to Maine Central for improvements. In 1922 the SR&RL entered receivership. Paved highways began to penetrate Franklin County, and passenger and freight business went to cars and trucks. In July 1926 the former K&DR was cut back to Carrabasset, and in 1931 service was discontinued north of Phillips. On July 8, 1932, the SR&RL stopped operating and stored its equipment. On April 17, 1933, the road resumed operating with the assurance of traffic from a plywood mill. Operations were profitable for a time, largely because maintenance was deferred — cars and locomotives were simply run till they ran no more — but in June 1935 the line was sold to H. E. Salzberg & Co., railroad scrappers. The last day of operation was June 29, 1935.

The other 2-foot-gauge lines in Maine were:

● The Bridgton & Saco River Railroad was chartered in 1881 to build a railroad from the town of Bridgton to a connection with the Portland & Ogdensburg (later Maine Central) at Bridgton Junction, in the town of Hiram. Instrumental in organizing and building it was George Mansfield. In 1898 it was extended north five miles to Harrison. Bridgton and Harrison are summer resort towns, and much of the business for the railroad was carrying people from "away" or "out of state" (good Maine words that cover a lot of territory). Maine Central bought control of the line in

295

1912. In 1927 a group of mortgage holders took control back from MEC, and in June 1930 the railroad was sold to the Bridgton & Harrison Railway. Three months later the extension to Harrison was dismantled. During the Depression freight traffic disappeared almost completely, and the B&H turned to passenger traffic, largely summer folk and railfans — the road survived into the era of organized railfan activity. The passenger business was not enough to keep the road going, and the town of Bridgton sold its stock in the road in the fall of 1941. The equipment was scrapped almost immediately.

- The Monson Railroad, the "Two by Six," was built from slate quarries at Monson to the nearest point on the Bangor & Piscataquis, six miles away, in 1883. The road was abandoned in 1943 because of declining business and highway competition. It was the last two-footer.

- The Wiscasset & Quebec Railroad was chartered in 1854 to build a railroad north from the seaport of Wiscasset. Construction began in 1894, and the rails reached the Belfast branch of the Maine Central (now the Belfast & Moosehead Lake Railroad) at Burnham in 1897. Maine Central refused to let the W&Q cross. The narrow gauge pulled back to Albion, 44 miles from Wiscasset, and formed a new company to build a line to Farmington to connect with the Sandy River. That effort got as far as Winslow, across the Kennebec River from Waterville, and the whole enterprise was reorganized as the Wiscasset, Waterville & Farmington Railroad in 1901. Business gradually trickled away to trolleys, then to

cars and trucks. On June 15, 1933, the morning train from Albion to Wiscasset derailed at Whitefield. The crew walked on in, and the road's owner left the train where it was and closed up shop.

- The Kennebec Central Railroad was opened in 1890 from Randolph to Togus, five miles. Its principal business was hauling coal to the National Soldiers' Home at Togus. Operation ceased in 1929 when the government gave the coal business to truckers.

Some of the locomotives and cars of the Maine 2-footers were rescued in the mid 1940s by Ellis D. Atwood, who built the Edaville Railroad around his cranberry farm in South Carver, Mass. It is still in operation.

Location of headquarters: Phillips, Maine
Miles of railroad operated: 1929 — 96; 1933 — 43
Number of locomotives: 1929 — 13; 1933 — 10
Number of passenger cars: 1929 — 20
Number of freight cars: 1929 — 156
Number of other cars: 1929 — 140
Number of cars: 1933 — 309
Recommended reading:
The Maine Two-Footers, by Linwood W. Moody, published in 1959 by Howell-North Books, 850 North Hollywood Way, Burbank, CA 91505
Ride the Sandy River, by L. Peter Cornwall and Jack W. Farrell, published in 1973 by Pacific Fast Mail, P. O. Box 57, Edmonds, WA 98020

SAVANNAH & ATLANTA RAILWAY

George M. Brinson began constructing a railroad northwest from Savannah, Georgia, in 1906. The railroad — the Brinson Railway — reached Newington, Ga., 43 miles from Savannah, in 1909. Brinson then acquired the Savannah Valley Railroad, which had a line from Egypt, Ga., through Newington and Sylvania to Mill Haven. At that point he ran out of money. Control of the railroad was acquired by a New York bank, though Brinson remained president. Construction continued and the road reached Waynesboro and a connection with the Central of Georgia in 1911 and St. Clair and a connection with the Georgia & Florida in

1913. The road was renamed the Savannah & Northwestern in 1914.

The Savannah & Atlanta was incorporated in 1915 to build a connecting link between St. Clair and the Georgia Railroad's main line near Camak. Upon completion in 1916 it formed the shortest route between Atlanta and Savannah. In 1917 the S&A absorbed the Savannah & Northwestern. The road entered receivership in 1921 and emerged with its name unchanged in 1929. The line's principal business was to serve as a Savannah extension of the Georgia Railroad. The railroad was purchased by the Central of Georgia Railway in 1951 but continued to operate separately until the formation of the Central of Georgia Railroad, a subsidiary of the Southern, in 1971. In 1961 S&A abandoned 36 miles of

C. M. Clegg

Savannah & Atlanta train 2, the southbound mixed, pulls out of Sardis, Ga., about halfway between Camak and Savannah, behind Mikado 503.

line between Sylvania and Waynesboro and initiated joint operation with CofG, using S&A track between Savannah and Ardmore and CofG track between Ardmore and Waynesboro.

Savannah & Atlanta is remembered today chiefly for Pacific 750, purchased from the Florida East Coast in 1935 and given to the Atlanta Chapter of the National Railway Historical Society in 1962. Number 750 is a regular participant in Norfolk Southern's annual program of steam-powered excursion trains.

Location of headquarters: Savannah, Georgia
Miles of railroad operated: 1929 — 142; 1969 — 167
Number of locomotives: 1929 — 13; 1969 — 11

Number of passenger cars: 1929 — 7
Number of freight cars: 1929 — 58; 1969 — 781
Number of company service cars: 1929 — 46; 1970 — 23
Reporting marks: SA
Recommended reading: *Central of Georgia Railway and Connecting Lines*, by Richard E. Prince, published in 1976 by Richard E. Prince
Successors:
Central of Georgia
Southern Railway System (TWG)
Portions still operated: Savannah-Sylvania; Waynesboro-Camak: Central of Georgia (Southern Railway System)

SEABOARD AIR LINE RAILWAY

The Portsmouth & Roanoke Rail Road was formed in 1832 to build a railroad from Portsmouth, Virginia, to Weldon, North Carolina, on the Roanoke River, shortcutting a long, three-sided water route. The line reached Weldon in 1837. The new road was not successful, and in 1846 it was purchased by the Virginia State Board of Public Works, leased to the town of Portsmouth, and reorganized as the Seaboard & Roanoke Railroad. In the early 1850s control of the road was acquired by a group of Philadelphians who also controlled the Richmond, Fredericksburg & Potomac and the Richmond & Petersburg railroads.

The Raleigh & Gaston Railroad was completed in 1840 between Raleigh and Gaston, N. C. — not present-day Gaston but a town a few miles up the Roanoke River from it. In 1853 it was extended a few miles east to Weldon, connecting there with the Seaboard & Roanoke and several other railroads. During the Civil War portions of the railroad were torn up by both Union and Confederate troops; parts were rebuilt and used by both sides, although it was not a particularly strategic railroad. In 1871 the Raleigh & Gaston acquired control of a line under construction south from Raleigh, the Raleigh & Augusta Air-Line Railroad. By 1877 that line had reached Hamlet, N. C., and a connection with the Carolina Central, a line from Wilmington through Charlotte to Shelby. By 1875 the Seaboard and the two Raleigh roads were headed by one man, John M. Robinson, who was also president of the RF&P and the Baltimore Steam Packet Co. In 1881 Robinson gained control of the Carolina Central. The Robinson roads were known as the Seaboard Air-Line System.

The Seaboard had connected at Charlotte with the Atlanta & Charlotte Air Line Railway. In 1881 that came under control of the Richmond & Danville, predecessor of the Southern. The Seaboard began construction in 1887 of a line from Monroe, N. C., between Hamlet and Charlotte, to Atlanta — the Georgia, Carolina & Northern Railway. It reached the Georgia capital in 1892. In the late 1890s the Richmond, Petersburg & Carolina Railroad was completed between Norlina, N. C., and Richmond, Va., and in 1900 that line was named the Seaboard Air Line Railway.

In 1896 John Skelton Williams of Richmond and a group of associates obtained control of the Georgia & Alabama Railway, a line completed in

David W. Salter

Seaboard's line through central Florida offered a view (it still does to Amtrak passengers) of agricultural country quite different from the resort areas along the coasts. Train 58, the *Silver Meteor*, rolls north near Citra. Even as late in the passenger era as 1965 an observation car brings up the rear of the 21-car streamliner.

1891 between Montgomery, Ala., and Lyons, Ga. Williams leased and built lines to extend the G&A east to Savannah. In 1898 Williams acquired control of the Seaboard group of railroads, and in 1899 he took over the Florida Central & Peninsular Railroad, which had a line from Columbia, South Carolina, through Savannah and Jacksonville to Tampa, and another from Jacksonville west through Tallahassee to a junction with the Louisville & Nashville at the Chattahoochee River.

The Florida Central & Peninsular traced its ancestry to the Tallahassee Railroad, organized in 1834 to build a line from Tallahassee to the Gulf of Mexico — the 22-mile line was opened in 1836. The Jacksonville-Talla-

hassee route, opened in 1860, was built by two companies that were eventually united as the Florida Central & Western Railroad.

The Florida Railroad was opened in March 1861 from Fernandina through Baldwin and Gainesville to Cedar Key, Fla., to form a land bridge (to use current terminology) from the Atlantic to the Gulf. It became the Atlantic, Gulf & West India Transit Company, then the Florida Transit Railroad ("transit" having its older, less-specific meaning, rather than referring to streetcars, nickel fares, and frequent service). In 1883 it was consolidated with two other companies to form the Florida Transit & Peninsular Railroad; in 1884 that company and the Florida Central & Western merged to form the Florida Railway & Navigation Company, which was succeeded in 1889 by the Florida Central & Peninsular Railway. In 1890 a line of the FC&P was extended south to Tampa, and in 1893 it built a line north to Savannah, where it connected with the recently opened South Bound Railroad to Columbia, S. C.

In 1900, 91 miles of new construction between Columbia and Cheraw, S. C., connected the Georgia & Alabama and Florida Central & Peninsular with the "old" Seaboard. Williams proposed to build north from Richmond to connect with the Baltimore & Ohio, because the Richmond, Fredericksburg & Potomac was controlled by the Atlantic Coast Line. The Pennsylvania Railroad and the state of Virginia, both owners of portions of the RF&P, applied pressure, and the Seaboard was allowed to sign a traffic agreement with the RF&P — and with the Pennsy, too.

Williams was out at the end of 1903 — he went on to assemble the Georgia & Florida — but he had begun an extension west to Birmingham, Ala., by a combination of new construction and the acquisition of the East & West Railroad. In the early part of the twentieth century the Seaboard acquired a number of branches and short lines. SAL entered a brief receivership in 1908, and the corporation underwent a reorganization in 1915 when the subsidiary Carolina, Atlantic & Western Railway was renamed the Seaboard Air Line Railway and took over the previous Seaboard Air Line. In 1918 SAL opened a new line from Charleston, S. C., to Savannah. In conjunction with an existing line from Hamlet, N. C., to Charleston it formed a freight route with easier grades than the main line through Columbia. About that same time SAL began to gather up short lines in the agricultural and phosphate mining area of central

Some railroads were loyal to a single locomotive builder; others believed in spreading their business around. An assortment of Baldwin, Electro-Motive, and Alco power leads a Seaboard freight out of Montgomery, Ala., in August 1959. Seaboard's winding main line was responsible in part for the design of the Baldwin Centipede in the lead — ironically, Seaboard's route included the longest tangent in the U. S., nearly 79 miles from Hamlet to Wilmington, N. C., and another 57-mile straight stretch across Florida.

Florida: the Tampa & Gulf Coast (Tampa to St. Petersburg and Tarpon Springs), the Charlotte Harbor & Northern (Mulberry to Boca Grande), and the Tampa Northern (Tampa to Brooksville).

SAL's principal project in Florida during the land boom of the early 1920s was a line from Coleman, just south of Wildwood, southeast to West Palm Beach and Miami. SAL's first passenger train arrived in Miami on January 8, 1927; a few months previously SAL had opened an extension down the west coast to Fort Myers and Naples. In 1928 Seaboard acquired the Georgia, Florida & Alabama Railway, a 194-mile line from Richland, Ga., south through Tallahassee to the Gulf.

The Florida land boom collapsed in 1926, just as SAL was finishing up its lines to Miami and Naples, and the stock market crashed in 1929. The Seaboard was not a strong road, and it was located between the Atlantic Coast Line and the Southern, both prosperous and well-established railroads. Overextended by its expansion program in Florida, it collapsed

into receivership in December 1930. Government loans helped the road begin a modernization program, and revenues from the busy years of World War Two lifted the road back to profitability and permitted it to install block signals and centralized traffic control — the lack of automatic signals on most of SAL's lines had caused several accidents during the war. The Seaboard was reorganized as the Seaboard Air Line Railroad in 1946.

During the decade after WWII Seaboard prospered along with nearly every other railroad. Seaboard's position was bolstered by industrial development in the South and healthy traffic in phosphate rock — nearly one-fifth of Seaboard's tonnage — used in the production of fertilizers. Seaboard's passenger business was also healthy, thanks to heavy traffic between the Northeast and Florida.

In 1958 SAL absorbed the Macon, Dublin & Savannah, which it had long owned, and in June 1959 SAL purchased the Gainesville Midland, a 42-mile line connecting the mill town of Gainesville, Ga., with the Seaboard at Athens.

Merger of the Seaboard with parallel — and rival — Atlantic Coast Line was proposed in 1958. The benefits of the Seaboard Coast Line merger, which took effect July 1, 1967, derived largely from eliminating duplicate lines and terminals.

Location of headquarters: Norfolk, Virginia

Miles of railroad operated: 1929 — 4,490; 1966 — 4,123
Number of locomotives: 1929 — 726; 1966 — 551
Number of passenger cars: 1929 — 474; 1966 — 414
Number of freight cars: 1929 — 22,483; 1966 — 28,778
Number of company service cars: 1929 — 1,055; 1966 — 1,003
Reporting marks: SAL
Notable named passenger trains: *Orange Blossom Special, Silver Meteor* (New York-Miami, operated north of Richmond by Pennsylvania and Richmond, Fredericksburg & Potomac)
Historical and technical society: Southeastern Railroad Technical Society, 1552 Highcrest Drive, Valrico, FL 33594
Recommended reading: *Seaboard Air Line Railway*, by Richard E. Prince, published in 1969 by Richard E. Prince (SBN 9600088-1-0)
Subsidiaries and affiliated railroads, 1966:

Gainesville Midland
Richmond-Washington Co. (which owns controlling interest in Richmond, Fredericksburg & Potomac — 16.7%)
Predecessor railroads in this book: Macon, Dublin & Savannah
Successors:
Seaboard Coast Line
Seaboard System (TWG)
Portions still operated: The only major portions of the Seaboard Air Line that have been abandoned are: Andrews-Lanes, S. C.; Charleston-Pritchard, S. C.; Abbeville-Fitzgerald, Ga.; Sprague-Luverna, Ala.; Waldo-Cedar Key, Fla.; Tarpon Jct.-Tarpon Springs, Fla.; Arcadia-Manatee, Fla.; Hull-Boca Grande, Fla.; Fort Ogden-Naples, Fla. The remainder is operated by Seaboard System.

SEABOARD COAST LINE RAILROAD

In retrospect the Seaboard Coast Line seems to have been an intermediate phase in the creation of Seaboard System. Merger of the Seaboard Air Line and the Atlantic Coast Line was proposed in 1958 and took effect July 1, 1967. The merger permitted some duplicate lines to be eliminated, such as SAL's line between Charleston and Savannah, most of the ACL route into the Norfolk-Portsmouth area, and much of the dense network of track in central Florida.

The most prevalent objection to the creation of SCL was over Atlantic Coast Line's control of Louisville & Nashville. Both Southern and Illinois Central asked to purchase ACL's interest in L&N. The Southern and ACL plus SAL were about the same size, roughly 10,000 miles, and adding 6,000-mile L&N to either would create a large railroad. Southern presumably felt that if one railroad was to be considerably larger than its competitor, it wanted to be the big one. Southern later dropped its objection when it gained control of the Central of Georgia. Illinois Central was about the same size as L&N but had long been eager to penetrate the Southeast. Other protesters were Florida East Coast, which said that ACL-SCL would surround it, and Gulf, Mobile & Ohio.

On July 1, 1969 SCL purchased the Piedmont & Northern, a former interurban line owned by the Duke interests, and on September 1, 1976 SCL purchased the Durham & Southern, obtaining easier access to Durham, North Carolina.

About 1974 SCL's advertising began to refer to SCL, Louisville & Nashville, Clinchfield, Georgia Railroad, and the West Point Route as "The Family Lines," but the title was simply a marketing device, not the name of a corporation. The reference usually included a list of the members of the family. By then two other alliances south of the Ohio and east of the Mississippi had been formed: Southern-Central of Georgia-Georgia & Florida-"old" Norfolk Southern; and Illinois Central-Gulf, Mobile & Ohio. Unification of the members of the Family Lines could proceed. On November 1, 1980, Seaboard Coast Line and Chessie System were merged into the CSX Corporation. On December 29, 1982, Louisville & Nashville was merged into SCL to form the Seaboard System Railroad.

Location of headquarters: Jacksonville, Florida
Miles of railroad operated: 1967 — 9,306; 1982 — 8,772
Number of locomotives: 1967 — 1,235; 1982 — 1,255
Number of passenger cars: 1967 — 729; 1970 — 448
Number of freight cars: 1967 — 63,405; 1982 — 59,335

Continued on next page

Curt Tillotson Jr.

Two GP40s lead a fast piggyback train through Neuse, N. C., a few miles north of Raleigh on the former Seaboard main line, in June 1979.

Number of company service cars: 1967 — 2,156; 1982 — 2,392
Reporting marks: SCL
Notable named passenger trains: SCL continued to operate the trains of its predecessors and at the same high standards. When airplanes were being hijacked to Cuba, SCL seized the opportunity to advertise the inability of a train to be hijacked.
Historical and technical society: Southeastern Railroad Technical Society, 1552 Highcrest Drive, Valrico, FL 33594
Predecessor railroads in this book:
Atlantic Coast Line
Seaboard Air Line
Piedmont & Northern
Successors: Seaboard System (TWG)
Portions still operated: See entries for Atlantic Coast Line, Seaboard Air Line, and Piedmont & Northern

John C. Illman

A pair of ex-Burlington Northern F7s leased from a Tacoma scrap dealer bring Seattle & North Coast's twice-weekly Port Angeles-Port Townsend freight along the shore of Discovery Bay in January 1984.

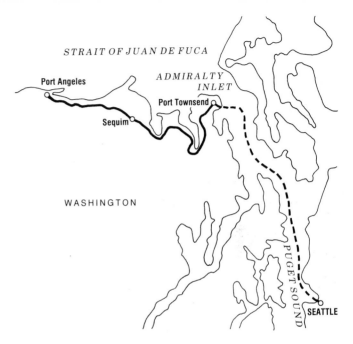

SEATTLE & NORTH COAST RAILROAD

On March 1, 1980, the Milwaukee Road withdrew from the Pacific Northwest. One portion abandoned was the isolated line on Washington's Olympic Peninsula from Port Townsend to Port Angeles. The line had been established in 1915 as the Seattle, Port Angeles & Western Railroad, and within three years the Milwaukee Road had taken it over. It became one of the road's most profitable branches, bringing out lumber and wood products from area forests. In recent years, though, the Milwaukee Road wanted to abandon the line.

North Coast Lines, a locomotive leasing company, was seeking a short line to purchase and operate. They negotiated with Milwaukee Road to lease the Port Townsend-Port Angeles line, closed the deal the day before the Milwaukee shut down, and, delayed by union injunctions, began service on March 24, 1980. Traffic consisted largely of outbound newsprint, kraft paper, lumber, and plywood and inbound chemicals.

The road's only connection with the rest of the North American rail system was by a 45-mile barge haul along Admiralty Inlet and Puget Sound to Seattle, where S&NC owned a one-fourth interest in Whatcom Yard near Pier 27. Beset by high expenses and truck competition, the road declared bankruptcy and shut down June 30, 1984. The Milwaukee Road regained control of the line in early 1985, retrieved all of the rolling stock that had been trapped since S&NC shut down, and once again sought a buyer to either operate or scrap the Olympic Peninsula line.

Location of headquarters: Seattle, Washington
Miles of railroad operated: 1980 — 50; 1984 — 50
Number of locomotives: 1980 — 6; 1984 — 7
Number of passenger cars: 1984 — 3
Number of freight cars: 1980 — 200; 1984 — 299
Reporting marks: SNCT
Predecessor railroads in this book: Chicago, Milwaukee, St. Paul & Pacific

SOUTHEASTERN RAILWAY
(Ferrocarril del Sureste)

Mexico's Southeastern Railway was constructed by the Ministry of Communications and Public Works (Secretaria de Comunicaciones y Obras Publicas, abbreviated SCOP). It was completed in 1950 from Allende, Veracruz, on the Rio Coatzacoalcos, to Campeche, where it connected with the United Railways of Yucatan. The UdeY line from Campeche to Merida was standard-gauged between 1953 and 1957. The Sureste bridged the Rio Coatzacoalcos in 1962, completing a rail connection between Yucatan and the rest of Mexico.

In 1969 the Southeastern and the United of Yucatan were merged to form the United South Eastern Railways (Ferrocarriles Unidos del Sureste). The railroad is owned by the Mexican government.

Location of headquarters: Coatzacoalcos, Veracruz
Miles of railroad operated: 1950 — 457; 1968 — 455
Rolling stock figures are unavailable
Reporting marks: SCOP, SE
Successors:
United South Eastern Railways (TWG)
National Railways of Mexico (TWG)
Portions still operated: Coatzacoalcos-Campeche: National Railways of Mexico, which is merging United South Eastern Railways
Map: See United Railways of Yucatan

Kalmbach Publishing Co.: Linn H. Westcott

A passenger train waits in the siding at Francisco Rueda, in the state of Tabasco, 77 kilometers east of Allende, while a mixed train rolls by on the main line in this 1952 scene. The sides of the Alco FA2 are lettered for the Sureste; the nose still carries SCOP initials.

SOUTHERN PACIFIC COMPANY — NARROW GAUGE LINES

The Carson & Colorado Railroad was conceived in 1880 at the height of the Nevada gold and silver boom. It was intended to run from Carson City to the Colorado River. Construction began at Mound House, Nev., east of Carson City on the standard gauge Virginia & Truckee, and rails reached Keeler, California, 299 miles from Mound House, in 1883. At that point William Sharon, its promoter, asked Darius Mills, its financier, what he thought of it. Mills answered, "Either we have built the railroad 300 miles too long or 300 years too soon."

In 1900 Southern Pacific purchased the line — and the town of Tonopah, Nev., began to boom. The Nevada & California Railway, an SP subsidiary, built a connection from Hazen, on SP's Sacramento-Ogden main line, to Churchill on the C&C, bypassing the Virginia & Truckee, then standard-gauged 137 miles of the C&C from Mound House to Tonopah Junction. SP merged the Carson & Colorado into the N&C in 1905.

SP's standard gauge "Jawbone" line from Mojave to Lone Pine was completed in 1910, largely to carry construction materials for the Los Angeles Aqueduct. At Lone Pine it connected with the narrow gauge. There were proposals to standard-gauge the former Carson & Colorado from Lone Pine to Tonopah Junction to form a route from Los Angeles via Hazen to Ogden, but doubt over the status of Southern Pacific control of Central Pacific kept the project from fruition.

In 1943 SP removed the narrow gauge rails between Mina, Nev., and Laws, Calif., having in 1938 ceased service between Tonopah Junction and Benton. The Laws-Keeler segment of the line was dieselized in 1954 and remained in operation until April 29, 1960, carrying minerals and livestock.

Location of headquarters: San Francisco, California
Miles of narrow gauge railroad operated: 1929 — 160; 1959 — 71
Number of locomotives: 1929 — 9; 1959 — 1
Number of passenger cars: 1929 — 9
Number of freight cars: 1929 — 284; 1953 — 222
Reporting marks: SP
Historical and technical society: Southern Pacific Historical & Tech-

nical Society, 218 Norton, No. 6, Long Beach, CA 90805
Recommended reading: *Southern Pacific Narrow Gauge*, by Mallory Hope Ferrell, published in 1982 by Pacific Fast Mail, P. O. Box 57, Edmonds, WA 98020
Portions still operated: Churchill-Mina, Nev.: Southern Pacific (standard gauge)
Map: See Tonopah & Goldfield

F. J. Peterson

Southern Pacific narrow gauge Ten-Wheeler 22, from the Florence & Cripple Creek by way of the Nevada-California-Oregon, rolls a short freight through the Owens Valley near Keeler, Calif.

The founders of the Central Pacific Railroad, the western portion of the first transcontinental railroad, were known as the Big Four. Leland Stanford, C. P. Huntington, Mark Hopkins, and Charles Crocker were respectively president, vice-president, treasurer, and general superintendent of the Central Pacific when it was completed in 1869. Three were born in upstate New York, and the fourth moved there early in his life. All four owned mansions atop San Francisco's Nob Hill. None founded a railroad dynasty: Huntington and Hopkins died childless, though Huntington adopted a niece and Hopkins raised the son of one of his household employees, and Stanford outlived his only son.

LELAND STANFORD (1824-1893)

was born in Watervliet, N. Y., across the Hudson River from Troy, and was educated at the Clinton Liberal Institute and the Cazenovia Seminary. In 1848 he married Jane Lathrop, the daughter of an Albany storekeeper, and left New York to set up a law practice in Port Washington, Wisconsin. When fire destroyed his office in 1852, he returned to Albany, then moved to California (the prospect of gold there had attracted several of his brothers), where he established a grocery business. In 1855, having amassed a fortune, he returned to Albany to rejoin his wife. He found the pace of Eastern life too slow and soon returned to California.

Stanford was elected governor of California in 1862; at the end of his two-year term he turned his energies completely to railroads. In 1885 he became president of Southern Pacific, was elected to the U. S. Senate, and founded Stanford University (officially the Leland Stanford Junior University) at Palo Alto as a memorial to his son, who had died in 1884 at age 15 of typhoid fever. Stanford's other interests included race horses and a vineyard and distillery for the production of medicinal brandy.

COLLIS P. HUNTINGTON (1821-1900)

was born in Harwinton, Connecticut. At age 14 he began to earn his own living as a clock peddler. He and his brother opened a general store in Oneonta, N. Y. In 1844 he married Elizabeth Stoddard, and early in the California gold rush he moved west and set up a hardware store in Sacramento, Calif., in partnership with Mark Hopkins. The two men were joined by Leland Stanford and Charles Crocker in forming the Pacific Associates to build the Central Pacific Railroad east from Sacramento. Huntington then expanded south with the Southern Pacific.

Huntington's wife died in 1884 and he soon remarried. Like Hopkins, Huntington had led a frugal existence; his second wife persuaded him to live as befit his means. In 1885 Huntington and Stanford had a falling out: After the Southern Pacific, perhaps the biggest force in California politics, had pledged support for the election of Aaron Sargent (a friend of Huntington's) to the U. S. Senate, Stanford decided he wanted the office himself. Huntington forced Stanford to resign as president of SP in exchange for the railroad's support, became president of SP himself, and assured SP's board of directors that he would work for them, not for his own political advancement. Huntington then turned his attention east and became a major force in the completion of the Chesapeake & Ohio. He briefly assembled a coast-to-coast railroad system.

Huntington died at his summer camp on Raquette Lake in the Adirondack Mountains of New York. On his death, Huntington's fortune passed to his second wife, who in 1913 married Huntington's nephew, Henry E. Huntington, southern California traction magnate.

MARK HOPKINS (1813-1878) was born at Henderson, N. Y. By age 15 he was a clerk in a store; he joined C. P. Huntington in founding Huntington & Hopkins in 1856 in Sacramento, Calif. He married a cousin, Mary Sherwood, in 1854. Although wealthy, Hopkins and his wife lived quietly, almost ascetically (Hopkins was a vegetarian) until the early 1870s when Hopkins yielded to pressure from his wife, purchased half a city block on Nob Hill in San Francisco from Stanford, and built a mansion. Hopkins did not live to see the completion of the mansion; after a winter during which he had been crippled by rheumatism, he made a trip to inspect SP's lines in Arizona, hoping that warmth and sunshine would relieve his pain. He died aboard the train in Yuma. (Do not confuse this Mark Hopkins with the educator of the same name, who lived from 1802 to 1877.)

CHARLES CROCKER (1822-1888) was born in Troy, N. Y. He left school at age 12 to form a newspaper sales agency, with which he supported his mother and sister while his father and four brothers established a farm in Indiana. In 1836 the family was reunited in Indiana. Crocker worked in a sawmill, then established a small ironworks. In 1849 he and two of his brothers joined the California gold rush; they were not successful prospectors, but they soon became successful storekeepers in Sacramento. In 1852 he returned to Indiana to marry Mary Deming, daughter of the owner of the sawmill where he had worked. Ten years later he sold his dry goods store and joined Huntington, Hopkins, and Stanford to found the Central Pacific Railroad and Crocker & Company, which built the road.

Soon after completion of the railroad Crocker sold his interest to his three partners. The Panic of 1873 prevented his partners from making their payments to him; Crocker returned to the railroad as a director and vice-president. He remained active in the affairs of Central Pacific and Southern Pacific throughout his life, and in the mid-1880s turned his attention to the construction of the Del Monte, a resort hotel owned by SP near Monterey, Calif. Crocker was always large of stature, but as he aged his girth became a medical concern and, complicated by diabetes, caused his death at the Del Monte in 1888.

Recommended reading: *The Big Four*, by Oscar Lewis, published in 1938 by Alfred A. Knopf, Inc., New York, N. Y.

SOUTHERN PACIFIC RAILROAD COMPANY OF MEXICO

In 1881 and 1882 the Santa Fe built the Sonora Railway north from Guaymas, the principal Gulf of California port in the Mexican state of Sonora, to Nogales, a new city straddling the U. S. border. The Santa Fe had built southwest from Kansas to Deming, New Mexico; trackage rights over SP to Benson, Arizona, and a Santa Fe line, the New Mexico & Arizona, from there to Nogales, Ariz., plus the Sonora Railway gave the Santa Fe an outlet to the Pacific.

Santa Fe also built west from Albuquerque to Needles, California, where it connected with an SP line from Mojave. Santa Fe realized the Needles-Mojave line could provide an entrance to California. Southern Pacific, interested in Mexico, worked a trade: Santa Fe got the line from Needles to Mojave and SP got the Sonora Railway, leasing it on July 15, 1898, and purchasing it outright December 27, 1911.

The Southern Pacific of Mexico (Sud Pacifico de Mexico) was incorporated in 1909 and acquired the rights, property, and franchises of the Cananea, Rio Yaqui & Pacific, under which name the Southern Pacific had extended the railroad south from Empalme, near Guaymas, and built branches east of Nogales. In 1912 the Sonora Railway was consolidated with SPdeM. Indian uprisings and the Mexican Revolution hampered construction and operation of the railroad. When soldiers and Indians finally permitted construction, the wild, rough barranca country south of Tepic impeded progress. The line finally reached a connection with National Railways of Mexico at Orendain Jct. in April 1927 and obtained trackage rights for the remaining 24 miles to Guadalajara. Further revolutionary activity destroyed bridges and interrupted service in 1929.

The SPdeMex was a consistent money-loser for its parent, and at the beginning of 1940 Southern Pacific withdrew support, forcing Southern Pacific of Mexico to live on its own income. Losses continued partly because of labor laws and partly because heavy tariffs imposed by the U. S. on produce from Mexico stifled traffic. Mexican authorities operated the line during a strike in 1947 and 1948. The status of foreign-owned hold-

Consolidation No. 3453 leads a short freight train through the barranca country on the Southern Pacific of Mexico between Tepic and Guadalajara.

Herb and Dorothy McLaughlin

ings in Mexico became questionable, and there was a possibility of expropriation. In December 1951 SP sold the railroad to the Mexican government. It was renamed the Ferrocarril del Pacifico (Pacific Railroad).

Location of headquarters: Guadalajara, Jalisco, Mexico
Miles of railroad operated: 1929 — 1,370; 1950 — 1,331
Number of locomotives: 1929 — 104; 1950 — 93
Number of passenger cars: 1929 — 129; 1950 — 88
Number of freight cars: 1929 — 1,513; 1950 — 618
Number of company service cars: 1950 — 202
Reporting marks: SPM
Successor companies: Ferrocarril del Pacifico (TWG)
Portions still operated: Nogales-Guadalajara, Nogales-Del Rio, Cananea-Naco: Ferrocarril del Pacifico

SPOKANE INTERNATIONAL RAILWAY

The Spokane International was built by D. C. Corbin from Spokane, Washington, north to the Canadian border at Eastport, Idaho, and Kingsgate, British Columbia. There it connected with Canadian Pacific's Kettle Valley route. The southern half of the line, from Spokane to Sandpoint, was parallel and within a few miles of Northern Pacific's main line; from Sandpoint to Bonners Ferry it virtually duplicated Great Northern's main line. The SI began operation on November 1, 1906. It gave CPR a route to Spokane — or in conjunction with Soo Line, which it controlled, a route from St. Paul, Minnesota, to Spokane in competition with James J. Hill's Great Northern and Northern Pacific. CPR purchased control of the SI in 1917.

Spokane International entered bankruptcy proceedings in 1933, and

Most of Spokane International's business was — and is — bridge traffic, but the lumber industry provided much of its local business. In this 1951 scene the first three cars behind the RS1 of Extra 205 are loaded with forest products.

reorganization (as the Spokane International Railroad) in 1941 wiped out CPR's stock interest. During World War Two business increased and revenues climbed to give the railroad Class 1 status (then, $1 million or more). After the war it needed and got extensive rebuilding and dieselization. More than 80 percent of its business was bridge traffic between CP and the connecting railroads at Spokane.

Union Pacific acquired control of SI on October 6, 1958, by acquisition of nearly 99 percent of its stock, and gradually acquired the remainder. Spokane International still exists, but Union Pacific run-through freights make the road look like just another piece of the Union Pacific.

Location of headquarters: Spokane, Washington
Miles of railroad operated: 1929 — 166; 1958 — 150
Number of locomotives: 1929 — 11; 1958 — 12
Number of passenger cars: 1929 — 6
Number of freight cars: 1929 — 263
Number of company service cars: 1929 — 18
Number of freight and company service cars: 1958 — 201
Reporting marks: SI
Successors: Union Pacific
Portions still operated: Spokane, Wash.-Kingsgate, B. C.; Coeur d'Alene Jct.-Coeur d'Alene, Idaho
Map: See opposite page

SPOKANE, PORTLAND & SEATTLE RAILWAY

James J. Hill announced in 1905 that he intended to build a railroad along the north bank of the Columbia River, partly to block the Milwaukee Road from doing the same and partly to invade Oregon, territory that belonged almost exclusively to E. H. Harriman's Union Pacific and Southern Pacific. The Portland & Seattle Railway was incorporated in 1905, and in 1908 Spokane was added to its name. The railroad was completed during 1908 from Pasco, Washington, to Portland, Oreg., along the north bank of the Columbia River, and in 1909 the line was opened from Spokane to Pasco. Jointly financing the construction of the SP&S were Great Northern and Northern Pacific, both under Hill's control.

Hill had already acquired a line along the south bank of the lower part of the Columbia River west of Portland; that plus Northern Pacific's line from Portland to Goble, Oreg., formed a route from Portland to Astoria, where connection was made with Hill's steamships to San Francisco.

Between Portland and Pasco SP&S's line followed the north bank of the Columbia River. The combination of easy curves and negligible grades made it the fastest stretch of railroad in the Northwest, even before the construction of dams along the Columbia necessitated line relocations which improved SP&S's alignment.

SP&S had three subsidiaries: Oregon Electric Railway, Oregon Trunk Railway, and United Railways.

SP&S acquired Oregon Electric in 1910, two years after it had been opened between Portland and Salem. The main line was extended south to Eugene in 1912; among the several branches was a freight-only line to a logging area on the western slope of the Cascades. The last passenger service was discontinued in 1933, and the road was dieselized in 1945.

Like many other parts of the Hill empire, the OE was characterized by head-on competition with Harriman, in this case with Southern Pacific's electric lines in the Willamette Valley.

The Oregon Trunk was incorporated in 1909 and opened in 1911 between Wishram, Wash., on the Columbia River, and Bend, practically in the center of Oregon, 152 miles. Both Oregon Trunk and the Oregon-Washington Railroad & Navigation Co. (Union Pacific) built south up the canyon of the Deschutes River. The two railroads, backed by Hill and Harriman, respectively, fought over occupancy of the canyon and eventually came to terms — trackage rights over portions of each other's line and abandonment of duplicate track. Oregon Trunk's bridge over the Crooked River north of Bend is tied with Southern Pacific's Pecos River bridge for the honor of highest common-carrier railroad bridge in the U. S.

In 1906 the United Railways Company was incorporated and purchased the properties of Oregon Traction Company, which had a line from Linnton to Keasey, Oreg., 54 miles. The line was operated primarily as a steam railroad and was notable for a 4,100-foot tunnel west of Portland. SP&S absorbed the company in 1943.

For most of its life the SP&S functioned as an obscure extension of its two parents. Its steam locomotives for the most part were acquired secondhand from GN and NP. The road acquired a distinct identity during the diesel era with its heavy reliance on Alco power and a new slogan, "The Northwest's Own Railway." SP&S was merged into Burlington Northern along with its parents, Northern Pacific and Great Northern, and Chicago, Burlington & Quincy on March 2, 1970.

Location of headquarters: Portland, Oregon

Miles of railroad operated: 1929 — 555 (915 with subsidiaries); 1969 — 922

Number of locomotives: 1929 — 99; 1969 — 112

Number of passenger cars: 1929 — 100; 1969 — 54

Number of freight cars: 1929 — 698; 1969 — 3,216

Number of company service cars: 1929 — 252; 1969 — 355

Reporting marks: SPS

Subsidiaries and affiliated railroads, 1929:
Oregon Electric Railway (154 miles, 10 locomotives, 76 passenger cars, 25 freight cars, 27 service cars)
Oregon Trunk Railway (152 miles, 3 locomotives, 10 service cars)
United Railways (54 miles, 6 passenger cars, 62 freight cars, 6 service cars)

Successor companies: Burlington Northern (TWG)

Portions still operated: all except Astoria-Seaside, Banks-Keasey, Sweet Home-Dollar, Grey Corvallis, and Oregon Electric's passenger route between Portland and Beaverton: Burlington Northern

STATEN ISLAND RAPID TRANSIT RAILWAY

The least-known borough of New York City is Richmond, or Staten Island. Geographically it is much closer to New Jersey than to New York, and until the completion of the Verrazano Bridge in 1964, it was connected to the rest of New York — city and state — by ferries from St. George, at the north end of the island. In 1885 Baltimore & Ohio purchased the Staten Island Rapid Transit Railway, which had a short line of its own between Tompkinsville and Clifton on the northeast shore of Staten Island and leased the Staten Island Railway, a line from Clifton to Tottenville, at its southern tip. (The railway had been completed in 1860 and was one of Cornelius Vanderbilt's early properties.) B&O's intention was to build freight and passenger terminals on Staten Island; purchase of SIRT gave B&O waterfront property on New York Bay. SIRT built a line west to the Arthur Kill Bridge in 1889 at the same time the Baltimore & New York, another B&O subsidiary, constructed a connecting line from Cranford Jct. on the Central Railroad of New Jersey. SIRT built a short line from Clifton to South Beach in 1892.

In anticipation of a tunnel under the Narrows to Brooklyn and a connection there with the New York subway system, SIRT electrified its

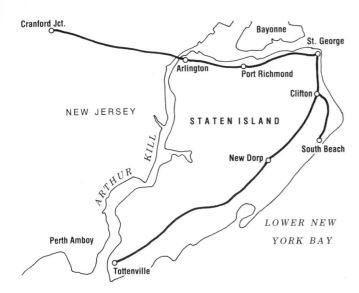

Herman Rinke

A single electric car operating on the line to Arlington passes through the U. S. Gypsum plant between New Brighton and Sailor's Snug Harbor on Staten Island's north shore. The standard-size hopper car, small by present-day standards, shows how small the electric car is.

lines in 1925 using third-rail power distribution and cars similar to those of the Brooklyn-Manhattan Transit Co. The electrification brought no big increase in traffic, and the tunnel was never built.

In 1944 SIRT purchased the property of the Baltimore & New York and merged the Staten Island Railway. In 1948 the road discontinued its ferry service between Tottenville and Perth Amboy, N. J. The terminal at St. George was destroyed by fire in 1946; a modern replacement was opened in 1951. SIRT discontinued passenger service on the lines to Arlington and South Beach in March 1953 because of city-operated bus competition.

On January 1, 1970, New York City's lease of the St. George-Tottenville line was terminated; after that date the city reimbursed the railroad for its passenger deficits. On July 1, 1971, operation of the Tottenville line was turned over to the Staten Island Rapid Transit Op-

erating Authority, a division of the state's Metropolitan Transportation Authority, and the line itself was purchased by the city of New York. Later that year the name of the railroad was changed to Staten Island Railroad Corporation. In 1985 the Staten Island Railroad was purchased by the Delaware Otsego System.

Location of headquarters: New York, New York
Miles of railroad operated: 1929 — 24; 1970 — 12
Number of locomotives: 1929 — 4; 1970 — 7
Number of passenger cars: 1929 — 95; 1970 — 48

Continued on next page

Number of freight cars: 1929 — 1; 1970 — 7 (cabooses)
Number of company service cars: 1929 — 21; 1970 — 6
Number of ferries: 1929 — 3
Reporting marks: SIR
Historical and technical societies:
Baltimore & Ohio Railroad Historical Society, P. O. Box 13578, Balti-
more, MD 21203
Affiliation for Baltimore & Ohio System Historical Research, 536
Clairbrook Avenue, Columbus, OH 43228
Portions still operated:
St. George-Tottenville: Staten Island Rapid Transit Operating Authority
Cranford Jct., N. J.-Clifton: Staten Island Railroad

SUMPTER VALLEY RAILWAY

The Sumpter Valley was incorporated in 1890 to tap the forests of the Blue Mountains of eastern Oregon. Much of the rolling stock for the line came from Union Pacific 3-foot-gauge lines in Utah and Idaho that had just been standard-gauged. The first portion of the line from Baker to McEwen opened for service in 1892, and the line reached the town of Sumpter (which was in the midst of a gold-mining boom) in 1897. The line reached Austin in 1905 and Prairie City, a cattle-raising center, in 1910. There were proposals to extend the line to Burns and also southwest to a connection with the Nevada-California-Oregon, which was building north from Reno, Nevada. That would have created a narrow gauge route all the way from California's Owens Valley to Baker, except for a short stretch of the standard gauge Virginia & Truckee, and it would have traversed some of the emptiest country in the U. S. Prairie City is as far as the SV got, but it did connect with an extensive network of logging railroads centered on Austin.

In 1932 the western 20 miles of the line from Bates to Prairie City were abandoned. In 1940 the SV bought two 2-6-6-2 articulateds from the Uintah Railway. SV converted them from tank engines to tender engines and used them for seven years.

By 1946 a reduction by the U. S. Forestry Service in the amount of timber that could be cut and the necessity to transfer lumber from narrow gauge to standard gauge cars at Baker caused the Sumpter Valley to petition for abandonment, even though it was still profitable and free of debt. The last scheduled run was on April 11, 1947, and official abandonment came on August 31, 1948. The articulateds were sold to International Railways of Central America.

H. R. Griffiths

Sumpter Valley 2-6-6-2 No. 250 rolls a long train of lumber along the Powder River in the Blue Mountains of eastern Oregon in 1946.

314

A two-mile portion of the railroad at Baker remained in switching service until the end of 1961. The sole remaining locomotive, a 30-ton Davenport diesel switcher built in 1937, was sold to the Denver & Rio Grande Western in 1963 for service at Durango as D&RGW No. 50.

Location of headquarters: Baker, Oregon
Miles of railroad operated: 1929 — 80; 1945 — 3
Number of locomotives: 1929 — 11
Number of passenger cars: 1929 — 4

Number of freight cars: 1929 — 236
Number of company service cars: 1929 — 24
Number of freight and company service cars: 1945 — 227
Reporting marks: SVRy
Recommended reading: *Rails, Sagebrush and Pine*, by Mallory Hope Ferrell, published in 1967 by Golden West Books, P. O. Box 80250, San Marino, CA 91108
Map: See page 311

SUSQUEHANNA & NEW YORK RAILROAD

The ancestor of the Susquehanna & New York was the Towanda & Franklin Railroad, which changed its name to the Barclay Railroad & Coal Company before construction began in 1855. The purpose of the railroad was to carry coal from mines at Barclay, Pennsylvania, to canal boats and later the Lehigh Valley Railroad at Towanda, about 15 miles.

Around the turn of the century the mines played out and floods destroyed the railroad. By then lumber had replaced coal in the economy of the area and there was still a need for a railroad. The line was rebuilt and

William Moedinger

Susquehanna & New York Ten-Wheeler 119 and a former gasoline-powered railcar form the daily local at Masten, Pa. The 4-6-0 was purchased from the Huntingdon & Broad Top Mountain. Upon the demise of the S&NY it was stored for several years and eventually purchased by the Clarion River Railway.

extended southwest over the divide between the Susquehanna and its West Branch to a connection with the Northern Central (Pennsylvania Railroad) north of Williamsport. The railroad emerged from several corporate changes in 1903 as the Susquehanna & New York Railroad. In 1907 the road began construction of a terminal at Williamsport and negotiated for trackage rights over the Northern Central for 22 miles.

By 1940 the forests along the line were depleted, and there were no towns of any size along the S&NY to create local business. The owner, United States Leather Co., weighed the railroad's deficit against its scrap value. The last train ran on May 22, 1942. The Lehigh Valley purchased the Towanda-Monroeton portion of the line, over which it had operated on trackage rights.

U. S. Leather owned two other short lines in northwestern Pennsylvania, the Tionesta Valley and the Clarion River. The Tionesta Valley was a 3-foot-gauge logging railroad from Sheffield to Hallton, Pa. It was abandoned in 1942. The Clarion River was a 12-mile standard gauge line opened in 1891 from Hallton to connections with the Buffalo, Rochester & Pittsburgh and the Ridgway & Clearfield (later Pennsylvania) at Car-

man, Pa. It came under the control of the Pittsburg, Shawmut & Northern and was sold to the Tionesta Valley in 1926. In the late 1930s the Clarion River was purchased by Clawson Chemical Company to maintain service to its plant at Hallton. Susquehanna Chemical Co. bought Clawson in 1946. The Clarion River was abandoned in 1948.

Location of headquarters: Williamsport, Pennsylvania
Miles of railroad operated: 1929 — 68; 1940 — 68
Number of locomotives: 1929 — 6; 1940 — 6
Number of passenger cars: 1929 — 3
Number of freight cars: 1929 — 69
Number of company service cars: 1929 — 7
Number of cars: 1940 — 31
Reporting marks: S&NY
Recommended reading: *Story of the Susquehanna & New York*, by Edward L. Kaseman, published in 1963 by Edward L. Kaseman, 819 Park Avenue, Williamsport, PA 17701
Portions still operated: Towanda-Monroeton, Pa.: Towanda-Monroeton Shippers' Lifeline

TALLULAH FALLS RAILWAY

The Northeastern Railroad was chartered in 1856 to build from Athens to Clayton, Georgia. Rails reached Tallulah Falls in 1882 shortly after the company was sold to the Richmond & Danville system (Southern Railway). The portion of the line north of Cornelia was sold again in 1887 to the Blue Ridge & Atlantic Railroad. The road entered receivership in 1892 and was reorganized as the Tallulah Falls Railway in 1897. Construction resumed, and Clayton finally got its railroad in 1904. The Southern reacquired the line in 1905 and extended it north to Franklin, North Carolina, in 1907.

In 1908 the TF weathered a brief receivership, and in 1923 it entered receivership again for keeps. The road petitioned for abandonment in 1933. The Georgia Public Service Commission recommended that the ICC deny the petition; the ICC approved it, but the railroad kept running.

Passenger service ended in 1946 when a truck hit the passenger train, damaging the locomotive slightly but putting the road's sole coach out of service. The road dieselized in 1948. The Tallulah Falls appeared in the 1950 movie, *I'd Climb the Highest Mountain*, and in 1955 Walt Disney used it as the setting for *The Great Locomotive Chase*. The Tallulah Falls made its last run on March 25, 1961, a victim of the paved roads it had carried the materials for. The line was dismantled later that year.

Location of headquarters: Cornelia, Georgia
Miles of railroad operated: 1929 — 57; 1960 — 57
Number of locomotives: 1929 — 5; 1960 — 2
Number of passenger cars: 1929 — 5
Number of freight cars: 1929 — 41
Number of company service cars: 1929 — 9
Number of cars: 1960 — 12
Recommended reading: *Memories of a Mountain Shortline*, by Kaye Carver and Myra Queen, published in 1976 by The Foxfire Press, Rabun Gap, GA 30568

William J. Husa Jr.

Seventy-tonner No. 502 hauls freight northward across the lake formed by a dam at Tallulah Falls, Ga., in December 1959.

TEMISCOUATA RAILWAY

The Temiscouata Railway was chartered in 1885 to bring forest products from northwestern New Brunswick to the St. Lawrence Valley. By the beginning of 1889 the line was in operation from Riviere du Loup, Quebec, southeast to Edmundston, N. B., and less than two years later an extension west along the St. John River to Connors, N. B., was opened. Edmundston had been reached by the New Brunswick Railway (later Canadian Pacific) from McAdam a decade before.

When the Temiscouata was built, it was proposed to continue the line east past Edmundston to Moncton, and Connors was intended to be a junction with the Quebec Central. The Moncton-Edmundston line was built not by the Temiscouata but by the National Transcontinental Railway (later Canadian National) in 1911 as part of its Moncton-Winnipeg

J. Norman Lowe

The Temiscouata acquired this motor-car-and-trailer set from Canadian National in 1934.

line. Quebec Central got no closer than Lac Frontiere on the Quebec-Maine border.

The road survived a couple of reorganizations, and Canadian National nursed it along with favorable divisions of interline revenue. In 1941 the Temiscouata abandoned 14 miles of its line between Edmundston and Baker Brook in favor of trackage rights on CN's parallel Edmundston-Quebec line.

The Temiscouata Railway was purchased by the Canadian government in 1949 and operation was taken over by Canadian National Railways on January 1, 1950. The portion of the Connors line beyond Clairs was abandoned in 1960.

Location of headquarters: Riviere du Loup, Quebec
Miles of railroad operated: 1929 — 113; 1949 — 113
Number of locomotives: 1929 — 7; 1949 — 7
Number of passenger cars: 1929 — 10; 1949 — 17
Number of freight cars: 1929 — 148; 1949 — 87
Number of company service cars: 1929 — 14; 1949 — 23
Reporting marks: TMC
Successor companies: Canadian National (TWG)
Portions still operated: Riviere du Loup-Edmundston, Baker Brook-Clairs (CN)

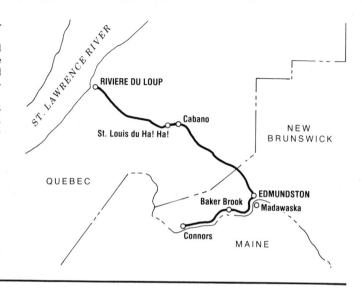

TENNESSEE, ALABAMA & GEORGIA RAILWAY

Construction of the Chattanooga Southern Railway began in 1890 and was completed in 1891, creating a new line between Chattanooga, Tennessee, and Gadsden, Alabama. Backing the project was Russell Sage, a New York financier. The company entered receivership in 1892 and was reorganized as the Chattanooga Southern Railroad in 1896. Receivers again took it over between 1907 and 1910; it was reorganized in 1911 as the Tennessee, Alabama & Georgia Railway — which followed the lead of its predecessors in 1920. During the 1920s the ICC approved a proposal to extend the line southwest to a connection with Seaboard's Atlanta-Birmingham line, but the idea never bore fruit.

The TA&G was sold, reorganized, and sold again, this time to a syndicate headed by W. H. Coverdale of Coverdale & Colpitts, the railroad engineering firm. The new management immediately undertook a long-needed rehabilitation. Much of the line was still laid with the original 56-pound rail; it was upgraded with 100-pound rail. As business increased, TA&G had to replace its small, low-drivered Consolidations with secondhand Mikados and a pair of ex-Boston & Albany Berkshires. The road was reorganized again in 1937.

The original purpose of the road was to tap the iron, coal, and timber resources of northeastern Alabama, but gradually the TA&G's principal purpose came to be serving the steel mills at Gadsden and furnishing a northward outlet for them.

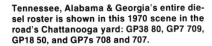

Tennessee, Alabama & Georgia's entire diesel roster is shown in this 1970 scene in the road's Chattanooga yard: GP38 80, GP7 709, GP18 50, and GP7s 708 and 707.

William J. Husa Jr.

On January 1, 1971, Southern Railway purchased the TA&G. The middle portion of the TA&G was abandoned about 1980. The remainder is operated as part of the Southern system.

Location of headquarters: Chattanooga, Tennessee
Miles of railroad operated: 1929 — 95; 1970 — 87
Number of locomotives: 1929 — 8; 1970 — 5
Number of passenger cars: 1929 — 2 (motor)
Number of freight cars: 1929 — 8; 1970 — 94

Number of company service cars: 1929 — 20; 1970 — 8
Reporting marks: TA&G
Recommended reading: *Central of Georgia Railway and Connecting Lines*, by Richard E. Prince, published in 1976 by Richard E. Prince
Successors: Southern (TWG)
Portions still operated: Chattanooga, Tenn.-Hedges, Ga.; Ewing, Ala.-Gadsden, Ala.: Southern
Map: See page 316

TENNESSEE CENTRAL RAILWAY

The Tennessee & Pacific Railroad was organized in 1871 and built eastward from Nashville to Lebanon, Tenn. By 1894 the line had extended east to Monterey with the intention of tapping coal mines; by 1900 the line had been pushed east to a connection with the Southern (Cincinnati, New Orleans, & Texas Pacific) at Emory Gap by the Tennessee Central Railway (the road's history includes several Tennessee Central companies, railroads, and railways). In 1904 the TC was complete, with a 2-mile extension from Emory Gap to Harriman and an 83-mile line quickly constructed from Nashville northwest to Hopkinsville, Kentucky.

The TC was the only direct route from Nashville to eastern Tennessee, albeit through topography requiring 3-percent grades, 10-degree curves, and several spectacular trestles. The road was intended to be a coal car-

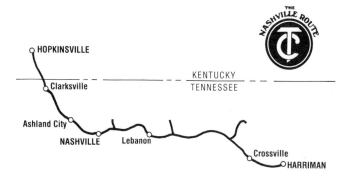

A westbound extra freight rolls out of a tunnel near Rockwood, Tenn., at the eastern end of the Tennessee Central.

rier — and by 1950 the principal commodity carried by the TC was indeed coal, but more coal was received from connecting railroads than was originated on line. TC provided access to Nashville for Illinois Central from Hopkinsville and for Southern from Harriman. Its tracks formed a belt line around Nashville, a city that was otherwise the exclusive province of Louisville & Nashville and its subsidiary Nashville, Chattanooga & St. Louis. During World War Two TC's traffic was boosted considerably by the Army installation at Fort Campbell, near Hopkinsville.

Between a brief receivership in 1904 and a longer one from 1913 to 1917 the road was divided at Nashville and operated by IC and Southern, but neither IC nor Southern wished to continue the arrangement. The road was reorganized in 1922, and in 1946 control was assumed by a group of investors from Philadelphia. Net operating income moved to the deficit side of the ledgers in 1963; in the decade from 1957 to 1966 the TC posted a net profit for only two years, 1958 and 1959. In May 1968 the ICC authorized abandonment of the Tennessee Central. Segments of its main line were acquired by other roads: Hopkinsville-Nashville — Illinois Central; Nashville-Crossville — Louisville & Nashville; and Cross-

ville-Harriman — Southern. IC has since abandoned its portion of the TC; the portion from Ashland City to Nashville has become the Nashville & Ashland City Railroad.

Location of headquarters: Nashville, Tennessee
Miles of railroad operated: 1929 — 296; 1966 — 280
Number of locomotives: 1929 — 41; 1966 — 21
Number of passenger cars: 1929 — 33
Number of freight cars: 1929 — 663
Number of company service cars: 1929 — 96
Number of freight and company service cars: 1966 — 557
Reporting marks: TC
Recommended reading: *Ghost Railroads of Tennessee*, by Elmer G. Sulzer, published in 1975 by Vane A. Jones Co., Indianapolis, Ind.
Portions still operated:
Ashland City-Nashville: Nashville & Ashland City
Nashville-Crossville: Seaboard System
Crossville-Harriman: Southern Railway

TEXAS & PACIFIC RAILWAY

The southernmost of the routes surveyed between 1853 and 1855 for a transcontinental railroad led across central Texas. It was the shortest and lowest route between the Atlantic and the Pacific and the one least subject to the rigors of winter, but the Civil War eliminated it from consideration. After the war, though, a transcontinental route between the thirty-second and thirty-fifth parallels was again feasible and desirable. In 1871 Congress chartered the Texas Pacific Railroad to build from Marshall, Tex., to San Diego, California, via El Paso, Tex. The name of the company was soon changed to Texas & Pacific Railway; its first president was Thomas Scott, who had been vice-president and general manager of the Pennsylvania Railroad, and its first chief engineer was Grenville M. Dodge, former chief engineer of the Union Pacific.

The new road purchased the properties and franchises of two early railroads, including a rail line in operation between Shreveport, Louisiana, and Longview, Tex. Construction west from Longview, begun in October 1872, was plagued by low water in the Red River (hindering the transportation of supplies), an epizootic that killed off the mules, and yellow fever. Even so, the line reached Dallas in less than a year.

By the beginning of 1874 the T&P was operating from Shreveport west to Dallas, from Marshall north to Texarkana, and from Sherman east to Brookston (near Paris). In July 1876 the line from Shreveport reached Fort Worth. (To keep its charter in effect, the T&P had to reach Fort Worth before the state legislature ended its session; Fort Worth's representative kept the session going for several extra days.) Less than a month later the Texarkana-Sherman line was completed.

Fort Worth remained T&P's western terminus for several years. In January 1880 Jay Gould and Russell Sage joined T&P's board of direc-

T&P

The 2-10-4 wheel arrangement was a natural development of Lima's Super-Power 2-8-4, and it was named "Texas" for the Texas & Pacific, its first user. T&P eventually amassed a stable of 70 of these machines, one of which is shown lifting a freight up Baird Hill in west Texas.

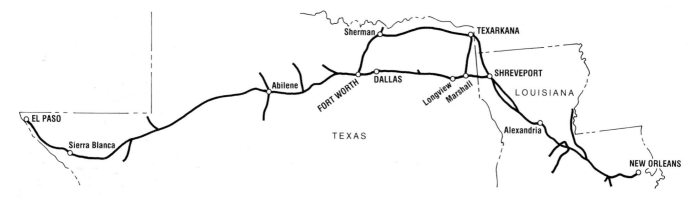

tors; in April of the next year Scott sold his interests in the T&P to Gould, who became president of the road. Construction had resumed in 1880, and the line proceeded rapidly across west Texas. On December 15, 1881, at Sierra Blanca, about 90 miles east of El Paso, the T&P met the Southern Pacific which had been building east from Los Angeles, completing the second transcontinental rail route.

By September 1882 T&P had purchased and built a line east from Shreveport to New Orleans, essentially completing the road. In the decades before and after the turn of the century T&P upgraded some of the hastily constructed portions of its main line and acquired a number of short branches, but nothing to alter the basic shape of its map.

The T&P was in receivership from 1885 to 1888 and entered receivership again in 1916. Fortunately for T&P, oil was discovered at Ranger, Tex., in 1918. T&P's revenues from the oil boom underwrote a rehabilitation program and put the road back in the black in 1924. Oil continued to be a major item of traffic until the completion of pipelines in the late 1940s.

In 1962 the Muskogee Co. authorized the sale of all its railroad stocks to the Texas & Pacific. In September 1964 T&P acquired control of the three Muskogee roads but immediately sold the Oklahoma City-Ada

Atoka to the Santa Fe. Midland Valley was merged into T&P on April 1, 1967, and the same happened to Kansas, Oklahoma & Gulf exactly three years later.

During reorganization in 1923 Texas & Pacific issued preferred stock to Missouri Pacific in exchange for mortgage bonds held by MP. By the beginning of 1930 MP owned all T&P's preferred stock and more than half its common stock. After many years of controlling T&P, MoPac finally merged the Texas & Pacific on October 15, 1976.

Location of headquarters: Dallas, Texas
Miles of railroad operated: 1929 — 1,956; 1975 — 2,139
Number of locomotives: 1929 — 372; 1975 — 153
Number of passenger cars: 1929 — 234
Number of freight cars: 1929 — 9,517; 1975 — 13,366
Number of company service cars: 1929 — 1,465; 1975 — 263
Reporting marks: T&P, TP
Historical and technical society: Missouri Pacific Historical Society, 9726 Whitestone Terrace, St. Louis, MO 63119
Recommended reading: *Texas & Pacific*, by Don Watson and Steve Brown, published in 1978 by Boston Mills Press, R. R. 1, Cheltenham, ON, Canada L0P 1C0 (ISBN 0-919822-83-5)

Subsidiaries and affiliated railroads, 1975:
Fort Worth Belt (60%)
Texas & Pacific-Missouri Pacific Terminal Railroad of New Orleans (50%, jointly with Missouri Pacific)
Abilene & Southern
Texas-New Mexico
Weatherford, Mineral Wells & Northwestern
Predecessor railroads in this book:
Kansas, Oklahoma & Gulf
Midland Valley
Successors: Missouri Pacific (TWG)
Portions still operated: Missouri Pacific operates all of the T&P except for the following lines, which have been abandoned: Donaldsonville-Napoleonville, La.; Lettsworth-Ferriday, La.; Melville-Port Barre, La.; Church Point-Crowley, La.; Melville-Bunkie, La.; Longbridge Jct.-Marksville, La.; Ville Platte-Eunice, La.; Cypress-Reisor, La.; Shreveport, La.-Texarkana, Tex.; Grand Saline-Alba, Tex. (Texas Short Line); Mineral Wells-Graford, Tex. (Weatherford, Mineral Wells & Northwestern); Hamlin-Abilene and Winters-Ballinger, Tex. (Abilene & Southern); Cisco-Throckmorton, Tex. (Cisco & Northeastern)

Ed Robinson

As T&P streamlined and dieselized its passenger trains, the *Eagle* colors were also applied to steam power, such as Pacific No. 706, shown at Jonesville, Tex., in 1951 on train 24.

TIDEWATER SOUTHERN RAILWAY

The Tidewater Southern was conceived as an interurban between Stockton and Fresno, California, although almost from the beginning there was talk of extension south to Los Angeles. Construction began in 1911, and in October 1912 the road began steam passenger service between Stockton and Modesto, 33 miles. The line was electrified in 1913. It was extended to Turlock in 1916, and a branch was built to Manteca in 1918, but these lines were never electrified nor did they offer passenger service. Passenger service ended in 1932, but wires remained over the tracks in Modesto until 1950. The city forbade the operation of steam locomotives in the streets, and electric locomotives (diesels after November 1947) pulled trains, steamer and all, through the city.

The Western Pacific obtained control of the road in 1917. The Tidewater Southern offered WP access to the rich agricultural and wine-producing area at the north end of the San Joaquin Valley and became a profitable feeder for WP. Regular operations of the Tidewater Southern were dieselized in 1948. One steam locomotive was retained for service during the heavy shipping season — and also out of deference to a bridge remaining from TS's light-rail interurban days — until 1955.

Tidewater Southern maintained its identity more firmly than did Sacramento Northern, WP's other ex-interurban, and hung on even after WP was absorbed by Union Pacific. It was mid-1983 before the *Official Guide* dropped its listing for Tidewater Southern — at the end it was a dead-end reference to Western Pacific — and even in 1985 the road was still listed in *The Pocket List of Railroad Officials* — although most of Tidewater

Southern's officials were located in Omaha and none were in Modesto.

Location of headquarters: San Francisco, California

Miles of railroad operated: 1929 — 65; 1981 — 56

Number of locomotives: 1929 — 1

Number of passenger cars: 1929 — 3

Number of motor freight cars: 1929 — 2

Number of freight cars: 1981 — 3

Reporting marks: TS

Recommended reading: *Western Pacific's Diesel Years*, by Joseph A. Strapac, published in 1980 by Overland Models, Inc., R. R. 12, Box 445, Muncie, IN 47302 (ISBN 0-916160-08-4)

Successors: Union Pacific

Portions still operated: UP operates all the TS except for the long-abandoned passenger trackage into downtown Stockton.

Map: See page 283

The refrigerator cars standing in front of the packing shed at Turner, Calif., and the fields beyond explain Tidewater Southern's value as a feeder to parent Western Pacific. RS1 747, once on the roster of Spokane International as No. 205, has just picked up three loaded reefers and is ready to leave for Stockton in this 1972 scene.

R. T. Sharp

TOLEDO, PEORIA & WESTERN RAILROAD

The Peoria & Oquawka Eastern Extension Railroad was chartered in 1852 to build from Peoria to the Illinois-Indiana state line at Effner. Construction began at East Peoria in 1855; a bridge over the Illinois River between East Peoria and Peoria was opened in 1857, and the entire line was completed at the beginning of 1860. It was renamed the Logansport, Peoria & Burlington Railroad in 1861, sold at foreclosure in March 1864, and reorganized as the Toledo, Peoria & Warsaw Railway. By new construction and absorption of the Mississippi & Wabash Railroad (Warsaw-Carthage, Ill.) TP&W was able to extend its line west to the Mississippi River in 1868, and to bridge the Mississippi to Keokuk, Iowa, in 1869. In 1871 it built a short branch from La Harpe to Lomax, Ill., and negotiated for trackage rights over the Chicago, Burlington & Quincy from Lomax to Burlington, Iowa.

In 1880 the road was reorganized as the Toledo, Peoria & Western Railroad and leased to the Wabash, St. Louis & Pacific for a term of 49½ years — the lease lasted until 1884. The TP&W Railway was chartered in 1887 to take over the railroad. In 1893 the Pennsylvania and a predecessor of the Burlington each acquired large stock interests in the TP&W. In 1927 the TP&W established a connection with the Santa Fe at Lomax, Ill.

In 1927 George P. McNear Jr. purchased the road at foreclosure. He saw the road's potential as a bridge route bypassing the congestion of Chicago and St. Louis, and he began to improve the physical plant. In 1941 McNear refused to go along with an industry-wide pay increase, proposing instead hourly wages and the elimination of inefficient practices. A bitter strike ensued, followed by government operation of the road during World War Two and the 1947 murder of McNear. That year new management took over and the railroad resumed operation after a 19-month work stoppage.

The modern Toledo, Peoria & Western was incorporated in 1952, succeeding at least three previous roads with the same name. In 1960 the Santa Fe purchased the railroad and sold half to the Pennsylvania — TP&W formed a Chicago bypass for traffic moving between the two. The formation of Conrail changed traffic patterns, and TP&W didn't fit into Conrail's plans. In 1976 TP&W bought the former Pennsylvania line from Effner to Logansport, Ind., where it could interchange traffic with Conrail and Norfolk & Western. In 1979, the Pennsylvania Company, a subsidiary of the Penn Central, sold its half interest in the TP&W back to the Santa Fe. Merger with Santa Fe took place December 31, 1983.

Location of headquarters: Peoria, Illinois

J. P. Lamb Jr.

Eastbound local freight No. 24 is safely in the siding at Forrest, Illinois, to meet westbound hotshot No. 21.

Miles of railroad operated: 1929 — 239; 1983 — 301
Number of locomotives: 1929 — 24; 1983 — 29
Number of passenger cars: 1929 — 13
Number of freight cars: 1929 — 348; 1983 — 382
Number of company service cars: 1929 — 43
Reporting marks: TPW
Historical and technical societies: TP&W Historical & Technical So-ciety, RR 1, Box 174B, Morocco, IN 47963
Recommended reading: *The Peoria Way*, by Joe McMillan and Robert P. Olmsted, published in 1984 by McMillan Publications, 3208 Halsey Drive, Woodridge, IL 60517
Successors: Atchison, Topeka & Santa Fe (TWG)
Portions still operated: Logansport, Ind.-Keokuk, Iowa; La Harpe-Lomax, Ill.; Hamilton-Warsaw, Ill.

TONOPAH & GOLDFIELD RAILROAD

In 1900 the discovery of silver in south-central Nevada created a boom town — Tonopah. The mining boom in turn created a demand for rail transportation. There were several proposals, including a branch of Southern Pacific's narrow gauge Carson & Colorado and southward extensions of the Nevada Central, the Eureka & Palisade, and even the Nevada Northern. A preliminary survey was made in early 1903, and on July 25, 1903, the Tonopah Railroad was organized by the Tonopah Mining Co., headquartered in Philadelphia. Work began promptly from Tonopah Junction, nine miles south of Mina on the C&C, and the 3-foot-gauge track reached Tonopah, 60 miles from the junction, on July 23, 1904. One week later a cloudburst washed out part of the line. More rain followed, and it was September 7 before service was restored (the engineer who located the line was one of many Easterners who thought it never rained in the desert).

In October 1904 SP began standard-gauging its line from Mound House, the junction with the Virginia & Truckee, to Mina. The Tonopah Railroad proceeded to standard-gauge its own line, and when completed on August 15, 1905, it marked the end of one of the shortest-lived narrow gauge operations on record.

Meanwhile, in 1902 gold had been discovered south of Tonopah, creating another boom town, Goldfield. The board of directors of the mining company declared the company had no interest in Goldfield affairs and declined to invest mining company or railroad assets in an extension to Goldfield. As individuals, however, they did — and organized the standard gauge Goldfield Railroad. On September 12, 1905, the first train rolled into Goldfield. At that point the same directors decided that it would be better to have one railroad than two, and the Tonopah & Goldfield Railroad was incorporated on November 1, 1905. The consolidated railroad did well enough to pay a 30 percent dividend in June 1907, but there were no dividends for the next five years, and when dividends resumed they were more modest.

Also in 1905 T&G interests organized the improbably named Bullfrog Goldfield Railroad to build south to Beatty to head off the Las Vegas & Tonopah and the Tonopah & Tidewater. It reached Beatty in April 1907, six months after the Las Vegas & Tonopah had arrived; the LV&T pushed on north parallel to the BG and arrived in Goldfield in October 1907 — just in time for the collapse of the mining boom and the nationwide business slump. In 1908 the Tonopah & Tidewater took over operation of the Bullfrog Goldfield.

There followed a long period of declining business and belt-tightening, through which the T&G continued to operate at a profit, if not a large one. The Las Vegas & Tonopah ceased operation in 1918, and the last Bullfrog Goldfield train left Goldfield on January 7, 1928, leaving the T&G alone in Goldfield. The T&G endured a receivership from 1932 to 1937, and in 1942 the Tonopah Mining Co. sold its interest in the railroad to Dulien Steel Products of Seattle. Scrapping appeared likely.

In 1942 the Army Air Force established an air base at Tonopah. Business once again boomed on the Tonopah & Goldfield, with movements of troops and aviation gasoline. Management problems prevented the railroad from taking advantage of the business to put the line into better

C. M. Clegg

World War Two brought a last surge of business to the Tonopah & Goldfield: Tank cars of aviation gasoline for the air base at Tonopah require the efforts of Consolidations 56 and 57 on the southbound mixed train a few miles out of Tonopah Junction.

shape, and when the air base was deactivated at the end of the war and the Army asked for the return of the three Alco RSD1s T&G had leased, all the steam locomotives needed repairs. The railroad embargoed traffic on October 1, 1946, and began handling mail and express by truck. Operators of mines protested the abandonment and promised carloads of ore if the road could be saved, but the railroad said that it could not exist on an occasional carload of ore with most other commodities going by truck. The Tonopah & Goldfield was formally abandoned on October 15, 1947.

Location of headquarters: Goldfield, Nevada

Miles of railroad operated: 1929 — 104; 1946 — 100
Number of locomotives: 1929 — 7; 1946 — 7
Number of passenger cars: 1929 — 1; 1946 — 2
Number of freight cars: 1929 — 104
Number of company service cars: 1929 — 7; 1946 — 10
Reporting marks: T&G
Recommended reading: *Railroads of Nevada and Eastern California, Volume I,* by David F. Myrick, published in 1962 by Howell-North Books, 850 North Hollywood Way, Burbank, CA 91505

In the late 1920s the owners of the Tonopah & Tidewater tried to develop Death Valley as a winter tourist resort. Part of their program was the purchase of a gas-electric baggage-coach, which would cost less to operate than a conventional steam-powered passenger train. Another part of the effort to attract tourists was the operation of a Pullman sleeping car twice a week between Los Angeles and Death Valley Junction. Union Pacific handled the sleeper between Los Angeles and Crucero.

Collection of Arthur C. Davis

TONOPAH & TIDEWATER RAILROAD

Francis Marion Smith's Pacific Coast Borax Co. had a borate mine in the Funeral Mountains east of Death Valley, California. The nearest railroad was the California Eastern at Ivanpah, Calif. (that line became a branch of the Santa Fe, with which it connected at Goffs; it was abandoned in 1921). Smith built a wagon road 100 miles north to the Lila C. Mine, and tried out a steam traction engine as a replacement for his 20-mule teams. The traction engine lasted all of 14 miles. Smith decided a railroad was necessary.

The Tonopah & Tidewater Railroad was incorporated on July 19, 1904, to build to Rhyolite, Calif. After several surveys, construction began on May 29, 1905, at Las Vegas, Nevada, a location suggested by Senator William Clark, the Montana copper magnate and builder of the San Pedro, Los Angeles & Salt Lake (later Union Pacific). Clark, after hearing of silver and gold discoveries in the Tonopah area, refused to let the T&T connect with the SPLA&SL, and started his own line to Tonopah, the Las Vegas & Tonopah.

Smith moved his base of operations to Ludlow, Calif., on the Santa Fe east of Barstow, and started construction in the fall of 1905. The relocated T&T crossed the SPLA&SL at Crucero, opened a branch from Death Valley Junction to the Lila C. Mine on August 16, 1907, and reached Gold Center on October 30 that year. The remaining two miles to Beatty were

on the rails of the Bullfrog Goldfield. By then the Panic of 1907 was in progress, and Rhyolite was already losing population. (Except for the former LV&T station and a few scattered buildings in Rhyolite, Beatty is all that remains today of the Rhyolite-Bullfrog-Gold Center-Beatty cluster of mining boom towns.)

In June 1908 ownership of the Tonopah & Tidewater and the Bullfrog Goldfield was transferred to a common holding company, with the blithe hope that the profits and losses of the two lines would offset each other. In 1914 the Lila C. Mine closed and the owners moved the borax operations to a new location at Ryan. The branch to the Lila C. Mine was abandoned and a new 3-foot-gauge railroad, the Death Valley Railroad, was built from Ryan to the T&T at Death Valley Junction. Also in 1914 the BG shifted its allegiance to the Las Vegas & Tonopah and the two roads consolidated their parallel lines between Beatty and Goldfield into a single line. When the LV&T ceased operation in 1918, the Tonopah & Tidewater once again took over the Bullfrog Goldfield and in 1920 acquired the majority of its stock.

The borax mines, which provided nearly all the T&T's traffic, were nearly exhausted by the late 1920s. The Bullfrog Goldfield was abandoned in 1928, and the Death Valley Railroad, which had been operated as a branch of the T&T, was closed in 1931. Traffic on the T&T continued to decline, but Borax Consolidated continued to pay interest on the bonds and make up the deficits. In 1933 T&T abandoned the Ludlow-Crucero portion of the line and moved the shop facilities from Ludlow to Death Valley Junction.

Over the years floods had occasionally disrupted service on the line. A major flood in March 1938 destroyed much of the south end of the T&T, and in December 1938 the road petitioned to discontinue service. Operation ceased on June 14, 1940, and the railroad was scrapped in 1942 and 1943.

Location of headquarters: Los Angeles, California
Miles of railroad operated: 1929 — 169; 1939 — 143
Number of locomotives: 1929 — 5; 1939 — 5

Number of passenger cars: 1929 — 5; 1939 — 5 (including 1 motor car)
Number of freight cars: 1929 — 29; 1939 — 29
Number of company service cars: 1929 — 13; 1939 — 9
Reporting marks: T&T
Recommended reading: *Railroads of Nevada and Eastern California, Volume II*, by David F. Myrick, published in 1963 by Howell-North Books, 850 North Hollywood Way, Burbank, CA 91505
Map: See page 327

Uintah 50 and sister 51 carried their water in large rectangular tanks alongside the boiler and their coal in a bunker behind the cab. Sumpter Valley converted them to conventional tender locomotives.

Collection of H. L. Broadbelt

UINTAH RAILWAY

The Uintah Basin in northeastern Utah contains the world's only commercially workable deposit of gilsonite, an asphalitic substance used in paint, roofing materials, sealing compounds, electrical insulation, fuels, and paving materials. In 1885 when it was recognized that gilsonite had commercial possibilities, the nearest railroads were the Rio Grande and the Union Pacific, about 100 miles south and north, respectively; a railroad into the Uintah Basin was necessary to carry the gilsonite out. General Asphalt Company and a subsidiary, Barber Asphalt Paving Co., first approached the Denver & Rio Grande about building a branch. D&RG declined, saying that such a branch would be useless if the market for gilsonite dried up. Barber decided to build its own railroad and because of the rugged terrain chose to build a 3-foot-gauge line, starting at Mack, Colorado, on the D&RG west of Grand Junction.

The Uintah Railway was incorporated in 1903, and the rails reached Dragon, site of the mining operation, in October 1904. The line over Baxter Pass, named for brothers who were the general manager of the rail-

LUCIAN C. SPRAGUE (1885-1960) began his railroad career as a callboy on the Burlington at age 14 and progressed to fireman, then engineer. He worked in the mechanical departments of the Great Northern and the Baltimore & Ohio and by the early 1920s was working for the Denver & Rio Grande Western as an independent engineering consultant. In 1923 he became the superintendent and in 1924 general manager of the Uintah Railway. Also in 1924 he married the daughter of a former superintendent of the Uintah. His tenure on the Uintah is remembered for the pair of 2-6-6-2T locomotives

he helped design to conquer the 7.5-percent grades and 66-degree curves of Baxter Pass.

In 1935, after several years of work in New York and three years with the Missouri-Kansas-Texas, he was appointed receiver of the Minneapolis & St. Louis. He realized that the road needed modern locomotives, more traffic, and cooperation from the employees. He restored employee morale, initiated programs to upgrade the track and the motive power, and fought off a plan proposed by John Barriger to partition the M&StL among eight neighboring railroads.

When new management headed by Ben Heineman took over the M&StL in 1954 Sprague turned to a career as a consulting engineer. His interests beyond railroading included baseball, fishing, antique automobiles, and a stable of trotting horses.

road and the surveyor who laid out the line, had 5 miles of 7.5-percent grade on the south slope (the grade on the north slope was easier, 5 percent) and curves as sharp as 66 degrees. (That curve has a radius of 87 feet, which translates to 12 inches on an HO scale model railroad — or to put it another way, sharper than North Shore's *Electroliners* had to contend with. Two percent is considered a stiff grade on a mainline railroad.)

In 1911 news broke that the Uintah would convert to standard gauge, tunnel under Baxter Pass, extend north to Vernal, Utah (a rumor that continued during much of the Uintah's existence), and become an extension of the Colorado Midland. What was constructed was a 12-mile, 3-foot-gauge extension to Watson and Rainbow, Utah.

In the early 1920s a business recession reduced the demand for gilsonite and highways penetrated the Uintah Basin, connecting the region with the Denver & Salt Lake at Craig, Colo. In 1923 Lucian Sprague became superintendent of the railroad and in 1924 general manager. He is remembered chiefly for helping to design a pair of articulated locomotives with a 2-6-6-2T wheel arrangement to replace Uintah's aging Shays.

The gilsonite business held up fairly well during the Depression, but improved highways began to threaten the line. In 1937 the highway between Vernal, Utah, and Craig was paved, and that same year the Barber company announced plans to move its mining operations from Rainbow to Bonanza, 15 miles north of the end of the railroad. From Bonanza it was easier and cheaper to truck gilsonite east to the D&SL than to truck it to the Uintah, carry it over Baxter Pass to Mack, and transfer it to standard gauge cars there. By mid-1938 the Uintah Railway had nothing to carry, and the few towns along the line were deserted. In August of that year the road petitioned for abandonment. Mesa County was concerned about the abandonment because of the loss of tax revenues for the schools; the ICC examiner stated that taxes were not a sufficient reason to keep a losing business going. In its last few months the railroad operated only one round trip a week, and the last train ran on May 16, 1939. Little remains of the Uintah and the towns it served.

The two articulateds were sold to the Sumpter Valley Railway in eastern Oregon in 1940; they went to Guatemala in 1947.

Location of headquarters: Mack, Colorado
Miles of railroad operated: 1929 — 70; 1938 — 70
Number of locomotives: 1929 — 10; 1938 — 8
Number of passenger cars: 1929 — 3; 1938 — 3
Number of freight cars: 1929 — 123; 1938 — 123

Number of company service cars: 1929 — 14; 1938 — 14
Recommended reading: *Uintah Railway*, by Henry E. Bender Jr., published in 1970 by Howell-North Books, 850 North Hollywood Way, Burbank, CA 91505
Map: See page 111

ULSTER & DELAWARE RAILROAD

In 1866 the Rondout & Oswego Railroad was chartered to build west from Rondout, New York, now part of the city of Kingston. In those days Rondout was a separate town and, more important, the east terminal and headquarters of the Delaware & Hudson Canal. The railroad's goal was not Oswego, on Lake Ontario, but a connection with the Albany & Susquehanna (later Delaware & Hudson) near Oneonta. Construction began in 1866. By late 1870 32 miles of line were in service.

The rails continued to push westward — over the Catskills and into the valley of the East Branch of the Delaware, then up and over into the valley of the West Branch at Stamford. In 1872 the company was reorganized as the New York, Kingston & Syracuse Railroad, and in 1875 it was sold and reorganized again as the Ulster & Delaware Railroad.

The Catskill Mountains were rapidly developing into a summer resort area. The Stony Clove & Catskill Mountain Railroad was organized in 1881 by Ulster & Delaware management to build a 3-foot-gauge line from Phoenicia on the U&D to Hunter, with a branch, the Kaaterskill Railroad, to serve the Hotel Kaaterskill and the Catskill Mountain House. Service on the SC&CM began in mid-1882, and the Kaaterskill line opened in June 1883. That same month the West Shore opened between Jersey City and Kingston, giving the Ulster and Delaware a direct rail connection to New York.

In the mid-1880s work resumed to extend the U&D over another divide and into the valley of the Susquehanna River. While that was in progress the U&D merged its two narrow gauge subsidiaries in 1893, and standard-gauged them in 1899. In July 1900 the U&D finally arrived in Oneonta, where it connected with the Delaware & Hudson. The D&H Canal

had ceased operation only two years before, and the U&D acquired some of its coal traffic. Coal traffic soon came to provide the bulk of U&D freight revenue.

Ulster & Delaware's peak passenger year was 1913. Paved highways began to penetrate the Catskills, and the huge mountain hotels closed one by one as tastes in vacationing changed. U&D management approached the New York Central, asking if they'd like to buy a railroad through the Catskills; NYC replied they wouldn't. Then the ICC added NYC takeover of the U&D (which entered receivership in 1931) to the conditions under which it would approve absorption of Michigan Central and Big Four (Cleveland, Cincinnati, Chicago & St. Louis) by NYC. On February 1, 1932, the Ulster & Delaware became the Catskill Mountain Branch of the New York Central.

In 1940 the Hunter and Kaaterskill branches, the former narrow gauge lines, were abandoned. Passenger service was discontinued in early 1954. Coal traffic from the D&H disappeared, and in 1965 NYC cut back the west end of the line from Oneonta to Bloomville. Conrail completed abandonment of the line in September 1976, but three short portions survive as tourist railroads.

Location of headquarters: Kingston, New York
Miles of railroad operated: 1929 — 129; 1931 — 129
Number of locomotives: 1929 — 29; 1931 — 29
Number of passenger cars: 1929 — 54; 1931 — 53
Number of freight cars: 1929 — 168; 1931 — 153
Number of company service cars: 1929 — 12; 1931 — 11
Recommended reading: *The Ulster & Delaware*, by Gerald M. Best, published in 1972 by Golden West Books, P. O. Box 80250, San Marino, CA 91108
Successors:
New York Central
Penn Central
Conrail
Portions still operated:
Kingston-Kingston Point: Trolley Museum of New York
Phoenicia-Mount Pleasant: Catskill Mountain Railroad
Kelly's Corners-Arkville-Highmount: Delaware & Ulster Rail Ride

Charles A. Elston

It's 10:15 a.m. on August 2, 1947: Both line and locomotive are former Ulster & Delaware property as New York Central train 530 stops at Kortright to pick up a box of eggs destined for down-country points.

UNADILLA VALLEY RAILWAY

The Utica & Unadilla Valley Railroad was incorporated in 1888 to build south along the Unadilla River from the Delaware, Lackawanna & Western's Utica branch at Bridgewater, New York. Construction began in 1889, and the road was opened as far as West Edmeston, nine miles, in 1894. That year it was reorganized as the Unadilla Valley Railroad. The railroad used Lackawanna rolling stock until it purchased its own locomotive and car in 1895, the same year it was extended another 11 miles to New Berlin and a connection with the New York, Ontario & Western.

In 1904 control of the road was obtained by Lewis Morris, who reorganized it as the Unadilla Valley Railway. The railroad became prosperous, and the principal commodity it carried was milk. In the early 1930s Morris purchased a gravel bed, then sold it to the railroad as a potential traffic source; the gravel from it, however, did not meet the specification of the state highway department. The gravel bed and the quarrying equipment became an expensive millstone around the Unadilla Valley's neck.

In 1936 the railroad (minus the quarry) was purchased by the H. E. Salzberg Co., a scrap dealer and railroad dismantler — but rather than dismantle the UV, Salzberg set out to see if it could be made profitable. One of Salzberg's first actions was to call on shippers up and down the line to reassure them that the road would not be scrapped. In the late 1930s the road was the subject of an article in *Fortune* magazine.

In October 1941 the railroad bought the New York, Ontario & Western's New Berlin Branch from Edmeston through New Berlin to New Berlin Junction (East Guilford), 29 miles, with trackage rights 3 miles farther on NYO&W's main line into Sidney.

In 1956 the Dairyman's League plant at Mount Upton closed. It had provided 35 percent of the Unadilla Valley's revenue. The UV cut back the south end of the line from New Berlin Junction to Mount Upton — and in 1957 the NYO&W was abandoned. The UV continued to operate, running up deficits. Its abandonment petition was approved, and the line was closed on December 23, 1960.

Location of headquarters: New Berlin, New York
Miles of railroad operated: 1929 — 19; 1960 — 48
Number of locomotives: 1929 — 3; 1960 — 1

John Pickett

Unadilla Valley 2-6-2 No. 5 leads a train of Lackawanna milk cars along the Unadilla River at Leonardsville, N. Y., in June 1947.

Number of passenger cars: 1929 — 4
Number of freight cars: 1929 — 18; 1960 — 2
Number of company service cars: 1929 — 7; 1960 — 17
Reporting marks: UV
Recommended reading: *Days Along the Buckwheat & Dandelion*, by Fred Pugh, published in 1984 by Fred Pugh, Box 26, West Edmeston, NY 13485 (ISBN 0-914821-04-0)
Map: See page 331

333

United Railways of Yucatan 251, a narrow gauge 4-4-0 built by Baldwin in 1916, scurries through a field of sisal on its way to Merida with train 56 from Sotuta in 1964. UdeY's roster included wood-burners until 1960; both standard and narrow gauge 4-4-0s operated until the mid-1960s.

Frank Barry

UNITED RAILWAYS OF YUCATAN
(Ferrocarriles Unidos de Yucatan)

The first railroad in Mexico's state of Yucatan was the standard gauge Ferrocarril Progreso a Merida (Progreso to Merida Railway), authorized in 1874 and opened in 1881 between the city of Merida and the port at Progreso, 24 miles away. Most of the railroad's business was in hauling sisal, a fiber from which rope is made. Two other railroads were begun about the same time, the Ferrocarril Merida a Valladolid (Merida to Valladolid Railway), and the Ferrocarril Peninsular, which completed a line to Campeche in the state of the same name in 1898. Both these lines were 3-foot gauge. The three railroads were combined in 1902 as the United Railways of Yucatan, and a fourth, the 3-foot-gauge Ferrocarril de Merida a Peto, was added in 1909. A third rail for narrow gauge trains was added to the Merida-Progreso line between 1958 and 1960.

The UdeY was isolated until 1950, when the Southeastern Railway

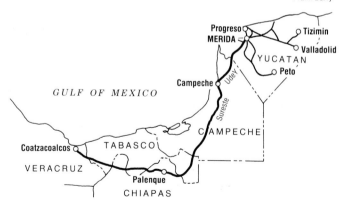

334

(Ferrocarril del Sureste) was completed from Allende, Veracruz, on the Rio Coatzacoalcos, to Campeche. The line from Campeche to Merida was standard-gauged between 1953 and 1957, and the Rio Coatzacoalcos was bridged in 1962, finally connecting Yucatan by rail with the rest of Mexico.

In 1969 the Southeastern and the United of Yucatan were merged to form the United South Eastern Railways (Ferrocarriles Unidos del Sureste), now being absorbed by National Railways of Mexico. Some of the former UdeY lines south and east of Merida are still narrow gauge.

Location of headquarters: Merida, Yucatan
Miles of railroad operated: 1929 — 535; 1968 — 392 (264, standard gauge; 128, 3-foot gauge)
Number of locomotives: 1929 — 58; 1968 — 49

Number of passenger cars: 1929 — 119; 1968 — 81
Number of freight cars: 1929 — 747; 1968 — 294
Number of company service cars: 1929 — 58; 1968 — 55
Recommended reading: *Mexican Narrow Gauge*, by Gerald M. Best, published in 1968 by Howell-North Books, 850 North Hollywood Way, Burbank, CA 91505
Successors:
United South Eastern Railways (TWG)
National Railways of Mexico (TWG)
Portions still operated: Merida-Progreso; Merida-Valladolid; Dzitas-Tizimin; Merida-Peto; Acanceh-Sotuta; Merida-Campeche: National Railways of Mexico

UTAH-IDAHO CENTRAL RAILROAD

The Ogden, Logan & Idaho Railway was created in 1914 by the merger of two Utah city streetcar systems, Ogden Rapid Transit and Logan Rapid Transit. Both were owned by the Eccles interests. The Ogden company had a suburban line extending north to Brigham City, and the Logan company by then extended from Wellsville, Utah, north through Logan to Preston, Idaho. Several routes for a connecting line were surveyed, and the longest (by 20 miles) was chosen because it would serve several towns in the sparsely settled area. The connection was constructed quickly, forming a through line from Ogden to Preston that closely paralleled the Union Pacific line north out of Ogden. It used much of the abandoned right of way of the narrow gauge Utah & Northern, which UP had taken over and relocated in the process of standard-gauging.

Approximately halfway between its terminals, a Utah-Idaho Central train tops Collinston Divide at Summit, Utah.

Fred Fellow

In 1920 the Ogden city lines were spun off as a separate company, Utah Rapid Transit (Ogden streetcar service ended in December 1935). The Logan city lines were replaced by buses in 1924. At the same time UIC bought three highway buses for Ogden-Preston service by a considerably shorter route than the rail route.

Utah-Idaho Central was reorganized in 1926 and in 1937. By the end of World War Two parallel highways had taken most of the railroad's traffic, rail passenger schedules were down to one train a day, and the UIC had several years of deficit operation on its books. On December 26, 1946, the UIC petitioned to abandon, and the last passenger train ran on February 15, 1947 — freight service lasted two weeks longer. The Bamberger Railroad purchased half a mile of UIC track in Ogden, but the remainder of the line was dismantled and scrapped.

Location of headquarters: Ogden, Utah
Miles of railroad operated: 1929 — 113; 1944 — 121
Number of locomotives: 1929 — 7; 1944 — 6
Number of motor cars: 1929 — 29; 1944 — 12
Number of other cars: 1929 — 197; 1944 — 122
Reporting marks: UIC
Recommended reading: *Interurbans of Utah*, by Ira L. Swett, published in 1954 by Interurban Press, P. O. Box 6444, Glendale, CA 91205
Map: See page 42

Virginia & Maryland 200, an Alco C420 acquired from the Long Island, leads a freight consisting mostly of covered hoppers of feed near Painter, Va.

Edward A. Lewis

VIRGINIA & MARYLAND RAILROAD

The New York, Philadelphia & Norfolk, a subsidiary of the Pennsylvania Railroad, completed a line down the Delmarva Peninsula from Wilmington, Delaware, to Cape Charles, Virginia, in 1884. In conjunction with a car ferry across the mouth of Chesapeake Bay to Norfolk the line formed a route to the south that bypassed the congestion and restrictive freight clearances of Baltimore and Washington.

In the 1960s the line's status declined, and Penn Central continued the process of neglect during its brief stewardship. At one point the Southern Railway was interested in the line for access to the chemical industry at Wilmington, but SR could not reach an agreement with one of the unions.

In 1976 Conrail took over the main line as far south as Pocomoke City, Maryland, but the branches on the Delmarva Peninsula were classified as light density by the United States Railway Association and therefore not included in Conrail. However, Conrail operated the branches for a time with federal subsidy.

The branches in Delaware and Maryland were taken over by the Maryland & Delaware Railroad, which is still in operation. On April 1, 1977, the Virginia & Maryland Railroad took over the line between Pocomoke City and Cape Charles and undertook extensive rehabilitation of the track. At the end of October 1981 a new company under local control, the Eastern Shore Railroad, took over from the Virginia & Maryland.

Location of headquarters: Cape Charles, Virginia
Miles of railroad operated: 1977 — 145; 1980 — 96
Number of locomotives: 1977 — 3; 1980 — 3
Number of freight cars: 1980 — 37
Reporting marks: VAMD
Predecessor railroads in this book: Pennsylvania Railroad
Successors: Eastern Shore
Portions still operated: Pocomoke City, Md.-Norfolk: Eastern Shore

VIRGINIA & TRUCKEE RAILWAY

During the California gold rush of 1849 Nevada was simply a place to pass through on the way west. In 1849 the Mormons established a settlement at Genoa, east of Lake Tahoe. Gold placers were discovered nearby, followed by the discovery of the Comstock Lode and the establishment of Virginia City, and the boom was on. The miners were hampered by large amounts of a blue rock surrounding the gold, and for some time no one realized that the blue rock was silver ore.

By 1865 the Comstock mines were ready to produce on a larger scale. Machinery and timbers for deeper workings were expensive. William Sharon, local representative of the Bank of California, recognized the need for a railroad to take ore to reducing mills located along the Carson River and to bring in mining machinery and timbers. He asked an engineer if a railroad could be built from Virginia City to the Carson River. The engineer said "Yes."

The Virginia & Truckee Railroad was incorporated on March 5, 1868. Construction began almost a year later, and the first train from Carson City rolled into Gold Hill, just south of Virginia City, on December 21, 1869, accompanied by the traditional noises: whistles, bands, cannon, and popping corks. A month later the line reached Virginia City. The line from Carson City to Reno and a connection with the Central Pacific was completed on August 24, 1872.

The railroad's fortunes followed those of Virginia City and its mines. The destruction of most of Virginia City by fire in 1875 simply brought more business in the form of building materials, but ore production began to decline toward the end of the decade. In 1880 the Carson & Colorado was chartered by some of V&T's directors. Its narrow gauge track took off from the V&T at Mound House, northeast of Carson City, to head south 300 miles through uninhabited country into California's Owens Valley. The C&C was acquired by the Southern Pacific in March 1900. Two months later silver was discovered at Tonopah, and the C&C became a key link in the route to Tonopah. SP standard-gauged the C&C as far south as Tonopah Junction, and the new Tonopah Railroad did the same. SP considered purchasing the V&T as a connection between the C&C and the main line at Reno, but the price V&T set was too high and SP instead built a connection south from Hazen, completely bypassing the V&T.

The railroad was reorganized in 1905 as the Virginia & Truckee Railway. In 1906 V&T opened a 15-mile extension south from Carson City to Minden, and there was talk of electrifying the Reno-Minden line. Mining continued, but the V&T came to depend more on agriculture than on mining.

In 1924 the road paid its last dividend. Motor cars and mixed trains replaced the passenger trains, and the Minden line became the main route. The Virginia City line became a branch. Traffic continued to dwindle and, following the death of Ogden L. Mills, sole owner of the road since

Train 2, the daily-except-Sunday mixed, rolls south alongside Route 395 between Steamboat and Carson City. The power is V&T second No. 5, a 2-8-0 purchased from the Nevada Copper Belt in 1947 and V&T's only 8-coupled locomotive.

A. C. Kalmbach

1933, the road entered receivership in 1938. The Virginia City line was abandoned in 1939, and the V&T sold some of its old-time rolling stock to Hollywood film companies (surplus rolling stock had simply been stored, and Nevada's dry climate prevented it from deteriorating). Railroad enthusiasts discovered the line, and their excursion trains reminded Nevadans that the V&T still existed. More equipment was sold to Hollywood, providing needed money for V&T's treasury. V&T showed a small profit in 1939, but operating losses resumed. The revenue derived from scrapping the line to Virginia City helped keep the V&T alive through World War Two. After the war the V&T was discovered by Lucius Beebe, who romanticized the railroad (and Virginia City and the Comstock Lode) all out of proportion.

It is open to question whether V&T's postwar management was intent on keeping the road alive or abandoning it. That was 35 years ago, and question or no, the V&T ended service on May 31, 1950.

In recent years a tourist railroad, also named Virginia & Truckee, has begun operating between Virginia City and Gold Hill, and the Nevada State Museum has opened the Virginia & Truckee Railroad Museum at Carson City.

Location of headquarters: Carson City, Nevada
Miles of railroad operated: 1929 — 67; 1949 — 46
Number of locomotives: 1929 — 8; 1949 — 3
Number of passenger cars: 1929 — 19; 1949 — 4
Number of freight cars: 1929 — 32; 1949 — 9
Number of company service cars: 1929 — 8
Reporting marks: V&T
Recommended reading: *The Silver Short Line*, by Ted Wurm and Harre Demoro, published in 1983 by Trans-Anglo Books, P. O. Box 6444, Glendale, CA 91205 (ISBN 87046-064-1)
Portions still operated: Virginia City-Gold Hill: Virginia & Truckee (1976)
Map: See page 327

338

VIRGINIAN RAILWAY

The Virginian was the creation of one man, Henry Huttleston Rogers, and was a one-commodity railroad — practically a conveyor belt to move coal from the mountains of West Virginia to ships at Norfolk, Virginia.

The Deepwater Railway was incorporated in West Virginia to build a line south into the mountains from Deepwater, W. Va., a station on the Chesapeake & Ohio 30 miles southeast of Charleston. By 1902 Henry Huttleston Rogers, vice-president of Standard Oil, had acquired an interest in the 4-mile line, which served lumber mills and coal mines. Neither C&O nor Norfolk & Western would agree on the matter of freight rates, so Rogers decided to build his own railroad from the coalfields to tidewater at Norfolk. He got the Deepwater's charter amended to allow construction to the Virginia state line, and he incorporated the Tidewater Railway in Virginia in February 1904 to build a railroad between Norfolk and the West Virginia state line.

In March 1907 the name was changed to Virginian Railway; in April of that year it acquired the property of the Deepwater Railway. The line was completed between Norfolk and Deepwater at the beginning of 1909. From Roanoke to Norfolk the railroad was as close as possible to a straight line and it had an almost constant gentle descent. West of Roanoke, though, lay the Blue Ridge Mountains, with grades in both directions. The steepest eastbound grade was 2 percent for 14 miles from Elmore to Clarks Gap, W. Va.

The Virginian was built as a heavy-duty railroad. Before World War One, when the normal coal car was a 50-ton hopper, Virginian was using 120-ton 12-wheel gondolas. In 1909 the road bought 2-6-6-0s, its first Mallets, and within a decade rostered 2-8-8-2s and 2-10-10-2s. Virginian even experimented with a 2-8-8-8-4 that was unable to generate steam fast enough for its six cylinders. In the 1920s the Virginian electrified its line between Roanoke, Va., and Mullens, W. Va. The new electrics could haul heavier trains than the best steam power and move them twice as fast.

In 1925 the Norfolk & Western agreed to lease the Virginian on approval of the ICC, which denied the application. Other suitors included the Pennsylvania, the New York Central, and the Chesapeake & Ohio. In 1929 the Virginian applied to the ICC for permission to build a one-mile line across the Kanawha River at Deepwater, W. Va., to connect with New York Central's Kanawha & Michigan Railway. The ICC approved, over the protest of the Chesapeake & Ohio.

Virginian was never a major passenger carrier. Even in 1930 mainline service was an all-stops daytime local west of Roanoke and two such trains, one day and one night, east of Roanoke. Luxury was confined to a Norfolk-Roanoke sleeping car and a Roanoke-Huntington, W. Va., parlor car, both gone by 1933, as was the Norfolk-Roanoke night train. January 29, 1956, marked the final run of the last passenger schedule, a Norfolk-Roanoke daytime local.

In 1948 Virginian received 4 two-unit electric locomotives to begin replacement of the aging side-rod motors; in 1956 and 1957 12 more electrics joined the roster. The new units were basically six-axle diesel hood units with Ignitron rectifiers instead of diesel engines. Shortly after they arrived Virginian dumped the fire on its last steam engine; the diesels that replaced steam were all Fairbanks-Morse products (except for a General Electric 44-tonner that had been on the roster since 1941).

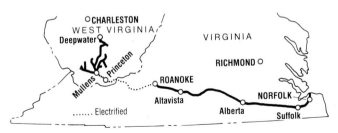

The Virginian and the Norfolk & Western hadn't forgotten the idea of merger. By 1959 the climate was different. The stockholders of the two railroads and the ICC approved, and on December 1, 1959, the two roads merged. An almost immediate casualty of the merger was Virginian's electrification. N&W developed a one-way traffic pattern to take advantage of the best grades, and the electrics had only eastbound work to do. The electrification was shut down at the end of June 1962.

Location of headquarters: Norfolk, Virginia
Miles of railroad operated: 1929 — 545; 1958 — 608
Number of locomotives: 1929 — 175; 1958 — 120
Number of passenger cars: 1929 — 62
Number of freight cars: 1929 — 10,273; 1958 — 17,143
Number of company service cars: 1929 — 368; 1958 — 184
Reporting marks: VGN
Recommended reading: *The Virginian Railway*, by H. Reid, published in 1961 by Kalmbach Publishing Co., 1027 North Seventh Street, Milwaukee, WI 53233 (ISBN 0-89024-558-4)
Successors: Norfolk & Western (TWG)
Portions still operated: The only major portion of the Virginian that has been abandoned is the main line east of Jarratt, Va., junction with Seaboard System's ex-Atlantic Coast Line route. The rest is operated by Norfolk & Western.

H. Reid

Three of Virginian's side-rod electrics lift eastbound coal toward the summit of Clark's Gap at Bud, W. Va., in 1950.

WABASH RAILWAY

The Wabash seems to have gone through more reorganizations and name changes than most railroads its size; I will use the term "Wabash" to refer to the company in this history, unless clarity requires the full title. The oldest part of the Wabash was the Northern Cross Railroad, chartered about 1837 to run from Quincy, Illinois, east to the Indiana state line. In 1851 the North Missouri Railroad was chartered to build northwest from St. Louis to the Iowa border at Coatesville, Mo. The line, completed in 1858, required a ferry crossing of the Missouri River at St. Charles, 19 miles from St. Louis, until a bridge was completed in 1871. In the 1860s the road acquired a branch to Brunswick; the town of Moberly was established at the junction and became the location of the road's shops. The Brunswick line was extended to Kansas City in 1868. The main route was extended north to Ottumwa, Iowa, in 1870, and construction of a line from Brunswick to Omaha was begun that same year (it reached Council Bluffs, Iowa, in 1879). These extensions were built by separate companies and leased to the North Missouri. The North Missouri ran into financial difficulty in 1871; it was succeeded in 1872 by the St. Louis, Kansas City & Northern Railroad.

In 1853 two railroads were organized: the Toledo & Illinois to build from Toledo, Ohio, to the Ohio-Indiana state line, and the Lake Erie, Wabash & St. Louis to continue the line across Indiana to Attica, following the route of the Wabash & Erie Canal. The two were merged as the Toledo, Wabash & Western Railroad in 1856, succeeded in 1858 by the Toledo & Wabash Railway. By then the line had absorbed the Great Western of Illinois (a successor to the Northern Cross) and reached all the way from Toledo to the Mississippi River at Quincy, Ill., and Keokuk, Iowa.

In 1879 Jay Gould merged the Wabash and the St. Louis, Kansas City & Northern to form the Wabash, St. Louis & Pacific Railroad. To it he soon added the Chicago & Paducah, a line from Streator to Effingham, Ill., crossing the Wabash at Bement. Gould organized another railroad to build into Chicago from a point on the Chicago & Paducah. That line was completed in 1880. About the same time Gould constructed a line from Butler, Ind., to Detroit. The Detroit line soon became the main route; the Toledo line lapsed into secondary status.

Gould continued to add short lines to the Wabash. By 1884 the Wabash had 3,549 miles of road extending from Detroit to Omaha and from Fonda in northwestern Iowa to Cairo, Ill. Financially the Wabash was overextended, and Gould's frequent rate wars with other railroads reduced the road's income. In May 1884 Wabash defaulted on interest payments and entered receivership, with Gould as the receiver. The leased lines — like the Des Moines North Western and the Cairo & Vincennes — were returned to their owners and the Wabash itself was reorganized as several separate railroads. In 1889 they were reunited as the Wabash Railroad.

In 1898 Wabash acquired trackage rights from Detroit through southern Ontario to Buffalo over the rails of the Grand Trunk. The Canadian

J. P. Lamb Jr.

The Chicago-St. Louis *Blue Bird* was perhaps the ultimate daytime streamliner, with a buffet car up front, a diner in the middle, a round-end observation car at the rear, and five Vista-Domes. However, the other Chicago-St. Louis day train, the *Banner Blue*, shown northbound at Mansfield, Illinois, in 1958, had a certain charm with its assortment of headend cars, comfortable rebuilt coaches, secondhand streamlined diner-lounge, and parlor car with brass-railed observation platform.

portion of the Wabash was connected with the rest of the system by ferries across the Detroit River between Detroit and Windsor. A line from Butler to New Haven, Ind., east of Fort Wayne, was opened in 1902, allowing Detroit-St. Louis trains to be routed through Fort Wayne, Huntington, and Wabash, Ind. The older, more direct route along the Eel River was sold to the Pennsylvania Railroad. In 1904 the Wabash reached Pittsburgh from Toledo over the rails of the Wheeling & Lake Erie and the Wabash Pittsburg Terminal (predecessor of the Pittsburgh & West Virginia). The WPT was part of George Gould's plan to try to assemble the transcontinental system that his father had almost put together. Wabash wasn't in Pittsburgh very long — receivership overtook it again in 1911, followed by reorganization in 1915 as the Wabash Railway.

Continued on page 343

JAY GOULD (1836-1892) was born in Roxbury, New York (various accounts give his name as "Jason" or "Jayson"). His first jobs were those of clerk, blacksmith, and surveyor; after starting a tannery he became a leather merchant in New York City. He began investing in railroads, starting with the Rutland & Washington, which was owned by his father-in-law. He sold it to a predecessor of the Delaware & Hudson at a profit. Spurred by his success, he got control of the
Cleveland & Pittsburgh, worked its price up, and sold it to the Pennsylvania. In 1867 Gould became a director of the Erie. With Daniel Drew, the Erie's treasurer, and James Fisk, another of its directors, he issued a large quantity of new shares of stock to prevent Cornelius Vanderbilt from getting control of the road. He engaged in further speculation and stock trading and left the Erie in 1872.

Gould then acquired an interest in the Union Pacific, becoming a director of the railroad in 1874. He bought control of the Kansas Pacific and the Denver Pacific, which together formed a route from Kansas City through Denver to Cheyenne that competed with UP's line from Omaha to Cheyenne. He pumped up their value and forced UP to buy the two smaller roads by exchange of stock. About that same time he got control of the Western Union Telegraph Company.

After toying with Union Pacific Gould turned his attention to the Missouri Pacific and the Wabash, to which he added the International & Great Northern, the St. Louis, Iron Mountain & South-ern, and the Texas & Pacific (forming the nucleus of the modern-day Missouri Pacific system) and the Missouri, Kansas & Texas. He also turned his attention eastward. He came within a hairsbreadth of uniting the Central of New Jersey, the Reading, the Philadelphia, Wilmington & Baltimore, and the Baltimore & Ohio to form a New York-Washington route, but the Pennsylvania got the PW&B, and Baltimore & Ohio had to build its own line from Baltimore to Philadelphia. Gould was also a major force on the Lackawanna and for a short time controlled the New York & New England.

Gould was a speculator, not a railroader, and for the most part his purpose in buying and selling railroads was to make money and get out. The one exception was the Missouri Pacific, which he held onto until the end of his life.

Recommended reading: *Jay Gould — His Business Career*, by Julius Grodinsky, published in 1957 by the University of Pennsylvania Press, Phildelphia, Pa.

GEORGE JAY GOULD (1864-1923) was the oldest son of Jay Gould. He inherited his father's railroad empire, which included Missouri Pacific, Texas & Pacific, Wabash, International & Great Northern, and St. Louis Southwestern, and he began to build them into a transcontinental system. He acquired the Denver & Rio Grande, the Wheeling & Lake Erie, and the Western Maryland. To reach the Pacific he built — or rather the Denver & Rio Grande built — the Western Pacific from Salt Lake City to Oakland, Calif.

The gap between Cumberland, Maryland, western terminal of the Western Maryland, and Wheeling, West Virginia, east end of the Wheeling & Lake Erie, was far more difficult to close and proved to be Gould's undoing. The Pennsylvania considered Pittsburgh its exclusive property and fought Gould all the way. Moreover, the Pennsy had already occupied the few good railroad locations in the area. Gould constructed the Wabash Pittsburgh Terminal Railway from Pittsburgh Junction on the W&LE a few miles west of Steubenville, Ohio, to a terminal in the heart of downtown Pittsburgh. The railroad was opened in 1904. It was an expensive railroad, almost entirely, it seemed, either in tunnels or on high bridges, and its terminal in Pittsburgh was more suitable for passengers than for freight.

Meanwhile, the Western Maryland was constructing an extension from Cumberland to Connellsville, Pennsylvania, reaching there in 1912, about the same time the Pittsburgh & Lake Erie (part of the New York Central System) did — and about the same time that the construction costs of the Wabash Pittsburgh Terminal bankrupted the Wabash and the construction costs of the Western Pacific bankrupted the Rio Grande. George Gould's empire crumbled away.

Much of the empire of the two Goulds has been reassembled: Union Pacific has merged Western Pacific and Missouri Pacific; MoPac had already absorbed Texas Pacific, International-Great Northern, and St. Louis, Iron Mountain & Southern. The Wabash, the Wheeling & Lake Erie, and the Wabash Pittsburgh Terminal (later Pittsburgh & West Virginia) all became part of Norfolk & Western in 1964. Western Maryland has become part of Chessie System and most of its lines have been abandoned. Only the Denver & Rio Grande Western remains independent.

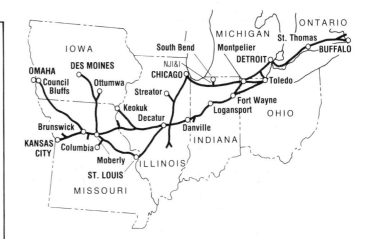

The automobile industry was growing and Wabash found itself in the middle of it. One of the road's biggest assets was its direct line from Detroit to Kansas City, bypassing Chicago and St. Louis. The key portion of the route was the Decatur, Ill.-Moberly, Mo., line. (Decatur was the hub of the Wabash system and site of its principal shops.) The Hannibal-Moberly portion of the line was built by the Missouri-Kansas-Texas, but in 1894 the Wabash made arrangements to operate the line jointly, with costs proportionate to use. Wabash found itself paying 90 percent of the costs and leased the line in 1923.

In 1925 the Wabash acquired control of the Ann Arbor, and by the end of 1962 Wabash owned all but a few shares of Ann Arbor's stock. In 1928 the Pennsylvania Company gained control of the Wabash, largely to protect itself after Wabash and Delaware & Hudson bought control of the Lehigh Valley.

Wabash passenger service had several distinct personalities. Between St. Louis and Kansas City, Wabash operated the easternmost segment of Union Pacific's *City of St. Louis* and its own *City of Kansas City*. That was

343

also mixed-train territory: Well into the 1960s several mixed trains a day connected the university town of Columbia, Mo., with the main line at Centralia, and in later years the St. Louis-Council Bluffs train was a mixed. On the Chicago-St. Louis run Wabash competed with Gulf, Mobile & Ohio and Illinois Central and had the best rolling stock in the form of the Vista-Dome *Blue Bird*. The second Chicago-St. Louis train, the *Banner Blue*, was one of the last trains to carry an open-platform parlor-observation car. Between Detroit and St. Louis the night and day trains were not glossy streamliners or extensions of someone else's train or plug locals — they were just plain, comfortable trains. In later years the daytime run acquired a legendary name from folk music, *Wabash Cannon Ball*.

The Wabash was unique in extending through the imaginary line dividing the country — a line from Chicago through Peoria to St. Louis, then down the Mississippi River to New Orleans. It was more a bridge railroad than an originator of traffic, a paradoxical situation in that most railroads had to shorthaul themselves to turn over traffic to the Wabash. The only major railroads that could give Wabash the long haul without sacrifice were the Union Pacific and the Kansas City Southern at Kansas City, UP at Council Bluffs, Iowa, and the Lackawanna and the Lehigh Valley at Buffalo.

At the end of 1963 the Pennsylvania Company owned nearly 87 percent of Wabash's stock. When the Pennsylvania and the New York Central planned their merger it was clear that Pennsy would not be allowed to include Wabash — Penn Central was large enough, and the ICC would probably deny it anyway. Wabash found a niche in the Norfolk & Western-Nickel Plate merger, but Wabash subsidiary Ann Arbor was kept in the Pennsy family (N&W didn't want it) by selling it to the Detroit, Toledo & Ironton on August 31, 1963. Wabash was leased to the expanded Norfolk & Western on October 16, 1964. On March 31, 1970, N&W acquired control from the Pennsylvania Company; by the end of 1980 N&W had almost complete ownership of the Wabash.

Location of headquarters: St. Louis, Missouri
Miles of railroad operated: 1929 — 2,524; 1963 — 2,422
Number of locomotives: 1929 — 660; 1963 — 307
Number of passenger cars: 1929 — 412; 1963 — 101
Number of freight cars: 1929 — 26,633; 1963 — 15,028
Number of company service cars: 1929 — 889; 1963 — 644
Reporting marks: WAB
Notable named passenger trains: *Blue Bird* (Chicago-St. Louis)
Historical and technical society: Wabash Railroad Historical Society, 3005 Softwind Trail, Fort Worth, TX 76116
Recommended reading: *Wabash*, by Donald J. Heimburger, published in 1984 by Heimburger House Publishing Co., 310 Lathrop Avenue, River Forest, IL 60305 (ISBN 0-911581-02-2)
Subsidiaries and affiliated railroads, 1963: New Jersey, Indiana & Illinois
Successors: Norfolk & Western (TWG)
Portions still operated: Buffalo, N. Y.-Windsor, Ont.; Suspension Bridge, N. Y.-Welland, Ont.; Detroit-St. Louis-Kansas City; Toledo, Ohio-New Haven, Ind.; Maumee, Ohio-Steubenville, Ind.; South Bend-Dillon, Ind.; Chicago-Bement, Ill.; Decatur, Ill.-Moberly, Mo.; Bluffs-Meredosia, Ill.; Moberly, Mo.-Des Moines, Iowa; Centralia-Columbia, Mo.: Norfolk & Western
Brunswick, Mo.-Blanchard, Iowa: Northern Missouri
Blanchard-Council Bluffs, Iowa: Colorado & Eastern

WASHINGTON & OLD DOMINION RAILWAY

The city of Alexandria, Virginia, in 1836 saw the Winchester & Potomac and the Baltimore & Ohio suddenly funnel to Baltimore the trade that had been coming down to Alexandria from the Shenandoah Valley. After an initial flurry of excitement and the chartering of a stillborn railroad, Alexandrians in 1853 chartered the Alexandria, Loudon & Hampshire Railroad to build west across the Blue Ridge to Winchester, Va. By 1858 the roadbed reached to Leesburg, and train service that far began in 1860. During the Civil War the road was not of any strategic value, but it suffered as much damage as if it had been.

In 1870 the AL&H set its sights on the Ohio River at Parkersburg,

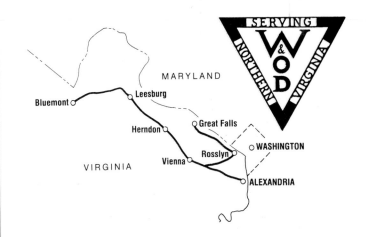

Herbert H. Harwood Jr.

By the 1950s the Washington & Old Dominion had shaken off the image of its interurban past and looked like most other short lines, right down to the GE 70-tonners, both of which are shown leading a freight through Sunset Hills, Va.

West Virginia, renamed itself the Washington & Ohio, and built a few miles further to Round Hill, about 50 miles from Alexandria. In 1877 the road slipped into receivership. It went through several more changes of name and goal before being swept into the Richmond & Danville system in 1886. With the rest of the R&D it became part of the Southern Railway family in 1894. In 1900 another four miles of track brought the road to Snickersville, which was renamed Bluemont when it achieved the lofty status of a town served by a railroad.

In the early years of the twentieth century John R. McLean (owner of the Washington *Post*) and Senator Stephen B. Elkins (developer of a coal, lumber, and railroad empire in West Virginia) bought a plot of land at the Great Falls of the Potomac, west of Washington, to develop as a park. They built the Great Falls & Old Dominion Railroad, a trolley line, to connect it with Washington. Both park and trolley line opened in 1906.

The enterprise prospered, and McLean and Elkins looked to expand. In 1911 McLean with Elkins's heirs (the senator had died earlier that year) organized the Washington & Old Dominion Railway to encompass the GF&OD, the Alexandria-Bluemont branch (leased from the Southern), and a newly-built connecting link. The W&OD hung trolley wires over most of the Alexandria-Bluemont line and began operating in 1912 as partly an electric railroad and partly a steam road, and partly rural, partly suburban. It quickly acquired a reputation for random and casual operation.

In the 1920s freight began to replace passengers as the principal revenue item, but the onset of the Depression put the road into receivership. In the mid-1930s the road cleaned house — scrapping old equipment, abandoning the park at Great Falls and the line to it, and reorganizing as the Washington & Old Dominion Railroad. The Purcellville-Bluemont

345

segment was taken up in 1938, and the trolley wires came down in 1941 with the end of passenger service.

Replacing the electrics were three 44-ton diesels. Passenger service was resumed during World War Two, first with a two-car streamlined gas-electric train from the Pennsylvania (originally one of Budd's early rubber-tired experimentals), then with assorted secondhand gas-electrics. Passenger service ended again in 1950 when the mail contract expired.

W&OD bought its Alexandria-Purcellville line from the Southern Railway in 1945, and in the early 1950s became solvent, almost prosperous. On November 6, 1956, Chesapeake & Ohio bought the W&OD because of the prospect of a power plant being constructed near its line (it did not happen). Between 1959 and 1961 business flourished, largely in construction materials for Dulles International Airport, although far more material came by truck than by train — the same was true for the construction of the community of Reston, built in the early 1960s. W&OD sold the Rosslyn branch in 1962 for highway use. In 1965 the W&OD petitioned to abandon the rest of the line, largely to sell its right of way for highway and power line use. The Washington & Old Dominion ceased operation on August 27, 1968. Most of the line has been rebuilt as a hiking-biking-horseback riding trail.

Location of headquarters: Rosslyn (Arlington), Virginia
Miles of railroad operated: 1929 — 72; 1967 — 48
Number of locomotives: 1929 — 4; 1967 — 3
Number of motor passenger cars: 1929 — 12
Number of motor freight cars: 1929 — 1
Number of freight cars: 1929 — 12
Recommended reading: *Washington & Old Dominion Railroad*, by Ames W. Williams, published in 1970 by Capital Traction Quarterly, Springfield, Va.

WASHINGTON, IDAHO & MONTANA RAILWAY

In 1905 the Potlatch Lumber Company moved its mill from Palouse, Washington, to Potlatch, Idaho. The Oregon Railway & Navigation Co. (Union Pacific) was reluctant to build a line to follow the lumber company, so Potlatch built its own line, through towns named Harvard, Yale, Princeton, Vassar, and so on. Construction reached Purdue, Idaho, end of the line — and considerably short of the goal implied by the name — in 1908.

In the early 1950s Potlatch Forests, successor to Potlatch Lumber, was using trucks to carry logs and had little further need for the railroad. However, other business had developed along the line. To tap this traffic source Milwaukee Road, which connected with the WI&M at Purdue, purchased the road in 1962. (The interchange point at some time was

There is little question about the principal item of Washington, Idaho & Montana's traffic. Number 21, an oil-burning 2-8-0, approaches Potlatch in May 1947 with a train that is carrying mostly lumber products.

Philip C. Johnson

shifted to Bovill, two miles south of Purdue.) Burlington Northern purchased the WI&M in March 1981 after Milwaukee Road abandoned its lines west of the Missouri River and integrated WI&M's operations with its own.

Location of headquarters: Potlatch, Idaho
Miles of railroad operated: 1929 — 49; 1980 — 50
Number of locomotives: 1929 — 5; 1980 — 1
Number of passenger cars: 1929 — 4
Number of freight cars: 1929 — 266
Number of company service cars: 1929 — 3
Successors: Burlington Northern
Portions still operated: Palouse-Bovill: Burlington Northern

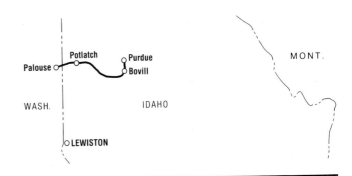

WATERLOO, CEDAR FALLS & NORTHERN RAILWAY

The Waterloo & Cedar Falls Rapid Transit Co. was incorporated in December 1895. In 1896 it purchased the Waterloo Street Railway. Faced with difficulty obtaining a franchise to operate in Cedar Falls, it arranged to electrify and operate over a branch of the Chicago Great Western. The CGW and the electric line were closely associated for several years.

In 1904 the electric line changed its name to Waterloo, Cedar Falls & Northern Railway. It expanded southeast in 1913 with a line to Cedar Rapids, and built a freight belt line around Waterloo to serve such industries as John Deere and Rath Packing Co. The WCF&N early recognized the benefits of interchanging carload freight with the steam railroads — indeed, it handled much of its freight with steam power until 1915 — and it actively promoted industrial development in Waterloo. By 1927 WCF&N's freight revenue exceeded its passenger revenue. WCF&N's passenger service was notable for its steam-road-size parlor-observation cars, which were later rebuilt as coaches, though they still retained the observation platform.

A fire in the Waterloo roundhouse in October 1954 destroyed most of the passenger equipment, several locomotives, and the shop machinery

William D. Middleton

Freight motor 182 leads a train across the Cedar River bridge south of Waterloo. The first car in the consist is a refrigerator car from the Rath plant in Waterloo.

347

that was necessary to maintain the electric cars and locomotives. WCF&N discontinued passenger service in 1956 (Waterloo city cars were replaced by buses in 1936; WCF&N operated the buses until 1953, when the cities of Waterloo and Cedar Falls took over the bus service). In March 1955 the stockholders approved sale of the line to the Waterloo Railroad, which was organized by the Illinois Central and the Rock Island that year. The Waterloo Railroad took over the property of the WCF&N on July 1, 1956. Diesel operation was phased in gradually, and electric operation ended in August 1958. Illinois Central purchased Rock Island's half interest in the Waterloo Railroad in July 1968, and in 1970 IC made the line simply a part of its Iowa division. Today it functions as a switching operation at Cedar Rapids and Waterloo and has nearly 700 freight cars (marked WLO).

Location of headquarters: Waterloo, Iowa
Miles of railroad operated: 1929 — 138 (track miles); 1955 — 98
Number of locomotives: 1929 — 7; 1955 — 10
Number of passenger cars: 1929 — 41; 1955 — 2
Number of freight cars: 1929 — 120; 1955 — 28
Number of company service cars: 1929 — 44; 1955 — 67

Reporting marks: WCF&N
Recommended reading: *Iowa Trolleys*, edited by Norman Carlson, published in 1975 by Central Electric Railfans' Association, P. O. Box 503, Chicago, IL 60690
Successor companies: Waterloo Railroad
Portions still operated: short portions of line at Waterloo and Cedar Rapids: Waterloo (Illinois Central Gulf)

WELLSVILLE, ADDISON & GALETON RAILROAD

The Wellsville, Addison & Galeton Railroad was incorporated in October 1954 by Murray M. Salzberg to purchase an orphan segment of the Baltimore & Ohio (formerly Buffalo & Susquehanna) from Galeton, Pennsylvania, to Wellsville, New York, Addison, N. Y., and Ansonia, Pa. Salzberg took possession on January 1, 1956. The purchase price included six ex-B&S 2-8-0s and a handful of cabooses, work cars, and snowplows. Salzberg, however, intended to operate the line with diesel power, and he acquired seven center-cab General Electric units built between 1937 and 1940 for Ford Motor Company's River Rouge works. WA&G also gathered a fleet of several hundred interchange freight cars, all secondhand — mostly outside-braced wood-sheathed box cars from Boston & Maine. They were rebuilt and repainted and given WA&G's new slogan, "The

Sole Leather Line," a reference to the tanneries sited along the railroad.

In 1959 the line to Addison was abandoned north of Elkland, Pa., because of a weakened bridge; the interchange at Addison was with the same railroad — Erie and later Erie Lackawanna — as the interchange at Wellsville. In 1964 the 26-mile Coudersport & Port Allegany, which connected with the Wellsville line, was purchased by Salzberg.

Eventually the GE diesels began to wear out and WA&G acquired a fleet of former Southern Pacific F7s in 1968 and 1969. About the same time the per diem rules changed and revenue from WA&G's fleet of box cars dropped. WA&G petitioned to abandon the Wellsville line and rely solely on interchange with Penn Central at Ansonia. (The C&PA ceased operation in December 1970.) Floods in 1972 ended service on the

Wellsville line, and it was officially abandoned in 1973. The road petitioned the ICC to discontinue service on the remainder of the line, and the last run was on March 16, 1979. The road's last two F7s were rebuilt for Pittsburgh-area commuter service operated by the Port Authority of Allegheny County; the others had previously been sent to the Louisiana & North West. GE centercab diesel 1700, the last of its type, has been preserved by the Lake Shore Railway Historical Society in North East, Pa.

Location of headquarters: Galeton, Pennsylvania
Miles of railroad operated: 1956 — 91; 1978 — 40
Number of locomotives: 1956 — 4; 1978 — 6
Number of freight cars: 1956 — 3; 1978 — 17
Reporting marks: WAG
Recommended reading: *Wellsville, Addison & Galeton Railroad*, by Edward A. Lewis, published in 1971 by Short Tracks Development Corp., 14 East Main Street, Arcade, NY 14009
Predecessor railroads in this book:
Buffalo & Susquehanna
Baltimore & Ohio
Map: See page 44

David H. Hamley

One of Wellsville, Addison & Galeton's GE centercab diesels has a string of the road's wooden box cars in tow at Ansonia, Pa., in March 1970.

WESTERN MARYLAND RAILWAY

On May 27, 1852, the Maryland General Assembly granted a charter to the Baltimore, Carroll & Frederick Rail Road to build a line from Baltimore northwest through Westminster, then west toward Hagerstown, Md. The name of the enterprise was soon changed to Western Maryland Rail Road. The line was opened as far as Union Bridge in November 1862, and it was seized briefly by the Union army during the Battle of Gettysburg in July 1863. Construction resumed in 1868. The line reached Hagerstown in 1872 and was extended a few miles to a connection with the Chesapeake & Ohio Canal at Williamsport in 1873.

In 1881 WM leased a line north to Shippensburg, Pennsylvania, and in 1886 established a connection there with a predecessor of the Reading. Also in 1886 WM gained a branch north from Emory Grove to Hanover and Gettysburg, Pa.; that line was soon extended southwest from Gettysburg to meet WM's main line at Highfield, Md. The main line was extended from Williamsport to Big Pool, Md., and across the Potomac River to Cherry Run, West Virginia, where it connected with the Baltimore & Ohio. B&O, WM, and Reading joined forces to operate a through freight route between Cumberland, Md., and Allentown, Pa., via Harrisburg.

WM's stock was largely owned by the city of Baltimore; the city also held its mortgage bonds. By the turn of the century WM's debt to Baltimore was substantial, and the city was seeking a buyer for the railroad. Bids were submitted in 1902. The syndicate representing George Gould was the lowest bidder but guaranteed full payment of WM's debt, extension west to Cumberland, and creation of a major tidewater terminal at Baltimore. On May 7, 1902, the city accepted the Gould syndicate's offer. WM immediately built the marine terminal, Port Covington, and began construction westward along the Potomac (where all the good locations had been taken by the Baltimore & Ohio Railroad, the Chesapeake & Ohio Canal, and the National Turnpike). The line reached Cumberland in 1906. There it met the Cumberland & Piedmont Railway, which with the West Virginia Central & Pittsburg, another Gould road, formed a route southwest from Cumberland through Elkins to Durbin and Belington, W. Va. In 1907 Gould acquired control of the Georges Creek & Cumberland Railway, which had a line from Cumberland north through the Cumberland Narrows.

B&O and Reading had broken their traffic agreement with WM in 1902, with the result that coal from Gould's West Virginia Central bypassed the WM and went instead over the Pennsy, which at the time controlled B&O. The rest of Gould's empire was in trouble too, and in 1908 the Western Maryland entered receivership, as did the Wabash Pittsburgh Terminal and the Wheeling & Lake Erie. The Western Maryland Railway took over the WM at the beginning of 1910 and immediately began construction of an 86-mile extension northwest from Cumberland to a connection with the Pittsburgh & Lake Erie at Connellsville, Pa.

When the Gould empire collapsed John D. Rockefeller acquired control of the Western Maryland. Because the ICC merger plan of 1921 grouped WM with Baltimore & Ohio, B&O bought Rockefeller's WM interest in 1927 and soon increased its WM holdings to 43 percent. Frank Taplin, who controlled the Pittsburgh & West Virginia, protested B&O's action. The ICC charged B&O with violating antitrust laws — in its effort to carry out the ICC merger plan. Pennsylvania Railroad interests acquired the P&WV in 1929 and offered to purchase WM, but B&O refused to sell, eventually placing its WM holdings in a nonvoting trust.

In 1944 WM acquired the Cumberland & Pennsylvania, a short coal road out of Cumberland. WM began dieselization in 1949, starting with the eastern end of the system, farthest from the coalfields it served. Passenger service — which consisted of coach-only local trains — lasted barely long enough to be dieselized.

As merger plans were formulated WM could see its traffic dry up. Merger of New York Central and Pennsylvania could throw traffic from the Pittsburgh & Lake Erie (part of the NYC system) onto the Pennsylvania. Norfolk & Western could easily reroute traffic from the P&WV onto N&W lines right to Hagerstown. WM decided to forsake independence and join the Baltimore & Ohio-Chesapeake & Ohio — after all, B&O was almost a half owner of WM. B&O and C&O applied to control WM, and the ICC approved their bid in 1967.

There was little evidence of C&O-B&O control until 1973, when the Chessie System was incorporated to own C&O, B&O, and WM. In 1973 WM applied to abandon 125 miles of main line from Hancock, Md., to Connellsville, Pa. WM's single track paralleled B&O's double-track line

A Class I-2 Decapod, one of 20 built by Baldwin in 1927, tugs hard on a westbound freight at Corriganville, Md., a few miles out of Cumberland, on August 23, 1952. Relegated to pusher service at the rear of the train is a 4-6-6-4, 13 years younger but no more powerful than the enormous 2-10-0.

R. F. Collins

and had easier grades and better clearances, but the expense of maintaining the line and building connecting lines outweighed any savings that might result from its lower operating costs. That same year WM's Port Covington coal terminal was abandoned in favor of B&O's newer pier in Baltimore. Gradually B&O absorbed WM's operations, and in late 1983 B&O merged Western Maryland.

Location of headquarters: Baltimore, Maryland
Miles of railroad operated: 1929 — 878; 1982 — 1,152 (the increase is due to operation over B&O on trackage rights)
Number of locomotives: 1929 — 259; 1982 — 109
Number of passenger cars: 1929 — 78
Number of freight cars: 1929 — 11,481; 1982 — 6,836
Number of company service cars: 1929 — 159; 1982 — 145
Reporting marks: WM

Historical and technical society: Western Maryland Railway Historical Society, P. O. Box 395, Union Bridge, MD 21791
Recommended reading: *The Western Maryland Railway*, by Roger Cook and Karl Zimmermann, published in 1981 by Howell-North Books, 850 North Hollywood Way, Burbank, CA 91505 (ISBN 0-8310-7139-7)
Predecessor railroads in this book: Cumberland & Pennsylvania
Successors: Chessie System (TWG)
Portions still operated:
Baltimore, Md.-York, Pa.; Porters, Pa.-Tonoloway, Md.; Hagerstown, Md.-Shippensburg, Pa.; Big Pool, Md.-Cherry Run, W. Va.; Cumberland-Frostburg-Mt. Savage, Md.; Carlos Jct., Md.-Dailey, W. Va.; Elkins-Pickens, W. Va.: Chessie System
Emory Grove-Cedarhurst, Md.; Westminster-Highfield, Md.: Maryland Midland

WESTERN PACIFIC RAILROAD

In 1900 the Gould railroads (Western Maryland, Wabash, Missouri Pacific, and Denver & Rio Grande chief among them) stretched from Baltimore to Ogden, Utah, with only a short gap in Pennsylvania. The Southern Pacific connection at Ogden furnished considerable traffic to the system, but that traffic vanished when E. H. Harriman obtained control of Union Pacific and Southern Pacific, effectively shutting Denver & Rio Grande out of the Ogden Gateway. At the same time California shippers and merchants considered themselves at the mercy of Southern Pacific, which had a virtual monopoly in the area.

From time to time railroads had been proposed and surveyed through the Sierra Nevada, the mountain range along much of the eastern boundary of California, via the Feather River canyon and Beckwourth Pass on a route 2,000 feet lower than the route the Central Pacific (later Southern Pacific) had taken over Donner Pass. One such survey had been made by W. H. Kennedy, assistant to the chief engineer of the Union Pacific when Jay Gould controlled UP. Arthur Keddie used the Kennedy survey to obtain a franchise for a railroad on that route. Keddie's partner, Walter J. Bartnett, signed an agreement with George Gould, Jay Gould's eldest son and successor, to take over the various surveys, franchises, and incorporations.

The Western Pacific Railway (the name chosen was also that of the railroad that originally extended the Central Pacific from Sacramento to Oakland) was incorporated in 1903 to build a railroad between Salt Lake City and San Francisco. Gould's Denver & Rio Grande underwrote $50 million in bonds for construction. The last spike was driven in 1909 on the Spanish Creek trestle at Keddie, Calif.

The new road had no branches to feed it, and as a result revenue didn't cover operating expenses and construction costs. WP entered bankruptcy in 1915 and pulled the Rio Grande in with it. At the same time the eastern end of Gould's empire collapsed as the cost of building the Wabash Pittsburgh Terminal (later Pittsburgh & West Virginia) bankrupted the Wabash. The Western Pacific Railway was sold in 1916 and reorganized as the Western Pacific Railroad.

In 1917 the WP purchased control of the Tidewater Southern, an inter-

urban that ran south from Stockton, Calif., and took over the south end of the narrow gauge Nevada-California-Oregon to gain entry to Reno, Nevada. Operation of WP by the United States Railroad Administration introduced paired track operation with Southern Pacific between Winnemucca and Wells, Nev., 182 miles. The arrangement was discontinued after the USRA relinquished control, but resumed in 1924. With the payment it received from the government for damages — chiefly the result of lack of maintenance — WP purchased control of Sacramento Northern, an electric line from Sacramento to Chico, Calif.

In 1926 Arthur Curtiss James acquired control of WP; he already had large holdings in Great Northern, Northern Pacific, and Burlington. WP

The steam era was ending as Mikado 308 waited with an eastbound freight train at Altamont, Calif., summit of WP's climb over the hills between San Francisco Bay and the Central Valley.

The westbound *California Zephyr* has just ducked under its own path in circling Williams Loop near Massack, Calif., in this July 1952 photo. The third car from the rear of the train is a through sleeper from New York via the New York Central.

purchased the San Francisco-Sacramento Railroad, an interurban between the two cities of its name, in 1927 and merged it with Sacramento Northern. Construction to link the railroad with the Great Northern at Bieber, Calif., was completed November 10, 1931, creating the Inside Gateway route and making the WP a north-south carrier in conjunction with GN and the Santa Fe line in the San Joaquin Valley. Western Pacific underwent voluntary reorganization in 1935.

After World War Two WP teamed up with Rio Grande and Burlington to operate the *California Zephyr* between Chicago and Oakland, Calif.

Plans for the train had been laid in 1937, but the war postponed their realization. The postwar period brought the Vista-Dome, and the *CZ* was the first long-distance train to carry Vista-Domes — five per train. Because of the routing, the train could not compete on the basis of speed against the Union Pacific-Southern Pacific-Chicago & North Western *City of San Francisco*, but the *CZ*'s schedule was planned to take full advantage of the Vista-Domes for viewing the scenery. The train was an immediate success. The secondary train on the route was replaced with a Budd Rail Diesel Car named *Zephyrette* (not to be confused with the *CZ*'s hostess, who had the same title). Western Pacific's segment of the *California Zephyr* left Oakland for the last time on March 21, 1970.

In 1962 Southern Pacific and Santa Fe sparred for control of Western Pacific; neither won. Western Pacific was merged with Union Pacific on December 22, 1981, giving UP the extension to San Francisco that it had surveyed so many years before. WP's identity quickly disappeared as the road became simply the Fourth Operating District of UP, then the Western Division of the South-Central District in 1983. In response to employee pressure it was renamed the Feather River Division when the South-Central District became the new Western District in 1985.

WP owned two switching roads on the east shore of San Francisco Bay jointly with Santa Fe: the Oakland Terminal Railway and the Alameda Belt Line. WP, Santa Fe, and Southern Pacific jointly owned the Central California Traction Co., which runs between Stockton and Sacramento.

Location of headquarters: San Francisco, California
Miles of railroad operated: 1929 — 1,055; 1981 — 1,436 (including Sacramento Northern and Tidewater Southern)
Number of locomotives: 1929 — 169; 1981 — 144
Number of passenger cars: 1929 — 86
Number of freight cars: 1929 — 9,470; 1981 — 6,077

Number of company service cars: 1929 — 396; 1981 — 219
Reporting marks: WP
Notable named passenger trains: *California Zephyr* (Oakland-Chicago, operated jointly with Denver & Rio Grande Western and Chicago, Burlington & Quincy)
Historical and technical society: Feather River Rail Society, P. O. Box 8, Portola, CA 96122
Recommended reading:
Portrait of a Silver Lady, by Bruce A. MacGregor and Ted Benson, published in 1977 by Pruett Publishing Co., 3235 Prairie Avenue, Boulder, CO 80301 (ISBN 0-87108-509-7)
Western Pacific's Diesel Years, by J. A. Strapac, published in 1980 by Overland Models, RR 12, Box 445, Muncie, IN 47302 (ISBN 0-916160-08-4)
Subsidiaries and affiliated railroads, 1981:
Sacramento Northern
Tidewater Southern
Alameda Belt Line (50%)
Central California Traction (33%)
Oakland Terminal (50%)
Successors: Union Pacific (TWG)

WHEELING & LAKE ERIE RAILWAY

The Wheeling & Lake Erie Rail Road was incorporated in 1871 to build a line from Martin's Ferry, Ohio, a few miles up the Ohio River from Wheeling, West Virginia, through the coalfields of southeastern Ohio and on to the Lake Erie ports of Sandusky and Toledo. Construction began in 1873. The road was unable to raise much capital, and the directors decided to build it as a narrow gauge line. In 1877 a few miles of track were completed between Norwalk and Huron, Ohio, but the only service was excursion trains for the stockholders. Construction ceased later that year, and the W&LE petitioned for dissolution.

In 1879 the stockholders tried again, about the time Jay Gould decided to build a line eastward from the Wabash. Construction resumed in 1881, this time standard gauge. In 1882 the W&LE acquired the Cleveland &

Marietta Railroad, and late that year service began between Toledo and Marietta. A year later, though, the C&M was in receivership and back on its own. The W&LE reorganized in 1886 and continued construction eastward, reaching Martin's Ferry in 1889 and Wheeling at the end of 1891. The new road prospered until the combination of a depression and a long strike by coal miners in 1896 threw it into receivership.

Myron T. Herrick, a Cleveland banker, was appointed receiver of the W&LE in 1897. He soon added to it the Cleveland, Canton & Southern, an often-reorganized, run-down, former narrow gauge line from Cleveland to Zanesville, Ohio. The shape of the map of the new railroad got it the nickname "Iron Cross." Turn-of-the-century prosperity embraced the new W&LE, largely because of coal traffic. In 1906 the W&LE chartered the Lorain & West Virginia Railway to build a line from Wellington to Lorain.

C. W. Burns

Wheeling & Lake Erie's Berkshires were close cousins of the Nickel Plate's 2-8-4s, but differed in details. Number 6404, a 1937 Alco product, wheels an 80-car coal train west through Harmon, Ohio, in September 1938.

In 1907 the Gould empire collapsed. The W&LE fell into receivership; in 1912 William McKinley Duncan (nephew of U. S. President William McKinley) was appointed receiver. His management style was conservative, allowing only improvements that promised a good return on investment. The road returned to profitability, but at the expense of unpainted buildings and unsignaled main lines. The growth of the automobile industry, however, deserves most of the credit for bringing the W&LE up from the depths. While coal continued to be the mainstay of W&LE's traffic, Detroit's factories were hungry for steel from mills at Canton and Massillon, roller bearings from the Timken plant at Canton, and other such goods; in addition, W&LE's line to Toledo bypassed much of the congestion there.

The Wheeling was one of the first railroads to drop passenger service — because of the automobile, which was so beneficial on the freight side of W&LE's ledgers. The last passenger train, a Cleveland-Wheeling run operated with Atlantics and wood cars, was discontinued in July 1938.

In 1927 the Nickel Plate, the Baltimore & Ohio, and the New York Central teamed up to buy the Wheeling & Lake Erie stock held by John D. Rockefeller. The Van Sweringen brothers, who controlled the Nickel Plate, bought more on their own to keep W&LE out of the reach of Leonor F. Loree of the Delaware & Hudson, who was trying to build a rail system to compete with NYC, B&O, Nickel Plate, and Pennsylvania. The Van Sweringens also sought to keep W&LE out of the hands of the Pittsburgh & West Virginia. The ICC investigated the matter and ordered B&O, NYC, and NKP to sell their W&LE stock. The Van Sweringens' Alleghany Corporation bought NYC's shares and traded its interest in the Buffalo, Rochester & Pittsburgh to the B&O for B&O's interest in the W&LE. By 1929 the Wheeling & Lake Erie was owned by the Van Sweringens, although they were not allowed to exercise control.

In 1946 and 1947 NKP purchased approximately 80 percent of the stock of Wheeling & Lake Erie, and on December 1, 1949, NKP leased the W&LE.

Location of headquarters: Cleveland, Ohio
Miles of railroad operated: 1929 — 512; 1948 — 506
Number of locomotives: 1929 — 185; 1948 — 161
Number of passenger cars: 1929 — 66
Number of freight cars: 1929 — 11,626; 1948 — 13,646
Number of company service cars: 1929 — 273; 1948 — 151
Reporting marks: WLE
Historical and technical society: Nickel Plate Road Historical &

Technical Society, P. O. Box 29822, St. Louis, MO 63129
Recommended reading: *The Nickel Plate Story*, by John A. Rehor, published in 1965 by Kalmbach Publishing Co., 1027 North Seventh Street, Milwaukee, WI 53233
Successors:
New York, Chicago & St. Louis (Nickel Plate)
Norfolk & Western
Portions still operated: Norfolk & Western operates all of the former Wheeling & Lake Erie except Orrville-Dalton, Ohio, and South Lorain-Wellington, Ohio.

WHITE PASS & YUKON RAILWAY

The White Pass & Yukon was born in the Yukon gold rush of 1898. A railroad was necessary to carry machinery and supplies from tidewater at Skagway, Alaska, over the Coast Mountains to the Yukon River in Canada's Yukon Territory. Construction of the 3-foot-gauge railroad began in 1898, and crews working from Skagway and from Whitehorse, Y. T., met at Carcross, Y. T., on July 29, 1900. The road's destination at one time was Fort Selkirk, Y. T., at the confluence of the Pelly and Lewes (or Upper Yukon) rivers.

WP&Y's corporate structure encompassed three railroads — the Pacific & Arctic Railway & Navigation Co. (Alaska, 20.4 miles), the British Columbia-Yukon Railway (British Columbia, 32.2 miles), and the British Yukon Railway (Yukon Territory, 58.1 miles) — all operated by the White Pass & Yukon.

The WP&Y prospered for a few years; then gold mining slackened and the company entered reorganization. The belligerence of Japan and the approach of World War Two roused the economy of the Yukon. The railroad's business increased and in 1937 it even inaugurated air services (WP&Y had operated steamboats between Whitehorse and Dawson and between Carcross and Atlin for many years).

The bombing of Pearl Harbor in 1941 triggered the construction of the Alaska Highway. One of the jumping-off places for construction crews was Whitehorse, the northern terminus of the railroad. The WP&Y found itself with too big a job to do, and the U. S. Army's Military Railway Service moved in to operate the line. The Army purchased locomotives from several narrow gauge lines in the U. S. to handle the increased traffic — in 1943 the road handled the equivalent of 10 years' worth of prewar tonnage.

After the war the WP&Y returned to its primary business of bringing the necessities of life into the Yukon and carrying out silver, lead, and zinc. In addition, the railroad developed a tourist business, connecting with cruise ships calling at Skagway. In 1951 the White Pass & Yukon Corp. was chartered to acquire ownership of the subsidiary companies.

To reduce the cost of transferring cargo between ship or truck and train, the White Pass developed a container that would fit on the narrow gauge cars and on flatbed trucks. In 1954 WP&Y designed and bought a ship, the *Clifford J. Rogers*, to carry the containers between Vancouver, B. C., and Skagway. WP&Y also owns an oil pipeline paralleling the railroad between Skagway and Whitehorse and a large trucking operation.

Much of the railroad's traffic in recent years had come from the Yukon mining industry, but a slump shut down the mines and WP&Y suspended operation in 1983 for lack of ore traffic and because of competition in the form of a new highway from Skagway to Whitehorse.

Location of headquarters: Seattle, Washington
Miles of railroad operated: 1980 — 111
Number of locomotives: 1980 — 20
Number of passenger cars: 1980 — 34
Number of freight cars: 1980 — 399
Number of company service cars: 1980 — 36
Reporting marks: WPY
Recommended reading: *The White Pass and Yukon Route*, by Stan Cohen, published in 1980 by Pictorial Histories Publishing Co., 713 South Third West, Missoula, MT 59801 (ISBN 0-933126-08-5)
Subsidiaries and affiliated railroads, 1980:
Pacific & Arctic Railway & Navigation Co.
British Columbia-Yukon Railway
British Yukon Railway
Map: See page 106

F. L. Jaques

White Pass & Yukon's tour trains stopped at Bennett for meals and to afford passengers a chance to stretch their legs.

WINSTON-SALEM SOUTHBOUND RAILWAY

The Winston-Salem Southbound was incorporated in 1905 — late as North American railroad history goes — to build a railroad from Winston-Salem, North Carolina, to the South Carolina state line. Construction began in 1909 after its principal connections, Norfolk & Western and Atlantic Coast Line, guaranteed its bonds and became its joint owners. The reason for the road's existence was probably to form a shortcut for coal moving south to fuel ACL locomotives and U. S. Navy ships at Charleston, S. C. WSS's rails reached Whitney in December 1910; a few months later the line was extended to Wadesboro, where it connected with ACL.

WSS depended on parent Norfolk & Western for maintenance of its line and for supervision of its operations, and it relied on Atlantic Coast Line for accounting and marketing. In the early 1950s WSS's motive power fleet consisted of two half-century-old ex-N&W 2-8-0s, two ex-ACL Mikados, and two similar 2-8-2s purchased new. In 1957 the Southbound replaced steam with four GP9s, two delivered in WSS's gray and maroon and two delivered at the same time in ACL black. About 1967 they disappeared, two each, into the roster of parents Norfolk & Western and Seaboard Coast Line. After that the Southbound leased power from its parents. Also by the end of 1967 WSS no longer had any interchange freight

357

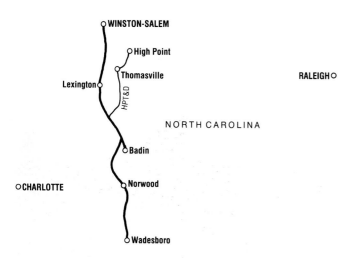

cars of its own, although three cabooses remain in service in 1985. I will use 1967 as the end date for the railroad, but it really marks transition to a paper railroad. WSS maintains a degree of independence even though its allegiance is split between the two giants of southeastern railroading, Norfolk Southern and CSX Corporation.

In 1960 Winston-Salem Southbound acquired control of the High Point, Thomasville & Denton Railroad, a 34-mile line from High Point to a connection with the WSS at High Rock.

Location of headquarters: Winston-Salem, North Carolina
Miles of railroad operated: 1929 — 98; 1967 — 95
Number of locomotives: 1929 — 11
Number of passenger cars: 1929 — 3
Number of freight cars: 1929 — 203
Number of company service cars: 1929 — 17; 1967 — 8

Winston-Salem Southbound time freights 209 and 212 meet at Eller, N. C., in 1956. Mikado 827, right, is ex-Atlantic Coast Line, but its tender is ex-Norfolk & Western. Mikado 300, approaching, was built for WSS to ACL specifications — the N&W pilot is a later modification.

Reporting marks: WSS
Subsidiaries and affiliated railroads, 1967: High Point, Thomasville & Denton
Portions still operated: Winston-Salem to Wadesboro and Whitney to Badin, N. C.

WRIGHTSVILLE & TENNILLE RAILROAD

Tennille, Georgia, 55 miles east of Macon on the Central of Georgia, was the starting point for the Wrightsville & Tennille. In 1884 it began and completed a 16-mile line south to Wrightsville. By furnishing materials for construction of the W&T, the Central Railroad & Banking Company gained control of the short line. In 1886 the W&T merged the Dublin & Wrightsville, which reached to the bank of the Oconee River opposite Dublin. In 1891 it bridged the Oconee, and in 1899 it acquired the Oconee & Western Railroad, from Dublin to Hawkinsville. In 1908 the W&T filled out its map by taking over the Dublin & Southwestern Railroad, which had a line from Dublin to Eastman.

The lines west and south of Dublin were abandoned in 1941. The Wrightsville & Tennille was merged with the Central of Georgia Railroad, a new Southern Railway subsidiary, along with its parent, the Central of Georgia Railway, on June 1, 1971. The Tennille-Dublin portion is still in operation.

The Wrightsville & Tennille was the largest of Central of Georgia's subsidiary short lines. The others were:
- Wadley & Southern, formed in 1906 to consolidate several railroads with lines from Wadley to Collins, 53 miles, and Wadley to Rockledge, 37 miles. By 1930 the road was down to a 20-mile route from Wadley to Swainsboro; that was abandoned in 1964.
- Louisville & Wadley Railroad, built in 1879 from Wadley north to Louisville, 10 miles. It was reorganized in 1961 as the locally owned Louisville & Wadley Railway. It is still in operation.
- Sylvania Central Railway, built in 1885 from Rocky Ford, on CofG's Savannah line, to Sylvania, on the Savannah & Atlanta, 15 miles. It was independent during some years of its history and a CofG subsidiary during other years. It was abandoned in 1954.

Location of headquarters: Dublin, Georgia
Miles of railroad operated: 1929 — 104; 1970 — 36
Number of locomotives: 1929 — 7; 1970 — 1
Number of passenger cars: 1929 — 10
Number of freight cars: 1929 — 33; 1970 — 1
Number of company service cars: 1929 — 3; 1970 — 1

W. F. Beckum Jr.

Wrightsville & Tennille train 1, the daily-except-Sunday mixed from Tennille to Dublin, pauses at Brewton on Washington's birthday, February 22, 1954.

Reporting marks: WTR
Recommended reading: *Central of Georgia Railway and Connecting Lines*, by Richard E. Prince, published in 1976 by Richard E. Prince
Successors: Central of Georgia (Southern Railway System)
Portions still operated: Tennille-Dublin: Southern
Map: See page 297

359

In 1940 Yosemite Valley train 3, a 4-4-0 trailing a steel baggage-mail car and a wood observation car, stands at El Portal, ready to carry passengers down the Merced River Canyon.

Millard Brown: Collection of Harre W. Demoro

YOSEMITE VALLEY RAILROAD

Yosemite National Park was established in 1890, and soon afterward railroad routes into the valley were surveyed. A group of men from San Francisco and Oakland incorporated the Yosemite Valley Railroad in 1902 and chose a route that simply followed the Merced River canyon into the park. Grading got under way in 1905 from the city of Merced, California, and early in 1906 service began as far as Merced Falls. In May 1907 the railroad reached a point about 12 miles from the east end of the valley and established a station named El Portal. From there the railroad built a wagon road into the park. Service over the full length of the line began on May 15, 1907.

By 1910 through Pullmans were being operated over the Southern Pacific from Los Angeles and Oakland to Merced; in 1912 the Yosemite Lumber Co. opened a sawmill at Merced Falls and a logging operation across the river from El Portal. The tourist business grew, and visiting royalty and Hollywood stars rode the YV.

The only major relocation of the railroad was required because of dam construction on the Merced River in the 1920s. Business peaked in 1925 — paved roads reached El Portal in 1926. Passenger traffic dropped 78 percent from 1925 to 1928, and the Yosemite Lumber Co. suspended operations in 1927.

The Depression drove YV into bankruptcy in 1935; the railroad was reorganized as the Yosemite Valley Railway. Freight traffic increased and the railroad showed a small profit, but a flood in December 1937 wiped out 30 miles of the line in the Merced River Canyon. Service resumed in 1938. The lumber company, which had resumed operations, closed permanently in 1942, and passenger traffic dropped to almost nothing during World War Two. The trustees of the road petitioned for abandonment on August 31, 1944. Another flood in February 1945 further weakened the road's finances, and a bridge fire in August of that year marooned some of the railroad's equipment. The last run was on August 24, 1945.

The railroad made a profit before fixed charges in 32 of its 38 years of operation; with proper financing it might have endured long enough to take advantage of California's postwar boom. Now, as the crush of automobile traffic threatens to destroy Yosemite National Park, many wish the YV were still around.

Location of headquarters: Merced, California
Miles of railroad operated: 1929 — 78; 1944 — 78
Number of locomotives: 1929 — 8; 1944 — 8

Number of passenger cars: 1929 — 8; 1944 — 7
Number of freight cars: 1929 — 255; 1944 — 73
Number of company service cars: 1929 — 10; 1944 — 8
Recommended reading: *Railroads of the Yosemite Valley*, by Hank Johnston, published in 1963 by Johnston-Howe Publications, 1244 Long Beach Boulevard, Long Beach, CA 90813

GLOSSARY

AAR: see Association of American Railroads.

Affiliate: a company effectively controlled by another or associated with others under common ownership or control.

Association of American Railroads (AAR): the coordinating and research agency of the American railroad industry. It is not a government agency but rather an organization to which railroads belong, much as local businesses belong to a chamber of commerce.

Bankrupt: declared legally insolvent (unable to pay debts as they fall due) and with assets taken over by judicial process to be distributed among creditors.

Bridge route, bridge traffic: Bridge traffic is freight received from one railroad to be moved by a second railroad for delivery to a third; for example, lettuce from California received by the Cotton Belt from Southern Pacific at Corsicana, Texas, for delivery to New York Central at East St. Louis. A bridge route is a railroad with more bridge traffic than traffic originating or terminating on line.

Capitalization: the total par value or stated value of the capital of a company. Overcapitalization means the value of the stocks and bonds exceeds the value of the physical properties of the railroad; conservative capitalization means the two values are close.

Centralized Traffic Control (CTC): a traffic control system whereby train movements are directed through remote control of switches and signals from a central control panel. The trains operate on the authority of signal indications instead of the authority of a timetable and train orders.

Charter: an instrument in writing from a state or country granting or guaranteeing rights, franchises, and privileges to a corporation. Obtaining a charter is a necessary part of incorporation.

Common carrier: a transportation company that offers — indeed, must offer — its services to all customers, as differentiated from a contract carrier, which carries goods for one shipper. The difference is like that between two buses, one signed "Main Street"; the other, "Charter."

Consolidation: the unification of two or more corporations by dissolution of existing ones and creation of a single new corporation.

Control: ownership by a railroad or by those sympathetic to its interests of enough of the securities of a second road to control its traffic policies.

Controlling interest: sufficient stock ownership in a corporation to exert control over policy.

CTC: see Centralized Traffic Control.

Degree: a measure of the sharpness of a curve. It is the angle through which the track turns in 100 feet of track. The number of degrees is equal to 5729 divided by the radius of the curve in feet.

Directed Service Order: an order issued by the Interstate Commerce Commission directing one railroad to handle the traffic of another, if the second is unable to by reason of strike, damage, abandonment, or other emergency.

Embargo: an order issued by a railroad or public regulatory agency prohibiting the acceptance of some or all kinds of freight for transportation on a railroad's lines or between specified points or areas because of traffic congestion, labor difficulties, or other reasons.

Financial interest: ownership of enough securities of a second road, short of control, to influence its traffic policies.

Foreclosure: a legal proceeding that bars or extinguishes a mortgagor's right of redeeming a mortgaged estate. In domestic terms, you mortgage your house as security on a loan for its purchase. If you fail to keep up payments, the mortgagee — the bank — can foreclose, which means the bank gets the house and you no longer have it. It's the same with a loan for construction of a railroad.

Grade: the inclination or slope of the track. It is usually measured as a percent — for example, a rise of 2 feet in 100 feet of track is 2 percent. Occasionally it is expressed as "1 in n," where n is the number of feet in which the track rises 1 foot. Both measures are ratios — 1 in 50 is the same as 2 percent. The steepest mainline grade in North America is 4.7 percent on a Southern Railway line near Saluda, North Carolina. The usual maximum for a main line in mountainous territory is about 2 percent.

Holding company: a company that owns other companies for purposes of control. The charter of one such company empowered it to acquire, hold, and dispose of stocks, bonds, and securities issued by corporations and government, state, and local authorities — in other words, do everything but coin money and administer the sacraments.

ICC: see Interstate Commerce Commission, below and page 164.

Incorporate: to form into a corporation recognized by law as an entity.

Interstate Commerce Commission (ICC): the agency of the federal government that carries out the provisions of the Interstate Commerce Act and other federal laws regulating interstate transportation — see page 164.

Interurban: an electric railroad running between cities, often of lighter construction than "steam" railroads and often operating in the streets of cities and towns instead of on private right of way. Interurbans had their rise and fall during the first four decades of the twentieth century.

Joint operation: operation of two railroads as one unit under two separate boards of directors.

Lease: the handing over of the property of a railroad in return for a specified yearly payment. The railroad must be returned in as good condition as when it was handed over. The most prevalent form of lease calls for the guarantee of the interest and principal of outstanding bonds of the lessor and a guaranteed percentage on the stock. The lessor company continues to exist and to retain ownership of its railroad property.

Line-haul railroad: a railroad that performs point-to-point service, as distinguished from a switching or terminal railroad.

Merger: the issuing of additional securities by a major company in payment for the securities of a minor company whose corporate existence is then ended; absorption by a corporation of one or more others.

Mixed train: a train carrying both freight and passengers, the latter either in passenger cars or in the caboose.

Operating contract: operation of a minor road in return for a payment to the major road for the service rendered. The minor company continues to exist and to retain ownership of its property.

Operating ratio: the ratio of operating expenses to revenue from operations. A railroad with an operating ratio of 80 or lower is doing nicely; a railroad that has an operating ratio over 100 is in trouble or soon will be.

Percent: the measure of slope or inclination of track — see Grade.

Per diem: daily rental paid by one railroad for the use of the cars of another.

Piggyback service: transportation of highway truck trailers and containers on flatcars.

Pooling agreement: Under a pooling agreement railroads are operated separately but all income is divided arbitrarily, irrespective of traffic carried.

Pound (rail): The unit of measure of rail size is weight per yard — a 3-foot length of 90-pound rail, for example, weighs 90 pounds.

Proprietary company: a corporation owning all or a controlling portion of the shares of another.

Purchase: payment of cash outright for all the property of a railroad, which may divide such proceeds as it wishes among its owners and then cease to exist as a corporation.

Receiver: a person appointed by a court to manage a corporation during a period of reorganization in an effort to avoid bankruptcy.

Receivership: management by a receiver.

Reorganization: the rehabilitation of the finances of a business concern under procedures prescribed by federal bankruptcy legislation.

Route mile: a mile of railroad line without regard to the number of tracks on that line. For example, the Milwaukee Road line from Chicago to Milwaukee is 85 route miles. The line is double track, so it includes 170 track miles for main track alone, not counting sidings and spurs.

Shorthaul: to move traffic a shorter distance than the maximum possible for a given railroad between two points. For example, Burlington Northern is said to shorthaul itself if it turns over Seattle-Chicago traffic to the Milwaukee Road at St. Paul rather than take it all the way to Chicago on its own rails.

Short line: a railroad with less than 100 miles of mainline track. There is no official or legal definition of the term; this is the criterion used by the railroad industry and the American Short Line Railroad Association.

Steam railroad: a term still used by regulatory bodies to differentiate ordinary railroads from "electric railways" — interurbans and streetcar companies.

Subsidiary: a company wholly controlled by another that owns more than half its voting stock.

Switching railroad or

Terminal railroad: a railroad whose business is not point-to-point transportation but rather pickup and delivery service for a connecting line-haul road. Switching and terminal companies usually receive a flat per-car amount for their services.

Trackage rights: rights granted by a railroad to another to operate on the tracks of the first, usually for a rental fee or a toll and usually without rights to service customers along that line.

Track mile: a mile of track — see Route mile.

USRA: United States Railroad Administration, the federal agency that took over operation of almost all U. S. railroads during World War One.

INDEX

The index lists the first appearance of subjects within each entry. *Italic* type indicates the primary entry for the principal railroads. Maps that are not with a railroad's primary entry are indicated by **boldface** page numbers. I have alphabetized letter by letter, treating "&" as "and" and omitting the words "railroad" and "railway" except where they fall in the middle of a name (like "Western Railway of Alabama"), and for purposes of alphabetizing I have treated "Pittsburg" as "Pittsburgh," whether or not the railroad in question did.

M

Mackinaw & Marquette, 123
Macon & Augusta, 21
Macon, Dublin & Savannah, *182*, **299**, 300
Madrid, 294
Mad River & Lake Erie, 212
Maine Central, 225, 285, 295
Main Line of Public Works, 5, 251
Manchester, 223
Manistee & Northeastern, 264
Manistique & Lake Superior, 19
Manitoba Great Northern, 144
Marietta & North Georgia, 180
Maryland & Delaware, 337
Mason City & Fort Dodge, 76
Master Car Builders' Association, *183*
Maysville & Big Sandy, 60
McAdoo, William G., 9
McGinnis, Patrick B., *223*
Memphis & Ohio, 178
Memphis, Clarksville & Louisville, 178
Memphis, Paducah & Northern, 60
Meridian & Memphis, 149
Metropolitan Transit Development Board (San Diego), 293
Mexican Central, 7
Mexican National, 7, 99, 112
Mexican Railway (Ferrocarril Mexicano), *183*
Mexico North-Western, *166*
Michigan Central, 78, *212*, 263, 332
Michigan Interstate, 19
Michigan Northern, 19, *186*
Michigan Southern, 209
Michigan Southern & Northern Indiana, 210
Middletown & Unionville, 229
Middletown, Unionville & Water Gap, 229
Midland, 223
Midland of Manitoba, 144
Midland Terminal, *187*
Midland Valley, *189*, 322

Millen & Southwestern, 141
Milwaukee Road, see Chicago, Milwaukee, St. Paul & Pacific, *81*
Mineral Range, 123
Minneapolis & St. Cloud, 144
Minneapolis & St. Louis, *191*, 330
Minneapolis Industrial, 193
Minnesota & International, 239
Minnesota & Northwestern, 75
Minnesota & Pacific, 144
Minnesota, Dakota & Pacific, 191
Minnesota Western, 191
Mississippi & Missouri, 87
Mississippi & Tennessee, 157
Mississippi & Wabash, 325
Mississippi Central Railroad, 176, *193*
Mississippi Central Railway, 156
Missouri & Arkansas, 195
Missouri & North Arkansas, *195*
Missouri-Kansas-Texas, 80, 191, 290, 342
Missouri, Oklahoma & Gulf, 139, 189
Missouri Pacific, 62, 65, 190, 286, 290, 322, 342
Mobile & Ohio, 44, 150, 156, *197*
Mobile, Jackson & Kansas City, 149
Moffat, David H., *115*
Mohawk & Hudson, 206
Mohawk & Malone, 14, 209
Mohawk Valley, 209
Monon, see Chicago, Indianapolis & Louisville, *78*
Monson, 296
Montana, 83
Montana Central, 144
Montgomery, 22
Montgomery & Eufala, 55
Montgomery & Mobile, 180
Montgomery & West Point, 22
Montpelier & Barre, 154, 199
Montpelier & Wells River, *198*, **281**, 285
Morris & Essex, 108

Mount Hope Mineral, 57
Mount Savage, 107
Muscle Shoals, Birmingham & Pensacola, 288
Muskogee Company, see Midland Valley, *189*

N

Nashville & Ashland City, 320
Nashville & Chattanooga, 200
Nashville & Decatur, 179
Nashville & Northwestern, 200
Nashville, Chattanooga & St. Louis, 30, 149, 180, *200*, 320
Natchez & Eastern, 193
National Railroad Passenger Corp. (Amtrak), 12
National Railways of Mexico, 7, 100, 184, 304, 308, 335
National Transcontinental, *50*, 317
Naugatuck, 225
Nevada & California, 305
Nevada-California-Oregon, 314, 352
Nevada Central, 326
Nevada County Narrow Gauge, *202*
Nevada Northern, *203*, 326
New Albany & Salem, 78, 212
Newfoundland, *204*
New Haven, see New York, New Haven & Hartford, *222*
New Haven & New London, 225
New Haven & Northampton, 225
New Jersey & New York, 132
New Jersey Midland, 229
New Jersey Southern, 56
New London Northern, 279
New Mexico & Arizona, 308
New Orleans & Northeastern, 205
New Orleans Great Northern, 42, 149, *205*
New Orleans, Jackson & Great Northern, 156
New Orleans, Jackson & Northern, 156
New Orleans, Mobile & Chicago, 149
New Orleans, Mobile & Texas, 180
New Orleans, St. Louis & Chicago, 156

ACKNOWLEDGMENTS

Many people read the entries for the railroads. They made corrections and provided additional material, and they kept the project moving with their encouragement. I owe them a considerable debt of gratitude, one that can't be discharged by simply printing their names here. If you need a group of friendly, helpful, knowledgeable railroad enthusiasts, here they are:

Russell Allen, J. Leonard Bachelder, John W. Barriger IV, John Barry, John Beach, Roger Bee, Henry E. Bender Jr., Ted Benson, George A. Berghoff, Marvin Black, Lawrence Bolton, Seth Bramson, Michael C. Brestel, Ken Brovald, Charles A. Brown, Wiley Bryan, John B. Corns, Peter Cox, Bruce Curry, Rob Danner, Harre W. Demoro, David W. DeVault, Larry DeYoung, Thomas W. Dixon, Gary W. Dolzall, Arthur D. Dubin, William G. Dulmaine Jr., Martin Evoy III, L. D. Farrar, Tom Fetters, Franklin Garrett, H. Arnt Gerritsen, Patrick J. Goedert, David Grandt, H. Roger Grant, John G. Gruber, E. J. Haley, Russell Hallock, John M. Ham, David H. Hamley, Robert M. Hanft, George E. Hardy Jr., Herbert H. Harwood Jr., Bob Hayden, Jim Hediger, George W. Hilton, Don L. Hofsommer, John C. Illman, Edward E. Immel, J. David Ingles, John S. Ingles, Richard W. Jahn, Norman C. Keyes, Tom King, Ken Kraemer, George Krambles, Frank Kyper, Roger Levenson, Edward A. Lewis, J. Norman Lowe, James J. D. Lynch Jr., Stanley H. Mailer, Louis A. Marre, Ken Marsh, Albro Martin, John B. McCall, Mel McFarland, Deane Mellander, William D. Middleton, William J. Miller, Arthur B. Million, Charles M. Mizell, David P. Morgan, David F. Myrick, Rolly Osmun, Robert C. Paoa, Bert Pennypacker, Keith Petersen, J. A. Pinkepank, John C. Plytnick, Tom Post, Frederick Pugh, John A. Rehor, H. Reid, Frank T. Reilly, Richard R. Reynolds, Louis Saillard, Willard Schultz, Jim Scribbins, Jim Shaughnessy, A. Gill Siepert, John Signor, Marjorie P. Silver, Mike Small, Charles M. Smith, Henry F. Sommers, Howard Speidel, Steve Steinkraus, Fred A. Stindt, Paul Stringham, Jim Teese, Jim Walker, R. R. Wallin, F. Hol Wagner Jr., John H. White Jr., Richard J. Wilhelm, M. Craig Wilson, Charles E. Winters, William Withuhn, and Dreat Younger.

For some railroads I sent the information to the appropriate historical or technical society. The society in turn referred it to its expert — the men are listed above. Thanks are also due to: Ann Arbor Railroad Technical & Historical Association, Anthracite Railroads Historical Society, Chesapeake & Ohio Historical Society, Great Northern Railway Historical Society, Hawaiian Railway Society, Illinois Terminal Railroad Historical Society, Missouri & Arkansas Railroad Museum, New Haven Railroad Historical & Technical Association, New York Central System Historical Society, Nickel Plate Historical & Technical Society, Northern Pacific Railroad Historical Association, Ontario & Western Railway Historical Society, Pacific Northwest Chapter of the National Railway Historical Society, Pittsburgh, Shawmut & Northern Railroad Co. Historical Society, Reading Company Technical & Historical Society, Sumpter Valley Railroad Restoration Inc., Ulster & Delaware Chapter of the National Railway Historical Society, and Western Maryland Railway Historical Society.

Similarly, this book would be considerably diminished without the efforts of the people whose names appear beneath the photographs. I thank them, too, and I'm glad we had their work in our files.

This army of experts has done its best to trap errors, and two editors have further screened the work. Any errors that have slithered past both experts and editors I hereby certify as my own work. — G. H. D.

UPDATE

Railroads continued to merge and their old identities continued to vanish while this book was being written. A brief list of recent disappearances and impending changes as of mid-December 1985 follows. The degree of disappearance of a railroad's identity differs depending on where you look. For example, the 1985 edition of *Moody's Transportation Manual* lists Missouri Pacific separately (although right after Union Pacific) and includes a MoPac map, but *The Official Guide* has just a single entry for Union Pacific System, which comprises the Union Pacific Railroad and the Missouri Pacific Railroad. MP's newest diesels are yellow with red lettering, just like UP's; they are lettered Missouri Pacific on the sides but have a UP shield on the nose. In the next few years many more railroad images will disappear in favor of system identities: Boston & Maine, Delaware & Hudson, and Maine Central into Guilford; and Southern and Norfolk & Western into Norfolk Southern, to name just two.

Amtrak continues to be a political football, battling annually for budget and for existence while carrying increasing numbers of passengers, upgrading its rolling stock and stations, and covering more and more of its expenses from fares.

Atchison, Topeka & Santa Fe and Southern Pacific are approaching merger at the railroad level; if the merger is approved by the ICC the new railroad will be named the Southern Pacific & Santa Fe. The parent companies, Santa Fe Industries and Southern Pacific Company, merged in 1983 as Santa Fe Southern Pacific Corporation.

British Columbia Railway, which was the Pacific Great Eastern until 1972, is now BC Rail.

British Columbia Hydro & Power Authority's rail operation, formerly British Columbia Electric Railway, has been renamed B. C. Hydro Rail.

Conrail is up for sale. Bids have been submitted by Norfolk Southern and by a consortium headed by Morgan Stanley and await approval by Congress; another faction advocates continued government ownership of the now-profitable railroad.

Illinois Central Gulf continues to sell its lines. In late 1985 ICG agreed

Ronald Johnson

Large-system images are replacing the images of their components: The big "G" for Guilford overshadows the Maine Central lettering.

A. G. Coppinger

Missouri Pacific SD50 No. 5002 is yellow and gray and carries a Union Pacific shield on its nose — but the Missouri Pacific lettering is a different type style from that used by UP.

to sell its Meridian-Shreveport (formerly the Alabama & Vicksburg and Vicksburg, Shreveport & Pacific) and Hattiesburg-Gulfport (formerly the southern portion of the Gulf & Ship Island) lines to MidSouth Rail Corporation. ICG's parent, IC Industries, continues to offer the ICG itself for sale.

The Milwaukee Road is now the official name of the railroad that was the Chicago, Milwaukee, St. Paul & Pacific. It is owned by Soo Line, and Milwaukee's orange and black diesels are being repainted red and white and relettered "Soo Line."

Missouri Pacific is still a separate railroad within the Union Pacific system, but UP's yellow paint is rapidly covering MP blue, and UP's shield is fast supplanting MP's eagle.

Southern Pacific moves toward merger with Santa Fe (see above). It is generally thought that Southern Pacific will receive about the same emphasis in the SP&SF image as Atchison and Topeka did with the AT&SF.

United Southeastern Railways maintains its own listing in *The Official Guide*, even though its lines are included in the maps and tables for National Railways of Mexico.